Joseph Maran, Carsten Juwig,
Hermann Schwengel, Ulrich Thaler (Hg.)

Constructing Power
Konstruktion der Macht

GESCHICHTE

Forschung und Wissenschaft

Band 19

LIT

Joseph Maran, Carsten Juwig,
Hermann Schwengel, Ulrich Thaler (Hg.)

CONSTRUCTING POWER

Architecture, Ideology and Social Practice

KONSTRUKTION DER MACHT

Architektur, Ideologie und soziales Handeln

LIT

Umschlagbild: E. Dupérac, The Exact Depiction of the Papal Majesty During the Celebration of the Divine Mass in the Sistine Chapel, 1578. Vatican City, Biblioteca Apostolica Vaticana.

Gedruckt mit Unterstützung des Ministeriums für Wissenschaft, Forschung und Kunst Baden-Württemberg.

Layout und Bildbearbeitung: Sveta Matskevich

Bibliographic information published by Die Deutsche Bibliothek
Die Deutsche Bibliothek lists this publication in the Deutsche Nationalbibliografie; detailed bibliographic data are available in the Internet at http://dnb.ddb.de.

ISBN 3-8258-9314-6

A catalogue record for this book is available from the British Library

Auslieferung/Verlagskontakt:
Grevener Str./Fresnostr. 2 48159 Münster
Tel. +49 (0)251–62 03 20 Fax +49 (0)251–23 19 72
e-Mail: lit@lit-verlag.de http://www.lit-verlag.de

Distributed in the UK by: Global Book Marketing, 99B Wallis Rd, London, E9 5LN
Phone: +44 (0) 20 8533 5800 – Fax: +44 (0) 1600 775 663
http://www.centralbooks.co.uk/acatalog/search.html

Distributed in North America by:

Transaction Publishers
New Brunswick (U.S.A.) and London (U.K.)

Transaction Publishers
Rutgers University
35 Berrue Circle
Piscataway, NJ 08854

Phone: +1 (732) 445 - 2280
Fax: + 1 (732) 445 - 3138
for orders (U. S. only):
toll free (888) 999 - 6778
e-mail:
orders@transactionspub.com

Table of Contents

Editors' Preface

The present volume is aimed at contributing to an understanding of the architecture of societies from prehistory to the present day, in most cases societies organized as states, as a source for social history and sociology. This endeavour is based on a notion of architecture as both document and precondition of social realities, both platform for the self-projection of those in power and an arena for a continuing renegotiation of power, both a medium of codified messages and a means of spatial ordering. The representative aspects of buildings, on which previous research has concentrated its attention, are not left undiscussed, but the focus of the majority of contributions is on an enquiry into how architectural space and social agency together not only communicated, but reproduced systems of values, views of the world and particular social roles. In highlighting this aspect, a new direction is taken, which is hoped to shed light on the different social effects of architecture and thus widen perspectives in the cultural sciences, in which the study of buildings often remains dominated by a concern with typology and stylistic history.

Most of the contributions to this volume were presented at the symposium *Constructing Power*, held from 18 to 20 July 2005 at the *Internationales Wissenschaftsforum Heidelberg* as part of a one-year-project under the title *Signs of Supremacy*, which was carried out jointly by the sociologist Hermann Schwengel (University of Freiburg) and the archaeologist Joseph Maran (University of Heidelberg) in the framework of the *Altertumswissenschaftliches Kolleg Heidelberg*. The *Altertumswissenschaftliches Kolleg* has been established to provide a platform for such interdisciplinary cooperations between representatives of those disciplines studying antiquity and scholars from other disciplines within the humanities as well as the social and natural sciences not regularly engaged in the study of the past, from the University of Heidelberg and from the other universities in the Federal State of Baden-Württemberg. In addition to these objectives of bridging gaps between disciplines of very different orientations and strengthening collaboration between the universities of Baden-Württemberg, it is also intended as an institutional framework for the academic exchange between researchers from Germany and abroad.

The editors would like to express their sincere gratitude to those who contributed to the success of the symposium and the publication of the resulting volume. In the first place, our thanks go to the Ministry of Science, Research and Art Baden-Württemberg, as without its generous funding it would never have been possible to set up the *Altertumswissenschaftliches Kolleg Heidelberg*. To the representatives of the latter, Tonio Hölscher and Stefan M. Maul, we are grateful for their support of and active participation in the project *Signs of Supremacy*. To the Rector's Offices of the Universities of Freiburg and Heidelberg, we extend our thanks for their assistance and their backing of the research work of the *Altertumswissenschaftliches Kolleg*. We also thank the board of trustees of the *Internationales Wissenschaftsforum* and in particular its director, Michael Welker, and manager, Theresa Reiter, for the opportunity to hold the symposium *Constructing Power* in this remarkable venue. For their help in the smooth running of the symposium, Geneviève Steinert and Claus Kropp deserve our thanks, while, over the course of a year, the project *Signs of Supremacy* as a whole has profited from active student participation and commitment. We are also grateful to Sveta Matskevich for her competent and diligent handling of the layout and image processing, and to Matthew Johnson for his advice and help in the editing of the English contributions in this volume. To the LIT-Verlag, our thanks are due for the good and professional collaboration in the publication of this volume. A special debt of gratitude is owed, finally, to the contributors to this volume, which was only made possible by their ideas.

British archaeologists who have worked within European archaeology, various historical processes are explored. These include the social processes resulting in the transformation of egalitarian communities into ranked hierarchies and state systems, or the processes of increasing economic diversity and intensification (where the existence of an interplay between both economic and social processes was accepted), or the processes that may have changed how people categorised, and thus worked, the material world. All such explanations have recognised the interplay between these different kinds of historical processes, although different writers have argued over which particular process may have operated as a prime mover in the formation of a particular historical sequence[6].

This brings me to the core of my argument. I am not interested in continuing the debate concerning which of the forces of history can claim a general primacy in causal explanations. For example, I find recent arguments over whether the development of the Neolithic was driven primarily by social or by economic processes, or by the adoption of new conceptual schemes as ludicrous: the world and the lives that people lived did not divide in this way[7]. What I would ask you to notice is that, in all the approaches we have touched upon, explanation seems always to involve uncovering that which is hidden, and the metaphor of uncovering obviously appeals to archaeologists whose work is dominated by the practices of discovery and excavation. But uncovering implies that a surface appearance hides something more profound, requiring us to pull that surface away to discover the hidden truth of an explanation[8]. In all these approaches, the description of a historical sequence is not the description of history as a process but merely the historical description of surface appearances: it is only the tracing of the consequences that arose from the engine-room of some underlying cause. The search for the causal mechanism of history then presents us with the options already described. Social forms may be claimed to rise upon the deeper foundation of economic logic, or social strategies may be believed to drive the economic process, and so on. And in all these accounts, there remains an infinite regress because each cause will require a further causal condition to stand as its explanation. Ultimately there appears no resolution to arguments that hinge upon the theorised assertions that this or that process must be primary to the historical process.

This reasoning is very unlike the archaeological reliance upon the less contentious, mechanical explanations for the formation of a stratigraphic sequence of soil deposits. While we cannot see the forces of history, we can observe the physical processes of site formation, and it is hardly surprising that many archaeologists would rather work with what they can see than with that which only emerges through theory. Thus we do not appear to observe the making of history in our material sequences but only its effects and the making of history remains available only through speculation[9].

Contrary to these arguments, let us propose quite simply that nothing is hidden. By this I mean that there is no deeper explanation underlying the form of things, there are no deeper levels to history than history itself. This is not to claim, as the empiricist would, that appearance and reality are one and the same, for if this were the case then the intellectual struggles of life would be at an end. Instead, my claim is that the history we seek is immanent to the material conditions we observe; it is embedded in that material rather than lying behind it. Such a history is not however brought immediately into view, not because it is hidden by its consequences, but because we do not look at the material aright. We do not see history because we approach the material from the wrong perspective. The challenge is therefore to find a path through the material that will provide a perspective that reveals history as practice and supports the point that I have just tried to make. This is not an argument that will necessarily convince you by means of its theoretical elegance: it will only convince you by revealing the fuller potential of the history of the period from the perspective from which we have chosen to observe the architectural remains at our disposal.

6 Systems analysis does not require the identification of a prime mover to explain change as Renfrew and others have demonstrated in their analysis of feedback processes, although the demand to explain change always seem to result in the search for a limited number of contributing factors (cf. Renfrew 1972). For a more refined understanding of complex systems see van der Leeuw and McGlade 1997.

7 Barrett 2006. For arguments concerning the drivers resulting in the adoption of the Neolithic see Thomas 1999 and Rowley-Conwy 2004. A more measured view remains Bender 1978.

8 Cf. Thomas 2004, 149-70.

9 This is why Binford's Middle Range Theory (e.g. Binford 1981, 1983) can allow us to observe site formation processes but will never be able to offer us historical explanations.

The Origins of the Neolithic

Archaeologists generalise by assigning material to particular periods of history, enabling us to see the character of those periods in the form of a material assemblage, and then to extend that characterisation to include the formation processes that could have produced such an assemblage. These generalisations are powerful. An assemblage of materials comes to represent an extinct set of processes, and a single component of that assemblage can be taken to represent the period as a whole. The fifth and fourth millennium earthen and stone long-mounds of western Europe are a case in point. They are among the characteristic monuments that are assigned to the Neolithic in these regions, and the Neolithic is the period in which agriculture was established. Long-mounds and agriculture therefore go together; indeed the establishment of the architecture of mounds and the establishment of agriculture are assumed to be connected in some way.

The Neolithic of Europe is the label applied to a geographically extensive and very diverse assemblage of material which is taken to encompass the history of Stone Age agriculture[10]. It is the occurrence of agriculture that gives the period its unity, and how that agriculture was established, from south-west Asia through Europe, is assumed to be somehow represented by the geographical and chronological sequences of material. There would therefore appear to be a unity of purpose – the emergence and development of agriculture – which determines the ways the artefacts and the monuments of the period are thought about. The image of material change is dominated by the assumption that it is driven by the east-to-west movement of domesticates across the continent, a process which has the appearance of dragging an associated package of cultural changes along with it. Thus the agenda for historical enquiry is set. Even when the hunter-gatherers of temperate Europe are treated as active participants in the process, it is as the recipients of agriculture and its associated material culture, and not as their instigators[11]. It appears that by uncovering the processes that animated the trajectory of material change we will automatically arrive at an explanation for the spread of domesticates; the story sought is thus the story of the arrival of agriculture.

One regional distinction between the central Europe assemblage and that of its western neighbours comes in the form of the built environment. The former is dominated by the domestic architecture of often massive timber long-houses characteristic of the *Linearbandkeramik* cultures (hereafter LBK)[12], while the latter, lacking such monumental domestic architecture, boasts the appearance of long-mounds, built variously of earth, timber and stone and distributed along the Atlantic seaboard and around the southern Baltic coastlands[13]. The assumption, now well established, is that the relationship between these two very different kinds of building, the one domestic and the other a form of mortuary monumentality, must tell us something about the transmission of agriculture to the west; all we need to know is how to read the signs. In this way, archaeologists begin to write the pseudo-histories that explain the appearance of these material things.

The view has long been held that the superficial similarity shared between the external form of the long-mounds and the long-houses and some of the components of their plans (Abb. 1) must imply that the builders of long-mounds were labouring to represent the long-houses either when standing or perhaps in a collapsed and ruined state[14]. The details of the argument have passed through a number of different versions although recent accounts share a common expectation: because long-mounds in their complex history of development are widely (but not entirely) associated with mortuary deposits, they

10 For a recent review of the European material see Price 2000.

11 For example, Whittle (1996) considers the ways exotic food resources may have been adopted by local populations rather than being introduced by colonizers. Consequently the beginning of the Neolithic is explained in terms of the mechanisms of resource transmission.

12 The origins for this material in south-central Europe are reviewed by Jochim (2000) and the cultural assemblage in north-central Europe (there termed "Linear Pottery") by Bogucki (2000).

13 The stone built cairns of Atlantic Europe have long been treated as a single phenomenon, first as a cultural dispersal of megalithic traditions, including a possible megalithic "religion" (Daniel 1963), and then as a common adaptive expedient (Renfrew 1984, 165-99). Midgley (2005) has argued that the phenomenon of monumental cemeteries in the Neolithic must also include the earth and timber mounds of lowland northern and western Europe.

14 The argument extends from Childe (1949) to Hodder (1984) and is summarised and developed by Bradley (1998, 3-14, 36-67). See also Sherratt 1990, 1995.

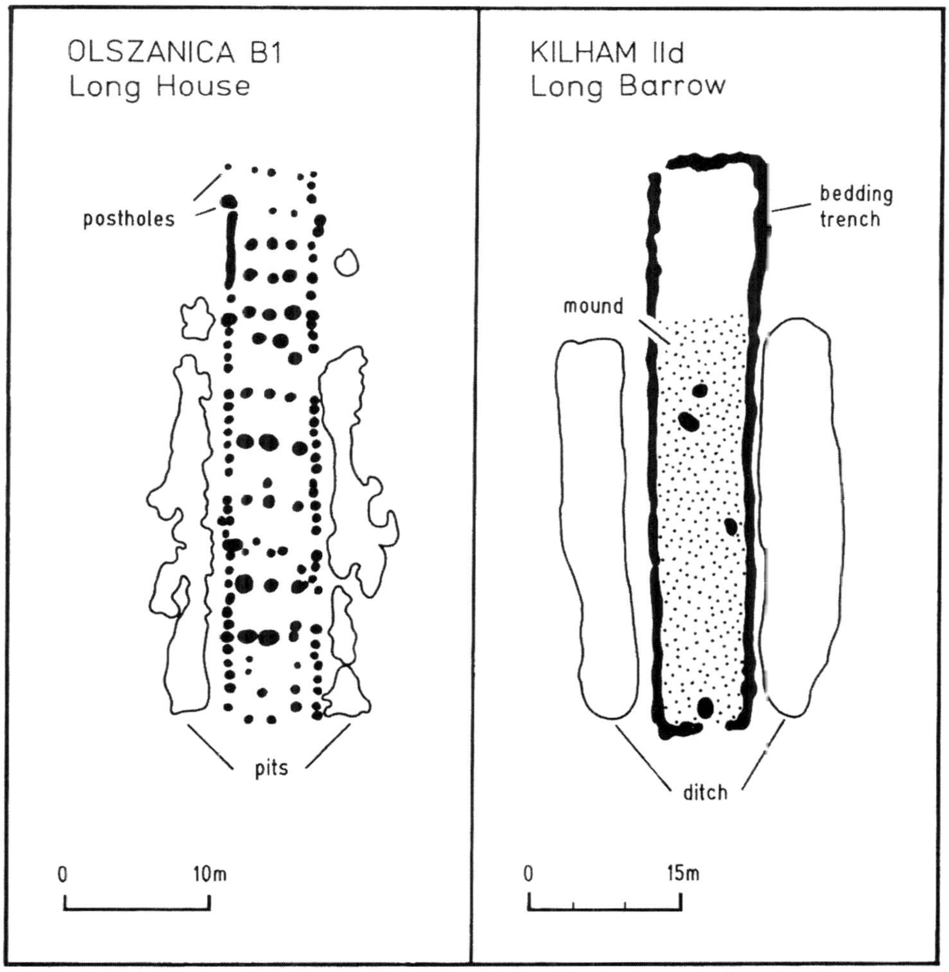

Abb. 1. The comparison drawn between the plan of the Polish LBK house at Olszanica and the English long-mound at Kilham. Note the differences of scale. After: Bradley 1998, fig. 13.

are assumed to have had a ritual function. The argument then follows that because ritual uses symbolism as a means to represent certain values or spiritual beings, then the ritual long-mounds can be regarded as 'symbolic' or 'representational' of some value or condition. Thus, the meaning of the mound will only be given to us, as it was to its original users, when we discover what the mound represented. By reducing the meaning of the monument to a question of representation, the archaeological solution has been to claim that the original reference to which the mound pointed was based upon its visual mimicking of the form of the house. The long-mound is a representational device that remains recognisable by us to this day.

If the two structural traditions did share a common outward form because the manifestation of the long-mound was derived from the house acting as a template, then this mimicry would be a historical phenomenon in need of an explanation. The chronological and geographical sequence between the two architectural traditions in the two regions appears to form part of a larger package of cultural and economic change. Indeed, the long-mound tradition emerged in the fifth millennium and developed through the fourth millennium, to the west and north-west of the sixth to fifth millennium heartlands of LBK settlement. The instigation of mound building is widely regarded as a manifestation of the westward extension of farming from that earlier LBK core region. Consequently, we are invited to accept that the reasons for the adoption of long-mounds to the west are connected to the mechanisms by which agriculture spread beyond that earlier frontier between agriculturalists and hunter-gatherers, although why long-mounds rather than houses were built as part of that process remains to be resolved.

Lengthy and complex chains of causality are clearly involved in these arguments. What evidence might support the derivation of long-mounds from long-houses? Perhaps we should expect to find an overlap in the distribution of the two types of monument with an indication of a succession where mounds replaced houses. Midgley has offered a sustained case for treating the earliest long-mound cemeteries of Poland and the Paris Basin as developing in close physical relationship with the domestic building traditions of the late and post-LBK communities in these regions[15]. In a few examples, we find mounds that have been built upon abandoned house sites, although this pattern of physical replacement is less easy to establish for the westward extension of the long-mound tradition. In Britain, for example, the mounds are separated by several hundreds of miles and by at least a millennium from their presumed domestic prototypes. If the case for such a domestic prototype is to hold good for all cases then we must assume that, by the time they had reached their widest distribution at the end of the fourth millennium, the mounds had taken on this symbolic significance in their own right and no longer by direct comparison with the original referent. In other words, for the observer, the mound could no longer have 'meant' a house if such meaning depended upon the direct comparison of the mound to the house. Western domestic architecture with its smaller buildings shares few characteristics of the earlier central European long houses[16]. Was this detachment from the original sources of its meaning achieved by a folk memory that bridged the geographical and chronological divide? Or could the observer have projected this particular meaning onto the mound from another perspective? It seems to me that such questions are beyond the hope of any satisfactory resolution.

The conclusion may be that the historical processes used to explain the history of these new architectural conditions in western Europe remain beyond reach empirically and can only be the subject of speculation. It *may* have been the case that some long-mounds represented near-contemporary or earlier houses, and that in doing so they also represented the values of the domestic world now transformed by the hunter-gatherer-cum-farming communities who provided them with ancestral associations, or that they marked the objectification of a kind of historical reasoning in which the collapsed and decayed form of the domestic structure was represented by the mound, or that the construction and the form of the mound bound together a new kind of labour force and by so doing converted hunter-gatherers to the new sensibilities of agriculture, … or then again it may not. All such speculative narratives share the commonly held assumption that historical explanations require us to specify the forces that drove historical processes and that these forces included the ways categories of experience were ordered. In the particular case of the 'spread' of long-mound architecture those same forces are assumed to have been connected with the introduction of agriculture.

Let us now take a different perspective. We will neither accept that the transmission of a cultural icon of domesticity from the central European house to the western European long-mound can explain the instigation of long-mounds with reference to long-houses, nor will we assume a necessary relationship between the building of the monuments and the spread of agriculture. In addition, rather than accepting that the similarities between the form of house and mound are significant, we will emphasise the differences between them.

The long-house was architectural in the traditional sense of the word: the buildings enclosed a series of interrelated spaces under one roof. Long-mounds are not architectural in the same sense. Many long-mounds were solid structures overlying earlier deposits, and where timber or stone chambers were built in the body of the mound many were sealed by the mound. In some cases, the stone chambers were linked by an access passage or gallery to the area beyond the mound, although this access may have been sealed for long periods of time and may have become permanently blocked at some stage of the monument's use. In almost all cases where they existed, the chambers were cramped, difficult of access and unlikely to have been occupied for any lengthy period. The house embraced the occupant whilst the long-mound sometimes tolerated difficult and restricted access but excluded most from entry. Long-mounds were largely solid structures, more reminiscent of monumental sculpture than of architecture.

15 Midgley 1985, 2005.
16 For a review of some of this material see Darvill and Thomas 1996.

The base-line for comparison between the house and the tomb might therefore be drawn more effectively from the perspective of human engagement than by the form of each structure. The house contained a hierarchy of performative fields within which participants will have regularly moved whilst the tomb did not provide a similar theatre of experience. The house enclosed and made possible the routine enactments of the values that operated between the lives of people. Enactments which referenced the long-mound on the other hand occurred in the labour organisation of its building and in occupying the ground beyond the structure. Only to a limited extent did some practitioners explore the architectural expression of the mound by entering the chambers contained by some of them. The difference between the two kinds of building can be effectively expressed as the difference between the place of performance and the place towards which performance was directed.

Now, of course, the distinction drawn here can still be accommodated by adopting the traditional argument that derives the form of the mound from the house. The symbolism of the tomb could be treated, if we so wished, as a non-functional representation of every-day domestic structures. In other words, the representation is not the same as the thing which is being represented. The house of the dead must, of necessity, have excluded the occupancy of the living. My point, however, is that the application of this structuralist logic has usurped the role of historical interpretation because it has failed to show how the logic could ever have arisen historically; it is simply accepted as given. Consequently, we are offered various speculative narratives of 'how it might have occurred'. I have already made the point that tomb building is assumed by these narratives to have been made 'meaningful' by virtue of its reference to the earlier (and mainly distant) house form, but the reference of one thing to another does not make that thing meaningful. Meaning is not a labelling exercise, it is not a matter of translation whereby one thing is found to stand for something else. Meaning is richer than this: it expresses 'how the world is' in statements and actions that link particular things and events to a more general scheme, where these statements or actions may be assessed for their accuracy and validity. Meaning is about living in the world rather than drawing up a catalogue of equivalences.

Archaeologists have recently introduced the presence of the human agent into their work in the hope of animating their understanding of historical sequences. All these attempts express the view that human agency is knowledgeable, implying that actions always have been meaningful because they expressed an understanding of the world. Whilst this assertion seems acceptable, it leads to the unfortunate situation that the agent is treated either as a spectator looking in upon a world, or as an author who has inscribed some message upon the material conditions of the world. This presents us with the duality of an 'inner' agent and 'outer' world and so with an agent/spectator who saw and understood the relationship between the form of the long-house in one part of Europe and the long-mound in another. In such cases the agent and their world are treated as the autonomous components of a single equation. But the only condition that could have made that agency possible, and thus the condition that made that agency's intentionality possible, was for it to have been part of the world and not its detached observer. Being in the world implies occupying a place from whose perspective action and experience were informed and meaningful. The agents' 'mindedness' was part of the world, enabling them not only to see the connection between things but also to work upon their own connection with those things. A perspective on the connections of life was the grammar that made the possibilities of life, and thus of things, meaningful. The statements or actions that generalised the significance of life's experience were meaningful but they were also vulnerable from a particular world-bound perspective and in the messiness of practical experience. Communities who shared these understandings did so by building, defending and justifying certain perspectives, they worked in ways that attempted to see the world aright[17].

From the end of the fifth and through the fourth millennium B.C., the communities of western and northern Europe built long-mounds, not because they thought such mounds looked like the houses they had never seen or had only heard tell, nor because they had learnt to adopt or convert to a cultural rule that required their adherence and was expressed by a complex sequence of constructional practices that created a long-mound. The issue for us is not to uncover an elegant metaphor, such as that suggested by Hodder, in which the mound gestured towards houses that represented the values of domestication (in

17 Much of this and of the argument which follows draws upon Luntley's important commentary on Wittgenstein (Luntley 2003).

Hodder's terms the values of the *domus*), and in so doing enabled the transference of those values from the living household to the house of the dead and so on to an ancestral past[18]. These mythical histories can be by-passed once we accept that things were meaningful not because they could be equated to what they might once have represented, but because people knew how to perform their lives in relation to them. Our task is to understand these performative (meaningful) strategies, if for no other reason than that it was through these strategies that history was made.

The historical role adopted by the long-mound was therefore to act as an enhancer of possible perspectives rather than as an encoded message. A particular perspective implies a point of view, for only from a perspective could certain connections between experience and things become visible. These connections held people and things together in the form of a structure, but this was a structure that only existed in the lives it sustained. It was a structure that through its development enabled practitioners to find the effectiveness of their place in the world. The notion of structure can too easily imply the existence of a transcendental framework of rules existing beyond the practices that gave it life. Instead, we might think of structure as a grammar of practice in which the participant was both implicated and empowered by seeing the world aright. The participants in the historical drama acted grammatically by claiming their occupancy of a perspective from which shared judgements of the adequacy of actions could be warranted and critically assessed.

The long-mound architecture may now be regarded not as the result of transferring a cultural motif from the farming communities of central Europe to the proto-agriculturalists to the north and west. It was not simply a modification of the physical form of the landscape but rather a modification of the landscape perspective achieved by hunter-gatherers in the lower river valleys, coastal basins and western uplands that stretched away from the hinterland of the fifth millennium agriculturalists. There is an irony in the way archaeologists have persistently denied hunter-gatherers cultural intent because of the apparent paucity of their cultural products. This has meant missing the conditions of possibility for these hunter-gatherers to ever have had their own histories. Consequently, the history of hunter-gatherers appears to be something that had to be downloaded from outside, either in the form of environmental determinism or as the transmission of economic or cultural traits from neighbouring agriculturalists. However, hunter-gatherers could only ever have entered upon the world, and indeed recognised the effectiveness of their own existence in that world, through a perspective that showed how their experiences fitted into the world and how their expectations could be validated; they entered the world in other words from a perspective that was entirely cultural.

Perspectives arise from somewhere because they are perspectives towards a particular condition. By marking those landscapes, perhaps by the modifications caused by the felling or burning of vegetation, or by the depositing of caches of materials (including perhaps the dead), or simply by the routines of congregation, places were created[19]. These places meant more than the simple labelling of a location by a particular activity, as in the form of a symbol marked on the ground as if upon a map. Place was that location to which prior expectations and experiences converged; places were drawn into view from the perspectives offered by those experiences. It was as if the spaces from whence experiences were gained were folded into a place as the diversity of journeys and histories that stretched through time and across space converged upon a place. And space also unfolded from these places as life extended forward into future fields of activity and as new panoramas were understood[20]. The power of the architecture of place was to contribute to the making of these perspectives and by so doing to inform the understandings by which landscape could be occupied. The distinction between the place of the house and the place of the mound is now clearer. The drama of performances lived out within and around the houses of central Europe was, as Hodder[21] has argued, the means by which the products of the widely distributed and engendered labours of procurement were reworked for a community of consumption. The spaces of agricultural life were in this sense enfolded into the house. Could a similar enfolding have been achie-

18 Hodder 1990.

19 The enormous longevity of the routine patterns of the use of post-glacial hunter-gatherer landscapes with the implications these histories have for plant and animal management needs to be recognised. See for example the work of Dark in Mellars and Dark 1998.

20 On this issue see Elden on the work of Heidegger (Elden 2001).

21 Hodder 1990.

ved at the site of a long-mound? It is at this point of his argument that Hodder seems to lose sight of his own idea. The *domus* was not some abstract notion to which the house pointed as a sign. The *domus* was embodied, it was lived out in the smoke-filled shell of the structure, in the smells, tastes and in the physical proximity of others, in the comforts (and discomforts) of those places. The long-mound on the other hand sealed the surface on which it stood, it was approached from outside and the perspectives it gave were realised in the paths of approach and in the vistas against which the mound was viewed. Instead of searching for a representational analogy by which to translate the significance of one place in terms of the other, why do we not accept the things as they were?

Such an acceptance would see the building of long-mounds as a complex practice of deposition, mortuary rites and physical modifications, intentionally selecting places where the adequacy of certain perspectives linking experience to the world could be evaluated. These monuments did not emerge as the representation of a transcendental image of reality, but as a palimpsest of physical labour seeking to assess the relationship between experience and ideal. Significantly, the visual dominance achieved by some mounds will have had the effect of closing down the perspectives from which divergent experiences were linked to that ideal, perhaps resulting in a greater level of coherency in communal discourse. Were these actions instrumental in delivering an agricultural economy to the western margins of Europe? Or did they arise from the economic foundations provided by agriculture? Perhaps the answer is neither. Rather, the arrival of agriculture arose out of a convergence between the restructuring of the various communities' perceptions of their place in the world and the availability of new economic resources. If this was indeed the case then we can allow for the agrarian economies of western and northern Europe to have been built by hunter-gatherers without the need either for their conversion by farmer missionaries or by their need to adopt symbolically the exotic values that had once been lived by others.

I have used my first case study to question the way archaeologists have employed the formal similarities between long-house and long-mound architecture to claim that these similarities arose out of the mechanisms that established agriculture in western Europe. My suggestion is that, whilst both kinds of construction may have played a part in developing the agricultural economies characteristic of each particular region, they did not do so as part of a mechanism designed to transmit agriculture westwards. Instead, they were the practical means to orientate a particular perspective towards the landscapes of these different regions. Fundamental to this argument is my desire to move away from explaining the adoption of a particular architectural style as indicative of the adoption of certain values, such as the conceptual distinctions between *domus* and *agrios*, or the presence of *ancestors*, or whatever. The mysterious transmission of these values cannot explain the transmission of agriculture. In place of this idealism, I have argued for architecture as making a perspective upon the world possible and thus providing the means of seeing the world aright. The architecture of place was a drawing together of experience and the provision of grounds for future expectations, thus providing for a coherent and practical engagement with the world. The primacy that I have given architectural form as a means of structuring action, rather than as a representation of some condition or value, means that we can discard claims that a causal relationship existed between the histories of the two architectural traditions and we can reject the suggestion that such a link could ever have represented the means by which agriculture 'spread' westwards. Indeed, equating long-mound building with the adoption of agriculture in the west is something that now needs to be demonstrated and not assumed. The implication is that each architectural tradition emerged as the structuring of landscape perception by its inhabitants and will have helped to facilitate the practices that sustained quite different kinds of agricultural organisation in the regions concerned.

STONEHENGE

Stonehenge is one of the most remarkable pieces of architecture in the ancient world. The surviving arrangement of stones was erected during the third millennium B.C., although I will argue that its full architectural achievement was finally reached early in the second millennium when only minor modifications to the monument took place[22]. The importance of this final stage is that it extended perspectives

22 The full publication of the monument's archaeology is now found in Cleal et al. 1995.

that were possible upon the world from the vantage point of place, but it may also have marked a limit as to what could be achieved using these architectural techniques.

Questions of origin, scale, and purpose have always dominated the scholarship of Stonehenge. It has long been accepted that the instigation of such a remarkable building programme required the precondition of cultural and technical competence, something that might be attested in the architectural antecedents to the monument. With no such prototypes present among the indigenous British cultures, Richard Atkinson famously turned to the Aegean to locate the source of its architectural inspiration, proposing that a Mycenaean architect must have directed the labours of indigenous barbarians in the erection of the monument[23]. The prototypic example Atkinson offered to attest to the ability to erect lintels across stone uprights was the Lion Gate at Mycenae. The unlikely nature of the comparison, along with the turn against diffusion as an explanation for cultural change in the 1960s and the damning realisation that Stonehenge was likely to predate any putative Aegean precursor meant that an indigenous origin for the monument was finally accepted[24]. With architectural antecedents still lacking, the background for the building project was now seen to lie in the emergence of a centralised social authority capable of mustering the necessary labour resources[25]. However, it is surely self-evident that both skill and organisation must have existed if Stonehenge was ever to be built, making it redundant to demonstrate the point archaeologically. And neither of these necessary conditions amount to an *explanation* for why such skills and resources were mobilised towards the building of this particular monument; this is a question of motivation.

The efforts invested in the construction of the final sarsen building were enormous, both in the moving and the preliminary dressing of the stones, and also in their erection along with the working necessary to set the lintels upon the uprights. Prior to all this effort there had occurred the transportation of the blue stones from south-west Wales to Salisbury Plain to be variously employed in the later phases of Stonehenge's development. These exotic stones had at some stage been erected as a monument employing on stone the timber-working techniques of tongue-and-groove and mortise-and-tenon jointing[26]. If antecedent techniques are to be sought for the blue stone monument and for the final building phases of Stonehenge then these would appear to lie in a combination of abilities involving the movement, dressing and erection of standing stones and the woodworking traditions of joinery. The simplest way to accommodate this rather odd amalgamation of procedures is as the imaginative deployment of necessary skills directed towards a building project whose style and scale had never previously been attempted.

The scale of effort in the construction of Stonehenge is not however matched by the scale of the monument itself. Visitors seeing Stonehenge for the first time will often express a sense of disappointment: the circle covers a relatively small area and from most perspectives the stones sit below, and are therefore visually obscured against, the near horizon. In the seventeenth century the antiquary John Aubrey likened Stonehenge to a parish church when set against the cathedral-like scale of the great chalk-cut enclosure and stone circles of Avebury. However, the comparison is misleading. Stonehenge is a complex stone circle that encloses a relatively small area and if comparisons are to be sought then they should be drawn with the northern and southern stone circles erected within the Avebury enclosure[27]. Another comparison for the scale enclosed by the circle would be the timber circles built inside the massive chalk-cut enclosure at Durrington Walls, some 3 km to the north-east of Stonehenge itself[28]. At Stonehenge, the stone circle was encircled by an earlier but relatively slight earthwork, quite different from the massive ditch and outer bank that gave both Durrington Walls and Avebury their grandeur. Allowing for the uniqueness of the structure and the scale of work involved, Stonehenge appears to be more closely comparable in terms of its size and its landscape context to the free-standing stone circles of northern and western Britain than it is to the large late Neolithic henges of southern Britain.

Do such comparisons as these help in our understanding of the history of the period? Not immediately, for what do we expect them to reveal? Let us now return to the point I have already attempted

23 Atkinson 1956, 84ff.
24 Renfrew 1968.
25 Renfrew 1984, 225-45.
26 Cleal et al. 1995, figs. 108, 116.
27 Smith 1965.
28 Wainwright and Longworth 1971.

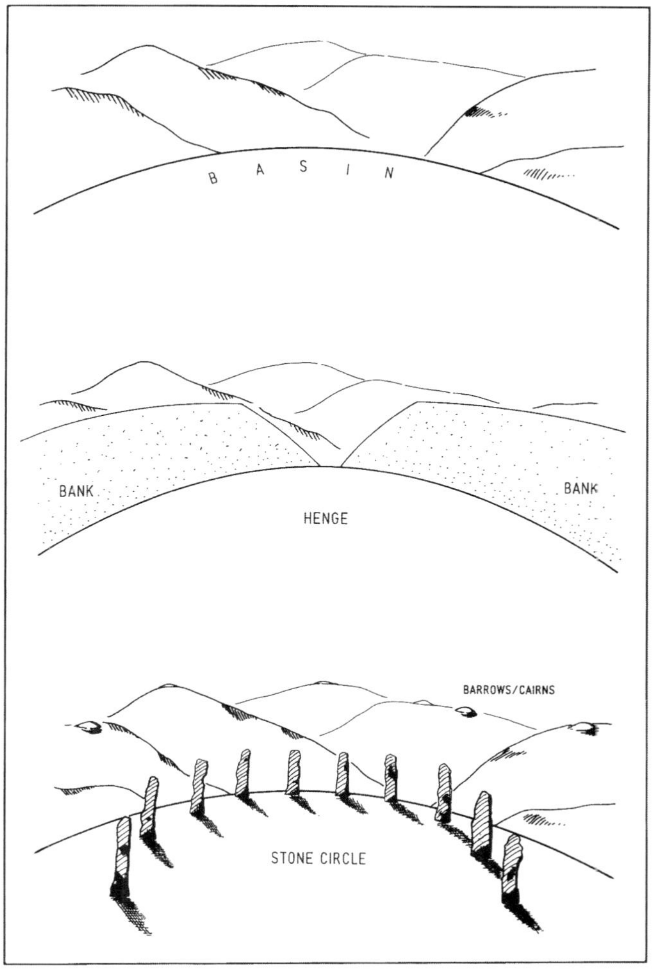

Abb. 2. The contrasting visual relationships between the interior of a henge and a stone circle and the surrounding topography. After: Bradley 1998, fig. 40.

to develop, that the architecture of place provided a perspective upon how to occupy the spaces of the world around that place, and that that to occupy such an architecture was to engage in the practicalities of seeing and acting in the world aright. This brings into view the ways these various monuments structured perception and the practices necessary for their occupation. A comparison may now be drawn between the complex timber and stone circles of Durrington and Avebury and the building of Stonehenge, for it is quite possible to recognise some basic architectural motifs that both timber and stone circles share[29]. At both Durrington and Stonehenge, we find avenues leading to and from the circle, a possible façade or outer demarcation immediately beyond the circle and the circle itself enclosing an inner setting of uprights. Not only do we encounter techniques of timber construction applied to stone but we also find the sharing, between timber and stone buildings, of similarities in design. These comparisons, along with the existence of an earlier timber building at Stonehenge have led Parker Pearson and Ramilisonina to suggest that the timber buildings at Durrington and the stone phase of construction at Stonehenge employed the contrast of timber and stone to represent the metaphorical transformation of organic existence into a state of permanence[30]. The result of this move in the third millennium was, according to Parker Pearson and Ramilisonina, to establish a relationship between the two locations of Durrington and Stonehenge as demarcating a passage between the transience of life and the timeless values associated with the dead and with ancestral time. In this way, a duality of places was created that

29 For a fuller development of this argument see Barrett 1994.
30 Parker Pearson and Ramilisonina 1998, see also Barrett and Fewster 1998.

Abb. 3. The approach to Stonehenge from along the Avenue. Photograph: author.

stood for the binary opposition between life (organic decay) and death (dry permanence), a geographical relationship which was deployed in the enactment of funerary rites evoking a journey between Durrington Walls and Stonehenge.

The problem with this suggestion is that it uses a summary of the final ordering of places to project back to the presumed and intellectualised motivations for the lengthy building programme. However, for a representation to exist, there has to be something that is seen to be represented, something that is grasped through experience, and this returns us to the central point of this paper: the primacy of material conditions, including architecture, lies not in their representational power but in their ability to orientate a perspective upon experience. I would therefore suggest that we should not assume that the life : death duality is timelessly given, only awaiting for various historically and culturally specific forms of representation to be applied to it, any more than that ancestors are necessarily a timeless presence in the prehistory of Europe[31]. Let us assume instead that life : death, and indeed ancestors themselves, are categories that have to be seen or grasped, they require a particular perspective if they are to be brought into view or made available to experience, and that this shared perspective has to be built if any communal appreciation of these values is to be effective.

Based on the contrast he draws between the architecture of the stone circles and that of the henge monuments of Britain, Bradley has suggested that each class of monument defined a different quality of place in the landscape by the nature of its enclosure[32]. The stone circles provided visual reference from place to topography, while the henges tend to secure a degree of visual closure by the erection of the bank (Abb. 2). One type of structure therefore looked outward, the other inward. Avebury and Durrington separated the ground that they enclosed from the surrounding landscapes, physically by the excavation of a massive internal ditch and visually by the erection of a bank that formed a near horizon between the observer and the sky. Stonehenge was to a certain extent visually permeable: the sky behind was glimpsed from the approach along the Avenue (Abb. 3), and the wider topographic horizon could be

31 This is to take up Whitley's objection to the application of ancestral values as a general feature applicable to numerous aspects of European prehistory (Whitley 2002).

32 Bradley 1998, 116-31. We should note the varied nature of the architecture of stone circles. In some, the stones stand high enough to intervene between the observer and the landscape beyond, as in the case of Stonehenge; in others, they are so low they merely enclose an area of ground.

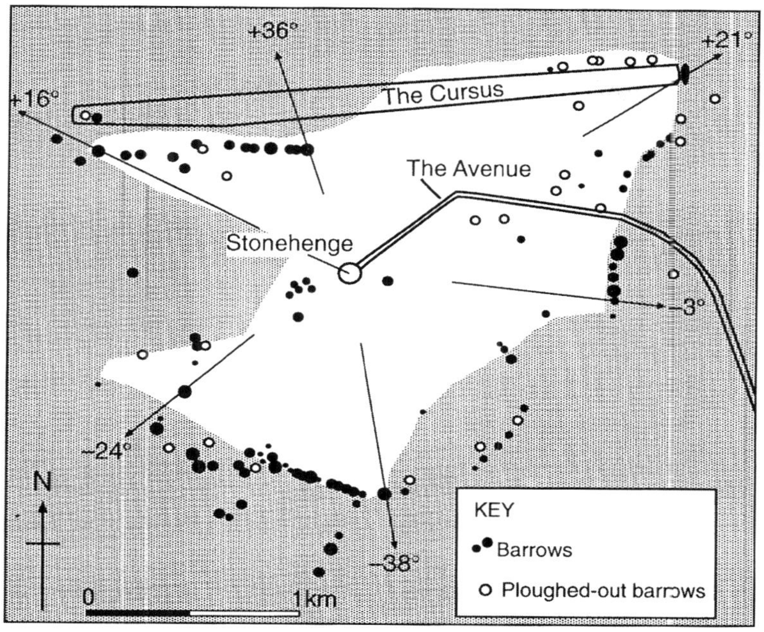

Abb. 4. The envelope of visibility formed by the near horizon around Stonehenge and marked by barrow cemeteries in the second millennium B.C. After: Ruggles 1997, fig. 8.

observed from the monument. It is that horizon, the so-called visual envelope around Stonehenge, which in the second millennium B.C. became embellished by a series of round barrow cemeteries running in a broad and discontinuous arc from the south-west to north-west of the monument (Abb. 4). These burial sites began to develop in the Beaker period but their full expression came with the construction of the large barrow mounds broadly contemporary with the rich early Bronze Age 'Wessex Culture' graves that were buried in some of the mounds. The open views from Stonehenge therefore provided one perspective around which a burial landscape emerged during the early second millennium B.C. This was some centuries after the stone structure had been erected and the main timber structures at Durrington had collapsed. Significantly, no barrow cemeteries were constructed to demarcate the horizon beyond the Durrington enclosure for the horizon from within the enclosure was defined by the bank. In light of this, it is also important to note that Woodward and Woodward have suggested that the barrow cemeteries around Avebury did not develop with visual reference from the henge monument itself but with visual reference from other locations beyond that enclosure[33]. Once again, the horizon from within the henge was demarcated by the bank rather than the surrounding topography. Perhaps the point of the contrast between these various types of monument is not so much between the uses of timber or stone as building material but, as Bradley has suggested, the contrasting perspectives on the landscape provided by the different kinds of enclosure. This contrast will have offered very different kinds of potential for developing the form of the local topography by the sighting of round barrows. Stonehenge does become an exemplary monument of the dead by the second millennium B.C., not as a representation but as providing a perspective upon that condition. This returns us to the approach I am arguing for here, that death has to be seen from a particular perspective before it can be represented effectively. Stonehenge appears to build such a perspective in the second millennium B.C.; whether it represented the dead in the previous millennium remains open to question.

33 Woodward and Woodward 1996.

REPRESENTATION

The paper has attempted to challenge the assumption that material culture should be treated primarily as a form of representation. We have touched upon the ways archaeologists have treated the European Neolithic as a period whose material conditions arose as a complex and interwoven structure of representations. The British literature is particularly full of studies that treat buildings, artefacts and buried deposits as ordered in such a way that they encoded particular meanings. I have already cited examples where the house is seen to have encoded values of domesticity, the long-mound as representing a conjunction of values associated with the domestic and the (ancestral) dead, and timber and stone buildings as representing the contrast between life and death. These examples could be extended to include other cases where patterns of deposition, including human bone, artefact debris and food residues, are confidently assessed to encode meanings, many of which we are, remarkably, still able to read. All such arguments accept the case that material culture is an expression of an understanding, a view of the world, without examining how that understanding was recognised or captured by the participant. Indeed the arguments go further, treating human motivation as fundamentally a motivation to communicate an intellectualised image of the world. Such a position raises obvious problems for those scholars who believe that historical interpretation should explain the causes for the things and events that occurred, for how are we to explain the causes of an agent's desire to communicate a particular understanding of their world?

All perception is from a point of view, which if shared may provide the basis for a common understanding and for communication. Such a point of view belongs within the world, partly constructed through the use and modification of material culture that contributes to a perspective before it can communicate an understanding that may arise from that perspective. My treatment of architecture has been as an embellishment of place, and as the construction of perspective, rather than as a medium of communication. Communication, to emphasise the point, is an act of trust in the commonly held views of the world. If this approach links architecture to the construction of power then that construction was one that empowered people to see the world and their place within it rather more than one that acted to communicate the power of a particular authority.

As I hope I have shown, to view the material in this way opens an alternative perspective upon the history of the Neolithic and upon the nature of historical interpretation. But it also raises an important question, for this argument does not deny that material culture was used to represent certain conditions, it simply questions the primacy given to such representations in current interpretations. The question that remains concerns when and how various forms of representation emerged. Do they occur as a secondary feature of the occupancy of material culture throughout its history, or do they emerge to dominate particular periods in socially and culturally specific ways? Any attempt to answer this question must involve a whole other study but I will offer one suggestion: that the distinction between the European Neolithic and European Bronze Age is not a matter of technological change, nor the passage from one stage of social evolution to another, but of the increasingly representational role taken by material culture. That role is seen in a number of media, from the complexity of the rock art of the period, through forms of dress, the representational decoration on metalwork, to the textual materials of Linear A and Linear B. We should not underestimate the significance of this development. Representations establish an ability to perceive things that are absent and by so doing they extend the effect of those things over time and space[34]. The media used might have facilitated the widespread convergence towards common forms of mythology, although such convergence must have necessitated the building of a shared perspective that the mythologies and oral traditions will have addressed[35]. Perhaps the single example of the Nebra disc might illustrate the scale and complexity of the changes that were occurring in the period. The composite metal disc appears to be a sky map, with the depiction of the horizon, the constellation of the Pleiades, the sun and the moon. It is the sky seen from a perspective but transferred, that is represented, by a medium that could be transported. Not only was the image of that portion of the sky available without the direct experience, but something of the perspective was preserved without actually 'being there'.

34 The relationship between presence and absence is intricate; many of the representational systems of the Bronze Age may have functioned in the context of oral narration (cf. Bennet 2004).

35 This paper was written before I was able to consider the issues raised in this connection by Kristiansen and Larsson 2005.

We are far too used to the contemporary political and economic structures of 'time-space distanciation' with the result that we all too easily miss the radical nature of mapping the sky for others to see. For such images to work they must have claimed a form of authenticity that was previously grounded upon direct experience, the perspective of a particular place. That authenticity had now become the ability to read the signs. Perhaps it is not a coincidence that, as such shifts towards complex forms of representation occurred, the architecture of the landscape began to change in western Europe and the monumental embellishments that characterised the authenticity of experience in the Neolithic were replaced by the architecture of settlement and community. The full implications of this transformation are only now beginning to emerge; they surely mark one of the most profound developments in the prehistory of Europe.

Bibliography

Atkinson, R.J.C. 1956. *Stonehenge*. London: Hamish Hamilton.

Barrett, J.C. 1994. *Fragments from Antiquity: An Archaeology of Social Life in Britain, 2900-1200* BC. Oxford: Blackwell.

—. 2006. "Material Culture, Humanity and the Beginnings of the Neolithic." In *Die Dinge als Zeichen: Kulturelles Wissen und materielle Kultur – Perspektiven einer kulturwissenschaftlichen Synthese*, edited by T.L. Kienlin, 111-24. Universitätsforschungen zur prähistorischen Archäologie 127. Bonn: Habelt.

Barrett, J.C., and Fewster, K. 1998. "Stonehenge: *Is* the Medium the Message?" *Antiquity* 72: 847-52.

Bender, B. 1978. "Gatherer-Hunter to Farmer: A Social Perspective." *World Archaeology* 10: 204-22.

Bennet, J. 2004. "Iconographies of Value: Words, People and Things in the Late Bronze Age Aegean." In *The Emergence of Civilisation Revisited*, edited by J.C. Barrett and P. Halstead, 90-106. Oxford: Oxbow Books.

Binford, L.R. 1962. "Archaeology as Anthropology." *American Antiquity* 28: 217-25.

—. 1981. *Bones, Ancient Man and Modern Myths*. New York: Academic Press.

—. 1983. *In Pursuit of the Past*. London: Thames and Hudson.

Bogucki, P. 2000. "How Agriculture Came to North-Central Europe." In Price 2000, 197- 218.

Bradley, R. 1998. *The Significance of Monuments: On the Shaping of Human Experience in Neolithic and Bronze Age Europe*. London: Routledge.

Childe, V.G. 1949. "The Origin of Neolithic Culture in Northern Europe." *Antiquity* 23: 120-35.

Clark, J.G.D. 1939. *Archaeology and Society*. London: Methuen.

—. 1974 Reprint. *Prehistoric Europe: The Economic Basis*. London: Methuen. Original edition, London: Methuen, 1952.

Clarke, D.L. 1968. *Analytical Archaeology*. London: Methuen.

Cleal, R., K. Walker, and R. Montague. 1995. *Stonehenge in its Landscape: Twentieth Century Excavations*. London: English Heritage.

Daniel, G. 1963. *The Megalith Builders of Western Europe*. London: Penguin Books.

Darvill, T., and J. Thomas. 1996. *Neolithic Houses in Northwest Europe and Beyond*. Oxford: Oxbow Books.

Dawkins, R. 1976. *The Selfish Gene*. Oxford: Oxford University Press.

Elden, S. 2001. *Mapping the Present: Heidegger, Foucault and the Project of a Spatial History*. London: Continuum.

Hodder, I. 1984. "Burials, Houses, Women and Men in the European Neolithic." In *Ideology, Power and Prehistory*, edited by D. Miller and C. Tilley, 51-68. Cambridge: Cambridge University Press.

—. 1990. *The Domestication of Europe*. Oxford: Blackwell.

Jochim, M. 2000. "The Origins of Agriculture in South-Central Europe." In Price 2000, 183-96.

Kristiansen, K., and T.B. Larsson. 2005. *The Rise of Bronze Age Society: Travels, Transmissions and Transformations*. Cambridge: Cambridge University Press.

Luntley, M. 2003. *Wittgenstein: Meaning and Judgement*. Oxford: Blackwell Publishing.

Mellars, P., and P. Dark. 1998. *Star Carr in Context*. Cambridge: McDonald Institute for Archaeological Research.

Midgley, M.S. 1985. *The Origin and Function of the Earthen Long Barrows of Northern Europe*. British Archaeological Reports International Series 259. Oxford: British Archaeological Reports.

—. 2005. *The Monumental Cemeteries of Prehistoric Europe*. Stroud: Tempus Publishing.

Parker Pearson, M., and Ramilisonina 1998. "Stonehenge for the Ancestors: The Stones Pass on the Message." *Antiquity* 72: 308-26.

Price, T.D., ed. 2000. *Europe's First Farmers*. Cambridge: Cambridge University Press.

Psillos, S. 2002. *Causation and Explanation*. Chesham: Acumen Publishing.

Renfrew, C. 1968. "Wessex without Mycenae." *Annual of the British School at Athens* 63: 277-85.

—. 1972. *The Emergence of Civilisation: The Cyclades and the Aegean in the Third Millennium BC*. London: Methuen.

—. 1984. *Approaches to Social Archaeology*. Edinburgh: Edinburgh University Press.

Rowley-Conwy, P. 2004. "How the West Was Lost: A Reconsideration of Agricultural Origins in Britain, Ireland and Southern Scandinavia." *Current Anthropology* 45: 83-113.

Ruggles, C. 1997. "Astronomy and Stonehenge." In *Science and Stonehenge*, edited by B. Cunliffe and C. Renfrew, 203-29. Oxford: Oxford University Press.

Sherratt, A. 1990. "The Genesis of Megaliths: Monumentality, Ethnicity and Social Complexity in Neolithic North-West Europe." *World Archaeology* 22: 147-67.

—. 1995. "Instruments of Conversion? The Role of Megaliths in the Mesolithic/Neolithic Transition in North-West Europe." *Oxford Journal of Archaeology* 14: 245-60.

Smith, I.F. 1965. *Windmill Hill and Avebury: Excavations by Alexander Keiller 1925-1939*. Oxford: Clarendon Press.

Thomas, J. 1999. *Understanding the Neolithic*. London: Routledge.

—. 2004. *Archaeology and Modernity*. London: Routledge.

van der Leeuw, S., and J. McGlade, eds. 1997. *Time, Process and Structured Transformation in Archaeology*. London: Routledge.

Wainwright, G., and I. Longworth. 1971. *Durrington Walls Excavations 1966-1968*. London: Society of Antiquaries.

Whitley, J. 2002. "Too Many Ancestors." *Antiquity* 76: 119-26.

Whittle, A. 1996. *Europe in the Neolithic*. Cambridge: Cambridge University Press.

Woodward, A.B., and P.J. Woodward. 1996. "The Topography of Some Barrow Cemeteries in Bronze Age Wessex." *Proceedings of the Prehistoric Society* 62: 275-91.

Der minoische ‚Hof' als Kulisse zeremonieller Handlung

Diamantis Panagiotopoulos

Abstract

The nature of Minoan palaces has recently become a matter of lively debate. The present paper takes a traditional approach to this problem in that it adheres to the premise that the Minoan palace did serve as a royal residence and focuses on its role as a backdrop for ceremonial performance. The fundamental architectural concept of this mega-structure lies in the distinction between 'inside' and 'outside', i.e. a private and a public sector. The clear division of urban space reflected and cemented social inequality. The Central Court, the 'luxury hearth' of Minoan society, with its highly sophisticated façades provided an adequate setting for ceremonial appearances of the king and was obviously accessible only to members of the elite. Such an area of restricted access, which was certainly invested with profound symbolic meanings, should not be downgraded to a simple place of assembly for any social group. The West Court, on the other hand, an open, public piazza in the immediate vicinity of the palace complex, was predestined to be a meeting point between the ruling elite and its subjects and played a crucial role in the legitimization of political power. The discussion closes with a re-evaluation of the miniature frescoes from Knossos, in which it is argued that this major iconographical source of information about performative action depicted events outside the palace complex.

Prolegomena

In der kretischen Neupalastzeit, jener Periode der minoischen Kultur, die uns am besten überliefert ist, findet die Frage nach der Konstruktion der Macht einen einzigen Adressaten, nämlich den minoischen Palast. Wegen des rätselhaften Fehlens von Tempelanlagen, königlichen Gräbern oder anderen repräsentativen Denkmälern aus der Neupalastzeit bleibt der Palast als Konzept, bautechnische Leistung und performativer Raum die einzige archäologisch fassbare Manifestation machtpolitischer Ansprüche. Die Auseinandersetzung mit den Mechanismen der Macht im minoischen Kreta ist im Bereich der Ägäischen Archäologie heute aktueller denn je, da sie im Mittelpunkt einer erst kürzlich entfachten Debatte über den Typ des minoischen Herrschaftssystems steht. Dem traditionellen, von Arthur Evans geprägten Paradigma einer monokratischen Herrschaft nach orientalischem Vorbild[1] steht seit kurzem ein neuer radikaler Ansatz gegenüber, der die Existenz eines Herrschers verneint, und an dessen Stelle ein nach oligarchischen Prinzipien aufgebautes politisches System vermutet, dessen Kern miteinander konkurrierende soziale Gruppen bildeten[2]. Die Organisation dieser als factions bezeichneten Gesellschaftssegmente soll auf einem schichtenübergreifenden, klientelähnlichen Abhängigkeitsverhältnis beruht haben. Den minoischen Palast verstehen die Anhänger der neuen Theorie nicht mehr als multifunktionale Herrscherresidenz, sondern als ein öffentliches Gebäude, das zeremonielle Zentrum der Stadt, das als

1 Den Grundgedanken einer Gottesherrschaft des mythisch überlieferten Minos, die der theokratisch fundierten politischen Autorität orientalischer Könige entsprach, erläutert Evans (1921, 1-4) in den ersten Seiten seines *opus magnum*; ferner Driessen 2002, 2-3.

2 Driessen 2002; Hamilakis 2002. Dieser Deutung der minoischen Paläste, die aus der Sicht der neupalastzeitlichen administrativen Dokumente die Existenz eines zentralistisch aufgebauten politischen System verneint, ist auch Schoep 2002 zugeneigt. Zu einer kritischen Sichtung des *factions*-Modells s. Day und Relaki 2002, 224-6.

performativer Schauplatz von identitätsstiftenden Ritualen der Gemeinschaft[3] bzw. als Arena politisch-ideologischer Konkurrenz fungierte[4].

Jenseits dieser divergierenden Meinungen herrscht heute ein breiter Konsens über die herausragende Bedeutung dieser Gebäudekomplexe als Schauplatz zeremonieller Handlung[5] sowie über die Quintessenz des minoischen Palastsystems: Nicht die Macht der Waffen, sondern der Glanz der Zeremonien war das, was dieses komplexe institutionelle Gefüge in seinem Inneren zusammenhielt. Es scheint daher lohnenswert zu versuchen, einen Blick auf den Palast als Schauplatz zeremonieller Handlung zu werfen, in der Hoffnung, dass es möglich sein wird, das Legitimationsprinzip eines antiken Herrschaftssystems zu ergründen, auch ohne sein ‚Gesicht' wirklich zu kennen. Folgende Überlegungen gehen von der Prämisse aus, dass die minoischen Paläste Herrscherresidenzen waren, die ihre engsten historischen Parallelen in den orientalischen Palästen finden[6]. Die Konzentration auf den Palast von Knossos (Taf. 1) – mit nur punktueller Berücksichtigung der anderen minoischen Paläste – ist keine Absicht, sondern eine Notwendigkeit, da man nur anhand dieses größten und wichtigsten minoischen Palastes seine Funktion als zeremonielle Kulisse sowohl auf der Ebene der historischen Realität als auch auf der Ebene der bildlichen Darstellung greifen kann[7].

DRINNEN – DRAUSSEN

Für das Verständnis des minoischen ‚Hofes' als sozial-politische Institution und Kulisse zeremonieller Inszenierung – der Begriff ‚Hof' ist hier nicht als architektonisches, sondern als gesellschaftliches Konstrukt zu verstehen[8] – hat die bauliche Gestaltung dieser Megastruktur eine grundlegende Bedeutung. Auch wenn der knossische Palast nur bis zur Höhe des Erdgeschosses erhalten ist, kann es keinen Zweifel daran geben, dass es ein introvertierter, in sich gekehrter Baukomplex war[9]. Sein ‚Herz' und Ausgangspunkt der baulichen Gestaltung bildete ein rechteckiger, nord-süd-orientierter Zentralhof (Taf. 1). Die einzelnen Raumeinheiten der den Hof umgebenden Flügel sprangen nach außen unregelmäßig vor[10]. Von innen gesehen, aus der Sicht derjenigen, die im Zentralhof verkehrten, bot der Palast durch seine reich gegliederten Fassaden eine prachtvolle architektonische Kulisse[11]. Aus der Sicht der – im wahrsten Sinne des Wortes – Außenstehenden war er allerdings, durch seine geschlossenen Außenwände mit wenigen, kleinen Eingängen, ein abgeriegelter Baukörper, der bloß durch Größe und Monumentalität imponierte. Dieser scharfe Gegensatz zwischen Drinnen und Draußen[12] wurde durch die Gestaltung der Westfassade noch stärker pointiert (Taf. 2.1). Aus der Sicht der Stadt war die West- zugleich die Hauptfassade. Da sich der Hügel, auf dem der Palast errichtet war, nur gegen Westen zu einem geräumigen Platz öffnete, spricht man hier berechtigterweise von der Stadtseite des Palastes. Diese Westfassade war eine hohe, blanke Mauer ohne ein großes Tor oder Propylon, statt dessen mit einem Eingang, der sich, wie Beyer bemerkte, eher unauffällig an der Seite des hier vorspringenden Teils der Westfassade öffnete[13]. Der bescheidene Charakter dieses Palasttores stand in keinem harmonischen Verhältnis zur

3 Driessen 2004, 75-6.

4 Driessen 2002, 8-13; Hamilakis 2002, 188. Im Zuge dieses neuen theoretisches Ansatzes werden anstelle des konnotativ belasteten Begriffs 'Palast' den neutralen Bezeichnungen *court-centred building* oder *court-compound* der Vorzug gegeben.

5 S. neben den oben erwähnten Ansätzen auch Vansteenhuyse 2002, 240-1.

6 Zum orientalischen Palast als Begriff und historisches Konzept s. Novak 1999, 313-22.

7 Die anderen kretischen Paläste haben nur spärliche oder keine Freskofragmente geliefert.

8 Zum Begriff des ‚Hofes' als soziales System in der Antike und der Neuzeit s. Winterling 1997.

9 S. Chapouthier und Demargne 1942, 71-2; Schachermeyr 1964, 119-20: „[...] auch deutet nichts darauf, dass die Paläste durch architektonisch geschlossene Fronten als etwas Besonderes zu wirken versuchten. [...] Die eigentliche „Front" der Paläste richtete sich daher nicht nach außen, sondern nach innen, nach dem Palasthof".

10 S. Graham 1987, 27, 238-9; Matthäus 2000, 57, 61.

11 Palyvou 2002, 171-2; 2004, 216.

12 Zu einem Versuch der schärferen Unterscheidung zwischen dem privaten und öffentlichen Bereich antiker Hofarchitektur am Beispiel frühhellenistischer Residenzen s. Hesberg 1996. Eine derart präzise Bestimmung des Privaten und Öffentlichen in den minoischen Palästen wäre wegen der misslichen Überlieferungslage *a priori* zum Scheitern verurteilt.

13 Beyer 1987, 214.

Größe und Monumentalität der Fassade und des Gebäudes im Allgemeinen[14]. Der Palast öffnete sich also dem Besucher als prunkvolle Architekturfassade erst von innen[15].

Wenn wir annehmen wollen, dass die Hauptfassade eines repräsentativen Gebäudes nicht nur praktische Funktionen erfüllte, sondern auch einen symbolischen Gehalt hatte, dann richtete die monumentale Westfassade[16] des knossischen Palastes eine unmissverständliche Botschaft an den Betrachter: Durch ihren nicht einladenden, sondern abgrenzenden Charakter fungierte diese hohe Mauer als Trennwand zwischen Innen und Außen, zwischen der höfischen Elite und der breiten Masse der Bevölkerung[17]. Der im Verhältnis dazu enge Südwest-Eingang ermöglichte einen streng regulierten Zugang in das Palastinnere und festigte auf symbolischer Ebene die Spaltung zwischen den beiden sozialen Sphären[18]. Es ist merkwürdig, dass diese Funktion der ‚Stadtseite‘ des knossischen Palastes als nicht zu überschreitende räumliche und gesellschaftliche Barriere bislang in ihrer Bedeutung nicht angemessen gewürdigt wurde[19].

DER ZENTRALHOF: *THE PLACE TO BE*

Nehmen wir die trennende Funktion der Westfassade als Ausgangspunkt und versuchen wir nun die beiden Höfe als Austragungsorte von Festen und Zeremonien zu betrachten. Beginnen wir – wie könnte es anders sein – mit dem Zentralhof. Die absolute Dominanz dieser unbebauten offenen Fläche stellt das wichtigste diagnostische Merkmal minoischer Palastarchitektur dar[20]. Die meisten orientalischen Paläste sind um ein kompliziertes System von Höfen gruppiert[21], doch in keinem Fall dominiert ein Zentralhof das Entwurfsschema einer Herrscherresidenz so erdrückend wie auf Kreta. Wie lässt sich die übermäßige Größe des minoischen Zentralhofes erklären? Versuche, diese Dimensionen durch bautechnische Überlegungen wie die Notwendigkeit der Lüftung, Belichtung und Kommunikation der Palastflügel zu begründen, mögen seine Existenz, jedoch nicht seine Größe erklären. Bedenkt man, dass ein abgeschlos-

14 Der geschlossene Charakter der Außenfassaden lässt sich auch in den anderen kretischen Palästen beobachten. Die einzige Ausnahme stellt der Palast von Phaistos mit der monumentalen Treppe im Nordteil der Westfassade dar. Diese überdimensionierte Freitreppe und die hintereinandergeschalteten Querräume des großflächigen Propylon stehen allerdings nicht im Einklang mit den drei engen, versetzten Eingängen, zu denen sie führen, und machen daher eine Funktion dieses Raumkomplexes als Passage sehr unwahrscheinlich (Noack 1908, 12-3). Die Vermutung von van Effenterre (1987, 86-7) und Marinatos (1987, 140), dass es sich dabei nicht um einen Prachteingang, sondern um eine Zuschauertribüne handelte, scheint demzufolge viel plausibler. Gestützt auf einige überlegenswerte Argumente ging Beyer 1987 sogar einen Schritt weiter und erkannte an diesem Raumkomplex des Palastes von Phaistos ein festes ‚Raummodul‘, das auch in Knossos, Mallia und Kato Zakros vorkommt und seiner Meinung nach als Tempel diente.

15 Diese exquisit ausgestalteten Fronten des Zentralhofes scheinen einen bildlichen Niederschlag in den knossischen Miniaturfresken gefunden zu haben, s. Nörling 1995, 57-8 Taf. 9, 1 und 9, 3; Boulotis 1990, 445-6; vgl. ferner die Architekturdarstellung auf einem SM II-zeitlichen knossischen Gefäßfragment, Nörling 1995, 58 Taf. 9, 4. Einen Eindruck, wie ein kretischer Palast von außen wahrgenommen wurde, vermittelt uns vielleicht der massive, turmartige Gebäudekomplex auf dem sogenannten *Master Impression* aus Chania, s. Hallager 1985, 19-21 Abb. 10-1, 15, 17; Nörling 1995, 70.

16 Zur Monumentalität der knossischen Westfassade s. Hägg 1987, 129, der allerdings hier die Existenz eines ‚Erscheinungsfensters‘ vermutet.

17 Die Trennung zwischen einem öffentlichen Vorhof (*babānu*) und einem intimen Wohn- und Festhof (*bītānu*) stellt ein Grundprinzip der Raumordnung assyrischer Palastarchitektur dar, s. Heinrich 1984, 186-7. Diese Spaltung beider gesellschaftlicher Sphären begegnet uns bereits im Palast von Mari (Heinrich 1984, 68-81). Der Unterschied zu den minoischen Palästen besteht darin, dass der öffentliche Hof keine offene *piazza*, wie in Kreta, sondern in das Baugefüge des Palastkomplexes eingegliedert ist.

18 S. Driessen 2004, 79: „[...] entering the complex implies a transition from one world, open to the view of the public, to another, hermetically closed off. The narrowness of the pathway to follow, with a funnel effect at the entrance implies a line-up of individuals and a selection process, whereas the wide open space of the courts themselves suggests much larger crowds“.

19 Nur van Effenterre (1987, 86) hat sich nachdrücklich für diese Funktion der Westfassade ausgesprochen: „In a word, the West side of a Minoan palace is a *front*, not a *façade*. It is intended to be looked at from the town as a stop, or to give a dominant and privileged view onto the esplanade, and the town behind, from the upper stories of the palace, without direct contact“; s. ferner Palyvou 2004, 214: „In this confrontation (sc. between town and palace domain) the palace has raised an imposing and impregnable façade, whereas the town is, in a sense, in retreat“.

20 Davis 1987, 161; Palyvou 2002, 167.

21 Heinrich 1984, *passim*.

sener Zentralhof nie zu den typischen Merkmalen minoischer Hausarchitektur gehörte[22], drängt sich die Frage um so stärker auf, warum ein so großer Teil des minoischen Palastkomplexes von einem offenen, von außen unsichtbaren Hof eingenommen wurde. Ausgehend von den obigen Überlegungen zu einer scharfen Trennung zwischen dem palatialen und ‚städtischen' Raum der kretischen Gesellschaft ist es legitim zu vermuten, dass diese Größe von der Bedeutung des Zentralhofes als höfischer Mikrokosmos bedingt war. Der überdimensionierte Platz im Herzen der Residenz bot einen ‚sterilen' Lebensraum für die Mitglieder der palatialen Elite, eine von außen abgeschottete Welt, die durch die monumentalen Fassaden abgeschlossen wurde. Diese Fassaden, die alle vier Seiten des Hofes umgaben, bildeten eine kompakte, geschlossene architektonische Kulisse. Es handelt sich dabei, wie bereits erwähnt, um die eindrucksvollsten Fassaden der minoischen Architektur mit Quadermauerwerk, Öffnungen, Säulen- und Pfeilerreihen, überdachten Stoas, Balkonen mit hölzernen Balustraden und Verandas, die zusammen aus dem Zentralhof den ‚Luxusherd' der minoischen Gesellschaft machten, einen adäquaten Raum für das Leben der ‚feinen Leute' und eine wirkungsvolle Kulisse für die Durchführung ritueller oder zeremonieller Handlungen[23]. Doch der Zentralhof war offensichtlich etwas mehr als ein exquisiter Lebensraum für die höfische Elite.

Die Frage nach seiner symbolischen Dimension rückte in den letzten Jahren immer deutlicher in den Mittelpunkt der wissenschaftlichen Aufmerksamkeit. Palyvou betonte seine Rolle als räumlicher und performativer Fokus des Palastes und folglich der minoischen Gesellschaft[24]. Driessen plädierte für eine Bedeutung als kosmologisches Zentrum der minoischen Kultur oder als rituelle Landschaft, die ein typisches kretisches Landschaftsbild, eine von Bergen umgebene Ebene, reproduzierte[25]. Shaw[26] and erst kürzlich Goodison[27] haben ferner die strenge Nord-Süd-Orientierung des Zentralhofes hervorgehoben, die möglicherweise von der Lage der rituellen Räume an den Hoffronten diktiert wurde, die nach Tageslicht und Sonnenlauf ausgerichtet waren. Seltsam ist allerdings, dass bislang niemand jene symbolische Dimension des Zentralhofes angesprochen hat, die wir als einzige vielleicht auch archäologisch fassen können, nämlich die eines Erinnerungsortes. Die Tatsache, dass sieben Meter unterhalb des Niveaus des Zentralhofs die Ruinen einer Siedlung des akeramischen Neolithikums liegen[28], der ältesten uns bekannten Siedlung auf der Insel, welche durch sechs Meter mächtige neolithische Schichten überlagert wird, ist zwar allseits bekannt, doch hat sie bei der Diskussion über den symbolischen Gehalt des Zentralhofes kaum eine Rolle gespielt. Es ist unwahrscheinlich, dass die Erbauer und Herren des Palastes diesen Bezug des Platzes zu Ur-Knossos nicht instrumentalisierten. Die Wiege der Stadt als unbebaute Gedenkstätte, die von der Palastelite in Alltag und Ritual besetzt wurde, könnte eine wirkungskräftige symbolische Grundlage zur Legitimierung von machtpolitischen Ansprüchen geboten haben. Nimmt man eine Bedeutung des Zentralhofs als Ort der Erinnerung an, dann liegt es nahe zu vermuten, dass sich die hier ausgeführten staatstragenden Rituale auf Gründungsmythen der Stadt bezogen haben. Die Tatsache, dass der Zentralhof von Knossos wahrscheinlich bereits seit der FM-Zeit[29] ein offener, unbebauter Platz im Zentrum einer ständig anwachsenden Stadt war, scheint die besondere Bedeutung dieses Areals zu bestätigen.

Zu den interessantesten Merkmalen der minoischen Zentralhöfe von Knossos, Phaistos und Mallia gehören ferner ihre Größen und Proportionen. Diese offenen Flächen zeigen in allen drei großen Palästen ein festes Länge-Breite-Verhältnis zwischen 1:2,2 und 1:2,5 und – noch wichtiger – trotz der unterschiedlichen Größe der Paläste ein sehr ähnliches Ausmaß (53 x 28 m)[30]. Der Zentralhof erweist sich also wegen seiner genormten Maße nicht bloß als offener Platz, sondern als Arena performativen Handelns[31], dessen Charakter wir leider nicht erschließen können. Die Bildmedien verewigen Feste, Prozes-

22 Palyvou 2002, 168-9.
23 Palyvou 2002, 171-3; Driessen 2004, 77.
24 Palyvou 2002.
25 Driessen 2004, 77, 80.
26 Shaw 1973, bes. 56-8.
27 Goodison 2004, bes. 342-6.
28 Evans 1994, 6 Abb. 3; Efstratiou u. a. 2004, 43-8 Abb. 1.3 Tabelle 1.1.
29 S. hierzu Driessen 2004, 78. Ausgehend von den Ergebnissen der Sondagen im Bereich des Zentralhofs datiert Evans (1994, 16) die ersten Nivellierungsarbeiten in die FM-Zeit.
30 S. Palyvou 2002, 171.
31 S. auch Driessen 2004, 75.

sionen, Faustkämpfe, ja sogar Stierspiele, die vor einer repräsentativen architektonischen Kulisse stattgefunden haben[32], doch für jede dieser Möglichkeiten fehlt der endgültige Beweis ihrer Lokalisierung am Zentralhof. Es ist jedenfalls realistischer anzunehmen, dass ein Stier durch die Gänge des Palastes zum Zentralhof für die Austragung des minoischen Stierspiels geführt wurde[33], als dass sich hier eine Menschenmasse versammelte, um einer Zeremonie oder einem anderen Spektakel beizuwohnen – eine Vermutung, die neuerdings immer beliebter wird[34]. Wie wahrscheinlich ist es, dass der knossische Zentralhof als Ort der Zusammenkunft einer größeren Menschengruppe diente? Eine solche Funktion stünde mit der, von verschiedener Seite propagierten, herausragenden symbolischen Bedeutung dieses Platzes in Widerspruch. Denn dadurch wird der Zentralhof vom performativen Raum zum Versammlungsort, vom Ort außeralltäglicher Erfahrungen zum einfachen Nutzungsraum degradiert. Zuschauermenge zum einen und symbolische Bedeutung bzw. Wirkung des Zentralhofs als Kulisse zum anderen sind meiner Meinung nach zwei entgegengesetzte Größen. Nur die Stoas und die Balkone könnten als Zuschauertribünen fungiert haben[35], allerdings für eine sehr kleine Gruppe von Menschen, nämlich der höfischen Elite. Der geschlossene Charakter des Palastes und nicht zuletzt die Tatsache, dass es auf dem Zentralhof keine festen Installationen gibt, die als Zuschauerränge hätten dienen können, machen es sehr unwahrscheinlich, dass sich hier zu bestimmten Anlässen eine größere Menschengruppe versammelte. Offener Raum ist in diesem Fall nicht mit öffentlichem Raum gleichzusetzen.

Der Westhof: eine Schnittstelle

Verlassen wir nun den inneren Kern des minoischen Palastes und richten wir unsere Aufmerksamkeit auf den gepflasterten Westhof (Taf. 2.1), der integraler Bestandteil aller drei großen Paläste war (Knossos, Phaistos und Mallia). Dabei handelte es sich eigentlich nicht um einen Hof, sondern um einen großen, offenen Platz ohne streng definierbare Grenzen, eine piazza pubblica, die offensichtlich einen liminalen Charakter hatte, da sie zwischen der urbanen und palatialen Sphäre eingebettet war[36]. Die wichtigsten Zeugnisse baulicher Ausgestaltung, die durch bestimmte zeremonielle oder rituelle Bedürfnisse diktiert war, sind neben der Pflasterung die Schautreppen, die wir aus Knossos und Phaistos kennen, und – wichtiger noch – die sogenannten Prozessionswege. Rechtwinklig angeordnete Schautreppen liegen in Knossos und Phaistos am Nordrand der Westhöfe[37]. In Knossos zeigen sie sehr flache Stufen, die nur als Stehtribüne hätten dienen können (Taf. 3)[38]. Wegen ihrer kleinen Größe ist davon auszugehen, dass hier ein erlesenes Publikum Platz hatte, um einen Ritus, einer Zeremonie oder einem athletischen Spektakel beizuwohnen.

Das auffälligste Merkmal des Westhofes sind allerdings die erhöhten Plattenwege, die in der Regel eine Breite von 1,0 m, auf dem knossischen Westhof 1,40 m, aufweisen (Taf. 2.2, 4, 5)[39]. Ihre besondere Funktion und Bedeutung wurden durch das verwendete Material intensiviert, da sie aus Licht reflektierenden weißen Kalksteinen bestanden, die sich farblich von den dunkleren Pflastersteinen einer Strasse oder eines Platzes hervorhoben[40]. In Knossos lief ein solcher Prozessionsweg mitten auf der *Royal Road*, einer schnurgeraden prachtvollen Strasse, die den *Little Palace* mit dem Westhof verband. Am Westhof zeigte er eine verzweigte diagonale Wegführung (Taf. 4). Der gerade Weg endete an der vorhin erwähn-

32 Nörling 1995, 51-64 Taf. 10, 1-3; VII, 1.
33 S. Graham 1957; Pelon 1982.
34 S. Driessen 2002, 9; Palyvou 2002, 176; ferner Gesell 1987, 126 Anm. 12, nach deren Berechnung der Zentralhof als potenzieller Versammlungsplatz für 1698 hockende und 5435 stehende Personen hätte dienen können. Gesell erkennt allerdings die Unzulänglichkeit solch statistischer Überlegungen, die den Zentralhof des Palastes von Knossos nur mit Zuschauern füllen und keinen Platz für den Grund ihrer Zusammenkunft übrig lassen.
35 S. auch Gesell 1987, 126 Anm. 12.
36 Damiani Indelicato 1982, 53-82; Preziosi 1983, 107; Driessen 2004, 79; Palyvou 2004, 214-5.
37 Evans 1928, 578-87 Abb. 362-5; Marinatos 1987, 139.
38 S. Marinatos 1987, 137.
39 Evans 1928, 577-8; Damiani Indelicato 1982, 29-32, 36, 38, 40, 42, 57-63, 66, 70, 107, 115-6, 118, 131, 155, Taf. II-VII, X-XIV; Palyvou 2004, 214; ferner Marinatos 1987, 137.
40 Palyvou 2004, 214.

ten Schautreppe, die von Evans als *Theatral Area* bezeichnet wurde (Taf. 5)[41]. Eine weitere Abzweigung führte direkt in den Südwest-Eingang des Palastes.

Diese Prozessionswege lagen nicht nur in der unmittelbaren Umgebung des Palastes, sondern waren auch Teile eines ausgedehnten Zirkulationsnetzes. Sowohl Palyvou[42] als auch Driessen[43], die vor kurzem unsere Aufmerksamkeit auf dieses ausgedehnte Netz von Plattenwegen lenkten, vermuteten hier eine primär praktische Funktion: Die erhöhten Plattenwege sollen den Stadtverkehr organisiert und eine gewisse Hierarchie der Zirkulation festgelegt haben. Als zentripetale Wegweiser lenkten sie, ihrer Meinung nach, den Besucher direkt an einen der Eingänge des Palastes und akzentuierten dabei die Rolle dieses Baukomplexes oder sogar des Zentralhofs selbst als Zentrum der Stadt.

Von besonderem Interesse ist, was mit diesen Plattenwegen an einer, aus architektonischer, administrativer und ritueller Sicht, sehr neuralgischen Stelle des Palastgebäudes geschah, nämlich seinem Eingang. Der verhältnismäßig breite Plattenweg, der zum Südwest-Eingang des Palastes führte, endete dort nicht, sondern wurde in den inneren Kern des Gebäudes fortgeführt. Palyvou, die diesem auffälligen Merkmal ihre besondere Beachtung schenkte, sprach sich für ein symbolisches Eindringen in das Gebäude durch die Stadt aus, das sie als ein weiteres Indiz für den öffentlichen Charakter dieses Gebäudes betrachtete[44]. Vor dem Hintergrund einer Interpretation der Westfassade des Palastes als Barriere in räumlicher und sozialer Hinsicht ließe sich allerdings genau das Gegenteil behaupten und eine kultisch-zeremonielle Funktion der Plattenwege annehmen. Die Tatsache, dass sie eine hervorgehobene Verkehrsführung markierten und die Grenze der palatialen Sphäre durchbrachen, indem sie in den Palast eindrangen, ist ein sprechendes Zeugnis für ihren königlichen oder zeremoniellen Bezug. Sie könnten die Wege des Königs markiert haben, wenn er sich außerhalb des Palastes bewegte, bzw. die Wege von königlichen oder kultischen Prozessionen. Dadurch würde der Unterschied zwischen König und Untertanen bzw. zwischen alltäglichem und außeralltäglichem Verkehr explizit gemacht. Sie könnten folglich wie ein roter Teppich fungiert haben, der bis ins Palastinnere ‚gerollt' war und nur an der Grenze des Zentralhofs endete, am absoluten Kristallisationspunkt der königlichen Präsenz, wo eine solche liminale Markierung sinnlos war[45]. Nicht die Stadt drang also in den Palast ein, sondern umgekehrt der Palast griff in die Stadt ein. Es war die königliche Präsenz, die durch Prozessionen und ihre steinerne Spur (die erhöhten Prozessionswege) ein zeremonielles Spinnennetz über die Stadt spannte, ein Netz, in dessen Zentrum die glanzvolle Manifestation des Königtums stand, nämlich der Palast.

Die Bildmedien

Unsere Möglichkeiten, den minoischen Hof als Schauplatz zeremonieller Handlung zu betrachten, wären an dieser Stelle ausgeschöpft, hätten wir nicht die bildlichen Quellen, die eine besondere Vorliebe für die Schilderung von Festen und Zeremonien zeigen. Zwei Miniaturfresken aus dem Nordflügel des Palastes, das sogenannte *Grandstand Fresco* und das *Sacred Grove and Dance Fresco* monopolisieren seit ihrer Veröffentlichung das wissenschaftliche Interesse und spielen eine Schlüsselrolle bei jedem Versuch, die Funktion des knossischen Palastes als zeremonielles Zentrum zu beleuchten[46]. In beiden Fällen handelt es sich um eine moderne Zusammenstellung von meist nicht zusammengehörigen Fragmenten. Die genaue Stelle der Fragmente im rekonstruierten Bild ist dadurch nicht gesichert. Nach einhelliger Meinung schildern beide Szenen eines oder verschiedene große Feste im bzw. am Palast von Knossos. Die beiden Bilder werden in der Regel als Ausdruck einer Dualität des performativen Raumes in Knossos betrachtet, als eine Darstellung des Drinnen und Draußen zeremonieller Aktivität in der minoischen

41 Zu einer ähnlichen räumlichen Beziehung zwischen Zuschauertribüne und Prozessionswegen am Westhof des Alten Palastes von Phaistos s. Marinatos 1987, 137.

42 Palyvou 2004, 213-6.

43 Driessen 2004, 79-80.

44 Palyvou 2004, 214-6.

45 S. hierzu Palyvou 2002, 173: „It is important to emphasize the fact that no causeways interrupt the unity of the central Court: there is no need to specify crossings from one point to another; the importance lies in being there. The absence of causeways in another indication of the non-urban nature of this open space".

46 Evans 1930, 46-80.

Hauptstadt: das *Sacred Grove and Dance Fresco* (Taf. 6.1) soll Feste oder Zeremonien verewigt haben, die unmittelbar außerhalb des Palastes stattgefunden haben, das *Grandstand Fresco* (Taf. 6.2) ähnliche Handlungen im Zentralhof desselben. Die Darstellung zahlreicher Zuschauer in beiden Bildern wird in der Forschung nahezu einmütig als Beleg für die Funktion beider Palasthöfe als Versammlungsorte einer größeren Menschengruppe betrachtet[47]. Wie richtig ist diese Sicht der Dinge?

Was die erste Szene anbelangt, in der die Darstellung einer vollen Zuschauertribüne im Mittelpunkt steht, hat man bereits richtig erkannt, dass der Ort des dargestellten Ereignisses der Westhof des knossischen Palastes gewesen sein muss[48]. Die erhöhten Prozessionswege und ihre Anordnung zeigen eine frappante Ähnlichkeit mit den vorhin angesprochenen Prozessionswegen, die heute noch auf dem Westhof des Palastes zu sehen sind. Der Schauplatz der zweiten Szene ist durch eine üppige architektonische Kulisse definiert: eine dreiteilige Struktur mit Säulen und Kulthörnern, ein Hof sowie Treppenanlagen mit Säulen. Auch hier werden die erhaltenen Teile der Szene durch das Publikum dominiert. Von den Zuschauerrängen heben sich Frauen in eleganter Bekleidung hervor, die entweder stehend oder sitzend dargestellt sind. Einer *communis opinio* zufolge weisen die reich gegliederte Front und der rechteckige Hof auf ein Ereignis hin, das sich am Zentralhof des Palastes abspielte[49]. An der dreigeteilten Fassade des Miniaturfreskos glaubte man sogar den ebenfalls dreigeteilten ,Zentralhofschrein' an der Westfront des Zentralhofs des Palastes erkennen zu können[50]. Die Annahme dieser gängigen Interpretation würde bedeuten, dass der Zentralhof des Palastes der Austragungsort von ,Veranstaltungen' war, denen eine größere Personengruppe beiwohnte. Auf den erhaltenen Fragmenten dieser Szene sind immerhin etwa 450 Zuschauer in kursorischer Weise wiedergegeben[51]. Wie realistisch ist es anzunehmen, dass der knossische Palast, dieses introvertierte Herrschaftsgebäude anlässlich eines großen Festes seine Tore für eine größere Gruppe von Leuten öffnete, die durch die engen Gänge den Zentralhof betraten, um dort den festlichen Höhepunkten beizuwohnen? Das Unbehagen, das ein solcher knossischer ,Tag der offenen Tür' auslöst, wird zwar durch die von mehreren Seiten geäußerte Vermutung gemildert, dass an diesen höfischen Festen im Palastinneren nur ein erlesener Kreis von Teilnehmern anwesend war[52]. Die Annahme eines elitären Publikums, das ein Zugangsrecht zum knossischen Palast hatte, findet aber keine ikonographische Bestätigung. Gegen die Vermutung einer förmlichen Versammlung von privilegierten Mitgliedern der herrschenden Elite spricht ferner die wahrscheinliche Präsenz von Kindern unter den Zuschauern[53].

Die hier dargestellten Zuschauer sind in derselben Weise wiedergegeben, wie das Publikum des *Sacred Grove and Dance Fresco*. Innerhalb einer der beiden Szenen wird allerdings zwischen den Zuschauern deutlich unterschieden: Die elegant gekleideten Frauen des *Grandstand Fresco*, die als wahre Blickfänger dienen, lassen sich durch die Kleidung, den prominenten Platz und die Bedeutungsgröße vom einfachen und kursorisch gezeichneten Publikum deutlich absetzen. Die Vermutung, dass hier ein Klassenunterschied zwischen Mitgliedern der palatialen Elite und Personen aus den niederen sozialen Schichten zum Ausdruck gebracht werden sollte, erscheint gerechtfertigt. Die Deutung dieser Szene als Schilderung eines Festes am Zentralhof hätte daher die Annahme einer ,offenen' Veranstaltung im Kern der Residenz als logische Konsequenz, was nach den obigen Überlegungen nicht plausibel ist.

Die gängige Deutung dieses Bildes stößt auf ein weiteres Problem, das aus der jetzigen Anordnung und Rekonstruktion der vorhandenen Freskofragmente hervorgeht. Diese und alle anderen Rekonstruktionsversuche setzen ins Zentrum des Geschehens keinen performativen Akt, sondern wieder ein Publi-

47 Bei der Gruppe, die den Ereignissen am Zentralhof beiwohnte, geht man generell von einem privilegierten Personenkreis, der Zugang zum Palastinneren hatte, aus, siehe z.B. Driessen 2004, 80.

48 Marinatos 1987, 141-2; Davis 1987, 157-9; Immerwahr 1990, 65.

49 Siehe z. B. Davis 1987, 159-60; Immerwahr 1990, 65; Nörling 1995, 58-9.

50 Evans (1930, 48) selbst hat sich zwar bei der Rekonstruktion der architektonischen Reste des 'Zentralhofschreins' an der Fassade des Freskos orientiert, vermied aber letztere als Darstellung ersterer zu deuten.

51 S. Davis 1987, 161.

52 Palyvou 2002, 176: „assembly of people with ruling power." Hier sei ferner auf die wilde Vermutung von Davis (1987, 160-1) hingewiesen, die am *Grandstand Fresco* ein Jugendtreffen von etwa 1000 Personen am Zentralhof des Palastes erkennen will.

53 Davis 1987, 159.

kum. Das Ergebnis ist eine sonderbare ikonographische Konstellation, die in der bisherigen Forschung meist kritiklos akzeptiert wurde: ein Publikum blickt auf ein anderes Publikum[54].

Sowohl auf der Ebene der Realität, als auch auf der Ebene ihrer Reflexion in den Bildmedien erheben sich Zweifel am traditionellen Verständnis des *Grandstand Fresco*. Lassen wir das Problem der Zuverlässigkeit der Rekonstruktion beiseite[55], das nur durch eine neue sorgfältige Untersuchung der Freskofragmente angegangen werden kann, und konzentrieren uns auf die Frage der Lokalisierung der dargestellten Handlung. Ist es möglich, das Festgeschehen an einem anderen Ort anzusiedeln? Palyvou hat erst vor kurzem hinter dieser dreiteiligen Struktur kein Heiligtum, wie Evans meinte, sondern eine Art Bildchiffre für den minoischen Palast vermutet[56]. Nach ihrer Meinung sei die Anzahl der Säulen (drei) nicht zufällig, sondern unterliege einer künstlerischen Konvention, um Vielzahl und dadurch eine ganze Säulenreihe zu versinnbildlichen. Diese Konvention ist uns aus der ägyptischen Ikonographie recht gut bekannt, in der Dreier-Gruppen als Sinnbild für den Plural gelten[57]. Palyvou hat eine sehr überzeugende Vermutung für die Logik aufgestellt, die hinter dieser verkürzten Darstellung steckte: Da der Zentralhof als leere Fläche nicht darstellbar ist, konnte man diesen symbolträchtigen Raum nur durch die ihn abschließenden Fassaden unmissverständlich abbilden: Die Säulenreihe war das diagnostische Merkmal des Zentralhofes, der Zentralhof das diagnostische Merkmal des Palastes, also symbolisierte die Säulenreihe den Palast selbst[58]. Infolge dieser einfachen, doch überzeugenden Gleichsetzung darf man vermuten, dass die Säule bzw. das dreiteilige Gebäude als Sinnbild des Zentralhofes und dadurch des Palastes verstanden werden konnten, das bildliche Äquivalent des mykenischen Qualitativs *wa-na-ka-te-ro* der Linear B-Schrift (dem König zugehörig). Wenn die dargestellte Fassade nicht 'wörtlich' als ein bestimmter Teil des Palastes, sondern als Bildmetapher das ganze Gebäude oder eine ganz andere Anlage in seiner unmittelbaren Nähe[59] repräsentiert, dann ist es möglich, das geschilderte Ereignis nicht im, sondern am Palast zu lokalisieren, wie bereits Marinatos, Warren und Shaw vermuteten[60].

Welche Zeremonie oder welches Spektakel könnten der Grund dieser Zusammenkunft der knossischen Elite und Stadtbevölkerung gewesen sein? Die hier dargestellten Säulen ermöglichen eine Verknüpfung dieses Bildes mit zahlreichen Szenen aus verschiedenen Medien der Neupalastzeit, die eine zeremonielle Handlung oder ein (rituelles) Spiel thematisieren. Was bezweckte diese erstaunlich konsequente Darstellung von einem markanten architektonischen Element im Zusammenhang mit rituellen, zeremoniellen oder sportlichen Handlungen? Nichts anderes als die unmissverständliche Lokalisierung der Handlung in einem definiten architektonischen Rahmen und unvermeidlich auch an einem definiten Zeitpunkt. In jedem dieser Fälle handelte es sich offensichtlich nicht um eine Versinnbildlichung der Handlung *per se*, nämlich einer Prozession, eines Stierspiels, eines Faustkampfes, sondern um die Schilderung eines konkreten Festes an einem konkreten Schauplatz.

Fazit

Am Beginn der hier ausgeführten Überlegungen stand der Gedanke, dass der minoische Palast durch seine Monumentalität und Geschlossenheit soziale Schranken aufbaute und das asymmetrische Verhältnis zwischen Elite und Stadtbevölkerung zementierte. Im Gegensatz zu neueren Ansätzen, die den Palast als ein im Prinzip urbanes Konzept ansehen, ein semi-öffentliches zeremonielles Gebäude, wurde hier eine diametral entgegengesetzte These vertreten, nach der dieser gewaltige Baukomplex vom Volk als eine ‚verbotene Stadt', das Nest des Herrschers und des ‚Hofstaates' wahrgenommen wurde – eine Deu-

54 Die Paradoxie dieser Rekonstruktion führt zu nicht weniger paradoxen Schlüssen, s. Immerwahr 1990, 65: „According to this topographical interpretation the „event" for which the crowds have gathered would not have been depicted in this particular painting".

55 S. hierzu die von Marinatos (1987, 139) geäußerten Zweifel.

56 Palyvou 2002, 175.

57 Bietak 2000, 224-6.

58 Möglich ist, dass auch einzelne Säulen als verkürzte Darstellung repräsentativer Säulenarchitektur und somit des Palastes selbst fungierten. Denn mit Ausnahme der anspruchsvollsten Villen, die selbst wie kleine Paläste gebaut waren, blieb die Säule ein exklusives Merkmal palatialer Architektur.

59 S. hierzu Shaw 1996, 187: „[...] built as display of pageantry and as a backdrop for grand occasions [...]".

60 Marinatos 1987, 139-40; Warren 1994, 192-4; Shaw 1996, 186-7.

tung, die mit dem Charakter von Palastanlagen von der Antike bis in die Gegenwart konform ist. Bei der separaten Behandlung von architektonischen Befunden und bildlichen Quellen ging es weniger um den Versuch einer definitiven Lösung, sondern viel mehr um eine bessere Gewichtung der Argumente. Denn für mich ist das bautechnische Konzept des Palastes ein handfesteres Argument als die Aussage eines Bildes, deren Rekonstruktion und Deutung mit einigen Problemen behaftet ist. Die architektonische Textur des knossischen Palastes scheint den Bedürfnissen eines introvertierten Lebensstils der höfischen Elite unterworfen worden zu sein. Der Zentralhof, dieser Ort des Besonderen, fungierte wohl als exklusiver Lebensraum für die ‚feinen Leute‘ und stellte bei Audienzen oder anderen Hofzeremonien eine standesgemäße Kulisse für die prachtvollen Selbstinszenierungen des Herrschers vor einem erlesenen Publikum dar. Der architektonische Befund leitet uns zur Vermutung, dass nur der Westhof des Palastes, dieser Ort der Zusammenkunft zwischen Herrscher und Beherrschten, einen geeigneten Schauplatz zur Visualisierung der königlichen Macht vor der Öffentlichkeit bot. Doch über die Problematik des Innen und Außen des minoischen Hofes hinaus steht fest, dass uns die Leute, die den Palast und die Stadt von Knossos in der Neupalastzeit bevölkerten, vor allem als eine Festgemeinschaft vor Augen treten. Hier kann es keinen Zweifel darüber geben, dass die Festlichkeiten ein Medium der Inszenierung kollektiver Identität waren. Durch ihre sozial-integrative Funktion festigten sie soziale Strukturen und bestätigten den politischen *status quo* der minoischen Gesellschaft. Abschließend lohnt es sich, unseren Blick noch einmal auf das bemerkenswerte Bild eines jubelnden Publikums zu richten, das im Kontext der Hochkulturen des 2. Jahrtausends v. Chr. und später noch eine singuläre Erscheinung bleibt. Diese Darstellungen hatten sicherlich keine propagandistische Absicht, denn sie stammten aus den inneren Palasträumen und waren daher nicht an die einfache Bevölkerung, sondern an einen elitären Kreis gerichtet, nämlich die Hausherren und ihre Gäste. Über ihren Realitätsgehalt könnte ein Skeptiker zweifeln. Was jedoch außer Zweifel steht, ist, dass sie ein sehr sprechendes Zeugnis für die Absichten der Mächtigen sind, die hinter der Veranstaltung von palatialen Festen und Zeremonien standen. Was hier versinnbildlicht wird, ist eigentlich das Bild eines freigiebigen, guten Königs, der sein Volk mit (Brot und) Spielen versorgte. Die einfachen Leute johlten vor Begeisterung am Tag des großen Festes, um dann – wie es Octavio Paz in seinem *Labyrinth der Einsamkeit* so treffend formulierte – „für den Rest des Jahres besser schweigen zu können“.

BIBLIOGRAFIE

Beyer, I. 1987. „Der Palasttempel von Phaistos.“ In Hägg und Marinatos 1987, 213-25.

Bietak, M. 2000. „The Mode of Representation in Egyptian Art in Comparison to Aegean Bronze Age Art.“ In *The Wall Paintings of Thera. Proceedings of the First International Symposium, 30 August – 4 September 1997, Petros M. Nomikos Conference Centre, Thera, Hellas*, herausgegeben von S. Sherratt, 209-46. Athen: Petros M. Nomikos and The Thera Foundation.

Boulotis, Chr. 1990. „Villes et palais dans l’art égéen du IIe millénaire av. J.-C.“ In *L’habitat égéen préhistorique. Actes de la Table Ronde internationale organisée par le Centre National de la Recherche Scientifique, l’Université de Paris I et l’École française d’Athènes (Athènes, 23-25 juin 1987)*, herausgegeben von P. Darque und R. Treuil, 421-59. Bulletin de Correspondance Hellénique Suppl. XIX. Athen: École Française d’Athènes.

Cadogan, G., E. Hatzaki, und A. Vasilakis, Hrsg. 2004. *Knossos: Palace, City, State. Proceedings of the Conference in Herakleion Organised by the British School at Athens and the 23rd Ephoreia of Prehistoric and Classical Antiquities of Herakleion, in November 2000, for the Centenary of Sir Arthur Evans’s Excavations at Knossos*. British School at Athens Studies 12. London: British School at Athens.

Chapouthier, F. und P. Demargne. 1942. *Fouilles exécutées a Mallia. Troisième rapport. Exploration du palais, bordures orientale et septentrionale (1927, 1928, 1931, 1932)*. Études Crétoises 6. Paris: Librairie Orientaliste Paul Geuthner.

Damiani Indelicato, S. 1982. *Piazza pubblica e palazzo nella Creta minoica*. Rom: Jouvence.

Davis, E. 1987. „The Knossos Miniature Frescoes and the Function of the Central Courts.“ In Hägg und Marinatos 1987, 157-61.

Day, P.M. und M. Relaki. 2002. „Past Factions and Present Fictions. *Palaces* in the Study of Minoan Crete." In Driessen u. a. 2002, 217-34.

Driessen, J. 2002. „‚The King Must Die'. Some Observations on the Use of Minoan Court Compounds." In Driessen u. a. 2002, 1-13.

—. 2004. „The Central Court of the Palace at Knossos." In Cadogan u. a. 2004, 75-82.

Driessen, J., I. Schoep, und R. Laffineur, Hrsg. 2002. *Monuments of Minos. Rethinking the Minoan Palaces. Proeccedings of the International Workshop „Crete of the hundred Palaces?" held at the Université Catholique de Louvain, Louvain-la-Neuve, 14-15 December 2001*. Aegaeum 23. Liège und Austin: Université de Liège, Histoire de l'art et archéologie de la Grèce antique and University of Texas at Austin, Program in Aegean Scripts and Prehistory.

Efstratiou, N., A. Karetsou, E. S. Banou, und D. Margomenou. 2004. „The Neolithic Settlement of Knossos; New Light on an Old Picture." In Cadogan u. a. 2004, 39-49.

Evans, A. 1921. *The Palace of Minos. A Comparative Account of the Successive Stages of the Early Cretan Civilization as Illustrated by the Discoveries at Knossos*. Band 1. London: Macmillan and Co.

—. 1928. *The Palace of Minos. A Comparative Account of the Successive Stages of the Early Cretan Civilization as Illustrated by the Discoveries at Knossos*. Band 2. London: Macmillan and Co.

—. 1930. *The Palace of Minos. A Comparative Account of the Successive Stages of the Early Cretan Civilization as Illustrated by the Discoveries at Knossos*. Band 3. London: Macmillan and Co.

Evans, J.D. 1994. „The Early Millennia: Continuity and Change in a Farming Settlement." In Evely u. a. 1994, 1-20.

Gesell, G. 1987. „The Minoan Palace and Public Cult." In Hägg und Marinatos 1987, 123-7.

Goodison, L. 2004. „From Tholos Tomb to Throne Room: Some Considerations of Dawn Light and Directionality in Minoan buildings." In Cadogan u. a. 2004, 339-50.

Graham, J.W. 1957. „The Central Court as the Minoan bull-ring." *American Journal of Archaeology* 61: 255-62.

—. 1987. *The Palaces of Crete*. Überarbeitete Neuausgabe. Princeton: Princeton University Press.

Hägg, R. 1987. „On the Reconstruction of the West Facade of the Palace at Knossos." In Hägg und Marinatos 1987, 129-33.

Hägg, R. und N. Marinatos, Hrsg. 1987. *The Function of the Minoan Palaces. Proceedings of the Fourth International Symposium at the Swedish Institute in Athens, 10-16 June, 1984*. Skrifter utgivna av Svenska Institutet I Athen 4°, 35. Stockholm: Paul Åströms Förlag.

Hallager, E. 1985. *The Master Impression. A Clay Sealing from the Greek-Swedish Excavations at Kastelli, Khania.* Studies in Mediterranean Archaeology 69. Göteborg: Paul Åströms Förlag.

Hamilakis, Y. 2002. „Too Many Chiefs? Factional Competition in Neopalatial Crete." In Driessen u. a. 2002, 179-99.

Heinrich, E. 1984. *Die Paläste im alten Mesopotamien*. Denkmäler antiker Architektur 15. Berlin: de Gruyter.

Hesberg, H. v. 1996. „Privatheit und Öffentlichkeit der frühhellenistischen Hofarchitektur." In *Basileia. Die Paläste der hellenistischen Könige. Internationales Symposion in Berlin vom 16.12.1992 bis 20.12.1992*, herausgegeben von W. Hoepfner und G. Brands, 84-96. Mainz: von Zabern.

Immerwahr, S.A. 1990. *Aegean Painting in the Bronze Age*. University Park u.a.: Pennsylvania State University Press.

Marinatos, N. 1987. „Public Festivals in the West Courts of the Palaces." In Hägg und Marinatos 1987, 135-42.

Matthäus, H. 2000. „Die minoischen Paläste. Architektur und Funktion." In *Im Labyrinth des Minos. Kreta – die erste europäische Hochkultur*, herausgegeben von H. Siebenmorgen, 57-72. Archäologische Veröffentlichungen des Badischen Landesmuseums 2. München: Biering & Brinkmann.

Noack, F. 1908. *Ovalhaus und Palast in Kreta. Ein Beitrag zur Frühgeschichte des Hauses*. Leipzig u.a.: B.G. Teubner.

Nörling, T. 1995. *Altägäische Architekturbilder.* Archaeologica Heidelbergensia 2. Mainz: von Zabern.

Novak, M. 1999. *Herrschaftsform und Stadtbaukunst. Programmatik im mesopotamischen Residenzstadtbau von Agade bis Surra ma ra'ā*. Schriften zur Vorderasiatischen Archäologie 7. Saarbrücken: Saarbrücker Druckerei und Verlag.

Palyvou, C. 2002. „Central Courts: the Supremacy of the Void." In Driessen u. a. 2002, 167-76.

—. 2004. „Outdoor Space in Minoan Architecture: „Community and Privacy"." In Cadogan u. a. 2004, 207-17.

Pelon, O. 1982. „Le palais de Malia et les jeux de taureaux.“ In *Rayonnement grec. Hommage à Charles Delvoye*, herausgegeben von L. Hadermann-Misguich und G. Raepsaet, 45-57. Brüssel: Éditions de l'Université de Bruxelles.

Preziosi, D. 1983. *Minoan Architectural Design. Formation and Signification.* Approaches to Semiotics 63. Berlin: Mouton Publishers.

Schachermeyr, F. 1964. *Die minoische Kultur des alten Kreta.* Stuttgart: Kohlhammer.

Schoep, I. 2002. „The State of the Minoan Palaces or the Minoan Palace/State?“ In Driessen u. a. 2002, 15-33.

Shaw, J.W. 1973. „The Orientation of the Minoan Palaces.“ In *Antichità cretesi. Studi in onore di Doro Levi*, herausgegeben von G. Pugliese Carratelli und G. Rizza, Band 1, 47-59. Cronache di Archeologia 12. Catania: Universitá di Catania – Istituto di Archeologia.

Shaw, M.C. 1996. „The Bull-Leaping Fresco from Below the Ramp House at Mycenae: a Study in Iconography and Artistic Representation.“ *Annual of the British School at Athens* 91: 167-90.

Van Effenterre, H. 1987. „The Function of Monumentality in the Minoan Palaces.“ In Hägg und Marinatos 1987, 85-7.

Vansteenhuyse, K. 2002. „Minoan Courts and Ritual Competition.“ In Driessen u. a. 2002, 235-45.

Warren, P.M. 1994. „The Minoan Roads of Knossos.“ In *Knossos. A Labyrinth of History. Papers Presented in Honour of Sinclair Hood*, herausgegeben von D. Evely, H. Hughes-Brock und N. Momigliano, 189-210. London: British School at Athens.

Winterling, A. 1997. „„Hof“. Versuch einer idealtypischen Bestimmung anhand der mittelalterlichen und frühneuzeitlichen Geschichte“. In *Zwischen „Haus“ und „Staat“. Antike Höfe im Vergleich*, herausgegeben von A. Winterling, 11-25. Historische Zeitschrift, N.F., Beih. 23. München: Oldenbourg.

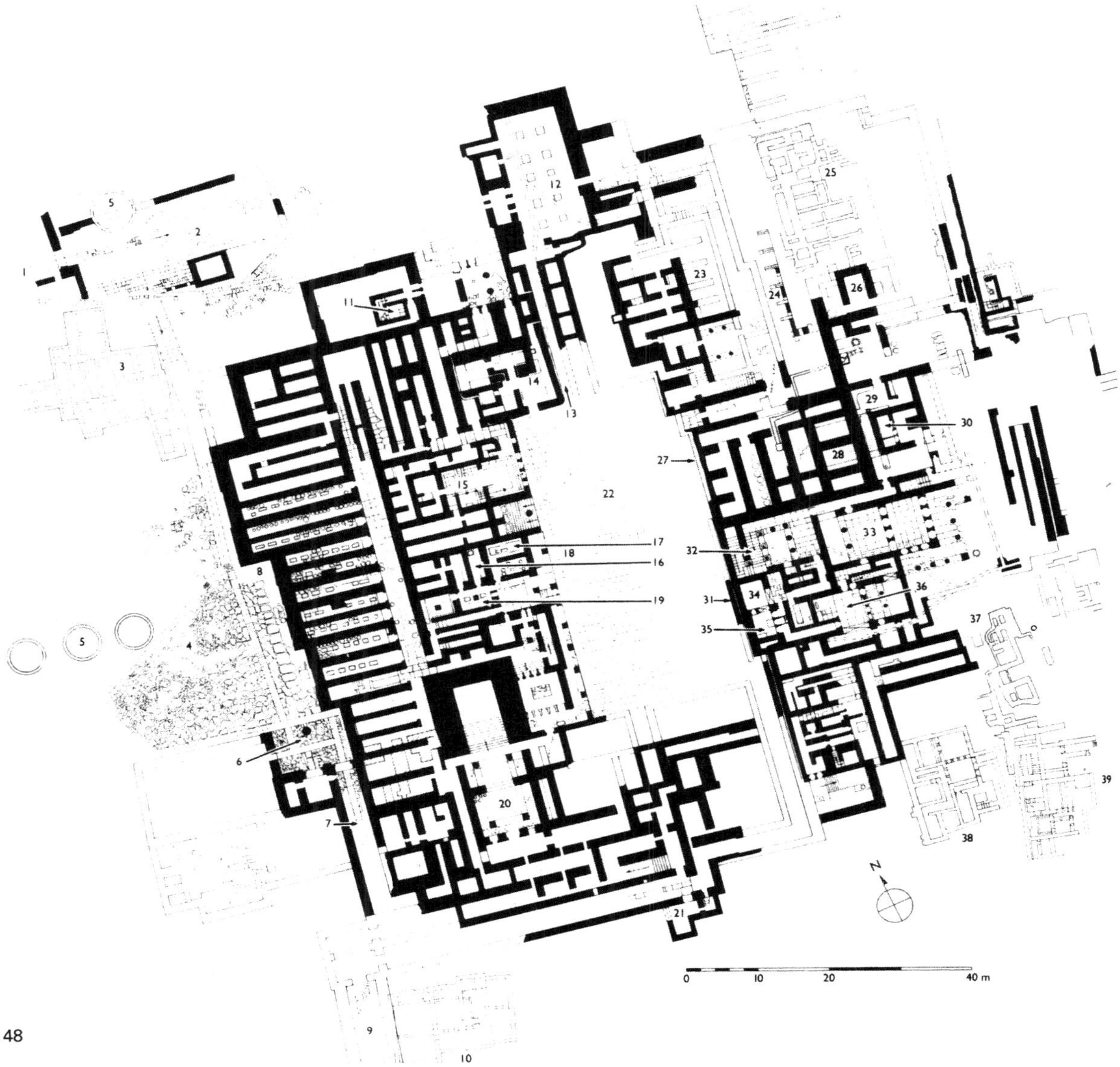

48

1 Prozessionsstraße
2 Schautreppe
3 Nordwestliches Schatzhaus
4 Westhof
5 Kouloures (Gemauerte Schächte)
6 Westliche Eingangshalle
7 Korridor mit Prozessionsfresko
8 Westmagazine
9 Stufenportikus (Südaufgang)
10 Südhaus
11 Lustralbassin
12 Nördliche Pfeilerhalle
13 Nordeingang
14 Pforte
15 Thronsaal
16 Vorratsraum
17 »Schatzgruben« im Zentralheiligtum
18 Dreiteiliges Heiligtum
19 Pfeilerkrypten
20 Südpropylon
21 Südliche Eingangshalle
22 Zentralhof
23 Nordostmagazine
24 Stallungen(?)
25 Magazine
26 Magazine
27 Osthalle
28 Wohnräume
29 Wohnräume
30 Werkstatt
31 Wohnräume
32 Großes Treppenhaus (»Grand Staircase«)
33 Halle der Doppeläxte
34 Wohnräume
35 Wohnräume und Bad
36 Halle der Königin
37 Pfeilerkrypta
38 »House of the Chancel Screen«
39 Südosthaus

Der minoische Palast von Knossos (Gesamtplan). Nach: Matthäus 2000, Abb. 48.

1. Westhof und -fassade des Palastes von Knossos (von NW). Aufnahme: Verfasser.

2. 'Prozessionsweg' auf dem Westhof des Palastes von Knossos. Aufnahme: Verfasser.

Knossos: Schautribüne (Theatral Area) am Westhof (von S). Nach: Evans 1928, Abb. 363.

Knossos: Royal Road mit Verzweigung der Prozessionswege (von O). Aufnahme: Verfasser.

Knossos: Royal Road mit Prozessionsweg. Im Hintergrund die Schautribüne (Theatral Area) am Westhof des Palastes (von W). Aufnahme: Verfasser.

1. Das *Sacred Grove and Dance* Fresco. Nach: Marinatos 1987, Abb. 7.

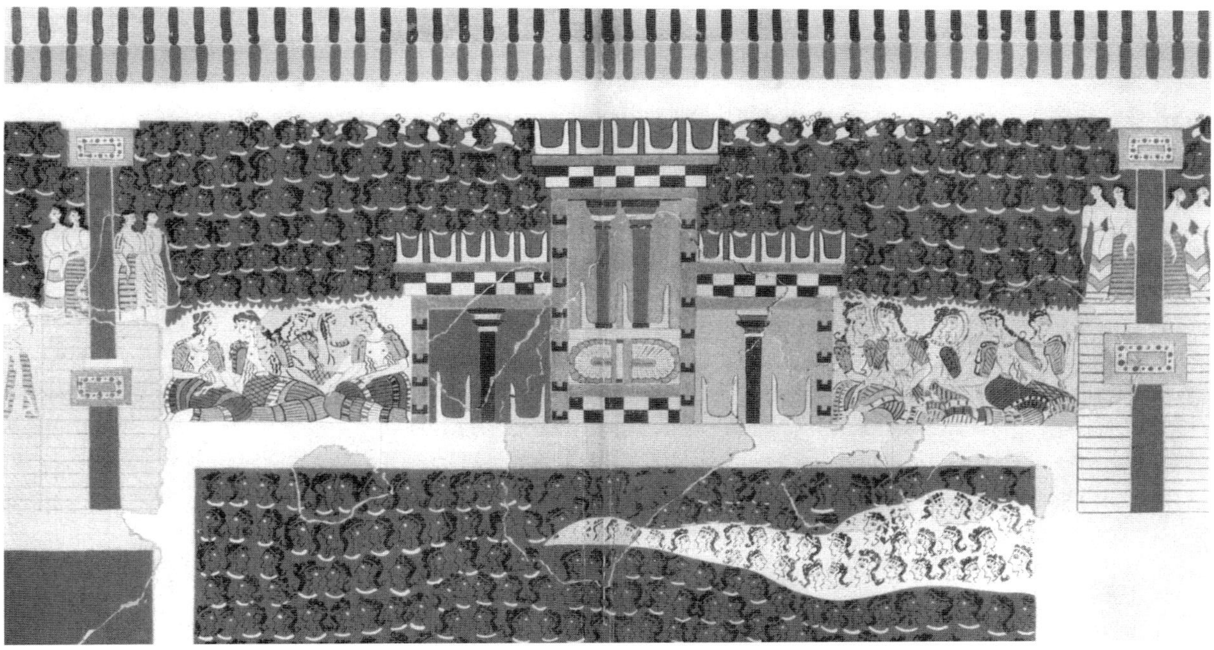

2. Das *Grandstand Fresco*. Nach: Evans 1930, Taf. XVI.

The Social Production of Space and the Architectural Reproduction of Society in the Bronze Age Aegean during the 2nd Millennium B.C.E.

James C. Wright

Introduction[1]

As a study of the human past, the primary method of archaeology is the placement of its subjects in space and time. Since the subjects are material, the remains of the built environment are obviously central to this task. In its analytical and interpretive mode archaeology focuses on how humans in the past produced space through building. In this sense, space and time are not universal abstracts but rather, as E. Casey states, "contained in places"[2]. Place is for him an existing "plenary presence permeated with culturally constituted institutions and practices"[3]. Archaeological places, then, are the remnants of these institutions and practices located in a fragmentary spatio-temporal grid. How archaeologists make sense of such a fragmentary past is a question of general hermeneutics[4]. Preeminent to this is architecture, which, as Connerton observes, is an "incorporating practice", that is, one that defines and is defined by the movements and actions of humans[5]. The trick for archaeologists is to try to discover something about the practices incorporated within architecture. These are, of course the practices of its occupants and the interpretations of its passersby, which are relative, continuous, and multiple[6]. The task therefore is further constrained by the limitations of our ability to understand the many intentions of creators, users, and viewers of architecture over a span of time we can usually only guess at[7].

I am grateful to Joseph Maran for inviting me to participate in this conference, for hosting me at Heidelberg and for so generously sharing his ideas about the problems addressed in this paper. Much of my interest in this topic was stimulated by my son Nicolaus, to whom I am indebted for his insights on Heidegger's thoughts about building and dwelling. I also wish to acknowledge the help in organizing my thoughts of students who participated in my seminar: Ulrich Thaler, Tobias Mühlenbruch, Malgorzata Siennicka, Bogdan Atanassov, Theodoros Giannopoulos and Jan Trenner. I also thank Matthew Johnson, John Barrett, Diamantis Panagiotopoulos, John McEnroe, Mary Dabney, Dimitris Nakassis, Donald Haggis, Jack Davis and John Bennet. Not least, I am indebted to the participants in the Heidelberg conference whose stimulating papers and excellent discussion, aided me in sharpening my ideas.

1 Abbreviations used in the text are EM – Early Minoan (Early Bronze Age), MM – Middle Minoan (Middle Bronze Age), LM – Late Minoan (Late Bronze Age), EH – Early Helladic (Early Bronze Age), MH – Middle Helladic (Middle Bronze Age), LH – Late Helladic (Late Bronze Age).

2 Casey 1996, 33.

3 Casey 1996, 46.

4 Connerton (1989, 14) on the possibility of an historical reconstruction; (1989, 95-6) on Schleiermacher's idea of a general hermeneutic.

5 Connerton (1989, 100-1) on the difference between 'inscribed practice' and 'incorporated practice'; see also Casey 1996, 21.

6 Eco 1980, 27-34.

7 Even as Baedekers were dispensing authoritative information for tourists, Mark Twain was mercilessly deconstructing them and showing how often the history of a monument has been rewritten and reinvented, see for example Twain (1899, 1: 177-9) on Notre Dame and on his visit to the holy monuments of Jerusalem (Twain 1899, 2: 327-47).

A Theory of Human Space

Although the experience of space is biological, its production is socio-cultural and its perception is inculcated[8]. Thus, the explanations different persons give of their experiences vary according to their individual and social perceptions. Yet the biological experience of space is fundamentally the same: movement through nature and movement through the built environment, which supplements and constrains that movement for human purposes. Through movement, the senses organize space in time: the past is background and the present foreground. The production of architecture organizes the experience of movement into the rhythm of constructed time. Architecture therefore is instrumental in the creation and organization of memory. As Connerton argues, the process of remembering in a social sense requires the bodily practice of commemoration[9]. This is something we do daily, as when we set an alarm clock, toll bells to mark different times of the day, or broadcast the call to prayer. Likewise, calendars regulate society's commemorations. All of these devices remind us when to remember and direct us to go where commemoration takes place, that is to the locales where memory is embodied: work places, schools, places of worship, cemeteries, plazas, and so forth. These places invariably contain built objects that, through their form and shape and through visual devices that display the components of commemorative ceremony, figuratively and literally queue us in proper order and cue us how properly to commemorate.

Architecture, whether a stele or a building, reproduces society by defining social relations and thereby prompts performance. Performances are bodily actions that literally incorporate social, natural and cosmic relations. Performance in this sense is commemoration. Buildings facilitate commemorative performance by reproducing and producing social relations. They are entirely bound up with the production of memory. They contain it, preserve it and divide it. They direct us to places where it resides. They enframe us and the places of memory and thereby focus our attention on them. As intentional devices, buildings control movement and the production and reproduction of memory.

The first performance of architecture is its construction[10]. We all stop to watch as masons chisel stone blocks and as cranes lift them into place, or even as a bricklayer trowels his mortar for the next row, and a carpenter nails his beams into place. These are bodily practices. They are customary habits, even rituals, for building is a craft – a tradition that is taught by a master who inculcates through his example and explanation the right movement of body and muscle, until the movement is written into the sinews and marked on the bones. What is taught is an expression of values that is manifest in every element of the built form, from mortise and tenon to carved ronceau, from doorway to building plan[11].

Building takes place in a landscape in which and out of which the built thing will come into being. The acquisition of materials requires transportation through the landscape, transformation of the materials into things for building (mud or clay for brick, wood for timbers, lime for cement, etc.) and then again a selection among them for each construction. A builder has to know his materials and, as Lefebvre emphasizes, his matériel (the processes, procedures, instruments of production, directions, and agenda – also termed the rules)[12]. In a non-specialist setting this knowledge involves for the builder wide-ranging practices throughout and within a region, such as making tools, knowing where the best stone is

8 The following discussion is informed by my reading of Casey (1996), Connerton (1989), Tuan (1977), and Heidegger (1954).

9 Connerton 1989, 72-3.

10 See Lefebvre's (1991, 113) discussion of the production of an object and emphasis on understanding the inseparability of object and productive labor.

11 Heidegger 1954, 147-9. As a craft, the construction of architecture materially reproduces, either explicitly or implicitly, the multiple dimensions of being – not just Heidegger's 'das Geviert' (earth, heaven, humans, divinities) but also Tuan's (1977, 34-50) human-centered experience of place: front, back, left, right, up, and down. This framing of space constrains it. No longer are the heavens above and the earth below; instead they are outside, and thus walls, floors, and ceilings by the act of enclosing also separate and distance. Just so, Heidegger (1954, 158-9) observes, a bridge materializes the relation between one realm and another. But this physical act of dwelling does not lead inevitably to Cartesian dualism. Taylor (1993, 333) emphasizes in his appreciation of Heidegger's achievement in philosophy that Being, or in this case Dwelling as engaged agency, is not Dwelling without there being a context, and the context is not neutral, as rationalists claim, rather *ursprünglich* (natural and primordial) and *zuhanden* (ready to hand). See also Casey 1996; Merleau-Ponty 1962, 421, passim.

12 Lefebvre 1991, 71, 104-5; for rules see Glassie 1975; see also McEnroe 1990, 197-8.

located, even planning ahead and planting trees, for example cypresses for roof beams. Thus, the act of building is also one that in different ways integrates and reflects the landscape. Little wonder then, how one senses in the architecture of a region its local flavors and peculiarities and how various yet integrated they are as they range from simple hut to grand edifice[13]. In this way, builders incorporate the landscape into their works, and this leaves behind important information about the social meaning of buildings and of the relationship and value of the landscape in buildings.

What of the things built? As dwelling, buildings house people, animals, foodstuffs, tools, clothes, the dead, and memories and metaphors (as Bachelard showed)[14]. In this way, buildings house many practices. Those not within the dwellings are outside, but their place is in relation to the building. These practices may be immediately in front of the building or behind it, at one side or the other, or under or over it. They may be outside but enclosed by a wall or enclosed within a structure outside the dwelling. Or the practice may be elsewhere – not in relation to the dwelling alone but in relation to it and other dwellings (such as a communal oven) or the entire community (a springhouse). As one extends farther outside, there are practices that are assigned to the landscape (farming, herding, timbering), but, for the house dweller and the village dweller, the landscape is in relation to the built spaces of dwelling. The rows of cypresses that mark out the Tuscan landscape in relation to its *casa colonica*, the hedges and field walls of the English landscape, the section lines and barbed wire fences of the American Midwest are all in relation to the places of dwelling. Even the desert, as a metaphor of absence, is perceived as without dwelling.

Archaeological Implications

For archaeology, the implications of these considerations lead us to a sharper understanding of what methods can be derived for the recovery and study of the material remains. I assert that past societies can be studied and partially understood from a study of the built environment by paying attention to the practice of building and to buildings as evidence of social practice. This is often considered metaphorically as the 'reading of texts', but built things are neither merely texts nor symbols. The craft of the builder is much less explicit than that of the writer, if only because the builder is not trained to think he is making something that will be 'read'; instead he builds something that will be used and inhabited, likely for generations. The durability of the built environment opens it up to multiple, continuing and adaptive uses; therefore, its 'meaning' is only graspable by studying its use over time and in changing contexts.

To do this we must remember that our explanations must reflect the spatial and temporal dimensions of the evidence we have, notably that our explanations be couched in language that is active rather than static. By starting with study of the evidence for the craft of building, we can trace out its practice through time and space. In this way local and external as well as vernacular and high style craft will be distinguished, their relation to each other recognized, and the dynamics of social processes identified. From such a beginning, we proceed to the study of building remains, first an attempt at a contextual, and then a functional assessment. Then we can examine how the remains of the built environment manifest social relations, political economy, ideology, and belief systems. Finally, through examination of changing practices and concepts in the use and deployment of the built environment, broader historical and comparative conclusions may be drawn.

As examples, I will explore and contrast the two traditions of architecture in the Aegean during the sec[illegible] millennium B.C.E., namely those of the so-called Minoan society on the island of Crete and the s[illegible] Mycenaean society on the mainland of Greece. The accompanying timeline clarifies the rela[illegible] between the two cultures (Abb. 1). The floruit of the Cretan is marked by two phases known as [illegible] and Neopalatial, namely periods when centralization is characterized by the formation of regional [illegible]e building complexes. These were successive and spanned approximately the first two-thirds of the

13 No wonder also, that in our modern world, this sense of the local is disturbed by the introduction into the built landscape of wholly foreign structures constructed from nothing local and owing their style and plan not to the community but to a globalized community largely alienated from its materials and relations of production.

14 Bachelard 1964.

Crete = Minoan	Mainland = Mycenaean
EM • ca. 2800-2000	*EH* • ca. 2800-2000
MM I-IIB = Protopalatial • ca. 1900-1750	*MH* • ca. 1900-1600
MM III –LM II = Neopalatial • ca. 1750-1450	*LH I-II = Early Mycenaean* • ca. 1700-1450
LM III = Postpalatial • ca. 1450-1200	*LH IIIA-B = Palace period* • ca. 1450-1200

Abb. 1. Timeline of Minoan and Mycenaean cultures.

second millennium B.C.E. The Mycenaean culture is in large part derived from the Minoan and its 'palatial' phase follows that of Neo-palatial period Crete, covering only about 250 years in the latter half of the second millennium B.C.E. It is important to keep this temporal and dependent relationship in mind when comparing the practices of building and interpreting the social dimensions of buildings and their uses in these different societies.

The Production of Space in Minoan Society

MORTUARY FACILITIES

I begin with a brief analysis of the mortuary facilities of Early and Middle Bronze Age Crete. In general, mortuary custom was to house the dead in collective structures built some distance from places of habitation[15]. In fact, the degree of centralization at mortuary sites seems much greater than that of habitation sites, such that it may be ventured that the location of mortuary complexes provided a central social locus for the burying groups[16]. The architecture of these places reflects the general structure of social relations. At the site of Koumasa, we find built spaces that on the one hand enclose and contain and on the other provide a formal place for assembly (Taf. 7.1). The round tombs function like storage jars for holding undifferentiated items. The pavings outside them are places of commemoration. Both are constructions that retain memory. They are places where the dead reside together in a past of memory and where the living congregate to recall the past through the habits of customary practices, which are performed on the open space of the pavings and within the enclosed spaces of the tombs. Some of the paved plazas are approached by a built path, as at Myrtos-Pyrgos[17], and the path directs the procession to the tombs, and thereby prescribes the bodily practices inherent in procession. The repetition of all these practices (from building to burying) instantiates memory and thereby provides the necessary background against which the individuals of a community and the community as a collective act in and experience the present[18].

Other instances of built mortuary facilities, at Mochlos and at Palaikastro for instance, exhibit a different structure for containing the dead, although with the same purpose of col-lective storage. These are rectangular receptacles that permit expansion by the closing of rooms and the addition alongside of others (Taf. 7.2). Although this practice was employed in the round structures, as seen in examples at Kamilari and Lebena, the advantage of working with rectangular forms was recognized by the builders, as demonstrated in the Roussolakos complex at Palaikastro[19]. In the mortuary complex at Chrysolakkos

15 Branigan 1992, 80-95, 124-7; Soles 1992, 243-55; Sakellarakis and Sakellaraki 1997, 246-52.
16 Branigan 1992, 127-41.
17 Cadogan 1978, 71-4, figs. 4-5.
18 Connerton 1989, 79-88; Heidegger 1954; Taylor 1993, 325-9, passim.
19 Branigan 1970, 154-9.

at Mallia, built during the Protopalatial Period[20], we see large-scale storage of the dead in a monumental complex (Taf. 7.2). The monumentalization of this traditional form of deposition of the dead is an elevation in scale, magnitude, and craftsmanship. Surrounding the large building is a paved passage that at the east is flanked by columns or pilasters. The masonry consists of cut stone orthostates, some reused but bearing drill cuttings for dowels, so that we are permitted to think that in one stage of this building shaped wooden beams were attached to the orthostates to secure the superstructure, a practice well known in palatial construction[21]. The same development and transformation of mortuary practices and architecture are well known from Archanes, where the round tombs of the early custom are found alongside the rows of added rectangular storerooms, and even a so-called Pillar Crypt, commonly employed in the palaces, is part of the complex[22]. At Archanes during its Neopalatial phase, the dwelling of the dead and the dwelling of the living merge in architectural practice.

It is significant that many of these mortuary facilities continue to be used throughout the time during which the first palaces come into being, i.e. down into MM II, or, as in the case of Archanes, even through the Neopalatial period. In spatial terms, they signal continuity of a place in the landscape for the dead, something Dabney has suggested signals continuing claims of landholdings by local gentry[23]. The maintenance of commemorative spaces at these complexes signals the stability of habits and customs performed through bodily practices to preserve and carry forward collective memory. This is especially evident at Kamilari where, over the long life of this tomb, hundreds of up-ended conical cups and other offerings found on the paved court beside the mortuary building testify to the durability of Minoan social practices and local custom[24]. Another enlightening example is Tomb 19 at Archanes, which Maggidis has shown contained many generations of a lineage or family group and where the similarity of the kinds of objects deposited over time attests the continuity of the practice of commemoration of the dead[25].

SETTLEMENT ARCHITECTURE

I have claimed that building is an important bodily practice, and now I assert that the process of carrying forward the craft is an act of memory both in the institution of apprenticeship and in the production of space. The production of space is first an act of craft, for it is the craft persons who create a specific cultural or social built space that is part of the larger production and practice of collective memory. This they accomplish by deploying what are for them the familiar elements of their practice: site, plan, elevation, materials, forms, and techniques. I have suggested that two primary aspects of Minoan mortuary architecture reflect core characteristics of the Minoan social structure, namely the design of mortuary receptacles as collective containers of the dead and the construction of external pavings to facilitate the approach and gathering of the living for commemorative ceremonies for the dead. Now I wish to consider the built spaces of settlements.

Although there is a contentious history of interpretation of the meaning of the layout of the EM settlement of Fournou Korifi[26], it is surely uncontroversial to claim that the agglomerative plan of the settlement is better understood as resulting from a strong sense of communal relations than as one of independent (and self-subsisting) families. In a broad sense, the hamlet may be viewed as a container, possibly with a central gathering place at the interior. At Vasiliki, the EM remains outline the plan of basement rooms and therefore are not a reliable guide to the architectural plan, but it is surely significant that an early phase has a well-paved court adjacent at the west side (Taf. 7.3)[27]. In the domestic dwellings of the Middle Bronze Age, these two features are also recognizable. The best place to examine them is at Mallia, where examples can be studied from the earliest phases of the Protopalatial down through the Neopalatial (MMIA-LM IB). First, I observe how the rectangular form of additive storage

20 Constructed atop a building of MMIA date, the mortuary complex could be as early as MMIB, more likely MM II; Demargne 1945, 40-2.
21 Demargne 1945, 40-2; Shaw 1973, 70, ns. 3-4.
22 Sakellarakis and Sakellaraki 1997, 177.
23 Dabney and Wright 1990, 46.
24 Levi 1961-62, 18-9, 80-91.
25 Maggidis 1998.
26 Branigan 1975, 117; Warren 1972, 266-7; Whitelaw 1983, 324, 331-7; Tenwolde 1992.
27 Zois 1976, 44-5, 90-3.

room employed in the tombs of Eastern Crete (Mochlos, Palaikastro, and Zakros) was incorporated into domestic plans. In Quartier Mu, all of the buildings have storerooms of parallel magazines located inside the outer walls of the buildings (Taf. 8.1). This form of room also makes up the bulk of the plan of the Crypte Hypostyle (Taf. 8.2) and is found in the first phase of the palace[28]. The overall plan of the buildings, even as they become larger, more elaborate and more differentiated, is one that is more heterarchical than hierarchical, more agglutinative than linear, and has high values of integration in terms of space syntax analysis focusing on the courts as access points[29].

PALACE SETTLEMENT ORGANIZATION

Outside the buildings, attention is drawn to paved walkways that connect the buildings to the large paved plaza alongside the west façade of the palace and the so-called 'agora' plaza ringed around by clusters of small buildings (Taf. 8.2). How would people accustomed to gathering on pavings before collective burial chambers feel when seeing and walking on paved walkways that lead from building to building and that lead to grand open paved courts, such as the 'agora'[30]? Was the employment of these architectural techniques, materials and forms a natural, unplanned action of the builders (whether elites or craft persons) of these architectural ensembles? Or was it a conscious deployment of traditional elements of the built environment to aid in the establishment of a new order of power relations during this first period of the Minoan palaces? As an American who hails from a country with a very shallow building history and in which there are few organically evolved courts or plazas (Native American ones aside), I might think the Minoan courts must have been designed. But as a frequent visitor in Europe, especially in villages and towns with deep continuous histories, I recognize that these spaces are equally the products of collective practices. They are material expressions built by craft persons working in largely local traditions, and they come out of the web of social relations and structures through the repetition of historical performances of a social, religious, political and economic nature, and particularly the practice of commerce in agricultural and craft goods. It is hard to think, when looking at the complex of buildings of MM period Mallia (and thinking also of the early examples at Ayia Fotia, as well as smaller entities such as at Vasiliki) that they were the object of conscious design any more than the natural expression of existing practices[31]. I say this cognizant of the changing nature of the political economy from one characterized, as Haggis has termed it, of clustered, horizontally integrated networks of social relations towards extractive, vertical, and hierarchical ones[32]. In terms of social relations and social structures, the Middle Minoan palaces and their Late Minoan successors evince spatial forms and organizations that bespeak the long tradition of collective performance at common spaces. This tradition of building and using spaces in Bronze Age Crete has at its core procession to and gathering in a paved area before proceeding into the built space[33]. Originally, this was an expression of the collective structure of village society. In the periods of the palaces, these built forms embodied these collective practices and were instrumental in maintaining the collective spirit of society, even as a hierarchical, extractive political economy was being instituted.

This is why, I believe, the palaces and the 'mansions' and the simple houses are organized heterarchically, which is to say in a non-linear way[34]. There is, of course, a focused movement, from outside court through the architectural shell to the inner central court, and in this regard the focus of Minoan buildings – certainly of the palaces – could be considered to be linear and centripetal; however, since

28 Amouretti 1970, 25-6, plan I; Pelon 1980, 1982, 1986.

29 Hillier and Hanson 1984, 108-9.

30 van Effenterre and van Effenterre 1969, ix-xii, 141-5; Damiani Indelicato 1982, 23-4, 41-50.

31 Tsipopoulou 1990 on A. Fotia; on planning see McEnroe's (1990, 198-99) comparison of the similarities and differences in the vernacular houses of Gournia and Pseira.

32 Haggis 2002, 122-5, 129-33.

33 McEnroe (1990, 198; 2001, 43-6) provides vernacular examples in the paved vestibules of Pseira.

34 I originally conceived this as 'centrifugal' following a similar observation by John McEnroe in an unpublished study that he shared with me, and this was based on the notion that from a central point (i.e. the central court) movement through Minoan buildings dispersed outwards. Although this is true it neglects the obvious centripetal movement both from outside to the center of the court as well as from within the rooms of a building to its center, as argued by Palyvou (1987). Reconsidering this, I realized that the opposition of heterarchy to hierarchy (see Crumley 1995), where heterarchy is defined as a non-linear ordering of otherness was more apt.

the inner court is a gathering place or a theatral place[35], it is not conceived in social terms as a space focused upon audience or confrontation with a person (or deity) of high rank. This lack of focus on the individual, also much observed in Minoan iconography[36], leads me to suggest that the construction of space in Minoan society reflects a lack of emphasis on the individual and on individual relations and stresses instead activities of a more collective nature. Hence, persons coming into Minoan buildings, whether houses or palaces, first are directed to a central space and then choose different routes that disperse outwards into the specialized and segmented built spaces that are joined under a common roof (Taf. 8.2)[37]. This is also why an iconography of space is created by elite builders. Painted on frescoes, carved on reliefs, engraved on seals, and painted on pottery, the iconography represents the constructed space of walkways, courts, theatral areas, corridors, and central courts as active processions and gatherings, often focused on performances (such as bull leaping) or on architectural façades, such as 'tripartite shrines' where epiphanies occurred[38]. When we explore these in more detail, we see how, as the political economy of the palaces developed, there emerged a consciously constructed architectural vocabulary that was reiterated throughout the architecture controlled by the elite and through the representation of architecture, and was spread across the island as a part of the 'civilizing process' that created the uniform material culture we term Minoan.

John McEnroe has illustrated how vernacular forms are distinguishable from high style ones in his study of the architecture of Neopalatial Pseira[39]. This distinction is also seen at Kommos, where the LM I House with the Snake Tube sits on top the agglutinative arrangement of houses destroyed at the end of MMIII[40]. The contrast between the two signals the new organization of traditional space into a formal and ideologically structured plan, which succeeds by its incorporation of many of the elements of the traditional spatial arrangement. In like manner, the formalization of raised walkways and of paved courts, notably at Phaistos and Knossos, testifies to the formalization of commemorative ceremonies in and around the palaces. At Knossos, the miniature frescoes provide an explicit glimpse of the performance of ceremonies in such spaces, since they show, even when looking only at the fragments and not the restoration, indoor and outdoor scenes of formal gathering in relation to the palace. The so-called Sacred Grove Fresco is a gathering of males and females in an outdoor place marked out by raised walkways (Taf. 8.3). The indoor scene of the so-called Grandstand Fresco shows a crowd gathered on steps, next to columns, within a wall-surrounded court, and around a Tripartite Shrine[41]. These frescoes point also to the unusual Minoan practice of using architectural elements as icons. Columns, column capitals, altars, tripartite façades, raised walkways, gates or doors, the Minoan 'metope-triglyph', and 'horns of consecration' are all deployed separately or in combination in frescoes, in relief carvings, and on signet rings and seals[42]. Even terracotta models of buildings were common[43]. In the society of the Minoan palaces, the built environment was coded and was itself the code for social integration; it determined and was determined by the commemorative practices that defined and redefined age-old relationships, which themselves were deeply tied to a collective sense of belonging, not merely to other humans but also to the deities above and below.

35 Driessen (2002, 9-10) argues that the central court is for communal ceremonial gatherings, but Panagiotopoulos (this volume) argues that it is a place of performance and not of gathering; he believes that the central court was a place for restricted groups to view ritual ceremony.

36 Davis 1995; Younger 1995.

37 Sinos 1971, 48-9, 51, 62, 71; Palyvou 2002, 171-2; 1987, 195-203.

38 Palyvou (2002, 169) makes a good case for the courts as the creation of the governing elite; for tripartite shrines see Shaw 1978.

39 McEnroe 1990, 43-6.

40 House with the Snake Tube: McEnroe 1996, 199-202; Middle Minoan buildings: Wright 1996, 189-99.

41 Davis 1987, 157-61; Marinatos 1987, 141-2.

42 Krattenmaker 1991, 295-330; Boulotis 1990; Palyvou 2002, 175.

43 Lebessi 1976; Mersereau (1991, 55-90, 200-58) examines the corpus of Minoan models and in particular offers a re-examination of those from the Loomweight Basement that shows, in short, that the many fragments found by Evans likely belong to a full model, like that from Archanes.

SPACE, PERFORMANCE AND RELIGION

Epiphanies of deities occurred in Minoan religious practice, according to Hägg and Niemeier, who have argued for this form of ritual practice on the basis of iconography of seals and architectural settings, and it seems that 'tripartite shrines' were an important place for such rituals[44]. Connerton makes it clear that commemoration requires bodily practices that are recurrent performances outside of time, in which the practice in the present merges with the practice in the past. Modern humans, caught up in the quantified and commoditized cadence of capitalist production and consumption, do not easily comprehend how the representation of the epiphany of a deity is not a mere objective representation but instead a recurrent real event in which actors participate and actually engage with the deity. As Connerton puts it, these scenes are an "exact reproduction" of myth ready to come alive at the time prescribed by the calendar in a ritual performance in which the elites and others will re-enact the appropriate gestures, movements, processions, and other commemorative acts[45]. In like manner, the painted Minoan processions, scenes of bull jumping, or massed gatherings in a central court before a tripartite shrine are not things to observe, but events occurring in 'real time'. We lack only the verbal scripts and musical accompaniments (but just barely when we examine the Harvester Vase from Ayia Triada with its sistrum rattling singer) that provide the rhythm and auditory space for the repetition and reinforcement of collective memory for the participants[46].

The calendar that governs these re-enactments is unknown to us, although work by Catherine Trümpy indicates that indeed calendars that probably were derived from Late Bronze Age practice were used in the early Iron Age, and surely the cycle of seasons, special celestial events, and the cycle of the human condition from birth to death were moments for commemoration that were not confined to palaces and mortuary places[47]. A further integration of the landscape was effected through ceremonies from place to place, and here we have evidence to argue that many of the familiar markers were employed in these acts too. Built paved roads leading outwards from the palaces connected them with satellite communities and probably also to sanctuaries, not least to peak sanctuaries and caves[48]. These commemorations are depicted in frescoes, on relief vessels (likely used in these very rituals), and on signets and seals, and thus were present reminders of the continuing cycle of commemoration and reaffirmation of the cosmos and the position and duties of individuals within it.

The Production of Space in Mycenaean Society

The rituals and objects of Minoan society and the crafting of their representation were known to mainland visitors already during the Protopalatial period. As Minoan society evolved, the involvement in Cretan affairs of persons from the Greek mainland increased, and the signs of the impact of life in the Minoan courts on these visitors are registered in the material culture of the beginning of the Late Bronze Age, famously in the richly furnished tombs of the Shaft Graves at Mycenae. Hence, any study of the material remains of the so-called Mycenaean society that was emerging at this time must take account of the influence of Minoan culture on it. That notwithstanding, the material evidence of the Mycenaeans provides a complex picture of social groups that had their own well defined customs onto which they selectively grafted an eclectic mixture of Minoan cultural elements.

44 Hägg 1983; Niemeier 1986; Shaw 1978.

45 Connerton 1989, 66; see for example Geertz's (1980) famous description of the mortuary ritual for the dead Balinese king.

46 Connerton 1989, 61-71; Driessen 2002, 8-9; Marinatos 1987.

47 Trümpy (2001, esp. 237-41) on non-Doric and Mycenaean correlates; I thank Joseph Maran for bringing this work to my attention.

48 Peatfield 1987; Warren 1994, 207-10; Sakellarakis and Sakellaraki 1997, 71-3; Niemeier and Knoblauch 1992, 324-8; Chryssoulaki 1990; Tzedakis et al. 1990a, 1990b; Marinatos 1987, 137; Damiani Indelicato 1982; see also Cavanagh 2001.

MORTUARY ARCHITECTURE

The differences are immediately apparent in the architecture of mortuary customs. Beginning in the late Early Bronze Age burial on the mainland was individual, within a pit or cist, and by the end of the Middle Bronze Age the individuality of mortuary receptacles was emphasized in the development of large built cists, which could receive successive burials, and their placement in some instances at the bottom of deep shafts. At the same time, membership in social groups was emphasized by the placement of burials in cemeteries or in mounds or restricted grave circles. Although the construction of mounds and of built cists that could be opened for additional burials indicates the marking of burials, unlike the practice in Crete, there is no evidence of formalized construction of gathering places, such as pavings, for commemoration of the dead. Only at Mycenae, where carved limestone stelae were erected over some of the richest and most elaborate burials of the grave circles, is above ground architecture present[49]. Of course, this hardly means that the burying groups did not gather to commemorate the dead; it simply implies that whatever memorial activities they practiced were not considered to need a built space for their performance. This may mean, as I have written previously[50], that commemoration was primarily associated with the acts leading up to and including internment, or that subsequent commemoration was not marked in a material way that we have been able to trace. Since we do know that these mortuary receptacles (and those subsequently developed by the Mycenaeans) were reopened for later interments, it is worth questioning why there was not more marking of tombs or tomb sites than we recognize. The answer, I believe, is found in observing that Mycenaean mortuary practice consisted of clusters of individual burial receptacles for small burying groups whose memorial activities were largely focused on the underground architecture of these tombs.

As the so-called Mycenaean culture develops, two underground burial receptacles are introduced: *tholos* tombs, which are elaborate stone-built corbelled chambers, the tops of which are covered by a distinctive mound, and chamber tombs carved out of the hard marl or loosely cemented conglomerate. Both are for successive deposition, but whereas *tholos* tombs are restricted in number for use by the ruling elite, chamber tombs were the more ubiquitous, being the receptacle for officials and the lower orders, and they are arranged in cemeteries (Taf. 9.1). Both of these burial types are a linear architecture, expressed by the long entrance passageways cut into the slope-side, often more or less parallel to the others. As containers for successive depositions, they express linear relations within a family or kin group – quite different from the undifferentiated Minoan tombs with ossuaries. Aside from the remains found within the chambers that inform us of the practice of successive interment, the entrance passageways (known as *dromoi*, singular *dromos*) preserve evidence of having been reopened. Within them broken drinking vessels and other objects (including other interments, even in some instances horse burials) are frequently found, and these are strong evidence that commemorative ceremonies did take place and that they were performed by the limited burying group associated with each tomb. Thus the architectural and other evidence of Mycenaean mortuary custom, unlike that of the Minoans, leads to the hypothesis that the social structure of the Mycenaeans was focused on discrete groups, most likely families and their kin[51].

Chamber and *tholos* tombs are also sometimes built as house tombs. The entrance passage ends at a façade, which frequently has a doorframe cut into the rock face around the entrance. In elaborate ones, these façades carry cut relief depicting the beam ends of a roof above a door defined by inset jambs and a lintel[52], while the most elaborate of the *tholos* tomb entrances are flanked by highly decorative half-columns, which support another story of columns, beam ends and elaborately carved relief bands – possibly even figural scenes in relief – above the doorway (Taf. 9.2)[53]. Some of the chambers of these tombs are carved in the form of the interior of buildings with gabled roofs and even have fresco decora-

49 Some tombs of the Middle Bronze Age were marked: Dickinson (1983, 59) cites 16 of the c. 230 at Lerna as marked and, of course, tumuli by their nature were visible, but with the advent of chamber tombs marking seems largely to have disappeared.
50 Wright 1987, 174-6.
51 Dickinson 1983, 63-5.
52 See for example the recently excavated tombs at Ellenika north of Kalamata: Koumouzelis 1996.
53 E.g. the Treasury of Atreus at Mycenae: Wace 1949, figs. 49-51; Mylonas 1966, fig. 114.

TOMB	POSITION							TECHNIQUE	
	Chamber	Lintel	Stomion	Façade	Dromos base at façade only	Entire base of dromos	Entire dromos	Hammered	Sawn
Cyclopean									
Epano Phournos									
Aegisthus 1st		●							
Panagia		●	●		●				
Aegisthus 2nd		●			●				
Kato Phournos		●	●	●				●	
Lion		●	●	●				●	
Genii	●	●	●	●	●	●		●	●
Atreus	●	●	●	●	●	●	●	●	●
Klytemnestra	●	●	●	●	●	●	●	●	●

Abb. 2. Distribution of Conglomerate among tholoi at Mycenae.

ted benches as furnishings[54]. In this manner, the mainlanders expressed the importance of the individual and the household and in the elaborate tomb façades utilized architectural elements borrowed from the Minoans to express the power relations embedded in the palace as seat of power and authority.

CRAFT TRADITIONS

As was the case in Crete, we are able in examination of the architectural craftsmanship of Mycenaean mortuary construction to identify local practices that are elaborated and incorporated into the high style architecture of the palaces. First is the rapid spread of the *tholos* form. Invented in Messenia at the end of the Middle Bronze Age, it proliferated there during the first phase of the Late Bronze Age (LH I) but was otherwise only exceptionally employed elsewhere[55]. Beginning in LH IIA this form was adopted throughout the Peloponnese and Central Greece. The technical competence necessary to construct these monumental underground corbel-vaulted chambers with their entrances covered by massive monolithic lintels implies specialized knowledge and craft persons who traveled from place to place, either as independent or dependent workers. In some instances, elements of construction provide evidence of this, for example at Peristeria, where the limestone ashlar façade of *Tholos* 1 bears an incised sign of a double axe, which likely was the sign of a Minoan mason[56]. At Mycenae, there is abundant evidence to show that local masons developed a distinctive style of construction for the *tholos* tombs built there[57]. As Wace showed, the engineering knowledge of the masons improved as they became more familiar with the strength of the materials they used, and thus they increased the size of the tombs and elaborated the decorative qualities of the tombs. Local quarries were opened for the fine-grained soft limestone (*poros*) preferred for dressing façades and for the harder conglomerate preferred for monolithic blocks, primarily lintels. As the accompanying Abbildung 2 illustrates, as the masons became more proficient in the use of these stones, they employed them more extensively throughout the tombs. Of particular interest is the increase in the employment of conglomerate blocks in the Kato Phournos and Lion Tombs; in the latter these blocks are dressed in isodomic courses to create a very impressive entranceway into the

54 For example the tombs at Aidonia, esp. Tombs 7, 9 (Krystalli-Votsi 1996, 27, 31), the frescoed tombs at Thebes (Spyropoulos 1972) and some of the tombs at Ellenika (unpublished); it is important to point out, however, that there is much variety in the architectural form of the chamber, and Cavanagh and Mee (1998, 48, 65-70, 77) believe this is due to local conditions.

55 Cavanagh and Mee 1984; 1998, 48.

56 Vermeule 1964, 41, fig.6.

57 A total of nine tholos tombs were built between LH IIA and LH IIIB and, based on constructional techniques, they were categorized into types by A.J.B. Wace in 1923 (Wace et al. 1921-23, 283-402; Wace 1949, 16-9, 119-31); he ordered his types chronologically, and subsequent study has verified this stylistic developmental scheme.

chamber. This experiment led in the final phase to the construction of the entire tomb (entrance corridor, façade and entranceway, and chamber) of carefully dressed ashlar blocks of conglomerate. Details, for example the recessed frames around the door, were cut with saws, leaving a very smooth surface[58].

AN ARCHITECTURAL STYLE OF POWER

In the so-called Klytemnestra and Atreus tombs, this locally developed style was elevated to monumental proportions to aggrandize the status of the person or persons for whom it was intended (Abb. 2). The tombs represent the highest form of the individualistic expression of Mycenaean mortuary customs. As already mentioned, their façades explicitly utilize architectural elements of the palaces and thereby provide a strong visual link between palace as seat of the living ruler and tomb as seat of the dead. This built expression was extended in the plan and form of the famous Lion Gate entrance to Mycenae. Its approach is flanked on both sides by high walls of massive courses of dressed conglomerate, creating an entrance passage like that of the tombs. The façade wall with its monolithic threshold, doorjambs, and lintel of conglomerate, surmounted by the Lion Gate relief, echoes the façades of the tombs and, presumably adumbrates the doorways leading into the main rooms of the palace atop the citadel.

The significance of architecture as an icon of power, already identified in Minoan architecture, is evident in the Lion Gate relief, where the rampant felines face and frame a column, which is based on two Minoan altars[59]. Following Wace, George Mylonas suggested that this was a kind of heraldic device symbolizing the ruling family, with the columns representing the royal palace[60]. Boulotis was even more specific: the flanking felines represent the ruling dynasty at Mycenae and the column and altar symbolize their control not only of the palace at Mycenae but also of the religious basis of its authority[61]. I think the relief also declares Mycenae's supreme control after the downfall of Knossos[62]. Whether or not this interpretation is accepted, the evidence of the deployment of the conglomerate masonry style abundantly illustrates how a local style of craftsmanship can be used to make powerful statements of control. Aside from the use of conglomerate in the late *tholos* tombs (perhaps as early as LH IIIA2) and gate entrance to the citadel by the mid 13th century B.C.E. (LH IIIB1), this stone is systematically employed for key decorative elements in and around the palace – for column and anta bases, for thresholds and door jambs[63]. Notable is the inclusion of a gate in the processional path from the Cult Center, presumably leading up to the Grand Staircase entrance to the main part of the palace[64]. A map of the disposition of constructions using conglomerate at Mycenae outlines a processional order of power (Taf. 10.1). It begins with the outer boundaries of the citadel as one approaches by road, for first is the bridge, built partially of conglomerate, over the ravine below the church of Ayios Georgios[65]. As one proceeds up the ravine the massive conglomerate-built terrace of the Atreus tomb catches the eye, and then the tomb itself, since

58 Wace 1949, 31, 37, 43, 138; Küpper 1996, 14-6.

59 Shaw 1986, with references to earlier studies.

60 Mylonas 1966, 173-5; Wace 1949, 53.

61 Boulotis 1990, 456-7; a thorough discussion of this motif is in Krattenmaker 1991, 304-9, passim.

62 The altars used as bases for the columns are specifically Minoan, see for example their actual discovery at Archanes (Sakellarakis and Sakellaraki 1997, 80-2) and the discussion by Krattenmaker (1991, 127-34), who agrees with M. Shaw (1986) that these altars are associated with entranceways; the column depicted is the Mycenaean version of the Minoan: contrast the columns with echinus capitals from the Treasury of Atreus (Mylonas 1966, fig. 114) with any number from Minoan painting (Wesenberg 1971, 3-27; updated and discussed by Krattenmaker 1991, 45).

63 Cavanagh and Mee (1999, 94) argue for a date of LH IIIA2 for the Atreus tomb, which places it and the more or less contemporary Klytemnestra tomb significantly earlier than the Lion Gate, West Wall, Great Ramp, Grave Circle A, and final palace constructions, which belong in mid IIIB and slightly later. Wace (1956) established a sequence for these that was modified by Mylonas (1961, 199-200; 1965, 100, 109, 114-21, 128-9) as a result of his studies of the fortification walls, gates, and other structures within the citadel; see also Hope Simpson and Dickinson 1979, 36. For column bases, antae and thresholds see Küpper (1996, 115-7), although, as J. Maran pointed out to me, the identifications of conglomerate blocks by Küpper (1996, fig. 220) is inaccurate: at Tiryns the SW column of the Great Propylon is of conglomerate while the two interior anta of the interior (W) porch are not; in the Small Propylon the NE column is conglomerate as are the two antae at NE and NW; at Mycenae plans indicating where conglomerate blocks were discovered were made under Wace's direction (Wace et al. 1921-23, pl. II; 1949, figs. 4, 32) and additional notations were made by Mylonas (1968, 17, 21, 38, figs. 20-1). Altogether these show a consistent use of conglomerate for antae, column bases and thresholds throughout the palace and associated structures atop the hill, from the NW Propylon over to the House of the Columns.

64 Mylonas 1972, 19, pl. I (at "K").

65 Wright 1982, 192-3; 1987, 177-83.

it must have been open in anticipation of the deceased. Next are the Klytemnestra tomb and then the entrance into the world of the living through the Lion Gate. Finally, after coming within the circuit of the citadel walls, one encounters the decorative elements that mark the processional paths to the palace, including the gate to the Cult Center and the propylon to the palace, and, finally, the decorated entrances to the palace rooms. There were, of course, many other signs of power that adorned these spaces, but the consistent appearance of these traditional masonry practices forms the backbone of this display.

THE MYCENAEAN PALACE

In a previous study, I had tentatively suggested that the appearance of this masonry style elsewhere might mark the claim by the rulers at Mycenae to control other places in the Argolid[66]. Both Küpper and Maran in their reexamination of the evidence for the use of conglomerate at Tiryns have more strongly emphasized this point; notably Maran thinks that the citadel at Tiryns was never an autonomous settlement and only takes on its monumental form at this time of expansion by Mycenae[67]. As he suggests, mapping the deployment of conglomerate (and other specially cut blocks) at Tiryns describes a processional route that leads to the center of power. In fact the 'megaron' at Tiryns is marked out by architectural elements that direct, enframe and focus the attention of the visitor in a fashion more elaborate than anywhere else (Taf. 10.2). First, one notices the strict axial alignment of the building to the court before it, surrounded by its colonnade supported by bases of conglomerate and microcrystalline limestone[68]. Then one's attention is drawn to the front of the 'megaron', marked out by the hard red limestone of the lowest step, a stone found in this region, and it is framed by the massive sawn conglomerate antae flanking the porch. The base of the walls on either side of the porch is decorated with revetments of gypsum carved with the 'Minoan triglyph rosette' motif[69] – devices that otherwise are only known from Knossos, where they were perhaps used in a similar manner[70]. Progressing inwards, one crosses into the vestibule through the 'polythyron' with its three doorways with thresholds of conglomerate and then proceeds across another conglomerate threshold into the inner chamber. There, the visual elements are the fresco-painted floor, the colonnade around the central hearth, the throne at the right, and fresco painted walls.

The floor is decorated with squares painted with dolphins and octopuses, a motif that is borrowed from Minoan painting and widely used for the floors of major rooms of Mycenaean palaces (also at Pylos and Gla) where it focuses attention on the throne[71]. Other elements of Minoan painting are utilized in wall frescoes, but primarily as devices within a thoroughly Mycenaean iconography. In selecting Minoan themes, whether for wall frescoes, relief carving, or engraving on signets and seals, the masters of the Mycenaean citadels did not choose to place in the foreground representations of processions and gatherings of large groups, scenes of deities and votaries before shrines, and scenes of outdoor shrines, of towns, palaces and individual buildings. Instead, they fashioned an iconography of themselves that, while it did not neglect the procession, displayed the individual foremost. This is witnessed in the well-known preference for scenes of hunting and combat, as well as in representation of individuals – in portraits, as helmeted warriors, as priests, and as riding in chariots[72]. Surely this is why most scholars, when examining the layout of the palaces, are led naturally to the presumption that the central placement of the throne within the 'megaron' means that it was the seat of a ruler, presumably the *wanax*[73].

66 Wright 1987, 183.

67 Küpper 1996, 115-8; Maran (this volume).

68 Müller 1930, 193-200; Wace 1949, 137.

69 Schliemann 1976, 284-92; Müller 1930, 139-43. Gale et al. (1988, 69-70) show that the gypsum used at Mycenae comes from central Crete while that at Tiryns does not, but rather originates in Triassic deposits, either those recognized in western or eastern Crete, in the Ionian islands, or in Lakonia; see also Higgins and Higgins 1996, 104, 203, 205.

70 Krattenmaker (1991, 121-6) reviews the carved examples of the 'triglyph rosette' from Knossos and Evans' idea that they were associated with entrance areas, which she does not deny, but cautions that they do not have in situ contexts and, unlike the Mycenaean ones, were not placed as dadoes at the base of walls; see also Immerwahr 1990, 144.

71 Hirsch (1980, 459-61) argued that the dolphin and octopus frescoes at A. Triada must be Mycenaean since they are unique in Minoan floor painting where as common in Mycenaean, however, as Militello (1998, 331-2) in his study of the frescoes points out the precedents for these motifs and refines the date to LM IIIA1.

72 Davis and Bennet 1999, 107-1; Immerwahr 1990, 109, 122.

73 Skepticism that there were thrones is voiced by Rehak (1995a) on the basis of a thorough, critical review of all the evidence.

As I have argued elsewhere, the entire spatial organization of the palaces is one of a progressive movement through concentric rings of space to a central point, the monumental hearth at the center of the 'megaron'[74]. As Maran has recently clarified, this organization has its most perfect expression in the planning and layout of the final palace at Tiryns[75]. At this time, LH IIIB – the 13th century B.C.E., the uniform plan of the Mycenaean palace with the 'megaron' at its heart spreads throughout the mainland (Taf. 10.2), and, in a lesser form – the corridor house defined by Hiesel – spreads across the Aegean[76].

THE MONUMENTALIZATION OF THE DOMESTIC

At the core of this plan is the abstracted notion of the structure of a Mycenaean house. Essential to this concept is the long tradition in mainland domestic architecture of an axial, freestanding building. Despite considerable variability in plan and form[77], the linearity and individuality of mainland domestic architecture are its paramount characteristics, especially when contrasted with Minoan buildings. The obvious difficulty, when expanding the size and number of rooms of such a plan, is with its internal divisions, since additional rooms will be strung out in a line, with each successive one reachable only through the preceding ones. This is why the Mycenaeans developed the plan of a flanking corridor with rooms off it as a solution that preserved the core structure of the traditional house while permitting the addition of rooms for storage and specialized activities[78]. This act demonstrates unequivocally the fundamental importance for the builders of these structures of the domestic unit as an architectural expression. Its concomitant monumentalization in the form of the hearth-centered 'megaron' of the palaces is surely a statement about the socio-political organization of the Mycenaean palace-states, namely one of power and authority vested in the superior lineage or lineages of the community. Unlike Minoan society, the Mycenaeans had a long tradition of accentuating the individual family and its lineage and of according status to individuals of high rank, who attained and maintained this status through acts of prowess, apparently hunting and fighting, since these are ubiquitously represented from the inception of the MH through the end of the Mycenaean era. The linear organization of the architecture of mainland households during the Middle and Late Bronze Ages frequently was focused on a central stone built hearth, often with a column in the middle of the main room. The monumentalization of these elements in the palaces was an invention of tradition by the ruling elite, one that would be recognized for its expression of widely held values throughout the communities of the mainland[79]. In terms of craft, the selection of these architectural elements was also a natural choice, elevating traditional and widely shared elements of construction to the realm of specialized craftsmanship. The result was an architectural invention of what was probably a newly defined (or redefined) relationship between the ruler and his subjects and between the ruler, possible seated on a throne, and the deities worshipped around the hearth[80].

We do not have direct evidence of what acts of commemoration and what performances of worship (or of political or economic authority) took place within the 'megaron'. At Pylos, the singular placement of a symmetrically painted octopus before the throne and the basin-like depression in the plaster that has a drain running off it has led many to suspect an act of libation, while other evidence seems to

74 Wright 1994, 56-60.

75 If he is correct (as I believe he is ; see Maran 2004, 275) in arguing that this was built by the rulers at Mycenae, then I think that the purposeful incorporation of Minoan architectural elements into the heart of this design is probably a signal of Mycenae's hegemony over the Aegean after the destruction of Knossos in the 14th century B.C.E.

76 The uniform palace plan is recognized at Pylos, Tiryns, Mycenae, possibly Athens (see Nylander 1962; Iakovides 1962, 173-8), and probably Thebes. The Corridor House, a kind of secondary administrative seat, is found at this time (LH IIIA2-B) at the Menelaion outside Sparta (mansion 2-3), in secondary buildings around Mycenae and Tiryns (e.g. the Ivory Complex, buildings of the Cult Center; Buildings V and VI in the Unterburg), at Gla, Dimini, Phylakopi on Melos, Gournia on Crete, and possibly at Rhodes, Miletos, and Korakou (M. Siennicka kindly shared with me an unpublished paper in which she argues for such a building at Korakou on the basis of the conglomerate threshold found there; see Blegen's "megaron" [1921, 95-6, fig. 125]).

77 Hiesel 1990, 203-4, 239-50; Wright 2005, 20.

78 Hiesel 1990, 205.

79 Where the invention took place is unclear: one argument is that it is to be found in Mansion I of the Menelaion (LH II), from where it was adapted in LH IIIA in the Argolid (Rutter 2005, 27-8; Wright 2005, 20); Hiesel (1990, 205-9) also argues that the Menelaion is the earliest example of what he dubs the "Korridorhaus".

80 Wright 1994, 50-6. Rehak (1995a, 117) plausibly suggests that instead of a throne the area was used for rituals of drinking and libation.

support the notion of ritualized drinking or offerings of drink around the hearth[81]. More recently, studies of feasting provide evidence of commemorative ceremonies, and it may be characteristic of Mycenaean society that the architectural evidence for the places of these commemorations is harder to come by[82]. It seems that only in the latest phase of Mycenaean society, i.e. only during the 13th century B.C.E., did the Mycenaeans begin to construct formal places of assembly. These are evident in specialized constructions that are not generalizable, as is the case on Minoan Crete with the ubiquitous courts, walkways, theatral installations, and tripartite shrines. Most evident on the mainland are the courts before the 'megaron', but they are not universal, not appearing for example at Gla or around most of the corridor house complexes (with the apparent exception of Dimini). The formal arrangement laid out at Tiryns of successive courts reached through propyla is unique, although it may be argued that the renovation of the palace complexes at Mycenae and Pylos followed similar principles[83]. Likewise, the construction of roadways, ramps, and processional corridors in the latest phase of the Mycenaean palaces, especially at Tiryns and Mycenae, demonstrates a concern to use architecture to interconnect, direct, and focus commemorative acts. Perhaps the singular nature of Mycenaean commemorative practice is best illustrated in the construction of the Lion Gate and its coordination with structures that would now be housed within the circuit of the fortification walls.

The long history of occupation by a ruling elite at Mycenae, perhaps only matched at Pylos and Thebes, surely created many places of historical memory at which monuments were constructed. Without doubt, the carved stone stelae of Grave Circles A and B are the oldest, and during the last phase of reconstruction of the citadel their reinstallation within the artificially raised circular terrace enclosed by a stone-slab circle was a conscious act of re-commemoration[84]. As I have suggested elsewhere, the orientation of the entrance to the grave circle to the Lion Gate was a purposeful alignment in order to draw the attention of the visitor to this place where the honored ancestral dead were buried[85]. The overall reorganization of the approach to the citadel (the addition of the Lion Gate and its powerful relief, the orientation of the Grave Circle entrance to it, and the construction of processional routes to the palace and to and from the Cult Center) was the core of an integration of previously disparate (or at best loosely linked) elements and places of ceremony into a coordinated spatial statement. But this master plan was uniquely developed for the historical situation at Mycenae; at the other palaces different circumstances and different histories created different forms of spatial integration[86]. Unlike the uniform and universal application of architectural forms across the settlements and palace centers of Minoan Crete, the singularity of constructions at the mainland centers represents the historical contingency of rule at the Mycenaean palaces. Performance and commemoration were much more inventions of tradition for the purpose of creating a societal identity than organically evolved expressions of social structure.

81 Säflund 1980; Rehak 1995a; Stocker and Davis 2005.

82 On Mycenaean feasting see Wright 2005; on the problematic identification of architectural spaces, see Bendall (2004, 126-8) who suggests a hierarchy of three spaces in and around the palace complex at Pylos; and Thaler (2005), whose analysis confirms a shift in focus during the last phase of the palace at Pylos to courts 58 and 63. Comparable evidence from the other palaces is not available and the evidence of group ceremony (qua feasting, sacrifice and worship) at other sites, e.g. Tsoungiza, A. Konstantinos-Methana, Maleatas Terrace-Epidauros, comes primarily from deposits of artifacts and organic remains rather than from built spaces.

83 Müller 1930, 193-200; Nelson 2001, 207-12.

84 Wright 1987; Gates 1985.

85 The construction of the Granary took place after the original constructions of the Lion Gate, Great Ramp, grave Circle and West Circuit wall as argued by Wace (1956) and demonstrated in great detail by Mylonas (1965, 100, 109, 114-21, 128-9, see supra n. 63) as a result of his extensive investigations of the entire building complex.

86 At Tiryns, as Maran now argues (supra n. 67), the reformation followed an abstract formality with little historical precedent; at Pylos a long history of construction preceded the latest palace plan (Nelson 2001, 194-206) but even the latest was subjected to radically contingent revision (Wright 1984; Shelmerdine 1987; Thaler 2005).

CONCLUSIONS

A commonplace in some scholarship attempting to reconstruct the form and structure of the pre- and protohistoric societies of the Aegean has been to essentialize the interpretation of the material remains into stylistic narratives about the dichotomous nature of 'Minoans' and 'Mycenaeans', as if these names were actual designations acceptable to the long dead persons and societies they purport to describe and as if the sorting of material remains into conceptually bounded types corresponded to actual geographic as well as social boundaries. Perhaps the most prominent scholar in the study of Aegean art to be identified with this approach was Friedrich Matz, who saw in the artistic styles of these archaeologically recognized cultures a deeply embedded aesthetic structure[87]. Despite racist implications of this way of thinking, this approach continues to appeal[88]. What is most injurious in such structuralist attempts is their ahistorical assumption that the character of these ancient peoples was deep-seated and immutable, written as it were in their genetic code[89]. Furthermore, such structuralism fails to ask how such a social nature came into being or about attendant historical processes[90]. Instead the 'just so' of ontological classification objectifies the persons and institutions of antiquity into dehumanized antiquarian categories and rarely questions the assumptions on which it is founded.

The approach taken here assumes that individuals are part of and act within the collective of social relations, that their actions can be both those of consciously acting individuals and of members of institutions[91]. Within this framework, I have tried to show how the actions of individuals as builders and as planners are crafted within a social and historical context of traditions of practice, performance and commemoration. My position is that the remains of the built environment, when analyzed for variation and regularity across broad spatial horizons and temporal spans permit us to distinguish patterns that can be explained hypothetically in terms of traditional customs, on the one hand as craft traditions handed down from master to apprentice, on the other as social traditions of commemoration and performance that bind societal memory in institutional forms. In structuralist terms, these patterns are rules of expression, and these rules are mutable. They are subject to manipulation by individuals aiming at specific goals and to adjustment by changing techno-economic circumstances, macro-economic forces, ecological change, or combinations of any of these.

Many analysts of the built environment claim that it is a product of social structure as well as its producer[92]. In this sense, built remains are thought to be an expression of that structure. But for archaeologists to assume naively that they can simply 'read' the structure from the remains misunderstands that the practice of social acts is not directly tied to the construction of material forms, whether the objects used or built spaces that contain. In fact, it is commonly the case that the built form does not conform with (and may even seem to contradict) the actual practice. In order to make sense of architectural

87 This approach is the methodological foundation of his masterful study of Minoan glyptic (Matz 1928, 2-3, 28-9, 261-70) and underlies his racist study of Greek art under National Socialism (Matz 1939, 5-8, passim). After the war, Matz (1951, 1014-5) restated the structuralist principles in his study of torsion in Aegean art, and finally, in a modified form in his study of Aegean art and culture (1962). This approach was common in the study of ancient art, e.g. Schweitzer 1969, esp. 191-203.

88 E.g. Walberg 1976, 1986; Bouzek 1992; and discussions by Morgan (1985, 9-10, n. 8) and Crowley (1989).

89 Matz admitted the error of his 1939 National Socialist publication and explained it as a 'compensation' for having two half-Jewish in-laws (1974, 67-8): "Die Tatsache, daß ich zwei halb-jüdische Schwäger hatte, erwies sich auf die Dauer als Belastung. Jedenfalls verlangte sie nach einer Kompensation in irgend einer Form. Ich war kurzsichtig genug, um eine Möglichkeit dafür in der Bestrebungen zur Stützung des humanistischen Gymnasiums zu sehen, die es damals auch von nationalsozialistischer Seite gab. Für eine Schriftenreihe, die den Obertitel trug 'Auf dem Wege zum nationalpolitischen Gymnasium', verfaßte ich eine kleine griechische Kunstgeschichte um so eher, als ich damals noch annahm, daß Formstruktur und Volkstum (1939) innerlich verhaftet seien. Genützt hat natürlich das Schriftchen gar nichts. Wenn es überhaupt ein Ergebnis brachte, so war es für mich die dann zunehmend sich festigende Einsicht, daß es mit dieser Art der Beziehungen zwischen künstlerischer Form und Volkstum ein Irrtum ist." Compare this to the harsh judgment rendered by Jung 2000.

90 Throughout Matz's (1962, 23, 67-9, 146-8, 157-9, 179-80, 209) writings diffusion through migration, especially "Indo-German" migration, is used as an explanation of the process of change, and in the latest work a much richer archaeological-historical picture is painted that tempers the structuralist assertions, although they are still present.

91 Giddens 1984, 214-21; Wylie 2002, 127-35.

92 Rapoport 1969, 47; Hillier and Hanson 1984, 6-25; Giddens 1984, 162-93.

remains as evidence of social practices and social structure, I argue it is necessary to identify in the archaeological record material forms that recur over space and time in ways that indicate they were intended or used in similar ways, in other words that the producers and users of these spaces intended or performed similar social performances in them. What I have tried to show in the instances of 'Minoan' and 'Mycenaean' approaches to building spaces is that, in each tradition, there are archaeologically related material remains whose formation and transformation can be explained in similar functional terms because the are consistently found within reasonably coherent spatial contexts. In both societies, furthermore, these built forms continue to be constructed, although often in more elaborate manner, as the societies are transformed by the creation of more complex levels of local socio-political integration, such as occurs in states. At that point, the archaeological record is sufficiently well documented in spatial and temporal terms as to be treated historically. My conclusion is that the remnant places of the built environment of the past retain the structures of the primary forms of social relations that were important in the formation of social polities and their political economies.

BIBLIOGRAPHY

Amouretti, M.-C. 1970. *Fouilles exécutées a Mallia: Le centre politique*. Vol. 2, *La Crypte Hypostyle (1957-1961)*. Études Crétoises 18. Paris: École française d' Athénes.

Bachelard, G. 1964. *The Poetics of Space*. Boston: Beacon Press.

Bendall, L. 2004. "Fit for a King? Hierarchy, Exclusion, Aspiration, and Desire in the Social Structure of Mycenaean Banqueting." In *Food, Cuisine and Society in Prehistoric Greece*, edited by P. Halstead and J. Barrett, 105-35. Sheffield Studies in Aegean Archaeology 5. Oxford: Oxbow.

Blegen, C. 1921. *Korakou: A Prehistoric Settlement near Corinth*. New York: American School of Classical Studies at Athens.

Boulotis, C. 1990. "Villes et palais dans l'art égéen du IIe millénaire av. J.-C." In Darcque and Treuil 1990, 421-59.

Bouzek, J. 1992. "The Structure of Minoan Representational Art." In *Eikon: Aegean Bronze Age Iconography: Shaping a Methodology: Proceedings of the 4th International Aegean Conference/4e Rencontre egénne internationale, University of Tasmania, Hobart, Australia, 6-9 April 1992*, edited by R. Laffineur and J.L. Crowley, 175-8. Aegaeum 8. Liège: Université de Liège, Histoire de l'Art et Archéologie de la Grèce Antique.

Branigan, K. 1970. *The Foundations of Palatial Crete*. London: Routledge and Kegan Paul.

—. 1975. Review of *Myrtos: An Early Bronze Age Settlement in Crete*, by P. Warren. *Classical Review* 25: 116-18.

—. 1992. *Dancing with Death: Life and Death in Southern Crete c. 3000-2000 B.C.* Las Palmas: Adolf M. Hakkert.

Cadogan, G. 1978. "Pyrgos, Crete, 1970-77." *Archaeological Reports* 24: 70-84.

Casey, E.S. 1996. "How to Get from Space to Place in a Fairly Short Stretch of Time: Phenomenological Prolegomena." In *Senses of place*, edited by S. Feld and K.H. Basso, 13-52. Santa Fe: School of American Research Press.

Cavanagh, W. 2001. "Recent References to Bronze Age Roads in the Aegean." In *Urbanism in the Aegean Bronze Age*, edited by K. Branigan, 180-1. Sheffield Studies in Aegean Archaeology 5. London: Sheffield Academic Press.

Cavanagh, W., and C. Mee. 1984. "Mycenaean Tombs as Evidence for Social and Political Organisation." *Oxford Journal of Archaeology* 3: 45-64.

—. 1998. *A Private Place: Death in Prehistoric Greece*. Studies in Mediterranean Archaeology 125. Jonsered: Paul Åströms Förlag.

—. 1999. "Building the Treasury of Atreus." In *Meletemata: Studies in Aegean Archaeology Presented to Malcolm H. Wiener as He Enters His 65th Year*, edited by P.P. Betancourt, V. Karageorghis, R. Laffineur, and W.-D. Niemeier, 93-102. Aegaeum 20. Liège: Université de Liège, Histoire de l'art et archéologie de la Grèce antique et al.

Chryssoulaki, S. 1990. "L'urbanisme minoen. A: le réseau routier urbain." In Darcque and Treuil 1990, 371-80.

Connerton, P. 1989. *How Societies Remember*. Cambridge: Cambridge University Press.

Crowley, J.L. 1989. "Subject Matter in Aegean Art: The Crucial Change." In *Transition: Le monde égéen du Bronze moyen au Bronze récent: Actes de la deuxième Rencontre égéenne internationale de l'Université de Liège, 18-20 Avril 1988*, edited by R. Laffineur, 203-14. Aegaeum 3. Liège: Université de l'Etat à Liège.

Crumley, C.L. 1995. "Heterarchy and the Analysis of Complex Societies." In *Heterarchy and the Analysis of Complex Societies*, edited by R.M. Ehrenreich, C.L. Crumley, and J.E. Levy. Arlington: American Anthropological Association.

Dabney, M.K., and J.C. Wright 1990. "Mortuary Customs, Palatial Society and State Formation in the Aegean Area: A Comparative Study." In *Celebrations of Death and Divinity in the Bronze Age Argolid: Proceedings of the Sixth International Symposium at the Swedish Institute at Athens, 11-13 June, 1988*, edited by R. Hägg and G.C. Nordquist, 45-53. Skrifter utgivna av Svenska Institutet i Athen 4°, 40. Stockholm: Swedish Institute in Athens.

Damiani Indelicato, S. 1982. *Piazza pubblica e palazzo nella Creta Minoica*. Rome: Soc. Editoriale Jouvence.

Darcque, P., and R. Treuil, eds. 1990. *L' habitat égéen préhistorique: Actes de la table ronde internationale, Athènes, 23-25 juin 1987*. Bulletin de correspondance Hellénique Supplément 19. Athènes: École française d'Athènes.

Davis, E. 1987. "The Knossos Miniature Frescoes and the Function of the Central Courts." In Hägg and Marinatos 1987, 157-61.

—.1995. "Art and Politics in the Aegean: The Missing Ruler." In Rehak 1995b, 11-22.

Davis, J.L., and J. Bennet 1999. "Making Mycenaeans: Warfare, Territorial Expansion, and Representations of the Other in the Pylian Kingdom." In *POLEMOS: Le contexte guerrier en Égée á l'âge du Bronze: Actes de la 7e Rencontre égéenne internationale, Université de Liège, 14-17 Avril 1998.*, edited by R. Laffineur, 105-20. Aegaeum 19. Liège: Université de Liège, Histoire de l'art et archéologie de la Grèce antique et al.

Demargne, P. 1945. *Fouilles exécutées a Mallia: Exploration des nécropoles (1921-1933)*. Études Crétoises 7. Paris: Librairie Orientaliste Paul Geuthner.

Detournay, B., J.-C. Poursat, and F. Vandenabeele. 1980. *Fouilles éxecutées a Malia: Le Quartier Mu*. Vol. 2, *Vases de pierre et de métal, vannerie, figurines et reliefs d'appliqué, éléments de parure et de décoration, armes, sceaux et empreintes*. Études Crétoises 26. Paris: Librairie Orientaliste Paul Geuthner.

Dickinson, O.T.P.K. 1983. "Cist Graves and Chamber Tombs." *Annual of the British School of Archaeology* 78: 55-67.

Driessen, J. 2002. "'The King Must Die.' Some Observations on the Use of Minoan Court Compounds." In Driessen et al. 2002, 1-14.

Driessen, J., I. Schoep, and R. Laffineur, eds. 2002. *Monuments of Minos: Rethinking the Minoan Palaces: Proceedings of the International Workshop: Crete of the Hundred Palaces? Held at the Université Catholique de Louvain, Louvain-la-Neuve, 14-15 December 2001*. Aegaeum 23. Liège: Université de Liège, Histoire de l'art et archéologie de la Grèce antique et al.

Eco, U. 1980. "Function and Sign: The Semiotics of Architecture." In *Signs, Symbols, and Architecture*, edited by G. Broadbent, R. Bunt, and C. Jencks, 11-69. New York: Wiley.

Gale, N.H., H.C. Einfalt, H.W. Hubberten, and R.E. Jones. 1988. "The Sources of Mycenaean Gypsum." *Journal of Archaeological Science* 15: 57-72.

Gates, C. 1985. "Rethinking the Building History of Grave Circle A at Mycenae." *American Journal of Archaeology* 89: 263-74.

Geertz, C. 1980. *Negara: The Theatre State in Nineteenth-Century Bali*. Princeton: Princeton University Press.

Giddens, A. 1984. *The Constitution of Society: Introduction of the Theory of Structuration*. Berkeley: University of California Press.

Glassie, H.H. 1975. *Folk Housing in Middle Virginia: A Structural Analysis of Historic Artifacts*. Knoxville: University of Tennessee Press.

Hägg, R. 1983. "Epiphany in Minoan Ritual." *Bulletin of the Institute of Classical Studies* 30: 184-5.

Hägg, R., and N. Marinatos, eds. 1987. *The Function of the Minoan Palaces: Proceedings of the Fourth International Symposium at the Swedish Institute in Athens, 10-16 June, 1984*. Skrifter utgivna av Svenska Institutet i Athen 4°, 35. Stockholm: Swedish Institute in Athens.

Haggis, D.C. 2002. "Integration and Complexity in the Late Pre-Palatial Period: A View from the Countryside in Eastern Crete." In *Labyrinth Revisited: Rethinking Minoan Archaeology*, edited by Y. Hamilakis, 120-42. Oxford: Oxbow Books.

Heidegger, M. 1954. "Bauen Denken Wohnen." In *Vorträge und Aufsätze*, edited by M. Heidegger, 145-62. Pfullingen: Verlag Günther Neske.

Hiesel, G. 1990. *Späthelladische Hausarchitektur: Studien zur Architekturgeschichte des griechischen Festlandes in der späten Bronzezeit*. Mainz am Rhein: Philipp von Zabern.

Higgins, M.D., and R. Higgins. 1996. *A Geological Companion to Greece and the Aegean*. Ithaca: Cornell University Press.

Hillier, B., and J. Hanson. 1984. *The Social Logic of Space*. Cambridge: Cambridge University Press.

Hirsch, E.S. 1980. "Another Look at Minoan and Mycenaean Inter-Relationships in Floor Decoration." *American Journal of Archaeology* 84: 453-62.

Hope Simpson, R., and O.T.P.K. Dickinson. 1979. *A Gazetteer of Aegean Civilization in the Bronze Age*. Vol. 1, *The Mainland and the Islands*. Studies in Mediterranean Archaeology 52. Göteborg: Paul Åströms Forlag.

Iakovides, S. 1962. *Η Μυκηναϊκή Ακρόπολις των Αθηνών*. Athens: Πανεπιστήμιον Αθηνών, Φιλοσοφική Σχολή.

Immerwahr, S.A. 1990. *Aegean Painting in the Bronze Age*. University Park: Pennsylvania State University Press.

Jung, R. 2000. "Das Megaron: Ein Analogie(kurz)schluß der ägäischen Archäologie." In *Vergleichen als archäologische Methode: Analogien in den Archäologien. (Mit Beiträgen einer Tagung der Arbeitsgemeinschaft Theorie (T-AG) und einer Kommentierenden Bibliographie)*, edited by A. Gramsch, 71-93. British Archaeological Reports International Series 825. Oxford: Archaeopress.

Koumouzelis, M. 1996. "A Monumental Chamber Tomb at Ellenika." In *Atti e memorie del secondo Congresso internazionale di micenologia, Roma-Napoli, 14-20 ottobre 1991*, edited by E. De Miro, L. Godart, and A. Sacconi, 1221-8. Incunabula Graeca 98. Roma: Gruppo editoriale internazionale.

Krattenmaker, K. 1991. "Minoan Architectural Representation." Ph.D. diss., Bryn Mawr College.

Krystalli-Votsi, K. 1996. "The Excavation of the Mycenaean Cemetery at Aidonia." In *The Aidonia Treasure: Seals and Jewellery of the Aegean Late Bronze Age*, edited by K. Demakopoulou, 21-31. Athens: Ministry of Culture.

Küpper, M. 1996. *Mykenische Architektur: Material, Bearbeitungstechnik, Konstruktion und Erscheinungsbild*. Internationale Archäologie 25. Espelkamp: Verlag Marie Leidorf.

Lebessi, A. 1976. "Ο οικίσκος των Αρχανών." *Αρχαιολογική Εφημερίς*: 12-23.

Lefebvre, H. 1991. *The Production of Space*. Oxford: Blackwell.

Levi, D. 1961-62. "La tomba a tholos di Kamilari presso a Festòs." *Annuario della Scuola Archeologica di Atene e delle missioni italiane in Oriente* 39-40: 7-148.

Maggidis, C. 1998. "From Polis to Necropolis: Social Ranking from Architectural and Mortuary Evidence in the Minoan Cemetery at Phourni, Archanes." In *Cemetery and Society in the Aegean Bronze Age*, edited by K. Branigan, 87-102. Sheffield Studies in Aegean Archaeology 1. Sheffield: Sheffield Academic Press.

Maran, J. 2004. "Architektonische Innovation im spätmykenischen Tiryns – Lokale Bauprogramme und fremde Kultureinflüsse." In *Althellenische Technologie und Technik. Tagungsband 21.-23.3.2003 Ohlstadt*, 261-88. Weilheim: Verein zur Förderung der Aufarbeitung der Hellenischen Geschichte.

Marinatos, N. 1987. "Public Festivals in the West Courts of the Palaces." In Hägg and Marinatos 1987, 135-43.

Matz, F. 1928. *Die frühkretischen Siegel: Eine Untersuchung über das Werden des minioschen Stiles*. Berlin, Leipzig: Walter de Gruyter.

—. 1939. *Die griechische Kunst: Auf dem Wege zum nationalpolitischen Gymnasium*. Beiträge zur nationalsozialistischen Ausrichtung des altsprachlichen Unterrichts 9. Frankfurt a.M.: Verlag Moritz Diesterweg.

—. 1951. *Torsion: Eine formenkundliche Untersuchung zur aigaiischen Vorgeschichte*. Akademie der Wissenschaften und der Literatur Mainz, Abhandlung des Geistes- und Sozialwissenschaftlichen Klasse 12. Wiesbaden: Franz Steiner Verlag.

—. 1962. *The Art of Crete and Early Greece: The Prelude to Greek Art*. Translated by A.E. Keep. New York: Greystone Press.

—. 1974. *Archäologische Erinnerungen aus sechs Jahrzehnten (1910-1970)*. Marburg: Privately published.

McEnroe, J.C. 1990. "The Significance of Local Styles in Minoan Vernacular Architecture." In Darcque and Treuil 1990, 195-202.

—. 1996. "The Central Hillside at Kommos: The Late Minoan Period." In Shaw and Shaw 1996, 199-237.

—. 2001. *Pseira*. Vol. 5, *The Architecture of Pseira*. Philadelphia: University of Pennsylvania Museum of Archaeology and Anthropology.

Merleau-Ponty, M. 1962. *Phenomenology of Perception*. New York: Humanities Press.

Mersereau, R. 1991. "Prehistoric Architectural Models from the Aegean." Ph.D. diss., Bryn Mawr College.

Militello, P. 1998. *Haghia Triada*. Vol. 1, *Gli affreschi*. Bottega d'Erasmo 9. Padova: Aldo Ausilio Editore.

Morgan, L. 1985. "Idea, Idiom and Iconography." In *L'iconographie minoenne: Actes de la Table ronde d'Athènes (21-22 Avril 1983)*, edited by P. Darcque and J.-C. Poursat, 1-17. Bulletin de correspondance Hellénique Supplément 11. Athens: Ecole française d'Athènes.

Müller, K. 1930. *Die Architektur der Burg und des Palästes*. Tiryns: Die Ergebnisse der Ausgrabungen des Instituts 3. Augsburg: Benno Filser.

Mylonas, G.E. 1961. "Η ακρόπολις των Μυκηνών." *Αρχαιολογική Εφημερίς* [1958]: 153-207.

—. 1965. "Η ακρόπολις των Μυκηνών, II: Οι περίβολοι, αι πύλαι και αι άνοδοι." *Αρχαιολογική Εφημερίς* [1962]: 187-99.

—. 1966. *Mycenae and the Mycenaean Age*. Princeton: Princeton University Press.

—. 1968. *Mycenae's Last Century of Greatness*. Australian Humanities Research Council Occasional Paper 13. Sydney: Sydney University Press.

—. 1972. *Το θρησκευτικόν κέντρον των Μυκηνών*. Πραγματείαι της Ακαδημίας Αθηνών 33. Athens: Ακαδημία Αθηνών.

Nelson, M. 2001. "The Architecture of Epano Englianos, Greece." Ph.D. diss., University of Toronto.

Niemeier, W.-D. 1986. "Zur Deutung des Thronraumes im Palast von Knossos." *Mitteilung des Deutschen Archäologischen Instituts, Abteilung Athen* 101: 63-95.

Niemeier, W.-D., and P. Knoblauch. 1992. "Der Weg nach Knossos." In *Amnisos nach den archäologischen, historischen und epigraphischen Zeugnissen des Altertums und der Neuzeit*, edited by J. Schäfer, 323-8. Berlin: Gebr. Mann.

Nylander, C. 1962. "Die sogennanten mykenischen Säulenbasen auf der Akropolis in Athen." *Opuscula Atheniensa* 4: 31-77.

Palyvou, C. 1987. "Circulatory Patterns in Minoan Architecture." In Hägg and Marinatos 1987, 195-203.

—. 2002. "Central Courts: The Supremacy of the Void." In Driessen et al. 2002, 167-72.

Peatfield, A. 1987. "Palace and Peak: The Political and Religious Relationship between Palaces and Peak Sanctuaries." In Hägg and Marinatos 1987, 89-93.

Pelon, O. 1980. *Fouilles exécutées a Mallia: Le palais de Malia*. Vol. 5. Études Crétoises 25. Paris: Librairie Orientaliste Paul Geuthner.

—. 1982. "L'épée à l'acrobate et la chronologie maliote." *Bulletin de correspondance Hellénique* 106: 165-90.

—. 1986. "Un dépôt de fondation au palais de Malia." *Bulletin de correspondance Hellénique* 110: 3-19.

Persson, A.W. 1942. *New Tombs at Dendra near Midea*. Lund: C.W.K. Gleerup.

Rapoport, A. 1969. *House Form and Culture*. Foundations in Cultural Geography Series. Englewood Cliffs: Prentice-Hall.

Rehak, P. 1995a. "Enthroned Figures in Aegean Art and the Function of the Mycenaean Megaron." In Rehak 1995b, 95-118.

—, ed. 1995b. *The Role of the Ruler in the Prehistoric Aegean: Proceedings of a Panel Discussion Presented at the Annual Meeting of the Archaeological Institute of America, New Orleans, Louisiana, 28 December 1992. With Additions*. Aegaeum 11. Liège: Université de Liège, Histoire de l'art et archéologie de la Grèce antique et al.

Rieger, A., and W. Böser. 1990. "Das neue Kartenwerk von Tiryns." In *Tiryns: Forschungen und Berichte*. Vol 11, 165-71. Mainz: Philip von Zabern.

Rutter, J. 2005. "Southern Triangles Revisited: Lakonia, Messenia, and Crete in the 14th-12th Centuries BC." In *Ariadne's Threads: Connections between Crete and the Greek Mainland in Late Minoan III (LM IIIA2 to LM IIIC): Proceedings of the International Workshop held at Athens, Scuola Archeologica Italiana, 5-6 April 2003*, edited by A.-L. D'Agata, J. Moody, and E. Williams, 17-50. Tripodes: Quaderni della Scuola Archeologica Italiana di Atene 3. Athens: Scuola Archeologica Italiana di Atene.

Säflund, G. 1980. "Sacrificial Banquets in the 'Palace of Nestor'." *Opuscula Atheniensa* 13: 237-46.

Sakellarakis, Y., and E. Sakellaraki. 1997. *Archanes: Minoan Crete in a New Light*. Vol. 1. Athens: Ammos Publications.

Schliemann, H. 1976. Reprint. *Tiryns: The Prehistoric Palace of the Kings of Tiryns*. New York: Arno Press. Original edition, London: John Murray, 1886.

Schweitzer, B. 1969. "Das Problem der Form in der Kunst des Altertums." In *Allgemeine Grundlagen der Archäologie: Begriff und Methode, Geschichte, Problem der Form, Schriftzeugnisse*, edited by U. Hausmann, 163-203. München: C.H. Beck.

Shaw, J.W. 1973. "Minoan Architecture: Materials and Techniques." *Annuario della Scuola Archeologica di Atene e delle missioni italiane in Oriente* 49 (n.s. 33): 7-265.

—. 1978. "Evidence for the Minoan Tripartite Shrine." *American Journal of Archaeology* 82: 429-48.

Shaw, J.C., and M.C. Shaw, eds. 1996. *Kommos: An Excavation on the South Coast of Crete*. Vol. 1, *The Kommos Region and Houses of the Minoan Town*. Pt. 2, *The Minoan Hilltop and Hillside Houses*. Princeton: Princeton University Press.

Shaw, M.C. 1986. "The Lion Gate Relief of Mycenae Reconsidered." In *ΦΙΛΙΑ ΕΠΗ εις Γ.Ε. Μυλωνάν*. Vol. 1, 108-23. Βιβλιοθήκη της εν Αθήναις Αρχαιολογικής Εταιρείας 103. Athens: Αρχαιολογική Εταιρεία.

Shelmerdine, C.W. 1987. "Architectural Change and Economic Decline at Pylos." In *Studies in Mycenaean and Classical Greek Presented to John Chadwick*, edited by J.T. Killen, J.L. Melena, and J.-P. Olivier, 557-68. Minos 20-22. Salamanca: Universidad de Salamanca.

Sinos, S. 1971. *Die vorklassischen Hausformen in der Ägäis*. Mainz: Verlag Philipp von Zabern.

Soles, J.S. 1992. *Prepalatial Cemeteries at Mochlos and Gournia and the House Tombs of Bronze Age Crete*. Hesperia Supplement 24. Princeton: American School of Classical Studies at Athens.

Spyropoulos, T. 1972. "Αρχαιότητες και μνημεία Βοιωτίας-Φθιωτίδος: Μεγάλο Καστέλλι." *Αρχαιολογικόν Δελτίον* 27 (Χρονικά): 309-12.

Stocker, S., and J.L. Davis. 2005. "Animal Sacrifice, Archives, and Feasting at the Palace of Nestor." In Wright 2005, 59-75.

Taylor, C. 1993. "Engaged Agency and Background in Heidegger." In *The Cambridge Companion to Heidegger*, edited by C. Guignon, 317-36. New York: Cambridge University Press.

Tenwolde, C. 1992. "Myrtos Revisited: The Role of Relative Function Ceramic Typologies in Bronze Age Settlement Analysis." *Oxford Journal of Archaeology* 11: 1-24.

Thaler, U. 2005. "Narrative and Syntax: New Perspectives on the Late Bronze Age Palace of Pylos, Greece." In *Space Syntax: 5th International Symposium*, edited by A. van Nes, 323-39. Delft: Techne Press.

Trümpy, C. 2001. "Die kretischen und kyprischen Monatsnamen als Zeugen für die Geschichte und Religionsgeschichte im frühen ersten Jahrtausend v.C." In *Kreta und Zypern: Religion und Schrift von der Frühgeschichte bis zum Ende der archaischen Zeit. 26.-28.2.1999, Ohlstadt / Oberbayern - Deutschland*, edited by A. Kyriatsoulis, 233-43. Altenburg: DZA Verlag für Kultur und Wissenschaft.

Tsipopoulou, M. 1990. "Νέα στοιχεία για τη μινωϊκή κατοίκηση στην περιοχή της πόλης της Σητείας." In *Πεπραγμένα του ΣΤ' Διεθνούς Κρητολογικού Συνεδρίου*. Vol. A2, edited by V. Niniou-Kindeli, 305-15. Chania: Φιλολογικός Σύλλογος 'Ο Χρυσόστομος'.

Tuan, Y. 1977. *Space and Place: The Perspective of Experience*. Minneapolis: University of Minnesota Press.

Twain, M. 1899. *The Innocents Abroad or The New Pilgrim's Progress*. 2 vols. Hartford: American Publishing Company.

Tzedakis, G., S. Chryssoulaki, and L. Kyriopoulou. 1990a. "Ο δρόμος στη μινωϊκή Κρήτη." In *Πεπραγμένα του ΣΤ' Διεθνούς Κρητολογικού Συνεδρίου*. Vol. A2΄, edited by V. Niniou-Kindeli, 403-14. Chania: Φιλολογικός Σύλλογος 'Ο Χρυσόστομος'.

Tzedakis, Y., S. Chryssoulaki, Y. Veniéri, and M. Avgouli. 1990b. "Les routes minoennes: Le poste de Hiromandres et le controle des communications." *Bulletin de correspondance Hellénique* 114: 43-62.

van Effenterre, H., and M. van Effenterre. 1969. *Fouilles exécutées a Mallia: Le centre Politique*. Vol. 1, *L'Agora (1960-1966)*. Études Crétoises 17. Paris: École française d'Athénes.

Vermeule, E.T. 1964. *Greece in the Bronze Age*. Chicago: University of Chicago Press.

Wace, A.J.B. 1949. *Mycenae, an Archaeological History and Guide*. Princeton: Princeton University Press.

—. 1956. "The Last Days of Mycenae." In *The Aegean and the Near East: Studies Presented to Hetty Goldman on the Occasion of her Seventy-fifth Birthday*, edited by S.S. Weinberg, 126-35. Locust Valley: J.J. Augustin.

Wace, A.J.B. C.A. Boethius, W.A. Heurtley, L.B. Holland and W. Lamb. 1921-23. "Excavations at Mycenae." *Annual of the British School of Archaeology* 25: 1-434.

Walberg, G. 1976. *Kamares: A Study of the Character of Palatial Middle Minoan Pottery*. Boreas 8. Stockholm: Almqvist and Wiksell.

—. 1986. *Tradition and Innovation: Essays in Minoan Art*. Mainz am Rhein: Verlag Philipp von Zabern.

Warren, P.M. 1972. *Myrtos: An Early Bronze Age Site in Crete*. Annual of the British School in Athens Supplement 7. London: Thames and Hudson.

—. 1994. "The Minoan Roads of Knossos." In *Knossos: A Labyrinth of History: Papers Presented in Honour of Sinclair Hood*, edited by D.H. Evely, H. Hughes-Brock, and N. Momigliano, 189-210. Oxford: Oxbow Books.

Wesenberg, B. 1971. *Kapitelle und Basen: Beobachtungen zur Entstehung der griechischen Säulenformen*. Beihefte der Bonner Jahrbücher 32. Düsseldorf: Rheinland.

Whitelaw, T. 1983. "The Settlement at Fournou Korifi Myrtos and Aspects of Early Minoan Social Organization." In *Minoan Society: Proceedings of the Cambridge Colloquium 1981*, edited by O. Krzyszkowska and L. Nixon, 323-45. Bristol: Bristol Classical Press.

Wright, J.C. 1982. "The Old Temple Terrace at the Argive Heraeum and the Early Cult of Hera in the Argolid." *Journal of Hellenic Studies* 102: 186-201.

—. 1984. "Changes in Form and Function of the Palace at Pylos." In *Pylos Comes Alive: Industry and Administration in a Mycenaean Palace*, edited by C.W. Shelmerdine and T.G. Palaima, 19-29. New York: Archaeological Institute of America.

—. 1987. "Death and Power at Mycenae." In *Thanatos: Les coutumes funéraires en Egée à l'âge du Bronze: Actes du colloque de Liège, 21-23 avril 1986*, edited by R. Laffineur, 171-84. Aegaeum 1. Liège: Université de Liège, Histoire de l'Art et Archéologie de la Grèce Antique.

—. 1994. "The Spatial Configuration of Belief: The Archaeology of Mycenaean Religion." In *Placing the Gods: Sanctuaries and Sacred Space in Ancient Greece*, edited by S.E. Alcock and R. Osborne, 37-78. Oxford: Clarendon Press.

—. 1996. "The Central Hillside at Kommos: The Middle Minoan Period." In Shaw and Shaw 1996, 140-99.

—, ed. 2005. *The Mycenaean Feast*. Princeton: American School of Classical Studies at Athens.

—.2005. "The Formation of the Mycenaean Palace." In *Ancient Greece from the Mycenaean Palaces to the Age of Homer*, edited by S. Deger-Jalkotzy and I.S. Lemos, 7-51. Edinburgh Leventis Studies 3. Edinburgh: Edinburgh University Press.

Wylie, A. 2002. *Thinking from Things: Essays in the Philosophy of Archaeology*. Berkeley: University of California Press.

Xanthoudides, S. 1924. *The Vaulted Tombs of Mesará: An Account of Some Early Cemeteries of Southern Crete*. Translated by J.P. Droop. London: Hodder & Stoughton.

Younger, J.G. 1995. "The Iconography of Rulership in the Aegean: A Conspectus." In Rehak 1995b, 151-211.

Zois, A.A. 1976. *Βασιλική*. Vol. 1, *Νέα αρχαιολογική έρευνα είς το Κεφάλι πλήσιον του χωριού Βασιλική Ιεράπετρας*. Athens: Αρχαιολογική Εταιρεία.

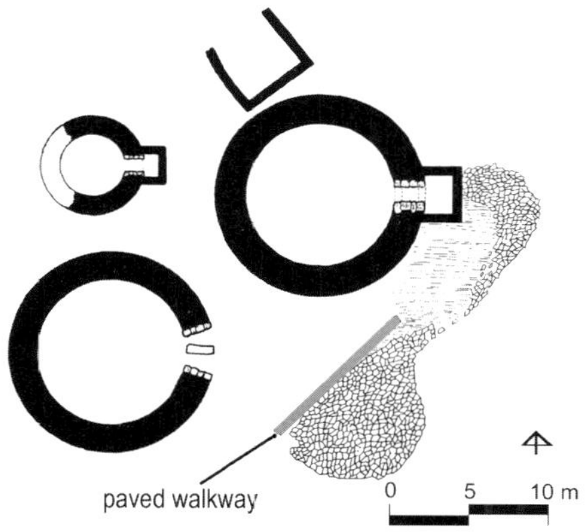

1. Plan of tombs at Koumasa. Adapted from: Xanthoudides 1924, pl. LXI.

2. Plan of tomb of Chrysolakkos. Adapted from: Demargne 1945, pls. XXXVIII.1.

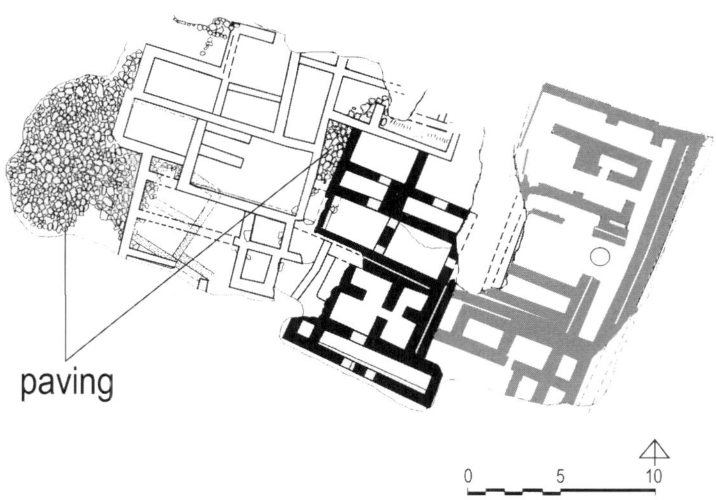

3. Plan of buildings at Vasiliki. Adapted from: Zois 1976, plan III.

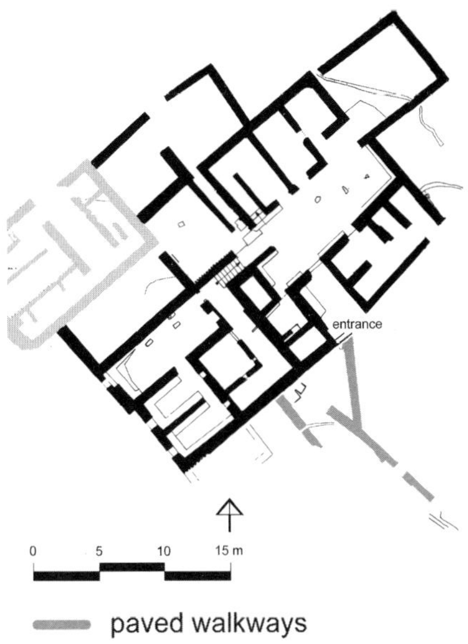

1. Plan of Quartier Mu, building B. Adapted from: Detournay et al. 1980, plan I.

3. Sacred Grove Fresco. Adapted from: Driessen 2002, plate 1

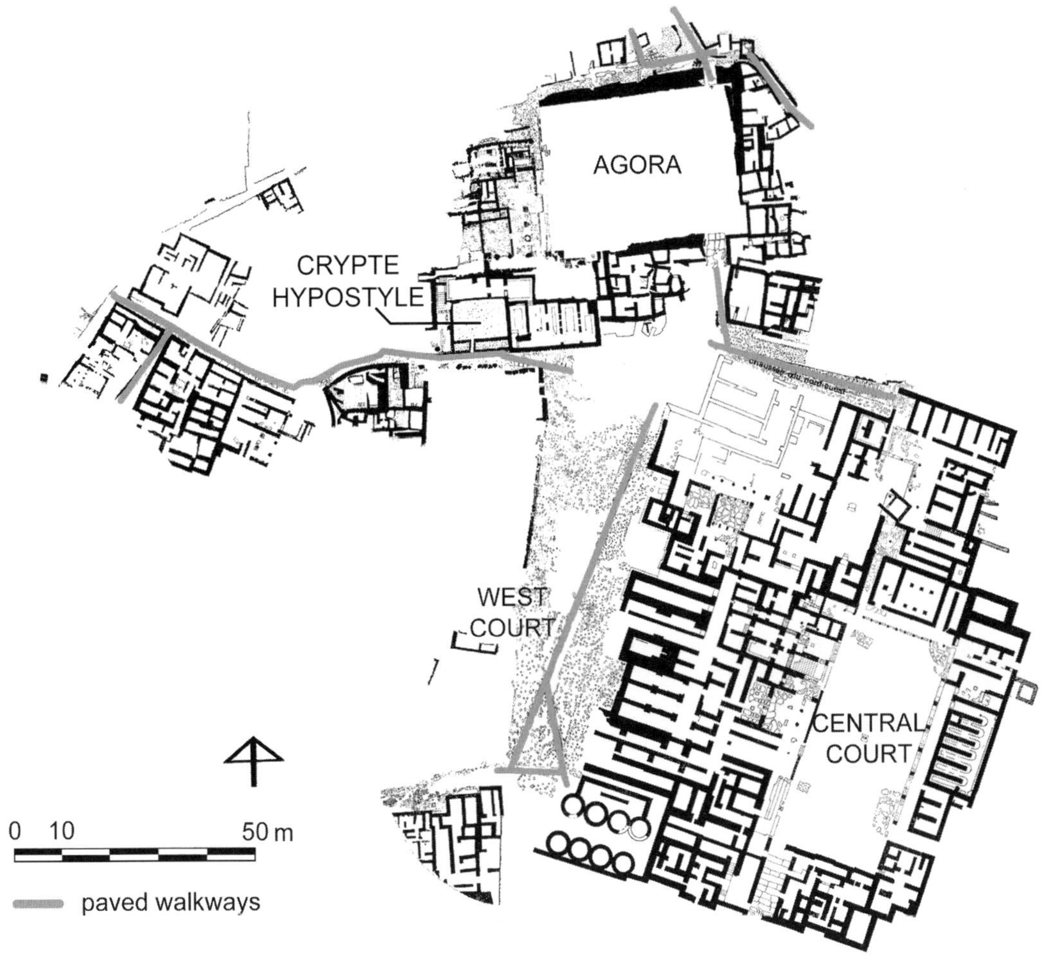

2. Plan of Mallia agora and palace. Adapted from: Effenterre and Effenterre 1969, plan I.

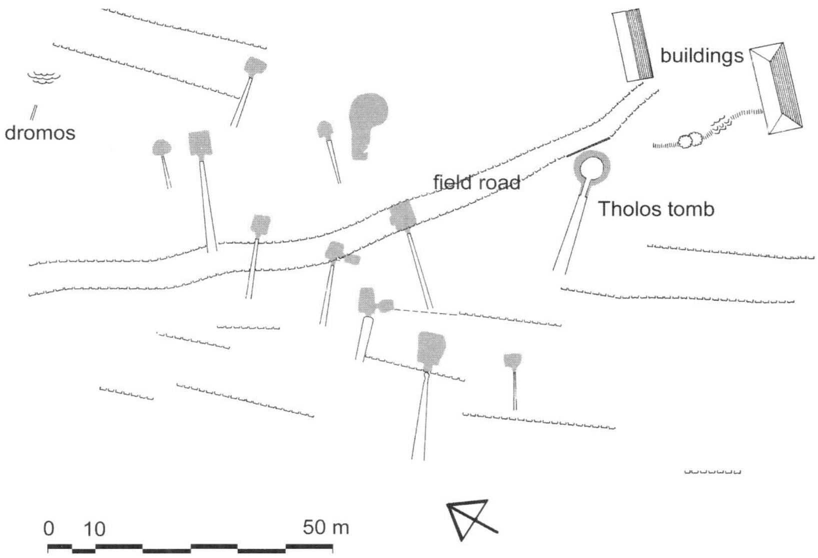

1. Chamber tomb cemetery. Adapted from: Persson 1942, figure 17.

2. Atreus façade. Adapted from: Wace 1949, figure 51.

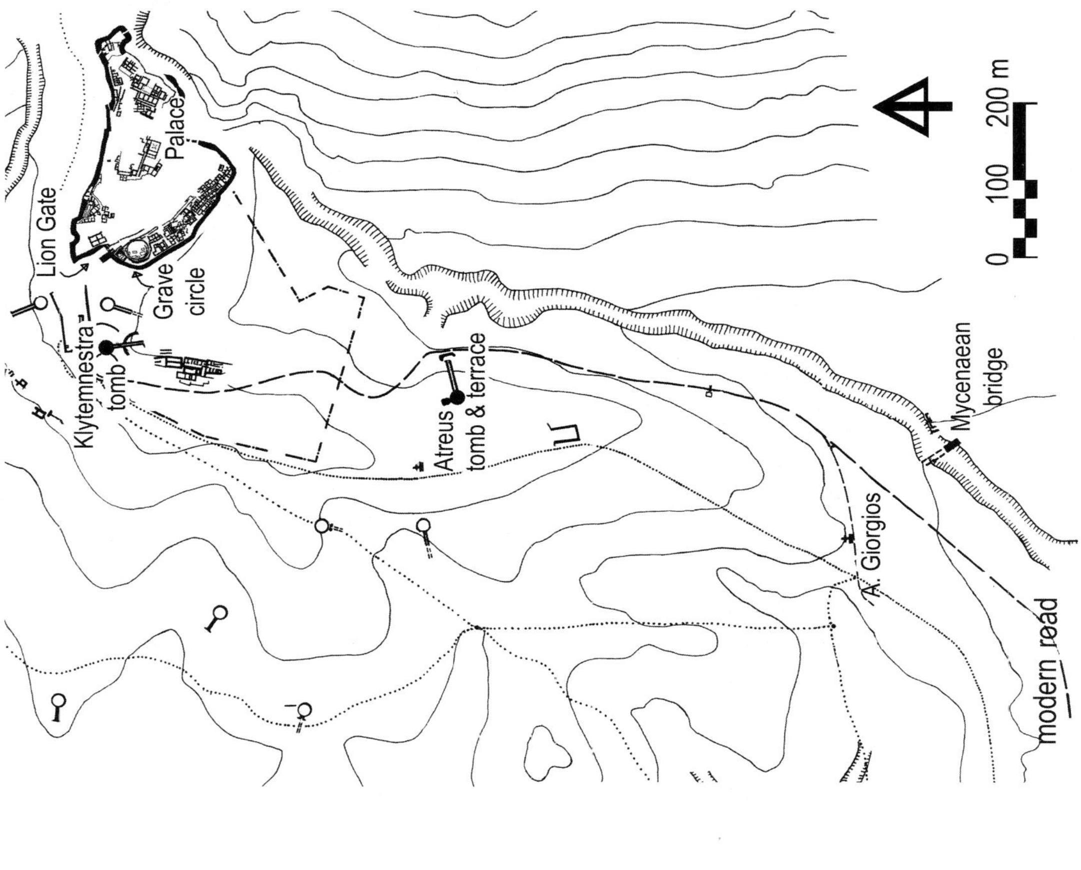

1. Map of Mycenae. Adapted from: Wace 1949, figure 2.

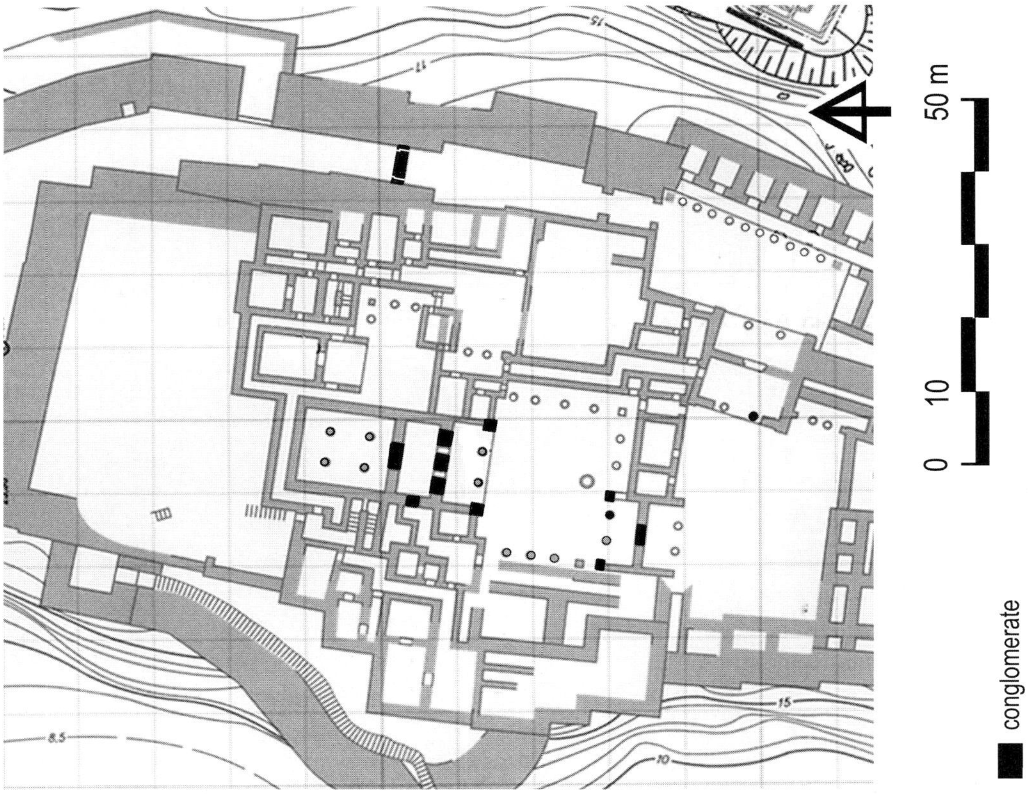

2. Map of Tiryns. Adapted from: Rieger and Böser 1990, foldout plate at 1:1000.

Mycenaean Citadels as Performative Space

Joseph Maran

Every society creates the kind of built environment which it regards as adequate for expressing the particular social relations between individuals. Due to the reflexive relationship between architecture and society, the previous sentence can also be turned around, inasmuch as architectural space contributes to the continuous process of creating society through social practice. This special relation linking society with its built environment derives from the fact that architecture is part of the structure of social systems and thus subject to what Anthony Giddens has called the duality of structure. This means that, to quote Giddens, "the structural properties of social systems are both medium and outcome of the practices they recursively organize"[1]. For this reason, to regard architecture as a mere reflection of specific ideological and political circumstances is insufficient, insofar as it does not consider the dynamic relation between society and architecture. At least in the 'emic' perspective, also the expression 'propaganda' does not adequately describe the way in which monumental architecture works. Its significance rests on the existence of a common set of shared values and worldviews which pervades a given society[2] and on which its members do not usually reflect, because it is ingrained in their habitus. This set of shared values and worldviews, however, can tear apart and let hidden conflicts come to the surface.

The citadels and palaces of Mycenaean culture belong to the World Cultural Heritage and they impress today's visitor by their huge Cyclopean walls, the astonishing corbel-vaulted structures and former decoration with beautiful frescoes. But in this context, my emphasis will be on the question of how certain forms of social practice and architectural space may have interacted in these citadels.

In dealing with British late medieval castles, Matthew Johnson has made clear that in order to gain new insights into such structures a change in perspective is necessary. Research had hitherto focused, he argues, on the definition of the manifold military functions of the castles, on the differentiation of typological groups according to the classification of their plans and on the inference of possible influences of other building traditions mirrored in the ground plans[3]. In contrast to this, the social significance of the castles and their integration into the surrounding landscape can only be understood, if their symbolic meaning and the combination with the forms of social interaction taking place in and around them are considered. The prerequisite for grasping aspects of the perception of the built environment will be to switch from the bird's-eye view on architecture and the associated thinking in ground plans to an approach which takes the perspective of the visitor into account. The analysis of case studies leads Johnson to the conclusion that the way in which different parts of the castles were linked through passageways reflects an architectural staging of the access to the castle, through which the architecture gradually revealed itself to the visitor, while he or she was drawn deeper and deeper into the innermost part of the structure. The spaces of the different buildings and courts the visitor had to pass through, he points out, served as stages for interaction in the social and theatrical sense of that term[4].

The reason why I cited in detail some of the observations of Matthew Johnson on performative aspects of medieval fortification architecture is that in several respects striking similarities to Mycenaean citadels emerge. On a general level, one of these consists in the aspect that these citadels were mostly examined from the viewpoint of fortification and warfare. Only recently, this has begun to change and attempts have been made to determine symbolic aspects of Mycenaean architecture and to link this architecture with social practices possibly taking place in it. In this regard, I particularly want to mention the contributions of James Wright, which have significantly added to our knowledge of the peculiarities

1 Giddens 1984, 24.

2 For the inappropriateness of the term 'propaganda' see already Zanker (1987, 11-4) in the context of the imagery and architecture of early imperial Rome.

3 Johnson 2002, 1-18.

4 Johnson 2002, 51-2.

of the 'staging of power' in Mycenaean Greece[5]. In order to relate architectural space with social practice it is instructive to turn to the concept of 'performative space'. According to Erika Fischer-Lichte, a 'performative space' has the quality of opening up, structuring and organizing possibilities for relations between actors and the audience, for movement and perception[6]. It is important to note, though, that the use of space and the realization of actions are not determined by a 'performative space', and on the contrary, the very meaning of this space is subject to change in the course of the interaction between the actors as well as between them and the audience. In my opinion, a terminology which derives from performance theory and the theatrical connotation of the term "staging" is useful to understand not only medieval castles, but also Mycenaean citadels, whose configuration deserves to be interpreted under the viewpoint of performative esthetics, as described by Fischer-Lichte[7].

It could be objected that the much-used comparison between theatre and life can be applied to all actions and especially to those taking place in public[8]. This is certainly the case, but nevertheless I will try to show, based on previous studies, like those of Wright, that Mycenaean citadels represent a particularly good example for a concept of architecture which is intimately linked to the performance of social interaction. Before turning to case studies, it is necessary to address the nature of the archaeological sources, because it imposes limitations on an interpretation in the sense of 'performative space'. When we apply the terminology developed by Edward T. Hall and Amos Rapoport[9], we have in archaeology parts of the fixed-feature elements of the ground floors of buildings like walls, floors, gates, column-bases and hearths at our disposal, and, if carefully excavated and documented, we get a small number of semifixed-feature elements. Most of the latter elements, like furniture and gardens, however, are almost inevitably lost, which is particularly regrettable since the semifixed realm is crucial for understanding the 'fine-tuning' of spatial arrangements[10]. Finally, the people ('nonfixed-feature elements') who originally moved in these spaces usually do not leave any traces. The analysis of the structure of the architectural remains allows hypothesis on what Rapoport[11] has called "the meaning designed into an environment", and by analyzing how architectural space contributed to the control and the preconfiguration of movement, we can make inferences about the potential for specific patterns of action. Moreover, the observation of the arrangement of architecture enables us to grasp facets of its perception and to recognize possible architectural cues which were decoded by people who had the necessary cultural knowledge. As we will see, in the case of the Mycenaean citadels of the 13th century BC such an investigation leads to the conclusion that they were planned down to details and designed for certain sequences of action. Whether, however, this built environment was ever used in the way it was planned and which associations the inhabitants and users had when they looked at the architecture and its cues, we cannot determine. Moreover, the dynamics of the continuous shift in the meaning of the built environment becomes noticeable to archaeologists only in retrospect, when changes in the layout of the built environment occur.

Some of the characteristic features of Mycenaean palatial architecture were recognized quite early in the history of research. When Heinrich Schliemann and Wilhelm Dörpfeld uncovered the first such palace in Tiryns in 1884 and 1885, they found that at its centre stood an imposing building with its front opening onto a court. The building had a plaster floor with painted decoration and it was structured into three parts, a porch, a vestibule and a main room furnished with a huge round hearth and next to it, at the right-hand wall of the room, a narrow rectangular field lined with small stone blocks. What he found in Tiryns reminded Dörpfeld of the description of the Homeric 'megaron' and accordingly he transferred this designation to the central building of a Mycenaean palace which he also called "Männerwohnung", that is the place where the noble men resided[12]. Dörpfeld's assumption that the megaron represents a

5 Wright 1987; 1994; (forthcoming).
6 Fischer-Lichte 2004, 187.
7 Fischer-Lichte 2004. On specific performative aspects of Mycenaean palatial centres see already Frizell 1997-98; for Minoan palatial architecture Marinatos 1987, 129-42; 1995, 45-7; Goodison 2001, 81-7.
8 Goffman 1959, 71-4; Turner 1982, 102-22; Schechner 2003, 174-7.
9 Hall 1966, 95-105; Rapoport 1982, 87-101.
10 Rapoport 1982, 101.
11 Rapoport 1982, 21.
12 W. Dörpfeld in Schliemann 1886, 215, 253. For a critical assessment of Dörpfeld's use of the term 'megaron' see Jung 2000.

specific feature of Mycenaean imposing architecture was vindicated when only a few years later remains of an almost identical building came to light in the palace of Mycenae[13]. Almost 60 years had to pass, until in the early 1950s the excavation in Pylos in Messenia provided the final evidence that such tripartite central buildings with a round hearth, which we still call 'megaron'[14], were not restricted to the Argolid but rather a general element of Mycenaean palatial architecture.

Not only distinctive features of Mycenaean palaces but also the differences between the latter and Minoan palatial architecture began to emerge already in an early stage of research. The excavations of Sir Arthur Evans in Knossos gave evidence for a palace which did not have a specific building, but a great rectangular court at its centre, an architectural configuration which later proved to be attested in other Cretan sites. In Knossos, bordering on the Central Court a sequence of rooms was found which yielded an elaborate seat with plaster decoration placed against the right-hand wall[15]. This find had a repercussion on the interpretation of the Mycenaean palaces, inasmuch as it suggested that the rectangular stone-lined field on the right-hand wall of the main room of the megaron of Tiryns might have been used as a foundation for a place of a throne[16]. The latter view gained general acceptance when it became evident that the main room of the megaron of Pylos was furnished with a shallow rectangular installation situated exactly at the same spot as in Tiryns[17].

Dörpfeld's approach to use the Homeric poems to interpret Mycenaean imposing architecture had a long-lasting impact on the course of research. But his views were also important, insofar as he introduced the notion of using specific architectural features to identify the whole. When we use the expression 'megaron palaces' today, we follow this line of reasoning. The tendency of segmenting Mycenaean architecture has been intensified due to the fact that research founded its judgments on the analysis of ground plans while the visitor's perspective was rarely taken into consideration. Such a typological approach runs the risk of conceiving an architectural ensemble, like a Mycenaean citadel, as a mere addition of separate architectural modules. To perceive architecture in such a way is consistent with the widespread view of likening space to a container, which is filled with objects and people and forms the background of action. In contrast to this, dynamic concepts of space, like the notion of a "duality of space" of Martina Löw[18], have emphasized that space is not independent from action, but rather constituted through the observation of continuously changing arrangements of social goods and living beings in places[19]. The relevance of such dynamic concepts of space for the interpretation of architecture in general and Mycenaean citadels in particular can be underlined by an example. On the basis of the spatial separation of palace and Cult Centre in Mycenae, Spyridon E. Iakovidis has recently drawn the conclusions that the king cannot have played an important role in religion and that the Cult Centre must have been independent from the palace[20]. If, however, the constitution of space is directly linked with action, then through movement different parts of a settlement could have been connected, and in the eyes of the participants a coherent space may have emerged which was not congruent with a specific architectural module[21]. In my opinion, this point of view is crucial for understanding sites like Tiryns and Mycenae.

As early as 1930, Kurt Müller underlined the necessity to see these citadels as an integral whole and to include the visitor's perspective in the analysis of architecture[22]. Müller's approach is distinguished by the attempt to avoid analogies to Homer and to understand Mycenaean architecture in its own right by carefully observing how it expresses itself. Based on this strict methodology, he was able to gain insights which, although he wrote long before Linear B would be deciphered, still stand up to scrutiny. The ana-

13 Tsountas and Manatt 1969, 44-66.

14 Jung (2000) and Darcque (1990; 2005, 318-9), however, have argued in favor of an abandonment of this term.

15 Evans 1964, 901-20.

16 Müller 1930, 145, 198 with n. 1.

17 Blegen and Rawson 1966, 87-8.

18 Löw 2001, 166-72.

19 Löw 2001, 152-79.

20 Iakovidis 2004, 14, 28-9. See already Mylonas 1977, 75 for a similar view. In contrast to Iakovidis and Mylonas I would agree with those who have argued in favor of a cultic function of the megaron: Dietrich 1973; 1974, 136-9; Wright 1994; Albers 2001, 132-4; see also Maran and Stavrianopoulou (forthcoming).

21 For the linkage of different points of ritual significance within the citadel of Mycenae see Kilian 1992, 17; Albers 1994, 122; Stavrianopoulou 1995.

22 Müller 1930, 167, 193-8.

lysis of the last magnificent phase of palatial rebuilding in Tiryns, which, as we know today, was carried out around 1250 BC, convinced Müller that there had existed the wish to stage through architectural and esthetical means a route connecting the main entrance with the main room of the megaron. Müller was also the first to counter Dörpfeld's interpretation of the megaron as a "Männerwohnung"[23]. Instead, he identified the building with the seat of a ruler, because he had recognized the function of the rectangular stone-line field next to the hearth as the place of a throne.

The increase in knowledge about Mycenaean society gained since the decipherment of Linear B makes it possible to carry on where Müller left off and to combine his ideas with what we know about the political structure and ideology of Mycenaean kingdoms. An example for these new approaches to Mycenaean architecture are studies by Wright, in which he described the organizing principle of the main passageways in the citadels of Tiryns and Mycenae as centripetal and focused on the *wanax*, the Mycenaean king[24]. As the goal and culmination of this organizing principle, he identified the throne-room with the monumental hearth serving as some sort of *axis mundi*[25]. The spatial relation between throne and hearth was interpreted by Wright as a reflection of the involvement of the king in rituals focusing on the hearth-fire and its connection to supernatural powers. That is why he preferred to speak of a "hearth-wanax-ideology" rather than simply of a "wanax ideology", a term coined by Klaus Kilian[26]. Wright went on to link the centripetal direction of passageways in Mycenae and Tiryns with the performance of processions, which he presumed to have formed an integral part of palatial cult activities[27]. The importance of processions in Mycenaean religion was emphasized by Robin Hägg who applied Fritz Graf's[28] basic differentiation between centripetal and centrifugal processions to Mycenaean Greece and supplemented it by the definition of cyclical processions[29].

There are indeed several reasons to assume that processions were a crucial element of Mycenaean rituals. First, processions form the most common iconographical subject of Mycenaean fresco painting of the palatial period. On the right-hand wall of the vestibule of the megaron of Pylos, such a procession leads in the direction of the throne-room[30], a feature which was interpreted by Hägg as a sign of the performance of centripetal processions[31]. Second, the Linear B sources contain indications of processions. Thus, the tablet Tn 316 from Pylos has been interpreted by Anna Sacconi as referring to a yearly ritual procession in honor of several deities[32]. According to Eftychia Stavrianopoulou, the text describes a centrifugal procession from Pylos through several intermediary stations probably to the sacred precinct of Sphagianes[33]. She argued that the movement of this centrifugal procession led to an imagined unification between palace and cult precinct and to a reversal of the existing bipolarity.

Indeed, the defining principles of the organization of Mycenaean citadels cannot be fully understood if we do not consider processions to be a central category of ritual practice[34]. In this context, I will focus on Mycenae and Tiryns during the late palatial period of the 13th century B.C., since these are currently the only Mycenaean palatial sites where the integration of a palace in its wider architectural surroundings can be studied. I will thus focus on the assessment of two synchronous phases of two citadels and not on the long-term dynamics. Needless to say, that I will rely on results previously presented by other colleagues and will add some supplementary observations.

23 Müller 1930, 171, 198.
24 Wright 1994, 60.
25 Wright 1994, 57-8; (forthcoming). For the architectural symbolism of an *axis mundi* see Rapoport 1982, 116.
26 Kilian 1988.
27 Wright (forthcoming).
28 Graf 1996, 56.
29 Hägg 2001. Already Dietrich (1993, 117) made a similar distinction between directions of processional movement, without using the terms 'centripetal' and 'centrifugal'.
30 McCallum 1987, 138-40.
31 Hägg 1985, 216; 2001, 144.
32 Sacconi 1987. For the interpretation of the crucial verb *i-je-to* see Ruijgh 1967, 322 with n. 139; Lejeune 1971, 306-7 with n. 88.
33 Stavrianopoulou 2003
34 The stimulating attempts of Neve (1993, 21-3, fig. 44; 2001, 18-9, 47) to regard the particular layout of the system of gates and passageways in Boğazköy as the reflection of processions which were carried out on certain occasions remind us that a similar situation may have prevailed in the Hittite sphere.

It has to be stressed that, due to the lack of a Linear B archive, the political structure of the Argolid during the Mycenaean palatial period cannot be determined. Undoubtedly, the Argive plain shows the highest density of Mycenaean centers in the whole of Greece, since in addition to Mycenae and Tiryns there are also Argos and Midea. This high density of major sites is particularly noteworthy in light of the lack of clear-cut geographical subdivisions, like mountain ranges or major rivers, in the rather small Argive plain[35]. Nevertheless, the scholarly opinions on the political geography of the Mycenaean palatial period in this region differ significantly. Views interpreting the site distribution as the reflection of rivaling petty kingdoms[36] are found alongside others arguing that the sites were under the rule of the same king. Already Müller opted in favor of this second interpretation and expressed the belief that Mycenae was the capital of a strong and unified kingdom[37]. I fully agree with him and will gather archaeological evidence supporting this assessment.

Any attempt to look at Mycenaean citadels as performative space has to tackle the question of how they originally may have appeared to a visitor. Regrettably, the question of the setting of Mycenaean palatial centers in the landscape and their position in relation to features of the natural environment is rarely considered[38]. In the following, first some aspects of the outer appearance of Mycenae and Tiryns will be discussed, and then we will gradually move on to their interior[39].

From the outside, the Mycenaean citadels of the Argolid were distinguished by the use of un-plastered Cyclopean stone blocks. The impact of this megalithic masonry on an observer must have been enhanced by the fact that the normal contemporary settlement architecture was characterized by open settlements consisting of houses built with stones of small size and mud-bricks[40]. Without denying the practical defensive significance of such Cyclopean fortifications[41], which has been emphasized in the literature, it is likely that this building technique also conveyed to the observer symbolic messages like hardness, inapproachability and unlimited power[42]. This impression was increased by the rather uniform appearance of the Cyclopean walls, which, unlike medieval castles, did not have a façade broken up by protruding towers, windows and architectural ornaments.

The outer appearance of Mycenaean fortifications is particularly obvious in Tiryns. It is not a coincidence that this site is almost always photographed from an elevated position, because on the ground level even from some distance its impression is so uniform that it cannot be adequately depicted. Arguably, nowadays the impression of Mycenaean sites is overly dominated by their fortification because the buildings in the interior of the citadels are only preserved in the lowermost courses of their foundations. But it has to be stressed that in the case of Tiryns even initially most parts of the interior buildings were not visible from the outside, since they were hidden behind the huge walls. The sole exception is the palace, which must have been visible from far away. Revealingly, the part of the acropolis on which the palace stood was not only the highest part of the hill, but also directed towards south, thus ensuring that the palace was seen as a landmark from the sea[43]. In the case of Mycenaean Tiryns, the wish to ensure a maximum of visibility seemingly concerned the palace in general but not the actions taking place in its interior because all palatial courts were surrounded by buildings. This in turn made it impossible for

35 Darcque 1998, 108-9.

36 Cf. Bintliff 1977, 288-9, 345-7; Carlier 1984, 35; Kilian 1988, 296. For a criticism of applying such a 'Homeric model' to the Mycenaean palatial period see Müller 1930, 217; Darcque 1998, 110-2; 2005, 402.

37 Müller 1930, 216-7; Mylonas 1983, 89; Wright 1987, 183; Lauter 1987, 225 with n. 12; Albers (forthcoming); Hope Simpson 2003, 233-4; Maran 2004, 275.

38 An exception is the contribution by Spencer (1995) dealing with the possible visual relation of monuments in the Pylos region. He did not, however, discuss how the palace may have been perceived from different topographical points in its vicinity.

39 We will choose an approach which in the literature has been called 'phenomenological': Tilley 1994; Bender 1998, 22-6, 35-8. See also Barrett 1994, 32-7; Johnson 2002, 1-18. The layout of the ritual topography immediately outside of the fortification of Mycenae and its possible symbolic significance has already been analyzed by Wright (1987), and I will leave aside this aspect.

40 For a comprehensive discussion of building materials and techniques see Darcque 2005, 65-129.

41 Shelmerdine 1999, 407.

42 Iakovidis 1983, 2, 108-9; 1999, 203; Wright 1994, 51; Albers (forthcoming); see also Rapoport 1982, 117 for such a symbolic meaning of the built environment.

43 This is probably also the main reason why the Early Helladic Circular Building of Tiryns was built at exactly the same spot about a millennium prior to the first Mycenaean palatial megaron: Marzolff 2004a, 84.

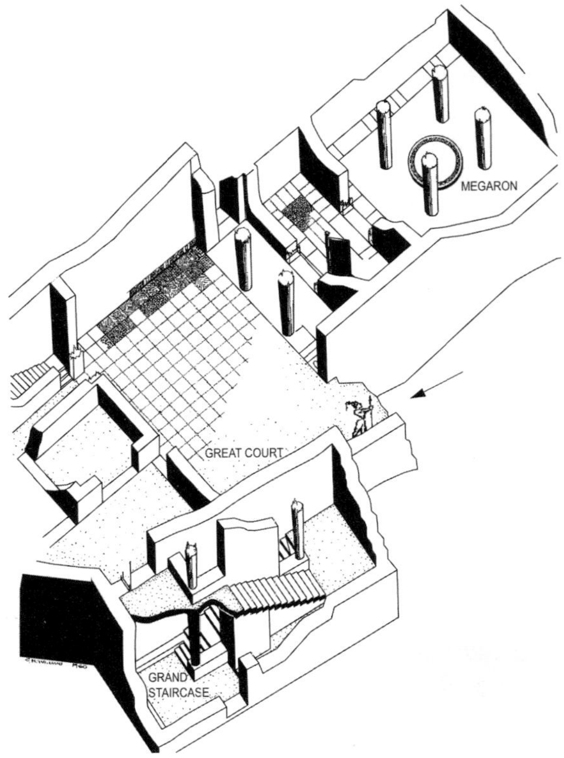

Abb. 1. Mycenae. The approach to the Megaron via the Grand Staircase. After: French 2002, fig. 23. Mycenae Archive, Charles K. Williams II.

people standing in the courts to look outside[44]. William Cavanagh has put forward the hypothesis that these rather closed courts functioned as arenas which may have been overlooked by spectators in the surrounding buildings[45].

The architectural compactness and inapproachability of Tiryns fits well into the usual picture of a marked difference between Minoan and Mycenaean culture as regards the participation of the general population in festivities. Clearly, the central courts of the always-unfortified Minoan palaces offer room for larger numbers of people, and that such impressive gatherings of people indeed took place in the courts is suggested not only by the openness and accessibility of the palaces from the outside, but also by the depiction of crowds of spectators in Minoan fresco painting[46]. In contrast to this, as G. Albers and W. Cavanagh have pointed out[47], the courts of Mycenaean palaces, due to their small size and the architectural restriction of access, are likely to have been intended only for small numbers of selected people.

But what if in the Mycenaean Argolid the communal participation expressed itself differently and took place only in specific sites? It seems to me that in this regard Mycenae may represent a very interesting case. Its megaron with the accompanying court is situated on a lower terrace of the summit of the hill directly above the Chavos ravine (Taf. 11.1-2). This position reminds us that not in all Mycenaean palatial centers the most important building stood on the highest topographical point. Nevertheless, as far as I know, the palaces were always built on topographically exposed spots. The southern side of the court in front of the Mycenae megaron is thought to have been provided with a parapet interpreted in the literature as a means to allow a view from the inside of the palace to the outside[48]. As Cavanagh

44 Cavanagh 2001, 124.
45 Cavanagh 2001, 124.
46 Marinatos 1987; but see Panagiotopoulos (this volume) for a differing position.
47 Albers 2001, 136-8; Cavanagh 2001, 124, 130.
48 Mylonas 1966, 63-4; 1983, 98; Iakovidis 1983, 60; French 2002, 98. A.J.B. Wace was hesitant to decide whether the south wall of the court was high or low, because he argued that the "lords of Mycenae may have preferred safety to scenery"

rightly noted, this view must have been curtailed by the upper part of the Grand Staircase connecting the megaron with the cult centre[49]. Only immediately to the east of the Grand Staircase there seems to have been room for such an opening to the outside (Abb. 1). The unique positioning of the megaron, the court and the Grand Staircase on the edge of a high and very steep rock may bear witness for a magnificent architectural staging in which not so much the view to the outside, but rather *from* the outside played the decisive role. Already from far away the eye of the visitor, who reaches Mycenae on the topographically most important approach, is fixed upon the area of the Grand Staircase and the megaron terrace (Taf. 11.1-2). Thus, like in Tiryns the palace was arranged in order to be seen from a considerable distance. But in contrast to Tiryns, in Mycenae this may have also been done in order to allow a view on what was going on inside the citadel. I suggest this because the lower slopes of the surrounding hills lend themselves to being used, and indeed may have been used, as some sort of an open-air theatre for spectators who observed processions leading to the megaron or to the cult centre[50]. In this context, the mentioned opening between the Grand Staircase and the megaron may have served as a 'window' of appearance (Abb. 1). In addition, further opportunities to be seen from the outside may have existed, if the walls of the Grand Staircase were provided with large openings[51].

When we move towards the citadels, we note a common point between Tiryns and Mycenae inasmuch as the main gates of both sites were architecturally concealed from being seen from a distance. The main gate of Tiryns, which corresponds in its measurements and its way of construction with the Lion Gate[52], was not the main entrance to the site. Instead, it seals off a long and narrow passage, which we will turn to later. Although in Mycenae the Lion Gate served simultaneously as the citadel's main gate and entrance, it was not immediately visible because it was shielded by a protruding rectangular bastion. Accordingly, a visitor notes this gate only in the last part of her or his way to the citadel. Architecturally, the imposing character of the main gates of Mycenae and Tiryns was enhanced by their placement within ascending approaches, in Mycenae a ramp, in Tiryns a passage. Good strategic reasons can be put forward for concealing and elevating the main gates of citadels[53]. Nevertheless, when we look at the further course of the passageway inside the citadel these features may also be read in a different way, namely to reveal to the visitor only gradually and in a steady heightening of tension the mysteries of the sites. In no other citadel the attempt to stage through architectural means the ascent to the palace is as evident as in the already mentioned case of the approach connecting the main entrance with the throne-room in Tiryns (Taf. 13 [yellow]). After the initial description by Müller[54], this way has been the subject of a thorough analysis by Michael Küpper[55]. I will pick up the thread of his comments and will first provide an overview over the course of the way.

The visitor who walked up a ramp to the main entrance and, after turning right, passed through it must have been amazed by the extreme width of the Cyclopean wall, a point already emphasized by Küpper[56]. After entering the narrow passage and turning sharply to the left, one was confronted at a distance with the main gate, which sealed off the ascending gateway and recalled the Lion Gate. This is the first architectural reference to Mycenae which we observe in Tiryns. Behind the main gate, the passage slightly widened and after about 30 m the visitor reached, probably behind an additional narrow gate[57], a wider space formed by an exterior forecourt with a stoa. After another sharp turn to the right,

(Wace 1949, 75; see also Wace et al. 1921-23, 189).

49 Cavanagh 2001, 124.

50 Already Albers (2001, 138) concluded that the general population of a Mycenaean kingdom may have assembled outside of the citadels to follow from a distance as spectators religious ceremonies like processions. Frizell (1997-98, 114) reached a similar conclusion regarding spectators standing outside the citadel of Mycenae along what she called the "via triumphalis", to observe the transport of the huge conglomerate blocks from the quarries to Mycenae

51 Monumental exterior staircases with oversized openings allowing a view from the outside are known from residences of the Renaissance period, cf. Biller and Großmann 2002, 166 (Schloss Hartenfels); Gascar et al. 1979, 16 (Châteaux Blois). I would like to thank Ulrich Thaler for drawing my attention to these buildings.

52 W. Dörpfeld in Schliemann 1886, 218; Müller 1930, 70-3. Müller (1930, 73) even considered that the same architect was responsible for the building of the two gates.

53 Iakovidis 1999, 202.

54 Müller 1930, 193-6; see also Kilian 1984, 45-6; 1987, 25.

55 Küpper 1996, 111-8.

56 Küpper 1996, 112.

57 Müller 1930, 25, fig. 47, pls. 2, 4.

one was faced with the outer hall of the Great Propylon. The intention to lead the visitor in a specific direction manifests itself by the fact that this Propylon is slightly turned northwards, so that someone standing in its inner hall could already see the Little Propylon on the other side of the interior forecourt[58]. After passing through this forecourt and after sharply turning to the right, one walked through the two halls of the Little Propylon, and saw on the opposite side of the Great Court the porch of the Great Megaron, whose main axis was shifted towards east in relation to the one of the Little Propylon. This meant that in order to enter the megaron centrally one again had to change direction. Over two shallow steps, the visitor finally reached, through the porch and the vestibule, the throne-room of the Great Megaron.

Decisive for the interpretation are, however, the details of execution of this passageway, suggesting an attempt to preconfigure the bodily movement and to symbolically 'charge' the ascent to the palace through the intentional use of architectural cues. Of special significance are points which I would like to designate as 'liminal' (Taf. 13)[59]. To this group belong the main entrance, the main gate, all propyla and the porch of the Great Megaron. Not only are they placed at the transition from one zone to the other, but they also yield architectural evidence for an attempt to make one aware of the fact that he or she was about to enter a zone of different meaning. In order to reach these points the direction of movement had to be changed[60]. The visitor took a new position, passed through the point and was faced with the next gate. The liminal points were accentuated on the one hand by monolithic thresholds which had to be crossed, and on the other hand by the structure of the propyla which led the visitor from one hall supported by two columns to another one. The porch of the Great Megaron resembles with its two columns the halls of the propyla[61], thus emphasizing its transitory character. In all known cases, the porch of a Mycenaean palatial megaron is placed opposite to the main access to the court, but not once is it aligned along the same axis[62].

Probably the most remarkable aspect distinguishing the way to the Tirynthian Great Megaron consists in the use of huge conglomerate blocks, which, other than on the route to the throne room, were not systematically used in Tiryns (Taf. 12). While already Müller had recognized that these blocks derive from quarries near Mycenae, which are more than 20 km away[63], it was Wright who first realized the particular symbolic significance of the appearance of this 'Mycenaean' stone material[64]. In investigating the distribution of the conglomerate blocks in Tiryns, Küpper has found them to be employed in a well-considered manner, and in addition he stated that semantically this stone material signified the most important points of access[65]. Unfortunately, he made some mistakes in determining the stone material and that is why his plan[66] showing the appearance of such blocks needs to be corrected (Taf. 12). Thus, not all liminal points were emphasized by conglomerate. Instead, these conglomerate construction elements are concentrated on the main gate, which entirely consists of this stone, and then again on the last and most important part of the way between the Little Propylon and the throne room[67]. Whether other stone materials used in the construction of the Tirynthian palace were also employed because they were symbolically 'charged' is more difficult to say. At least in the case of the entrance to the Great Megaron the alternation of light gray lime-sandstone for the lower step and reddish limestone for the upper step documents a deliberate choice of raw materials (Taf. 12)[68], but this may have been done for the color-

58 Müller 1930, 194; Küpper 1996, 112, fig. 219.

59 Turner 1982, 20-43; Schechner 2003, 58-62. Already Wright (1994, 54) compared such points to boundaries which one had to pass.

60 Mühlenbruch 2003, 480 fig. 1, 482-3.

61 Iakovidis 1983, 14.

62 It seems insufficient to try to explain this merely by pointing to the need to lead the visitor past the altar in the Great Court of Tiryns (Küpper 1996, 113), since in Mycenae and Pylos, where no such installation seems to have existed, the same phenomenon can be observed.

63 Müller 1930, 177, 216. For the considerable labour effort involved in transporting and using these huge blocks as building material see Santillo 1989; Frizell 1997-98.

64 Wright 1987, 174-83.

65 Küpper 1996, 115-8.

66 Küpper 1996, fig. 220.2.

67 After a detailed discussion, Küpper (1996, 114-5) reached the conclusion that all conglomerate thresholds must have been visible, and that probably also the conglomerate blocks used in the front of the antae-walls of the Great Megaron had remained unplastered.

68 Müller 1930, 195.

effect only[69]. At first sight, the use of the reddish limestone for all column bases of the Great Megaron points in a similar direction, but Küpper has convincingly argued that the material of the stone was concealed by plaster[70].

It is likely that in addition to symbolic cues the play with opposite esthetical experiences contributed to the staging of the way to the throne-room. First of all, there is the experience of narrow vs. wide and dark vs. light. The way leads from the narrowness of the passage, which Müller likened to a ravine[71], to the wideness of the different courts[72]. During daylight, the experience of walking this way must have been characterized by the alternation between hypaethral parts lightened by the brightness of the sun and the darkness of the roofed parts[73]. But probably a different esthetical factor exerted the greatest influence on a visitor. While the walls of the narrow gateway consisted of huge, rough stone-blocks, somewhere behind the Great Propylon the colorful images of the frescos adorning the walls must have suddenly set in. Neither in Tiryns nor in Mycenae we are able to reconstruct the fresco program but it is certain that depictions of processions formed the most important iconographical topic.

The whole structure of the way exemplifies an attempt to prescribe by architectural means the movement of a visitor and to draw her or him into the depth of the citadel, until the goal of the movement, the Great Megaron, was reached. This is not the only aspect of performative space in which Mycenaean citadels resemble the circumstances in British medieval castles described by Matthew Johnson. Other similarities are the significance of "twists and turns at critical moments, when one crosses a threshold into a space of different social status"[74], and the fact that the hall situated in the centre of medieval castles was placed in a way that a visitor entering the courtyard would immediately notice it[75].

It should be mentioned that, besides the described centripetally directed way, there exists in Tiryns also a quite direct access to the palace which is distinguished by different features. In approaching the citadel from the harbor and through the western Lower Town, a visitor could have directly entered the citadel through a postern gate and then could have moved onwards to reach the west wing of the palace via the West Staircase and the Middle Citadel (Taf. 13 [pink]). This connection, however, does not exhibit any of the mentioned signs for an architectural staging of the ascent, and I think it is likely that it served as a more private access for the staff and dignitaries of the palace[76].

When we try to identify in Mycenae a way resembling in its architectural staging and the use of symbolic cues the described connection between the main entrance and the megaron in Tiryns, then the likely choice is the passageway which starts at the Lion Gate, climbs up the ramp and winds up the west slope of the hill, to finally reach after crossing gates and other entrances with monolithic conglomerate thresholds[77] the court of the megaron[78]. As in Tiryns, the main axis of the propylon of Mycenae is shifted in a way that a visitor is optically guided to the next liminal point, thus emphasizing the centripetal direction of this way. Besides this centripetally directed access there exists in Mycenae another way to reach the megaron, namely via the already mentioned Grand Staircase. In contrast to the West Staircase of Tiryns which connected the palace with the Lower Town, the Grand Staircase of Mycenae was integrated in the circulation within the citadel. It is part of what Georgios E. Mylonas has called the procession way, because it provides a connection between the megaron and the cult centre, and then onwards to Grave Circle A[79]. The concept of this way differs in several respects from what we find in Tiryns. Along the way, there were several stations to be reached, and its orientation can be designated 'centrifugal' just as well as 'centripetal'. In fact, I would agree with Mylonas that in this case the centrifugal direction is more pronounced. This way provided an imposing connection between the seat of

69 Müller 1930, 195.
70 Küpper 1996, 113-4.
71 Müller 1930, 73 ("beklemmende Enge"), 193 ("schluchtartige Enge"). On the importance of light effects in the staging of power in Minoan palaces see Goodison 2001.
72 Küpper 1996, 112-3.
73 Müller 1930, 167-8, 193-5, fig. 75.
74 Johnson 2002, 83.
75 Johnson 2002, 75.
76 Kilian 1984, 46.
77 Mylonas 1966, 16-20; Küpper 1996, 115-6, fig. 220.1.
78 Mylonas 1966, 66-78; Iakovidis 1983, 57-9; Wright 1994, 51-4.
79 Mylonas 1977, 26-8; 1983, 138-41; Albers 1994, 16-7, 122.

the king, the seat of the gods and the seat of the ideologically elevated ancestors[80]. Moreover, it allowed a continuation of processions outside the walls of the citadel to the tholos graves and to other points in the closer or further vicinity of Mycenae. The population of the kingdom may have been able to follow from the outside as spectators some of the events going on. As mentioned, the upper part of the way from the megaron to the Cult Centre could have been overlooked from the surrounding hills, while the view on the lower part of the way, between the Cult Centre and the Lion Gate was probably blocked by the Cyclopean wall. Outside of the Lion Gate, on the other hand, the population may have again had the opportunity to follow the events[81].

That the way over the Grand Staircase to the megaron does not find any comparison in Tiryns is only one of a series of features by which Mycenae is set apart from all other Argive sites. To these features belong the Cult Centre, Grave Circle A and a unique concentration of tholos tombs[82]. These differences lead us back to the decisive question of the political relation between Mycenae and Tiryns. I agree with Gabriele Albers that the very special ritual topography of Mycenae bears witness for supremacy of this site during the palatial period[83]. This was the main seat of the king's family, where on certain occasions and with the possible integration of the population rituals were carried out which exemplified the connection between the ruling, the gods and the ancestors and thus were of central significance for bolstering the then prevalent world-view. In my opinion, in Tiryns most of these elements are missing, because it served as a second palace of the same king, in which only specific rituals were carried out. This would explain why we get in Tiryns symbolic references to Mycenae, like the copy of the Lion Gate and the conglomerate thresholds, which are likely to have been understood by the initiated[84]. Similar to the use of porphyry as a sign of papal or imperial power in the European Middle Ages[85], conglomerate may have been regarded as the kingly stone of the Argolid during the Mycenaean palatial period. If we interpret Tiryns as the second palace of the same ruler, it becomes understandable why at this site, on the basis of the architectural staging of the mentioned passageways, only a centripetal, but not a centrifugal direction can be inferred. This is so, I would argue, because the Tirynthian megaron served as the goal, but not the starting point of processions. We can speculate that the king and/or the queen traveled on certain occasions from Mycenae to Tiryns in order to perform certain rituals, to reside and to receive high guests coming from over the sea. Possibly the kingly pair itself led the procession or it entered the Great Megaron through the West Staircase and the corridors of the West Wing of the palace and waited there for the procession to arrive. The whole importance of campstools in contemporary iconography and the iconographical attestation of sedan-seats[86] may derive from the institution of an 'itinerant monarchy'.

The assumption that the *wanax* and the queen only occasionally visited Tiryns would also help to explain some exceptional features of its palace. The equipment of the so-called bathroom with one of the largest monoliths used in Tiryns consisting of a unique stone material of unknown provenance (Taf. 12), as well as the connection, albeit indirect[87], between this room and the vestibule of the Great Megaron point to an extraordinary importance of the bathroom. This may have been the place where the king or the queen after their arrival underwent a ritual purification before entering the Great Megaron[88]. Another feature possibly reflecting the status of Tiryns as a second palace is the curious doubling of megaron-buildings which in this clarity is unparalleled in other Mycenaean palaces[89]. As is well known, the Little Megaron resembles in most respects a miniature version of the Great Megaron. Its floors were decora-

80 Wright 1987, 179-81; Albers 1994, 122; Stavrianopoulou 1995, 432.

81 Albers 2001, 138.

82 Wright 1987, 177-82.

83 Albers (forthcoming). See also Albers 2001, 131, 139-41.

84 See already Müller 1930, 216-7.

85 De Blaauw 1991. On color symbolism in medieval towns see Marzolff 2004b.

86 Dimakopoulou 1989.

87 Contrary to the original interpretation of W. Dörpfeld (in Schliemann 1886, 260), Müller (1930, 148-50) has shown that the 'bathroom' was only accessible from the north-south oriented Corridor XII, but not from Corridor IX which led directly to the side-entrance of the porch of the Great Megaron. But if Müller was correct in assuming a connection between Corridors IX and XII (Müller 1930, 148, pl. 1), bathroom and megaron would have nevertheless been linked. For a different viewpoint see Küpper 1996, 117.

88 A ritual function of the Tiryns bathroom was already postulated by H.B. Siedentopf (in Jantzen 1975, 34), Kilian (1987, 25) and Papadimitriou (2001, 42).

89 Already Müller (1930, 168-71) spoke of a "Doppelpalast".

ted, it had a court, a porch and a main room furnished with a central hearth and a rectangular field on its right which is likely to have served as the place of a throne. Although the Little Megaron stood next to the Great Megaron, no connection between the two buildings seems to have existed and instead the Little Megaron had a totally separate system of access branching off from the main route in the inner hall of the Great Propylon[90]. This way also exhibits some of the already described features of the architectural staging of movement, like the importance of twists and turns before reaching monolithic thresholds or doorways and the alternation of open and roofed spaces. Still, it lacks the monumentality and the powerful symbolic cues of the main passageway, such as the use of conglomerate and the integration of propyla. Kilian identified the Little Megaron as the seat of the *lawagetas*[91]. This may indeed have been the case, but I would argue that whoever resided in the Little Megaron is likely to have done this in their function as the deputy of the *wanax* in Mycenae.

It was my aim to show that the whole significance of architecture only reveals itself if one tries to link it with social practice and to grasp aspects of what Martina Löw calls the "duality of space". In this regard, the archaeologist is faced with a dilemma. She or he can never get a direct glimpse on actual social practices, but can at the most recognize indirectly aspects of these, exactly because space and action are mutually related and facets of the pattern of movement are mirrored in the built environment in its function as performative space. In the case of the Mycenaean citadels, processions are likely to have been the kind of interaction which left the most marked imprint on the layout of architecture. During the processions, the meaning encoded in certain architectural cues was recalled by the participants and integrated by them into ritual practice through which the social order and the relation to supernatural powers were simultaneously expressed and newly constituted.

BIBLIOGRAPHY

Albers, G. 1994. *Spätmykenische Stadtheiligtümer: Systematische Analyse und vergleichende Auswertung der archäologischen Befunde*. British Archaeological Reports International Series 596. Oxford: Tempus Reparatum.

—. 2001. "Rethinking Mycenaean Sanctuaries." In Laffineur and Hägg 2001, 131-41.

—. Forthcoming. "Re-Evaluating Mycenaean Sanctuaries." In *Celebrations: Sanctuaries and the Vestiges of Cult Practice: Symposium Held at the Norwegian Institute at Athens, 12-16 May 1999.*

Barrett, J.C. 1994. *Fragments from Antiquity: An Archaeology of Social Life in Britain, 2900-1200 BC*. Oxford et al.: Blackwell.

Bender, B. 1998. *Stonehenge: Making Space*. Oxford et al.: Berg.

Biller, T., and G.U. Großmann. 2002. *Burg und Schloss: Der Adelssitz im deutschsprachigen Raum*. Regensburg: Schnell und Steiner.

Bintliff, J.L. 1977. *Natural Environment and Human Settlement in Prehistoric Greece*. British Archaeological Reports Supplementary Series 28. Oxford: British Archaeological Reports.

Blegen, C.W., and M. Rawson. 1966. *The Palace of Nestor at Pylos in Western Messenia*. Vol. 1, *The Buildings and their Contents*. Princeton: Princeton University Press.

Carlier, P. 1984. *La royauté en Grèce avant Alexandre*. Strasbourg: AECR.

Cavanagh, W. 2001. "Empty Space? Courts and Squares in Mycenaean Towns." In *Urbanism in the Aegean Bronze Age*, edited by K. Branigan, 119-34. Sheffield: Sheffield Academic Press.

Darcque, P. 1990. "Pour l'abandon du terme 'megaron'." In *L'habitat égéen préhistorique: Actes de la Table ronde d'Athènes, 23-27 juin 1987*, edited by P. Darcque and R. Treuil, 21-31. Bulletin de Correspondence Hellénique Supplement 19. Paris: Boccard.

—. 1998. "Argos et la plaine argienne à l'époque mycénienne". In *Argos et l'Argolide: Topographie et urbanisme: Actes de la Table ronde internationale, Athènes – Argos, 28/4-1/5/1990*, edited by A. Pariente and G. Touchais, 103-15. Recherches franco-helléniques 3. Athens: École française d'Athènes.

90 Müller 1930, 167-9, fig. 75.
91 Kilian 1987, 32.

—. 2005. *L'habitat Mycénien: Formes et fonctions de l'espace bâti en Grèce continentale à la fin du IIe millénaire avant J.-C.* Bibliothèque des Écoles françaises d'Athènes et de Rome 319. Athens: École française d'Athènes.

de Blaauw, S. 1991. "Papst und Purpur: Porphyr in frühen Kirchenausstattungen in Rom." In *Tesserae: Festschrift für Josef Engemann*, edited by E. Dassmann, 36-50. Jahrbuch für Antike und Christentum Ergänzungsband 18. Münster: Aschendorffsche Verlagsbuchhandlung.

Dietrich, B.C. 1973. "A Religious Function of the Megaron." *Rivista storica dell'antichità* 3: 1-12.

—. 1974. *The Origins of Greek Religion*. Berlin et al.: de Gruyter.

—. 1993. "Uniformity and Change in Minoan and Mycenaean Religion." *Kernos* 6: 113-22.

Dimakopoulou, K. 1989. "Πήλινο ομοίωμα φορείου της μυκηναϊκής εποχής από την Τίρυνθα." In *ΦΙΛΙΑ ΕΠΗ εις Γ.Ε. Μυλωνάν*. Vol. 3, 25-33. Athens: Archaeological Society of Athens.

Evans, A. 1964. *The Palace of Minos at Knossos*. Vol. 4. New York: Biblo and Tannen.

Fischer-Lichte, E. 2004. *Ästhetik des Performativen*. Edition Suhrkamp 2373. Frankfurt am Main: Suhrkamp.

French, E. 2002. *Mycenae: Agamemnon's Capital: The Site in its Setting*. Stroud: Tempus.

Frizell, B.S. 1997-98. "Monumental Building at Mycenae: Its Function and Audience." *Opuscula Atheniensia* 22-23: 103-16.

Gascar, P. 1979. "Königssitze." In *Die schönsten Burgen und Schlösser Frankreichs*, 8-49. Zürich et al.: Verlag Das Beste.

Giddens, A. 1984. *The Constitution of Society: Outline of the Theory of Structuration*. Berkeley et al.: University of California Press.

Goffman, E. 1959. *The Presentation of Self in Everyday Life*. Garden City: Doubleday.

Goodison, L. 2001. "From Tholos Tomb to Throne Room: Perceptions of the Sun in Minoan Ritual." In Laffineur and Hägg 2001, 77-88.

Graf, F. 1996. "Pompai in Greece: Some Considerations about Space and Ritual in the Greek Polis." In *The Role of Religion in the Early Greek Polis: Proceedings of the Third International Seminar on Ancient Greek Cult, organized by the Swedish Institute at Athens, 16-18 October 1982*, edited by R. Hägg, 55-65. Stockholm: Åström.

Hägg, R. 1985. "Pictorial Programmes in Minoan Palaces and Villas." In *L'iconographie Minoenne: Actes de la Table Ronde d'Athènes (21-22 avril 1983)*, edited by P. Darcque and J.-C. Poursat, 209-17. Bulletin de Correspondance Hellénique Supplément 11. Paris: Boccard.

—. 2001. "Religious Processions in Mycenaean Greece." In *Contributions to the Archaeology and History of the Bronze and Iron Ages in the Eastern Mediterranean: Studies in Honour of Paul Åström*, edited by P.M. Fischer, 143-7. Vienna: Österreichisches Archäologisches Institut.

Hägg, R., and N. Marinatos, eds. 1987. *The Function of the Minoan Palaces: Proceedings of the Fourth International Symposium at the Swedish Institute in Athens, 10-16 June, 1984*. Stockholm: Åström.

Hall, E.T. 1966. *The Hidden Dimension: Man's Use of Space in Public and Private*. London et al.: The Bodley Head.

Hope Simpson, R. 2003. "The Dodecanese and the Ahhiyawa Question." *Annual of the British School of Archaeology at Athens* 98: 203-37.

Iakovidis, S.E. 1983. *Late Helladic Citadels on Mainland Greece*. Monumenta Graeca et Romana 4. Leiden: Brill.

—. 1999. "Late Helladic Fortifications." In Laffineur 1999, 199-204.

—. 2004. "The Cult Centre of Mycenae." In *I culti primordiali della Grecità: Convegno Internazionale alla luce delle scoperte di Tebe, Roma, 24-25 febbraio 2000*, 13-30. Rome: Academia Nazionale dei Lincei.

Jantzen, U. 1975. *Führer durch Tiryns*. Athens: Deutsches Archäologisches Institut.

Johnson, M. 2002. *Behind the Castle Gate: From Medieval to Renaissance*. London et al.: Routledge.

Jung, R. 2000. "Das Megaron – Ein Analogie(kurz)schluss der ägäischen Archäologie." In *Vergleichen als archäologische Methode: Analogien in den Archäologien*, edited by A. Gramsch, 71-95. British Archaeological Reports International Series 825. Oxford: Tempus Reparatum.

Kilian, K. 1984. "Pylos – Funktionsanalyse einer Residenz der späten Palastzeit." *Archäologisches Korrespondenzblatt* 14: 37-58.

—. 1987. "Zur Funktion der mykenischen Residenzen auf dem griechischen Festland." In Hägg and Marinatos 1987, 21-37.

—. 1988. "The Emergence of *wanax* Ideology in the Mycenaean Palaces." *Oxford Journal of Archaeology* 7: 291-302.

—. 1992. "Mykenische Heiligtümer der Peloponnes." In *KOTINOS: Festschrift für Erika Simon*, edited by H. Froning, T. Hölscher, and H. Mielsch, 10-25. Mainz: Zabern.

Küpper, M. 1996. *Mykenische Architektur: Material, Bearbeitungstechnik, Konstruktion und Erscheinungsbild.* Internationale Archäologie 25. Espelkamp: Leidorf.

Laffineur, R., ed. 1999. *POLEMOS: Le contexte guerrier en Égée à l'âge du Bronze: Actes de la 7e Rencontre égéenne internationale, Université de Liège, 14-17 avril 1998.* Aegaeum 19. Liège: Université de Liège et al.

Laffineur, R., and R. Hägg. eds. 2001. *POTNIA: Deities and Religion in the Aegean Bronze Age: Proceedings of the 8th International Aegean Conference, Göteborg, Göteborg University, 12-15 April 2000.* Aegaeum 22. Liège: Université de Liège et al.

Lauter, H. 1987. "Nouveaux aspects du palais de Mycènes au HR IIIB." In *Le système palatial en Orient, en Grèce et à Rome: Actes du Colloque de Strasbourg, 19-22 juin 1985*, edited by E. Lévy, 219-25. Leiden: Brill.

Lejeune M. 1971. *Mémoires de philologie mycénienne: Deuxième série (1958-1963).* Incunabula Graeca 42. Rome: Edizioni dell'Ateneo.

Löw, M. 2001. *Raumsoziologie.* Suhrkamp Taschenbuch Wissenschaft 1506. Frankfurt am Main: Suhrkamp.

Maran, J. 2004. "Architektonische Innovation im spätmykenischen Tiryns – Lokale Bauprogramme und fremde Kultureinflüsse." In *Althellenische Technologie und Technik. Tagungsband 21.-23.3.2003 Ohlstadt*, 261-88. Weilheim: Verein zur Förderung der Aufarbeitung der Hellenischen Geschichte.

Maran, J., and E. Stavrianopoulou. Forthcoming. "Πότνιος Ανήρ - Reflections on the Ideology of Mycenaean Kingship." In *KEIMELION: The Formation of Elites and Elitist Lifestyles from Mycenaean Palatial Times to the Homeric Period*, edited by E. Alram and G. Nightingale.

Marinatos, N. 1987. "Public Festivals in the West Courts of the Palaces." In Hägg and Marinatos 1987, 135-42.

—. 1995. "Divine Kingship in Minoan Crete." In *The Role of the Ruler in the Prehistoric Aegean: Proceedings of a Panel Discussion Presented at the Annual Meeting of the Archaeological Institute of America, New Orleans, Louisiana 28 December 1992*, edited by P. Rehak, 37-48. Aegaeum 11. Liège: Université de Liège et al.

Marzolff, P. 2004a. "Das zweifache Rätsel Tiryns." In *Macht der Architektur – Architektur der Macht: Bauforschungskolloquium in Berlin vom 30. Oktober bis 2. November 2002 veranstaltet vom Architektur-Referat des DAI*, edited by E.-L. Schwandner and K. Rheidt, 79-91. Diskussionen zur Archäologischen Bauforschung 8. Mainz: Zabern.

—. 2004b. "Roter Turm und Weißes Tor. Die 'farbige' Stadt des Mittelalters." In *Die vermessene Stadt: Mittelalterliche Stadtplanung zwischen Mythos und Befund*, edited by M. Untermann, 173-9. Mitteilungen der Deutschen Gesellschaft für Archäologie des Mittelalters und der Neuzeit 15. Paderborn: Deutsche Gesellschaft für Archäologie des Mittelalters und der Neuzeit.

McCallum, L.R. 1987. "Decorative Program in the Mycenaean Palace of Pylos: The Megaron Frescoes." Ph.D. diss., University of Pennsylvania.

Mühlenbruch, T. 2003. "Zu vorderorientalischen Parallelen der mykenischen Palastrchitektur." *Archäologisches Korrespondenzblatt* 33: 479-91.

Müller, K. 1930. *Tiryns: Die Ergebnisse der Ausgrabungen des Instituts.* Vol. 3, *Die Architektur der Burg und des Palastes.* Augsburg: Filser

Mylonas, G.E. 1966. *Mycenae and the Mycenaean Age.* Princeton: Princeton University Press.

—. 1977. *Μυκηναϊκή Θρησκεία.* Πραγματείαι της Ακαδημίας Αθηνών 39. Athens: Athens Academy.

—. 1983. *Πολύχρυσοι Μυκήναι.* Athens: Ekdotiki Athinon.

Neve, P. 1993. *Hattuša – Stadt der Götter und Tempel: Neue Ausgrabungen in der Hauptstadt der Hethiter.* Mainz: Zabern.

—. 2001. Die Oberstadt von *Hattuša: Die Bauwerke.* Vol. 2, *Die Bastion des Sphinxtores und die Tempelviertel am Königs- und Löwentor.* Boğazköy-Hattuša: Ergebnisse der Ausgrabungen 17. Mainz: Zabern.

Papadimitriou, A. 2001. *Τίρυνς: Ιστορικός και αρχαιολογικός οδηγός.* Athens: Ekdoseis Esperos.

Rapoport, A. 1982. *The Meaning of the Built Environment: A Nonverbal Communication Approach*. Beverly Hills et al.: Sage Publications.

Ruijgh, C.J. 1967. *Études sur la grammaire et le vocabulaire du grec mycénien*. Amsterdam: Hakkert.

Sacconi, A. 1987. "La tavoletta di Pilo Tn 316: Una registrazione di carattere eccezionale?" In *Studies in Mycenaean and Classical Greek Presented to John Chadwick*, edited by J.T. Killen, J.L. Melena, and J.-P. Olivier, 551-5. Minos N.S. 20-22. Salamanca: Universidad di Salamanca.

Santillo, R. 1989. "Il blocco da 120 tonnellate nell'antichità. Problemi e soluzioni di trasporto e di posizionamento." *Edilizia Militare* 25-26: 47-64.

Schechner, R. 2003. *Performance Studies: An Introduction*. London et al.: Routledge.

Schliemann, H. 1886. *Tiryns: Der prähistorische Palast der Könige von Tiryns*. Leipzig: Brockhaus.

Shelmerdine, C.W. 1999. "Pylian Polemics: The Latest Evidence on Military Matters." In Laffineur 1999, 403-8.

Spathari, E. 2001. *Μυκήνες: Ιστορικός και αρχαιολογικός οδηγός*. Athens: Ekdoseis Esperos.

Spencer, N. 1995. "Heroic Time: Monuments and the Past in Messenia, Southwest Greece." *Oxford Journal of Archaeology* 14: 277-92.

Stavrianopoulou, E. 1995. "Die Verflechtung des Politischen mit dem Religiösen im mykenischen Pylos." In *POLITEIA: Society and State in the Aegean Bronze Age: Proceedings of the 5th International Aegean Conference, University of Heidelberg, Archäologisches Institut, 10-13 April 1994*, edited by R. Laffineur and R. Hägg, 423-433. Aegaeum 12. Liège: Université de Liège et al.

—. 2003. "Neue Erkenntnisse zur frühgriechischen Religion: Der Beitrag der mykenischen Texte." Inaugural lecture, University of Heidelberg, 4 June 2003.

Tilley, C. 1994. *A Phenomenology of Landscape: Places, Paths and Monuments*. Oxford et al.: Berg.

Tsountas, C., and J.I. Manatt. Reprint 1969. *The Mycenaean Age: A Study of the Monuments and Culture of Pre-Homeric Greece*. Chicago: Argonaut Publishers. Original edition, London: Macmillan, 1897.

Turner, V. 1982. *From Ritual to Theatre: The Human Seriousness of Play*. New York: PAJ Publications.

Wace, A.J.B. 1949. *Mycenae: An Archaeological History and Guide*. Princeton: Princeton University Press.

Wace, A.J.B., C.A. Boethius, W.A. Heurtley, L.B. Holland, and W. Lamb. 1921-23. "Excavations at Mycenae." *Annual of the British School at Athens* 25: 1-434.

Wright, J.C. 1987. "Death and Power at Mycenae: Changing Symbols in Mortuary Practice." In *Thanatos: Les coutumes funeraires en Egee a l'age du bronze: Actes du colloque de Liège (21-23 avril 1986)*, edited by R. Laffineur, 171-84. Aegaeum 1. Liège: Université de Liège et al.

—. 1994. "The Spatial Configuration of Belief: The Archaeology of Mycenaean Religion." In *Placing the Gods: Sanctuaries and Sacred Space in Ancient Greece*, edited by S.E. Alcock and R. Osborne, 37-78. Oxford: Clarendon Press.

—. Forthcoming. "The Formation of the Mycenaean Palace." In *Ancient Greece from the Mycenaean Palaces to the Age of Homer*, edited by S. Deger-Jalkotzy and I.S. Lemos. Edinburgh Leventis Studies 3. Edinburgh: Edinburgh University Press.

Zanker, P. 1987. *Augustus und die Macht der Bilder*. München: Beck.

1. Mycenae. View of the site and its surroundings from the south-west. Photograph: author.

2. Mycenae. View of the Megaron Terrace. After: Spathari 2001, Fig. 37.

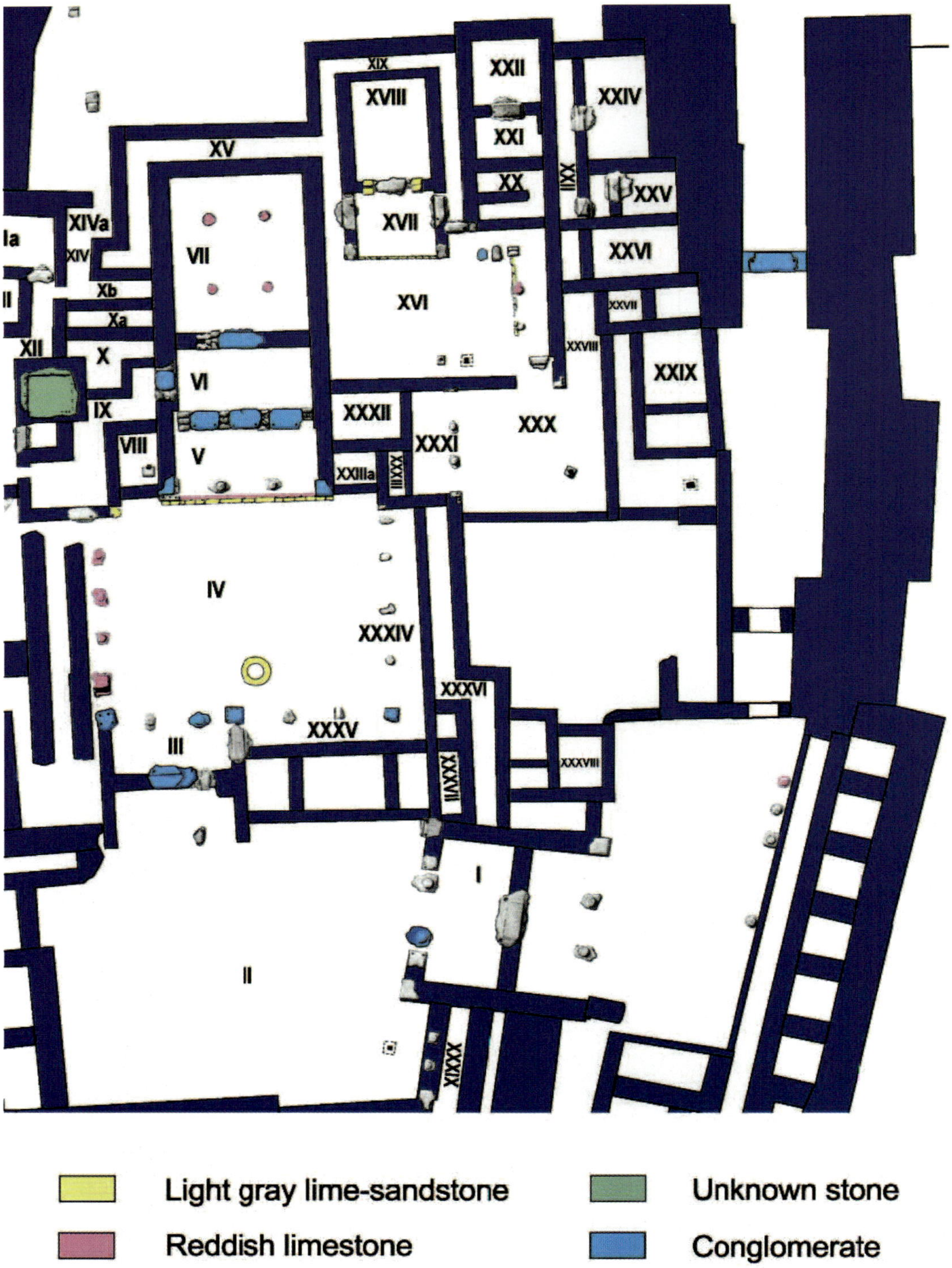

Tiryns. Plan of the Upper Citadel with special stone materials marked with colors. After: Müller 1930, Pl. 1; modifications: author.

Tiryns. Plan of the Upper Citadel with passageways (yellow and pink) and "liminal" points (green circles). After: Müller 1930, Pl. 1; modifications: author.

Constructing and Reconstructing Power
The Palace of Pylos

Ulrich Thaler

Introduction

While the construction of power is the subject matter of this interdisciplinary volume, its reconstruction is what this contribution will be concerned with in particular. Yet, there are two different aspects or 'modes' of reconstruction that will have to be dealt with: the archaeological and the social reconstruction of power. The need to reflect on the former directly results from the limitations of archaeological data as sources for an enquiry into past social realities: as archaeologists, we can never directly observe the social processes we are interested in, but have to reconstruct them from the patterning of the material traces they have left.

Since social power, however, is never static, but is constantly renegotiated as the relationships which it orders are lived and acted out[1], architecture cannot be understood adequately as a petrified expression of power. Therefore, a consideration of the social construction of power by architectural means needs to go hand in hand with a discussion of its social reconstruction; along with the plan of a building, we need to discuss the changes of its plan. In trying to do so, we may find, that – in clear contrast to the limitations of its data – archaeology's inherently diachronic perspective offers opportunities not necessarily encountered in disciplines studying the present.

In correspondence with the two modes of the reconstruction of power, the archaeological and the social, this contribution can be broadly divided in two parts. In the first, I will outline a conception of space as constituted on different levels of definition and, correspondingly, analysis, which provides a framework for the integration of different perspectives on and approaches to the study of social space. In a second step, I will aim to bring together, within this framework, the results of different analyses of the palace of Pylos (Abb. 1) on the ridge of Ano Englianos in Messenia, Greece, so that in the end, we can arrive at a coherent reconstruction of the reconstruction of Late Bronze Age social order. Since models, theories and paradigms in archaeology tend to fail (even) more quickly in application than under philosophical scrutiny, it will be to the second, practical part that I will devote more… space.

Archaeologically Re-Constructing Power: An Integrative Perspective

"Social archaeology", as Lin Foxhall reminds us, "encounters a fundamental theoretical dilemma. […] The dynamic flow of social life is speedy and its time scales are short-term"[2]. The archaeologist, therefore, is forced to deal with time spans which in themselves are anything but archaeological. Architectural structures, in contrast, appear to be comparatively stable social constructs. But if we want to capture their social effects and functioning more fully, we will be best served by a conception of space which

I would like to express my sincere gratitude to Joseph Maran, who made possible my involvement in the *Zeichen der Herrschaft* project of the *Altertumswissenschaftliches Kolleg Heidelberg*, which for a year not only provided the funding needed to continue work on my PhD dissertation, but also an extraordinarily stimulating environment in which to do so. I also owe and acknowledge a debt of gratitude to those who contributed to this atmosphere, among whom I would like to mention in particular the visiting scholars we had the privilege to welcome in Heidelberg, Susan and Andrew Sherratt, John Barrett, Matthew Johnson and Jim Wright.

1 Tilley (1982, 37) and the contributors to a volume edited my Miller and Tilley (1984) were among the first – if not, indeed, they were the first – to introduce this perspective into archaeology.

2 Foxhall 2000, 484-5.

Abb. 1. View along the axis of the megaron and the Main Building from the south-east. Blegen and Rawson 1966, fig. 9 (courtesy of the Department of Classics, University of Cincinnati).

takes into account the differential diachronic stability of different elements of the built or otherwise (wo)man-made environment – whether these be certain architectural elements with their distinctive life cycles or spatially and architecturally situated social practices of different duration. Although he does not put as clear an emphasis on the dimension of time, the architectural theoretician Amos Rapoport offers a conception of space which allows us to do just this in distinguishing fixed-feature, semifixed-feature and nonfixed-feature elements of the build environment, i.e. elements such as, firstly, buildings, floors and walls, secondly, furniture and furnishing of various kinds and, thirdly, human beings and their actions and behaviour[3].

Rapoport's definitions of these offer a greater clarity than the distinction of fixed-feature, semifixed-feature and informal space developed by Edward Hall in his proxemic studies[4], on which they are based. For Hall subsumes both physically present structures and their learned internalizations[5] under the notion of fixed-feature space, even in cases where the former have been lost; as an example, he points to the dining area in contemporary American living rooms, to which the rules and norms formerly developed in the architecturally separate dining room still apply, even when they diverge from those valid in the rest of the living room. Valuable though this observation is, it seems clearer conceptually to subsume such rules and norms under the notion of nonfixed-feature space as defined by Rapoport; the latter, accordingly, encompasses a wider spectrum of human practices and forms of behaviour than Hall's informal space, under the heading of which little more than situationally specific interpersonal distances is discussed[6].

The archaeologically decisive idea of differential diachronic stability, on the other hand, is developed more clearly by Steward Brand than in Rapoport's work. Brand's distinction of site, structure, skin, serv-

3 Rapoport 1982, 88-101; 1990, 13.
4 Hall 1966, 94-105.
5 Hall 1966, 100.
6 Hall 1966, 107-22.

ices, space plan and stuff[7] – optionally to be complemented by the seventh 's' of souls[8] – has resulted, however, from considerations of present-day building and its practicalities and problems. Brand is less concerned with a historical perspective than with the realization that it is inadvisable to embed a heating system, as a services-element, in a floor, as part of the structure, if the floor can be expected to last for 50 years while the heating system is likely to become outdated in a mere 10 years. While this latter consideration may not be of immediate archaeological relevance, it does make good archaeological sense to integrate the idea of finer subdivision, which takes into account diachronic stability or flexibility, into Rapoport's scheme. Accordingly, I want to suggest and apply a distinction between (diachronically) stable fixed-feature elements, e.g. the walls of a building, and (diachronically) unstable fixed-feature elements, e.g. frescoes.

Since nonfixed-feature elements in Rapoport's sense do not usually feature as *explanans* in an archaeological situation, as fixed- and semifixed-feature elements do, but rather as *explanandum*, as part of the social situation to be clarified, archaeological analysis can be based on a revised concept of three levels of spatial definition: stable fixed-feature elements, unstable fixed-feature elements and semifixed-feature elements – alternatively and more simply, we may refer to these as a first, second and third level of spatial analysis. Within this scheme, greater diachronic flexibility coincides with and corresponds to a clearer definition of specific social situations, but also with a greater scope for manipulation through social practices and individual acts. In clear contrast, diachronically stable elements are less easily modified by social agents in the short term and offer the more basic spatial definition of any situation, within which the more detailed definition through more flexible elements unfolds. This, of course, raises problems for archaeological praxis; the most serious of these is that, while the archaeological record is characterized by destruction and abandonment contexts, the destruction or abandonment of a building does not represent its characteristic form of use, the social situation typically associable with it. Accordingly, it is most of all with respect to the diachronically most sensitive, and thus from a socio-historical perspective most interesting, elements that archaeologists often need to ask themselves whether the situations they can reconstruct from these belong within the field of everyday or of exceptional activities. Fortunately, the present case study entails little difficulties in this respect.

The above conceptual framework permits not only, as stated at the outset, the integration of different perspectives and methodological approaches into a coherent account in general terms. It should also, more specifically, allow us to considerably strengthen particular interpretations through triangulation as outlined by Alison Wylie[9]; Wylie explains that a convergence of differently based arguments in their results and conclusions permits a more forceful corroboration or rejection of an interpretative position than a single line of argument could. In the present case study, the different levels of analysis can be conceived as such independent lines of argument.

In what follows, I will discuss the application of the framework thus outlined to the study of the Bronze Age palace of Pylos. But while the framework of three analytical levels provides a basic structure not only for research, but also for its written account, I will not always follow this structure in a strictly linear fashion. There are two main reasons for this; the first of these is the methodological one that some types of analysis deal with material which can be ascribed to different levels; this reflects the simple fact that the three levels can be distinguished conceptually and analytically, but are experienced simultaneously. The second reason is that – whatever the structuring framework of archaeological reconstruction – the social reconstruction of power constitutes contexts of meanings to which its analytical account will have to make some reference in its structure.

7 Brand 1994, 13.
8 Brand 1994, 17.
9 Wylie 2000, 232.

SOCIALLY RE-CONSTRUCTING POWER: THE CASE STUDY OF ANO ENGLIANOS

What makes the palace on the ridge of Ano Englianos[10] near present-day Pylos in Messenia an exceptional case for the study of the architecture of the Mycenaean culture, the first civilization on the European mainland, and what allows us to consider the reconstruction of power during its lifetime, is our ability to distinguish the state of the building at two successive points in time[11]. The earlier building state (Taf. 14) can be dated to the beginning of the ceramic phase Late Helladic IIIB at around 1300 B.C., when the palace was built or possibly rebuilt in the general layout preserved today. The later state (Taf. 15) is datable to the end of Late Helladic IIIB, around 1200 B.C., when the Pylian palace was destroyed by fire and Mycenaean palatial civilization came to an end in a series of upheavals which involved the entire Eastern Mediterranean, but unfortunately remain poorly understood.

This possibility to assess, at least in its outcome, the architectural development of the palace over the century or so of its existence forms the basis both for the present study and for a widely accepted narrative which interprets the architectural changes as evidence of a long-term economic decline preceding the eventual catastrophic end of the Pylian palace and state[12]. According to this view, a concentration of economic activities within the palace building complex indicates difficulties in maintaining central authority in the region controlled by the palace administration. In addition, remodelling within the palace is linked implicitly or explicitly to the extensive contemporary fortificatory activities at the palatial centres in the Argolid, such as the eponymous site of Mycenae. The observation or assumptions underlying this view have been most clearly stated by Cynthia Shelmerdine: "Looking at the general pattern of these changes to the palace, it is evident that they consistently do three things: 1) diminish spaciousness and elegance of the complex in its original form; 2) add storage and workroom space; and 3) restrict access and circulation"[13].

In what follows, it will be my aim to, on the one hand, disprove these assumptions and thus the hypothesis built on them and, on the other, to sketch an alternative explanation of architectural change in Ano Englianos, which focuses attention on, firstly, changes in the forms of representation and legitimization of supreme rule and, secondly, a development towards a functionally more favourable layout for a building complex serving as the centre of an early state.

FIRST LEVEL: STABLE FIXED-FEATURE ELEMENTS

The first level of spatial analysis encompasses the basic architectural definition of social space, on which a more fine-grained later definition of specific social situations quite literally builds. It may not come as a surprise, therefore, that this level can be dealt with quite comprehensively with recourse to a single coherent methodological approach; I am referring to the space syntax analysis developed at the Bartlett School of University College London[14].

For such an analysis, the ground plan of the building under study has to be transformed into a graph in which spatial units are represented by a circle and their respective links, such as doors, are rendered as connecting lines. As the relative positions of two spatial units are no longer conceived geometrically, but purely topologically as the minimum number of interposed steps, spatial units within the dendritic graph can be ordered in rows according to their distance from a particular space. Usually, the exterior of the building, referred to as the 'carrier space', is chosen as this root. The resulting representation is called a 'justified graph', or 'j-graph' for short (Abb. 2). On its basis, a number of numeric indicators of spatial properties can be developed for the 'integration' of any spatial unit, i.e. its connectedness with the remainder of the structure as well as with the carrier space. Likewise, indicators can be calculated for the building as a whole; these express the difficulty or ease of access to and movement within the

10 Blegen and Rawson 1966; Lang 1969; Blegen et al. 1973.

11 Wright (1984) was the first to offer a coherent discussion of phasing. The following study is based on plans of two building states which have been revised with regard to the results of recent re-excavations (Nelson 2001; preliminary reports cited therein); I will discuss these more fully in my PhD dissertation (Thaler (forthcoming a)).

12 Palaima 1984, 33; Wright 1984; Shelmerdine 1987.

13 Shelmerdine 1987, 564.

14 Hillier and Hanson 1984; Hillier 1996; Hanson 1998; cf. Markus (this volume).

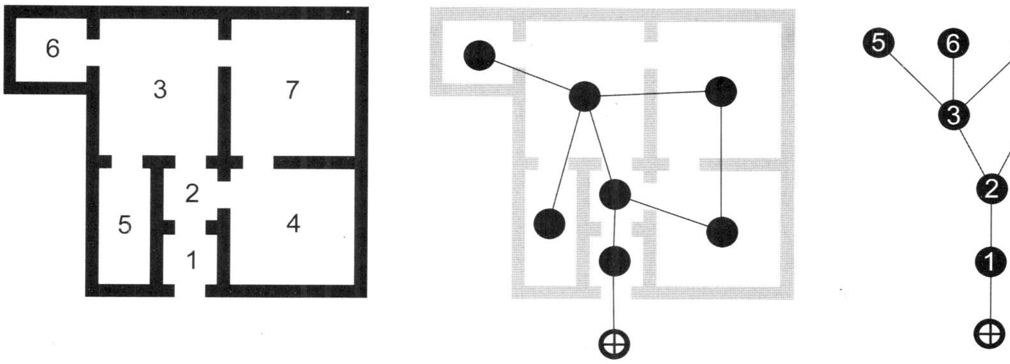

Abb. 2. From left to right: plan, topological graph and j-graph of a building. Drawing: author.

building. Therefore, Shelmerdine's third assumption, i.e. that "changes to the palace [...] restrict access and circulation"[15], can be directly assessed through this methodology[16].

Indeed, the palace is found to be a little less integrated with its surroundings in the later building state, access from outside does become a little more difficult. But even then, the integration of the carrier space retains a value which is close to the average of integration, i.e. on average any room within the building is as easily reached from outside the palace as from another room inside it. In clear contrast, the carrier space in, e.g., medieval castles is often the least integrated unit, its integration value representing the minimum for the building complex. Hence, the association of the 'restriction of access' with fortificatory intentions cannot be sustained[17]. It seems to make better sense to ascribe the slight change to a growing differentiation between the palace and the surrounding settlement, especially since, contrary to Shelmerdine's assumption, which as a whole has to be rejected, internal integration does not change noticeably, i.e. circulation within the palace became neither easier nor more difficult in the later building state. We may reasonably assume that such a differentiation will have had both functional and social aspects.

Space syntax analysis also allows us to trace a differentiation in the area dubbed "entrée des fournisseurs"[18] by Klaus Kilian, which is characterised by the juxtaposition of pantries (rooms 18-22), the wine magazine (rooms 104-105) and storerooms for oil (rooms 25-25, probably 27). Both in a mapping of areas of primary access for the three points of entrance to the palace area (Taf. 16.3) and in a corresponding mapping of areas of primary control[19] for the three most integrating courts (Taf. 16.4), this area at the back of the Main Building shows up as a clearly definable, coherent economic unit in the later building state; nothing like this is observable in the earlier building state. In addition, we may note that the building complex as a whole is relatively deep from this direction, i.e. routes of access via the corresponding point of entrance are comparatively long for many rooms. But a 'tradesman's entrance' need not provide easy access to a building as a whole, but only to a limited part of it – and indeed the storerooms in the economic unit become more easily accessible from the outside, which facilitated deliveries to the palace, and even become more integrated internally in the later building state.

A similar channelling of visitors towards a single route can be observed for the megaron, the central suite of rooms including room 6, the throne room. In the earlier building state, two alternative shortest routes lead to the core of the palace; the canonical access to the throne, via the propylon (rooms 1-2), the megaron court 3, porch 4 and vestibule 5, proves longer than these by one step (Taf. 16.1). In the later buildings state, however, a channelling of visitors towards the now relatively shorter canonical access

15 Shelmerdine 1987, 564.
16 A more comprehensive discussion of the space syntax analysis of Pylos is found in Thaler (2005).
17 In contrast to earlier studies, in which it is merely implied, a military connotation is explicitly stated by Shelmerdine (1999, 406-8).
18 Kilian 1987, 207.
19 These two forms of representation, which derive from Hanson's (2000, 108-10) mapping of step-depth, do not form part of the standard repertory of space syntax methodology, but are based on basic spatial properties in the terms of space syntax.

to the megaron is apparent; one of the shorter routes of the earlier state is cut off, the other is lengthened through the interposition of additional spaces (Taf. 16.2). At the same time, the integration of the megaron and its depth from the carrier space do not change noticeably; yet, we do find evidence that its 'perceived distance' from the exterior of the palace grew. This will emerge more clearly from second level analysis than from a discussion of space syntax.

The channelling of traffic to the throne is closely linked to the development of court 58, in front of the Main Building, which, as the mapping of primary access shows, in the later phase comes to control all traffic to the palace that did not use the 'tradesman's entrance'. This 'other' traffic will have included formal visitors, such as those approaching the megaron as the centre of the palace and notionally of the state, as well as the more formal economics dealings of the palace with the territory under its rule. The latter is indicated by the fact that the palace archive falls within the area of primary control of court 58; the same is true of the Northeastern Building (rooms 93-100), traditionally referred to as the "Palace Workshop"[20], to which I will return later.

Further light is shed on the development of court 58 by a comparison with court 63 with regard to their respective topological positions. Both belong to the most integrating courts, on which the mapping of areas of primary control is based, and both form part of an undifferentiated ring of outdoor spaces around the Main Building in the earlier building state. But while court 58 shifts, in the course of the thirteenth century B.C., to a configurational position that ensures control of access from outside the palace, court 63 becomes further removed from the outside, despite the fact that it retains its role as the most integrating space for circulation within the palace. These hubs of, respectively, visitor access and internal circulation continued, however, to share certain functions in the later buildings state; this is evident in the fact that pantries were closely connected with both, as indeed with courts 3 and 88 as well. The association of the rich inventories of these pantries with palatial feast is commonly accepted; so is the recognition of courts as locales for such feasts. What the present analysis now permits to suggest is that in the different topological positions of these courts a differentiation between social groups can be identified. Only few would have been allowed to celebrate in court 3, which, by virtue of its close association with the megaron, would have been the most prestigious of these locales, whereas court 58 as the outermost court would have welcomed the widest and least privileged group of participants. Court 63 occupied an intermediary position, as it was deeper within the building complex than 58 and fronted the main suite of rooms in the Southwestern Building, rooms 64 and 65, comparable but second to the megaron. As part of the economic unit oriented towards the 'tradesman's entrance', court 88 is difficult to position in this scheme; we will see later that there is no reason to try.

Despite its considerable analytical potential, space syntax methodology by no means tells us all there is to know about the first level of analysis. In particular for Pylos, a discussion of architectural archetypes[21] is of further interest; while a ground plan cannot capture what experiencing these in their social contexts meant, it is at least suited to their archaeological identification. The Mycenaean megaron, which constituted, in its canonical form with porch, vestibule, flanking corridors and a central hearth surrounded by four columns, the core of the Late Helladic IIIB palaces, has long been viewed as such an archetype with a tradition stretching back into the Middle Helladic period[22]. While the underlying typology can be and recently has been questioned[23], I want to make it the starting point of my considerations. Due to its long tradition, the megaron can be understood as an architecture which came to transcend its role as a medium for the structuring of communication and, through reference to the social knowledge of its users, became a medium of communication itself[24]. Accordingly, we may ask whether changes to

20 Or simply the "Workshop" (Blegen and Rawson 1966, 299).

21 The way I employ the term 'archetype' needs to be clearly distinguished from, e.g., Thiis-Evensen's (1987, esp. 17 on the history of the term in architectural theory) use of the same word. Thiis-Evensen's archetypes – floor, wall and roof – are basic structural elements, the concrete form of which shows variations in terms of themes and motifs. Starting from the archaeological notion of 'type', I will understand 'archetype' to mean a form of building or expression which is characterized by a long tradition and, due to this, a high potential for identification and strong connotations with certain social practices and conventions.

22 Hiller 1986; Kilian 1987; Barber 1992; Werner 1993. Hiller (1986, 85-6) even assumes a tradition stretching back to the Early Helladic period.

23 Jung 2000, esp. 85-6; Wright 2005; cf. Wright 1990, 350.

24 Cf. Broadbent 1980, esp. 145.

the Pylian palace may have affected traditional elements and thus have potentially changed some of the messages communicated. Indeed, this appears to have been the case: when the south-western corridor was walled off to provide additional pantries, this did not merely contribute to the formation of the economic unit oriented towards the 'tradesman's entrance'; it also led to a dissociation of the storerooms at the back of the megaron from the suite of staterooms itself. The close connection of the main room and the storerooms behind, however, is one of the characteristics of the postulated typological sequence[25]. The changes may have been made for purely functional reasons, to adapt a monumentalized traditional layout to the needs of a palatial centre, but they may also have expressed a change in the self-image of the person enthroned in the megaron. Regardless of intentions, they will have changed actual experience, as matters of state and everyday economic activities became more clearly separated.

It would, however, be an inappropriate simplification to equate the built structure of the megaron with specific meanings and attribute these to those who built and rebuilt it or had others do so. While certain intended meanings, e.g. in the present case an architecturally stated claim to 'Mycenaean-ness', may be assumed when an established archetype is employed in an elite context, something more subtle than conscious signification will have come into play here: the megaron did not merely express a 'Mycenaean' identity, but made it possible; it allowed its users to act 'Mycenaean' and thus become and be 'Mycenaean'[26]. By elaborating the traditional form of domestic architecture into the representative core of their residences, the Mycenaean rulers must have been able to draw on a whole set of culturally embedded social practices and conventions – a social resource they, however, had to share with their visitors. If we accept the typological derivation of the megaron from Middle Helladic house forms, a discussion of these practices and conventions will have to start from the notion of *oikos*[27]. If we follow the critics in questioning this long tradition, we can still see in the Mycenaean palatial megara the rapid establishment of a clearly defined building type with which certain practices and conventions were associated. But in the latter case, these would be more likely to have focussed on membership of the elite rather than on Mycenaean identity.

A last issue to be addressed on the first level of analysis is Shelmerdine's first assumption, i.e. that changes to the palace of Pylos diminished "the spaciousness and elegance of the complex in its original form"[28]. Quite obviously, such a statement overlooks certain aspects of the later additions. One may doubt the excavators' verdict, who saw in the late ramp 59, between room 60 and the Main Building, "a somewhat imposing canyon"[29]. One could also disagree with Kilian's suggestion that planning aimed at an impressive effect is evident in the fact that the opening of the outer porch of the propylon, room 1, was twice as wide as ramps 59 and 91, which flanked the Main Building[30]. It seems very difficult, however, to escape the conclusion that court 58, onto which the propylon and the ramps opened, underwent extensive remodelling during the thirteenth century B.C. which considerably enhanced its impressiveness[31]: the Northeastern Building was fronted by a pillared hall and we may confidently assume the presence of a pillared building in the area of the south-western stairway to the plateau on the opposite site of the court, although its form remains unknown due to the poor preservation of remains in this area[32].

Still, for Shelmerdine the loss of elegance reveals itself already in building technique. She admits, though, that room 82, which was built with rubble walls early in the thirteenth century B.C., does not fit her chronological assumptions[33]; neither does room 60, which was built at a later stage in a technique

25 Hiller 1986, 86; cf. Hiesel 1990, 206; Werner 1993, 66-8.
26 On "Making Mycenaeans" cf. Davis and Bennet 1999, esp. 111-4.
27 Barber 1992, 22.
28 Shelmerdine 1987, 564.
29 Blegen and Rawson 1966, 236.
30 Kilian 1984, 43.
31 Indeed, it is only through the additions to the complex that 58 becomes a court in the proper sense; for the earlier building state the term 'square' might be more appropriate. A comparison with the different forms of outdoor space discussed by Palyvou (2004) indicates that, again, we can see in this evidence for a growing differentiation between the palace and the surrounding settlement.
32 Blegen and Rawson 1966, 228, fig. 412; Blegen et al. 1973, 40, fig. 306.
33 Shelmerdine 1987, 561 n. 24.

closely resembling that employed in the Main Building[34]. To my mind, it makes better sense to consider the relative 'frontality' of the different parts of the complex, i.e. whether they were meant to be seen or accessed by 'the public': room 82 was built in a back area, the same in which the 'tradesman's entrance' later developed; room 60, like the south-western façade of the Main Building, borders court 58.

The rubble walls of courts 42 and 47, on the other hand, which were erected in front of the ashlar-built north-eastern façade and cut off the access to the columned porch 41 provide much better, indeed probably the best evidence for the loss of elegance described by Shelmerdine, as photographs taken during excavation vividly illustrate[35]. But even here, difficulties arise with her interpretation: firstly, Michael Nelson's evaluation of re-excavations undertaken in the 1990s resulted in an earlier dating of the ashlar façade, which no longer appears to be an original element of the Late Helladic IIIB palace, but is seen as a re-used Late Helladic IIIA structure[36]; secondly, Nelson's reconstruction indicates that, even in early Late Helladic IIIB, the view of the façade would not have been unimpeded by other buildings, as previously assumed[37]; thirdly and most importantly, we have to remember that what looks like a bare wall to the archaeologist may often have looked differently to the inhabitant. In a number of places within the palace where no plaster is preserved on the walls, the surviving floors turn upwards before reaching the walls, clearly indicating the erstwhile presence of some kind of wall plaster. In courts 42 and 47, there are only scant remains of wall plaster, but these seem to be, like the more extensively preserved stucco floors, of comparatively good quality for unroofed spaces[38]. But in discussing wall plaster and stucco floors, we are already moving ahead to the second level of analysis.

SECOND LEVEL: UNSTABLE FIXED-FEATURE ELEMENTS

Different forms of surface treatment of walls, floors and – unfortunately a hypothetical point in the present case study – ceilings offer different visual, potentially also different tactile stimuli. Different sensory stimuli or, more precisely, the resulting changes in sensory perception, offer important cues as to, in general terms, socially and situationally adequate and expected behaviour and, more specifically, the importance of transitions between spatial units[39]. A simple example may illustrate this: walking along a hotel corridor done out in silk tapestries and finding at its end two open doors giving access to two rooms, one furnished with the same silk tapestries, the other showing walls of bare concrete, only the more enterprising spirits (and those who feel seriously out of place to start with) would choose concrete over silk. There are two elements here which result in a heightened 'perceived threshold' between silken surroundings and concrete construction: firstly, the simple fact that there is a change in sensory perception; secondly, that the different wall treatments offer different social connotations.

In accordance with these considerations, it is possible to map different forms of wall and floor treatment in the palace of Pylos and, from this mapping, develop simple numeric expressions for the 'height' of thresholds (Taf. 17.2)[40]. In so doing, I presume that a qualitative progression from clay via plain and painted stucco to figural wall-painting does not merely connote different status for today's archaeologists, but was correspondingly connoted for the Bronze Age inhabitants and visitors of the palace. The decorative use of certain stones or building techniques, which occurs in a small number of places within

34 Blegen and Rawson (1966, 236-44) and Blegen et al. (1973, figs. 303, 306) suggested a later date in comparison to the Main Building, which, amongst others, Wright (1984, 22) accepted. Shelmerdine (1987, 561) considered room 60 a relatively early addition, while Nelson (2001, 208, fig. 82) dates it in his Late Helladic IIIB early phase. But neither would this necessarily make it a part of the building complex as it stood at the beginning of the thirteenth century B.C., nor is the latter probable.

35 Blegen and Rawson 1966, fig. 28.

36 Nelson 2001, 204, 207, fig. 81.

37 Nelson 2001, figs. 81-2.

38 Blegen and Rawson 1966, 182-4, 207; Lang 1969, 205, 211. A plan by Kilian (1984, 38 fig. 1) even indicates painted stucco for the outside face of the wall around courts 42 and 47; the reasons for this elude me.

39 Rapoport 1982, esp. 26-7, 57-9; Sanders 1984, esp. 341-3; 1990.

40 The methodology closely follows the one applied by Sanders for Myrtos (1984, 405, 483-484, fig. 93; 1990). A mapping of surface treatment by Kilian (1984, 38 fig. 1) could unfortunately not be used for analysis, as correspondence to the information in the excavation reports (Blegen and Rawson 1966; Lang 1969) seemed only partial.

the palace, is treated as 'equal' to the use of non-figural frescoes, in which it is occasionally imitated[41]. In addition to this, the thresholds indicated in the plan take account of two further characteristics: on the one hand, whether a space was unroofed, roofed but open on one side or roofed and enclosed by walls on all sides; on the other, changes in floor level, which are weighted doubly if they surpass eye level, as in staircases (Taf. 17.1).

Unavoidably, the resulting mapping remains incomplete – not just because of the incompleteness of archaeological data, but also because the sheer number of sensory changes which could potentially be mapped defies any aspiration to completeness. For example, the visual impact of the respective width of different rooms would be of interest, while, of course, our perception is only dominated by the visual, but never exclusively visual: changes of temperature may be associated with the hearths in the megaron and room 46 as well as with areas of light and shade; olfactory perception can offer important clues as well. Such characteristics can hardly be mapped for the building complex as a whole, but we may profitably give them some consideration in the discussion of individual contexts. This allows us to interpret a mapping of thresholds like the one presented here with some confidence, as does, more importantly, the realization that sensory markers in the built environment always, but particularly so in more public spaces, tend towards redundancy, i.e. the transmission of the same messages in different media[42].

The lengthening of the 'perceived distance' between the outside of the palace and the megaron in the later building state has already been mentioned in the discussion of space syntax analysis, but is picked up more clearly be the mapping of 'perceived thresholds': along the canonical route to the throne room, sensory perception constantly changes, i.e. distance is stressed as the visitor constantly has to negotiate marked thresholds. Interestingly, thresholds are as high or even higher when a visitor wants to diverge from the route to the megaron once inside the Main Building, e.g. to enter the archive rooms 7 and 8[43]. The trend towards a channelling of visitors in the later building state is even more apparent here than the perceptual distancing of the throne.

Elements which were not mapped both strengthen and modulate the described effects; the so-called 'sentry-stands' in rooms 1, 4 and 5 offer the most instructive example[44]. Accepting their interpretation as places where guards stood, we can see them as strongly accentuating the transitions from the outer to the inner porch of the propylon, the megaron's porch to its vestibule and the vestibule to the throne room for the entering visitor, while not contributing to the thresholds perceived by the visitor returning from the throne room. If, conversely, we follow the less plausible, but possible alternative interpretation that the 'sentry-stands' indicate the positions of incense burners, the resulting effect would be reversed.

The economic unit in the north-west offers a completely different picture: in the area of the pantries and storerooms at the back of the Main Building, relatively few changes of sensory perception occur at the transition from one room to the other; indeed, this area of relative uniformity stretches even further into the north-eastern part of the Main Building. While the available data is pitifully incomplete and does not allow definite statements, it seems plausible to presume a comparable degree of uniformity for the outdoor spaces behind the Main Building. If this holds true, the only noticeable thresholds in this area had to be crossed when entering a building from a court. This could directly correspond to limited rights of access for those who delivered oil or kylikes to the palace, who would have been allowed to come right up to the doors of pantries 20 and 21 in court 88, but would not have been permitted into the pantries themselves and the storerooms behind.

Though mainly in methodological terms, we can also profit from a consideration of the Southwestern Building, where the uniformity of the area north-east of rooms 64 and 65 at first appears to be the result of poor preservation or even an artefact of methodology. But on closer inspection, the fact that the preserved stucco floor continues unbroken from room to room[45] provides a clear indication that the area was indeed comparatively uniform in appearance and that, in this case, the loss of information can

41 Cf. McCallum 1987, 76-7. This concerns, most of all, court 3. Since in the outdoor spaces bordering on the north-eastern ashlar façade different forms of wall treatment also occur, these could not be assigned a single form of wall treatment in the corresponding mapping (Taf. 17).

42 Hall 1966, 96; Rapoport 1982, 84, 149-52; Sanders 1984, 93, 439-40, 545.

43 Cf. McCallum's (1987, 143) suggestion that the frescoes of porch 44 clearly set it apart from the access to the megaron.

44 Blegen and Rawson 1966, 57, 68, 74-5.

45 Blegen and Rawson 1966, 259-76.

be explained as a loss of redundancy. In clear contrast, the transition from the figural wall-paintings of room 64 to the plain mud-plaster of the rooms to the north-west is not represented at all in the mapping – for the simple reason that the little 'room' 66 does and did not actually have any walls, its four sides all being occupied by doors. What I want to illustrate with these two examples is that the mapping of surface treatments provides a helpful overview, but, like any architectural plan in archaeology, cannot and is not meant to replace the more detailed consideration of individual contexts.

A further qualification needs to be made in that these observations apply to the later building state only. The same holds true – with one possible exception to be discussed later – for considerations of the decorative program of the palace frescoes, despite Lucinda McCallum's unconvincing attempt to ascribe these wall-paintings to the earlier building state[46]. Yet, there is no doubt that, while a more detailed understanding of it eludes us, a certain temporal depth is documented in the frescoes, most obviously in those places where several superimposed layers of stucco have been preserved; at least, this confirms the classification of frescoes and other forms of surface treatment as fixed-feature, but unstable elements of the built environment.

The problematic association of the decorative program with a supposedly original architectural design notwithstanding, McCallum's study of the megaron frescoes[47] remains the starting point for any consideration of the decorative program. McCallum clearly stated the central importance of the depiction of a procession leading towards the political and spiritual centre of the kingdom in the throne room and clarified its connection with the banqueting scene which can be plausibly reconstructed in the throne room itself[48]. That the presence of a sacrificial animal in the latter scene, a bull trussed up on an altar in McCallum's reconstruction, has recently been questioned[49] may, however, caution us against overstating parallels with later Greek cult practice.

Another, potentially very illuminating aspect of the megaron's decoration is touched upon by McCallum, but not discussed in detail: the apparent incongruence of motifs in the north-western and south-eastern halves of the throne room[50]. To the left of the throne[51], there is the already mentioned banqueting scene including a lyre player, the procession approaches from this direction, too; to the right of the throne, wild and in part mystical beasts are depicted. While McCallum suggests that the ruler's role in cult and his strength are represented here as two aspects of his personality, I think we might be better advised to read this juxtaposition motifs in terms of a binary opposition of concepts. Ian Hodder's terms *domus* and *agrios*[52], though developed in discussion of the Neolithic, provide interesting templates in this context: the same contrast between a domesticated or civilized sphere and the untamed nature opposed to it can be observed in the Pylian megaron; even the inversion through which the sphere of nature is transferred to a deep position within the building and thus enclosed and controlled by the sphere of civilization is present. That a table of offerings and the probable libation installation next to the throne were found in the inner half of the throne room may guide further interpretation; it is at odds, however, with McCallum's proposition that the cultic aspect of the ruler's personality is expressed in the outer half of the room.

More relevant again is McCallum's remark that neither the dichotomy of the decorative concept nor the preserved frescoe fragments leave any space for the reconstruction of a pair of heraldic animals antithetically opposed to the lion and griffin which have been partially preserved to the right of the throne[53]. Consequently, we might want to reconsider the idea that the compositional scheme of the frescoes was only completed by the ruler's taking seat on the throne flanked by the animals[54]. A last suggestion of

46 McCallum 1987, 19-20, 66, 147.
47 McCallum 1987.
48 McCallum 1987, 108-9.
49 Stocker and Davis 2004, 190.
50 McCallum 1987, 138-40.
51 From the point of view of the enthroned ruler.
52 Hodder 1990, 83-7.
53 McCallum 1987, 97-101. The second aspect actually seems problematic if McCallum's own reconstruction drawing (McCallum 1987, pl. 9) is taken into account, in which there seems to be ample room for another lion and another griffin. But already Reusch (1958, 339, cf. 336) doubted the reconstruction of an antithetical composition.
54 Bennet 2001, 34. Already Reusch (1958, 346-8, 352-3, 356) developed a comparable argument with regard to the Knossian throne room, but doubted is appropriateness for the Pylian megaron.

Abb. 3. Reconstruction of part of the battle scene (22 H 64) in porch 64 by Piet de Jong. Lang 1969, pl. M (courtesy of the Department of Classics, University of Cincinnati).

McCallum's that is relevant to the present study is the idea that certain frescoes, e.g. a single human figure she reconstructs in the outer porch of the propylon, may have served as 'signposts'; this might reflect the efforts to channel visitors towards certain routes[55].

One instance in which the frescoes preserved in the palace may permit diachronic comparison of decorative programs after all has been pointed out by Jack Davis and John Bennet, who contrasted the sedate processional and festive themes of the Main Building with the battle scenes of room 64 (Abb. 3) in the Southwestern Building[56]. Here, we might be able to distinguish not just different aspects of a kingly ideal and royal self-representation, but also a change over time. Two assumptions underlie such a suggestion: firstly, that rooms 64 and 65 of the Southwestern Building were erected in Late Helladic IIIA, some time before the Main Building[57], which is plausible; secondly, that either the original frescoes in these rooms or at least their themes were preserved until the end of the thirteenth century, which at first sight appears to be the more problematic assumption. That we cannot rule out the possibility of an extended life span of the frescoes themselves is indicated by the fact that the chequerboard border found in room 64 finds its only parallel in material from dumps predating the palace's destruction[58]. That there is some likelihood of a preservation of their themes in some locations and certainly in this one is evidenced by the fact that the naval theme of these dumped fragments is echoed by the recently announced reconstruction of the representation of a ship from material preserved in room 64[59].

55 McCallum 1987, 70-1, cf. 119, 121.
56 Davis and Bennet 1999, 115-6.
57 Most recently Nelson 2001, 201, fig. 81; cf. Davis and Bennet 1999, 108 n. 11.
58 Shaw 2001, 42.
59 Tracy 2006.

Any discussion of the second analytical level would remain incomplete without at least brief reference to the traces of fixed installations preserved in a number of rooms, which provide relatively unambiguous evidence of former functions: the throne and hearth of the megaron, evidence for shelves in several pantries, the built-in larnax in the bathroom and the built stands into which pithoi were set, e.g. in the oil magazines. Indeed, even the large pithoi in the wine magazine, although freestanding rather than set in such stands, may reasonably be called fixed-feature elements. The traditional functional labels of rooms, which I have – pre-emptively – made reference to in my discussion of the first level of analysis, are partly based on such unstable fixed-feature elements and partly on finds, which have to be classified as semifixed-feature elements.

THIRD LEVEL: SEMIFIXED-FEATURE ELEMENTS

Two fundamental difficulties underlie the discussion of the third analytical level: firstly, any furniture which could be profitably studied as semifixed-feature elements of social space is entirely absent. The above-mentioned shelves and the throne were not movable, i.e. they were fixed, while of movable, presumably wooden pieces of furniture nothing remains but some ivory inlays, which do not permit relevant conclusions for the present discussion[60]. Accordingly, third level analysis by necessity remains limited to smaller movable objects, notably small finds, pottery and animal bones. Secondly, the latter two of these categories of material rarely occur in use contexts, but mainly in storerooms or as refuse.

That, nevertheless, a discussion of the third analytical level can contribute considerably to the analysis of the Pylian palace is owed to a number of studies of different groups of material, which have been published in the past few years and which have shifted the focus of enquiry from the individual finds context to the social context of finds. In contrast to the first level of analysis, where space syntax offered a coherent single approach, less methodological coherence characterizes third level analysis, for which a review of literature comes to be the 'methodology' of choice.

The small finds have been discussed by Susan Hofstra with regard to identifications of workshop areas within the palace complex suggested in earlier studies[61]. Her results are unambiguous: if the finds from alleged workshops are matched against previously formulated criteria for their identification, such as the presence of tools, raw materials, half-finished products and waste, but also fixed installations, then none of the claims for the identification of a workshop can be upheld on present evidence. This is as true for suggestions which were advanced with some reservations originally – often to turn into factoids only a little later –, such as the "lapidary workshop" in room 55[62], as it is for supposedly stronger candidates. Most importantly, and this point is confirmed by Georgia Flouda[63] and Lisa Bendall[64] in contextual studies of administrative records found there, i.e. clay nodules and Linear B-tablets, the Northeastern Building does not live up to its designation as the "Palace Workshop". Instead, as Bendall formulates most clearly, it can now be identified as a clearinghouse for the redistributive palatial economy[65].

It is informative, at this point, to take another look at the mapping of areas of primary control presented in the discussion of the first analytical level, which makes clear that, like the palace archive, this clearinghouse lies within the frontal area focussed on court 58. This means that both groups of rooms dedicated to the official economic relations between the palace and the territory under its rule are oriented towards the court which in the later building state comes to serve as the distributor of official visitors to the palace.

As to the narrative of economic decline *sensu* Shelmerdine, we may note that with the 'loss' of the palace workshop(s) yet another indication of the alleged crisis is lost. Interestingly, Hofstra makes no mention in her account of implausible identifications of the perfume workshop which Shelmer-

60 This is particularly regrettable, since Palaima's (2000, 237) observations on inventories of furniture used during banquets, from which he deduces a seating order in pairs as shown in the frescoes, hints at the informative potential of this analytical level.

61 Hofstra 2000.

62 Blegen and Rawson 1966, 224.

63 Flouda 2000.

64 Bendall 2003. In this article, Bendall (2003, 225-6) calls for a reassessment of the architectural development of Pylos in the light of new evidence and the difficulties which the latter raises with regard to the narrative of economic decline.

65 Bendall 2003, 181, 225; cf. Flouda 2000, 215, 235.

Abb. 4. Floor of pantry 22 with ceramic vessels found *in situ*. Blegen and Rawson 1966, fig. 103 (courtesy of the Department of Classics, University of Cincinnati).

dine sought to locate in court 47[66]. But the hypothetical nature of this suggestion was clearly stated by Shelmerdine herself[67]; and even if we were to accept it, an outdoor workspace without fixed installations could just as easily be explained as an *ad hoc*-measure of very late date as by reference to a long-term decline.

With regard to pottery, feasting and conspicuous consumption have come to play an important role in our understanding of the finds. Just how conspicuous the consumption of pottery remains even for today's archaeologists is indicated by the conservative estimate that at the time of destruction no less than 8540 ceramic vessels were in use in the palace[68] – about half of which are accounted for by a single form of drinking vessel, the kylix. A remarkable convergence of results is evident between a survey of pantry inventories (Abb. 4) presented by Bendall[69] and the space syntax analysis discussed above. In the former study, Bendall contrasts the somewhat lesser quality of ceramic vessels in pantry 60 with better wares found in pantries 67 and 68 as well as in the area of pantries 18 to 22. Thus, she is able to trace a differentiation between courts 58 and 63, in which she sees a hierarchy of locales used for feasting within the palace – as has been suggested here on the basis of space syntax analysis. At the top of this hierarchy, however, Bendall places not the megaron court, but the megaron itself, where precious metal finds point to the use of metal drinking vessels. On the other hand, the exclusion of court 88, onto which pantries 20 and 21 open, from the hierarchy of feasting locales is corroborated by Bendall's results. These show that the inventories of rooms 18 to 22, which are dominated by drinking vessels, and rooms 67 and 68, which also comprise cooking pots and related forms, are complementary; together, these groups of vessels, which presumably were used in – or in relation to activities in – court 63, encompass a range of shapes which is paralleled in a coarser ware in pantry 60, which in turn probably served court 58.

Pantries account for the majority of late additions to storage capacities; room 60 is certainly late, as is the remodelling of rooms 18 to 22, which may not have been used to store pottery before. Todd Whitelaw has pointed out that not only these, but also all other obviously late additions to the palace's storage capacities are explained more easily and convincingly with reference to needs and consumption of the palace than by the assumption that a surplus extracted from the dependent territory was hoarded

66 Shelmerdine 1984, 86-8; 1985, 59-62.
67 Shelmerdine 1987, 561 n. 21.
68 Whitelaw 2001, 52.
69 Bendall 2004, 112-24. Whitelaw (2001, 58-60) offers an alternative, but to my mind less convincing, interpretation of the different fabric qualities.

in these rooms[70]. And since what was stored there were ceramic vessels and comestibles, we may more plausibly seek the reason for storage in the preparation of feasts hosted by the palace's inhabitants than in an economic crisis.

The large scale of such feasts is further attested by Linear B-documents detailing quantities of wine and quality foodstuffs provided by the palace administration[71], although the preserved records refer to events outside the palace[72], and by the finds of animal remains from within the palace. The study of individual find contexts of cattle bones indicates that upwards of two tons of beef were available for consumption on single occasions[73]. It is also interesting to note that the animals slaughtered were of larger than average size and that a majority of them were males[74]; one might speculate at least about a connection to the pairs of expensive and well-cared-for plough oxen on which the palace administration kept a watchful eye[75]. The contextual association of burnt cattle bones and miniature vessels in room 7 of the palace archive suggests that the administrators also monitored the consumption of beef in feasts and the sacrificial rites which may have been associated with it[76].

Reconstructing the Reconstruction: Results and Perspectives

Where do these considerations lead us in our efforts to archaeologically reconstruct the social reconstruction of power? In terms of the concept of space employed in this study, we seem to have reached the limits of archaeological inference *sensu stricto*: archaeological data will not usually permit an analysis of the next level of spatial definition, the nonfixed-feature elements. Where relevant textual sources are available, the historian may continue the archaeologist's enquiry; where these are missing, analogical arguments may help to carry on the enquiry beyond the ostensible limits of archaeological analysis. The surviving documents in the Linear B script, found nowhere in greater numbers than in Pylos, do not, unfortunately, shed any light on the social functioning of Mycenaean palaces as architectural structures. Yet, contemporary Hittite palatial architecture, e.g., about the use of which cuneiform texts do inform us, offers a most interesting comparison[77].

In methodological terms, we have less than no reason to assume that we have reached the limits of what can be done archaeologically. One of the particular strengths of the conception of space as interacting with social practices on different levels lies in the fact that it facilitates the integration of further perspectives in a coherent framework. To offer but one example of an approach that has not been touched upon in, but may profitably supplement the above analysis, I would like to point to the study of relationships of intervisibility. This can be brought to bear both on the intra-contextual analysis of a building complex, such as the present study, and on considerations of such a complex in its wider local and regional context, which I consider, despite my confidence in the results presented here, as a necessary complement to an intra-contextual perspective.

Intervisibility exists, for example, between the palace on the ridge of Ano Englianos and a group of Middle Helladic grave-tumuli on the neighbouring ridge of Tragana[78], but also, in the immediate surroundings of the palace, between porch 41, the monumental north-eastern stairway to the plateau of Ano Englianos, which dates to Late Helladic I, and Tholos IV, an important tomb a little further to the north-east. That this line of sight and a procession route which we may plausibly connect with it were cut off

70 Whitelaw 2001, 54.
71 Palmer 1994, 187-95.
72 Or, perhaps, especially since the preserved records refer to occasions outside the palace, which we might assume to have been surpassed by those hosted in Ano Englianos itself.
73 Halstead and Isaakidou 2004, 147. From this, Halstead and Isaakidou (2004, 148) deduce that around 3000 guests could be (plentifully) provided for. Weilhartner (2002, 49-50), on the basis of textual evidence, suggests a similar number of participants in palatial feasts. Whitelaw (2001, 58) assumes that 500 to 800 celebrants could be (closely) seated in courts 63 and 88; I do not, however, consider the latter court a locale for feasting.
74 Halstead and Isaakidou 2004, 146.
75 Halstead 1999, 321, 323-4.
76 Stocker and Davis 2004, 193.
77 Thaler (forthcoming b).
78 Spencer 1995, 284.

by the exterior wall of court 42 in the later building state provides an interesting parallel to the development of Grave Circle A at Mycenae. The latter was, in the course of the thirteenth century B.C., first integrated into the citadel and presumably palatial representation with considerable architectural effort, only to apparently loose its representative importance again some time before the palace was destroyed at the turn of the twelfth century B.C.[79].

Leaving aside conceptual and methodological concerns, this study has to prove its value through the relevance and power of conviction of its results in terms of an archaeological reconstruction of the social reconstruction of power. What conclusions, then, can we propose with regard to changes in relationships of power and how they were both documented and preconditioned by the built structure of the Pylian palace?

To begin with, we may note that certain elements of the self-image and self-representation of the rulers apparently lost in importance over time: reference to the ancestors of the living ruler, as indicated by the considerations immediately above, appears to have been one of these elements, as does the 'militarism' expressed in the battle scenes painted in room 64. The clarity with which an esteem of military prowess can be discerned in the choice of grave goods for early Mycenaean elite burials may point to a traditional connection between a military and an ancestral element in the self-legitimization of elites. But an adequate discussion of long-term continuities, trends and developments from the Shaft Grave to the Palatial period remains beyond the scope of this article.

A clear growth in importance, which is mirrored in architecture as well as in other fields, can be observed for the hosting of feasts and acts of conspicuous consumption[80]; but it is not feasting *per se* which becomes characteristic for the palace, but forms of feasting which highlight und confirm social differences[81]. In the contrast between the latter development and the diminishing importance of real or assumed links to the ancestors and of the idea of a warrior elite, the changes in the relative importance of different forms of the legitimization of supreme rule, which were referred to at the outset, are evident.

Besides such ups and downs in the significance of different forms of representation, a development towards a functional differentiation and towards functional improvements of the palace as a 'machine for ruling' has been identified as a second element of a new explanatory approach dealing with architectural changes in Ano Englianos. In the contextual discussion, I have highlighted the channelling of visitors towards certain routes and into certain areas of the palace: both the 'tradesman's entrance' for supplying the palace with everyday goods of consumption and the area focussed on court 58, in which the archive and clearinghouse bear witness to the more official economic dealings between the palace and the territory under its inhabitants' rule, deserve our attention in this respect, as does the carefully and lavishly designed access route to the throne room.

We also need to ask ourselves how this development towards differentiation and functional improvements fits with our more general ideas about the development of the Pylian kingdom. Indeed, what has been suggested here may lead us to question current assumptions about Pylian territorial expansion, most importantly the supposition that the kingdom had reached its full and final extent by the beginning of Late Helladic IIIB[82]. While the corresponding scenarios suggested by Bennet are plausible in themselves, there are but two points of reference for the actual chronology of the growth of the Pylian territory: the first of these is the establishment of control over the micro-region immediately surrounding Ano Englianos by the end of Late Helladic II, the other is the extent of the kingdom at the time of the palace's destruction at the end of Late Helladic IIIB[83]. What happened in between and, in particular, at what point or over what period of time the so-called 'further province' was incorporated into the palatial territory is still largely a matter of conjecture. The architectural development of the palace during the

79 Laffineur 1990.

80 Wright (2004) provides a useful and up-to-date overview of studies in this field.

81 Halstead and Isaakidou (2004, 150) put this most succinctly when they suggest that "the distinctive feature of Mycenaean palatial feasting is [...] neither its existence or its scale, but rather its cultural elaboration and highly inegalitarian social context."

82 Bennet 1995, 1999. In accordance with these studies, Davis and Bennet (1999, 106) have suggested to see "a new capital for a newly expanded kingdom" in the palace at Ano Englianos.

83 Even these points of reference are not beyond doubt; interestingly, Shelmerdine (2001, 127-128) argues, on the basis of the same survey data which Bennet uses, that Pylos established its control over surrounding settlements such as Beylerbey no earlier than in Late Helladic IIIA.

ceramic phase Late Helladic IIIB provides good reasons to consider the possibility that the Pylian kingdom may still have been in the course of expansion during this time and that the changes to the building complex at Ano Englianos reflect the changing needs of the political and administrative centre of this expanding early state.

Furthermore, we may want to reflect on the degree to which changes in the forms chosen to represent and reconstruct power in social discourse were correlated with changes in relationships of economic power. On the basis of rank-size considerations of Messenia's Late Bronze Age settlement structure, David Small has suggested that the term 'estate' may better capture the socio-economic organization of the Pylian 'kingdom' than the term 'state' can[84]. While I do not see my results in direct accordance with Small's argument, the possibility remains that the changes to the building complex at Ano Englianos reflect the transformation of a social organization which started out as an (over)extended household to true statehood – a statehood which, however, was not to last. A more detailed and thorough discussion of how architectural and socio-economic developments may have been interrelated in the Mycenaean period has recently been presented by James Wright[85].

In this respect as well, the next step has to be to extend our frame of reference beyond the confines of the palace as a building complex in order to confirm and complement the picture of changes in the importance of forms of representation and of growing social and functional differentiation outlined in this study. Archaeological data should permit us to do so, whereas the assumption of a long-term economic decline can no longer stand up even to the intra-contextual scrutiny presented here:

In the course of the thirteenth century B.C., architectural elegance may have been lost in some places within the building complex of Ano Englianos, in others it was only brought forth through architectural alterations. Storage capacities were indeed enlarged – not, however, to prepare for times of adversity, but in order to transform economic into social capital in acts of consumption, not to attain direct control over goods, but indirect control over human agents. No new workshops were established. The flow of outside visitors was channelled rather than barred. Circulation within the building remained as easy at the end of the century as it had been at its beginning.

Bibliography

Barber, R.L.N. 1992. "The Origins of the Mycenaean Palace." In *ΦΙΛΟΛΑΚΩΝ: Lakonian studies in honour of Hector Catling*, edited by J.M. Sanders, 11-23. London: British School at Athens.

Bendall, L.M. 2003. "A Reconsideration of the Northeastern Building at Pylos: Evidence for a Mycenaean Redistributive Center." *American Journal of Archaeology* 107: 181-231.

—. 2004. "Fit for a King? Hierarchy, Exclusion, Aspiration and Desire in the Social Structure of Mycenaean Banqueting." In Halstead and Barrett 2004, 105-35.

Bennet, J. 1995. "Space through Time: Diachronic Perspectives on the Spatial Organization of the Pylian State." In *Politeia: Society and State in the Aegean Bronze Age*, edited by R. Laffineur and W.-D. Niemeier, 587-602. Aegaeum 12. Liège: Université de Liège et al.

—. 1999. "Pylos: The Expansion of a Mycenaean Center." In Galaty and Parkinson 1999, 9-19.

—. 2001. "Agency and Bureaucracy: Thoughts on the Nature and Extent of Administration in Bronze Age Pylos." In Voutsaki and Killen 2001, 25-37.

Blegen, C.W., M. Rawson, W. Taylor, and W.P. Donovan. 1973. *The Palace of Nestor at Pylos in Western Messenia*. Vol. 3, *Acropolis and Lower Town, Tholoi, Grave Circle, and Chamber Tombs, Discoveries outside the Citadel*. Princeton: Princeton University Press.

Blegen, C.W., and M. Rawson. 1966. *The Palace of Nestor at Pylos in Western Messenia*. Vol. 1, *The Buildings and Their Contents*. Princeton: Princeton University Press.

Brand, S. 1994. *How Buildings Learn: What Happens after They're Built*. New York: Penguin.

Broadbent, G. 1980. "The Deep Structure of Architecture." In *Signs, Symbols, and Architecture*, edited by G. Broadbent, R. Bunt, and C. Jencks, 119-68. Chichester: John Wiley & Sons.

84 Small 1998; 1999.
85 Wright (forthcoming).

Davis, J.L., and J. Bennet. 1999. "Making Mycenaeans: Warfare, Territoriality, Expansion and Representation of the Other in the Pylian Kingdom." In Laffineur 1999, 105-20.

Flouda, G. 2000. "Inscribed Pylian Nodules: Their Use in the Administration of the Storerooms of the Pylian Palace." *Studi Micenei ed Egeo-Anatolici* 42: 212-45.

Foxhall, L. 2000. "The Running Sands of Time: Archaeology and the Short-Term." *World Archaeology* 31: 484-98.

Galaty, M.L., and W.A. Parkinson, eds. 1999. *Rethinking Mycenaean Palaces: New Interpretations of an Old Idea.* Los Angeles: Cotsen Institute of Archaeology.

Hall, E.T. 1966. *The Hidden Dimension: Man's Use of Space in Public and Private.* London: The Bodley Head.

Halstead, P. 1999. "Surplus and Share-Croppers: The Grain Production Strategies of Mycenaean Palaces." In *Meletemata: Studies in Aegean Archaeology Presented to Malcolm H. Wiener as He Enters His 65th Year*, edited by P.P. Betancourt, V. Karageorghis, R. Laffineur, and W.-D. Niemeier, 319-26. Aegaeum 20. Liège: Université de Liège et al.

Halstead, P., and J.C. Barrett, eds. 2004. *Food, Cuisine and Society in Prehistoric Greece.* Sheffield Studies in Aegean Archaeology 5. Oxford: Oxbow.

Halstead, P., and Isaakidou, V. 2004. "Faunal Evidence for Feasting: Burnt Offerings from the Palace of Nestor at Pylos." In Halstead and Barrett 2004, 136-54.

Hanson, J. 1998. *Decoding Homes and Houses.* Cambridge: Cambridge University Press.

Hiesel, G. 1990. *Späthelladische Hausarchitektur: Studien zur Architekturgeschichte des griechischen Festlandes in der späten Bronzezeit.* Mainz: von Zabern.

Hiller, S. 1986. "Early and Late Helladic 'Megara': Questions of Architectural Continuity in Bronze Age Greece." In *Early Helladic Architecture and Urbanization*, edited by R. Hägg and D. Konsola, 85-9. Studies in Mediterranean Archaeology 76. Göteborg: Paul Åströms Förlag.

Hillier, B. 1996. *Space is the Machine: A Configurational Theory of Architecture.* Cambridge: Cambridge University Press.

Hillier, B., and J. Hanson. 1984. *The Social Logic of Space.* Cambridge: Cambridge University Press.

Hofstra, S. 2000. "Small Things Considered: The Finds from LH IIIB Pylos in Context." Ph.D. diss., University of Texas at Austin.

Jung, R. 2000. "Das Megaron: Ein Analogie(kurz)schluß der Ägäischen Archäologie." In *Vergleichen als archäologische Methode: Analogien in den Archäologien*, edited by A. Gramsch, 71-95. British Archaeological Reports International Series 825. Oxford: Archaeopress.

Kent, S., ed. 1990. *Domestic Architecture and the Use of Space: An Interdisciplinary and Cross-Cultural Study.* Cambridge: Cambridge University Press.

Kilian, K. 1984. "Pylos: Funktionsanalyse einer Residenz der späten Palastzeit." *Archäologisches Korrespondenzblatt* 14: 34-48.

—. 1987. "L'architecture des résidences mycéniennes: Origine et extension d'une structure de pouvoir politique pendant l'Âge du Bronze récent. " In *Le système palatial en Orient, en Grèce et à Rome*, edited by E. Lévy, 203-17. Leiden: Brill.

Laffineur, R.1990. "Grave Circle A at Mycenae: Further Reflections on Its History." In *Celebrations of Death and Divinity*, edited by R. Hägg and G.C. Nordquist, 201-6. Skrifter utgivna av Svenska Institutet i Athen 4°, 40. Stockholm: Paul Åströms Förlag.

—, ed. 1999. *Polemos: Le contexte guerrier en Égée à l'Âge du Bronze.* Aegaeum 19. Liège: Université de Liège et al.

Lang, M.L. 1969. *The Palace of Nestor at Pylos in Western Messenia.* Vol. 2, *The Frescoes.* Princeton: Princeton University Press.

McCallum, L.R. 1987. "Decorative Program in the Mycenaean Palace of Pylos: The Megaron Frescoes." Ph.D. diss., University of Pennsylvania.

Miller, D. and C. Tilley, eds. 1984. *Ideology, Power and Prehistory.* Cambridge: Cambridge University Press.

Nelson, M.C. 2001. "The Architecture of Epano Englianos, Greece." Ph.D. diss., University of Toronto.

Palaima, T.G. 1984. "Scribal Organization and Palatial Activity." In Palaima and Shelmerdine 1984, 31-9.

—. 2000. "The Pylos Ta Series: From Michael Ventris to the New Millennium." *Bulletin of the Institute of Classical Studies* 44: 236-7.

Palaima, T.G., and C.W. Shelmerdine, eds. 1984. *Pylos Comes Alive: Industry and Administration in a Mycenaean Palace*. New York: Fordham University.

Palmer, R. 1994. *Wine in the Mycenaean Palace Economy*. Aegaeum 10. Liège: Université de Liège, University of Texas at Austin.

Palyvou, C. 2004. "Outdoor Space in Minoan Architecture: 'Community and Privacy'." In *Knossos: Palace, City, State*, edited by G. Cadogan, E. Hatzaki, and A. Vasilakis, 207-17. British School at Athens Studies 12. London: British School at Athens.

Rapoport, A. 1982. *The Meaning of the Built Environment: A Nonverbal Communication Approach*. London: Sage Publications.

—. 1990. "Systems of Activities and Systems of Settings." In Kent 1990, 9-20.

Reusch, H. 1958. "Zum Wandschmuck des Thronsaales in Knossos." In *Minoica: Festschrift zum 80. Geburtstag von Johannes Sundwall*, edited by E. Grumach, 334-358. Deutsche Akademie der Wissenschaften zu Berlin, Schriften der Sektion für Altertumswissenschaft 12. Berlin: Akademie-Verlag.

Sanders, D.H. 1984. "Behavior and the Built Environment: An Interpretive Model for the Analysis of Architecture in an Archaeological Context and Its Testing on Material from the Aegean Bronze Age Site of Myrtos, Crete." Ph.D. diss., Columbia University.

—. 1990. "Behavioral Conventions and Archaeology: Methods for the Analysis of Ancient Architecture." In Kent 1990, 43-72.

Shaw, M.C. 2001. "Symbols of Naval Power at the Palace at Pylos." In *ΙΘΑΚΗ: Festschrift für Jörg Schäfer zum 75. Geburtstag am 25. April 2001*, edited by S. Böhm and K.-V. von Eickstedt, 37-43. Würzburg: Ergon.

Shelmerdine, C.W. 1984. "The Perfumed Oil Industry at Pylos." In Palaima and Shelmerdine 1984, 81-95.

—. 1985. *The Perfume Industry of Mycenaean Pylos*. Studies in Mediterranean Archaeology Pocket Book 34. Göteborg: Paul Åströms Förlag.

—. 1987. "Architectural Change and Economic Decline at Pylos." *Minos* 20-22: 557-68.

—. 1999. "Pylian Polemics: The Latest Evidence on Military Matters." In Laffineur 1999, 403-10.

—. 2001. "The Evolution of Administration at Pylos." In Voutsaki and Killen 2001, 113-28.

Small, D.B. 1998. "Surviving the Collapse: The *oikos* and Structural Continuity between Late Bronze Age and Later Greece." In *Mediterranean Peoples in Transition: Thirteenth to Early Tenth Centuries BCE*, edited by S. Gitin, A. Mazar, and E. Stern, 283-91. Jerusalem: Israel Exploration Society.

—. 1999. "Mycenaean Polities: States or Estates?" In Galaty and Parkinson 1999, 43-7.

Spencer, N. 1995. "Heroic Time: Monuments and the Past in Messenia, Southwest Greece." *Oxford Journal of Archaeology* 14: 277-92.

Stocker, S.R., and J.L. Davis. 2004. "Animal Sacrifice, Archives, and Feasting at the Palace of Nestor." In Wright 2004, 179-95.

Thaler, U. 2005. "Narrative and Syntax: New Perspectives on the Late Bronze Age Palace of Pylos, Greece." In *Space Syntax: 5th International Symposium*, edited by A. van Nes, 323-39. Amsterdam: Techne Press.

—. Forthcoming a. "Architektur der Macht – Macht der Architektur: Mykenische Paläste als Dokument und Gestaltungsrahmen frühgeschichtlicher Sozialordnung." Ph.D. diss., Ruprecht-Karls-Universität Heidelberg.

—. Forthcoming b. "Aḫḫiyawa and Ḫatti: Palatial Perspectives." In *Mediterranean Crossroads*, edited by S. Antoniadou and A. Pace. Oxford: Oxbow.

Thiis-Evensen, T. 1987. *Archetypes in Architecture*. Oslo: Norwegian University Press.

Tilley, C. 1982. "Social Formation, Social Structure and Social Change." In *Symbolic and Structural Archaeology*, edited by I. Hodder, 26-38. Cambridge: Cambridge University Press.

Tracy, S.V. 2006. Report on the work undertaken by the American School of Classical Studies at Athens in 2005, presented at the open meeting on the work of the school, 17 March 2006, Athens.

Voutsaki, S., and J. Killen, eds. 2001. *Economy and Politics in the Mycenaean Palace States*. Cambridge: Cambridge Philological Society.

Weilhartner, J. 2002. "Kultische Festbankette im mykenischen Pylos." In *Temenos: Festgabe für Florens Felten und Stefan Hiller*, edited by B. Asamer, P. Höglinger, C. Reinholdt, R. Smetana and W. Wohlmayr, 45-52. Wien: Phoibos Verlag.

Werner, K. 1993. *The Megaron during the Aegean and Anatolian Bronze Age: A Study of Occurrence, Shape, Architectural Adaptation, and Function*. Studies in Mediterranean Archaeology 108. Jonsered: Paul Åströms Förlag.

Whitelaw, T. 2001. "Reading between the Tablets: Assessing Mycenaean Palatial Involvement in Ceramic Production and Comsumption." In Voutsaki and Killen 2001, 51-79.

Wright, J.C. 1984. "Changes in the Form and Function of the Palace at Pylos." In Palaima and Shelmerdine 1984, 19-29.

—. 1990. "An Early Mycenaean Hamlet on Tsoungiza at Ancient Nemea." In *L'habitat égéen préhistorique*, edited by P. Darcque and R. Treuil, 347-57. Bulletin de correspondance Hellénique supplément 19. Paris: Boccard.

—, ed. 2004. *The Mycenaean Feast*. Hesperia 73.2. Princeton: American School of Classical Studies at Athens.

—. Forthcoming. "The Formation of the Mycenaean Palace." In *Ancient Greece from the Mycenaean Palaces to the Age of Homer*, edited by S. Deger-Jalkotzy and I.S. Lemos. Edinburgh Leventis Studies 3.

Wylie, A. 2000. "Questions of Evidence, Legitimacy, and the (Dis)unity of Science." *American Antiquity* 65: 227-37.

Plan of the palace of Pylos in the earlier building state, dating to around 1300 B.C. Preserved and certain structures are rendered in black, conjectural ones in grey. Points of access to the palace are indicated by arrows. Drawing: author.

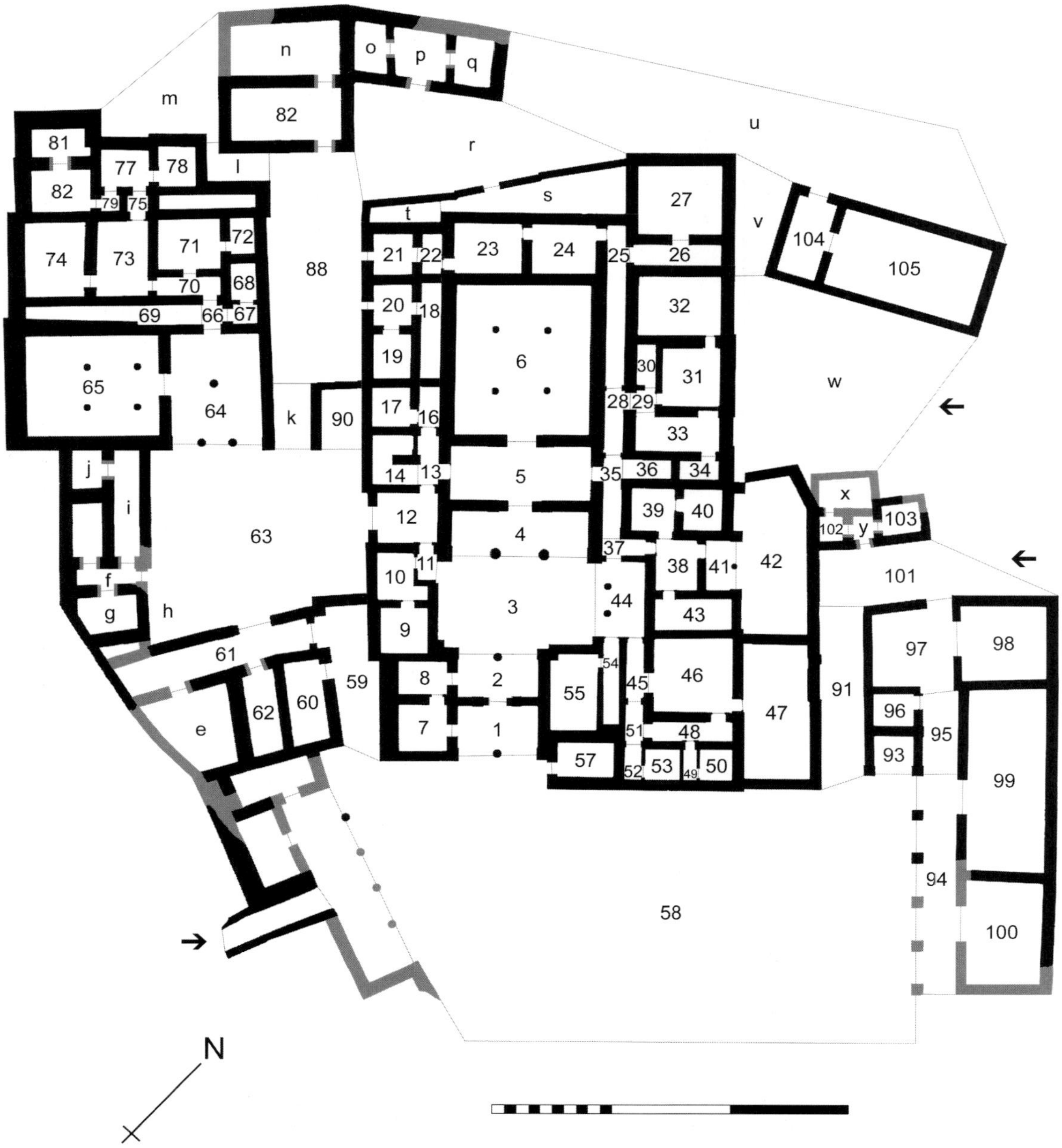

Plan of the palace of Pylos in the later building state, dating to around 1200 B.C. Preserved and certain structures are rendered in black, conjectural ones in grey. Points of access to the palace are indicated by arrows. Drawing: author.

1. Shortest routes of access to the throne room 6 in topological terms in the earlier building state, dating to around 1300 B.C.

2. Shortest routes of access to the throne room 6 in topological terms in the later building state, dating to around 1200 B.C.

3. Areas of primary access for entrances a, w and 101 in the later building state, dating to around 1200 B.C.

4. Areas of primary control for courts 58, 63 and 88 in the later building state, dating to around 1200 B.C.

Drawings: author.

1. Mapping of roofed spaces, roofed spaces open on one side and unroofed spaces in the later building state, dating to around 1200 B.C. Small white dots indicate moderate, larger white dots more pronounced changes of floor level. Drawing: author.

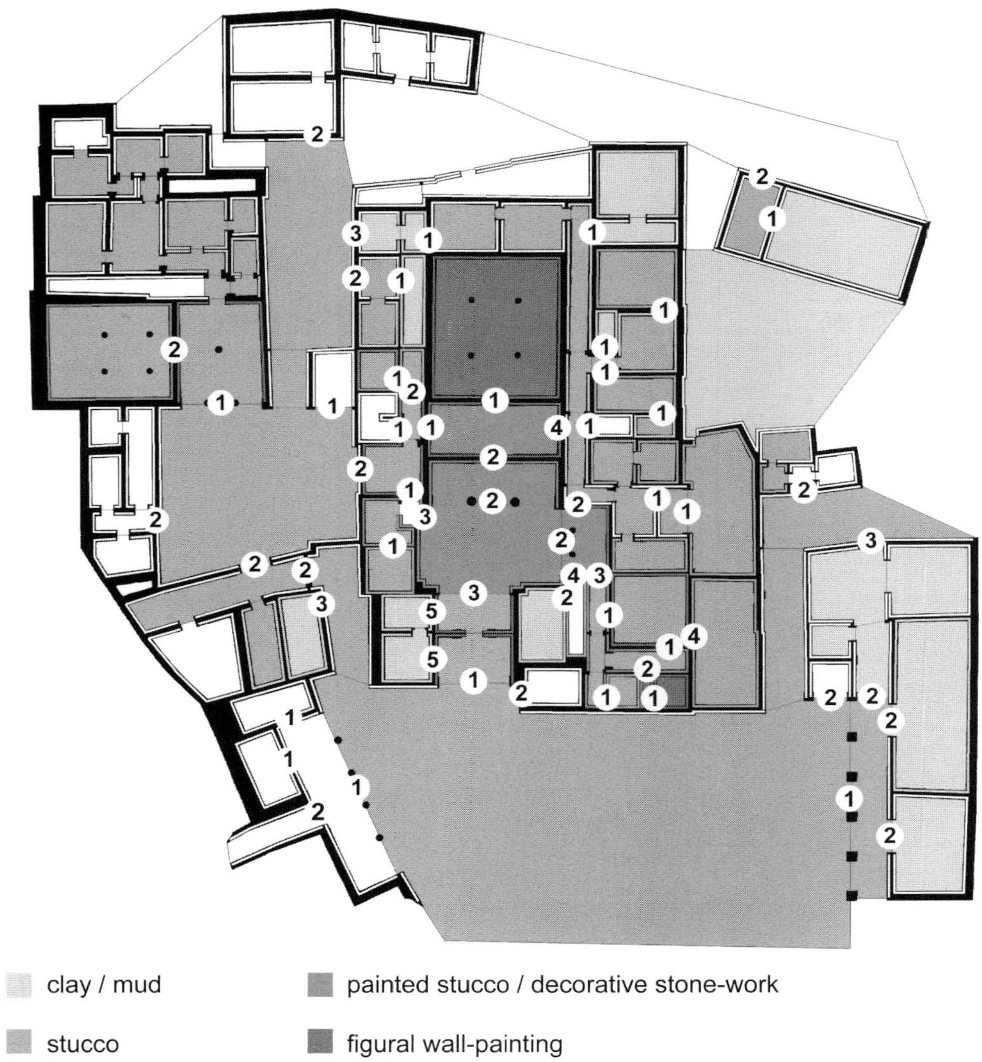

2. Mapping of surface treatment of walls and floors in the later building state, dating to around 1200 B.C. The inscribed numbers indicate the 'height' of perceived thresholds deduced from this mapping. Drawing: author.

Auf der Suche nach Konstruktionen der Macht. Die Festprozession des Osiris in Karnak

Andrea Kucharek

Abstract

The structures devoted to the cult of Osiris in the huge temple precinct of Amun-Re at Karnak are of conspicuously small size compared to the growing importance of the Egyptian god of the dead during the first millennium B.C. Moreover, most of them are confined, chronologically, to a time-span of about 250 years, and, geographically, to the rather peripheral northeastern sector of the temple precinct. Architecturally, most of these structures are more or less uniform, small chapels erected along the processional route of the god. This route, as definable by these chapels, does not follow the usual linear course but takes a wide curve towards the north and then back south to the 'tomb' of Osiris. I suggest that this route may have been a transposition of the processional route of Osiris at Abydos. Most of the chapels were built either by the 'god's consort of Amun', a female governor of the southern regions acting on behalf of the kings residing in the north, or jointly by the consort and the reigning king. In a number of these chapels, the major official of the consort is depicted, thus being present at the rituals performed by the god's consort. A considerable private influence on the erection of these chapels is suggested, thereby ensuring divine benevolence and secular prestige for the persons involved.

Einleitung

Das allgemeine Bild altägyptischer Architektur ist vor allem von monumentalen Strukturen geprägt. Die Pyramiden der Könige des Alten Reiches (um 2500 v. Chr.) galten bereits in vorchristlicher Zeit als Denkmäler des Größenwahns ihrer Erbauer. Herodot beschreibt im 5. Jahrhundert v. Chr. die Könige Cheops und Chefren, die Bauherren der beiden großen Pyramiden von Gisa, als gottlose Schurken, die die Tempel schlossen und das gesamte Volk für den Pyramidenbau in die Knechtschaft zwangen. Der Erbauer der dritten, sehr viel kleineren Pyramide hingegen, Mykerinos, sei gutherzig und gerecht gewesen[1]. Offensichtlich bemaßen Herodot bzw. seine Informanten die Schlechtigkeit des jeweiligen Herrschers in genauer Proportion zur Größe seiner Grabstätte.

Die Grabanlagen der Könige späterer Epochen waren unauffällig im Fels oder unter dem Erdboden verborgen. Nun aber wuchsen die Tempel der Götter zu Maßen heran, die die Welt erstaunten. Auch diese galten aber nicht allein als Zeugen großer Frömmigkeit. Noch heute sind die Kolossalstatuen ihrer Erbauer auffälliger Bestandteil eines Tempelensembles, und anhand eines gestürzten Kolosses lassen sich trefflich Überlegungen über die Eitelkeit des Machtanspruchs anstellen, man denke an Shelleys berühmtes Gedicht *Ozymandias*, dem die geborstene Riesenstatue Ramses' II. in seinem Totentempel in Theben als Sinnbild vergangener Größe bzw. vergänglichen Größenwahns diente[2].

Karnak

Ägypten war die monumentale Kultur des Altertums *par excellence*, und abgesehen von den Pyramiden von Gisa wird das wohl nirgendwo augenfälliger als in Karnak. Karnak, am Ostufer des Nils nahe dem heutigen Luxor, dem antiken Theben, gelegen, wird oft knapp als ‚Tempel' bezeichnet. Tatsächlich handelt es sich um ein hochkomplexes, über mehr als zwei Jahrtausende gewachsenes Gebilde aus zahllosen

1 Herodot *Historien* 2.124-8, 129-34.
2 Shelleys Beschreibung beruht auf Diodorus Siculus, *The Library of History* 1.47.

Gebäuden, Höfen und anderen Strukturen, das von einem Netz kulttopographischer und kulthistorischer Bezüge übersponnen ist. Karnak war der Haupttempelbezirk des ägyptischen Reichsgottes Amun-Re. Es gehört jedoch zum Wesen eines ägyptischen Tempels, dass er niemals nur einer einzigen Gottheit Wohnung bietet, sondern zumindest auch dessen engerer Familie. In einer Anlage von den Ausmaßen, der theologischen Bedeutung und historischen Tiefe Karnaks ist schlussendlich fast jede Gottheit im Rahmen eines Gastkultes irgendwie vertreten gewesen.

Betrachtet man einen Plan des Tempelbezirks (Taf. 18), stellt man fest, dass der Gedanke des Weges vorherrscht. So lässt sich vom Haupteingang der Tempelanlage über Hunderte von Metern – und, das sei hinzugefügt, in diachroner Perspektive über gut 2000 Jahre hinweg – eine schnurgerade, ununterbrochene Linie bis zum Barkensanktuar ziehen. Die Achse selbst lässt sich bis zum rückwärtigen Tor verfolgen. Weniger streng verläuft die rechtwinklig dazu angelegte Nord-Süd-Achse. Weitet man den Blick auf die Region Theben, so stellt sich heraus, dass die Wege nicht an den Mauern des Tempelbezirks enden, sondern Verbindungen herstellen mit anderen Tempeln und dass sie dabei auch den Nil überschreiten. Bemerkenswert ist die Kompromisslosigkeit, mit der Stadt, Feld und wüstes Land von den schnurgeraden Straßen durchschnitten wurden[3].

PROZESSIONEN

Diese Wege sind nicht die Wege der Menschen. Es sind die Wege der Götter[4]. In Ägypten bedeutete ein Götterfest zu feiern eine Prozession durchzuführen, wobei die Gottheit ihre Wohnung im Tempelinneren, das Sanktuar, verließ. Je nach Anlass fand die Prozession innerhalb des Tempels oder des Tempelbezirkes statt oder sie verließ diesen geheiligten Bereich und begab sich in den profanen Außenraum[5]. Ausgangs- und Endpunkt einer Prozession waren gewöhnlich Tempel. Der Festweg dazwischen war oft architektonisch gefasst. Die den Grundriss von Karnak geradezu beherrschenden, hintereinander gestaffelten Höfe entlang der Hauptachsen, die jeweils von einem breiten Torbau, dem Pylon, beschlossen werden, sind nichts anderes als architektonische Gestaltungen des Festweges, die im Verlauf von Jahrhunderten nach und nach an die bestehenden Strukturen angefügt wurden. Flankierende Reihen von Sphingen begleiteten die Prozessionsstraße außerhalb der Höfe. Oft ist eine besonders sorgfältige Pflasterung der Straße mit Steinplatten nachzuweisen. Bei längeren Wegstrecken boten so genannte Stationsheiligtümer Gelegenheit zum Darbringen von Opfergaben an die reisende Gottheit und zu weiteren rituellen Handlungen. Nicht zuletzt erlaubte die Rast einen reibungslosen Wechsel der Träger der gewichtigen Götterbarke.

Diese Elemente altägyptischer Festarchitektur treten in Karnak, der größten Tempelanlage Ägyptens, besonders deutlich zutage[6]. Sie sind aber an den meisten ägyptischen Tempeln nachzuweisen. Umso bemerkenswerter gestaltet sich der Befund einer Untersuchung des architektonischen Rahmens der Osirisprozession in Karnak.

OSIRIS

Osiris ist allgemein als der Totengott der Ägypter bekannt. Dieser Aufgabenbereich wird in seiner Mumiengestalt unmittelbar sichtbar. Krone und Szepter weisen hingegen unmissverständlich darauf hin, dass es sich bei Osiris auch um einen Herrscher handelt. Im Mythos war Osiris einst König von Ägypten gewesen. Nach seinem gewaltsamen Tod von der Hand seines Bruders Seth wurde er Herrscher des Jenseits[7]. Auch aus religionshistorischer Perspektive ist Osiris engstens mit dem Königtum verbunden,

3 Karten der thebanischen Prozessionsstraßen bei Cabrol (2001, Taf. 3-8).
4 Vgl. dazu Cabrol 2001, 712-5.
5 Zu Prozessionen in Theben, insbesondere in Karnak, s. Kemp 1989, 201-13; Fitzenreiter 2003, 143-7.
6 Eine minutiöse Studie der thebanischen Prozessionswege (ohne den hier vorgestellten) hat Cabrol (2001) vorgelegt.
7 Zum Osirismythos s. Assmann 1984, 149-77.

da sein Ursprung im königlichen Bestattungsritual der Frühzeit liegt[8]. Die Könige dieser Epoche wurden im oberägyptischen Abydos begraben, und Abydos blieb die zentrale Verehrungsstätte des Osiris.

Wenn auch im späteren Alten Reich die Zuständigkeit des Osiris sich vom königlichen Jenseits auf das Jenseitsschicksal aller Ägypter ausdehnte, bedeutete das keineswegs eine Abschwächung der herrscherlichen Identität des Osiris. Diese Herrschaft war im übrigen nicht auf das Totenreich beschränkt: Auch die Lebenden würden einmal sterben und damit schließlich Untertanen des Osiris werden, und als Ursprung der Nilüberschwemmung stand Osiris zudem am Ausgangspunkt sämtlicher Lebensmittelproduktion und damit des Lebens überhaupt im Nilland. Dieser letztgenannte Aspekt des Osiris, der im Lauf der Zeit immer mehr an Bedeutung gewann, wird im Folgenden noch eine wichtige Rolle spielen.

Jeder Verstorbene wurde, wie man sagt, ‚zu *einem* Osiris', er oder sie wurde dem Gott wesensverwandt. Ein Verstorbener wurde daher ‚Osiris NN' genannt. Insbesondere unter dem Aspekt der Generationenkontinuität, der Weitergabe von Wesen und Amt an die nachfolgende Generation, war das Osirismodell von großer Bedeutung[9]. Vorbild der Bindung zwischen Lebenden und Toten waren Osiris und sein Sohn Horus. Auch hier tritt wieder das Königtum in den Vordergrund. Osiris, der zu Lebzeiten König von Ägypten gewesen war, hatte seinem Sohn Horus dieses Königtum vererbt. Folglich war jeder lebende König eine Inkarnation des Horus, jeder verstorbene König ein Osiris.

Osiris in Karnak

Obwohl die Tempelanlage von Karnak über gut zwei Jahrtausende hinweg in Betrieb war und mindestens in der zweiten Hälfte dieses Zeitraums Osiris hier eine theologisch herausragende Stellung einnahm, sind die archäologischen Befunde für seinen Kult vergleichsweise spärlich, vor allem aber von so bescheidenen Ausmaßen, dass sie neben den sonstigen Tempelbauten praktisch verschwinden[10]. Sie konzentrieren sich im nördlichen, vor allem im nordöstlichen Bereich der Tempelanlage, der heute von einer gewaltigen Umfassungsmauer der 30. Dynastie umgeben ist, zum Zeitpunkt der Errichtung der Bauten aber noch außerhalb des abgeschlossenen Tempelbezirks lag (Taf. 19)[11]. In dieser Zone sind drei Gruppen osirianischer Strukturen auszumachen, bei denen es sich – von wenigen Ausnahmen abgesehen – um so genannte Osiriskapellen handelt. Nur die zentralen Elemente der kleinformatigen Bauten bestehen aus Stein, der Rest wurde aus Lehmziegeln aufgemauert. Jede der drei Gruppen besteht aus einigen mehr oder minder linear aneinander gereihten Kapellen. Die östlichste, aus vier Bauten bestehende Kapellengruppe (Taf. 19 [I]) besitzt darüber hinaus einen klaren gemeinsamen Bezugspunkt im Grab des Osiris (Taf. 19 [A]). Das Osirisgrab war ein wichtiges Ziel der Festprozession; hier wurde jedes Jahr eine kleine, aus Sand und Gipsstuck gefertigte Figur des Osiris bestattet, die während des abgelaufenen Jahres als Garant für die Fruchtbarkeit des Landes in einem Heiligtum bewahrt worden war[12]. Aufgrund neuerer Ausgrabungen lässt sich eine zunehmende Formalisierung der Grabanlage nachweisen. In den ersten Jahrhunderten (um 1000-600 v. Chr.) scheint eine oberirdische Markierung der einzelnen Grabstätten nicht stattgefunden zu haben; ohne erkennbare Ordnung liegen sie beziehungslos beieinander, so dass man wahrscheinlich lediglich von einer Art Einfriedung ausgehen kann, innerhalb derer die Figuren bestattet wurden. In einer zweiten Phase (ab 600 v. Chr.) wurde sukzessive ein merkwürdiges tunnelförmiges Gebilde aus Ziegeln angelegt, in dem die Osirisfiguren in kleinen Nischen abgelegt wurden (Abb. 1; Taf. 19 [A rechts]). Diese Grabanlage lag aller Wahrscheinlichkeit nach nicht unter freiem Himmel, sondern war von einem baumbestandenen Erdhügel überwölbt. In dieser Form ist das Osirisgrab in mehreren bildlichen und schriftlichen Darstellungen der Spätzeit – auch in Karnak – überliefert[13]. Erst in

8 Griffiths 1980; Wegner 1996, 9-59.

9 Vgl. Assmann 1991, 96-137.

10 Die kleinste der osirianischen Strukturen wurde als „le plus petit des monuments religieux de l'Égypte, perdu dans l'immensité de Karnak" beschrieben (Georges Legrain, nach Leclant 1965, 26).

11 Wie vor der 30. Dynastie die Umfassung jener Tempel und sonstigen Heiligtümer gestaltet war, die außerhalb des Amuntempelbezirks gelegen sind, ist noch weitgehend unerforscht. Die Osiriskapellen besaßen wohl eine einfache Lehmziegelumwallung, vgl. Coulon und Defernez 2004, 148 Abb. 7, 152.

12 Zu den Osirisgräbern in Karnak s. Coulon et al. 1995; Leclère und Coulon 1998; Leclère 2002; Leclère 2003.

13 Beispielsweise Coulon et al. 1995, Taf. 12.

Abb. 1. Das Osirisgrab der 2. Phase in Karnak. Nach: Leclère 1996, 10.

einer dritten Phase wurde gegen Ende des 3. Jahrhunderts v. Chr. ein rechtwinkliges, ungleich größeres Gebäude aufgeführt (Taf. 19 [A links]). Verlässlichen Rekonstruktionen zufolge enthielt diese Struktur nicht weniger als 720 Bestattungsnischen. Das Gebäude wurde in einer eigens angelegten Grube errichtet und war höchstwahrscheinlich, genau wie sein Vorgänger, überhügelt. Es fand also eine erhebliche Rationalisierung, aber auch eine Monumentalisierung statt, in der sich die stetig ansteigende Bedeutung des Osiriskultes spiegelte.

Südöstlich des Osirisgrabes, fast in der Achse des Haupttempels (Taf. 19 [T]) und von dieser aus zu betreten liegt ein etwas komplexerer Bau (Taf. 19 [B]), der dem in Karnak begrabenen Osiris geweiht war und in dem man vermutlich die dem Grab assoziierte Verehrungsstätte des Gottes erkennen darf[14].

Eine zweite Gruppe von Osiriskapellen liegt hinter der Umfassungsmauer des Tempels des Month nördlich des Amunbezirks (Taf. 19 [II])[15]. Ob neben der Ausrichtung auf den vor den Kapellen gelegenen Abschnitt des Prozessionsweges ein Bezugspunkt im Monthbezirk selbst vorhanden war, der den Standort der Kapellen am Weg bestimmte, ist nicht mehr festzustellen[16].

Ähnliches gilt für die dritte, westlichste Gruppe (Taf. 19 [III]): Die Fassaden der drei Kapellen sind auf den Prozessionsweg ausgerichtet, die Frage nach einem Bezugspunkt hinter den Kapellen ist ungeklärt[17]. Der Weg führt nach Süden auf den axial gelegenen Amuntempel zu.

Alle drei Gruppen sind offenkundig auf einen Weg hin ausgerichtet. Obwohl praktisch nur anhand der Kapellenorientierung[18] und daher nur sehr bruchstückhaft nachzuweisen, erscheint es plausibel,

14 Dieser Tempel ist bis auf einige Inschriften so gut wie unpubliziert, vgl. Porter et al. 1994, 207. Nur die beiden jüngsten osirianischen Strukturen in Karnak, das letzte, ptolemäerzeitliche Osirisgrab und der in seiner jüngsten Stufe römerzeitliche Tempel, sind in ihrer Ausrichtung streng auf den Haupttempel bezogen.

15 Auch diese Umfassungsmauer stammt, wie diejenige des Haupttempels, aus der 30. Dynastie und ist damit wesentlich jünger als die Kapellen.

16 Auch diese Kapellen sind faktisch unpubliziert, vgl. Porter et al. 1994, 13-5.

17 Im Verlauf der jüngsten Grabungen wurden hinter der mittleren Kapelle Reste eines Gebäudes freigelegt, das möglicherweise als Lebensmittelmagazin diente. Die Ausgräber vermuten einen direkten Bezug zu der Kapelle, die dem ‚Osiris, Herr der Speisen' geweiht war: Coulon und Defernez 2004, 160-90.

18 An einer Stelle sind geringfügige Reste der originalen Pflasterung nachweisbar, s. Coulon und Defernez 2004, 145.

diese Bruchstücke als Fragmente eines einzigen Wegverlaufs zu deuten. Die Kapellen gestalten den Weg nicht, sondern flankieren ihn lediglich abschnittsweise. Keinerlei monumentale Elemente wie Sphingen oder Säulenreihen lassen sich hier nachweisen, kein geradliniger Wegverlauf. Diese Straße fällt vollkommen aus dem rechtwinkligen Koordinatensystem der Tempelanlage heraus. Sie steht damit in auffälligem Gegensatz zur üblichen Führung von Prozessionswegen, wie sie innerhalb Karnaks und über Karnak hinaus in der Region Theben zu verfolgen ist.

Jede Kapelle ist einem bestimmten Aspekt des Osiris geweiht, der in einem Epitheton zum Ausdruck kommt, das zusammen mit dem Namen des Gottes in eine Königskartusche eingeschlossen ist. Die Epitheta betonen vor allem die bereits angesprochene Rolle des Osiris als Erhalter und Ernährer[19]. Sein Königtum wird durch die erwähnte Einschreibung des Namens in eine Kartusche (das einen Königsnamen umgebende Oval) hervorgehoben. Einige Beinamen wie ‚Herrscher der Ewigkeit' bezeichnen Osiris in seiner ursprünglichen Funktion als Totengott. Die Namen des Osiris in den Kapellen am Osirisgrab nehmen deutlich Bezug auf die Grabstätte[20], wohingegen für die beiden anderen Gruppen eine entsprechende Regelhaftigkeit nicht festzustellen ist.

Architektur und Dekoration der Kapellen sind bis auf sehr wenige Ausnahmen nur bruchstückhaft bekannt, doch kann bereits der Grundplan des steinernen Nukleus Aufschluss über die allgemeine Funktion dieser Bauten geben. Dass die Funktion eines Gebäudes seine Gestaltung bestimmt, ist eine triviale Beobachtung, die hier aber eine grundlegende Feststellung erlaubt. Was vorhin über die Tempelanlage von Karnak gesagt wurde, gilt im Einzelnen auch für einen ägyptischen Tempel ‚typischer' Ausführung: Er ist im Wesentlichen axial angelegt. Vom äußeren Tempeltor bis zum tief innen gelegenen Sanktuar führt ein schnurgerader Weg, der die Mittelachse des Tempelhauses bildet. Das innere Ende dieser Achse öffnet sich in das Barkensanktuar, von dem aus das Gottesbild zur Prozession aufbrach[21]. Damit verglichen weisen die Osiriskapellen einen grundlegenden Unterschied auf: Zwar besitzen die meisten von ihnen einen durch Säulen und Tore markierten, axial angelegten Zugang, der in vielen Fällen auch auf einen in der Mitte der Fassade des Tempelhauses befindlichen Eingang hinführt. Hinter der Fassade bricht das axiale Wegprinzip dann aber ab: Man befindet sich in einem Vorraum, von dem aus man seitlich in eine weitere Kammer gelangt[22]. Diese architektonischen Charakteristika zeigen, dass es sich bei den Osiriskapellen weder um vollwertige Tempel – mit einem zentralen (Barken)Sanktuar – handelt, noch um Stationskapellen, den für prozessionswegbegleitende Bauten üblichen Typ mit lang gestreckten Räumen zur Aufnahme der Prozessionsbarke. Das Prinzip der geknickten oder auch verschobenen Achse ist hingegen bei anderen Kapellen des Osiris, in denen alljährlich die Mysterien von Tod, Auferstehung und Herrschaftsübertragung im Verborgenen vollzogen wurden, die Regel (Abb. 2). Diese Merkmale erlauben den Schluss, dass die Osiriskapellen von Karnak nicht einem kontinuierlichen Kultbetrieb dienten, sondern nur anlässlich der Osirisfestlichkeiten aktiviert wurden. Die Kapellen waren nicht Wohnstätte, sondern Werkstätte der Gottheit mit einem eng definierten Aufgabenbereich[23].

Ein ‚klassischer' ägyptischer Tempel zeichnete sich, wie eben angesprochen, durch eine ausgeprägte Mittelachse aus, den Beginn des ‚Gottesweges'[24], auf dem sich die Gottheit zur Prozession begab. Ebenso geradlinig verliefen auch die Prozessionswege außerhalb von Tempelhaus und Tempelbezirk. Ein Gott ging keine krummen Wege, wenn es sich vermeiden ließ. Der Prozessionsweg des Osiris, zumindest

19 Beispielsweise ‚Osiris, Herr des Lebens' (mehrfach), ‚Osiris, der Lebensstifter', ‚Osiris, Herr der Speisen'.

20 ‚Osiris, der den Ischedbaum eröffnet', ‚Osiris inmitten des Ischedbaumes'. Isched war der Name des den Grabhügel des Osiris bekrönenden Baumes.

21 Es handelt sich hierbei, wie oben bereits angedeutet, um den Weg des Gottes, der von dem Weg des Priesters zu unterscheiden ist, der den Tempel durch Seiteneingänge betrat. Es ist außerdem zu unterscheiden zwischen dem Barkensanktuar und dem eigentlichen Kultbildsanktuar, das vor der Spätzeit oft seitlich hinter dem Barkensanktuar lag; s. zu beidem Fitzenreiter 2003.

22 Die sechs Kapellen der zweiten Gruppe weisen als ein weiteres Element, das sie von den zwei anderen Gruppen unterscheidet, einen den beiden Kammern vorgelagerten Raum auf. Der Kapelle des ‚Osiris, Herrscher der Ewigkeit' am Osirisgrab (Taf. 19 [I rechts]) wurde ein solcher Vorraum erst nachträglich angefügt.

23 Die Dekoration der einzigen publizierten Inneren Kammer einer Osiriskapelle (Leclant 1965, 33 Abb. 9, 34 Abb. 10-2) zeigt zum einen das Ritual des ‚Aufrichtens des Djed-Pfeilers', das eng mit der Bestattung des Osiris verknüpft ist, zum anderen Totenopfer und Verklärungen für Osiris in einer Darstellungstradition, die seit dem Alten Reich vor allem in Gräbern für Privatpersonen belegt ist, an eine Gottheit gerichtet m.W. jedoch einzig dasteht. Die ebenfalls abgebildeten Prozessionsstandarten reflektieren den formalen Rahmen des Geschehens.

24 So die ägyptische Bezeichnung des Prozessionswegs, vgl. Cabrol 2001, 61-4.

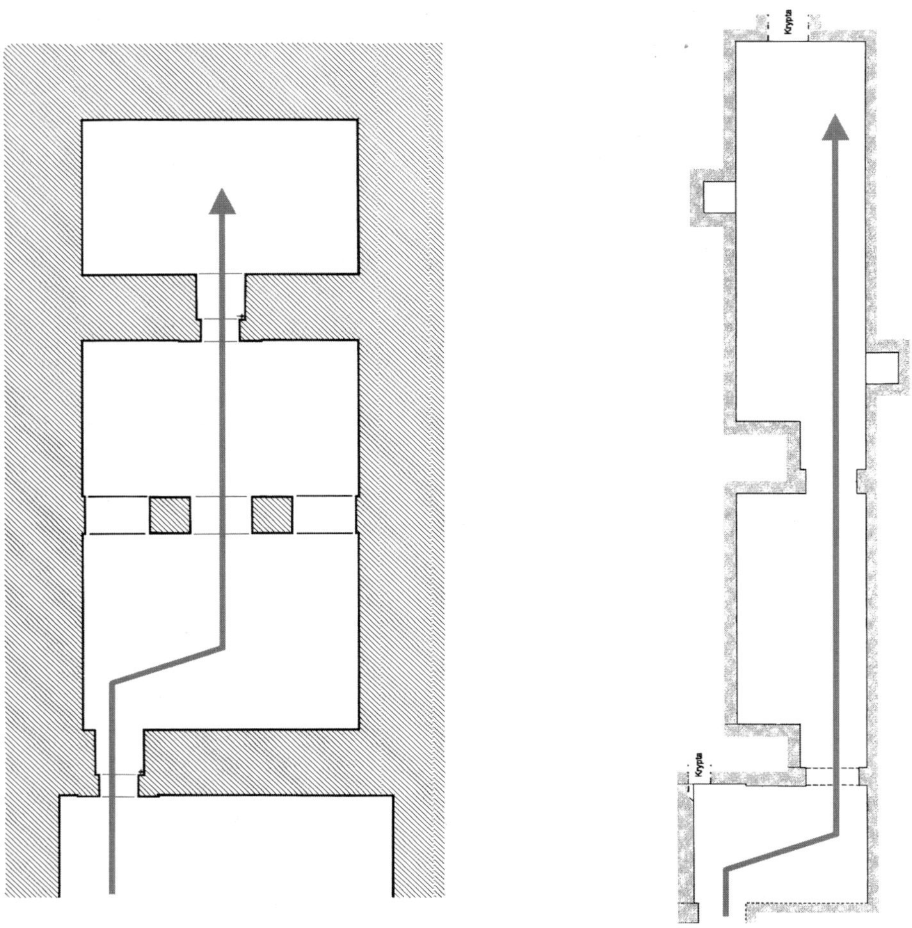

Abb. 2. Osiriskapellen auf den Dächern der Tempel von Dendera und Edfu. Nach: Cauville 1997, Taf. 2; Waitkus 1999, 159 Abb. 1.

der anhand der Kapellenanordnung nachvollziehbare Abschnitt hin zum Grab, verfolgte hingegen keineswegs eine gerade Linie. Er beschrieb vielmehr einen west-östlich orientierten, weit nach Norden ausgreifenden Bogen mit nur geringer Markierung des Weges (Taf. 19[25]). Über die Gründe für diesen exzentrischen Wegverlauf[26] lassen sich einstweilen nur Vermutungen anstellen. Möglicherweise liegt eine absichtliche Transposition der Prozessionstopographie von Abydos, dem Hauptkultort des Osiris, vor. Dort folgte der Festzug dem natürlichen Verlauf eines Wadi, eines ausgetrockneten Flussbettes, das ebenfalls einen Bogen nach Norden beschreibt (Taf. 20)[27]. Entsprechend der Lage am westlichen Nilufer verlief dort der Weg des Gottes von seinem Tempel zu seinem Grab in der alten Königsnekropole in ost-westlicher Richtung. Diese These einer Übertragung der ‚sakralen Landschaft'[28] gewinnt an Plausi-

25 Der eingezeichnete Wegverlauf kann und soll nur eine ganz allgemeine Vorstellung vermitteln, da sich – jedenfalls anhand des bislang publizierten Materials – keine detaillierteren Aussagen dazu treffen lassen.

26 Exzentrisch nicht nur wegen der nichtlinear angelegten Strecke, sondern auch wegen ihrer polaren Ausrichtung: Norden (hier ausgeprägt in der Lage nördlich des Haupttempels und der Ausbiegung nach Norden) und Osten (hier als Zielort = Grabstätte des Osiris) besaßen im ägyptischen Weltbild eine geringere Wertigkeit als Süden und Westen (s. Fitzenreiter 2004, 140-1). Auch diese Beobachtung spricht für die oben vorgetragene These einer Übertragung des Wegverlaufs.

27 S. Kucharek (im Druck).

28 Fitzenreiter (2003, 151) interpretiert die Struktur von Tell el-Amarna, der quasi aus dem Boden gestampften Residenzstadt des Echnaton, als „inverse Interpretation von Theben", Pamminger (1992, 115) die ungewöhnliche nordsüdliche Ausrichtung des Luxortempels als „Transposition der geographischen Realität und der theologischen Ideologie in Sakralarchitektur". Zur Einbindung der natürlichen Topographie in Kult und Politik Ägyptens s. Richards 1999. Die Transposition von mythischen Topographien auf sakrale Strukturen ist in Ägypten wohlbekannt. So ist jeder Tempel ein Abbild des ‚Urhügels', des ersten Schöpfungsortes, bzw. ruht auf ihm (Martin 1986).

Abb. 3. Die Prozessionsbarke des Osiris in Abydos im Giebelfeld der Stele Lyon H 1379. Im Barkenschrein der Abydosfetisch (eingerahmt). Nach: Fischer 1988, Taf. 18a.

bilität dadurch, dass es spezifisch der Osiris von Abydos war, der bei der Prozession in Karnak verehrt wurde. Konkret handelte es sich bei dem Prozessionsbild um den so genannten ‚Abydosfetisch', ein Gebilde letztlich ungeklärter Herkunft und Bedeutung, das für den Gott stand und bei den Osirisfeiern in Abydos in einer Prozessionsbarke erschien (Abb. 3). Ebendieser Abydosfetisch ist in Karnak in einigen Osiriskapellen sowie auf zahlreichen Tempelstatuen abgebildet, oft mitsamt den Tragstangen (Abb. 4). Er war offenbar ein zentrales Objekt der Prozessionsfeierlichkeiten, ohne dass seine genaue Funktion geklärt wäre[29].

Soziohistorische Dimension

Osirisfiguren wurden in Karnak spätestens seit Beginn des 1. Jahrtausends v. Chr. feierlich bestattet; diese Praxis wurde nachweislich noch unter römischer Herrschaft im 1. Jahrhundert n.Chr. ausgeübt[30]. Umso bemerkenswerter erscheint daher der vergleichsweise enge Zeitrahmen, in dem die Osiriskapellen errichtet wurden. Er umfasst die grob 400 Jahre von der 22. bis zur 26. Dynastie (945-525 v. Chr.). Es sind die Befunde dieser Zeit und vor allem der 25. und 26. Dynastie (ca. 750-525 v. Chr.), in deren Verlauf die meisten Osiriskapellen errichtet wurden, die der folgenden Darstellung zugrunde liegen.

Historisch betrachtet bildet der genannte Zeitraum keine einheitliche Epoche (Abb. 5). Nach der gängigen Einteilung wird die Zeit der 22.-25. Dynastie der sog. 3. Zwischenzeit zugerechnet, deren Beginn jedoch bereits die 21. Dynastie markiert. Die 21.-24. Dynastie wiederum bildet innerhalb der 3. Zwischenzeit die ‚Libyerzeit', da die Herrscher dieser Linie ursprünglich aus dem Westen eingewandert waren. Die letzte Libyerdynastie wurde von nubischen Eroberern abgelöst, den ‚Kuschiten', deren Herrschaft als 25. Dynastie gerechnet wird, die die 3. Zwischenzeit abschloss. Die letzte Dynastie, die in Karnak dem Osiriskult in hervorragender Weise Denkmäler setzte, war die der Spätzeit zugerechnete 26. Dynastie, deren Könige aus Sais im Delta stammten; diese Zeit wird daher oft als ‚Saitenzeit' bezeich-

29 Überlegungen bei Koemoth (2001) sowie Eaton (2004, 416-25).

30 Die ältesten Osirisgräber stammen aus dem frühen 1. Jahrtausend. Der Osiristempel am Grab (Taf. 19 [B]) wurde unter dem römischen Kaiser Tiberius letztmals erneuert. Ebenfalls aus römischer Zeit stammt ein Papyrus, in dem der Ritualablauf während der Osirisprozession in Karnak leitfadenartig aufgezeichnet ist (Barguet 1962).

Abb. 4. Die Statue des Hor (22. Dynastie) aus der Kapelle des ‚Osiris, der den Ischedbaum eröffnet' in Karnak. An der Seitenfläche eine Darstellung des Abydosfetischs mit Tragstangen und Prozessionsstandarten. Nach: Jansen-Winkeln 1985, Taf. 32.

net. Letztlich war freilich auch diese Dynastie libyscher Abstammung. In politischer Hinsicht war der gesamte Zeitraum eine unruhige Epoche, in der selten ein König unangefochten über ganz Ägypten herrschte[31].

Dieser historischen Heterogenität steht *ein* einender Faktor gegenüber. Genau in der Zeit, in der in Karnak Osiriskapellen errichtet wurden, regierte in Theben eine ‚Gottesgemahlin des Amun'. Diese Frau war stets eine Königstochter, die in aller Kürze als oberägyptische Statthalterin ihrer im Nildelta residierenden Dynastie charakterisiert werden kann. Als kultische Gemahlin des Hauptgottes von Karnak ging sie keine irdische Ehe ein und konnte daher keine eigene Dynastie begründen, sie besaß allerdings echten königlichen Status. In kultischer Hinsicht bedeutete das beispielsweise, dass sie eigenständig den Götterkult vollziehen konnte und in bildlichen Darstellungen diese Rolle alleine oder gleichberechtigt mit dem regierenden Herrscher ausfüllte. Die Vererbung ihres Amtes geschah durch Adoption einer Nachfolgerin. Die beiden letzten Amtsinhaberinnen übernahmen sogar die bis dahin stets von einem Mann ausgeübte Würde des Hohenpriesters des Amun, des höchsten geistlichen Amtes in Karnak.

Dass Osiriskapellen nur in der Epoche der Gottesgemahlinnen errichtet wurden, ist nachweislich kein zufälliges Zusammentreffen, da mit ganz wenigen Ausnahmen ebendiese Gottesgemahlinnen alleine oder zusammen mit dem regierenden König als Bauherrinnen der Kapellen firmieren.

Im Vergleich zu ihrer Machtfülle und in Anbetracht eines Amtes, das weit über 200 Jahre lang ununterbrochen ausgeübt wurde, fällt die Bilanz der Bauwerke der Gottesgemahlinnen eher bescheiden aus[32]. Wenn auch insgesamt die Epoche der 22. bis 26. Dynastie speziell in Oberägypten nicht eben von großer Baufreude geprägt war, sind doch in Hinsicht auf die Gottesgemahlinnen einige Besonderheiten zu registrieren. So tragen die Bauten dieser Zeit im Amunbezirk von Karnak selbst nur die Namen der regierenden Könige, die Gottesgemahlinnen finden dort keinerlei Erwähnung. Nur außerhalb des Amunbezirks ließen sie die bescheiden dimensionierten Kapellen aufführen, die alle einem einheitli-

31 Einen Überblick über diese bewegte Zeit unter besonderer Berücksichtigung des Aspekts der ‚Fremdherrschaft' gibt Jansen-Winkeln (2000).

32 Die einzigen Bauwerke, die den Gottesgemahlinnen abgesehen von den Kapellen in Karnak zugeordnet werden können, sind ihre Grabkapellen auf der Westseite von Theben in Medinet Habu. Obwohl ihr Herrschaftsgebiet deutlich über Theben hinausging, ist ihre Bautätigkeit praktisch auf diese beiden Punkte beschränkt geblieben. Lediglich in Medamud, einige Kilometer nördlich von Theben, sind noch Reste einer Kapelle der Gottesgemahlin Schepenupet II. gefunden worden, zusammen mit Blöcken einer etwa zeitgenössischen Osiriskapelle (unpubliziert, vgl. Coulon 2003, 56).

3. Zwischenzeit	21. Dynastie	Libyer	1070 - 715
	22. Dynastie		
	23. Dynastie		
	24. Dynastie		
	25. Dynastie	Kuschiten	745-655
Spätzeit	26. Dynastie	Saiten	664-525

Abb. 5. Chronologische Übersicht.

chen Schema verpflichtet waren und die überraschenderweise nicht dem Amun, dem göttlichen Gemahl der Bauherrinnen, geweiht waren, sondern Osiris[33]. Die Gründe für diese auffallende Einschränkung sind bislang ungeklärt.

Für die Tatsache der engen Bindung an Osiris insbesondere seitens der Gottesgemahlinnen kann hingegen eine zumindest partielle Begründung versucht werden. Hier spielt das seit dem Neuen Reich immer stärker hervortretende Wesen des Osiris als universaler Ernährer und Erhalter, als Herrscher nicht nur über die Toten, sondern auch über die Lebenden, eine gewichtige Rolle.

Amun-Re, der Hauptgott von Karnak, war eine Erscheinungsform des Sonnengottes, als dessen ‚Leichnam' Osiris galt. Der Sonnengott vereinte sich allnächtlich an der tiefsten Stelle der Unterwelt mit Osiris und erneuerte dadurch seine Lebenskraft. Zwischen Sonnenuntergang und Sonnenaufgang durchzog der Sonnengott auf einer westöstlichen Bahn das Totenreich, wobei er den Toten Licht und Leben spendete[34]. Diese enge Verbindung von Amun-Re und Osiris war sicherlich ein Auslöser der verstärkten Bautätigkeit für Osiris in Karnak. Gleichzeitig wuchs aber auch seine bereits angedeutete Position als *der* Lebensspender für Ägypten überhaupt, die sich im theologischen Bild der Verwesungsflüssigkeit des Osirisleichnams als Überschwemmungswasser ausdrückte[35]. In beiden Fällen ist das Motiv der Regeneration unübersehbar: Der – tagsüber gealterte – Sonnengott verjüngt sich durch die nächtliche Vereinigung mit seinem Körper in der Unterwelt und kann so am nächsten Morgen als Sonnenkind wieder im Osthorizont erscheinen und erneut seine Himmelsbahn beschreiten. Die periodisch auftretende Nilüberschwemmung aber, die die Äcker befruchtete und bewässerte, erhielt das ganze Land – von den Göttern bis zum letzten Wurm – am Leben. Die Gewährleistung der steten Wiederkehr der zyklischen kosmischen Phänomene von Sonnenlauf und Nilüberschwemmung und damit die Welterhaltung war Aufgabe des Herrschers, die er durch vorschriftsgemäß vollzogenen Kult erfüllte. Im Gegenzug verliehen die Götter dem König eine lange und erfolgreiche Regierung. Osiris wurde im Verlauf des 1. Jahrtausends v. Chr. zum Exponenten dieses Systems der Schöpfungserhaltung. Aus dem Jenseits heraus sorgte der König des Totenreiches für das Wohlergehen des Diesseits, vorausgesetzt, sein im regierenden Herrscher inkarnierter Sohn Horus sorgte durch Kult- und Festvollzug für seinen Vater Osiris. Diese Beziehung nimmt in den Osiriskapellen in Karnak Gestalt an, in denen im Verlauf der Osirismysterien der tote

33 Tatsächlich ist der Hauptgott von Karnak in der Wanddekoration der Kapellen stets mehr oder weniger prominent vertreten, an der Weihung an Osiris ändert dies jedoch nichts. Auch Statuen der Gottesgemahlinnen sind, soweit beschriftet, entweder mit einer Weihung an Osiris oder, bei Bronzestatuetten, mit Bildern des Osiris, des Abydosfetischs und/oder der ebenfalls in die osirianische Theologie eingebundenen Barke des Gottes Sokar versehen (Perdu 1996; Delange et al. 1998, 72-3).

34 Zur Verschmelzung osirianischer und solarer Theologie in der 3. Zwischenzeit in Theben vgl. Niwinski 1987-88.

35 S. Assmann 2003.

Gott belebt und zum Herrscher der Unterwelt erhoben wurde, bevor er am Ende des Prozessionsfestes zu Grabe getragen und dergestalt in sein jenseitiges Reich eingeführt wurde. Dank ihres königlichen Status konnte die Gottesgemahlin des Amun in die sonst dem König vorbehaltene Horusrolle eintreten. Erstaunlich bleibt bei allem die Anzahl der nachweisbaren Kapellen: Unter der Herrschaft von insgesamt sieben Gottesgemahlinnen entstanden etwa zwanzig der kleinen Bauten[36]. Eine Erklärung dafür ist, dass jede Gottesgemahlin jeder Kapellengruppe eine weitere Kapelle hinzufügen wollte. Ich möchte noch eine weitere Möglichkeit vorschlagen, die die erste Begründung nicht ausschließt.

Trotz des schlechten Erhaltungszustandes der meisten Kapellen und trotz der sehr unvollständigen Publikationslage ist ein höchst ungewöhnliches Element nicht zu übersehen: Die Präsenz von Privatpersonen. In einem bisher nicht dagewesenen Maß wurde der jeweils höchste Beamte einer Gottesgemahlin, der Obervermögensverwalter, der mächtigste Mann im Staat, in die Kapellendekoration mit einbezogen[37]. Schon seit Jahrhunderten hatte es das Institut der Tempelstatue gegeben, der durch königliche Gunst im Tempel aufgestellten Statue einer Privatperson. Sie sollte den Dargestellten für alle Zeiten in den Genuss der Opfergaben bringen, die der Gottheit im Tempel dargebracht wurden. Gleichzeitig übernahm die Tempelstatue eine Funktion, die zuvor der Grabanlage und ihrer Ausgestaltung zugekommen war: Sie verstetigte die Erinnerung an den Statuenbesitzer, was sich vor allem in den ausführlichen biographischen Inschriften dieser Statuen ausprägt[38]. In den Osiriskapellen aber manifestiert sich eine Steigerung sowohl des weltlichen Prestiges als auch des göttlichen Wohlwollens für die betreffende Person. Verglichen mit der unmittelbaren Gottesbegegnung, die die Gegenwart beim Götterkult impliziert, mutet die Bitte um Opfergaben und Gebete, wie sie für Tempelstatuen charakteristisch war, geradezu bescheiden an. Durch die Anbringung seines Namens auch an den von außen sichtbaren Toren der Kapelleneinfriedung blieb das außerordentliche Privileg des Obervermögensverwalters auch seinen Mitmenschen nicht verborgen[39].

Eine Vorstufe dieser erstaunlichen Entwicklung lässt sich durch einen glücklichen Zufall fassen. Die älteste datierbare Osiriskapelle in Karnak aus der 22. Dynastie, am Osirisgrab gelegen, enthält keine Darstellung oder Erwähnung einer Privatperson oder einer Gottesgemahlin[40]. Im Vorhof der Kapelle waren jedoch die Statuen eines hochrangigen Beamten und Priesters namens Hor (Abb. 4) und seiner Frau Schepensopdet aufgestellt[41]. In Art und Beschriftung entsprechen sie weitestgehend den zahlreichen sonstigen Tempelstatuen[42]. Die Statue des Hor trägt außerdem einen Schenkungsvermerk des Königs. Hor berichtet im autobiographischen Teil der Statueninschrift allerdings, dass er selbst die Kapelle erbaut habe, und nicht nur dies, sondern er bezeichnet sich ausdrücklich als ihr Urheber und Nutznießer: „Gott war es, der es (die Errichtung der Kapelle) in mein Herz gegeben hatte, damit meine Lebenszeit lang sei."[43] Kapelle und Statuen stehen, je für sich betrachtet, ganz im Rahmen der bestehenden Konventionen: Der Kultbau zeigt ausschließlich den König und die verehrten Gottheiten. Die Tem-

36 Abgesehen von den 14 Kapellen, die auf die drei in diesem Aufsatz behandelten Gruppen verteilt sind, sind noch einige vereinzelt stehende sowie diverse Blöcke von nicht mehr lokalisierbaren Kapellen bekannt.

37 Zum Obervermögensverwalter der Gottesgemahlinnen vgl. Graefe 1981.

38 Vgl. Guksch 1994, 16-7; Assmann 2004, 7.

39 Vorläufer dieser Erscheinung sind in der 21. Dynastie in Memphis bezeugt, wo Türstürze und Türpfosten eines kleineren Amunheiligtums Darstellungen bzw. Namen des Hohenpriesters von Memphis und des Priesters des Heiligtums tragen. Am selben Ort wurde auch ein entsprechend gestalteter Türsturz aus der Zeit Osorkons I. vom Beginn der 22. Dynastie gefunden (Porter et al. 1981, 853-4). Zwischen diesen und dem ersten Auftreten in Karnak liegt ein Zeitraum von ca. 200 Jahren.

40 Das Fehlen einer Gottesgemahlin in einer Osiriskapelle ist höchst ungewöhnlich, wenn auch nicht ganz einzigartig. Denselben Befund bietet die Dekoration der einzigen südlich des Amuntempels gelegenen, recht gut erhaltenen Osiriskapelle (Porter et al. 1994, 278), obwohl im Zeitraum ihrer Errichtung permanent Gottesgemahlinnen im Amt waren. Obervermögensverwalter der Gottesgemahlinnen sind erst seit der 25. Dynastie bezeugt.

41 Zu dieser Kapelle und den erwähnten Statuen vgl. Redford (1986), der auch auf eine dritte, *in situ* im Vorhof der Kapelle aufgefundene, fragmentarische Statue des Hor und der Schepensopdet eingeht; Coulon 2005, 334-6; Jansen-Winkeln 1985, 136-67, 506-14, 520-6, Taf. 30-3, 37-40.

42 In der chronologischen Abfolge der Privatstatuen tut sich mit der dem hier besprochenen Zeitraum unmittelbar vorangehenden 21. Dynastie (ca. 1070-945 v. Chr.) eine eklatante Lücke auf: Aus dieser Periode ist keine einzige Privatstatue bekannt (vgl. Eaton-Krauss und Jansen-Winkeln 2001, 3, 9). Erst mit der frühen 22. Dynastie setzt wieder eine umfangreiche Statuenproduktion ein.

43 Jansen-Winkeln 1985, 142. Die Worte „Ich bin gekommen, damit ich in [dieser Kapelle] bin" auf der Statue der Schepensopdet unterstreichen die Zusammengehörigkeit von Statue und Kapelle (Jansen-Winkeln 1985, 159).

pelstatue, die einer Privatperson als besondere königliche Gunstgabe zuteil wurde, ist zum Zeitpunkt der Kapellenerrichtung eine uralte Einrichtung. Erst aus der Kombination beider Objektgattungen ergibt sich eine neue Perspektive, aus der heraus die Osiriskapelle auch als privat initiiertes frommes Werk zu individuellem Nutzen verstanden werden kann.

Sehen wir uns im Vergleich die jüngste Osiriskapelle vom Ende der 26. Dynastie an[44]. Eine Statue des nunmehr waltenden Obervermögensverwalters Scheschonq ist nicht erhalten. Trotzdem kann am Anteil dieses Beamten an der Kapelle kein Zweifel bestehen. In praktisch jeder Szene, die seine Herrin, die Gottesgemahlin Anchnesneferibre, bei der Kultausübung vor einer Gottheit zeigt, ist auch Scheschonq anwesend: Er steht hinter der Gottesgemahlin und ist entsprechend seiner geringeren Würde in kleinerem Maßstab dargestellt[45]. Er partizipiert nicht handelnd am Kult, aber bereits die bloße Einbeziehung in die Kultsphäre des Göttlichen bedeutete für eine Privatperson allerhöchstes Privileg. Die Gottesgemahlin fungierte für ihn als ‚Mittlerin' zur Gottheit[46]. Nach außen hin verkündete der Name des Scheschonq an den Türpfosten unübersehbar seine Ausnahmestellung[47]. Das zwischen König bzw. Gottesgemahlin und Gott vonstatten gehende Kultgeschehen auf der einen Seite und die Präsenz einer Privatperson auf der anderen Seite sind nun nicht mehr separabel. Während Scheschonqs Vorläufer in der 22. Dynastie sich noch in Gestalt eines althergebrachten Mediums mit einer Position im Vorhof des Heiligtums begnügt hatte, waren im Verlauf der 25. Dynastie die Obervermögensverwalter in das Sanktuar selbst vorgedrungen. Die Frage, ob sie dies nur *in effigie*, im Bild taten oder ob sie leibhaftig an den Osirisriten teilnahmen, kann nicht eindeutig beantwortet werden. Es gibt aber durchaus Indizien, die dafür sprechen[48].

Wenn tatsächlich hochrangige Privatpersonen, vor allem Obervermögensverwalter, eine der treibenden Kräfte des Kapellenbaus waren, könnte dies eine Erklärung dafür liefern, warum mit dem Ende des Amtes der Gottesgemahlin des Amun auch die Errichtung von Osiriskapellen ein jähes Ende fand. Es ist bekannt, dass die Osirismysterien in Karnak noch im ersten nachchristlichen Jahrhundert vollzogen wurden, und aus der vorangehenden Ptolemäerzeit sind vereinzelt Priester der in den Kapellen verehrten Formen des Osiris belegt. Einer dieser Priester erweiterte sogar im eigenen Namen – nicht im Namen des Herrschers! – die älteste Osiriskapelle am Gottesgrab[49]. Die einzigartige Verquickung von königlicher und privater Initiative blieb aber auf die Epoche der Gottesgemahlinnen beschränkt und ist daher, so mein Vorschlag, in der spezifischen Herrschafts- und Verwaltungsstruktur der Zeit zu suchen.

Meine These lautet, dass die Osiriskapellen von Karnak ihre Existenz grundlegend der verstärkt im ersten vorchristlichen Jahrtausend erfolgten Wesensverschiebung bzw. -erweiterung des Totengottes Osiris hin zum allumfassenden Nährer und Erhalter der Schöpfung hin verdanken. An ihrer Lage und Architektur ist ihre Funktion als Stätte geheimer Rituale im Verlauf einer Festprozession ablesbar. Diese Rituale zielen auf die Wiederherstellung der königlichen Person des toten Gottes Osiris auf dem Weg zu seinem künftigem Herrschaftsbereich, dem Totenreich, und dienen gleichzeitig der Übertragung seines irdischen Königtums auf den regierenden Herrscher. Mit dem Grab des Osiris findet die Schnittstelle zwischen Diesseits und Jenseits eine konkrete Verortung. Der Prozessionsweg bildete vielleicht

44 Coulon 2003; Coulon und Defernez 2004.

45 S. beispielsweise Coulon 2003, 49 Abb. 2.

46 Zum Konzept des Mittlertums in Ägypten vgl. Radwan 1991, Pamminger 1996. Auf Stelen und im ägyptisch verwalteten Nubien ist der König als Mittler für eine Privatperson seit dem Neuen Reich belegt. In einem Tempel im ägyptischen Mutterland war dies zu jener Zeit nicht denkbar, wie die einzige Ausnahme zeigt: Die Darstellungen des hohen Beamten Senenmut im Totentempel der Königin Hatschepsut (18. Dynastie) in Deir el-Bahari (Theben-West) wurden zwar mit ihrer ausdrücklichen Erlaubnis, aber sämtlich an verborgenen Stellen angebracht (Dorman 1988, 6, 125).

47 Coulon und Defernez 2004, 157 Abb. 12.

48 So trägt der Obervermögensverwalter Harwa auf zwei seiner zahlreichen Statuen den Titel eines ‚Priesters des ‚Osiris, der Lebensstifter''. ‚Der Lebensstifter' war eine Form des Osiris, der eine zeitgenössische Osiriskapelle geweiht war. Die Vermutung, dass die beiden Statuen zur Kapelle gehörten und dass Harwa dort priesterliche Funktionen ausübte, liegt nahe. Zu den Statuen s. Gunn und Engelbach 1931, 803; Gunn 1934, 136, 141. Für die Osirisprozessionsfeste des Mittleren Reiches in Abydos (um 2000 v. Chr.) ist die Übernahme priesterlicher Ämter durch Verwaltungsbeamte für die Dauer des Festes bezeugt, vgl. Kucharek (im Druck).

49 Coulon 2005, 337-9.

die Kulttopographie des zentralen Osiriskultortes Abydos ab[50]. Die auffallende Anzahl der Kapellen kann durch die Pluralität ihrer Bezugspunkte erklärt werden, wobei bedauerlicherweise bei zwei der drei Gruppen dieser Bezugspunkt im Dunkel liegt. Eine weitere Motivation für die Errichtung mehrerer Kapellen innerhalb der Regierungszeit *einer* Gottesgemahlin ist vermutlich im privaten Sektor zu suchen. Für fast jeden Obervermögensverwalter der 25. und 26. Dynastie ist eine Beteiligung an einer Osiriskapelle nachzuweisen. In erheblicher Ausweitung des alten Privilegs der Tempelstatue erobern diese hohen Beamten den sakralen Raum, um dadurch göttliche Gunst und weltliches Prestige zu erlangen[51]. Letzteres wird durch die Lage der Kapellen außerhalb der Umfassungsmauern des Amuntempels auch für die Allgemeinheit deutlich fassbar. Die periphere Lage impliziert zwar zum einen einen minder sakralen Status, stellt aber zum anderen eine gewisse Öffentlichkeit sicher. An dieser Schnittstelle heiliger und profaner Räume stellten Gottesgemahlin und Obervermögensverwalter ihren Anspruch auf Gottesnähe zur Schau.

BIBLIOGRAFIE

Assmann, J. 1984. *Ägypten. Theologie und Frömmigkeit einer frühen Hochkultur.* Stuttgart: Kohlhammer.

—. 1991. „Das Bild des Vaters." In *Stein und Zeit. Mensch und Gesellschaft im alten Ägypten*, 96-137. München: Fink.

—. 2003. „Das Leichensekret des Osiris. Zur kultischen Bedeutung des Wassers im alten Ägypten." In *Hommages à Fayza Haikal*, herausgegeben von N. Grimal, A. Kamel und C. May-Sheikhholeslami, 5-16. Bibliothèque d'étude 138. Kairo: Institut français d'archéologie orientale.

—. 2004. „Die Konstruktion sakralen Raums in der Grabarchitektur des Neuen Reichs." *Archiv für Religionsgeschichte* 6: 1-18.

Barguet, P. 1962. *Le papyrus N. 3176 (S) au Musée du Louvre.* Bibliothèque d'étude 37. Kairo: Institut français d'archéologie orientale.

Cabrol, A. 2001. *Les voies processionnelles de Thèbes.* Orientalia Lovaniensia Orientalia 97. Löwen: Peeters.

Cauville, S. 1997. *Le temple de Dendara.* Band 10, *Les chapelles osiriennes.* 2 Bände. Kairo: Institut français d'archéologie orientale.

Coulon, L. 2003. „Un aspect du culte osirien à Thèbes à l'époque saïte . La chapelle d'Osiris Ounnefer ‚Maître des aliments'." *Égypte. Afrique et Orient* 28: 47-60.

—. 2005. „Trauerrituale im Grab des Osiris in Karnak." In *Abschied von den Toten. Trauerrituale im Kulturvergleich*, herausgegeben von J. Assmann, F. Maciejewski und A. Michaels, 326-41. Göttingen: Wallstein.

Coulon, L. und C. Defernez. 2004. „La chapelle d'Osiris Ounnefer Neb-Djefaou à Karnak. Rapport préliminaire des fouilles et travaux 2000-2004." *Bulletin de l'Institut français d'archéologie orientale* 104: 135-90.

Coulon, L., F. Leclère und S. Marchand. 1995. „‚Catacombes' osiriennes de Ptolémée IV à Karnak. Rapport préliminaire de la campagne de fouilles 1993." *Karnak* 10: 205-38.

Delange, E., A. di Mantova und J.H. Taylor. 1998. „Un bronze égyptien méconnu." *Revue du Louvre* 48.5: 67-75.

Dorman, P. 1988. *The Monuments of Senenmut. Problems in Historical Methodology.* London et al.: Kegan Paul International.

50 Der Stellenwert von Abydos lässt sich auch daran ablesen, dass dies außerhalb Thebens der einzige Ort war, an dem die oberägyptischen Herrscher der Libyerzeit nennenswerte Denkmäler hinterließen. In der folgenden 25. Dynastie wurden zudem zahlreiche weibliche Mitglieder des Königshauses in Abydos begraben.

51 Wahrscheinlich konvergieren hier mehrere Strömungen und Motive, die im vorliegenden Rahmen aber nicht diskutiert werden können. Erwähnt sei die bereits angedeutete Funktionsannäherung von Grab und Tempel seit dem späteren Neuen Reich, die sich zum einen in der Verehrung von Gottheiten im Grab niederschlug, zum anderen aber die so genannte ‚Sakralisierung des Diesseits', die sich im Wunsch des Verstorbenen nach zeitweiser Rückkehr in die Welt der Lebenden und insbesondere nach der Teilnahme an Götterfesten niederschlug. Gerade in der Sphäre des Totengottes Osiris, dem auch im Privatgrab eine prominente Rolle zukam, scheint die Möglichkeit einer Annäherung von Grab und Tempel besonders groß. Auf formale Vorläufer in der 21. und 22. Dynastie im Delta wurde oben verwiesen.

Dreyer, G. 1998. *Das prädynastische Königsgrab U-j und seine frühen Schriftzeugnisse*. Archäologische Veröffentlichungen 86. Mainz: Philipp von Zabern.

Eaton, K. 2004. „The Ritual Functions of Processional Equipment in the Temple of Seti I at Abydos." Dissertation, New York University.

Eaton-Krauss, M. und K. Jansen-Winkeln. 2001. „Der Würfelhocker des Hor aus der frühen 22. Dynastie." *Mitteilungen des Deutschen Archäologischen Instituts, Abteilung Kairo* 57: 1-13.

Fischer, H.G. 1988. „The Trumpet in Ancient Egypt." In *Pyramid Studies and Other Essays Presented to I.E.S. Edwards*, herausgegeben von J. Baines, T.G.H. James, A. Leahy und A.F. Shore, 103-9. London: Egypt Exploration Society.

Fitzenreiter, M. 2003. „Richtungsbezüge in ägyptischen Sakralanlagen – oder: Warum im ägyptischen Tempel das Sanktuar hinten links in der Ecke liegt (Teil I)." *Studien zur altägyptischen Kultur* 31: 107-51.

—. 2004. „Richtungsbezüge in ägyptischen Sakralanlagen – oder: Warum im ägyptischen Tempel das Sanktuar hinten links in der Ecke liegt (Teil II)." *Studien zur altägyptischen Kultur* 32: 119-48.

Graefe, E. 1981. *Untersuchungen zur Verwaltung und Geschichte der Institution der Gottesgemahlin des Amun vom Beginn des Neuen Reiches bis zur Spätzeit*. Ägyptologische Abhandlungen 37. Wiesbaden: Harrassowitz.

Griffiths, J.G. 1980. *The Origins of Osiris and his Cult. Studies in the History of Religion*. Supplement Numen 40. Leiden: Brill.

Guksch, H. 1994. *Königsdienst. Zur Selbstdarstellung der Beamten in der 18. Dynastie*. Studien zur Archäologie und Geschichte Altägyptens 11. Heidelberg: Orientverlag.

Gunn, B. 1934. „The Berlin Statue of Harwa." *Bulletin de l'Institut français d'archéologie orientale* 34: 135-42.

Gunn, B. und R. Engelbach. 1931. „The Statues of Harwa." *Bulletin de l'Institut français d'archéologie orientale* 30: 791-815.

Horneffer, A. und H.W. Haussig, Hrsg. und Übers. 1971. Herodot, *Historien*. Stuttgart: Kröner.

Jansen-Winkeln, K. 1985. *Ägyptische Biographien der 22. und 23. Dynastie*. Ägypten und Altes Testament 8. Wiesbaden: Harrassowitz.

—. 2000. „Die Fremdherrschaften in Ägypten im 1. Jahrtausend v. Chr." *Orientalia* 69: 1-20.

Kemp, B.J. 1989. *Ancient Egypt. Anatomy of a Civilization*. London: Routledge.

Koemoth, P.P. 2001. „À propos de la stèle d'Apollônios (Louvre N 328). Ophoïs, Osiris et Sérapis en Abydos." *Studien zur altägyptischen Kultur* 29: 217-33.

Kucharek, A. Im Druck. „Die Festprozession des Osiris in Abydos." In *Archäologie und Ritual. Auf der Suche nach der rituellen Handlung in den antiken Kulturen Ägyptens und Griechenlands*, herausgegeben von J. Mylonopoulos und H. Roeder. Wien: Phoibos.

Leclant, J. 1965. *Recherches sur les monuments thébains de la XXVe dynastie dite éthiopienne*. Bibliothèque d'étude 36. Kairo: Institut français d'archéologie orientale.

Leclère, F. 1996. „A Cemetery of Osirid Figurines at Karnak." *Egyptian Archaeology* 9: 9-12.

—. 2002. „Fouilles dans le cimetière osirien de Karnak – travaux récents." *Bulletin de la Société française d'égyptologie* 153: 24-44.

—. 2003. „Données nouvelles sur les inhumations de figurines osiriennes. Le tombeau d'Osiris à Karnak." In *Egyptology at the Dawn of the Twenty-First Century, Proceedings of the Eighth International Congress of Egyptologists Cairo, 2000*, herausgegeben von Z. Hawass, Band 1, 295-303. Kairo: The American University in Cairo Press.

Leclère, F. und L. Coulon. 1998. „La nécropole osirienne de la ‚Grande Place' à Karnak. Fouilles dans le secteur nord-est du temple d'Amon." In *Proceedings of the Seventh International Congress of Egyptologists*, herausgegeben von C.J. Eyre, 649-59. Orientalia Lovaniensia Analecta 82. Löwen: Peeters.

Martin, K. 1986. „Urhügel." In *Lexikon der Ägyptologie*, herausgegeben von W. Helck und W. Westendorf, Band 6, 873-5. Wiesbaden: Harrassowitz.

Niwinski, A. 1987-88. „The Solar-Osirian Unity as Principle of the Theology of the ‚State of Amun' in Thebes in the 21st Dynasty." *Jaarbericht Ex Oriente Lux* 30: 89-106.

Oldfather, C.H., Hrsg. und Übers. 2004. Diodorus of Sicily, *The Library of History. Books I-II.34*. Cambridge, Mass.: Harvard University Press.

Pamminger, P. 1992. „Amun und Luxor – Der Widder und das Kultbild.“ *Beiträge zur Sudanforschung* 5: 93-140.

—. 1996. „Magistrale Intervention. Der Beamte als Mittler.“ *Studien zur altägyptischen Kultur* 23: 281-304.

Perdu, O. 1996. „L'avertissement d'Aménirdis Ière sur sa statue Caire JE 3420 (= CG 565).“ *Revue d'Égyptologie* 47: 43-65.

Porter, B., R. Moss und E. Burney. 1981. *Topographical Bibliography of Ancient Egyptian Hieroglyphic Texts, Reliefs, and Paintings*. Band 3, *Memphis*. Teil 2, *Saqqâra to Dahshûr*. Oxford: Griffith Institute.

—. 1994. *Topographical Bibliography of Ancient Egyptian Hieroglyphic Texts, Reliefs, and Paintings*. Band 2, *Theban Temples*. 2. Auflage. Oxford: Griffith Institute.

Radwan, A. 1991. „Ramesses II as Mediator.“ In *Fragments of a Shattered Visage. The Proceedings of the International Symposium on Ramesses the Great*, herausgegeben von E. Bleiberg und R. Freed. 221-5. Monographs of the Institute of Egyptian Art and Archaeology 1. Memphis: Memphis State University.

Redford, D.B. 1986. „New Light on Temple J at Karnak.“ *Orientalia* 55: 1-15.

Richards, J.E. 1999. „Conceptual Landscapes in the Egyptian Nile Valley.“ In *Archaeologies of Landscape. Contemporary Perspectives*, herausgegeben von W. Ashmore und A.B. Knapp, 83-100. Malden: Blackwell.

Waitkus, W. 1999. „Die Dachkapellen des Edfu-Tempels.“ In *Edfu. Bericht über drei Surveys, Materialien und Studien*, herausgegeben von K. Dieter, 147-61. Die Inschriften des Tempels von Edfu, Begleithefte 5. Wiesbaden: Harrassowitz.

Wegner, J. 1996. „The Mortuary Complex of Senwosret III. A Study of Middle Kingdom State Activity and the Cult of Osiris at Abydos.“ Dissertation, University of Pennsylvania.

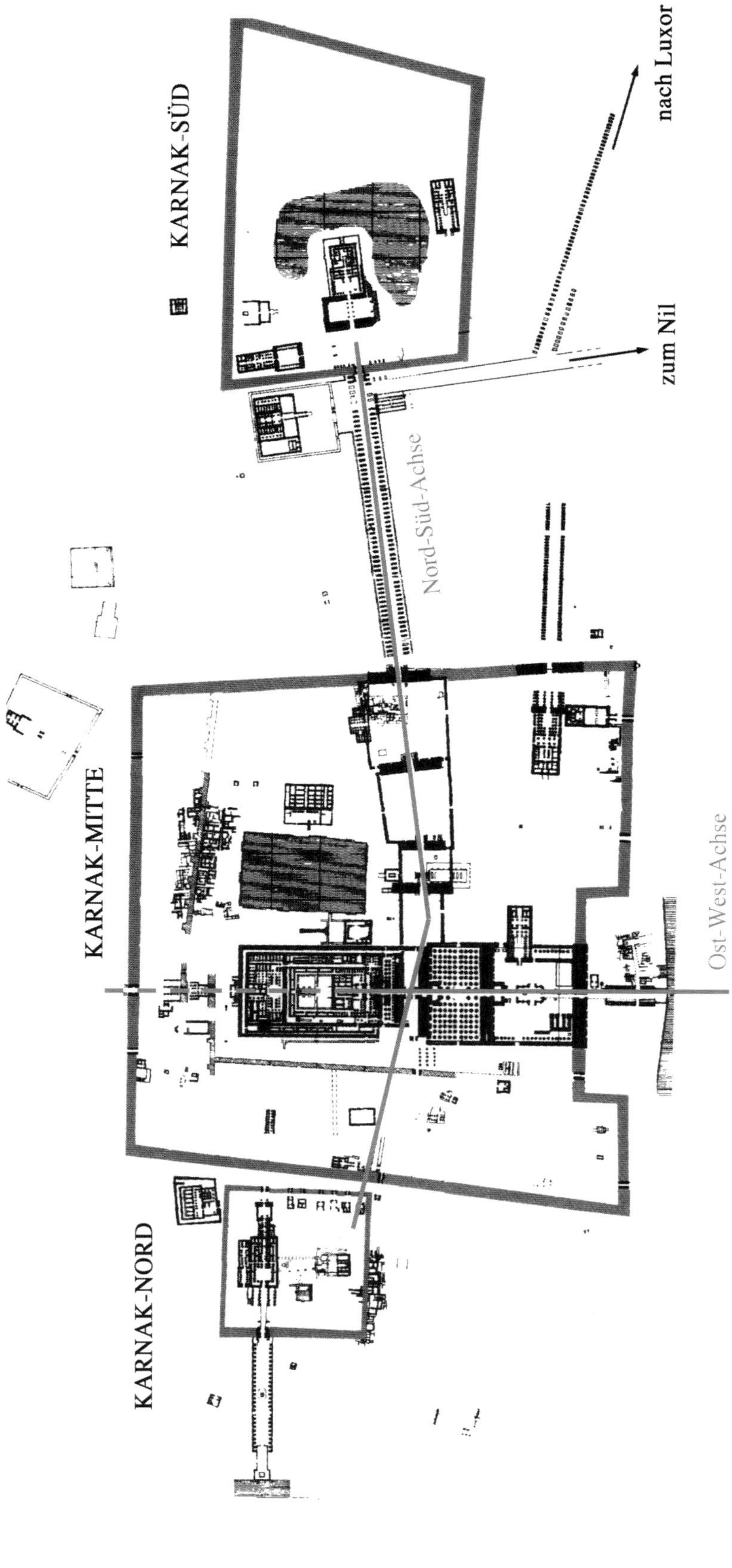

Die Tempelanlage von Karnak. Grundlage: Cabrol 2001, Taf. 2.

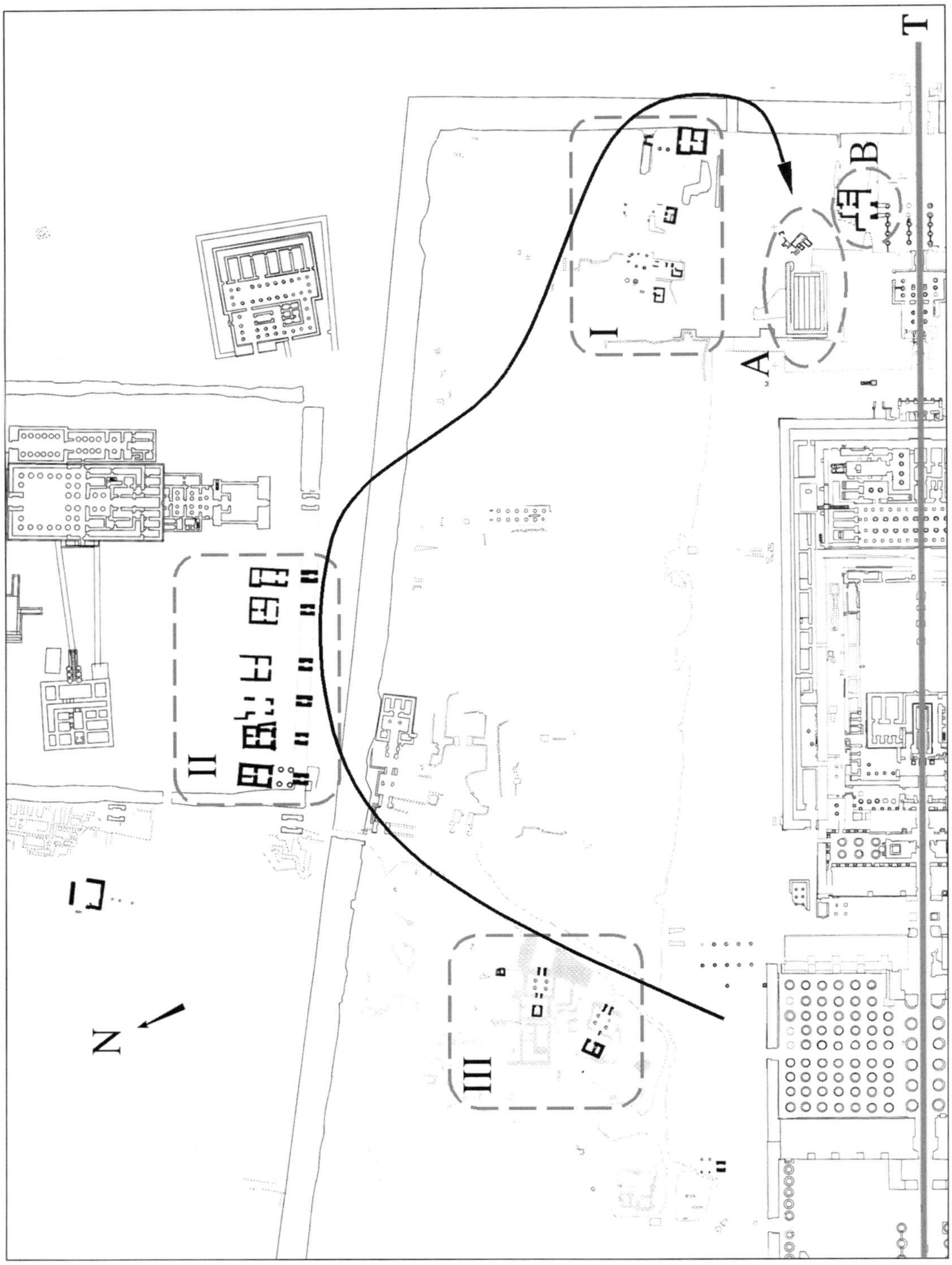

Osirianische Strukturen im nordöstlichen Bereich von Karnak. Grundlage: Coulon und Defernez 2004, 136 Abb. 1.

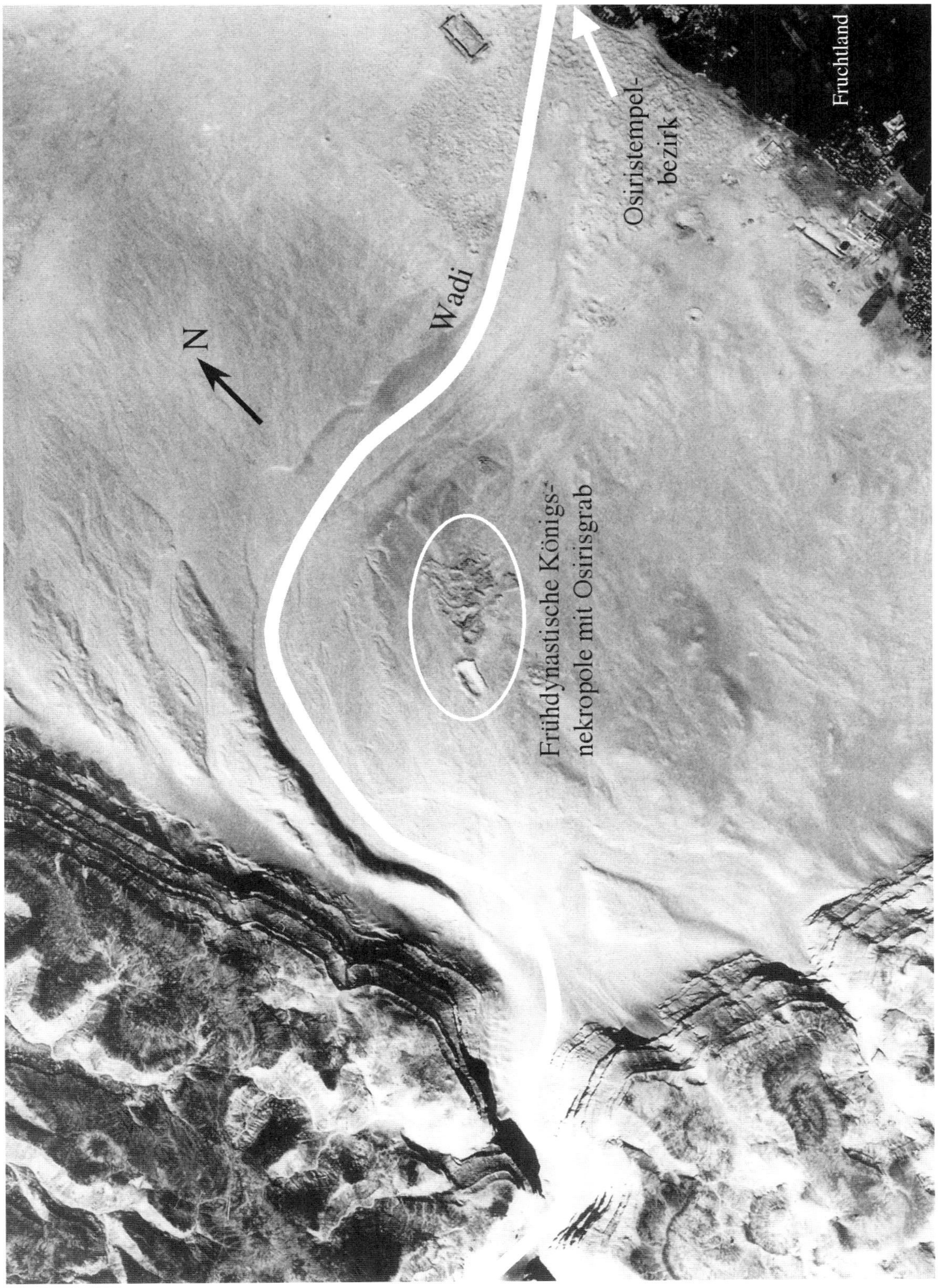

Luftaufnahme von Abydos. Grundlage: Dreyer 1988, Taf. 1.

Architektur und Raumordnung
Symbole der Macht, Zeichen der Mächtigen

MARLIES HEINZ

ABSTRACT

The history of building in the fourth millennium city of Uruk in southern Mesopotamia, Iraq, offers an opportunity to demonstrate that architecture and spatial order can be 'read' as signs of the prevalent social order.

The built form of the cultic and administrative centre of Uruk allows us to trace, over the course of four centuries, several phenomena: how formal traditions of building are, at first, handed down; how, later, new elements in architecture appear which result from disruptions of but do not negate formal architectural tradition; and, finally, how these new elements are in turn replaced by a return to traditional forms, which virtually erases all cultural memory of the 'new' interlude in Uruk society.

The 'new' in built and spatial order is seen here as the expression of a new political power in Uruk. The representatives of this power did not identify with and define themselves with reference to past traditions of Uruk society; accordingly, they needed new symbolic forms to represent the new social order and their position in it. That this break with tradition did not meet with unanimous approval is evident from the later history of building in the city.

URUK IN DER URUKZEIT – LEBENS- UND HERRSCHAFTSWEISEN IM WANDEL

Tiefgreifende Veränderungen in den Lebens- und Wirtschaftsweisen, ein Umbruch im politischen System und eine ‚Gesellschaft in Bewegung' umschreiben die Situation der urukzeitlichen Gesellschaft Südmesopotamiens im Übergang vom 4. zum 3. Jahrtausend v. Chr.

Mit Uruk entstand die erste ‚Großstadt' in Mesopotamien (Taf. 21). Die Vorgänge in Wirtschaft und Verwaltung erhielten eine Komplexität, die allein über mnemotechnische Maßnahmen nicht mehr bewältigt werden konnte. Aus einem frühen numerischen Notierungssystem entwickelte sich die Keilschrift und damit erstmals ein Aufzeichnungsinstrument für Sprache. Neue Funktionen entstanden im gesellschaftlichen Miteinander und wurden in institutionalisierter Form zu wirkungsmächtigen Instanzen im urbanen Kontext. Deren Vertreter präsentierten sich auf Siegelbildern, reliefierten Gefäßen und weiteren Bildträgern ebenso wie in der baulichen Gestaltung des Zentrums von Uruk. Neue Ausdrucksformen und neue Symbole der Herrschaft und des sozialen Miteinanders kamen auf, die gleichermaßen Ausdruck der Welt- und Selbstsicht der Herrschenden und ‚Identifikationsangebot' an die soziale Gemeinschaft waren. Mit der urbanen Lebensweise etablierte sich sowohl ein neues politisches System als auch eine neue Organisationsweise der Gemeinschaft, die im urbanen Zusammenhang anderen Regeln folgte als im dörflichen Verbund. Über die vielfachen Neuerungen und die veränderten funktionalen und organisatorischen Ansprüche der Gemeinschaft – so eine der Thesen hier – entwickelten sich neue, machtvolle Gruppen, die sich nicht mehr primär aus den traditionellen Elitekreisen des Kultbereiches rekrutierten.

Wie die ausgezeichnete Untersuchung von Algaze[1] gezeigt hat, setzte zu dieser Zeit zudem eine vom urbanen und politisch-kultischen Zentrum Uruk ausgehende und weit nach Osten, Norden, Nordosten und Nordwesten ausgreifende Expansionsbewegung ein, die sich archäologisch vor allem anhand der Neugründungen zahlreicher Siedlungen, „enclaves, outposts, stations"[2] in den genannten Regionen fassen ließ. Die materiellen Kulturbelege in den neugegründeten Siedlungen verwiesen direkt und

1 Algaze 1993.
2 Algaze 1993, 23-60.

eindeutig auf ihre Herkunft aus dem urukzeitlichen Südmesopotamien, das somit als Mutterland und Ursprungsregion der in der Ferne exterritorial siedelnden SiedlerInnen erkannt wurde.

Architektur und Raumordnung zur Urukzeit

Im Kontext dieser Entwicklung erfuhr das Zentrum von Uruk, Eanna, in den Schichten Uruk VI-IV mehrere große Umbauten, die in jeweils neuen Raumordnungen mündeten. Erstmals entstanden in der Peripherie des Kernlandes u.a. mit Habuba Kabira Handelsstationen und Enklaven unterschiedlicher Funktion und mit stark voneinander abweichenden Siedlungsstrukturen (Taf. 21).

Divergierende Raumordnungen – so der rote Faden hier – stehen als Indikatoren für divergierende Vorstellungen auch von sozialer und machtpolitischer Ordnung. Die Raumordnungen von Uruk symbolisieren die materialisierten Ordnungsvorstellungen verschiedener Interessensgruppen, die ihre jeweiligen Raum- und Ordnungsvorstellungen zu verwirklichen und sich darüber als die wirkungsmächtigen Akteure an der Spitze der jeweils herrschenden Ordnung zu präsentieren vermochten.

Der historische Kontext und die urbanen Lebens- und Siedlungsweisen, in dem die Planungen des Eanna stattgefunden hatten, boten spezifische Konditionen für den strukturellen Wandel der herrschenden Ordnungen, die auch die Zugangsmöglichkeiten zu machtvollen Positionen in der Gemeinschaft veränderten. Neue Gruppierungen, die nicht zu den ‚traditionellen' Eliten gehörten, erhielten die Chance, im Spektrum der Erfordernisse, die das urbane Leben an das Miteinander stellte, einflussreiche Positionen zu erlangen, die auch den Weg zur Herrschaft öffnen konnten. Die Raumplanung im Eanna hat – so unsere These – den Zugang neuer Gruppen zur Macht deutlich werden lassen, die zugleich in den Peripherien nicht den Gruppen entsprachen, die in Uruk neu zur Macht gelangt waren[3]!

In der Gestaltung des Eanna nahm insbesondere der Umgang mit den architektonischen Traditionen jeweils situationsspezifische und den Intentionen der Erbauer angepasste Formen an. Indem sich die Erbauer in die Tradition einer Gemeinschaft stellen bzw. sich von dieser ab- und dem Neuen zuwenden, treffen sie zugleich eine politische Aussage, die ihre Verbundenheit mit bzw. ihre Distanz zu bestimmten Überlieferungen vor Ort beleuchtet. Das Verhalten zu den Traditionen informiert u.a. über das Umfeld, aus dem die Erbauer des Eanna stammten.

Im Kontext der urukzeitlichen Entwicklung treten erstmals Bilder auf, die eine offenkundig omnipräsente Instanz als zuständig für alle politischen und kultischen Belange der Gemeinschaft wiedergeben. Zugleich liegen – allerdings aus jüngerer Zeit – Texte vor, die eher die Existenz zweier an der Machtspitze stehender Gruppierungen postulieren. Die Textaussagen stehen damit in Opposition zur Aussage der Siegelbilder, stützen aber zugleich das Szenario, das auch die Interpretation der architektonischen Belege zur herrschenden Ordnung in Uruk suggeriert. Über die Situation in den Peripherien informieren die Texte nicht.

Das Machtzentrum von Uruk – Der Befund

Mit Schicht Uruk VI wird im Eanna, dem Kultbezirk der Stadtgöttin Inanna, eine übergeordnete Bauplanung sichtbar, die in der Errichtung und Gestaltung eines Zentrums von bis dahin unbekannter Monumentalität mündet (Taf. 22)[4].

In den Schichten VI und V entstehen zunächst der sog. Steinstifttempel (VI) und der Kalksteintempel (V). Für Form und Typ des Letztgenannten sind Vorläufer aus der vorhergehenden Epoche der Ubaidzeit bekannt. Der in Uruk errichtete Bau ist aber ca. siebenfach so groß wie seine Vorgängerbauten in Eridu und Tepe Gawra in Nordmesopotamien[5]. In Schicht IVc/b kommen u.a. die Tempel F, G, H und Tempel A und B hinzu – alle in Typ und Bauprinzip dem Kalksteintempel entsprechend langrechteckig, durch-

3 Heinz 2005. In Uruk – so die These weiter – avancierten erfolgreiche Militärs zur politischen Macht, in Habuba Kabira war es den Kontrolleuren des Fernhandels gelungen, ihre wirtschaftliche in politische Macht zu transferieren.

4 Amiet 1977, 538-48.

5 Kubba 1998.

lässig, geprägt durch den Mittelsaal mit und ohne Kopftrakt und den links und rechts des Mittelsaals liegenden Raumreihen. Einige Hofkomplexe und Hallenbauten ergänzen das Bild.

Als letzter Bau der Schicht IVb entstand das sog. *square building*, das in seinem Grundriss von allen anderen Bauten abwich und als Bautyp singulär blieb. In Schicht IVb treten zudem erstmals die Siegel auf, die den sog. *Mann im Netzrock* als den für alle politischen Belange des Gemeinwesens Zuständigen in vielfältigen Handlungszusammenhängen wiedergeben[6].

Nach einer gewissen Zeit, deren Dauer absolut bisher nicht bestimmt ist, wurden die geplant errichteten Bauten des Kultzentrums abgerissen – mit einer Ausnahme: dem *square building*.

Eine Neuplanung des Eanna-Bezirkes begann und führte in Schicht IVa zu einer Gesamtanlage, deren Ausmaß in Monumentalität und Bauaufwand ohne Vorbilder war und auch später nicht mehr erreicht wurde.

Nach und nach entstanden als die wesentlichen Bauten der Tempel C, dessen Bautypus traditionellen Vorbildern folgt, Hallenbauten, kleinere Kultbauten und der Hof. Das *square building* bildete zunächst einen integralen Bestandteil dieser neuen Raumordnung. Im Verlauf der Schicht IVa musste der Bau dann aber zugunsten eines neuen Kultbaus, der nach traditionellem Zuschnitt errichtet war, weichen. Tempel D entstand. In seinen Maßen und im Bauaufwand blieb Tempel D einzigartig und übertraf alle bis dahin bekannten Gebäude im Eanna. Dagegen entsprachen sein Grundriss und Bautypus den traditionellen Kult- und Repräsentationsbauten. In Schicht IV traten zudem die ersten Belege für das neue Schriftsystem auf, das „mit Zahl- und Bildzeichen arbeitete und Tontafeln verwendete“[7]. Die Schicht IVa endet mit dem erneuten Abriss der gesamten Anlage.

Die Wirkungsmacht räumlicher Ordnung und ihre Instrumentalisierung durch die Mächtigen

„We must be insistently aware of how space can be made to hide consequences from us, how relations of power and discipline are inscribed into the apparently innocent spatiality of social life, how human geographies become filled with politics and ideology“[8]. „Space“, so die Ausführungen von Keith und Pile, ist „both the medium and the message of domination and subordination [...]. It tells you where you are and it puts you there“[9]. Architektur und Raumordnung, so kann dem hinzugefügt werden, wirken im gesellschaftlichen Zusammenhang dialektisch. Sie beeinflussen die Wahrnehmungsweisen, das Denken und Handeln der Menschen und zugleich ist es der Mensch, der seinerseits die räumliche Ordnung mittels seiner Bauten und Eingriffe in die Umwelt einprägt. Über die Aktion im Raum trägt der Mensch somit selbst zur Reaktion des Menschen auf den Raum bei.

In dieser Wirkungsmacht liegt der potenzielle Nutzen der Architektur und Raumordnung für die Mächtigen und in diesem Nutzen finden Architektur und Raumordnung in der Repräsentation der Mächtigen ihren Platz. Die Repräsentation soll die von den Eliten präferierten Sicht- und Wahrnehmungsweisen der Welt und des Miteinanders ‚gesellschaftsfähig‘ machen, die BetrachterInnen über die Repräsentationen an sich binden, Identitäten prägen, Loyalitäten aufbauen und die Legitimation der herrschenden Verhältnisse sowie der Ordnungsvorstellungen der Herrschenden sichern. Ein wesentliches Element auf dem Weg zum politischen Erfolg dürfte dabei die materialisierte Erinnerung gewesen sein, die von der Gegenwart, und je nach Intentionen der Mächtigen durchaus über ihren Bezug zur Vergangenheit, bis in die Zukunft dauerhaft zuverlässig und positiv konnotiert an die Erfolge der Auftraggeber, der Herrschenden und der Regierenden erinnern sollte.

Auch die Herrschenden in den altorientalischen (urbanen) Gemeinschaften hatten sich zum Ziel gesetzt, als erfolgreiche Herrscher in die Geschichte einzugehen. Auch damals wurden ‚medientaugliche‘ Ereignisse visuell, auch textuell aufbereitet und den ZeitgenossInnen wie nachfolgenden Generationen materialisiert und dauerhaft vor Augen geführt, um das, was an Aussagen jenseits des direkt Sicht- und

6 Nach Boehmer 1999 treten Siegel mit dem *Mann im Netzrock* sogar bereits ab Schicht Uruk V auf.
7 Amiet 1977, 538.
8 Soja 2003, 6.
9 Keith und Pile 1993, 37.

Greifbaren dennoch Teil des politischen Geschehens war, den Betrachtenden nahe zu bringen. Diese mussten glauben können (und wollen), was sie sahen. Per Visualisierung und Textualisierung sollte sich eine soziale Gemeinschaft bilden und das Betrachten des Visualisierten und das Lesen und Hören des Textualisierten den Eindruck der rechten Herrschaft, die die Ordnung sichert und für das gute Leben sorgt, fest im Gedächtnis der Angesprochenen verankern. Das Streben nach dauerhafter Erinnerung und Sichtbarkeit lässt zugleich die Ambivalenz von Architektur und Raumordnung als Symbole der Macht aufscheinen: Gebaute Umwelt als Medium der Mächtigen manifestiert die ‚Macht der Herrschenden' ebenso unübersehbar, wie sie das Wanken und Scheitern der ‚herrschenden Ordnung' dokumentiert. Die Schichten Uruk VI-IV illustrieren dies und dokumentieren über die Wirkungsmacht des sichtbar Erinnerten sowohl den Aufstieg, als auch den Fall der Mächtigen.

Uruk – Raumordnungskonzepte als Medien der materialisierten Erinnerung

Raumordnung als Symbol der Macht – mit diesem Parameter gingen die Erbauer des Eanna ebenso wie die Gestalter in den Peripherien in allen Planungsstadien offensiv um, erkennbar an den jeweils klaren Vorgaben der planenden Instanzen. Diese präsentierten sich zum einen über ein Bauprogramm, das auf traditionelle Architekturformen zurückgriff, diese u.a. durch Größe und Bauaufwand modifizierte und über diese Modifikation eine eigene Architektursymbolik prägte. Zum anderen stellten die Herrschenden den schon bekannten Bauformen vor allem mit dem *square building* eine neue Gebäudeform zur Seite und verwiesen damit explizit auf den Beginn einer neuen Architektur*sprache*. Dem Neuen war aber letztlich kein Bestand auf Dauer gewährt. Der Pflege des kulturellen Gedächtnisses stellte man statt dessen dauerhaft Tempel D zur Verfügung – wohl nicht zufällig ein Gebäude traditionellen Zuschnitts, das ungeachtet seiner konventionellen Bauweise in Größe und Bauaufwand alle bis dahin im Eanna errichteten Bauten bei weitem übertroffen hatte. Was also materialisiert erinnert wurde, unterstand der sorgfältigen Kontrolle der für die Raumplanung Zuständigen. Während Bauzustand IVb/IVa durch das Nebeneinander von modifizierter Tradition und Neuem hervortrat, wurde im nachfolgenden Bauzustand IVa das Neue ausgelöscht und die Repräsentation der Macht auf das Prinzip der Tradierung der Traditionen konzentriert. Von Planungszustand zu Planungszustand prägten Alternativen zur jeweils früheren herrschenden Ordnung den Raum – und wo Alternativen zur herrschenden Ordnung im Materiellen auftreten, so die Annahme hier, ist von alternativen Vorstellungen zur herrschenden Ordnung in den Köpfen derer, die diese alternativen Ordnungen ‚gebaut' haben, auszugehen. D.h., die für die Bauplanung Zuständigen präsentierten ihre Sicht auf Welt und die herrschende Ordnung mit jeweils eigenen, voneinander abweichenden Bauprogrammen. Die Repräsentation der Macht erfolgte dabei nicht durchgängig über Kontinuität und Ähnlichkeit, sondern ab Schicht IVb über eine formale Distanzierung und Absetzung. Zwei voneinander abweichende Prinzipien bildeten in Uruk die Grundlage der Repräsentation, die sich vor allem durch ihren Umgang mit den Traditionen unterschieden. In dem spezifischen Zugriff auf die Traditionen liegt u.a. unsere Annahme begründet, dass hinter dem formal Anderen das Wirken einer neuen Machtelite zu sehen ist und nicht die Innovationen einer traditionellen Elite, die ihrerseits neuen Erfordernissen des urbanen Miteinanders Rechnung trug.

Tradition, Raumgestaltung und die Symbolik einer neuen Macht

Tradition, d.h. die gemeinschaftliche Weitergabe gesellschaftsrelevanter Sachverhalte, konstituiert Gemeinschaft, schafft Identitäten und vermittelt Hoffnung auf bzw. erlaubt und ermöglicht Zugehörigkeit ebenso, wie sie diese potenziell auszuschließen vermag. Tradition suggeriert einer Gemeinschaft Kontinuität und Stabilität in ihrer Existenz. Tradition verspricht Ordnung und leistet Orientierungshilfe im Umgang miteinander. Tradition verpflichtet und Tradition ist normativ. Die Normativität und ‚Geschichtlichkeit' von Traditionen lässt Macht als ‚natürlich' erscheinen, oder, wie von Giddens umschrieben: „Tradition incorporates power relations and tends to naturalize them“[10]. Die Annahme, dass Gemeinschaftsmitglieder, die von einer Tradition profitieren, für den Erhalt dieser Tradition Sorge tragen werden, impliziert, dass es zugleich in allen Gesellschaften Individuen wie Gruppen gleichermaßen gibt, für deren Leben die gemeinschaftskonstituierenden Traditionen nicht förderlich sind. Letztgenannte Gruppierungen sind also in ihrer Existenz oder in der Umsetzung ihrer Interessen gerade deshalb nicht gesichert, weil die Traditionen Ordnungen zementieren, von denen sie gerade nicht profitieren.

Hinter dem Aufbrechen der traditionellen Bauweise, den Modifikationen des Tradierten und der Errichtung des in seiner Form einzigartigen *square building* sind Gruppierungen zu vermuten, die sich in den traditionellen Überlieferungen allein nicht wiederfanden. Offenkundig identifizierten sich die für die Planung Verantwortlichen nicht mehr primär mit den traditionellen Vorgaben an Architektur und Raumgestaltung, sondern bedurften zur Manifestation ihrer Herrschaft einer neuen Symbolik.

Das ‚Andere‘ in der Raumgestaltung steht für ‚die Anderen‘ an der Spitze des Gemeinwesens, für die allein die Tradierung der Tradition weder förderliches Mittel auf dem Weg zur Macht noch zur dauerhaften Erinnerung an ihre Herrschaft gewesen ist, die aber um die Traditionen vor Ort – und deren Wirkungsmacht – wussten, diese mit den positiv konnotierten Modifikationen geschickt in ihre Repräsentation integrierten und dennoch mit der Errichtung des *square buildung* das Neue, nämlich ihre Herrschaft, unübersehbar machten. Dem ‚richtigen‘ Umgang mit den Traditionen kam also eine wesentliche Macht auf dem Weg zum Erfolg zu – die Erbauer des Neuen, des *square building*, hatten diesen Zusammenhang offensichtlich ebenso erkannt wie die später für dessen Abriss Verantwortlichen. Indem sie das Neue an die Seite des Bewährten stellten, verschufen sie dem Neuen Akzeptanz und nahmen ihm zugleich das potenziell Bedrohliche. Als neue Ordnungsmacht griffen sie auf Symbole einer vermeintlich gemeinsamen Vergangenheit zurück, verankerten so die Gegenwart und die neue herrschende Ordnung in dieser Vergangenheit und versprachen über die Wahrung der Tradition eine gesicherte Zukunft. Ob die Anbindung der neuen Ordnung an die Vergangenheit und das Gewohnte dabei Konstruktion und geschickt dargestellte Fiktion oder ‚gelebte Realität‘ war, dürfte in dem Zusammenhang weniger bedeutsam gewesen sein.

Im Vordergrund – so die These hier – stand das Anliegen der neuen Mächtigen, über die Manifestation des Neuen und die Modifikation des Traditionellen die neue herrschende Ordnung sichtbar werden zu lassen, in der die traditionell gegebene Macht der religiösen Eliten, als solche benannt über die Kultbauten (scheinbar!) nicht negiert, dieser aber mit der Errichtung des *square building* offensiv und unübersehbar das Symbol einer neuen Macht zur Seite gestellt wurde.

MACHTWECHSEL IM KONTEXT URBANER ENTWICKLUNG – UND DIE AUSWIRKUNGEN AUF DIE GESTALTUNG DES RAUMES

Die Annahme, dass hinter der Abwendung von den Traditionen bzw. hinter der Modifizierung des Traditionellen das Auftreten einer neuen Gruppierung im Kreis der Mächtigen von Uruk zu vermuten ist, findet theoretische Unterstützung in den Studien der Stadtsoziologie, die sich mit den Entwicklungspotenzialen von Macht und Herrschaft in urbanen Kontexten befassen.

Im Kontext urbaner Entwicklung, so die Ergebnisse dieser Forschung, erhalten neue soziale Gruppen die Chance, aufgrund gefragter Fähigkeiten zu neuen Formen der Macht und darüber mitunter sogar zur Herrschaft zu gelangen. Erst die Stadt als Schmelztiegel heterogener Bevölkerungen ermöglichte es, dass sich über die Vielfalt der funktionalen Differenzierungen und der religiösen und kulturellen Spezialisierungen entsprechend differenzierte und spezialisierte Gruppen herauskristallisierten. Aus diesen Gruppenverbänden konnte den Herrschenden, je nach den gegebenen Umständen, erhebliche Konkurrenz erwachsen.

Dass Uruk im Prozess der Stadtwerdung und Uruk als Zentrum der Handelsexpansion eine Vielzahl entsprechender Gelegenheiten zur funktionalen Spezialisierung und darüber zur Ausbildung funktional spezialisierter Gruppen geboten hatte, zeigen die materiellen Belege ebenso wie die organisatorischen Erfordernisse – etwa die Anwendung geographischen Wissens für die Expansion und das exterritorial

10 Giddens 1994, 104. S. hierzu auch Beck u.a. 1994.

ausgelagerte Wirtschaftsgeschehen in den Peripherien und auch für die nur zu häufig mit den Expansionen verbundenen militärischen Aktivitäten. Bereiche also, die gesellschaftsrelevant und für das Prosperieren der Stadt Uruk von Belang waren und aus denen sich potenziell die VertreterInnen rekrutieren konnten, die über ihre Spezialisierung auf diesen Gebieten die Chance zur Macht und zur Herrschaft ergriffen und mit der Gestaltung des Eanna sichtbar gemacht hatten. „Group investments in authority", so Smith, „have an impact on the physical layout of the city as well as on members' social identy and economic success"[11]. Die Umsetzung der sozialen und machtpolitischen Verhältnisse in die Raumordnung von Uruk dürfte dem entsprochen haben. Und dass der sichtbaren Repräsentation der (noch) Herrschenden potenziell die ebenfalls sichtbare Repräsentation der schon machtvoll werdenden Gruppierungen gegenüber – bzw. wie im Fall von Uruk zur Seite – treten konnte, dürfte sowohl den Erbauern des *square building* als auch denen, die für seinen Abriss verantwortlich waren, bewusst gewesen sein.

Bild und Macht

Der rote Faden, dem die Interpretation der Raumordnung von Uruk folgt, besagt, dass Raumordnung und herrschende Ordnung eng miteinander verbunden waren. Der Wandel in der Raumordnung wird auf einen Wechsel in den dafür verantwortlichen Gruppierungen zurückgeführt. Die für die Gestaltung des Raumes Verantwortlichen rekrutierten sich aus unterschiedlichen funktionalen Kontexten (unserer These nach aus den Bereichen Militär und Kult).

Diese Annahme, dass es über die Ausbildung funktionaler Spezialisierung in Uruk bzw. in der Urukzeit zur Ausdifferenzierung verschiedener Machtsphären (weltlicher versus kultisch-religiöser) und letztlich zur Konkurrenz diverser Gruppen um die Herrschaft gekommen ist, gewinnt an Überzeugungskraft, wenn wir zwei weitere Quellen aus Uruk bzw. aus dem Umland von Uruk zur Interpretation der Machtverhältnisse heranziehen.

Die urukzeitlichen Siegelbilder dokumentieren (spätestens) ab Schicht IVb, der Schicht also, in der das *square building* entstand[12], den sog. *Mann im Netzrock*, einen ‚omnipräsenten' Herrscher, der als Krieger, als Sieger über menschliche Feinde, als Kämpfer gegen die Bedrohungen aus der Natur, als Ökonom und in kultischen Aktivitäten aktiv auch als Priester wiedergegeben wird (Taf. 23). Eine Instanz also, in der sich weltlich-politische und kultische Kompetenz in einer Person oder besser in einem Amt vereinten[13]. Vom Einfluss einer weiteren, primär religiösen Macht, die vorrangig als Mittler zwischen der Welt der Götter und der Menschen agiert hätte und deren Existenz die späteren Texte für die Urukzeit vermuten lassen, berichten die Bilder (soweit nach heutigem Kenntnisstand ersichtlich) nicht. Dass der *Mann im Netzrock* selbst nicht eine primär religiöse Instanz war, sondern ein weltlicher Herrscher, der auch Priesterfunktionen übernommen hatte, ist aus dem Spektrum seiner Zuständigkeiten abzuleiten. Während weltliche Herrscher zu allen Zeiten in den altorientalischen Gesellschaften auch kultische Funktionen übernommen haben, agierten-Priester nie als Krieger und Militärs.

Der *Mann im Netzrock* tritt erstmals mit der Urukzeit in Erscheinung; neu ist auch die Wiedergabe stets ein und desselben Protagonisten in der genannten Vielfalt von Handlungszusammenhängen. Die neuen Symbole der Herrschaft und die neuen Bilder der politischen Ordnung und des sozialen Miteinanders waren gleichermaßen Ausdruck der Ideologie der Herrschenden und ‚Identifikationsangebot' an die soziale Gemeinschaft. Als Repräsentationsmittel der Mächtigen geben die Bilder eine interessengebundene Sicht der Welt und der eigenen Position in dieser Welt wieder. Um die neue Ordnung in Uruk zu legitimieren und eine loyale Anhängerschaft aufzubauen, mussten die Bilder den BetrachterIn-

11 Smith, A.T 2003, 17.

12 Amiet 1977, 539.

13 Dass dem Herrscher Beratergremien zur Seite standen und einen nicht geringen Einfluss auf diesen ausübten, wie von Selz (1998, 281-344) in seiner Studie zu den altorientalischen Herrschaftssystemen im 3. Jahrtausend v. Chr. ausgeführt, widerspricht diesem System nicht. Rücksprache und Verhandlungen des Herrschers mit entsprechenden Beratern waren vermutlich gängige Herrschaftspraxis, ohne dass diese ‚Berater' offenkundig das Selbstbild der Herrschenden bestimmt oder diese sich entsprechend als Teil einer ‚Machtgruppe' präsentiert hätten. Zum Einfluss entsprechender Beratergremien im Mittelalter siehe auch Gerd Althoff (2003); zur Aktualität des Beraterwesens in der Politik der Neuzeit, siehe die Tagespresse!

nen zugleich ‚Identifikationsangebote' liefern, die das Neue als Bereicherung und nicht als Bedrohung sichtbar werden ließen. In der Architektur wurde dies offenkundig zunächst dadurch erfolgreich gelöst, dass Altes neben Neuem bewahrt wurde und beides zusammen die Raumordnung ergaben. Besonders wirksam wird die Selbst- und Weltdarstellung der Eliten also dort, wo es ihnen gelingt, geübte Seh- und Wahrnehmungsgewohnheiten anzusprechen, die die Betrachtenden als ‚schlüssig' erkennen und die es diesen so ermöglichen, Einvernehmen über die legitime Sichtweise der sozialen Welt herzustellen[14]. Wenn es den Eliten gelingt, diese ‚allen gemeinsame Einsicht' in die Darstellungen zu erzielen, dann kann es gelingen, ein allgemein gültiges Sinn*gebäude* zu errichten, das die „ganze Geschichte der Gesellschaft und das ganze Leben des Einzelnen" in einem Sinnsystem zusammenführt[15]. Verschiedene Wirklichkeiten werden dann begreiflicher, die Legitimation der herrschende Ordnung, und damit auch und vor allem die politische Ordnung, selbstverständlich.

Auf den urukzeitlichen Siegeln gelang die Ansprache von geübten Wahrnehmungsgewohnheiten dort, wo die Themenwahl die Verknüpfung von Erinnertem und Erfahrenem mit dem Neuen herstellte, also die Alltagserfahrungen der Gemeinschaft und somit eine Welt ansprach, mit der man sich identifizieren und deren gezeigte Ordnung man als schlüssig akzeptieren konnte (oder auch nicht). Im Idealfall ließ sich dieses Einverständnis auf ein Einverständnis mit dem neuen Protagonisten der Macht, *dem Mann im Netzrock*, übertragen. Anders ausgedrückt: „ (...) wo die Bilder den individuellen Erfahrungen eine öffentliche Existenz ermöglichen"[16], verband das Bild Erfahrenes und das Wissen der BetrachterInnen mit neuen Handlungszusammenhängen und Akteuren. Die Verbindung von Kult und Religion, Subsistenzsicherung und Schutz der Gemeinschaft mit dem erfolgreichen *Mann im Netzrock* dürfte die Akzeptanz des Neuen erleichtert haben.

Auch die Bilder verweisen also auf eine neue Ordnung in Uruk – sie kennen keine Vorläufer, ebenso, wie auch die Protagonisten und ihr Handlungs- und Verantwortungsspektrum erstmals in der hier gesehenen Weise abgebildet und der dauerhaften Erinnerung zur Verfügung gestellt werden. Mit der Konzentration der Kompetenzen auf diese Instanz findet also auch in den Bildern die Abweichung vom Traditionellen und die Propagierung einer neuen, stärker weltlich agierenden Macht statt.

Die Identifikation mit dem Neuen verläuft hier jedoch, anders als bei der Architektur, nicht über die Anknüpfung an bestehende formale (Bild-)Traditionen und nicht über das Nebeneinander von ‚Neu' und ‚Alt'. Vielmehr wird die Anknüpfung an Bekanntes über die Situierung des Protagonisten in Handlungszusammenhänge erreicht, die die Betrachtenden aus ihren Alltagserfahrungen kannten. Zeitlos gültige Handlungszusammenhänge prägen die Aussage. Was der *Mann im Netzrock* vollbrachte, verstand jede Betrachterin und jeder Betrachter, ob in Uruk, auf dem Lande, am mittleren Euphrat, in der Türkei oder im Iran; aus Sicht der heutigen Betrachtung also eine mehr als geschickte Bildgestaltung, in der sich alle(!) wiederfinden konnten – nicht über eine gemeinsame Geschichte und Tradition, über die sie vermutlich nicht verfügten, sondern über die allen gemeinsamen Alltagserfahrungen.

Das Neue in der Entwicklung der herrschenden Ordnung der Urukzeit wird so mittels zweier Parameter aufgezeigt (und in Erinnerung bewahrt): Architektur und Siegelbildern! Beide übermitteln hinsichtlich der herrschenden Ordnung durchaus differierende Botschaften, die sich, so die These hier, möglicherweise durch die Ansprache unterschiedlicher AdressatInnenkreise erklären lassen.

RAUMGESTALTUNG – BILDERWELTEN: REPRÄSENTATION UND DIE IDEOLOGIE DER MÄCHTIGEN

Unserer Interpretation der verschiedenen Quellen zufolge, hatte sich in Uruk zur Urukzeit eine Konkurrenz zwischen kultischer und weltlicher Elite entwickelt. Die neue herrschende Ordnung fand materiell, also sichtbar, in der Raumgestaltung des Eanna und in der Gestaltung der Siegelbilder ihren Niederschlag – aber, bei genauer Betrachtung, mit unterschiedlichen Aussagen zu den herrschenden Verhältnissen.

Mit der Gestaltung der Architektur und Raumordnung stellten die ‚Neuen', hier nun unter Verweis auf die Aussage der Siegelbilder als ‚weltliche Macht' angesprochen, ihre Symbole der Macht neben die

14 Barlösius 2001, 196-7; Körntgen 2003, 89.
15 Berger und Luckmann 1997, 103.
16 Bourdieu 2001, 17.

der alten Ordnung und präsentierten sich so gleichermaßen als Bewahrer der Tradition und der göttlichen Ordnung wie auch als Neuerer. Der Erinnerung an die ‚alte' Ordnung und damit auch an die Existenz der machtvollen Konkurrenz wurde explizit und weithin für jedermann sichtbar Raum eingeräumt. Ungeachtet der Veränderungen, die die baulichen Zeugnisse des religiösen Lebens erfahren hatten, suggerierte somit die gebaute Umwelt, dass die ‚Welt der Götter' und die von den Göttern bestimmten Ordnungen den weitreichenden Wandel der Urukzeit *sichtlich* unversehrt überstanden hatten. Mit dieser unübersehbaren Dokumentation der Wahrung religiöser Traditionen und der Integration der religiösen Symbolik der Vergangenheit in das politische Handeln der (urukzeitlichen) Gegenwart präsentierten sich die Herrschenden in der Architektur – anders als auf den Siegelbildern – zugleich als Neuerer und Bewahrer der von den Göttern bestimmten, traditionellen Ordnung – und dies in einer historischen Konstellation, in der von weitreichenden Veränderungen der gesellschaftlichen und politischen Ordnung auszugehen ist.

In der Gestaltung der Siegelbilder verfuhren die Zuständigen anders. Die Siegelbilder blenden die Erinnerung an alte Ordnungen, an eine gemeinsame Vergangenheit bzw. an das Wirken einer anderen, weiteren machtvollen Elite (nach unserer Beobachtung und Erkenntnismöglichkeit) gänzlich aus: Dem Bildprogramm zufolge hatte die neue herrschende Ordnung althergebrachte Traditionen auch in der Besetzung der Machtpositionen weitgehend hinter sich gelassen. Das Neue und die Symbole der neuen herrschenden Ordnung dominierten in den Bildern.

Divergierende Ansichten zur herrschenden Ordnung in Architektur und Bild: Ideologie der Macht – am AdressatInnenkreis orientiert und situationsspezifisch genutzt

Tradition wurde also dort offensichtlich gewahrt, wo ihre Sichtbarkeit unvermeidbar und die Gruppe der BetrachterInnen und damit die öffentliche Wirkungsmacht unkontrollierbar waren – also in der Gestaltung des öffentlichen Raumes. Die Ambivalenz der Botschaft in der gebauten Ordnung kann bei der Bedeutung, die der Tradition für das Gemeinschaftsleben zukam und damit der Gefahr, die unüberlegte Eingriffe in die Traditionen für die dafür Verantwortlichen nach sich ziehen konnte, als Versuch gewertet werden, dort, wo die Reaktionen der Betroffenen auf das Neue kaum kontrollierbar waren, die ‚wahren' Verhältnisse, also das hier postulierte Ausmaß der Machtverschiebung, zu kaschieren. Ungeachtet der Neuerungen im Miteinander von Uruk präsentierten sich die Herrscher weithin sichtbar als diejenigen, unter deren Herrschaft das ‚kultisch Notwendige' getan und damit das Wohlwollen der Götter für die Gemeinschaft gesichert wurde und verbanden so unauflösbar die eigene Herrschaft mit der Sicherung des Wohls der Gemeinschaft. Die gebaute Ordnung und die scheinbare Wahrung der Traditionen wären so auch als Ergebnis eines zielorientierten politischen Kalküls der neuen Elite zu verstehen, das es ihnen bei ihrer zunehmenden Machtfülle angeraten sein ließ, über die Pflege und Bewahrung der Bautradition sowohl die Macht der Götter und als auch deren Akzeptanz als die ultimativen Entscheidungsinstanzen in der Gemeinschaft offensiv zu bestätigen.

Die Botschaft der Siegel ist radikaler. Sie stellen die durchaus ‚revolutionäre' Botschaft, das Neue, prononciert in den Vordergrund. Grund für den radikalen Schnitt in der Ausblendung von Tradition und Vergangenheit und die Betonung nur einer zuständigen Machtinstanz dürfte auch hier – ebenso wie bei der Repräsentation der Macht über die Architektur angenommen – die Adressatengruppe gewesen sein. Die Siegel gingen primär durch die Hände der Verwaltung und erreichten darüber einen zunächst begrenzten und damit kontrollierbaren Nutzer- und BetrachterInnenkreis. In ihrem Wirken waren die Herrschenden auf eine loyale und funktionierende Verwaltung angewiesen; eindeutige Bilder hinsichtlich der Instanz, der die Verwaltung diente und die die Macht in Uruk ausübte, dürften überlebensnotwendig gewesen sein und erklären, warum die Siegelbilder den völlig anderen Umgang mit Tradition erforderlich gemacht hatten.

Die Ideologie der Macht, d.h. das Anliegen der Mächtigen, ihre Sicht der Welt und damit die kollektiven Interessen der herrschenden Elite in einer Weise zu präsentieren, die Allgemeingültigkeit beanspruchen und zum *common sense* avancieren konnten, wurde so in der Repräsentation über den geschickten Einsatz der verschiedenen Medien und orientiert an den potenziellen Rezipientinnen und Rezipienten zur Wirkung gebracht. Die Repräsentation funktionierte dabei als Mittel der Kommunikation und als solches als ‚symbolisch vermittelte Interaktion'. Diese wiederum funktioniert nach Habermas, weil die Kommunizierenden davon ausgehen, „wahre Aussagen über die objektive Welt"[17] auszutauschen. Dass die Regierenden heute wie die altorientalischen Eliten damals die Gültigkeit dieser Grundannahme auch für ihre (propagandistischen) Repräsentationsmaßnahmen voraussetzen, ist anzunehmen – dass Propaganda ihrem Wesen nach diese Grundannahme aber gerade konterkariert, ebenfalls!

Konkurrierende Mächte zur Urukzeit? – Texte und ihre Hinweise auf die herrschende Ordnung

Aus der Urukzeit selber liegen bisher keine Texte vor, anhand derer wir die Welt- und Selbstsicht der Herrschenden im Vergleich mit den Aussagen, die wir aus den Bildern und Bauten ableiten, rekonstruieren könnten. In einer Untersuchung zum „Herrentum und Königtum" befasst sich Heimpel[18] mit den Organisationsformen der politischen Herrschaft in Südmesopotamien im 3. Jahrtausend v. Chr. Hinweise auf die Formen der politischen Machtausübung in Uruk entnimmt Heimpel der Sumerischen Königsliste und Texten der frühdynastischen Zeit, Königsinschriften und Mythen, Hinweisen aus der Abstammungsgeschichte des Gilgamesh und den Ereignissen des Lugalbanda-Epos[19]. Insbesondere dort ist der Weg zur Herrschaft im urukzeitlichen Mesopotamien nachgezeichnet. Nachdem Enmerkar, der König von Uruk, vor Aratta (im Iran gelegen) versagt – er kann die Befestigungsmauern dieser Stadt nicht überwinden – und Lugalbanda die Rettung der Urukäer im Fremdland ermöglicht hat, wird der unfähige Machthaber abgesetzt und Lugalbanda aufgrund seines erfolgreichen Agierens durch die Göttin Inanna als Nachfolger und Herrscher von Uruk inthronisiert. Nicht das dynastische Prinzip, sondern der politische, wirtschaftliche und militärische Erfolg des Einzelnen, von Inanna – und das dürfte realiter gemeint haben, von der Inanna-Priesterschaft – wahrgenommen, ebneten den Weg zu Macht und Herrschaft. Erfolg und Versagen, nicht Herkunft, entschieden somit maßgeblich über das politische Geschick.

Die Texte und die Siegel aus bzw. die Befunde in Uruk, die uns hinsichtlich ihrer Aussagen zu den machtpolitischen Gegebenheiten hier interessiert haben, sind bislang chronologisch nicht miteinander zu verbinden. Das ist vorauszuschicken, bevor (dennoch) die aus den Texten gewonnenen Informationen als unterstützende Hinweise auf das oben interpretierte Bild der konkurrierenden Kräfte und ihrer Repräsentation in Raum und in den Bildern der Urukzeit herangezogen werden.

Raumordnungen und konkurrierende Mächte

TEXTE – BILDER – RAUMSTRUKTUR: EIN SZENARIO

Den Texten zufolge stehen zur Urukzeit zwei machtvolle Instanzen an der Spitze der Gesellschaft – die ‚traditionelle' Kultelite, die auch in prä-urbanen Kontexten zu den machtvollen Instanzen in den mesopotamischen Gesellschaften gehörte und die ‚neue' Macht, der von der Inanna-Priesterschaft zum ‚König' ernannte Krieger Lugalbanda – eine Machtinstanz, die erst durch die Benennung der ‚traditionellen Elite', der Priesterschaft, zu dieser Instanz ‚König' wird. Im urbanen Miteinander von Uruk, in dem die Expansion offenkundig wesentlich für den Machterhalt und die Machterweiterung des Zentrums gewesen war, bzw. für die Entwicklung der Stadt zur Stadt eine maßgebliche Rolle gespielt haben dürfte, werden neue Kompetenzen erforderlich. Das Militär, kampf- und landeskundig, stellt die Gruppierung dar, in deren Händen diese machtrelevanten Kenntnisse liegen. Diese neue weltliche Macht der Krieger und ‚*explorer*' wird für ihre militärischen und territorial sichernden Erfolge durch die kultische Elite, die Priester der Inanna, belohnt. Die Macht der weltlichen Elite steigt, aber die eigentliche Macht

17 Wiedergegeben nach Preglau 1997, 249.
18 Heimpel 1992.
19 Heimpel 1992, 10.

im Lande sind zur Zeit der Ernennung des Lugalbanda zum König von Uruk die Priesterschaften als die im Hintergrund, aber an entscheidender Stelle, agierenden ‚Königsmacher'.

Das Szenario erinnert in seinen Grundzügen erneut an die von der Stadtsoziologie erarbeiteten Erkenntnisse, denen zufolge im urbanen Kontext die Chance zur Machtergreifung durch neue gesellschaftliche Gruppen steigen und sich diese, wenn sie die Chancen wahrnehmen, schnell zur Bedrohung der alten Ordnung entwickeln können.

Auf die Verhältnisse in Uruk übertragen, wäre Lugalbanda einer der Repräsentanten der neuen Macht gewesen, der entsprechend dem soziologischen Modell in nachgerade klassischer Weise die Zeichen der Zeit erkannt und zur Umsetzung der eigenen politischen Ziele genutzt hatte. In der militärisch-weltlichen Macht wäre der traditionellen Kultelite die Konkurrenz erwachsen, die die vormals herrschende Ordnung abgelöst und diesen Wandel mit der Gestaltung des Eanna und der Bilder wirkungsmächtig zu dokumentieren verstanden hätte. Das Szenario zeigt ferner Anklänge an die oben ausgeführten Überlegungen zum Umgang der Mächtigen mit den Traditionen, wonach sich insbesondere die ‚neu in den Kreisen der Macht Etablierten' mit neuen Symbolen der Herrschaft – hier der Raumgestaltung des Eanna und den Neuerungen in den Siegelbildern – zu repräsentieren wussten.

In der Aussage anders als die Botschaft der Architektur und doch für die Repräsentation der Macht logisch war der Umgang mit den Bildern, die erstmals die omnipräsente Machtinstanz *Mann im Netzrock* zeigen und die allein diesen als Machtinstanz in Uruk wiedergegeben und dabei die ‚Königsmacher', den Texten zufolge die eigentliche politische Macht im Hintergrund – so unsere Interpretation –, ausblenden. Ambivalente Botschaften – so die Annahme hier – waren in der Ansprache der Verwaltung, also im Kontext der Siegelpraxis anders als in der Architektur und Raumgestaltung der Festigung der neuen Macht nicht förderlich.

Uruk, die bauliche Entwicklung der Schicht IVa – ein letzter Wandel, eine Renaissance der Traditionen – und das Ende einer Grossmacht

Die Raumordnung im Eanna von Schicht VI–IVa (Taf. 22) prägte das Nebeneinander von Alt und Neu, interpretiert als das Ergebnis des politischen Handelns einer neuen weltlichen Macht, die ihre Sicht auf die Welt zumindest zeitweise in Bauten und Bildern hatte in den Vordergrund stellen können.

In Schicht IVa wird das *square building* abgerissen, in IVa der monumentale Tempel D auf dem benachbarten Baugrund errichtet – ein Gebäude mit traditionellem Grundriss, aber größer und monumentaler als alles zuvor Gebaute in Eanna. Baulich wird mit dieser Aktion die Erinnerung an das ‚Neue' in Uruk ausgelöscht, ein *backlash* gleichsam zum vorausgegangenen Wandel in den Schichten VI-IVa, dem jetzt die vorrangige Betonung des Traditionellen folgt.

Dass die ehemals ‚Neuen' Altes neben Neuem akzeptiert hatten, wurde oben als geschickt kalkulierter Umgang der Neuen mit den Traditionen interpretiert. (Dass der Verzicht auf den Bruch mit dem Gewohnten aber auch anders interpretiert und als das Verdecken einer politischen Schwäche des Systems gesehen werden kann, das den Prozess des Wandels auf einem der wichtigsten Felder der Identitätsstiftung und der Stabilisierung der herrschenden Ordnung nicht hatte durchführen können, sei hier nur angemerkt).

Wenn wir der Baugeschichte des Eanna folgen und diese als roten Faden durch die Entwicklung der herrschenden Ordnung akzeptieren, dann hatte sich die ‚neue' Macht in Uruk nicht dauerhaft als dominante Kraft etablieren können. Mit der Errichtung des monumentalen Tempels D in Schicht Uruk IVa setzte sich vielmehr die Stärke der religiösen Tradition und der religiösen Elite durch, die die Tradierung der traditionellen symbolischen Formen auch über das Intermezzo des Wandels hinaus hatten sichern können. Eine sichtbare Anbindung an die Zeugnisse der jüngeren Geschichte war für die Repräsentation dieser Elite nicht von Nöten und die jüngere Bautradition offenkundig nicht in dem Maße positiv konnotiert, als dass sie für die Stabilisierung der Verhältnisse in Uruk IVa hilfreich gewesen wäre. Wo Wandel eintritt und sich die ‚neue' alte Macht, wie in Schicht Uruk IVa dokumentiert, nicht mehr über eine gemeinsame Vergangenheit und Tradition mit ihren Vorgängern legitimieren kann oder will, konnte sich gerade die Erinnerung an das Vergangene zum gravierenden Nachteil in der Etablierung einer neuen herrschenden Ordnung auswirken. Der Abriss des *square building* war vor diesem Hintergrund zwingend. Das Ausblenden der jüngeren Vergangenheit und die Monumentalität des neu gebauten Tempels erinnern in ihren Gründen an den Ausspruch Papst Nikolaus V. (15. Jahrhundert n. Chr.), dem Gründer des Vatikans, der über den Sinn des Bauens in Rom verlautbaren ließ, er habe die monumentalen Bauten errichten lassen „gegen Feinde von außen und gefährliche Neuerer im Innern"[20]. – Bauen als Warnung und Erinnerung!

Die Einbettung von Tradition in die Repräsentation der Macht war also ein ambivalentes Unterfangen. Die Herrschenden hatten (und haben) von Fall zu Fall zu entscheiden, ob es der Umsetzung der politischen Intentionen und der Repräsentation dienlich war, Traditionen aufzunehmen und fortzuführen, zu modifizieren oder diese zu brechen und durch neue (oder neue alte) Traditionen zu ersetzen. Der Umgang mit der Tradition war von jeher manipulativ, je nach Situation und Bedarf wurde die ‚Geschichte' der eigenen Herkunft und der herrschenden Ordnung aufgezeigt, unterdrückt, konstruiert und erfunden.

Mit Schicht Uruk IVa, so unsere Interpretation der späten Baugeschichte des Eanna, und dem Abriss des *square building* setzte der Niedergang der weltlichen Macht ein; damit verbunden waren sowohl eine kurze Renaissance der kultischen Traditionen als auch eine Wiedererstarkung der kultischen Eliten – wenn auch beides nur von kurzer Dauer. Die Hintergründe für den letzten großen Wandel in der herrschenden Ordnung, der mit dem Machtverlust der weltlichen Herrschaft in der Urukzeit sichtbar wird, fußt – so unsere Überlegung – in den wirtschaftlichen und politischen Veränderungen der späten Urukzeit. Das Ende der Schicht Uruk IV bedeutete wirtschaftlich das Ende der ehemals prosperierenden Stadt Uruk und den Zusammenbruch ihres weitverzweigten Netzwerkes von Enklaven und Umschlagplätzen. Die Entmachtung der weltlichen Herrscher in einem System, in dem diese ihre Machtpositionen (den Texten zufolge) dauerhaft nur über ihre sichtbaren Erfolge sichern konnten, scheint nach diesem Szenario nachgerade logisch.

BIBLIOGRAFIE

Algaze, G. 1993. *The Uruk World System*. Chicago: University of Chicago Press.

—. 2001. „The Prehistory of Imperialism: The Case of Uruk Period Mesopotamia." In Rothman 2001, 27-84.

Althoff, G. 2003. *Inszenierte Herrschaft. Geschichtsschreibung und politisches Handeln im Mittelalter*. Darmstadt: Wissenschaftliche Buchgesellschaft.

Amiet, P. 1977. *Die Kunst des alten Orient*. Freiburg: Herder.

Assmann, A. 1991. „Kultur als Lebenswelt und Monument." In Assmann und Harth 1991, 11-25.

Assmann, A. und D. Harth, Hrsg. 1991. *Kultur als Lebenswelt und Monument*. Frankfurt am Main: S. Fischer.

Assmann, J. 1991. „Gebrauch und Gedächtnis. Die zwei Kulturen des pharaonischen Ägypten." In Assmann und Harth 1991, 135-52.

—. 1999. *Das kulturelle Gedächtnis. Schrift, Erinnerung und politische Identität in frühen Hochkulturen*. 2. Auflage. München: C.H. Beck.

Attarian, Ch.J. 2003. „Cities as a Place of Ethnogenesis. Urban Growth and Centralization in the Chicama Valley, Peru." In Smith M.L. 2003, 184 - 211.

Barlösius, E. 2001. „Die Macht der Repräsentation." In *Gesellschaftsbilder im Umbruch*, herausgegeben von E. Barlösius, H.-P. Müller und S. Sigmund, 179-202. Opladen: Westdeutscher Verlag.

Beck, U., A. Giddens und S. Lash. 1994. *Reflexive Modernization. Politics, Tradition and Aesthetics in the Modern Social Order*. Cambridge u.a.: Polity Press.

Behrens, R. 2002. *Kritische Theorie*. Hamburg: Europäische Verlagsanstalt.

Ben-Amos, D. und L. Weissberg, Hrsg. 1999. *Cultural Memory and the Construction of Identity*. Detroit: Wayne State University Press.

Berger, P.L. und Th. Luckmann. 1997. *Die gesellschaftliche Konstruktion der Wirklichkeit. Eine Theorie der Wissenssoziologie*. Frankfurt am Main: S. Fischer.

20 Zitiert nach Kündiger 2001, 25.

Boehmer, R.-M. 1999. *Uruk. Früheste Siegelabrollungen.* Endberichte/ Ausgrabungen in Uruk-Warka 24. Mainz: von Zabern.

Bourdieu, P. 1992. *Die verborgenen Mechanismen der Macht.* Schriften zu Politik und Kultur 1. Hamburg: VSA-Verlag.

—. 2001. *Das politische Feld. Zur Kritik der politischen Vernunft.* Konstanz: UVK. Cassin, E., J. Bottéro und J. Vercoutter. 1965. *Die Altorientalischen Reiche I.* Fischer Weltgeschichte 2. Frankfurt am Main: S. Fischer.

Christian, S. 2004. *Before Lewis and Clark: the Story of the Chouteaus the French Dynasty that Ruled America's Frontier.* New York: Farrar, Straus and Giroux.

Crespi, F. 1991. „Kultur und soziale Praxis. Symbolische und gesellschaftliche Ordnung im Widerspruch." In Assmann und Harth 1991, 112-22.

Dietrich, M. und O. Loretz, Hrsg. 1998. *Dubsar anta-men. Studien zur Altorientalistik. Festschrift für Willem H. Ph. Römer.* Alter Orient und Altes Testament 253. Münster: Ugarit-Verlag.

Dobres, M. und J. Robb. 2000. *Agency in Archaeology.* London: Routledge.

Edelman, M. 1976. *Politik als Ritual. Die symbolische Funktion staatlicher Institutionen und politischen Handelns.* Frankfurt am Main u.a.: Campus.

Eichmann, R. 1990. *Uruk. Die Stratigraphie. Grabungen 1912 - 1977 in den Bereichen „Eanna" und „Anu-Ziqqurrat".* Endberichte/ Ausgrabungen in Uruk-Warka 3. Mainz: von Zabern.

Emberling, G. 2003. „Urban Social Transformations and the Problem of the „First City". New Research from Mesopotamia." In Smith M.L. 2003, 254-68.

Eisenstadt, S.N. 1991. „Die Mitwirkung der Intellektuellen an der Konstruktion lebensweltlicher und transzendenter Ordnungen." In Assmann und Harth 1991, 123-34.

Frayne, D.R. 1990. *Old Babylonian Period. The Royal Inscriptions of Mesopotamia.* Early Periods Volume 4. Toronto: University of Toronto Press.

Giddens, A. 1994. „Living in a Post-Traditional Society." In Beck u.a. 1994, 56-109.

Giesen, B. 1991. *Die Entdinglichung des Sozialen. Eine evolutionstheoretische Perspektive auf die Postmoderne.* Frankfurt am Main: Suhrkamp.

Graves-Brown, P. und S. Joanes. 1996. *Cultural Identity and Archaeology. The Construction of European Communities.* London u.a.: Routledge.

Heimpel, W. 1992. „Herrentum und Königtum." *Zeitschrift für Assyriologie* 82: 4-21.

Heinrich, E. 1982. *Die Tempel und Heiligtümer im alten Mesopotamien. Typologie, Morphologie und Geschichte.* Denkmäler antiker Architektur 14. Berlin: de Gruyter.

Heinz, M. 1997. *Der Stadtplan als Spiegel der Gesellschaft. Siedlungsstrukturen in Mesopotamien als Indikator für Formen wirtschaftlicher und gesellschaftlicher Organisation.* Berlin: Reimer.

—. 2005. „Bauen, Planen, Raumgestalten. Repräsentation der Macht via Architektur. Ein ambivalentes Unterfangen." In *Otium. Festschrift für Volker Michael Strocka,* herausgegeben von T. Ganschow und M. Steinhart, 123-42. Remshalden: Verlag Bernhard Albert Greiner.

Keith, M. und St. Pile. 1993. „Introduction Part 2. The Place of Politics." In *Place and the Politics of Identity,* herausgegeben von M. Keith und S. Pile, 22-40. London u.a.: Routledge.

Kocka, J. 1977. „Gesellschaftliche Funktionen der Geschichtswissenschaft." In *Wozu noch Geschichte?*, herausgegeben von W. Oelmüller, 11-33. München: W. Fink.

Körntgen, L. 2003. „Repräsentation – Selbstdarstellung – Herrschaftspräsentation." In Propaganda – Selbstdarstellung – Repräsentation im römischen Kaiserreich des 1. *Jahrhunderts n. Chr.*, herausgegeben von G. Weber und M. Zimmermann, 85-101. Historia, Einzelschriften 164. Stuttgart: Steiner.

Kubba, S.A. 1998. *Architecture and Linear Measurement during the Ubaid Period in Mesopotamia.* BAR International Series 707. Oxford: Hedges.

Kündiger, B. 2001. *Fassaden der Macht. Architektur der Herrschenden.* Leipzig: E.A. Seemann.

Kurtz, D.V. 2001. *Political Anthropology. Paradigms and Power.* Boulder u.a.: Westview.

Lim, W.S.W. 2004. *Architecture, Art, Identity in Singapore.* Singapore.

Lithwick, H. 2000. *Developing Frontier Cities. Global Perspectives – Regional Contexts.* Dordrecht: Kluwer Academic Publications.

Orthmann, W., Hrsg. 1975. *Der Alte Orient.* Propyläen Kunstgeschichte 14. Berlin: Propyläen.

Pollock, S. 1999. *Ancient Mesopotamia.* Cambridge: Cambridge University Press.

Preglau, M. 1997. „Kritische Theorie. Jürgen Habermas." In *Soziologische Theorie. Abriß der Ansätze ihrer Hauptvertreter*, herausgegeben von J. Morel, 240-64. München u.a.: Oldenbourg.

Ragotzky, H. und H. Wenzel, Hrsg. 1990. *Höfische Repräsentation. Das Zeremoniell und die Zeichen.* Tübingen: Niemeyer.

Reps, J. W. 1969. *Town Planning in Frontier America.* Princeton: Princeton University Press.

Roaf, M. 1990. *Cultural Atlas of Mesopotamia and the ancient Near East.* New York: Facts on file.

Rothman, M.S., Hrsg. 2001. *Uruk Mesopotamia and its Neighbors. Cross-cultural Interactions in the Era of State Formation.* Santa Fe: School of American Research Press.

—. 2001a. „The Local and the Regional. An Introduction." In Rothmann 2001, 3-26.

Schwarz, G. 2001. „Syria and the Uruk Expansion." In Rothman 2001, 233-64.

Selz, G. 1998. „Über Mesopotamische Herrschaftskonzepte. Zu den Ursprüngen mesopotamischer Herrscherideologie im 3. Jahrtausend." In Dietrich und Loretz 1998, 281-344.

Smith, A.T. 2003. *The Political Landscape. Constellations of Authority in Early Complex Societies.* Berkeley: University of California Press.

Smith, M.L., Hrsg. 2003. *The Social Construction of Ancient Cities.* Washington u.a.: Smithsonian Books.

Soja, E.W. 2003. *Postmodern Geographies.* 8. Auflage. London u.a.: Verso.

Stein, G. 1999. *Rethinking World-systems. Diasporas, Colonies, and Interaction in Uruk Mesopotamia.* Tucson: University of Arizona Press.

Urry, J. 2000. *Sociology Beyond Societies. Mobilities for the Twenty-first Century.* London u.a.: Routledge.

Wade, R.C. 1996. *The Urban Frontier. The Rise of Western Cities, 1790-1830.* Urbana: University of Illionois Press.

Winter, R. 2001. *Die Kunst des Eigensinns. Cultural Studies als Kritik der Macht.* Weilerswist: Velbrück Wissenschaft.

Zeder, M.A. 2003. „Food Provisioning in Urban Societies. A View from Northern Mesopotamia." In M.L. Smith 2003, 156-83.

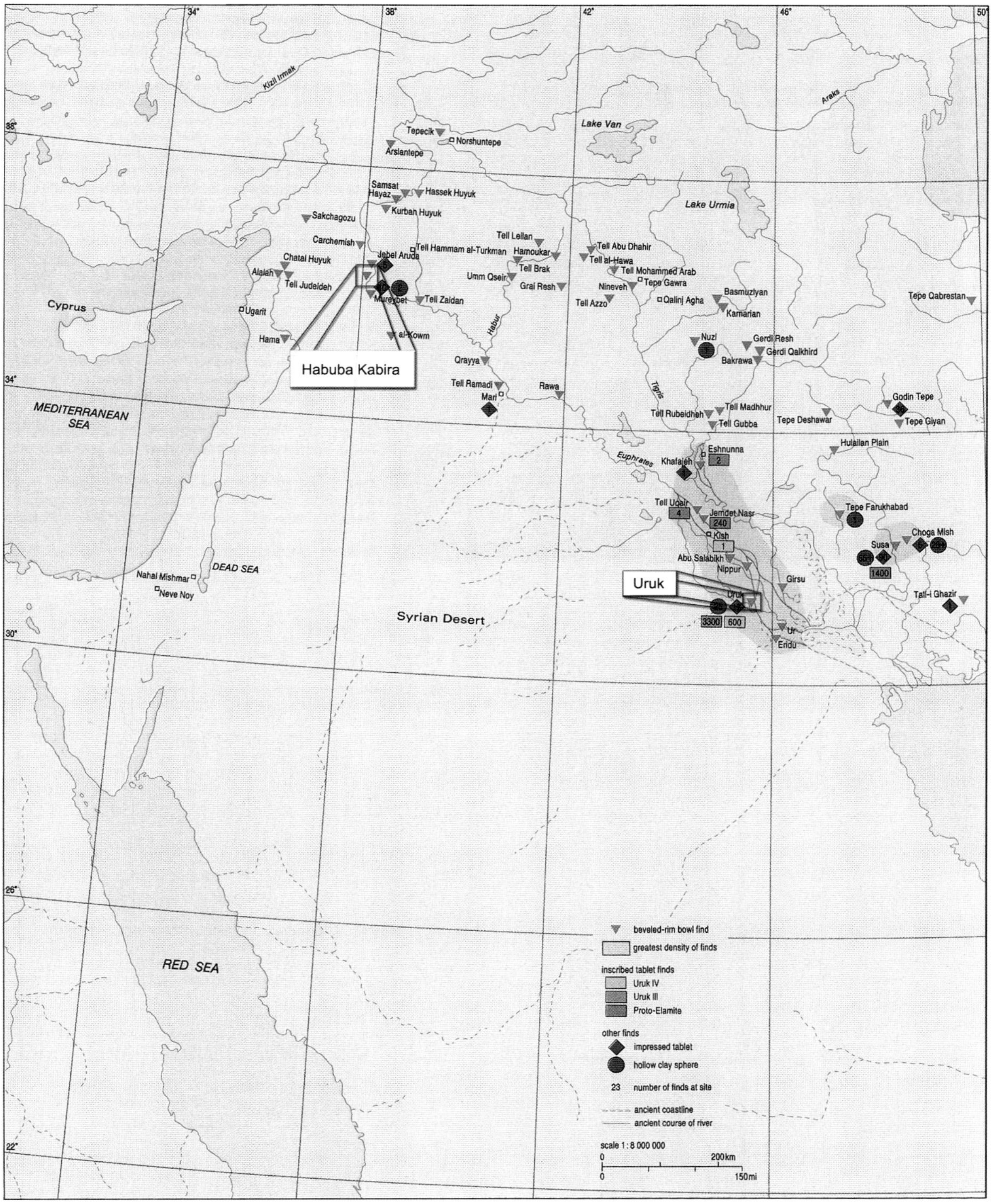

Karte. Nach: Roaf 1990, 65. Cultural Atlas of Mesopotamia and the ancient Near East. New York.

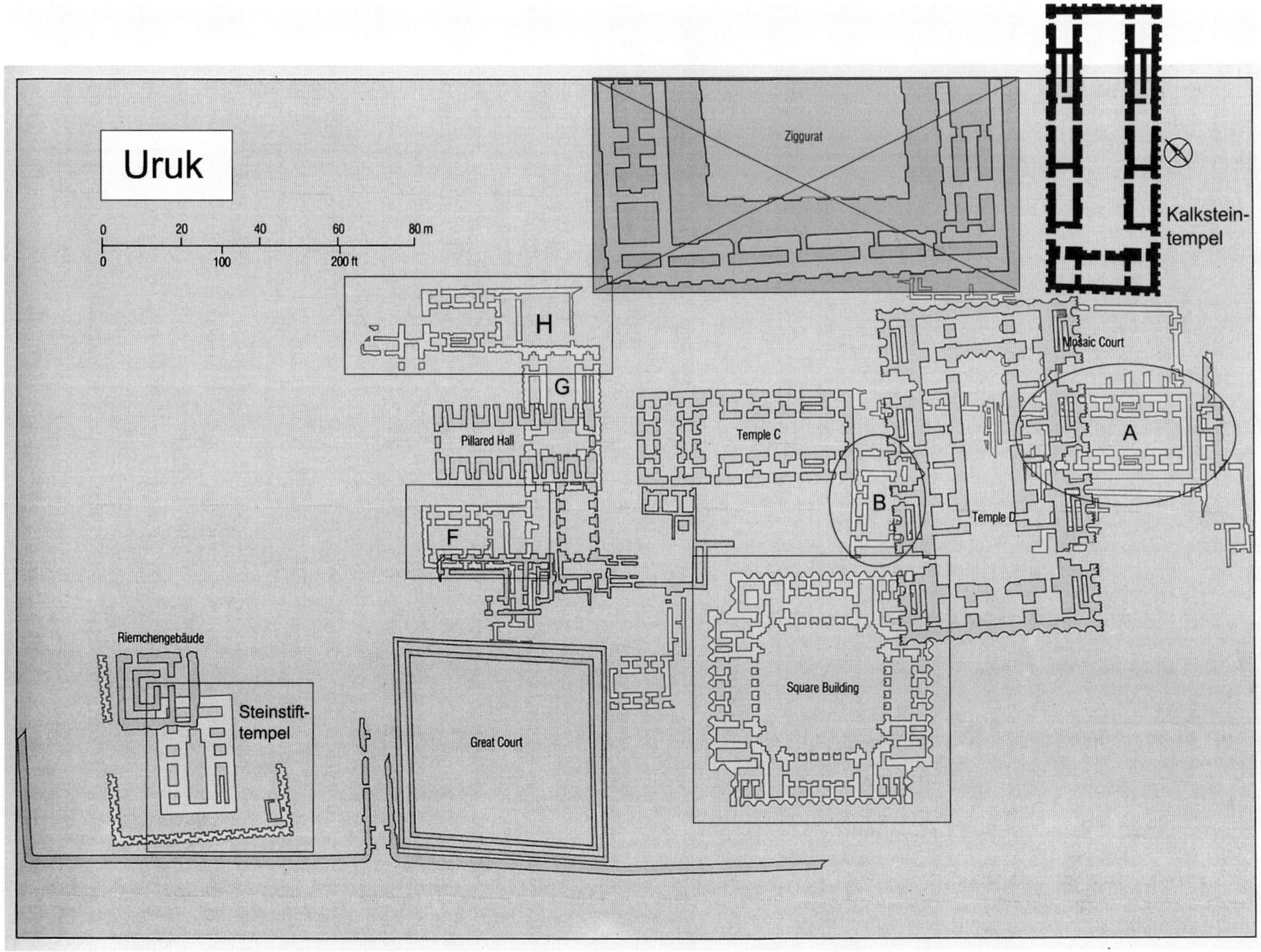

Der Eanna-Bezirk von Uruk. Nach: Roaf 1990, 64. Cultural Atlas of Mesopotamia and the ancient Near East. New York.

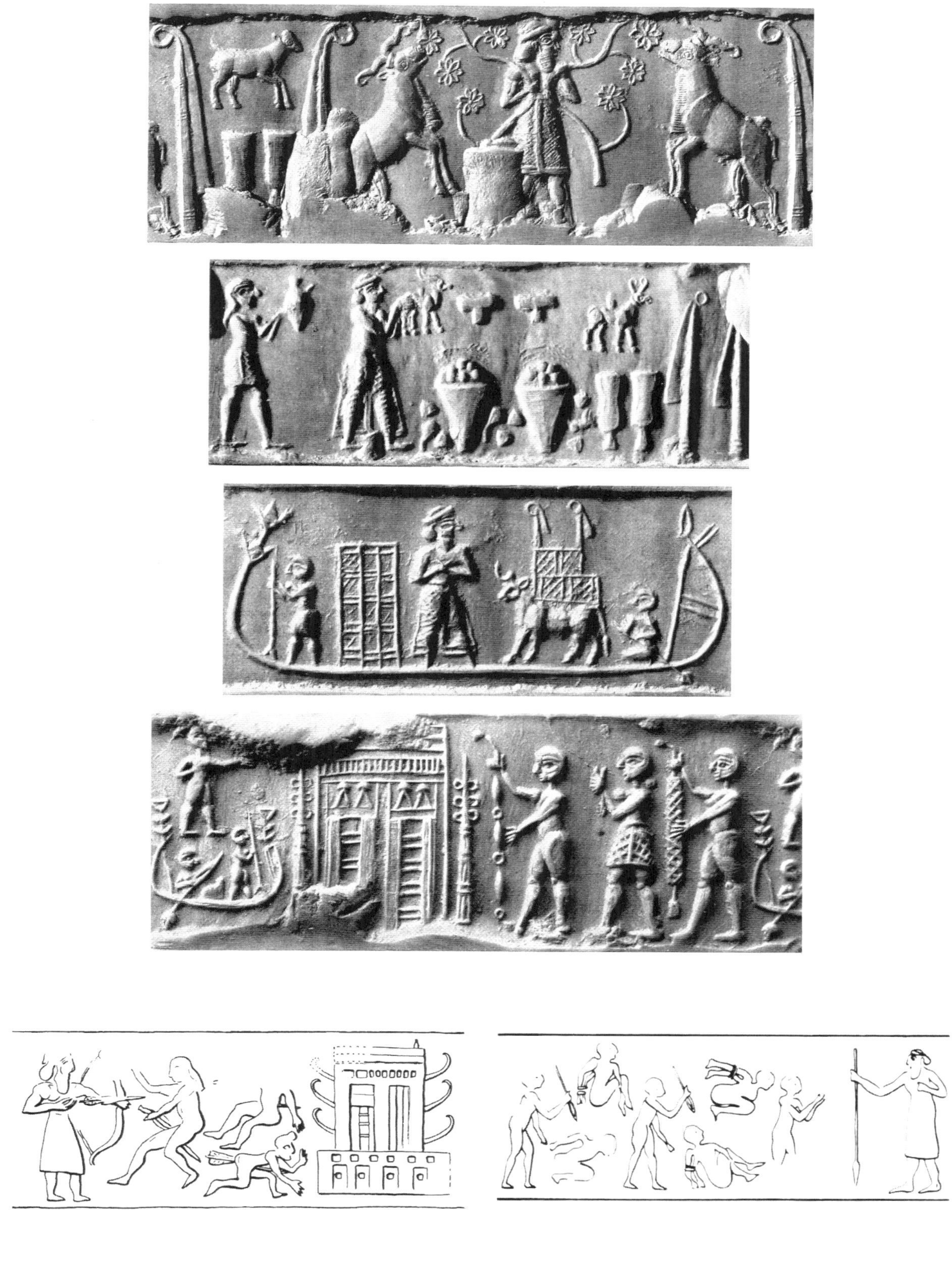

Der sog. Mann im Netzrock. Nach: Orthmann 1975, Fotos: Fig. 126a-d; Umzeichnungen: S. 223, Fig. 39c und 39d.

The Middle-Assyrian City of Ashur and Its State Architecture in the 14th and 13th centuries B.C.

Maria Gabriella Micale

Introduction

The significance of regimes throughout history, with respect to the impact of power on each person's life in terms of both space and time and taking into account the human ability to exercise power by transferring it to the arrangement of built space (and its representation), has been a matter of debate in historical research for decades and remains an open matter.

Among the different manifestations of power, architecture certainly is an ancient and direct one. Even though the relationship between architecture and power is a quite recent field of academic inquiry, no one has ever doubted the representative potential of architecture. Indeed, since it is an instrument in service of a greater and established order, it has always exercised this strength on the human agents who, more or less unconsciously, have been subjected to this order.

Both the employment and the reception of architecture as an instrument of power are well documented in archaeological and epigraphic documents from the ancient world and, as far as ancient Near Eastern cultures are concerned, from the historical and archaeological evidence of the Assyrian culture. For many centuries, what was known of the whole universe of ancient Assyrian culture was what the word of the Bible related. During the 19th century, however, Assyrian culture became a visible and tangible, in other words a 'material' presence in both European history and culture. As part of this new material world, architecture became, in the course of time, a fundamental subject of research for the understanding of the Assyrian world, in particular through helping to clarify the ideological connections between the foundation of the state on one hand and the exercise of power on the other.

It is true that the state of research favours analysis of Neo-Assyrian architecture. Nevertheless, a considerable quantity of information about Middle-Assyrian architecture is available, mostly due to the German excavations in Ashur undertaken at the beginning of the 20th century. This expedition was quite unsuccessful in terms of both sculptured slabs and monumental statues, which were what all European museums then aspired to obtain. By contrast, though, it produced an incomparable amount of scientific records that clarified the historical development of both Assyrian material culture in general and architecture in particular.

In academic studies, however, Middle-Assyrian architecture was relegated to a secondary or subordinate position with respect to the Neo-Assyrian one. Since Neo-Assyrian architecture had been the first brought to light, the interpretation of some Middle-Assyrian architectural elements depended on comparison with later and better-known features.

The Middle-Assyrian Empire

Since Assyria had been a great economic and political centre of power during a short period of the Middle Bronze age, its political revival represents, without any doubt, one of the most exceptional events of the second half of the second millennium. Assyria became a regional power due to its involvement in the system of political and diplomatic relationships among the Great Powers of that period: Egypt, Babylon and the Hittite empire[1].

1 The liberation of Assyria from the powers of that period, which exercised more or less direct control over Assyria, is narrated in Royal Inscriptions and in historical sources such as the correspondence between the Near Eastern powers and

The authors of this 'miracle' were some rulers who led Assyria from the 14th century B.C. onwards. Ashur-uballit I (1363-1328 B.C.) was the first of these and the letters he sent to the King of Egypt reflect the arrogance and ambition of a newly risen power[2]. On the one hand, these kings fully harnessed cultural expressions to making statements of political supremacy and ideological legitimacy; on the other hand, their support helped to bring about a floruit of cultural expression in media such as political literature and monumental architecture[3]. The temples and palaces already in existence were meticulously taken care of and continually restored, while new buildings and new foundations appeared. Characterized by political and religious symbolism, this intense activity is amply documented in royal inscriptions, which pay particular attention to it[4]. Thus, on the one hand, the text, the written message, represents the 'verbal' channel of propaganda by which political ideology is disseminated, while, on the other, architecture represents the non-verbal, 'material' stream, which aids the understanding of the propagandistic message, or at least its surface meanings[5]. Public buildings were probably visible from very far outside the city, so that the non-urban population could recognize the message as well.

Ashur as Monument of Assyria

Housing the most important temple of the national god Ashur, the city of Ashur witnessed the most intense building activity undertaken by Middle-Assyrian rulers (Abb. 1). It was situated on a roughly triangular spur of the Makhul range, overlooking the narrow Tigris valley.

Already occupied in the third millennium, Ashur formed the almost sole focus of attention of Assyrian rulers from the beginning of the second millennium, when the *ensi* of the city started to gain autonomy, until the accession of Shamshi-Adad I, when Ashur became one of several city-states he controlled[6].

Even though it was an isolated centre in an arid country and there was no agricultural hinterland of any importance[7], Ashur became at first the major centre of its region and later the capital of Assyria[8] thanks to several reasons. These were the natural defences, the presence of a river, the strategic location on upper-Mesopotamian trade routes, the ancient and uninterrupted presence of a sacred building of regional importance and, as a consequence, a traditional prestige. Indeed, from early on, the history of the city was linked to a sacred building dedicated to a goddess in the same place where the temple of Ishtar was to be sited later on[9].

As already stated, the ascension of Assyria in the international politics of its day was the direct result of the strategy of rulers who tried to build an Assyrian nation. They initiated projects in both foreign and home politics which aimed at developing nationhood in Assyria. At their time, the concept of Assyria as a region (*māt Aššur*) is first attested[10]. One of these projects, and maybe the most important, was the 'choice' of the capital. Certainly, it is possible to consider it a more or less 'natural' choice, given the significance the city had already acquired during its earlier history. It is possible to assume that, as a

the Egyptian kingdom. For an extensive analysis of the international political situation in which the Middle-Assyrian empire developed, see Liverani 1990, 1999; Grayson 1971; Artzi 1997.

2 Liverani 1990, 72. For an outline of the reign of Ashur-uballit I, see Harrak 1987, 7-60.

3 Grayson 1971, 318-9.

4 Matthiae 1994, 35-7.

5 Liverani 1979, 302; 1990, 28.

6 Larsen 1976. Even though the centrality of Old-Assyrian Ashur was not absolute, its role as the ideological centre of Assyria was reflected not only in the care Shamshi-Adad I took of the city's temples, but also in the fact that, according to the written sources, these temples were built and decorated with exotic precious materials. Moreover, this kind of narrative emphasizes the symbolic value of the temple. Actually, since it was constructed with exotic materials, it becomes an expression of the universal domain of both king and god and of their control over foreign places and resources (cf. Liverani 1990, 207).

7 Liverani 1995, 351-2; cf. Novák 1999, 107-10. After the defeat of the Mittanian kingdom, Assyrians attempted to colonize its cultivable lands; maybe this was motivated by the lack of an agricultural hinterland. For the Assyrian presence in Jazira, see Liverani 1988; Masetti-Rouault 1998.

8 Oates 1968, 19-21, 31-37.

9 The excavators of Ashur thought they had identified some traces of the archaic period in the temple of Ashur and compared these with the archaic phases of the temple of Ishtar (Haller and Andrae 1955, 9-14).

10 Larsen 1979a, 82.

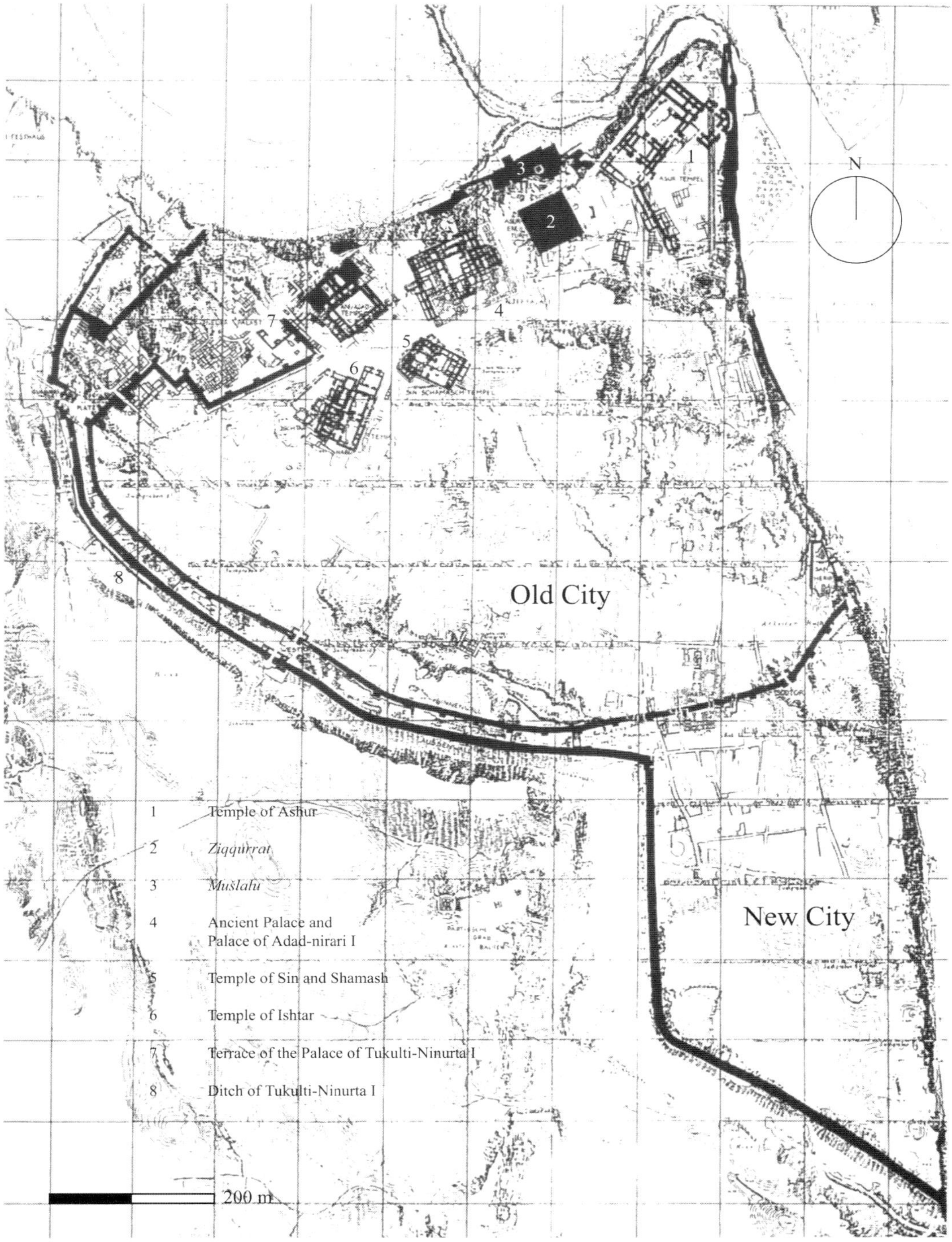

Abb. 1. Plan of Ashur. After: Andrae 1977; numbers and captions: author.

deified city that gave its name to the city god[11], Ashur was chosen as capital for the legitimating connection it established between the sacred sphere and worldly power. Considering sacredness as a hypostatic expression of social values[12] and 'sacred' as a synonym of 'Assyrian', it is clear that in reality Ashur was the codified expression of both Assyria and its society.

Thus, Ashur became the monumental capital during the Middle-Assyrian period, since at that time there existed an ideological need for both monuments and a capital. There appears to be no doubt about

11 Lambert 1983, 83-6.
12 Liverani 1979, 301.

this: the written documents testify an unprecedented increase in building activity; both the restoration of existing monuments and the building of new structures were the result of (or resulted in) transformation of the city itself, which was strongly linked to its change of status. Judging by the archaeological documentation, it is clear that this transformation occurred within the confines of an urban tradition which respected topographical constraints and had shaped the city from at least the Old-Assyrian period onwards. However, even though the city had already reached a considerable extension in the Old-Assyrian period and although written documents tell us that several well-known monuments of the later Middle-Assyrian period had precursors in that period[13], it can hardly be claimed that, from the 14th to the 12th century B.C., Ashur remained the city it had been before. There was one factor that changed both the appearance and the significance of the city, and this is its rank. Whereas Old-Assyrian Ashur was only a city-state, the aristocratic families of which traded along international, but limited routes, Middle-Assyrian Ashur was the capital of a state, which, as a political, social and military entity, had taken its position among the powers of the time – international relations make a nation. Even those architectural monuments which referred back to earlier ones had to appear in the light of this new strength, which was achieved through both a 'material' renewal (the reconstruction in an established topographic setting) and a symbolic-ideological renewal (the reoccupation of a historical and political context under changed circumstances).

The Monumental Architecture in Ashur from the 14th to the 13th Century B.C.

The long period after the unification of the Hurrian territories, when Assyria was only a vassal state, is reflected by a real gap in Assyrian documentary evidence. Furthermore, there is an almost complete lack of documents referring to building activity in Ashur during this period[14].

Whereas the historical and political developments during the Middle-Assyrian period are fairly well understood, it is more difficult to identify and follow the concomitant development of the most important expression of Ashur's new power, namely its monumental architecture.

In the middle of the 14th century, Ashur-uballit I was the first Assyrian ruler who abandoned his royal title of "servant of the god Ashur" and proclaimed himself "Great King" and "King of Assyria", *šar māt Aššur*[15]. Both his political and diplomatic activities are well known; he achieved a renascence in Assyria's power and fortunes. Despite the historical importance of his reign, his building activity is documented in just a few inscriptions. At Ashur-uballit's time, Ashur was already a fortified settlement comprising a few monumental buildings, which were concentrated in the north of the site, and several residential areas. Epigraphic evidence proves that the city of Ashur had already reached its greater historical expansion in the middle of the 14th century, when it probably consisted of two sectors, as it did, according to archaeological findings, in the Neo-Assyrian period[16]. It could be possible that the monumental core of the city was the northern triangle, which had an area of about 0.5 km^2[17], although Ashur-uballit already mentioned the so-called 'New City' (the southern sector), which had been constructed by Puzur-Ashur III[18]. This information may be confirmed by an inscription of Ashur-bel-nishesu[19] in which the ruler affirms that he completed the wall of the New City begun by Puzur-Ashur.

Bearing in mind the profound differences between the limited archaeological data and epigraphic evidence, it is possible to affirm that, during the reign of Ashur-uballit the city of Ashur was already fortified[20]. Moreover, there is no archaeological or epigraphic indication that this ruler constructed a city

13 As evidenced by names and in some cases topographic information.
14 Cf. some structures inside the Old Palace (Miglus 1986).
15 Grayson 1987, A.O.73.6.
16 Andrae 1913, 136; Miglus 1996, 56.
17 Larsen 1976, 60-3.
18 Grayson 1987, A.O.73.1; Larsen 1976, 61.
19 Grayson 1987, A.O.69.1.
20 Andrae 1977, 140-1.

wall. Traces of the earlier fortifications are archaeologically documented in some sections on the perimeter of the city, while no written documents predating the reign of Adad-nirari I were found in situ[21].

It is not clear which of these structures were preserved at that time. Actually, the latest document we have from an earlier period dates back to Ashur-nirari I[22], i.e. two hundred years earlier and, significantly, in the period of the first Mittanian pressure on Assyria's territory. However, it is possible to assume that the spatial development of the later structures was very similar to that of the earlier ones[23]. As to the city-gates, it is not easy to correlate archaeological and epigraphic data, since the latter mainly refer to a later period[24]. Probable remains of a western gate and a section of Old/Middle-Assyrian walls were located at the so-called Western and South Gates of the inner city wall[25]. Beyond the restoration of a palace previously built by Ashur-nadin-ahhe II[26] and possibly of a sector of the temple of Ishtar[27], which are only epigraphically documented, no building activity of Ashur-uballit I can be identified archaeologically. From an archaeological point of view, the city of that time seems to consist only of earlier monuments and to preserve its earliest appearance.

The so-called 'Old Palace' was located south-west of the *ziqqurrat* (Abb. 2)[28]. Even if it still stood unfinished in the 14th century B.C., it is possible that one of its sectors was restored by Ashur-uballit I. The possible activity of this ruler in the core of the monumental area is of great political and symbolic importance. According to an inscription, Ashur-uballit I renewed part of the so-called 'New Palace' previously built by Ashur-nadin-ahhe[29]. Since this inscription was found in the area of the Old Palace, it seems to be clear that Ashur-uballit operated in the core of the 'sacred city', an exceptional circumstance if we consider the 'national' political role of this ruler. Indeed, he issued the very first court edict[30], a clear sign of the importance of this new institution (the Palace) as well as being an index of political recovery of both capital and nation led by a ruler who abandoned his epithet as a servant and defined himself as a king. Bearing in mind that Ashur-uballit I asserted to have built a new palace in the New City as well[31], it is very significant that this ruler insists on the (re)construction of one or more palaces. This circumstance seems to be related to the new function that the palace assumed in the renovated political structure of Assyria[32]. Situated south-west of the Old Palace, the temple of Ishtar, probably the most ancient building of the city, does not show any trace of restoration which can be dated to the reign of Ashur-uballit, while only one written document testifies to such activity[33].

21 Andrae 1913, 3, 9, 95-8, 123-4. On the contrary, several documents were found in different contexts. They mentioned either the construction or the restoration of fortifications and walls before the 14th century B.C. (Andrae 1913, 10-2; Lackenbacher 1982, 21-2; Grayson 1987, A.O.32.2, A.O.60.5-6).

22 Grayson 1987, A.O.60.5-6.

23 At that time, the so-called mušlalu (literally step-gate) may already have been an important and singular part of the fortifications of Ashur. It was a kind of monumental gate, situated by the river in the northern section of the city wall; its nature and role are difficult to establish. The archaeological remains belonging to this structure were among the most exceptional and best preserved unearthed by the German archaeological expedition (Andrae 1913, 63-78). According to the Royal Inscriptions, Erishum I seems to have been its constructor (Grayson 1987, A.O.33.4), whereas, before Ashur-uballit I, Ashur-nirari I (Grayson 1987, A.O.60.4) and Puzur-Ashur III (Grayson 1987, A.O.61.1) had restored it (Lackenbacher 1982, 26). Thus, even if it is not possible to date exactly all the parts of the preserved structure, it might be assumed that in the middle of the 14th century B.C. this building was still standing (Andrae 1913, 64-7).

24 See Miglus 1982.

25 Andrae 1913, 53, 62.

26 Grayson 1987, A.O.73.1-2, 1002.

27 Grayson 1987, A.O.73. 4.

28 Preusser 1955, 6-12; Andrae 1977, 138-41; Heinrich 1984, 37-43. Cf. Margueron 1982, 390-6; Miglus 1986, 1989.

29 Cf. Grayson 1987, A.O.76.16.

30 Grayson 1971, 318.

31 Lackenbacher 1982, 41.

32 It has to be pointed out that, according to the sources, only Shamshi-Adad I claimed to have built a palace in Ashur before Ashur-uballit I. The references to the royal titles of Shamshi-Adad I seem to be quite significant: before Ashur-uballit, no one had designated himself šakin denlíl (appointee of the god Enlil). Eriba-Adad I, predecessor of Ashur-uballit I, had called himself šakin denlíl only in one of two of his known inscriptions (Grayson 1971, 313, 315-6). For the analysis of the relationship between the titles of the two rulers, see Grayson 1971, 313-4.

33 Grayson 1987, A.O.73. 4; Andrae 1922, 111-5; Larsen 1976, 59-60; Heinrich 1982, 197-8. For the analysis of the phases of the temple, see Andrae 1921, 1922, 1935; Bär 2003a, 2003b.

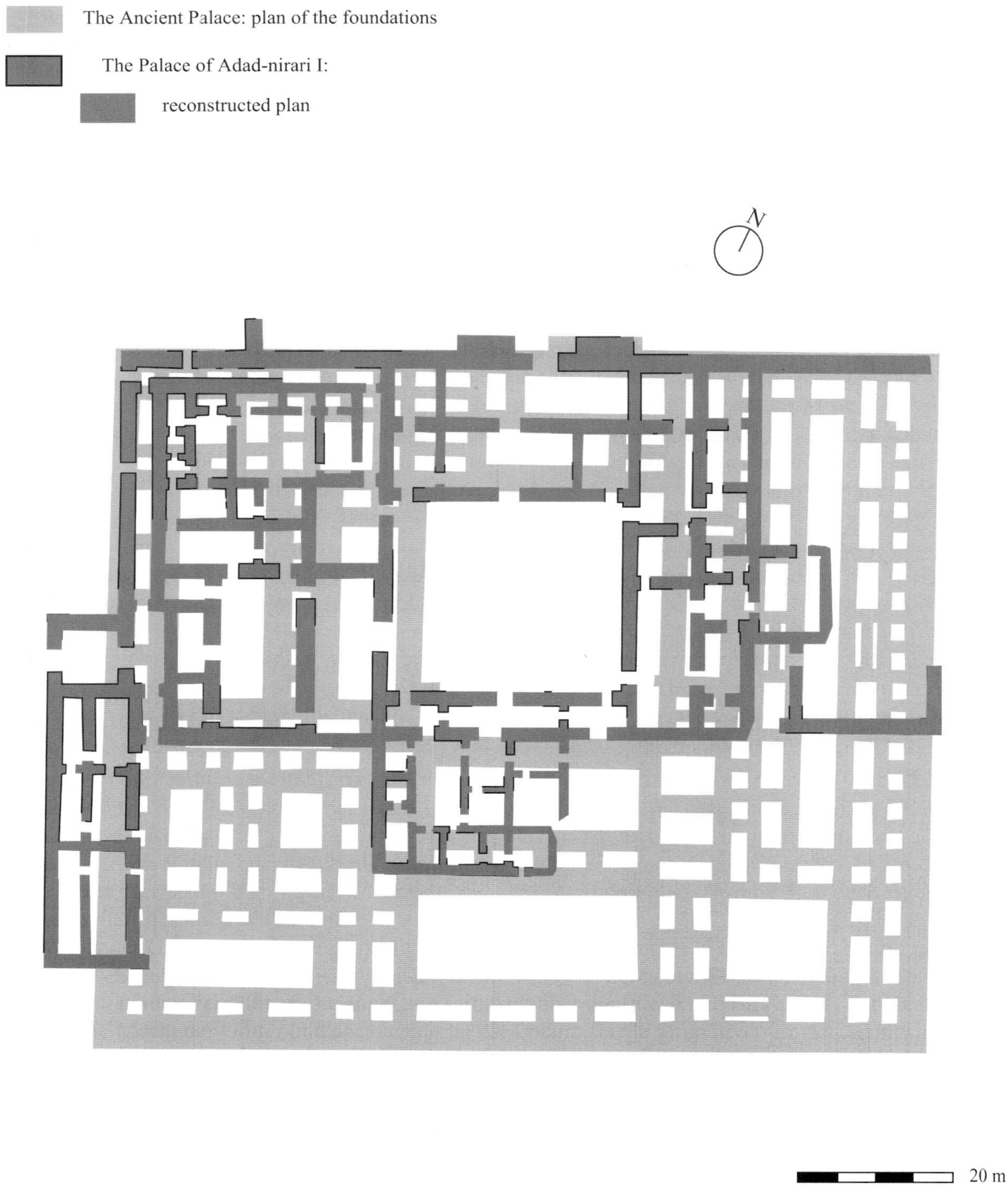

Abb. 2. The Ancient Palace and the Palace of Adad-nirari I. After: Preusser 1955, Pl. 3 and 4; drawing: author.

Even though it is possible that the northern sector of the city was already occupied by several other sacred buildings, as indicated by epigraphic sources informing us about an ancient temple of Adad[34],

34 Possibly already of Anu and Adad, see Andrae 1909, 1; Larsen 1976, 60; Lackenbacher 1982, 39-40.

archaeological data only document the presence of the older temples of Ashur[35] and Sin and Shamash[36] as well as the *ziqqurrat*[37] during the 14th century. Thus, although none of these temples was constructed or restored by Ashur-uballit I, it is possible, at least, that they were used at that time[38].

As to private and domestic buildings, archaeological research unearthed only a very few of these from any period of the city's history[39]. Thanks to a large set of trenches across the whole area of the city, it is possible to assume that Ashur had both several extensive residential sectors and that a few exceptional 'domestic' structures were built in the northern monumental sector.

The Middle-Assyrian residential area reached as far as the northern part of the New City. One may suggest that this growth is indicative of an increase of the urban population related to an increase of the bureaucratic and administrative activity. It is not always possible to recognize when and for how long these buildings were used. However, the structures in the eastern part of the 'Old City' surely date back to the 14th century B.C.[40].

There is no doubt that the residential quarter was inhabited by families linked to the central administration. Several factors allow us to conclude that the inhabitants were of some social status: the analysis of building technique and materials employed and, most importantly, the occurrence inside the houses of archives and libraries. Furthermore, these findings reveal an increase in the use of writing related to the development of the state administration. This suggests that the inhabitants of certain sectors, such as areas occupied by temples, used writing as a professional device[41].

The reign of Ashur-uballit I politically prepared the reign of Adad-nirari I, the ruler that finally submitted the Mittani kingdom[42]. Fully conscious of the political and military rise of Assyria, he took the heritage of his predecessor and carried out an unprecedented renovation of the city. Even though frenetic building and military activities went on at the same time, few archaeologically identified structures can be ascribed to Adad-nirari I. The written sources tell us about the renovation of the fortification wall, but only a short section of the eastern quay wall has been identified[43]. Furthermore, we read about the restoration of the temple of Ashur[44], probably also of the *ziqqurrat*[45] and of the temple of Ishtar[46], but the restoration of the palace is the only major work archaeologically documented[47]. Actually, Adad-nirari I built (although he says "restored") his palace on the foundations of the Old Palace (Abb. 2). While the palace is only partially preserved, it is the only fairly well known example of Middle-Assyrian secular architecture within the city. Moreover, it is the first important documented example of a wholesale change in plan of a building in the process of its reconstruction. Comparing the partially preserved reconstructed plan with the earlier one, a change in the spatial organization is clearly evident. Whereas the older plan can be understood as an expression of the Amorrean architectonic tradition, the New Palace seems to be influenced by the Mittanian one, as is evidenced by the functional differentiation of sectors which are now centred on the courtyards and connected by the state apartments[48]. Unfortunately, the lack of archaeological and epigraphic data does not allow a clear comprehension of this rebuilding

35 Schwenzner 1931-32, 1932-33, 1933-34; Haller and Andrae 1955, 5, 9-51; van Driel 1969, 19; Larsen 1976, 56-9; Lackenbacher 1982, 27-34.

36 Haller and Andrae 1955, 86, 92; Andrae 1977, 141-5; Lackenbacher 1982, 40-1.

37 Haller and Andrae 1955, 2-5; van Driel 1969, 11-5; Andrae 1977, 129-37.

38 Only one later source suggests that Ashur-uballit I restored part of the temple of Ashur as well (Lackenbacher 1982, 31; Grayson 1987, A.O.77.5).

39 Preusser 1954; Miglus 1996, 1997.

40 Miglus 1996, 57.

41 Pedersén 1985; 1997, 141-2, 150.

42 Harrak 1987, 61-131.

43 Andrae 1913, 149-53; Grayson 1987, A.O.76.8-9, 40.

44 van Driel 1969, 15; Grayson 1987, A.O.76, 19, 35-6, 42.

45 Grayson 1987, A.O.76.21, 24.

46 Grayson 1987, A.O.76.6, 15, 18, 37; Lackenbacher 1982, 35-6.

47 Preusser 1955, 13-8; Margueron 1982, 459-60; Grayson 1987, A.O.76.16, 29-31.

48 Cf. the Mittanian palace of Nuzi which, compared to the Amorrean ones, seems to be a 'modern' structure (Heinrich 1984, 85). If one accepts the Hurrian origin of the palace of Nuzi (cf. Henrich 1984, who denies this origin), it has to be admitted that the Hurrian influence has been the most important one in terms of the layout and functional organization of Adad-nirari's Palace.

which surely had to be the expression of an important political and social change affecting the new urban political reality, i.e. the Palace.

Thus, whereas at the beginning of Ashur-uballit's reign Ashur was probably the most prestigious city of the region, during Adad-nirari's time it already was the capital of a political and military power reborn. As stated before, archaeological and epigraphic data prove that most of the monumental buildings of Ashur were founded before the activities of these two rulers, which, reoccupying and reconstructing them, did not change their topographic relationships. Nevertheless, there is no doubt that the change of Ashur's status (from city to capital city) completely modified the significance of these buildings. Whereas until then, from the view of the common people, these monuments would only have been cultural symbols, they became symbols of Assyrian power when the Middle-Assyrian empire grew. Moreover, in accordance with the propagandistic use of state architecture, buildings were the tangible evidence of both the king's power and the favour of the deity towards the city and represented, at the same time, a 'request' for the total submission of the population.

During the first half of the 13th century B.C., under Shalmaneser I, the empire was still growing. However, also in this case, the great quantity of written sources referring to the building activity of this ruler contrasts with an almost absolute lack of archaeological evidence. The royal inscriptions, which pay more attention to building than to military activity, tell us about the restoration of the *ziqqurrat*[49], the temple of Ishtar[50], the palace[51] and other archaeologically unknown monuments. Archaeological research unearthed only one major piece of evidence for Shalmaneser's building activity, i.e. the reconstruction of the temple of Ashur after a fire. The inscriptions concerning this major event were numerous, giving different details[52]. Archaeological documentation proves that Shalmaneser did not change the older temple, but just enlarged it; a south-west courtyard was built with a monumental entrance and annexes (Abb. 3)[53].

Moreover, it is possible that Shalmaneser built the so-called *Westmassiv* on the arm of the Tigris, a quadrangular structure to the west of the *ziqqurrat*[54].

The most impressive archaeological evidence for the building activity of any Middle-Assyrian ruler comes from the reign of Tukulti-Ninurta I, to whom it is possible to ascribe the most extensive renovations.

One of the most important elements of his activity is the restoration of the fortification walls and the *ex novo* construction of a deep ditch in front of them: these made Ashur a kind of virtual island[55]. The western sections of both the city wall and the ditch are the only structures archaeologically documented. They include the newly erected so-called *Außenhaken* on a pre-existing natural height, i.e. a kind of fortified irregular space open towards the northeast, and the singular *Poternenmauer*[56]. Clear traces of a contemporary phase of the Tabira Gate have never been found, but the discovery of a nearby ramp renders its existence quite probable[57].

Concerning the temple of Ashur, Tukulti-Ninurta probably completed what his father Shalmaneser I had begun[58]. This activity is likely to have been linked to the construction of a new palace between the temple and the *ziqqurrat*, i.e. the 'King-Priest's Palace', although the latter is difficult to date (Abb. 3)[59]. Actually, Tukulti-Ninurta I tells us he rebuilt a palace his father had built in front of the *ziqqurrat*, even if there is no document to confirm that Shalmaneser was the original builder[60]. However, since it has been only partially unearthed, the building is not fully understood yet.

49 Grayson 1987, A.O.77.12, 23.
50 Grayson 1987, A.O.77.6.
51 Grayson 1987, A.O.77.10-1, 28.
52 Lackenbacher 1982, 31-4; Grayson 1987, A.O.77.1-5, 20-2.
53 Haller and Andrae 1955, 37-52; van Driel 1969, 15-9; Andrae 1977, 165-8; Heinrich 1982, 232-3.
54 Andrae 1913, 73-8.
55 Lackenbacher 1982, 25; Grayson 1987, A.O.78.19. cf. Lampl 1968, 17.
56 Andrae 1913, 108-10, 119-20, 124-6; 1977, 170-4.
57 Andrae 1913, 20-1, 30-2, 119.
58 Haller and Andrae 1955, 48; van Driel 1969, 19; Andrae 1977, 168-70; Lackenbacher 1982, 34.
59 Preusser 1955, 28-9; Heinrich 1984, 96.
60 Lackenbacher 1982, 46.

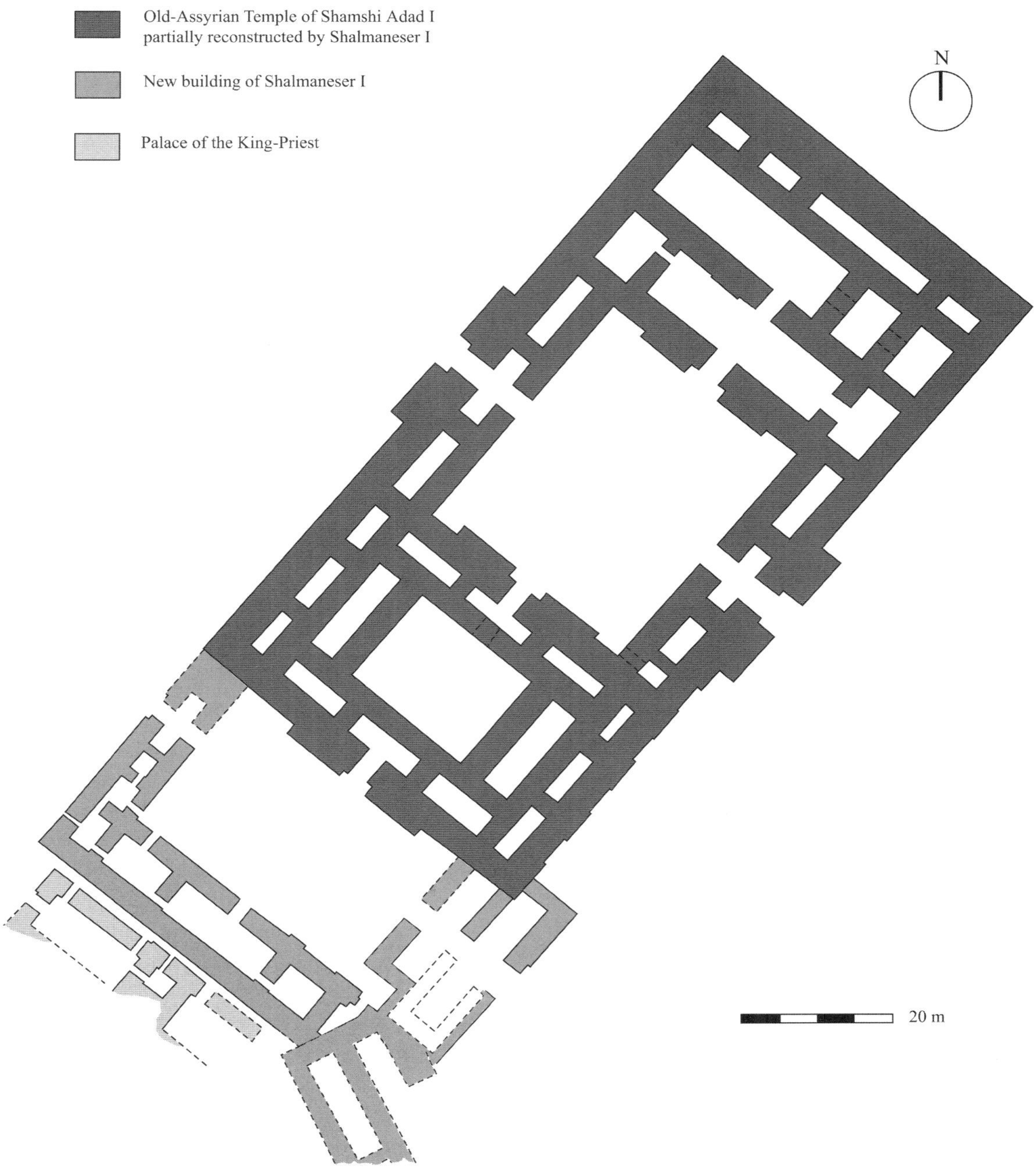

Abb. 3. The Temple of Ashur. After: Haller and Andrae 1955, Pl. 5; drawing: author.

As to the temple of Sin and Shamash, he rebuilt the monument following precisely the plan of the older construction. Situated south of the Old Palace, it was a rather unusual structure characterized by a front consisting of a stepped sequence of projecting towers. The first building phase which can be identified with certainty dates back to Ashur-nirari I, who declares himself the builder of the temple[61]. In fact, the reconstruction of Tukulti-Ninurta comprised no more than a reduction of the number of projecting towers belonging to the north-west façade[62].

61 Haller and Andrae 1955, 82-3; Grayson 1987, A.O.60.3.

62 Haller and Andrae 1955, 86-9; Heinrich 1982, 234-5. Some epigraphic sources tell us about Arik-din-ili (1319-1308 B.C.) restoring only the temple of Shamash. The analysis of one of these inscriptions allows us to suppose that he never completed the restoration work. It is very interesting that, according to these sources, the temple had entirely collapsed at the time of this ruler (Haller and Andrae 1955, 82; Lackenbacher 1982, 41).

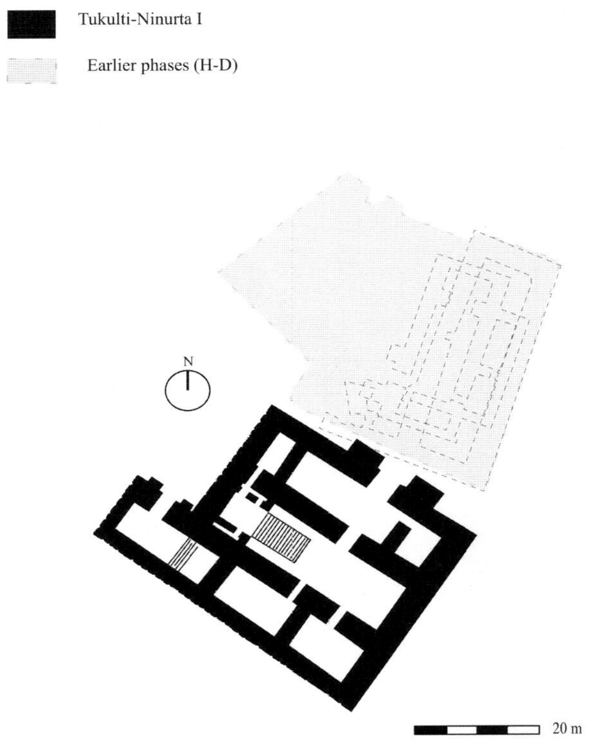

Abb. 4. The sacred area of Ishtar. After: Andrae 1935, Pl. 1; drawing: author.

In contrast, the temple of Ishtar underwent a reconstruction which we may term revolutionary (Abb. 4)[63]. Indeed, Tukulti-Ninurta I built a new structure in the area of the older sanctuary and although this structure recalls the previous layout, centred on the *cella* with a *bent axis* approach, it is typical of the wholesale architectural and topographic reformation of Tukulti-Ninurta I, in particular in its change of orientation. As it was common practice for a ruler to (re)construct a temple on the foundations of the previous structure in order to establish a direct connection with the first temple thought to have been founded by the deity itself[64], the construction of the new temple of Ishtar in the area of, but not on top of an older temple[65] is an innovation introduced by Tukulti-Ninurta I[66], who reveals himself as builder of what we have come to picture as Middle-Assyrian Ashur. In contrast to the case of the Old Palace, where the reconstruction of Adad-nirari was laid out on an earlier structure of sufficiently clear plan, the new temple of Ishtar cannot easily be compared with the earlier structure, since the latter is poorly understood. However, even if, as we have seen, the reconstruction of a building did not usually entail a complete change of layout, the reconstruction of the temple of Ishtar *ex novo* was completely consistent with the general renewal fostered by Tukulti-Ninurta. Thus, whereas the reconstruction of a building that followed the earlier plan could depend on a particular ideological or symbolic relationship between shape and function (this is the case of the temple of Sin and Shamash of Tukulti-Ninurta and a great part of the temple of Ashur of Shalmaneser I), the *ex novo* reconstruction of an old and celebrated building such as the temple of the Assyrian Ishtar necessarily corresponds to new political, social and consequently ritual requirements[67]. The intense and widely documented building activity of Tukulti-Ninurta reveals the specific character of his reign. On the one hand, he fostered expressions of cult and demonstrations of devotion; on the other, he realized what was needed for the exaltation of royalty and worldly

63 Andrae 1935, 15-35; Andrae 1977, 152-62; Heinrich 1982, 233-4.

64 Matthiae 1994, 34-7. For the later examples of Babylonian recovery of ancient ruins, see Winter 2000.

65 Miglus 1996, 142-4.

66 This change of site is documented in the Royal Inscriptions as well: Grayson 1987, A.O.78.12-13.

67 For instance, it is possible that, in this new structure, the lack of a court, which was the core of the sacerdotal administrative life of any temple, indicates the new – much more restricted – role of the sacerdotal class of Ashur during the reign of Tukulti-Ninurta: Baffi Guardata 1990, 28-9.

power. What results from this is a seemingly inconsistent image of his reign, between self-celebration and total submission to the god's will[68]. But it is clear that the submission to a deity is only a propagandistic expression and a facet of a wider self-celebration, typical of imperialist power.

After Tukulti-Ninurta's accession, Middle-Assyrian monarchy became more and more absolute, with even stronger universalistic ambitions[69]. He decided to construct for himself a new palace of unprecedented dimensions. It seems to be a first step towards the isolation he tried to achieve through the foundation of a new capital city, Kar-Tukulti-Ninurta, which, however, was still near to Ashur[70].

Mentioned several times in royal inscriptions[71], the construction of the new palace of Tukulti-Ninurta I was surely perceived as a revolution in urban planning. Not only did the new ruler seem to disregard the tradition symbolized by the place of residence, but he also chose a location far from the traditional 'sacred' area of the main temples. It seems to be in this phase that the historic disruption of the symbolic union between temple and palace occurs. This disjuncture is not so evident archaeologically, but indications of it can be found in a fair number of Middle-Assyrian inscriptions, which record that, according to a ritual, the gods went to the royal palace for an annual meeting[72]. This narrative clearly reveals that the gods did not live inside but outside the palace. The dimension of this new residence made the project only more unusual. In fact, the king's palace, É.LUGAL.U-MUN.KUR.KUR.RA, became the largest building of the city[73], surpassing the temple of the state god in size. Little remains of the great residence, which maybe was never completed, except for the impressive foundation terrace[74].

Tukulti-Ninurta represents the climax of the ideological and historical development of the Middle-Assyrian empire, at which, due to the foundation of Kar-Tukulti-Ninurta, Ashur lost the role as capital city for the first time.

STATE ARCHITECTURE OR THE EXPLOITATION OF ARCHITECTURE FOR THE PURPOSES OF THE STATE

Mesopotamian monumental buildings always expressed political power and social control. Nevertheless, comparing Middle-Assyrian architecture with the earlier one reveals a difference in meaning, since it was the effective expression of the power of a state which could be defined as an empire[75]. Undoubtedly, knowledge of the architectural arrangement of the capital of the Akkadian empire could lead to the development of a different notion of Near-Eastern monumental architecture and its evolution in the light of the relationship between power and its representation. However, for a full understanding of Ashur's Middle-Assyrian architecture as a state architecture, it is necessary to bear in mind that state architecture merely means the *exploitation* of architecture *for the purposes of* the State. Moreover, this exploitation encompasses not only the *construction of new buildings*, but also both *reconstruction* and *reoccupation* of buildings or places of symbolic and ideological value. Thus, bearing in mind what was stated before about the Middle-Assyrian city of Ashur and the intense building activity of its rulers, there is no doubt that what happened in Ashur between the 14th and 13th centuries and can be traced in each phase of the city represents a development which needs to be understood, first and foremost, not as architectural or in terms of town-planning but as conceptual. Indeed, even though we are aware of numerous interventions into the built structure of the city, Middle-Assyrian state architecture was at first realized, seemingly less 'actively', through reoccupation.

Thus, Ashur-uballit mainly *exploited* the *architecture* of Ashur which had survived from the periods of greater prestige of the city to the advantage of the state. Documented by an inscription that

68 Dolce 1997, 252-3.
69 For the relationship between military conquests and exaltation of the ruler, see Liverani 1988, 92-5.
70 For the foundation of Kar-Tukulti-Ninurta, see Dolce 1994, 1997.
71 Grayson 1987, A.O.78.1-10, 30.
72 Van Driel 1969, 165-7; Lackenbacher 1982, 138.
73 Lackenbacher 1982: 48, Grayson 1987, A.O.78.3.
74 Preusser 1955, 30; Heinrich 1984, 95-6; Andrae 1977, 162-3. For a discussion of remains of this building, see Miglus 1996, 90-93, plan 100.
75 It is possible to consider the Assyrian territorial expansion as the construction of an empire if one thinks about it as a structure of permanent political and economic control by the state over a multitude of different regions (Masetti-Rouault 1998, 226).

also records a partial restoration, the reoccupation of the Old Palace satisfied the usual propagandistic and ideological requirements of Mesopotamian rulers: either the establishment of a physical/structural link between with or the maintenance of ancestors' buildings was fundamental for the perpetuation of power through consensus[76]. But at the same time, the reoccupation determined the change of status of the palace itself: since it was occupied by the leader of a strong new political and administrative entity and ideationally transformed by the representative strength this power achieved, the palace became the real and symbolic centre of the power it was to represent from that moment onwards. Thus, bearing in mind the three modes of constituting a state architecture, occupation, reconstruction and foundation, the building activity of Tukulti-Ninurta represented a final stage because it was the extreme attempt of the ruler to subdue and transform architecture into a mere instrument of his power. Indeed, not only did he change the city of Ashur for centuries after (cf. the fortifications and the ditch, the new temple of Ishtar and the monumental building of the new palace by a city-gate), but also went on to found a new capital. In contrast to previous new foundations which had usually marked territorial conquests, this occurred at a late stage of his reign and, most significantly, in close proximity to the older capital city; this kind of new foundation could be the expression of an unsteady state[77].

Although those three modes of constitution form part of a unitary expression of the idea the exploitation of architecture by the state, it seems possible to recognize in them three distinct stages in the diachronic development of this single idea. Thus, the reoccupation represents a first, immediate and almost 'emotional' phase, whereas the foundation is the last one, in which the founding action of the king and its connotations with the divine power, which founds the cosmic order, makes the exploitation of the architecture complete.

Returning to the issues from which we started, the significance of regimes throughout history and the impact of power on human habitation, we can see that this kind of exploitation of architecture seems to be a recurring feature. Characteristically, the unfolding of the project of a state architecture takes place in several phases, as, for instance, with the initial stages of the building program in Rome under the Fascists several years after the advent of Fascism in Italy[78]. It of particular interest to point out that, in a striking parallel to Middle-Assyrian Kar-Tukulti-Ninurta, the Fascist foundation of a new capital on the outskirts of the 'eternal city', the EUR, a copy of the older one in which the Duce could create a 'new order', dates to 1942, that is to quite an advanced stage in the history of the dictatorship. Thus, it seems that the 'creation/foundation' stage is reached through elaboration and after some time only by a relatively established power. Similarly, the first and immediate act of exploitation of architecture in the modern case was the appropriation of an existing architecture which definitely and dramatically deprived the latter of its original significance: when Mussolini came into power, he took up residence in the Palazzo Venezia, a Renaissance palace in the centre of Rome, and made it the seat of his power; from this palace he decreed the construction of the EUR. Just as the Old Palace of Ashur had become the symbol of the new power of the new king Ashur-uballit, Palazzo Venezia became the symbol of the new power of the Duce, a power that, without any formal changes, made that building its symbol.

Conclusion - The Political Use of Architecture: A Message to an Inner Audience

As already seen before, the archaeological documentation offers an image of Ashur as a traditional city, with its urban plan shaped during an earlier period and in accordance with the topographic/natural setting of the site. The settlement was completely adapted to the environmental needs (for instance the fortifications) and the emplacement of the buildings in the various sectors of the city seems to meet natural requirements. It has to be noted that the main buildings are concentrated in the north, in a high and open position, far from the area facing the steppes and at the junction of two rivers. This last circumstance is very important since, on the one hand, it provided an easy water supply and, on the other, it created a double mooring place.

76 Matthiae 1994.
77 Dolce 1997, 254-5.
78 For the building activity in Rome during the Fascist dictatorship, see de Seta 1987, 79, 128-32; Frampton 1993, 252-4.

Thus, power did not completely transform the layout of the city (a layout that seems to have become a prototype[79]), but seems to have had more impact on what we may term the 'scenic effect'. Indeed, there is no doubt that the general increase of building activity was paralleled by a progressive change of each building at least in terms of increasing monumentality. As a consequence of needs of representation, buildings grew ever more monumental, even though the reconstruction of a building did not always entail changes of plan or even type. However, this representative power was certainly directed towards home politics, to involve not only the leading class materially and visually in the new empire, but also lower social classes. It is possible to assume that the latter were mainly employed as building-labour, which we may assume to have had profound effects on the social structure of a mainly rural population[80]. These workers would also have been 'emotionally' involved in their labour, probably persuaded they would gain advantages from working in a sacred city, fulfilling the will of both king and god. Moreover, if "knowledge is more important than action", as Mario Liverani asserts[81], what the empire was in reality was no more important than what its inner population assumed it was[82]. Thus, since the inner population knew the outside world exclusively through the ruler's conquests[83] and the inner world through the images the ruler provided, they could form an idea of the empire only by reference to appearances and the architecture formed part of these appearances.

Finally, bearing in mind the relationship between architecture, image and representation, it is necessary to mention, in the context of architectural representation, the relationship between power and representations of architecture. Indeed, the use of the architecture to the advantage of the state is clearly documented by representations of architecture; the representation of the places where society takes its shape through social action becomes in itself representative of power. Indeed, there are diverse examples of representations of architecture, mostly temples and fortifications, in Middle-Assyrian glyptic art. It is interesting to note that the image of those places was translated from the great monuments themselves into a smaller medium; it is equally worth noting that this medium, the seal, was in and of itself representative of the power of the state. Thus, in contrast to the representations of mainly foreign architecture in Neo-Assyrian reliefs, the narrative function of which lay in emphasizing and illustrating the conquering strength of the empire, the architectural images on the seals seem to have served the continuous reconfirmation of both inner power and social control.

Thus, power changes the meaning of the city. Independently from the restoration or reconstruction of individual buildings, archaeological evidence of which is not always available, the power of Assyria gives these buildings the meaning of state buildings. This could happen not only in a material way, i.e. through the continuous reconstruction which allowed buildings that were well preserved and visible to maintain their inner political and social message, but also in an invisible and immaterial way, i.e. through writing.

Ashur-uballit was the first Assyrian ruler who exploited writing to the full. This is documented not only by those documents which dealt with the building activities themselves, mainly royal inscriptions, but also by the correspondence with the King of Egypt, i.e. in a purely political and international context quite distinct from the sphere of administrative documents and internal affairs. Just as the king wears different dresses depending on the occasion, Ashur-uballit does not hesitate to designate himself 'Great

79 It is very interesting that the topographic arrangement of Ashur seemingly became a model of urban planning for several of the most important Assyrian cities, e.g. Nineveh (Novák 2004).

80 Beyond those cases in which deported prisoners were employed in building activities (as apparently Syrian ones in the construction of Kar-Tukulti-Ninurta), we have to remind ourselves that, if one was called into service, it did not always mean military service. And this labour was certainly needed in the building projects. In exchange for the service, the state allotted plots of land that could be treated almost as private while the tenant was employed in the service (van de Mieroop 2004, 172-3).

81 Liverani 1990, 47.

82 It seems that for the ruler, his prestige within the borders of the empire was more important than the prestige among international partners of the same rank (Liverani 1979, 299; 1990, 25, 224-9). For instance, since in reality the historical documentation seems to reveal that the reign of Tukulti-Ninurta was a time of crisis in international and mainly home politics, the foundation of Kar-Tukulti-Ninurta was a means to demonstrate the stability of the king's power mainly to an inner audience (Dolce 1997, 254).

83 Liverani 1990, 48.

King' in this correspondence and without any fear ventures to ask for gold for the construction of his palace, which, by means of the written word of international diplomacy, definitely and truly becomes the palace of the king of Assyria.

Bibliography

Andrae, W. 1909. *Der Anu-Adad-Tempel in Assur*. Wissenschaftliche Veröffentlichungen der Deutschen Orient-Gesellschaft 10. Leipzig: J.C. Hinrichs.

—. 1913. *Die Festungswerke von Assur*. Wissenschaftliche Veröffentlichungen der Deutschen Orient-Gesellschaft 23. Leipzig: J.C. Hinrichs.

—. 1921. "Die Ischtar-Tempel in Assur." *Mitteilungen der Deutschen Orient-Gesellschaft* 61: 4-21.

—. 1922. *Die archaischen Ischtar-Tempel in Assur.* Wissenschaftliche Veröffentlichungen der Deutschen Orient-Gesellschaft 39. Leipzig: J.C. Hinrichs.

—. 1935. *Die jüngeren Ischtar-Tempel in Assur.* Wissenschaftliche Veröffentlichungen der Deutschen Orient-Gesellschaft 58. Leipzig: J.C. Hinrichs.

—. 1977. *Das wiedererstandene Assur*. 2nd rev. ed. Edited by B. Hrouda. Munich: C. H. Beck.

Artzi, P. 1997. "The Middle-Assyrian Kingdom as Precursor to the Assyrian Empire." In Waetzoldt and Hauptmann 1997, 3-6.

Baffi Guardata, F. 1990. "Tradizione e innovazione nell'architettura assira del II Millennio a. C." In *Archeologia della Mesopotamia*, edited by F. Baffi Guardata and R. Dolce, 21-34. Roma: G. Bretschneider.

Bär, J. 2003a. *Die älteren Ischtar-Tempel in Assur: Stratigraphie, Architektur und Funde eines altorientalischen Heiligtums von der zweiten Hälfte des 3. Jahrtausends bis zur Mitte des 2. Jahrtausends v. Chr.* Wissenschaftliche Veröffentlichungen der Deutschen Orient-Gesellschaft 105. Saarbrücken: Saarbrücker Druckerei und Verlag.

—. 2003b. "Sumerian, Gutians and Hurrians at Ashur? A Re-Examination of Ishtar Temples G and H." *Iraq* 65: 143-60.

de Seta, C. 1987. *Architetti italiani del Novecento*. 2nd ed. Bari: Editori Laterza.

Dolce, R. 1994. "Città di fondazione e fondazione di città?" In *Nuove fondazioni nel Vicino Oriente antico: realtà e ideologia*, edited by S. Mazzoni, 131-64. Pisa: Giardini Editori e Stampatori.

—. 1997. "The City of Kar-Tukulti-Ninurta: Cosmic Characteristics and Topographical Aspects." In Waetzoldt and Hauptmann 1997, 251-8.

Frampton, K. 1993. *Storia dell'architettura moderna.* 3rd ed. Translated by F. Piccarreta. Bologna: Zanichelli Editore.

Grayson, A.K. 1971. "The Early Development of Assyrian Monarchy." *Ugarit-Forschungen* 3: 311-9.

—. 1987. *Assyrian Rulers of the Third and Second Millennia BC (to 1115 BC)*. The Royal Inscriptions of Mesopotamia, Assyrian Periods 1. Toronto: University of Toronto Press.

Haller, A., and W. Andrae. 1955. *Die Heiligtümer des Gottes Assur und der Sin-Šamaš-Tempel in Assur*. Wissenschaftliche Veröffentlichungen der Deutschen Orient-Gesellschaft 67. Berlin: Gebr. Mann.

Harrak, A. 1987. *Assyria and Hanigalbat.* Hildesheim: Georg Olms Verlag.

Heinrich, E. 1982. *Die Tempel und Heiligtümer im alten Mesopotamien.* Denkmäler Antiker Architektur 14. Berlin: de Gruyter.

—. 1984. *Die Paläste im alten Mesopotamien*. Denkmäler Antiker Architektur 15. Berlin: de Gruyter.

Lackenbacher, S. 1982. *Le roi bâtisseur: Les récits de construction assyriens des origines à Teglatphalasar III.* Paris: Editions Recherche sur les civilisations.

Lambert, W.G. 1983. "The God Aššur." *Iraq* 45: 82-6.

Lampl, P. 1968. *Cities and Planning in the Ancient Near East*. New York: Braziller.

Larsen, M.T. 1976. *The Old Assyrian City-State and Its Colonies*. Mesopotamia 4. Copenhagen: Akademisk Forlag.

—. 1979a. "The Tradition of Empire in Mesopotamia." In Larsen 1979b, 75-124.

—, ed. 1979b. *Power and Propaganda*. Mesopotamia 7. Copenhagen: Akademisk Forlag.

Liverani, M. 1979. "The Ideology of the Assyrian Empire." In Larsen 1979b, 297-317.

—. 1988. "The Growth of the Assyrian Empire in the Habur Middle Euphrates Area: A New Paradigm." *State Archives of Assyria Bulletin* 2: 81-98.

—. 1988. "Confine e frontiera nel Vicino Oriente del Tardo Bronzo: spunti di discussione e riflessione." *Scienze dell'Antichità* 2: 79-99.

—. 1990. *Prestige and Interest: International Relations in the Near East ca. 1600-1100 B.C.* Padova: Sargon s. r. l.

—. 1995. *Antico Oriente*. Bari: Editori Laterza.

—. 1999. *Le lettere di el-Amarna.*Vol. 2, *Le lettere dei 'Grandi Re'*. Brescia: Paideia.

Margueron, J.C. 1982. *Recherches sur les palais mésopotamiens de l'Age du Bronze*. Paris: Librairie Orientaliste Paul Geuthner S.A.

Masetti-Rouault, M.G. 1998. "Syriens at Assyriens dans la Djéziré, XIVème-Ixème siècle av. J.-C." In *About Subartu: Studies Devoted to Upper Mesopotamia*. Vol. 2, edited by M. Lebeau, 223-42. Subartu 4. Turnhout: Brepols.

Matthiae, P. 1994. *Il sovrano e l'opera: Arte e potere nella Mesopotamia antica*. Bari: Editori Laterza.

Miglus, P.A. 1982. "Die Stadttore in Assur: Das Problem der Identifizierung." *Zeitschrift für Assyriologie und Vorderasiatische Archäologie* 72: 267-79.

—. 1986. "Ein mittelassyrischer Anbau am Alten Palast in Assur." *Mitteilungen der Deutschen Orient-Gesellschaft* 118: 191-216.

—. 1989. "Untersuchungen zum Alten Palast in Assur." *Mitteilungen der Deutschen Orient-Gesellschaft* 121: 93-133.

—. 1996. *Das Wohngebiet von Assur*. Wissenschaftliche Veröffentlichungen der Deutschen Orient-Gesellschaft 93. Berlin: Gebr. Mann.

—. 1997. "Eine assyrische Stadt im Wandel: Einblicke in die Wohnarchitektur von Assur." In Waetzoldt and Hauptmann 1997, 317-24.

Novák, M. 1999. *Herrschaftsform und Stadtbaukunst*. Saarbrücken: Saarbrücker Druckerei and Verlag.

—. 2004. "From Ashur to Nineveh: The Assyrian Town-Planning Programme." *Iraq* 66: 177-85.

Oates, D. 1968. *Studies in the Ancient History of Northen Iraq*. London: British Academy.

Pedersén, O. 1985. *Archives and Libraries in the City of Assur.* Vol. 1. Uppsala: Uppsala University.

—. 1997. "The Use of Writing among the Assyrians." In Waetzoldt and Hauptmann 1997, 139-52.

Preusser, C. 1954. *Die Wohnhäuser in Assur*. Wissenschaftliche Veröffentlichungen der Deutschen Orient-Gesellschaft 64. Berlin: Gebr. Mann.

—. 1955. *Die Paläste in Assur*. Wissenschaftliche Veröffentlichungen der Deutschen Orient-Gesellschaft 66. Berlin: Gebr. Mann.

Schwenzner, W. 1931-32. "Das Nationalheiligtum des assyrischen Reiches: Die Baugeschichte des Aššur-Tempels Ehursagkurkurra." *Archiv für Orientforschung* 7: 239-51.

—. 1932-33. "Das Nationalheiligtum des assyrischen Reiches: Die Baugeschichte des Aššur-Tempels Ehursagkurkurra." *Archiv für Orientforschung* 8: 34-45, 113-23.

—. 1933-34. "Das Nationalheiligtum des assyrischen Reiches. Die Baugeschichte des Aššur-Tempels Ehursagkurkurra." *Archiv für Orientforschung* 9: 41-8.

van de Mieroop, M. 2004. *A History of the Ancient Near East*. Oxford: Blackwell Publishers.

van Driel, G. 1969. *The Cult of Aššur*. Assen: van Gorcum.

Waetzoldt, H., and H. Hauptmann, eds. 1997. *Assyrien im Wandel der Zeiten: XXXIXe Rencontre Assyriologique Internationale, Heidelberg 6.-10.Juli 1992*. Heidelberger Studien zum Alten Orient 6. Heidelberg: Heidelberger Orientverlag.

Winter, I.J. 2000. "Babylonian Archaeologists of the(ir) Past." In *Proceedings of the Ist International Congress on the Archaeology of the Ancient Near East, Rome, May 18th-23rd, 1998*, edited by P. Matthiae, A. Enea, L. Peyronel, and F. Pinnock, 1785-800. Roma: Università degli Studi di Roma 'La Sapienza'.

Enclosing Open Spaces: The Organisation of External Areas in Syro-Hittite Architecture

Marina Pucci

Introduction: Interpreting Architecture as a Cultural Feature

According to architectural theory[1], architecture is a three-dimensional space in which, looked at in one way, the building elements are the frame of a volume, and, seen in another way, the installations, décor and objects, which are in the space, combine to form it. In the semiotic studies of Greimas and Hammad[2], this three-dimensional volume includes not only all installations, objects and furniture, but also the people inside it. According to these scholars and others[3], architecture is a system of signs. The object of an architectural sign is its function[4], which is the reason why a specific space was formed. This function is a structure of forces which change from time to time and define a general attitude towards reality[5]. The link between space and function, i.e. between the sign and its object[6], depends on the concept and ideas of the people, as members of a community, who use this sign; it is consequently dependent on culture.

The analysis of architecture therefore provides us with information on the culture which produced it, allows us to determine influences on neighbouring cultural groups and is a main task of archaeological research. Archaeological excavations provide us with a space without humans, with few objects, partially destroyed installations, and partially preserved structures. Thus, the first archaeological step towards the interpretation of a structure is to reconstruct[7], according to the information gained during excavation, the volume of the structure itself, its decoration and its internal arrangement, and to analyse all these elements together.

Secondly, as spaces were neither built nor destroyed at once, but underwent several changes, interpreting the different phases of use of a structure is also a necessary step before we start to analyse a building as a sign.

The aim of this paper is to demonstrate that the architectural arrangement of external areas in Syro-Hittite town centres is a peculiar feature of these towns. I will attempt to shed light on their meaning, the object of the sign, to sketch out how this spatial organisation comes into being as the result of a fusion of two pre-existing traditions, to establish the cultural boundaries of this area and the differences to the neighbouring Assyrian culture. The two necessary steps leading to this analysis, i.e. the reconstruction of the sign and the sequence of the building periods, were the object of my PhD[8] work and form the basis of this further analysis.

1 Zevi 1997; Goldzamt 1976, 236-7; Clemente and de Rubertis 2001.
2 Greimas 1966; Greimas et al. 1970; Hammad 2003.
3 Cf. Broadbent 1980.
4 Eco 1980; Brusasco 1992.
5 Mukarovský 1989, 149.
6 Rapoport (1982, 35-53) affirms that architecture (the "built environment") always carries a meaning, which should be investigated through models of non-verbal communication. This meaning corresponds to the object of a sign.
7 About reconstructing the sign cf. also Pareyson 1988.
8 Pucci 2003.

Syro-Hittite Spatial Organisation

POLITICAL AND HISTORICAL SITUATION

The terms 'Syro-Hittite', neo-Hittite, Late Hittite or Aramean-Luwian are used to designate several urban centres which flourished during the first centuries of the early Iron Age in a geographical area limited by the river Halys (north), the river Khabour (east), the Ad-Duruz mountains (south) and the river Seyhan (west). The process of growth of these towns dates back to the late Bronze Age, when this geographical area was in large part under the political control of the Hittite Empire. Their decline coincides with the Assyrian conquest of this area over a period spanning the eighth and the seventh centuries B.C.[9].

During the early Iron Age, this geographical area was divided into several countries, characterised by the simultaneous use of two written languages, Luwian (a Hittite dialect) and Aramean[10], by the lack of definite boundaries separating them, as well as by fortified capitals, the seats of the rulers.

Archaeological investigations on these sites started at the end of the 19th century; first reports date back to 1893, with the publication of the first volume of the excavations in Zincirli[11]. In the following sixty years, reports of excavations in Syro-Hittite centres have been published continuously. At two sites, Zincirli and Tell Halaf, excavations uncovered most of the layout of the acropolis and provided us with the largest amount of detailed information. Therefore, the analysis focuses on spatial organisation at these two sites.

ZINCIRLI: THE FIRST BUILDING PERIOD

The general layout (Taf. 24) of the town of Zincirli is characterised by a walled lower town and a fortified acropolis[12]. The town wall consists of two concentric circular walls, with a gap of approximately 7 m between them. It was possible to access the town through three gates. All three gates (Taf. 24) follow a similar plan: an internal building with protruding towers consisting of two gate passages and a gate chamber, and an external structure with towers and one passage. This arrangement with a large enclosed area limited by the two walls fulfils obviously defensive functions: here the enemies could be trapped under the fire of defenders atop the town walls and the towers. The southern gate A stands out from the other ones due to its dimensions and décor. It consists of two separate structures: in each there were a gate chamber of approximately 100 m^2 and two passages. A total of six towers marked the structure. A long paved sloping gateway of 57 m led to the lower town.

The location of this gate on the same axis as the only entrance to the acropolis suggests that it was the main access to the town and therefore the six towers, visible from far away, emphasised the strength and the 'inaccessibility' of the town itself.

Carved orthostats and lion jambs enclosed the northern end of the internal courtyard (A/3), which extended over approximately 300 m^2[13]. The orthostats had carvings showing four different subjects: battle scenes, hunting, ceremonies and the underworld. None of the human figures carved on these orthostats can be identified as a specific individual. The hunting and war scenes can be interpreted as reflecting the power of the town and of its inhabitants over and in contrast to the outside world represented by both enemies and wild animals, and they fit within a location which physically marks the border between the 'we' (referring to the town) and the 'others' (referring to the wilderness outside the town). The fantastic figures represented the underworld. Here, the boundary between life and death was represented, again reflecting two opposing worlds (civilisation / wilderness, life / underworld, us / enemies). What is architecturally interesting is that these orthostats refer to and were visible only from this courtyard, and those located at the external corners and not visible due to the vicinity at this point of the external wall do not bear any reliefs.

9 For a general historical introduction see Hawkins 1982.
10 Hawkins 1995.
11 Luschan 1893.
12 Koldewey 1898, 103-31.
13 Luschan 1902, 202-8, pl. 34.

This enclosed space therefore acquires a second symbolic meaning. Due to the fact that it could contain a large number of persons, and that its formal architectural elements, such as the pebbled floor or the carved orthostats, imply that the space was not planned solely for military use, it is possible to propose the hypothesis that it might have been an area where rituals were performed. These rituals are connected to the context, to the space in which they were celebrated, i.e. to the boundary. They would strengthen the identity of the community[14] through the distinction between the community who leaves behind this border and the external world.

150 meters to the north, gate D[15] was the only access to the mound (Taf. 25.1); its general layout consisted of an internal passage room, two flanking towers and two sills. The imposing towers, the narrow passages (4.8 m) and the difference in height in comparison with the lower town (2.5 m) fulfil the expected defensive function. This structure, located at a higher position than the lower town, accessed by a sloping street, represented the acropolis, it was the representation of the powers which were ruling and living on the mound. The floor was pebbled and the thresholds consisted of square slabs, the gate had a non-covered drainage system, the sides of the walls were covered with square orthostats standing on stone bases.

There were two limited spaces inside this building: an external space (D/a) flanked by the towers, and a gate chamber (D/b). The two areas (D/a and D/b) are similar in size and formal architectural elements (floor, orthostats, drainage system). However, they differed with respect to two features: the orthostats in D/a are carved while those in D/b are plain, D/b was covered and therefore dark, while D/a was unroofed, allowing light to enter, and more accessible.

The themes represented in this external area are in part similar to those carved in gate A: battle scenes, hunting, funerary rituals and representations of gods[16]. On these orthostats, the funerary meal[17] again represents the two opposing worlds of death and life and fits within a place of passage as a gate. None of the human figures (hunters or warriors), as in the decorations of A, can be identified as representing a specific king, this time in contrast to the representation of the gods, who have identifying features[18]. These carved gods are represented moving into the same direction, performing a procession. We can also make a good case for assuming that the humans who acted as hunters and warriors and who were not identified represented members of the community. Here again, attention was focused on the religious elements, on the location as representing a boundary.

In the northwestern area of the acropolis, a third external space seems to represent the arrival point of the route (Taf. 25.1 and Abb. 1). Only stone lion jambs and a paved street leading through gate Q to courtyard M+R are preserved[19]. Here, the layout of the gate is reconstructed according to the archaeological remains: two flanking towers and one gate passage. No traces of means of closing the gate were found. This structure had the obvious function of marking out the entrance to an area, of monitoring those who were entering it and furthermore of emphasising that the space people were entering had a representative function. A standing statue was erected just to the north of the gate facing the extent outside the complex. The statue had a direct relationship with the area adjoining gate Q, limited to the west and to the south by the gate Q and building J. Several hollow cup marks were dug into the basis of the statue, revealing that libation[20] rituals were carried out in front of it. Due also to a lack of obviously divine features and to the presence of characteristics typifying funerary monuments, scholars such as D. Bonatz[21] suggested that statues of this kind were possibly funerary monuments. In this case, due to the size, to the fact that it rested on a lion base[22] and its location at an arrival point of a route, the statue probably represented an ancestor in the rulers' dynasty or indeed its founder, recognised through other inscriptions[23]. Thus, it is possible to make a case for the hypothesis that in this area a ritual took place, that the object of this ritual

14 For Syro-Hittite collective identity cf. Bonatz 2000, 161-5; Bonatz 2001.
15 Koldewey 1898, 122-7.
16 Luschan 1902, 208-29; Orthmann 1971, pls. 57-9.
17 Bonatz 2000, 60.
18 Such as lightning or a mirror (Black and Green 1992).
19 Luschan 1911, 362-9; Jacoby 1911, 288-9.
20 Ussishkin 1975; Jacoby 1911, fig. 194.
21 Bonatz 2000, 25-6; cf. Voos 1988.
22 Bonatz 2000, 105-6.
23 Hawkins 1982, 396.

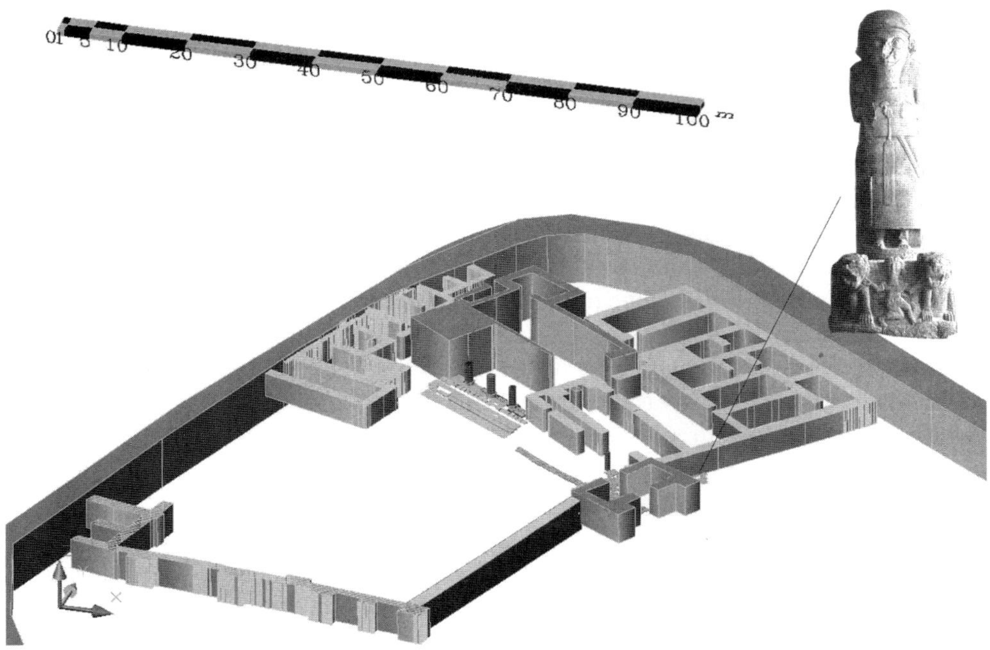

Abb. 1. Zincirli: 3D view of the northwestern area during the first building period. Drawing: author.

was an ancestor, and that this area might have been the last stop on a route coming from the southern gate of the town. Moreover, the subject, which was represented in each area, tended to reflect the identity of the town, to show the difference between 'us' and 'the others' and in addition to identify this 'us' as identical with the dynasty and the 'role' of the king, whose residence was clearly visible behind the statue. However, it remained a non-personal cult of the king, rather a worshipping of the figure of the founder, with whom identification was probably easier.

Religious representation is limited to these external areas. Once people entered the building complex they arrived in the large pebbled courtyard M+R[24] surrounded by four buildings (Abb. 1): the stone stairs leading to the columned porch of K and the original entrance of J to the north, the wall around the mound to the west, the long wall of Ab3 to the west and to the south, and Q to the east. The significance of this large courtyard was no longer linked to the community or to a common ancestor, but rather to the king who built it, and it celebrated his power through elevated representative and receptive structures of an imposing nature, and through self-representation at the entrances of the buildings[25]. The unroofed areas inside the complex remain the focus of this demonstration of power: through porticoes which in part show the structures, through the elevations of higher buildings which rise in the courtyard, and through orthostats depicting the king himself.

ZINCIRLI 2: THE CONSTRUCTION OF AN AREA BETWEEN THE GATES

In the course of time, the town suffered considerable destruction and underwent numerous architectural changes. The main changes concerning spatial organisation of the acropolis (Taf. 25.2) had to do with the construction of an internal wall around the mound, so that anyone entering the acropolis had to pass through a second gate (E). The area between both gates to the mound area was a large space (2400 m^2) surrounded by walls and accessible from two gates without internal constructions[26]. The main features of this area are the presence of an ash layer 1.5 m thick which starts at gate D and bridges the difference

24 Jacoby 1911, 267-88.
25 The carved and inscribed orthostat representing Kilamuwa was found at the entrance to building J (inscription KI: Tropper 1993, 27-46).
26 Koldewey 1898, 127-33.

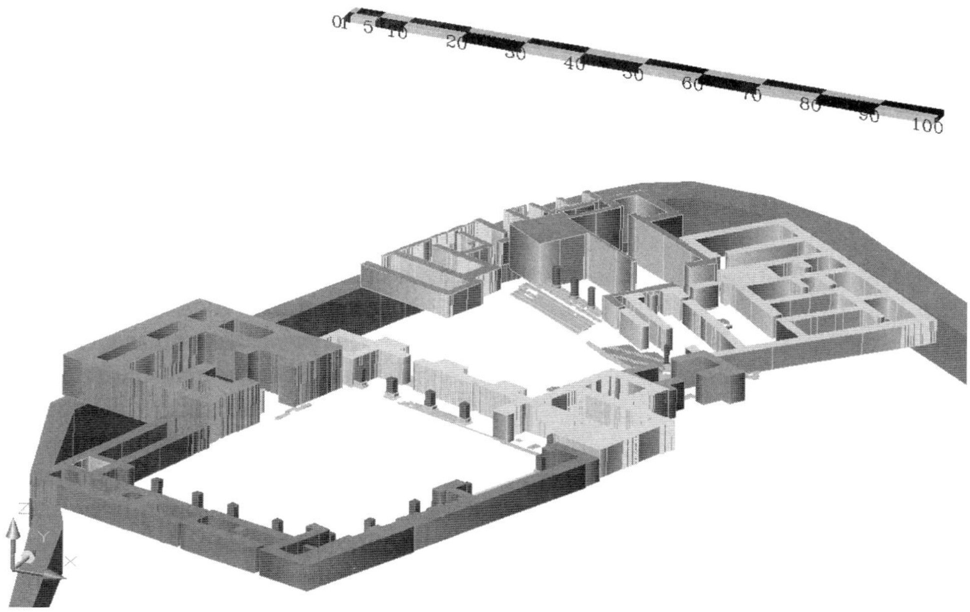

Abb. 2. Zincirli: 3D view of the northwestern area during the second building period. Drawing: author.

in height between the elevation of the paving in D and the elevation of the paving in E (over a distance of 25 m). Five statues of lions were found inside the ash layer, lying on one side, forming a semi-circle[27]. Next to the mouth of each statue was found a stone bowl. We can argue that the statues were buried as sacred figures. The ash surrounding them and the bowls near their heads are testimony to rituals in this area. There are no other clues available for investigating how this area was used after the statues were buried. However, the area near gate Q lost its ritual meaning as the statue previously standing there was buried next to its base, which then remained empty. Apparently, no other statue replaced the damaged one.

By contrast, the representative area to the west[28] gained a wider importance (Abb. 2): the area was divided into a working storage and private area to the north and a representative reception area to the south. The so-called "Nordwestlicher Hallenbau" (NWH in pl. 2B) to the south of courtyard M had bastions, which established a fortified limit to the courtyard; streets paved with different materials marked the routes crossing M; the porch façades of K and J constituted an open frame to the north. Similar attention to the architectural frames was applied in the layout of the southern court R: the frames limiting it were completely open with pillars sustaining the lintel of the buildings. Within this open and deep boundary, H III rose above the landscape, also visible from outside the mound. Building P, to the south, fulfilled a boundary function in order to represent an architectural stage effect for the court.

Like the decoration of the jambs of the so-called "Nordöstlicher Hallenbau"[29] (NÖH in pl. 2B), the external decoration of H III celebrates the kingship, the person of a particular king (Bar Rakib) and his residence[30]. We face in this case a shift in the meaning of spatial organisation: during the first building period the spatial organisation of the gate and of the areas external to the built complexes started from the town gate A through the gate of the mound area culminating in the area next to the representative complex on the northwestern edge of the mound. The location of the statue next to but outside the residence of the king 'quoted' a direct connection between the king as representative of a dynasty and member of a community, which was different from what it was outside. The king gained his power as a

27 Koldewey 1898, fig. 35.
28 Jacoby 1911.
29 Luschan 1911, 350-8; Orthmann 1971, 545-6, figs. F/1-9.
30 Luschan 1911, 338-45; Orthmann 1971, 547-8, figs. H/1-11.

member of this community. In a later period, the two elements (identity of the community and representation of the ruling class) are separated. The emphasis is still laid on the border, probably as a tradition, but a connection to kingship seems to be absent. The seat of the king is not the final destination or climax of a route; rather it represents the power of the ruler as such and not as part of a community. The ruler does not need to legitimise himself through identification with the community anymore.

THE SO-CALLED KAPARA PERIOD AT TELL HALAF

The site of Tell Halaf, which was excavated at the beginning of the 20th century, provides us with some elements of comparison with the spatial organisation of Zincirli. Both the lower town and acropolis (Taf. 26) were fortified[31] from the first building period onwards. During the second building period, which is most extensively preserved, the external area outside the southern gate was occupied by two structures: two rooms separated[32] from each other, each containing a statue seated above or near a pit with human ashes and funerary equipment. The represented figure bore no divine features[33], and probably showed the person buried directly below. Ash layers with votive objects found outside the grave pits near both statues suggest that religious worship took place here. The square surface of the statue and the cup held in its hands can be considered an offering table and a libation bowl for the ritual. This archaeological evidence may also confirm that an ancestral cult was part of the local religious tradition.

Adjacent to but separated from these graves by a wall, the southern and only entrance (ST) to the acropolis was accessible from a pebble-paved street bordered by walls on its eastern and western sides[34]. Two parallel large rooms with a paved passage, flanking tower and stone floor constituted the layout of the gate. After passing the gatehouse ST, one entered a large space constituting an 'intermediate area' between the gates, here indicated as ST/4, which extended over 4000 m^2 and was delimited by buildings on all sides. To the east, a mud-brick platform, approximately covering the distance between the southern gate and another internal one (approximately 30 m) and leaving a small corridor for reaching the eastern side of the acropolis, was the substructure of one or several buildings. Its access was not architecturally prominent: the ramp was not visible from the street, and anyone who entered the acropolis had to make a U-turn to climb to the top of the platform. Consequently, the structures on top of it were supposed to be visible but not accessible. The top of this platform was 6 m higher than the sill of the southern gate. It therefore gave an impression of dominance to those who entered the acropolis. Moreover, for those who were standing on the external street limited by the two walls, the difference in height was even greater; the walls flanking the street blocked the view of the smaller and nearer structures (G2, 1-3) behind them and adjoined the external side of the mound wall, so that the impending terrace dominated the view.

The Scorpion Gate[35] (SKT) and the building TP formed its northern limit. A pebbled street ran from the southern gate to the internal gate and crossed this area. To the north, the back wall of TP, decorated with small carved orthostats, dominated and restricted the view and limited the area. These orthostats were visible only from here, 1.2 m above the paving. Numerous scenes were carved on these orthostats: hunting, battle scenes, fantastic animals and a funerary meal, all of them suited to the concept of limits and boundaries as also in Zincirli.

By constructing this 'intermediate area' it was possible to fulfil two functions. Firstly, a second gate, as at Zincirli, guaranteed better control of the access to the acropolis and secondly, a bordering area with a wall 49 m long, standing on a higher level with carved orthostats[36], fulfilled a representative function and underlined a station on the way to the acropolis.

Once past the 'intermediate area', the northern gate SKT regulated access to the northwestern sector. Its layout was on a smaller scale, similar to the layout of ST: two large rooms, whose long axes were parallel, two towers flanking the entrance. The footings of the jambs in the southern entrance were covered

31 Oppenheim 1950.
32 Langenegger 1950, 159-67.
33 Bonatz 2000, 28-9 figs. B/4-5 and references.
34 Langenegger 1950, 130-41.
35 Langenegger 1950, 87-96.
36 Group A3 after Oppenheim 1955, 37-99.

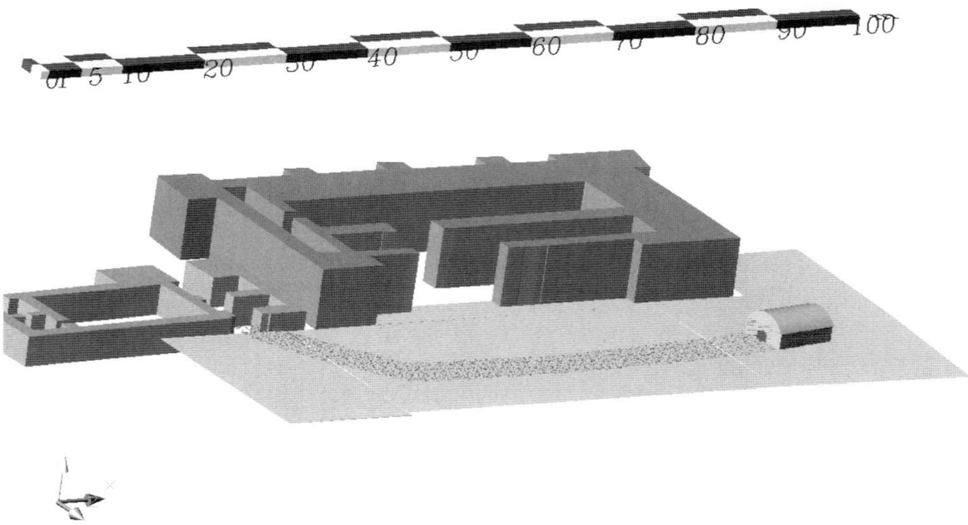

Abb. 3. Tell Halaf: 3D view of the area in Front of building TP before the Kapara period. Drawing: author.

with plain orthostats, alternately basalt and limestone slabs. The two northern orthostats of the southern passage represented two human-headed sphinxes with scorpion-tails looking south and occupied the last part of the jambs' footing. The orthostats' main function was formal: they were not structurally part of the building, this type of stone was not found in the region, and consequently was a luxury building material. This element together with the stones of the paving and of the sill gave an impression of power and richness.

The street leaving the structure SKT ran continuously to the north and after 15 m turned to the west. It was paved with pebbles and fragments of baked bricks (several were glazed), and larger stones bordered it.

When this sector was first built (Abb. 3), the street led to an underground structure (G3)[37], already in existence, whose vaulted roof was still visible from the ground. The square structure was not accessible, as its opening was walled and below ground level. A recess was built into the western wall 18 cm above the plastered floor. In front of the closed entrance, a pebbled external floor was connected to the structure: it could not give access to the structure, but instead led solely to the delimited area in front of the closed access. The structure was intact, and precious funerary equipment was found in the room, which was 5 m^2 in size. Therefore, we could assume that it was a cenotaph, a monument, and that the paved area in front of the entrance to the grave was used to carry out funerary rituals connected to the person buried in it. During this period, the entrance to a structure preceding TP was the southern limit of this area[38].

In a later period, this area was completely rearranged (Abb. 4) excluding the cenotaph to the west. Two terraces (T1 to the west and T2 to the east) 1.5 m higher than the entrance floor, a stone staircase, the small courtyard TP/A and a portico terrace constituted the external area of building TP. A wall separated them from the northern open area, glazed tiles and knobs decorated the external faces of the building.

Two small bastions flanked the stairs, and in front of the western one a basalt base was found still in place[39]. The surface of this slab was 0.6 m above the level of the paving in /A, and probably a statue stood here so that the already impressive effect caused by the bastions and the stone stairs was further enhanced.

37 Langenegger 1950, 100-8.
38 Langenegger 1950, 23-86.
39 Langenegger 1950, fig. 36, suppls. 1-3.

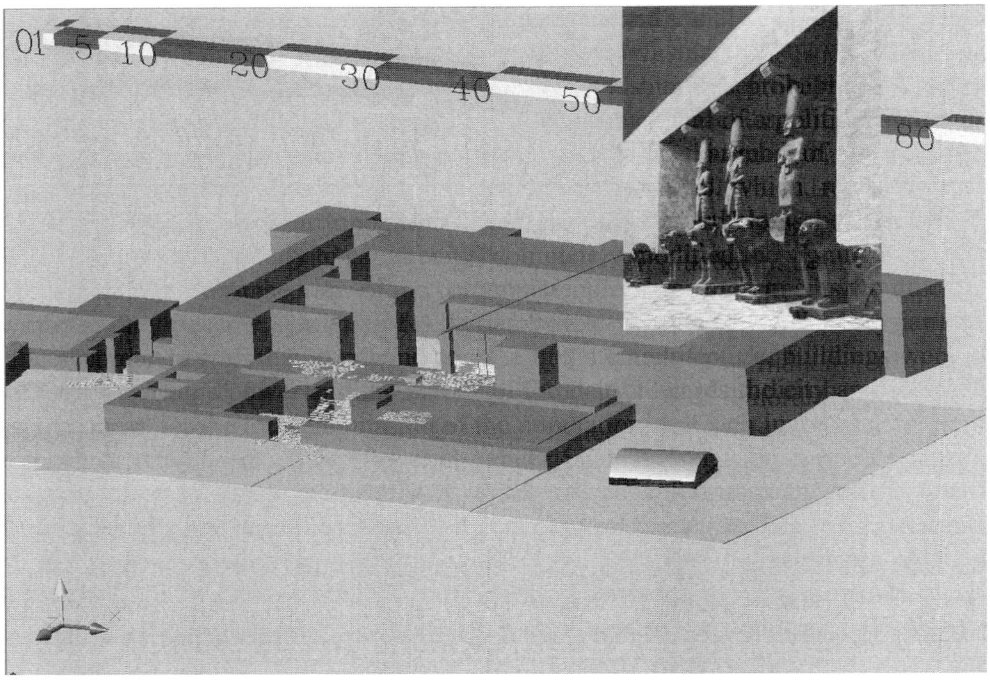

Abb. 4. Tell Halaf: 3D view of the area in front of building TP during the Kapara period. Drawing: author.

Two towers flanking the entrance to TP formed a recess and limited the southern side of TP/1. The niche formed by the towers and the entrance was covered with carved orthostats; here a rectangular installation built of glazed bricks depicting geometric patterns was located, directly in front of the second passage from the east. This installation was at least 1 m high and bore some similarities to the altar made of glazed bricks in the central court of the Nabu temple at Khorsabad[40]. The structure was thus probably used as an altar, which implies that worshipping took place at this altar in front of a divinity which was probably located on the façade of TP. There is an evident symmetry in the scenes carved on the orthostats: these represented, from west to east, 1. fantastic figures, 2. hunting, 3. a god, 4. a lion; this corresponded to the eastern sequence of scenes representing 4. a lion, 3. the sun, 2. hunting. Again, symmetry was visible in the statues supporting the roof spanning the entrance. The sequence sphinx-lion-bull-lion-sphinx highlighted the figure to which all architectural elements pointed: the god above the bull. It is worth pointing out that the symmetry of the decoration and of the architectural elements did not correspond to a real symmetry of the plan: the axis of the entrance was not located in the central axis of the building, so that the building was more developed to the west than to the east. This scenario was created to delimit an area with strong religious elements. Moreover, small supports were inserted in the floor in front of the statues, probably used to sustain libation bowls. Some of these installations bore a symbol with a double lightning[41] engraved into their surfaces. This symbol represented the storm god at all times and bore a religious significance. These elements had a correspondence in the inscription found on the small orthostats decorating the back wall of TP, emphasising that the structure was the house of the storm god Hadad. All elements would thus imply that we are facing a building dedicated to the weather god, and that the possibly funerary ritual connected to the western grave was abandoned in this period. However, the inscriptions which were carved on the statues and on the orthostats indicate that the building was the "house of Kapara son of Hadianu"; moreover, the internal arrangement of the structure did not have religious characteristics such as the external area: the smaller rooms were used as a storage area for a treasure and the central room probably fulfilled a reception function (also considering the presence of the fireplace). We may assume that there were various kinds of worshipping. The

40 Moorey 1994, 317.
41 Black and Green 1992.

ruler presented himself at the same level as a pantheon god through the reuse of orthostats, by making equal in inscription 'his house' to the house of the weather god, probably by living in a building whose external area was a place of worship for the god, by receiving guests in a structure with strong religious significance. As most of these elements show the function of the building during its last phase of usage, we might assume that the structure and the whole area underwent a change in its meaning. In the initial period, the concept of boundary and community was linked to a funerary practice, possibly referring to an ancestor, which may be a first step towards the ruler establishing celebrations of himself. In a second period, the emphasis was put on a specific king; the building became his seat. The whole area still kept its function in emphasising the boundary, but at the same time, the personal cult of a specific king gained the main space in the area.

The Arrangement of the External Areas as a Feature of Syro-Hittite Towns

The spatial organisation of the external areas at Zincirli and Tell Halaf bears great similarity to the spatial organisation at other Syro-Hittite sites (Taf. 27). Tell Tayinat[42] offers a further example of a stage effect and of clearly marked routes. A street leading to the acropolis passed through two gates (XI and VII), it branched off into two directions, to the south (building IX) and to the northwest (crossing gate XII). Here, another gate led to the internal area limited by surrounding isolated buildings. In the later phases, a stone paved street marked the access to the eastern buildings in the area. At Carchemish[43], a gate (the so-called King's Gate) led to an internal area, from which it was possible to reach the palace through another gate, standing on a higher terrace dominating the area. The walls limiting this area also bear carved orthostats representing both battle and hunting scenes as well as gods in procession. The importance of boundary structures was evident at Karatepe, Carchemish, Sagcagözu and Malatya, as mainly these structures bore carved orthostats.

It is thus possible to affirm that the builders paid great attention to the external space on the acropolis and gave special thought to the arrangement of these areas. The setting was formed by several elements which appear to be standard in all towns: 1. the construction of routes leading from the boundary of the town to a specific place on the acropolis; 2. the delimiting of open areas by porticoes, terraces, and decorated walls was created, as a result of which the gates obtained a major significance as they marked out the boundaries; 3. the fact that these open areas were not only empty spaces were people passed by, but places of worship and ritual. Through these ceremonies, the identity of the participants could be formed and strengthened.

Moreover, the figurative programme of the orthostats and statues erected at the base of the walls limiting these areas highlights several concepts: 1. marking the boundary of the community through the representation of scenes, which implied separating 'us' and the 'others' (as in battle and hunting scenes) and distinguishing 'us' (the inhabitants of the town) from the others; 2. the idea that passing the gate implied a passage from a system (the town) to another system in the outside world (such as the funerary meal scenes); 3. the protection of several gods from the pantheon who entered the town.

The statues, which probably represented deified ancestors or the founders of the towns but not a specific king or god, were also located in these limited external areas. Several other examples also appear at Carchemish, Karatepe, and Malatya[44]. These statues were the objects of rituals and considered sacred. The representation of the founder or ancestor as a god distinguished a particular town from another one, one particular community from another.

It is difficult to find a similar concept of space in the Late Bronze Age. We know from the Hittite tradition[45] that during festivities the statues of the gods were also brought in procession to the gate and worshipped there. However, the arrangement of several buildings in order to create a setting[46] is realised

42 Haines 1971.
43 Hogarth and Woolley 1914; Woolley 1921; Barnett and Woolley 1952.
44 Carchemish cf. Woolley 1921; Malatya cf. Delaporte 1940; Karatepe cf. Bossert et al. 1950.
45 Cf. Haas 1994.
46 About the scenic arrangement of Syro-Hittite architecture cf. Mazzoni 1997.

only during this later period. We might consider that after the collapse of the Hittite empire the inhabitants of this region mixed with the newly arrived nomads, the Arameans[47]. We know very little about the material culture of this people in the Late Bronze Age, but we know from later terminology of the region that they had a more family-based social structure (the countries being known by as 'House of [...]'). This social structure probably merged with the local tradition and at least at the beginning had a special importance in building the identity of the community which corresponded to the town. In the course of time, probably once the social and political status as independent city states with their own dynasty had become a tradition, single rulers[48] transferred the meaning of the ancestor/founder to their own person, by representing their residences and themselves as the objects of worship and as representatives for the town.

Among these towns, the architectural and iconographical ways of embodying the idea of a community are very similar: to judge from the excavated evidence, the structure of the architectural discourse in each town is identical, the differences between them are only formal (sometimes the style of the carvings, the materials employed in construction and consequently the shape of some buildings), but do not concern the structure or the symbols employed. Thus, the system of communication (sign system) employed at these sites appears to be the same: in order to communicate concepts such as the identity of a community or claims of legitimacy, they use the same 'architectural language' with the same signs. It is possible to define the cultural boundary between this 'architectural language' and the Assyrian one and mention the differences between them. The Assyrian architecture concentrated on constructing royal residences distinctly separated from outside. The propaganda and self-portrayal[49] of the king were also embodied by carvings on walls, but mainly focused on the figure of the ruling king, his courage and piety, which guaranteed him protection by the god and military success. The carvings were part of his residence and aimed at covered restricted spaces visible only by his court and guests. There was no effort in enacting rituals to strengthen the identity of a community. The main religious town Assur was not the residence of the king, who was the god's deputy and legitimised his power through the benevolence of the god. Each ruler built a new residence in a different place, as if he wanted to distinguish his image it from his predecessors. His architecture was instead focused on realising his personal secular power and mirrored the political status of the empire in contrast to the status of city-states.

When the Assyrians imported or documented that they had imported single elements of the architectural design of Syro-Hittite towns, they modified them to fit their concepts[50]. Several Assyrian rulers documented that they had built a Bit Hilani in a similar manner to the way palaces were built in the land of Hatti. In fact, they imitated only one element of the building (the porch) selecting the architectural sign and constructing it not in an external area but inside their palaces, thus changing the meaning of the sign. In this way, the porch lost its relevance as a module[51] for designing the external areas and became an exotic element inside the royal residence.

On the other hand, when the Assyrians conquered the Syro-Hittite towns they exported their architectural modules: at Zincirli for example, the large residence built on the top of the acropolis was isolated from the other structures, with restricted accessibility, a copy on a smaller scale of the royal residences in their homeland. In the case of the Bit Hilani, the architectural sign is selected, imported and changed in its meaning; in the second case, the architectural sign is imposed.

47 Mazzoni 1994; Lipinski 2000; Dion 1997.

48 Only few sites provide enough information to analyse this shift in meaning.

49 Cf. Matthiae 1996.

50 The origins and the features of the 'Hilani' have been debated for a long time. The term, used in Assyrian texts, was first used to refer to archaeological remains by Puchstein (1892). For a general bibliography cf. Novák 2004; Winter 1982.

51 The term 'module' indicates a part of a structure joined with others to make a building.

BIBLIOGRAPHY:

Barnett, R.D., and L.C. Woolley. 1952. *Charchemish*. Vol. 3. Oxford: Oxford University Press.

Black, J., and A. Green. 1992. *Gods, Demons and Symbols of Ancient Mesopotamia*. London: British Museum Press.

Bonatz, D. 2000. *Das syro-hethitische Grabdenkmal*. Mainz: von Zabern.

—. 2001. "Mnemohistory in Syro-Hittite Iconography." In *Proceedings of the XLVe Rencontre Assyriologique Internationale*. Pt. 1, *Historiography in the Cuneiform World*, edited by T. Abusch, P.A. Beaulieu, J. Huehnergard, P. Machinist, and P. Steinkeller, 65-77. Bethesda: Harvard University Press.

Bossert, H.T., H. Cambel, U.B. Alkim, and N. Ongunsu. 1950. *Die Ausgrabungen auf dem Karatepe*. Ankara: Türk Tarih Kurumu Basimevi.

Broadbent, G. 1980. "The Deep Structures of Architecture." In Broadbent et al. 1980, 205-12.

Broadbent, G., R. Bunt, and C. Jencks, eds. 1980. *Signs, Symbols and Architecture*. Bath: John Wiley.

Brusasco, P.L. 1992. *Architettura e imitazione*. Firenze: Alinea.

Clemente, M., and R. de Rubertis. 2001. *Percezione e comunicazione visiva dell'architettura*. Roma: Officina Edizioni.

Delaporte, L. 1940. *Malatya: Fouilles de la Mission Archéologique Francaise*. Vol. 1, *La Porte des lions*. Paris: De Boccard.

Dion, P.E. 1997. *Les Araméens à l'age du fer: Histoire politique et structures sociales*. Paris: Gabalda.

Eco, U. 1980. "Function and Sign: The Semiotics of Architecture." In Broadbent et al. 1980, 11-69.

Goldzamt, E. 1976. *W. Morris und die sozialen Ursprünge der modernen Architektur*. Dresden: VEB Verlag der Kunst.

Greimas, A.-J. 1966. *Sémantique structurale: Essai de methode*. Paris: Larousse.

Greimas, A.-J., R. Jakobson, M.R. Mayenowa, S.K. Šaumjan, W. Steinitz, and S. Żółkiewski, eds. 1970. *Sign – Language – Culture*. The Hague: Mouton.

Haas, V. 1994. *Geschichte der hethitischen Religion*. Leiden et al.: Brill.

Haines, R.C. 1971. *Excavations in the Plain of Antioch*. Vol. 2, *The Structural Remains of the Later Phases*. Chicago: Chicago Press.

Hammad, M. 2003. *Leggere lo spazio, comprendere l'architettura*. Roma: Meltemi.

Hawkins, J.D. 1982. "The Neo-Hittite States in Syria and Anatolia." In *Cambridge Ancient History*. Vol. 3, pt. 1, 372-441. 2nd ed. Cambridge: Cambridge University Press.

—. 1995. "Karkamish and Karatepe: Neo-Hittite City-States in North Syria." In *Civilisations of the Ancient Near East*. Vol. 2, edited by J.M. Sasson, 1295-307. New York: Charles Scribner's Sons.

Hogarth, D.G., and C.L. Woolley. 1914. *Carchemish*. Vol. 1. Oxford: Oxford University Press.

Jacoby, G. 1911. "VIII. Die Architektur der Grabung 1902." In *Ausgrabungen in Sendschirli*. Vol. 4, edited by F. v. Luschan, 267-324. Berlin: Reimer.

Koldewey, R. 1898. "Die Architektur von Sendschirli." In *Ausgrabungen in Sendschirli*. Vol. 2, *Ausgrabung und Architektur*, edited by F. v. Luschan, 103-200. Berlin: W. Spemann.

Langenegger, F. 1950. "Die Bauten und Schichten des Burghügels." In Oppenheim 1950, 3-324.

Lipinski, E. 2000. *The Arameans: Their Ancient History, Culture, Religion*. Leuven: Peeters.

Luschan, F. v., ed. 1893. *Ausgrabungen in Sendschirli*. Vol. 1, *Einleitung und Inschriften*. Berlin: W. Spemann.

—, ed. 1902. *Ausgrabungen in Sendschirli*. Vol. 3, *Die Thorskulpturen*. Berlin: Reimer.

—, ed. 1911. *Ausgrabungen in Sendschirli*. Vol. 4. Berlin: Reimer.

Matthiae, P. 1996. *L'arte degli Assiri*. Roma et al.: La Terza.

Mazzoni, S. 1994. "Aramean and Luwian New Foundations." In *Nuove fondazioni nel VOA: Realtá ed ideologia*, edited by S. Mazzoni, 319-39. Pisa: Giardini Editori.

—. 1997. "L'arte siro-ittita nel suo contesto archeologico." *Contributi e materiali di archeologia orientale* 7: 287-327.

Moorey, P.R.S. 1994. *Ancient Mesopotamian Materials and Industries: The Archaeological Evidence*. Oxford: Clarendon.

Mukarovský, J. 1989. *Kunst, Poetik, Semiotik.* Frankfurt am Main: Suhrkamp.

Novák, M. 2004. "Hilani und Lustgarten." In *Die Außenwirkung des Späthethitischen Kulturraumes*, edited by M. Novák, F. Prayon, and A.-M. Wittke, 335-72. Münster: Ugarit Verlag.

Oppenheim, M.F. v., ed. 1950. *Tell Halaf.* Vol. 2, *Die Bauwerke.* Berlin: de Gruyter.

—, ed. 1955. *Tell Halaf.* Vol. 3, *Die Bildwerke.* Berlin: de Gruyter.

Orthmann, W. 1971. *Untersuchungen zur späthethitischen Kunst.* Bonn: Habelt.

Pareyson, L. 1988. *Filosofia dell'interpretazione: Antologia dagli scritti.* Edited by M. Rovera. Torino: Rosenberg & Sellier.

Pucci, M. 2003. "Functional Analysis of Space in Syro-Hittite Architecture." Ph.D. diss., Freie Univeristät Berlin.

Puchstein, O. 1892. "Bit Hilani." *Jahrbuch des Deutschen Archäologischen Instituts* 7: 3-25.

Rapoport, A. 1982. *The Meaning of the Built Environment.* Beverly Hills: Sage Publications.

Tropper, J. 1993. *Die Inschriften von Zincirli.* Münster: Ugarit Verlag.

Ussishkin, D. 1975. "Hollows, Cup-Marks, and Hittite Stone Monuments." *Anatolian Studies* 25: 85-103.

Voos, J. 1988. "Studien zur Rolle von Statuen und Reliefs im syrohethitischen Totenkult während der frühen Eisenzeit." *Ethnographisch-Archäologische Zeitschrift* 29: 347-62.

Winter, I.J. 1982. "Art as Evidence of Interaction: Relations between the Assyrian Empire and North Syria." In *Mesopotamien und seine Nachbarn*, edited by H.J. Nissen and J. Renger, 355-82. Berlin: Reimer.

Woolley, L.C. 1921. *Carchemish.* Vol. 2. Oxford: Oxford University Press.

Zevi, B. 1997. *Saper vedere l'architettura.* Torino: Einaudi.

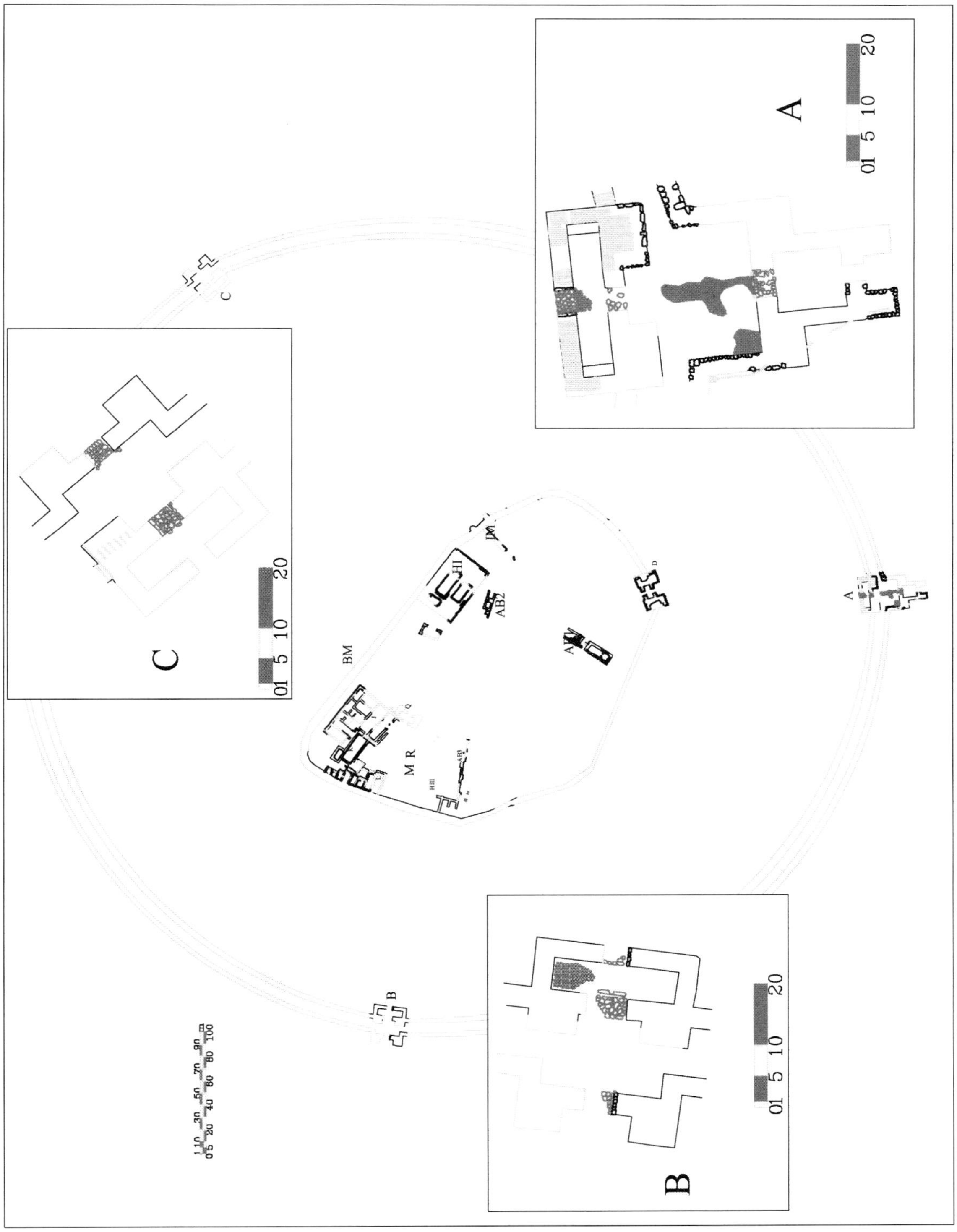

Zincirli: plan of the town with town gates. Drawing: author.

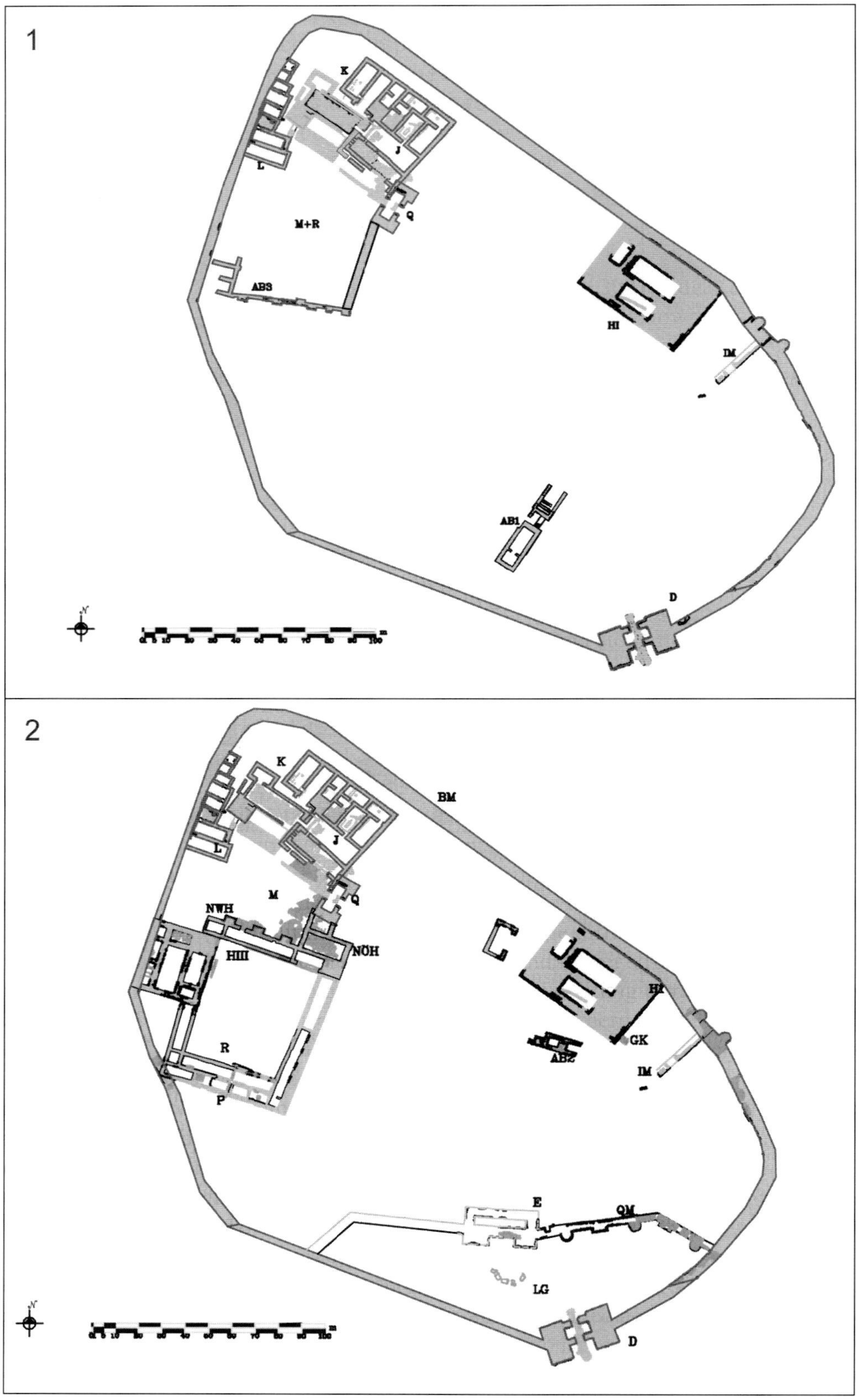

Zincirli: Plan of the Structures on the mound during the First (1) and Second (2) Building Period. Drawing: author.

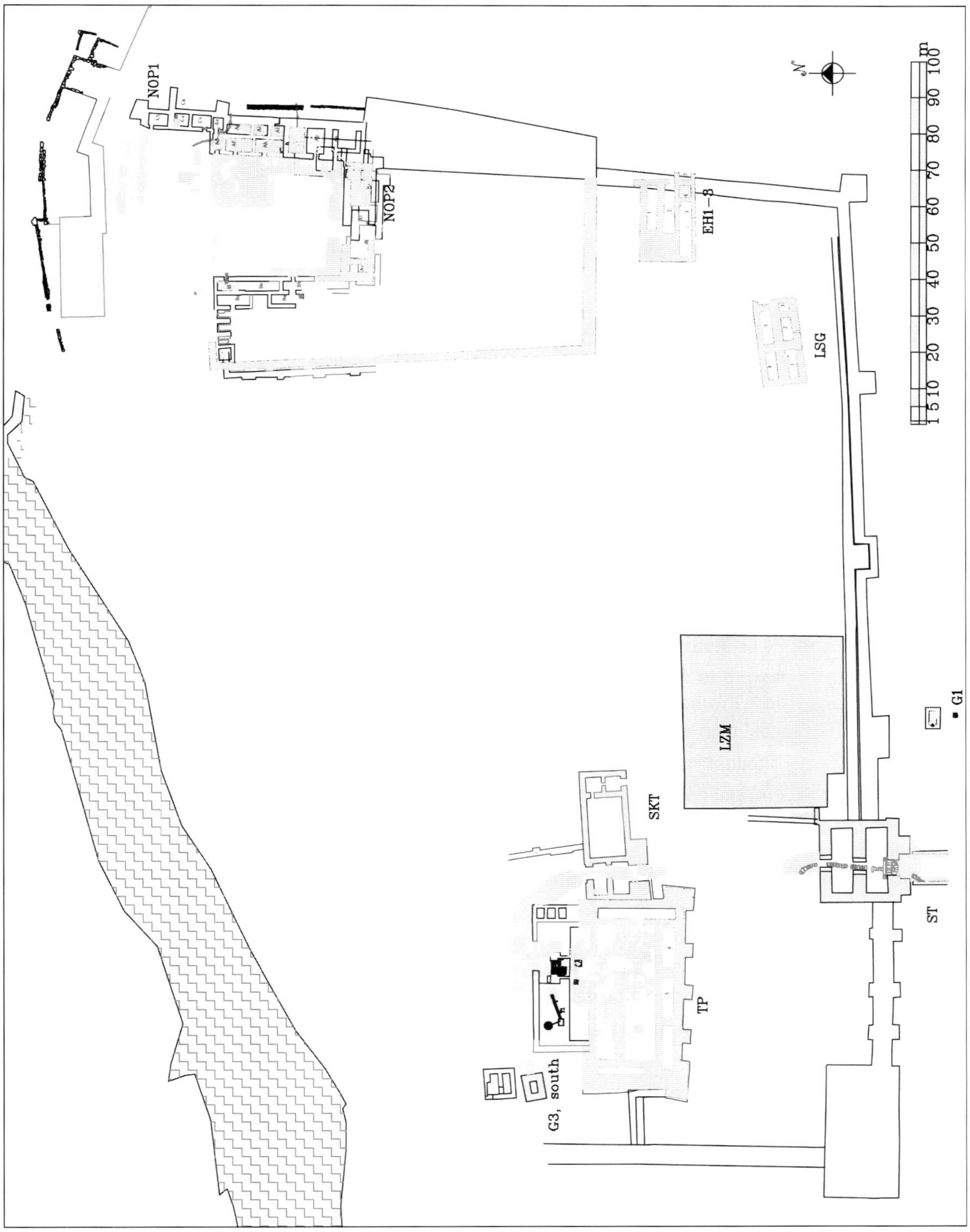

Tell Halaf: plan of the acropolis during the „Kapara Period“. Drawing: author.

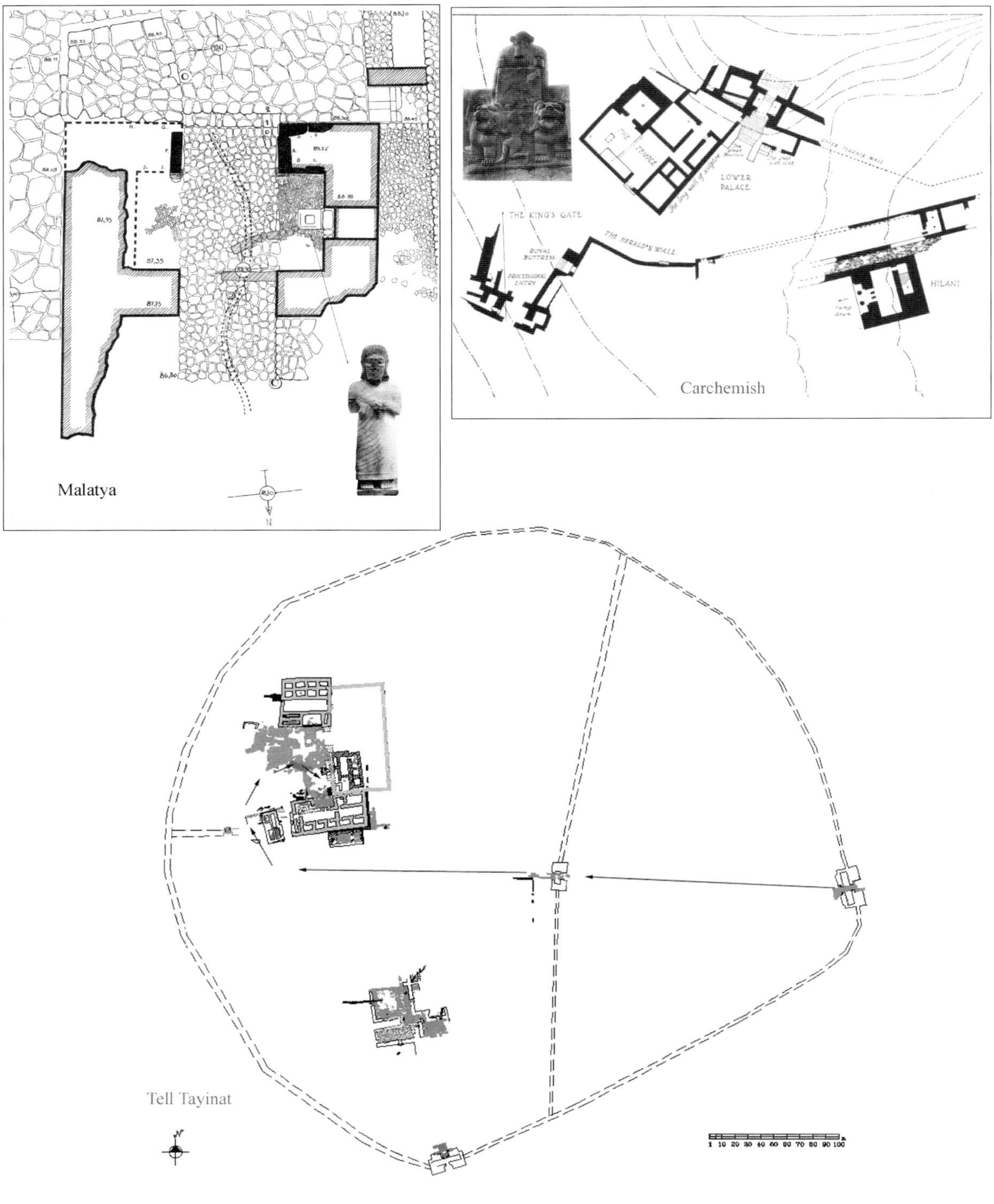

Carchemish, Malatya and Tayinat: organisation of the external spaces. After: Barnett and Woolley 1952, pl. 41a; Woolley 1921, pl. B25; Delaporte 1940, pls. XII, XXIX.

Macht, Raum und visuelle Wirkung: Auftritte römischer Kaiser in der Staatsarchitektur von Rom

Tonio Hölscher

Abstract

The exercise of political power affords efficient strategies for presencing statesmen and rulers in public spaces. Among such strategies, the most vigorous means are political appearances on significant public stages. In ancient Rome, first the leading republican statesmen, then the emperors exploited these possibilities to an extreme degree. In the period when Rome became the capital of an expanding territorial empire, the city developed into a complex spatial organism of highly ideological character: with a sacred borderline dividing the inner order from the outer world of war, with a public centre charged with the dignity of political issues, with sacred spaces of veneration for the community's essential ideals and values, and with places of commemoration of the city's glorious past. These were the spaces where the community of citizens and its leaders performed their collective rituals of domination, passing from outside to the inside, particularly in the great triumphal processions. The use of the temples of state gods for meetings of the senate was clearly ideological in purpose. And the most conspicuous of architectural stages were used for manifestations of ambitious protagonists of power.

The rituals and ceremonies of the emperors were particularly effective. Public speeches were made and state sacrifices performed in front of temples; the speakers' platforms and the altars were integrated in the architecture of the façade. The political space of the Forum as well as the sacred space of the Capitoline temple were used for mass rituals in which the positioning of different social groups in space reflected their positions within the community; a strong hierarchy created a visible panopticum of the Roman state, with the emperor at the apex. Arrivals and departures of the emperor, political manifestations and religious rites, and last but not least the solemn court funerals were staged as overwhelming spectacles in a meaningful political, religious and commemorative topography. Thus, politics were shaped to a considerable extent by significant public manifestations in which architecture and spaces became powerful factors and the living participants played roles of highly ideological character. Significant spaces and actions were integrated into performances of great visual impact.

1. Einleitung: Macht, Raum und Medien

Politische Macht und Herrschaft muss zum einen durch Ausübung von Gewalt und Überlegenheit durchgesetzt und bestätigt, zum anderen durch ideelle Handlungen begründet und manifestiert werden. Im antiken Rom war dies doppelte Gesicht der Herrschaft, insbesondere der Macht des Kaisers, stark ausgeprägt.

An der Ehrensäule des Traian, an der ein spiralig gewundenes Reliefband die Kriege dieses Kaisers gegen die Daker (im heutigen Rumänien) in über hundert Szenen schildert, werden einerseits militärische Handlungen vorgeführt, wie der Bau von Festungen und Straßen, Vormarsch, Schlacht, Eroberung und Zerstörung von Siedlungen und Bestrafung von Feinden, in denen der Kaiser seine Macht *konkret* zur Geltung bringt, andererseits Szenen von ideeller Bedeutung, wie Beratungen des Kriegsrats, feierliche Opfer des Bittens und der Reinigung zu Beginn des Feldzugs, Ansprachen an das Heer vor der Schlacht und nach dem Sieg, Verteilung von Geschenken an die Soldaten, wodurch der Kaiser sich *symbolisch* als höchste menschliche Instanz einer von den Göttern geschützten, guten und gerechten Weltordnung in

Szene setzt[1]. Damit wird die Ausübung der Macht eingebettet in die Begründung und Manifestation von legitimer ‚Herrschaft'. An der Traians-Säule, und ähnlich an der Säule des Marc Aurel, der die Kriege dieses Kaisers gegen nördliche Feinde darstellt, halten sich die Szenen der faktischen Ausübung von Macht und der ideellen Manifestation von Herrschaft die Waage.

Selbstverständlich ist diese Polarität von faktischer Macht und ideeller Herrschaft niemals exklusiv: Jede konkrete Ausübung von Gewalt hat auch eine ideelle Seite: ‚gerechte' Herrschaft über die Untertanen, ‚gerechter' Sieg oder ‚gerechte' Strafe über die Feinde. Und jeder ideelle Akt der Herrschaft impliziert zugleich einen tatsächlichen Erweis der Macht: die stellvertretende Kulthandlung für das Kollektiv der Untertanen, die einseitige richtungweisende Rede an das Heer. Die Realität ist voller Ideologie, die Ideologie prägt die Realität.

Um einer Handlung des Herrschers, über die konkreten Zwecke der Erteilung von Befehlen und Ausübung von Gewalt hinaus, die Signifikanz eines symbolischen Aktes der ‚Herrschaft' zu vermitteln, bedarf es wirkungsvoller Medien. Sie dienen dazu, den konkreten Handlungen die Emphase und Signifikanz der ‚Herrschaft' zu geben. Es muss unmittelbar evident werden, dass und warum mit der Handlung Macht ausgeübt wird. In Rom wurden solche Medien seit alter Zeit allgemein zur Heraushebung von bedeutenden religiösen und gesellschaftlichen Handlungen und Ritualen als auch zur Begründung und Inszenierung von staatlicher Macht eingesetzt.

Wenn man versucht, diese Medien in eine systematische Ordnung zu bringen, so sind mehrere Ebenen zu unterscheiden. Zunächst sind es die Grundkategorien von Raum und Zeit, in denen die Präsenz der Macht sich entfaltet.

- Die gegliederte Zeit, mit dem kosmisch vorgegebenen Rhythmus der Jahreszeiten und Monate und der historisch gewachsenen Folge der Götterfeste, besaß eine Semantik, die den Aktivitäten der religiösen und politischen Repräsentanten spezifische Bedeutungen verlieh. In Rom war der religiöse Kalender seit früher Zeit ein Machtinstrument der Herrscher und der herrschenden Klasse[2]. Die Anlässe, zu denen Magistrate und Machthaber auftraten, definierten und legitimierten ihre öffentliche Rolle.

- Die gegliederten Lebensräume bildeten einen Rahmen und eine Bühne von hoher Signifikanz für symbolische Handlungen der Religion und Politik. Die strukturellen Gliederungen in öffentliche und private, sakrale und profane Räume, in städtisches Drinnen und außerstädtisches Draußen, und die topographischen Orte der Tempel, öffentlichen Plätze und Staatsgebäude, prägten das Leben in allen Aspekten. Die Räume und Orte, an denen Magistrate und Machthaber öffentliche Handlungen ausführten, determinierten deren ideelle Bedeutung.

Im Rahmen der signifikant gegliederten Zeiten und Räume entfalten die verschiedenen Medien ihre unterschiedlichen Wirkungen. Die Sprache wird vor allem zur expliziten Begründung von Macht eingesetzt; dagegen vermitteln die akustischen, sensorischen und visuellen Wirkungen der Musik, der Gerüche und der bildhaften Formen der *Darstellung* und *Erfahrung* von Macht emotionale Kraft.

- Sprache wird in symbolischen Handlungen der Macht an zentraler Stelle eingesetzt: Ankündigungen durch Herolde, mit denen eine Handlung des Machthabers öffentlich gemacht wird; Reden des Herrschers, mit denen er eine Maßnahme, etwa eine Geldverteilung, proklamiert; Ansprachen an das Heer; Gebete an die Götter, Hymnen in poetisch gestalteter und musikalisch gefasster Form, die als solche zentrale Teile der herrscherlichen Handlung sind; und so fort.

- Sehr viel emotionaler wirken zumeist Stimulierungen der Sinne. Akustische Wirkungen werden vor allem durch Musik erzielt: Bei kultischen Festen und anderen öffentlichen Veranstaltungen wurden regelmäßig die staatlichen Musikkollegien mit Trompeten, Horn, Flöten und Kithara eingesetzt; in bildlichen Darstellungen wird ihre Bedeutung häufig betont[3].

Daneben können Gerüche, etwa Weihrauch, am Ort und zur Zeit des Aktes eine festliche Atmosphäre verbreiten. Vor allem bei religiösen Ritualen wurde kostbares Räucherwerk verbrannt; die dafür verwendeten Kandelaber sind nicht nur im Fundgut erhalten, sondern erscheinen auch häufig in der Dekoration verschiedener Architekturen, denen dadurch eine sakrale Atmosphäre vermittelt wird[4].

1 Baumer u.a. 1991; Hölscher 2002, 132-40; Seelentag 2004, 368-404.
2 Rüpke 1995.
3 Fless 1995.
4 Cain 1985; Hölscher (im Druck c).

Mit Musik und Gerüchen werden bestimmte Zeiten und Räume als bedeutungsvoll ausgezeichnet. Sie werden aus dem Fluss der insignifikanten ‚natürlichen' Zeit und aus dem Kontinuum des ‚natürlichen' Raumes herausgehoben. Zu der Zeit und an dem Ort, da die Musik zu hören und der Geruch wahrzunehmen ist, haben die Handlungen die Signifikanz des Rituals, des Festes, des Zeremoniells.

- Besonders starke Wirkungen wurden mit den Medien der visuellen Gestaltung, durch Inszenierungen und Signale der Macht erreicht. Dabei geht es zum einen um eindrucksvolle Präsentation der Orte und Räume, mit ihren Monumenten, Fassaden und Kulissen, an denen die Handlungen stattfanden, zum anderen um die formale Gestaltung der Handlungen und Vorgänge selbst, die Choreographie der Rituale und Auftritte an diesen Orten und in diesen Räumen.

Aus diesem gesamten Feld können hier nur die Räume und die Handlungen der Macht in ihren visuellen Aspekten in den Blick genommen werden. Der theoretische Weg, der damit beschritten wird, kann mit folgenden Punkten bezeichnet werden[5]:

- Kulturelles Handeln spielt sich in spezifischen kulturellen Räumen ab. Jede Gesellschaft konstruiert ihre kulturellen Räume nach den Konzepten und für die Anforderungen ihres kulturellen Handelns.
- Die kulturellen Räume prägen und stabilisieren umgekehrt das kulturelle Handeln der betreffenden Gesellschaften.
- Kulturelle Räume sind nicht rein physisch, als leere Dimensionen, sondern konzeptuell, als potentielle Bühnen kulturellen Handelns definiert. Sie geben der Lebenswelt eine ‚sinn'-hafte, ideelle Struktur, die den kulturellen Handlungen in diesen Räumen ihren ‚Sinn' vermittelt.
- Die mediale Erscheinung der kulturellen Räume und Handlungen ist visuell. Grenzen und Gliederungen der Räume werden durch visuelle Zeichen und formale Gestaltung sichtbar gemacht. Kulturelle Handlungen in diesen Räumen werden durch formale Gestaltungen – als Rituale und Zeremonien, programmatische Auftritte oder spektakuläre Events – ‚in Szene' gesetzt. Räumliche Zeichen und kulturelle Handlungen schließen sich zu ‚Bildern' zusammen.
- In diesem Zusammenhang können Bildwerke eine hohe sinn-stiftende Bedeutung gewinnen. Kulturelle Räume, etwa Heiligtümer, öffentliche Plätze, Grabbezirke, wurden mit Bildwerken ausgestattet, die den Räumen einen expliziten Sinn verliehen. Sie stellten Götter und mythische Helden, berühmte Staatsmänner oder die toten Vorfahren vor Augen und definierten damit die Räume als sakral, politisch, sepulkral und so fort[6]. Zugleich aber traten die Bildwerke mit der Gemeinschaft der lebenden Menschen in Kontakt und ergänzten sie zu einer idealen Gemeinschaft der Götter, der Lebenden und der Toten. Kulturelles Handeln der lebenden Menschen wird bildhaft zur Wirkung gebracht als Zusammenspiel von visuell gestalteten Handlungen in der Präsenz von sinnstiftenden Bildwerken und im Rahmen von sinn-haft gestalteten kulturellen Räumen.

Diese Systematik der Medien gilt nicht nur für Handlungen der Macht. Jedes kulturelle Handeln bedeutet, dass ‚natürliches' Handeln zu ‚kultureller Signifikanz' umgeformt und gesteigert wird: die Nahrungsaufnahme zum ‚Mahl', Körperverletzung und Mord zur ‚Rache' oder ‚Strafe' oder zum ‚Verbrechen'. Das zweckgebundene ‚natürliche Handeln' wird zur bedeutungsvollen ‚kulturellen Handlung'. Durch kulturelles Handeln werden die ‚natürlich' sich erstreckenden Dimensionen von Raum und Zeit zu signifikanten ‚kulturellen' Strukturen gegliedert. Die ‚natürlich' handelnden Menschen werden zu ‚kulturellen Rollen' verdichtet.

Bei den kommunikativen Medien bedeutet die kulturelle Steigerung den Wandel von der zweckgebundenen sprachlichen Mitteilung zur kulturellen ‚Botschaft', vom akustischen Signal zur Musik. In ganz besonderer Weise aber können visuelle Inszenierungen und Signale als Indikatoren von kultureller Signifikanz eingesetzt werden: Der Vorgang wird zum ‚Bild'.

2. Semantik der Räume: Religiöse und politische Topographie

Antike Städte hatten eine klar gegliederte Topographie, die für alle kulturellen Handlungen nicht nur einen festen Ort vorgab, sondern ihnen auch eine kollektiv verständliche Bedeutung vermittelte.

5 S. hierzu auch J. Maran in der Einleitung zu diesem Band.
6 Zanker 1979; Gazda 1991; Stemmer 1995.

Zum einen gab es strukturierte *Räume*, die den Status der verschiedenen Lebensräume bestimmten.

- Die Stadt als Siedlungsraum der Bürgergemeinde war durch eine sakrale Grenze, das Pomerium, von dem Umraum des Territoriums getrennt. Drinnen war der Raum *domi*, der bürgerlichen Ordnung, draußen der Raum *militiae*, des Krieges. Es waren zugleich Bereiche verschiedener Kompetenzen von politischen und religiösen Amtsträgern. Einige Kilometer weiter außerhalb gab es eine weitere Grenze, markiert durch Heiligtümer an den wichtigsten Zugangsstraßen, die eine stadtnahe Zone von dem weiteren Territorium abtrennte[7]. An diesen Grenzen wurden Rituale der Annäherung an die Stadt, insbesondere bei der Heimkehr vom Krieg, vollzogen.

- Drinnen wie draußen gab es öffentliche und private Räume, mit unterschiedlicher, juristisch geregelter Zugänglichkeit und Zuständigkeit.

- Ebenfalls drinnen wie draußen gab es sakrale und profane Räume, mit unterschiedlichen Nutzungen und Verhaltensregeln.

Diese Strukturen beruhen auf primordialen Kategorien, die bei der Entstehung der städtischen Lebensordnungen geschaffen wurden und seither grundsätzlich unverändert zur Gliederung der Lebensräume angewandt wurden.

Zum anderen gab es signifikante *Orte*, die für die Gemeinschaft eine kollektive Bedeutung entwickelten.

- Tempel und Heiligtümer waren Gottheiten geweiht, deren Kulte Bedeutung für bestimmte Bereiche des Lebens hatten, etwa Krieg, Erntereichtum und so fort. Seit der Zeit der römischen Expansion im 4. bis 3. Jahrhundert v. Chr. wurden dann zunehmend Tempel von den siegreichen Heerführern nach ihren siegreichen Feldzügen gestiftet. Die Gottheiten, denen diese Tempel errichtet wurden, waren höchst signifikant. Zum Teil wiesen sie auf Umstände des Sieges hin: Iuppiter Stator, der die Feinde aufgehalten hatte; die Tempestates, die den Römern günstigen Meeresstürme. Andere Gottheiten verkörperten politische Leitbilder: Concordia, die politische Eintracht; Salus, das Heil des Staates; Spes, die politische Zuversicht; Fides, die außenpolitische Vertrauenswürdigkeit; Honos und Virtus, Ehre und Mannhaftigkeit; Pietas, die Pflichterfüllung gegen die Götter. Mit den Tempeln blieb die Erinnerung an die Stifter und die glorreichen Anlässe gewöhnlich fest verbunden. Dadurch erhielt Rom eine religiöse Topographie, die semantisch, d. h. zugleich memorial und ideologisch aufgeladen war, und die durch regelmäßige Staatskulte für die Teilnehmer an den Ritualen erfahrbar gemacht und von ihnen internalisiert wurde[8].

- Plätze, Orte und Gebäude des öffentlichen Lebens waren für festgelegte Funktionen bestimmt, die auch ideelle Bedeutungen annahmen. Im Lauf der Zeit wurden diese Bedeutungen so fest mit den Orten assoziiert, dass sie ihnen einen kulturellen oder ethischen Charakter gaben, der auch die Verhaltensweisen prägte. Das Forum wurde zum Platz der Politik: Schon am Ende des 4. Jahrhunderts wurde es durch Ausweisung der Händler als Raum der politischen ‚Würde' nobilitiert; bald darauf wurde es durch ein Denkmal des Silens Marsyas zum Platz der bürgerlichen ‚Freiheit' erhoben; Augustus hat die Würde des Platzes noch einmal gesteigert durch die Vorschrift, hier nur in der feierlichen Staatstoga zu erscheinen[9]. Ähnliches gilt für andere Orte der Stadt, wie den Palatin oder das Kapitol.

- Stätten des Gedächtnisses an die ruhmreiche mythische Frühgeschichte der Stadt wurden überall verehrt und gepflegt. Am Tiber zeigte man die Höhle, in der die Wölfin die Stadtgründer Romulus und Remus gesäugt hatte; auf dem Palatin bewahrte man die Hütte des Romulus; auf dem Forum lokalisierte man das Hin und Her der Schlacht zwischen Römern und Sabinern nach dem Raub der Sabinerinnen; an der Quelle der Iuturna gedachte man des ersten Sieges der Römer gegen die Latiner, nach dem die göttlichen Zwillinge der Dioskuren hier ihre Pferde getränkt haben sollen. Die ganze Stadt war ein vielfältiges Zeugnis ihrer großen Vergangenheit[10].

Insgesamt hatte Rom damit eine religiöse, politische und memoriale Topographie, die ein reiches Spektrum an ideellen und ideologischen Wertsetzungen und Sinngebungen zur Anschauung brachte. Diese signifikanten Orte konnten für öffentliche Handlungen der verschiedensten Art genutzt werden:

7 Mommsen 1887-8, Band 1, 67-75.

8 Ziolkowski 1992; Hölscher 2001, 198-9.

9 Ausweisung der Lebensmittelhändler und neue ‚Würde' des Forums: Varro, bei Nonius 532. –Marsyas: Coarelli 1999a. – Verordnung des Augustus: Suet. Aug. 40.

10 Hölscher (im Druck a, b).

Man konnte entweder einen einzigen Ort für eine statische Aktion, eine Rede oder eine Geldspende, wählen, man konnte aber auch eine größere Zahl von Orten für vielfältige oder dynamische Aktionen, etwa Prozessionen oder Rituale mit mehreren Etappen, zusammenstellen. In diesen Räumen und Orten erhielten die Vorgänge des öffentlichen Lebens eine spezifische, kollektiv verständliche Bedeutung: nicht zuletzt die symbolischen Handlungen der Politik und der Staatsreligion.

3. Traditionelle Rituale und Manifestationen der Macht: Republik und Kaiserzeit

Die konzeptuellen Räume der Stadt Rom waren konstitutiv für alte Rituale der Macht und Herrschaft. Vor allem die Rückkehr von Feldzügen war ein Vorgang, der sehr deutlich als Übergang von dem ‚Draußen' des Krieges in das ‚Drinnen' des geschützten Siedlungsraumes verstanden und gestaltet wurde, bei dem zugleich der Feldherr seine militärische Befehlsgewalt ablegte. Die Grundidee war, dass der Heerführer mit seinem Heer durch ein rituelles Stadttor in die Stadt hinein und von dort über eine sakrale Straße über das Forum zum Kapitol zog, um dem obersten Staatsgott Iuppiter Optimus Maximus ein großes Dankesopfer darzubringen. Dazu wurde unter den verschiedenen Zugängen zu der Stadt ein bestimmtes Tor ausgewählt, an dem solche Durchgänge symbolisch vollzogen wurden.

TRIUMPH (Abb. 1)

In der Frühzeit, als das Stadtgebiet von Rom noch klein war, lag der rituelle Eingang zur Stadt, das Tigillum Sororium, anscheinend im Osten, wo die damals wichtigste Straße, die Via Latina, zu den damals wichtigsten Partnern, den Latinern führte. Hier wurden Rituale des Wechsels zwischen Drinnen und Draußen lokalisiert, die einerseits der Initiation der Jugendlichen, andererseits der Reinigung der rückkehrenden Krieger dienten. Von diesem Durchgang zog sich die Via sacra als Prozessionsweg zum Forum, dem politischen Zentrum der Stadt[11].

Als dann im 6. Jahrhundert v. Chr. die Stadt unter der Herrschaft des Königs Servius Tullius erweitert wurde, waren die Etrusker jenseits des Tiber zu den wichtigsten politischen Partnern geworden. Damals wurde ein neues rituelles Stadttor zum Tiber und zum Übergang in das etruskische Gebiet nach Westen hin positioniert: die Porta Triumphalis beim Forum Boarium, durch die die siegreichen Heere in die Stadt einzogen, in einem großen Umgang um den Palatin, wo sie dann im Osten wieder den Beginn der Via sacra erreichten. Von dort zogen sie zunächst zu dem politischen Zentrum des Forums und dann zu dem zentralen Staatskult des Iuppiter Optimus Maximus auf dem Kapitol[12].

Schließlich wurde im späteren 4. Jahrhundert v. Chr., als die römische Expansion sich vor allem in Richtung auf den griechisch geprägten Süden Italiens richtete, noch einmal ein neuer ritueller Zugang in die Stadt festgelegt. Damals wurde, nach einem Sieg gegen die Samniten, eine neue Reiterparade, die Transvectio equitum, eingeführt, die bei einem Heiligtum des Mars an der Via Appia begann, der großen neuen Überlandstraße in den Süden, von dort durch die Porta Capena in die Stadt eintrat, und weiter ebenfalls im Osten des Palatin zum Beginn der Via sacra führte. Auch dieser Reiterzug bewegte sich dann zum Forum, wo er bei dem Tempel der Dioskuren, der Reitergötter, vorbeizog und schließlich ebenfalls auf das Kapitol stieg[13].

In diesen Prozessions-Ritualen wurden die ideellen Gliederungen der Lebensräume, Drinnen und Draußen, sakral und politisch, in konkreter Bewegung erfahren. Im rituellen Vollzug wurde die Herrschaft über diese Räume realisiert und stabilisiert.

Die entscheidenden Etappen dieser Gliederung der Räume waren mit signifikanten Architekturen markiert. Der Übergang über die sakrale Stadtgrenze, das Pomerium, führte beim Triumphzug durch die Porta Triumphalis. Ein Relief von einem Triumphbogen des Kaisers Marc Aurel macht deutlich, welch starke bildhafte Wirkung bei diesem Ritual entwickelt wurde (Taf. 28.1): Die Porta schließt sich mit der Fassade eines signifikanten Tempels, wohl der Kriegsgöttin Fortuna Redux, zu einer Kulisse zusammen,

11 Coarelli 1999b.
12 Coarelli 1968. Dazu demnächst eine Untersuchung von S. Schipporeit.
13 Weinstock 1937, 2179-80.

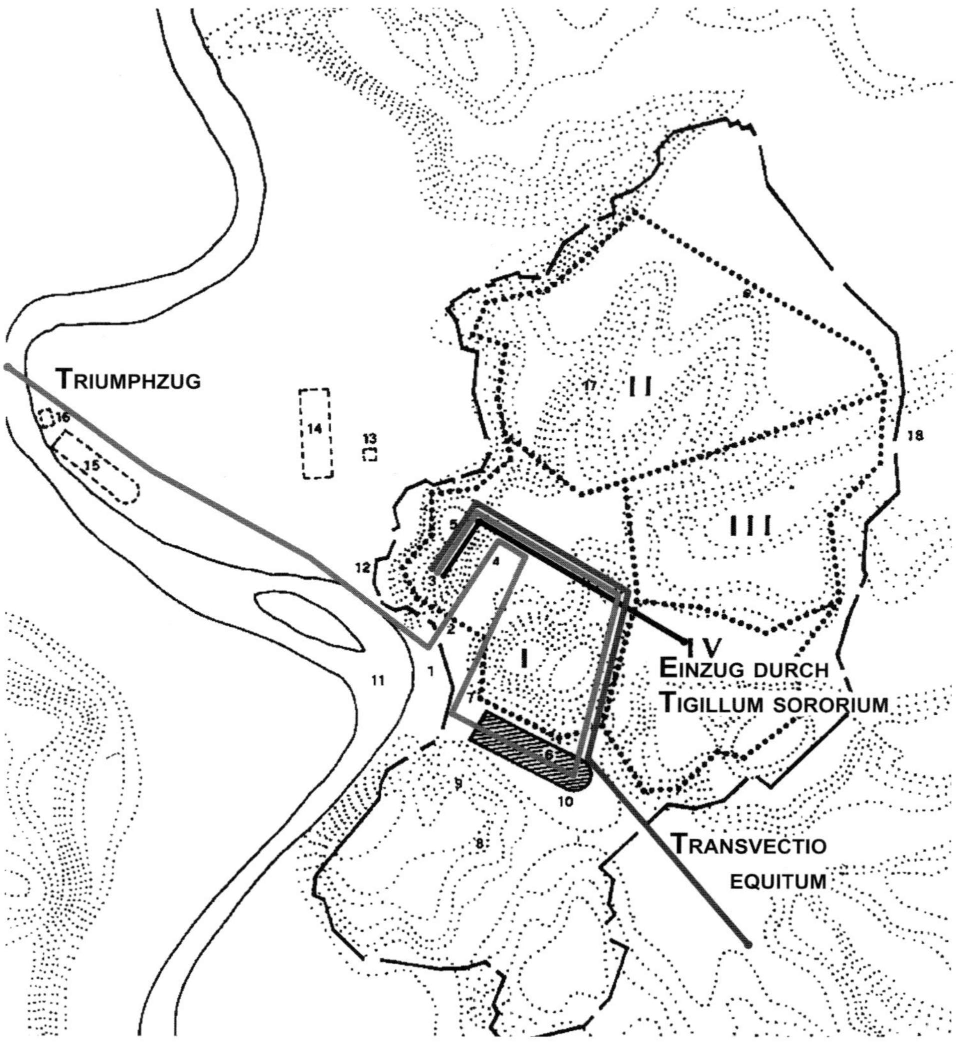

Abb. 1. Rom mit Wegstrecken der frühen Einzugs-Rituale.

vor der der Einzug des siegreichen Kaisers inszeniert wird[14]. Eine explizite Bildwirkung wurde dadurch erreicht, dass der Zug durch Theaterbauten geführt wurde, wo große Mengen von versammelten Zuschauern Ausschnitte der Prozession vor der Wand des Bühnengebäudes betrachten konnten. Ein Relief, das eine entsprechende Szene der Circusprozession im Theater zeigt, kann diesen Charakter der Performanz vor Augen führen (Taf. 29.1)[15]. Schließlich erreichte das Ritual seinen Höhepunkt bei dem feierlichen Opfer auf dem Kapitol, das auf einem weiteren Relief des Marc Aurel dargestellt ist (Taf. 28.2). Hier erscheint der Kaiser bei der Opferhandlung vor der Fassade des Iuppiter-Tempels, in dessen Giebel der oberste Gott über einem Adler thront: Der Herrscher über das Universum und der Kaiser des römischen Weltreichs sind in dem zentralen Sakralraum Roms in einer bildhaften Inszenierung zueinander in Beziehung gesetzt[16].

In allen diesen rituellen Szenen sind die Bauwerke weit mehr als nur topographische Angaben über den Ort des Geschehens. Sie markieren die signifikanten Räume, in denen die Handlungen vollzogen werden, und geben den Handlungen dadurch ihren Sinn. So gesehen, sind die Bauwerke ‚aktive' Träger religiöser und politischer Bedeutung[17].

14 Ryberg 1967, pl. IX; Andreae 1973, Abb. 532.
15 Ciotti 1950; La Rocca 1995.
16 Ryberg 1967, pl. XV; Andreae 1973, Abb. 533.
17 Allgemein zu Architekturen in römischen Staatsreliefs: Maier 1985; Quante-Schöttler 2002.

STAATSOPFER

Der Abschluss des Triumphs auf dem Kapitol weist auf eine andere Gruppe von Ritualen römischer Machthaber, die nicht dynamisch Räume der Herrschaft erschlossen, sondern statisch bestimmte Orte und Räume besetzten: die großen Opfer für die Staatsgötter.

Nicht erst beim Triumph, sondern schon beim Auszug zum Krieg wurden symbolische Räume aktiviert. Der Feldherr vollzog bereits die Eingeweideschau zur Einholung günstiger Vorzeichen auf dem Kapitol, wie es auf einem Relief in Paris dargestellt ist[18]. Anfang und Ende des Krieges waren damit in demselben Raum fixiert.

Auf einem Sesterz des Kaisers Caligula erscheint der Herrscher bei einem feierlichen Staatsopfer vor der Fassade eines Tempels (Taf. 29.3). Es ist der Tempel für den vergöttlichten Augustus, den Vor-Vorgänger des Caligula, dessen Fertigstellung und Einweihung mit diesem Ritus gefeiert wird. Tempelfront und Staatsritus gehen hier eine enge Verbindung ein. Der in dem Tempel verehrte Augustus war als Dynastiegründer die Legitimationsfigur des lebenden Kaisers. Er erscheint in der Mitte des Giebels als ideale Gestalt und noch einmal auf dem First in einer triumphalen Quadriga, gerahmt von den Gründerheroen Roms, Aeneas und Romulus, über den Giebelecken. Der Tempel repräsentiert seinen Inhaber, im Gefolge seiner mythischen Leitfiguren. Der Nachfolger besetzt den symbolischen Raum vor dem Tempel, im Münzbild wie im tatsächlichen Ritual. Die bildhafte Inszenierung hebt in prägnanter Weise die legitimierende Kraft hervor, die von dem göttlichen Begründer der Herrschaft ausgeht[19].

Der semantische Zusammenhang von Raum, Architektur, Gottheit und Herrschaft lässt sich an einer Kette von Bildzeugnissen erweisen. Dass der Tempel für die Gottheit steht, zeigt sich an vielen Beispielen, in denen in der Fassade das Kultbild erscheint, obwohl es normalerweise in der verschlossenen Cella nicht zu sehen war: so etwa in einem Münzbild mit dem Tempel der Concordia in Rom (Taf. 29.4)[20]. Deutlicher war diese Botschaft in den Fällen, in denen die Gottheit im Giebel oder auf dem First des Tempels noch einmal dargestellt war, wie etwa am Tempel des Mars Ultor auf dem Forum des Augustus (Taf. 29.2). Die Gottheit übte hier in ihrem Bild sichtbar die ‚Oberhoheit' über den sakralen Raum ihres Tempels und die darin vollzogenen Kulthandlungen aus[21]. Noch eine Stufe weiter geht es, wenn die Gottheit als lebende Gestalt an einer sakralen Handlung teilnehmend gezeigt wird, z.B. Iuppiter beim Abschluss von Verhandlungen zwischen dem Kaiser Traian und nördlichen Barbaren, oder die Göttin Concordia beim Opfer zweier Personen (Taf. 29.5)[22]. Der sakrale Raum, die Architektur des Tempels, das Bild der Gottheit und ihre ‚lebende' Erscheinung beziehen sich wechselseitig aufeinander und treten für einander ein.

Die bildhafte Wirkung, die in solchen Szenen liegt, wurde nicht nur bei der Darstellung in Bildwerken, sondern auch in der konkreten Inszenierung der Rituale selbst gesucht. Grundsätzlich lag es in Heiligtümern mit architektonisch aufwendigen Kultbauten nahe, dass die Opferhandlungen für die Gottheit vor der Fassade vollzogen wurden. In der Frühzeit, vor allem in Griechenland, finden sich zwar vielfach und aus verschiedenen Gründen Abweichungen von diesem Brauch, etwa auf der Akropolis von Athen oder im Zeus-Heiligtum von Olympia, wo die Altäre exzentrisch im Verhältnis zu den Tempeln lagen; aber bei neu geplanten Tempeln wurde es immer mehr zur Regel, die Altäre in die Mittelachse vor der Fassade zu legen. Für die Teilnehmer und Betrachter der Opfer muss sich dabei von selbst eine visuelle Beziehung zwischen der Architektur und dem Ritual ergeben haben. Der Vorplatz des Tempels stellte einen funktionalen Raum für den Kult dar, der durch die Fassade eine repräsentative Monumentalität erhielt. In Griechenland waren es gewöhnlich spezielle Priester, die dabei als Protagonisten agierten; in Rom traten weitgehend Repräsentanten des Staates in diesen rituellen Räumen auf, die Magistrate, später die Kaiser, als Vertreter der Gemeinschaft gegenüber den Staatsgöttern.

Diese gewissermaßen ‚natürliche' Zuordnung von Ritual und Architektur wurde aber noch zur Zeit der römischen Republik intentional neu gestaltet. Bei dem Tempel des Iuppiter am Forum von Pompeii, der sich nach römischer Art auf einem hohen Podium erhebt, wurde der Altar um 80 v. Chr. in

18 Ryberg 1955, fig. 69, a-b; Koeppel 1985, 204-12, Nr. 50.
19 Nash 1961 Band I, Abb. 177.
20 Nash 1961 Band I, Abb. 347.
21 Ryberg 1955, fig. 36 d; Zanker 1970, Abb. 45 und 46.
22 Traian und Barbaren: Hassel 1966, Taf. 6, 1 unten. – Zwei Kaiser beim Opfer: z. B. Hölscher 1990, Nr. 136.

Abb. 2. Rom, Tempel des Mars Ultor, Fassade (Rekonstruktion). Nach: Kockel 1995, Abb. 121.

die monumentale Freitreppe integriert[23]. In Rom ist der Tempel des Mars Ultor auf dem Forum des Augustus ein besonders eindrucksvolles Beispiel für diese Gestaltung, die sich dann bei vielen Tempeln der römischen Kaiserzeit findet (Abb. 2)[24]. Dadurch wurde die Opferhandlung wie auf eine Bühne hoch über die Zuschauer gehoben und fest in die Kulisse der Tempelfassade integriert. Das Ritual, mit den Machthabern des Staates im Zentrum, wurde zum Schauspiel, zum plakativen Bild der politischen Frömmigkeit, der *pietas*.

Diese Gestaltung von Tempelfassaden als Szenario von Staatsopfern gehört in dieselbe Zeit, in der die *pietas* gegenüber den Staatsgöttern zu einem zentralen Leitbild römischer Staatsmänner erhoben wurde. Im Jahr 191 v. Chr. wurde Pietas als Göttin in Rom mit einem Tempel und staatlichem Kult etabliert. Jedes öffentliche Opfer, vom Kaiser oder anderen Würdenträgern vollzogen, wurde als Demonstration der *pietas* verstanden. In vielen offiziellen Opferszenen erscheint die Göttin Pietas als Verkörperung dieses politischen Leitbilds anwesend.

4. Öffentliche Auftritte von Staatsmännern der Republik

Die Praxis, symbolträchtige Orte zu besetzen und damit den Anspruch auf Macht und Herrschaft sichtbar zu machen, wurde in der späten Republik und der Kaiserzeit auf weitere Vorgänge ausgedehnt, die nicht in alten religiösen Ritualen festgelegt waren.

Senats-Sitzungen

Seit dem 2. Jahrhundert v. Chr. wurde der Senat nicht mehr ausschließlich in dem angestammten Bau der Curia Hostilia am Forum einberufen, sondern zum Teil auch in verschiedenen Tempeln[25]. Dass dafür Kultbauten verwendet wurden, war zunächst deswegen angezeigt, weil Senatssitzungen in inaugurierten, d. h. religiös definierten Räumen stattfinden mussten, wie es auch für die Curia galt. Der Beschluss,

23 Pompeii: Ulrich 1994, 235-43, s. bes. die Wiedergabe auf dem Relief fig. 40. – Ähnlich der gleichzeitige Forum-Tempel von Paestum in seiner spätrepublikanischen Erneuerung (nach 80 v. Chr.): Ulrich 1994, 107-15; s. auch den Fortuna-Tempel von Pompeii: Ulrich 1994, 244-8.

24 Kockel 1995, fig. 117, 120, 121.

25 Zum Folgenden s. Taylor und Scott 1969, 557-72; Ulrich 1994, 57-69, 81-107; Bonnefond-Coudry 1989, 65-136, m. E. allzu skeptisch, was die ideologische Bedeutung bei der Wahl der Tempel betrifft: Wenn die Quellen darüber nicht viel

außerhalb des Senatsgebäudes zusammenzukommen, war jedoch nicht nur von äußeren Notwendigkeiten, sondern vor allem von inhaltlichen, vielfach religiösen und ideologischen Vorgaben geprägt. Man wählte Tempel, deren Gottheiten dem Anlass angemessen waren.

Bei der Beratung über die Verleihung eines Triumphs an einen siegreichen Feldherrn entsprach es zwar zunächst praktischen Bedürfnissen, dass man außerhalb der rituellen Stadtgrenze tagte, denn der Heerführer durfte zu diesem Zeitpunkt die Stadt noch nicht betreten. Immerhin aber wählte man dafür den Tempel des Apollo, dem die rituelle Reinigung des Heeres nach dem Krieg oblag, oder den der Bellona, die eng mit den Ritualen des Kriegsbeginns verbunden war; dasselbe gilt für den Empfang fremder Gesandter. Innerhalb der Stadt wurden die Stätten der Senatsversammlungen offenbar in der Regel nach ideellen Gesichtspunkten festgelegt. Man kam im Tempel der Concordia zusammen, wenn es um Fragen der inneren Eintracht ging, etwa auf dem Höhepunkt der Verschwörung des Catilina, und noch unter Tiberius bei der Verkündigung des Todesurteils gegen Seian. Dort konnte man politische Kontrahenten ermahnen, zur Eintracht zu finden und damit die Göttin Concordia zu ehren, „in deren Tempel sie zusammengekommen waren."[26] Der Tempel des Castor war ein Ort von Sitzungen, in denen unter dem Schutz der Dioskuren die Angelegenheiten der adligen Führungsschicht verhandelt wurden. Im Tempel des Iuppiter auf dem Kapitol fanden regelmäßig die Sitzungen am 1. Januar statt, wenn die Gelübde für das kommende Jahr proklamiert wurden, dazu an anderen Tagen, wenn Kriege eröffnet wurden, wenn sonstige große politische Entscheidungen anstanden oder wenn der Staat in seinen Grundfesten zum Thema wurde. Besonders spektakulär müssen dort die Vorgänge um die Ermordung des Tiberius Gracchus gewesen sein, mit der Volksversammlung vor dem Tempel des Iuppiter und der Versammlung des Senats im nahen Tempel der Fides, womit das politische Vertrauen wieder beschworen werden sollte. Seit der frühen Kaiserzeit wurden Beratungen über Krieg und Triumph in den Tempel des Mars Ultor gelegt. Dagegen war die Senatssitzung, bei der über Caesars Begräbnis verhandelt wurde, in den Tempel der Tellus verlegt worden, der Göttin der Erde, in der seine sterblichen Überreste bestattet werden sollten. Dass dabei immer die betreffende Gottheit mit involviert wurde, zeigt sich darin, dass die Senatoren ihr vor Beginn der Sitzung ein Opfer darbrachten. Das höchste Organ des römischen Staates nutzte somit die symbolischen Räume zur ideologischen Sicherung seiner Macht.

POLITISCHE AUFTRITTE

Ebenfalls schon zur Zeit der Republik wählten ambitionierte Staatsmänner die Szenerie von Tempeln als Orte für politische Auftritte. Der konservative Staatsmann Sulla benutzte mehrfach das hohe Podium des Castor-Tempels für seine Aktivitäten auf dem Forum. Darin lag allem Anschein nach eine politische Intention, denn die Dioskuren waren als Patrone der Reiterei die traditionellen Schutzgötter der adeligen Führungsschicht, deren politischer Exponent Sulla war. Darum war es umgekehrt ein spektakulärer Akt, als der revolutionäre Clodius mit seiner Schlägerbande zwei Jahrzehnte später eben diesen symbolischen Ort der Nobilität besetzte. Der Kampf um die ideologischen Orte traf die Gegner ins politische Herz[27].

Noch provokativer war ein Vorgang, in dem Caesar seine prätendierte politische Machtstellung in Szene setzte. Wenige Monate vor seiner Ermordung beschloss der Senat für ihn ein Bündel völlig exzeptioneller Ehrungen, die ihn schon zu Lebzeiten auf eine Stufe mit den Göttern stellten. In einer feierlichen Prozession zog die ehrwürdige Körperschaft, angeführt von den Konsuln, zu dem neuen Forum, das Caesar gebaut hatte, mit einem Tempel für seine göttliche Ahnherrin Venus, von der er seine einzigartige Stellung ableitete. Abweichend von der Norm, hatte der Bau keine frontale Treppe, sondern seitliche Aufgänge, so dass die Front sich scheinbar unzugänglich über dem hohen Podium erhob: offenbar als Ehrfurcht einflößender Ort für Auftritte hoch über der Volksmenge. Dort oben empfing Caesar die

aussagen, so kann eine solche Bedeutung doch oft aufgrund der historischen Situation plausibel angenommen werden. Überzeugend zur Wahl des Concordia-Tempels für politische Manifestationen: Döbler 1999, 48-62.

26 Ermahnung zur Eintracht: Dio Cassius 46, 28. S. auch Köb 2000, 50-1 (mit weiterer Literatur).

27 Ulrich 1994, 100-5.

devoten Senatoren – im Sitzen, ohne sich zu erheben. Es war eine Inszenierung, in der die Gestalt des Staatsmannes zwischen den Säulen wie ein Bildwerk vor dem Kultbild der Venus im Inneren des Tempels gewirkt haben muss. Damals wurde ihm dies Verhalten als Übermaß an Anmaßung angelastet. Aber er leitete damit unmittelbar Verhaltensweisen der Kaiser ein[28].

5. Öffentliche Auftritte der Kaiser

Die römischen Kaiser entwickelten ein breites Spektrum von Möglichkeiten, Staatsakte in bestimmten öffentlichen Räumen der Hauptstadt zu vollziehen. Verschiedene Typen von Handlungen wurden an jeweils spezifischen Orten ausgeführt; aber auch derselbe Typus von Handlungen konnte an verschiedenen Orten vollzogen werden, wenn er einen unterschiedlichen Sinn erhalten sollte.

Augustus beging seinen Amtsantritt als Konsul, indem er am 1. Januar vor dem Capitolinischen Iuppiter-Tempel auf der *sella curulis* saß, bevor er das Amt an einen Suffektkonsul weitergab[29]. Diese Szene muss eine starke bildhafte Wirkung gehabt haben. Für ihn und seinen Feldherrn Agrippa wurden Bildnisstatuen in der Vorhalle des Pantheon aufgestellt, eines Tempels zur Verehrung aller großen Gottheiten zusammen mit Iulius Caesar. Sie standen dort gewissermaßen im Wartestand zur Aufnahme unter die Götter, die nach ihrem Tod wie für Augustus' vergöttlichten Vater vorgesehen war[30]. Die visuelle Wirkung muss ähnlich der gewesen sein, die der lebende, statisch sitzende Caesar zwischen den Säulen des Venus-Tempels und Augustus vor dem Iuppiter-Tempel ausgeübt hatten. Der hypertrophe Kaiser Caligula hat sich dann tatsächlich im Tempel der Dioskuren thronend zwischen den Kultbildern der beiden Götter gezeigt[31]. Später hielt Hadrian im Pantheon Hof, zwischen den Standbildern der Götter[32]. Hier ist der Unterschied zwischen lebenden Gestalten und Bildwerken weitgehend aufgehoben.

Wie bei den Opferhandlungen, so wurde auch bei den politischen Reden die bildhafte Wirkung vor der Fassade des Tempels bewusst durch die architektonische Gestaltung gesteigert. Seit dem 2. Jahrhundert v. Chr., offenbar zum ersten Mal bei einem Neubau des Dioskuren-Tempels auf dem römischen Forum (Abb. 3), wurde vielfach das Podium der Tempel über die Säulenreihe der Front nach vorne gezogen, so dass sich eine hohe Plattform für Redner ergab, auf die man nicht von vorne, sondern von der Seite oder von hinten aufstieg. Die Redner traten dann vor der Kulisse der Fassade in ähnlicher Inszenierung auf wie die Opfernden an den in die frontale Treppe integrierten Altären[33].

Für Staatsakte, die das ganze Volk betrafen, wurde mit Vorrang das Forum gewählt (Abb. 4). Nero inszenierte die Selbst-Unterwerfung des Armenier-Königs Tiridates im Jahr 66 n. Chr. in einem gewaltigen Schaubild, das Sueton unter die von diesem Kaiser veranstalteten *spectacula* zählt: Vor allen Tempeln standen Kohorten von Soldaten und hoben die sakralen Zonen des Platzes hervor. Von deren Militärkleidern setzte sich die stadtrömische Bevölkerung in weißen Gewändern ab, die den Platz, nach Ständen geordnet, füllte. An der Westseite, zu Füßen des Kapitols, erschien der Kaiser, gefolgt von Senatoren und Prätorianern, nahm auf der hohen Rednerbühne Platz, gerahmt von Feldzeichen und Standarten. Dort vollzog er ein theatralisches Ritual, in dem der fremde König sich unterwarf und daraufhin mit der Vasallenherrschaft belehnt wurde. Die Menge bekam ein inszeniertes Bild des kaiserlichen Ruhmes vorgeführt, und war selbst zu einem inszenierten Bild des römischen Volkes und Heeres geordnet[34].

Welche Bedeutung dabei der Architektur und den Monumenten des Platzes beigemessen wurde, ist an einem Paar von Reliefs zu erkennen, den sog. Anaglypha Traiani, die zwei Staatsakte des Kaisers Traian auf dem Forum darstellen (Taf. 30.1 und 30.2.): die Verkündigung eines Geldgeschenks an die stadtrömische Bevölkerung und den Erlass von Schulden an die Staatskasse durch die öffentliche Verbrennung von Schuldtafeln. Beide Szenen sind vor der Kulisse der Staatsbauten an der Südseite des

28 Livy, Per. 106; Suet. Iul, 78, 1; Plut. Caes. 60, 4; App. BCiv. 106-7; Dio Cass. 44, 6,4–8,4. Dazu Ulrich 1993, bes. 77. Hölscher 2004, 86-7..

29 Suet. Aug. 26, 3.

30 Dio Cass. 53, 27, 2-3. Dazu Coarelli 1983.

31 Suet. Cal. 22, 2. Dazu Winterling 2003, 139-52.

32 Dio Cass. 69, 7.

33 Ulrich 1994 passim. Strocka 2005, mit Skepsis über die Funktion der meisten Tempelpodien als Rednerbühne.

34 Sueton Ner. 13, 1-2; Köb 2000, 124-5.

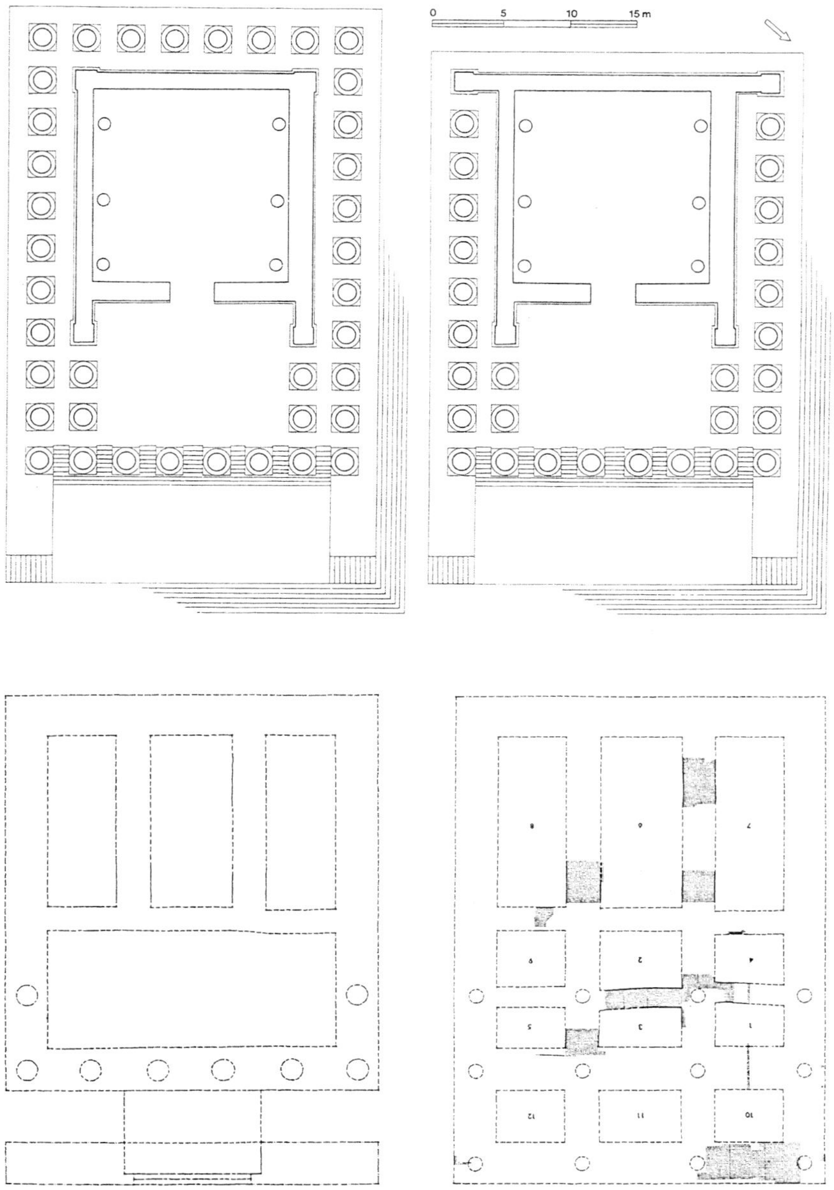

Abb. 3. Rom, Tempel des Castor, Phasen des 2. Jh. v. Chr. (Rekonstruktion). Nach: I. Nielsen und J. Zahle in: Ulrich 1994, Abb. 15.

Forums entfaltet. Traian hat für seine Ansprache die Rednerbühne vor dem Tempel des vergöttlichten Caesar gewählt und damit die Autorität des kultisch verehrten Archegeten der römischen Kaiser für sich mobilisiert. Die Menge steht auf dem Platz um ein Denkmal herum, das einen weiteren kaiserlichen Akt der Fürsorge für das Volk, die Unterstützung kinderreicher Familien, rühmt. Im Hintergrund stehen ein Feigenbaum, der an die Gründerheroen der Stadt, Romulus und Remus, erinnerte, und die Statue des Silens Marsyas, die ein Symbol der Bürgerfreiheit war. Liberalitas, die Freigebigkeit des Kaisers, und Libertas, die Freiheit der Untertanen, sollten aufeinander bezogen erscheinen. Auf dem zweiten relief mit der Verbrennung der Schuldtafeln, auf dem die Architekturkulisse des Forums sich fortsetz, aber thront auf der gegenüberliegenden Rednerbühne, gerade noch in Resten erkennbar, eine weibliche Gottheit, die nur Concordia sein kann, welche dort ihren Tempel hatte. Die Göttin der Eintracht, die das politische Ziel der kaiserlichen Maßnahmen darstellt, wird als aktive Kraft in das Geschehen eingeführt. Der politische Raum entsteht hier durch ein vielschichtiges Zusammenwirken von semantisch sprechender

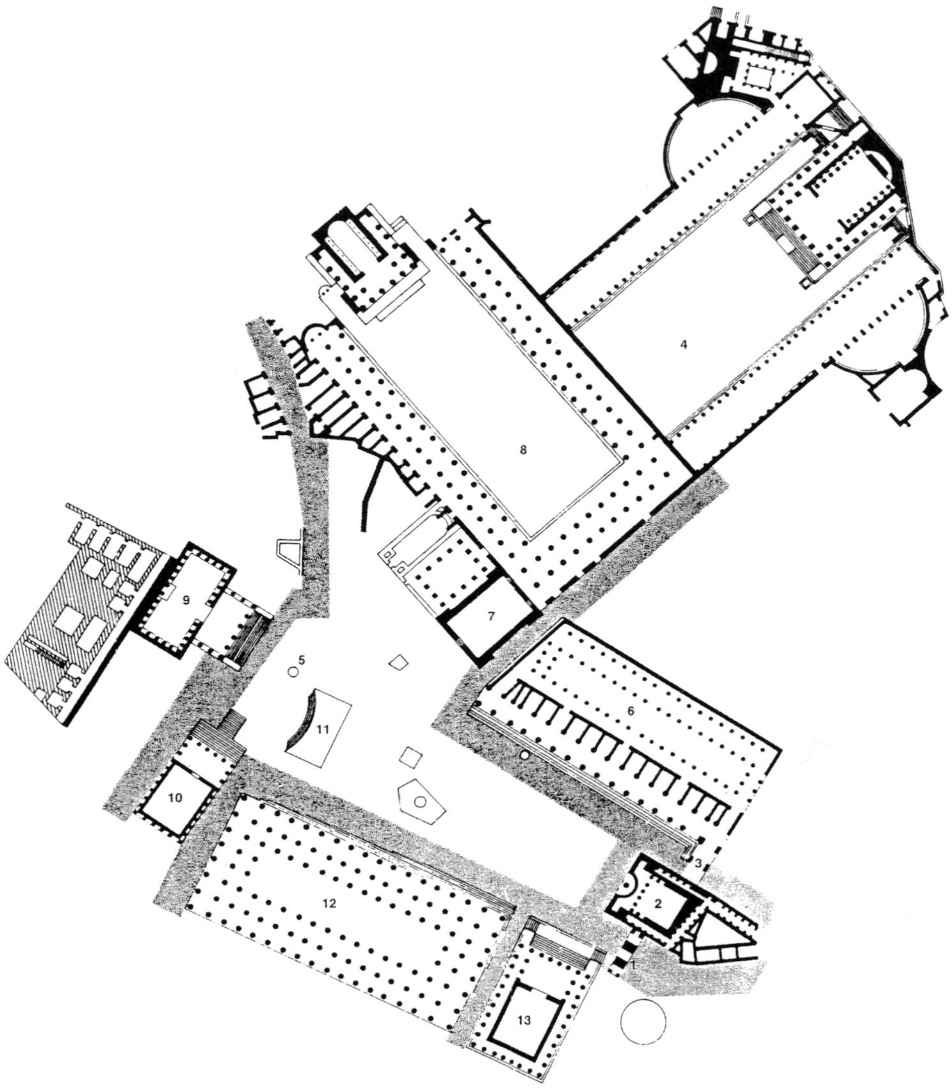

Abb. 4. Rom, Forum Romanum. Zeichnung: H. Vögele.

Architektur, ideologisch bedeutsamen Bildwerken, ‚präsenter' Gottheit, programmatisch handelndem Herrscher und real begünstigter Bevölkerung[35].

Noch bildhafter wird die berühmte Ansprache Konstantins auf dem Forum nach dem Sieg bei der Milvischen Brücke 312 n. Chr. in Szene gesetzt. Ein Relief vom Ehrenbogen dieses Kaisers zeigt die Rednerbühne auf der Westseite des Platzes, darauf in der Mitte den Kaiser als Redner, umgeben von Gefolge (Taf. 30.3). Das zuhörende Volk ist auf die Seite gerückt, so dass sich eine hierarchische Abstufung ergibt. Zu beiden Seiten auf der Bühne aber stehen Sitzstatuen früherer Kaiser, Hadrian und Marc Aurel, offenbar Vorbilder des Herrschertums, zwischen denen auch der Kaiser in seiner frontalen Stellung wie ein Bildwerk erscheint. Und hoch über der Szene erheben sich fünf Säulen mit Standbildern des Iuppiter und jener vier Herrscher, der Tetrarchen, die eine Generation zuvor die kaiserliche Macht neu begründet hatten und in deren Nachfolge Konstantin eintreten wollte. Auch hier ist der politische

35 Rüdiger 1973; Koeppel 1986, 17-24; Köb 2000, 130-9.

Raum im tatsächlichen Ritual wie im Bild in einer unauflösbaren Verschränkung von Architektur, Bildwerken und handelnden Menschen ideologisch besetzt[36].

Der letzte, aber spektakulärste Auftritt des Kaisers auf der Bühne der Hauptstadt war sein Begräbnis. Die Leichenfeier des Augustus wie aller späteren Kaiser wurde zur höchsten Wirkung gesteigert, weil der Tod des Herrschers eine strukturelle Krise der Herrschaft bedeutete, die durch die Übertragung der Macht auf den Nachfolger bewältigt werden musste. Der Ort für die wichtigsten Rituale war das Forum: der genuine Raum der gesamten Bevölkerung. Hier hatten schon in republikanischer Zeit die führenden Familien ihre großen öffentlichen Totenfeiern ausgerichtet; dies Ritual wurde beim Tod des ersten Kaisers, Augustus, zu einer überwältigenden Manifestation der Herrschaft ausgestaltet[37].

Der Leichnam wurde in einer feierlichen Prozession aus dem Palast auf das Forum getragen und auf der Rednertribüne im Westen des Platzes aufgestellt. Die architektonische Umgebung war im höchsten Maß suggestiv. Sämtliche Bauten des Forums waren unter Augustus neu errichtet worden. Es war ein umfassendes Bauprogramm, das von Augustus gesteuert wurde, zu dem er selbst aber nur wenige Bauten beitrug. Die politische Pointe lag nicht darin, dass er als der alleinige übermächtige Bauherr auftrat, sondern dass er alle führenden Kräfte Roms mobilisierte, einen Beitrag zur Neugestaltung des politischen Zentrums der Hauptstadt zu leisten und als Auftraggeber der Bauten zu firmieren: Angehörige des Kaiserhauses, alte politische Mitkämpfer, ursprüngliche Anhänger des Antonius, die dann zu ihm übergegangen waren, kooperierende Familien der alten Nobilität, Angehörige neuer aufstrebender Schichten, nicht zuletzt Senat und Volk. Alle sollten mitmachen, in einer großen konzertierten Aktion des Konsenses. Da die Namen der Erbauer fest mit den Bauwerken verbunden blieben, waren sie alle in der Kulisse der Leichenfeier präsent[38].

Der Sarg, der auf der Rednerbühne an der Westseite des Platzes aufgestellt wurde, trat in eine besondere Beziehung zu der Architektur. Schräg darüber, als bildhafte Kulisse des Staatsaktes, erhob sich die breite Front des Tempels der Concordia. Der Kult dieser Göttin war in republikanischer Zeit in enger Verbindung zur Stätte der Volksversammlung mit der Rednerbühne eingerichtet worden, als Beschwörung der Eintracht der politischen und sozialen Gruppen. Der Neubau unter Augustus, von seinem vorgesehenen Nachfolger Tiberius errichtet, galt der vorbildlichen *concordia* im Kaiserhaus als Muster für die Eintracht des ganzen Reiches. In diesem ideologischen Szenario des Konsenses und der *concordia* entfaltete sich der Übergang von dem toten Herrscher zum Nachfolger in seiner ganzen Prägnanz[39].

Dabei spielten Bildwerke als ideologische Sinnträger und als Vermittler zwischen Architektur und Akteuren eine eminente Rolle. Über dem geschlossenen Sarg war ein Bildnis des Kaisers im Triumphornat zu sehen; ein zweites Bildnis, vielleicht in der Tracht des Konsuls, wurde aus dem Senatsgebäude gebracht, ein drittes zeigte ihn auf dem Triumphwagen[40]. Sie alle dienten als konkrete Bezugspunkte für die Rituale. Später wurde beim Begräbnis des Kaisers Pertinax ein Knabe eingesetzt, der mit einem Fächer die Fliegen von dem Bildnis vertrieb: Die Grenzen zwischen Bild und lebender Person waren aufgehoben[41]. Als Bildwerke schlossen sich diese Darstellungen des toten Kaisers mit den Ehrenstatuen großer Staatsmänner und Feldherren zusammen, von Sulla bis Iulius Caesar, die auf der Rednerbühne und im näheren Umkreis aufgestellt waren und den politischen Charakter dieses Ortes bezeichneten. Unter diese wurde nun auch der Verstorbene eingereiht.

Aber auch die lebenden Teilnehmer der Prozession hatten Bildwerke mitgetragen: seine Vorfahren und früh verstorbenen Verwandten, berühmte Gestalten der Vorzeit wie Romulus und solche der jüngsten Vergangenheit wie Pompeius; dazu Personifikationen der von ihm unterworfenen Länder. Die Gemeinschaft der gesamten *res publica* trat hier in einem gewaltigen Schaubild auf: Die lebenden Vertreter der Bevölkerung stellten sich nach Ständen geordnet auf, visuell unterscheidbar durch ihre farblich unterschiedenen Trachten; dazu traten in Bildwerken die Mitglieder der Gemeinschaft, die aus zeitlicher und räumlicher Distanz einbezogen wurden: die berühmten Vorfahren wie die unterworfenen Völker am

36 L'Orange und von Gerkan 1939, 80-9; Koeppel 1990, 56-60; Köb 2000, 141-5.
37 Zanker 2004, 20-40.
38 Zanker 1972; Hölscher 2000, 249-51.
39 Zum Tempel der Concordia s. Gasparri 1979.
40 Dio Cass.56, 34-6, bes. 34, 1-2.
41 Dio Cass. 75, 4, 3.

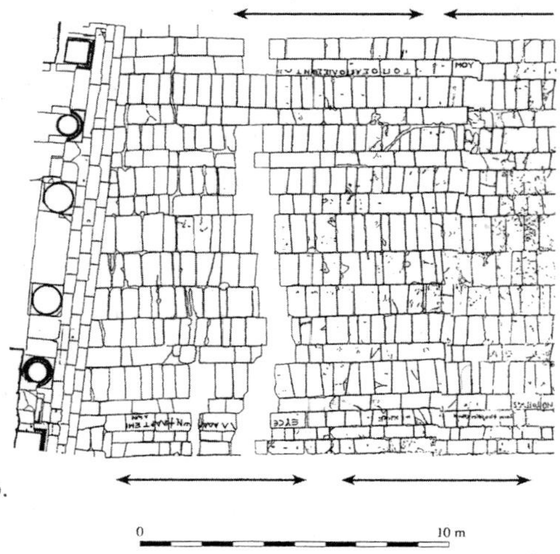
b.

Abb. 5. Magnesia am Mäander. Markierung der Standplätze für Prozessionen am Eingang zum Heiligtum der Artemis. Nach: von Hesberg 2005, Abb. 59b.

Rand des Reiches. Architektur, Bildwerke und lebende Teilnehmer stellten ein unauflösbares Bild vor Augen, das zugleich hoch ideologisch aufgeladen und sehr konkret erfahrbar war.

Dies Szenario wurde schließlich durch zwei Leichenreden aktiviert. Zunächst hielt der Enkel Drusus eine Rede auf Augustus aus der ‚privaten' Sicht der Familie, anschließend aber sprach der politische Nachfolger Tiberius über seine politische Größe in Bezug auf Untertanen und Reich. Für die familiäre Rede wählte man die traditionelle Rednerbühne im Westen, wo schon seit Jahrhunderten die Leichenbegräbnisse der großen Familien begangen worden waren. Die Rede des Nachfolgers fand dagegen auf der Rednerbühne im Osten vor der Front des Tempels des vergöttlichten Caesar statt. Hier erschien der neue Kaiser in einer genealogischen Filiation über den verstorbenen Augustus an dessen göttlichen Vater angeschlossen, dessen Stern im Giebel des Tempels zu sehen war.

Nach so viel ideologischer Aufladung zog die gesamte versammelte Bevölkerung in einer hierarchisch gegliederten Prozession durch das Triumphtor hinaus auf das Marsfeld zu dem zu Lebzeiten erbauten Mausoleum, wo der Leichnam auf einem riesigen Scheiterhaufen verbrannt wurde, in dessen Flammen man den Kaiser zum Himmel aufsteigen zu sehen meinte: ein eklatantes Fanal, in dem die aufgestaute Hochspannung sich löste.

Wie bewusst dafür gesorgt wurde, dass die Teilnehmer an solchen Ritualen in den öffentlichen Räumen durch ihre Aufstellung eine bildhafte Ordnung darstellten, ist nicht nur aus den Schriftquellen zu erschließen. Im Heiligtum der Artemis von Magnesia am Mäander, wie auch in anderen Städten, waren die vorgeschriebenen Standplätze einzelner Gruppen von Besuchern, Berufsvereinen und dergleichen, oder auch von Klinen für das Gelage auf dem Pflaster durch Inschriften markiert (Abb. 5)[42]. Unterschiede in der Tracht und in der aktiven Beteiligung am Ritual müssen die Anschaulichkeit solcher Szenarien noch gesteigert haben.

7. Wirklichkeit und Bild

Die Demonstration von Macht und die Inszenierung von Herrschaft in symbolischen Räumen bediente sich in hohem Maß visueller Wirkungen[43]. Die realen Handlungen, vielfach in rituellen Formen, wurden als ‚Bilder' gestaltet; dadurch schlossen sie sich mit den bildhaften Ausstattungen und Gestaltungen der Räume, mit Architekturen und Bildwerken, zu visuellen Gesamteindrücken zusammen. Dennoch fallen beide Sphären, gestaltete Bildwerke und gestaltete Lebensformen nicht identisch zusammen. Die

42 Kern 1900, 146 Nr. 237-238; Bingöl 1998, 42-3, Abb. 55; Hesberg 2005, 233-4.
43 Zum Folgenden s. Hölscher 1995, bes. 27-9.

Realität der Lebenswelt ist zwar in hohem Maß, aber nicht unbegrenzt nach kulturellen und ideellen Konzepten gestaltbar. In dieser Hinsicht hat die Bildkunst Mittel zur Verfügung, die über die Realität hinausgehen.

Eine Opferhandlung oder eine politische Rede vor einer Tempelfassade kann in der konkreten Durchführung durch Hebung auf ein Podest sichtbar gemacht und inszeniert werden, aber die Proportionen zwischen Mensch und Architektur und die Sichtbedingungen im konkreten Raum lassen sich nicht wesentlich verändern. Das Bild dagegen kann das Bauwerk und die menschliche Figur in ein Verhältnis zueinander setzen, das die ideellen Beziehungen deutlicher macht, etwa durch Vergrößerung der Protagonisten, wie auf der Münze des Caligula[44]. Andere Bildwerke gehen noch weiter in dieser Richtung. Auf der Ehrensäule des Marc Aurel empfängt der Kaiser eine Delegation unterwürfiger Gegner vor dem zentralen Feldherrngebäude eines Militärlagers, das den römischen Herrschaftsraum anzeigt; der Giebel überhöht die Szene wie ein Tempel und gibt dem Vorgang eine sakrale Aura, die nur durch die Bildgestaltung entsteht[45]. Auf der Traianssäule wird der Aufbruch des römischen Heeres zu einem Angriff vor einem befestigten Lager so in Szene gesetzt, dass ein Torbogen den Kopf des Kaisers wie ein Nimbus umgibt[46]. Auch diese Hervorhebung kann sich aus keiner ‚natürlichen' Perspektive ergeben, sondern nur im Bild gestaltet werden.

Die Bildkunst wie die Gegenständlichkeit des konkreten Lebens sind Medien, die der Mensch nach kulturellen und ideellen Konzepten gestaltet. Aber die beiden Medien stehen unter verschiedenen Bedingungen. Die Bildkunst hat das größere Potential an Gestaltung. Die Lebenswelt aber ist der Raum, in dem mit visuellen Manifestationen Macht und Herrschaft ausgeübt werden.

BIBLIOGRAFIE

Andreae, B. 1973. *Römische Kunst.* Freiburg: Herder.

Baumer, L., T. Hölscher und L. Winkler. 1991. „Narrative Systematik und politisches Konzept in den Reliefs der Traianssäule. Drei Fallstudien." *Jahrbuch des Deutschen Archäologischen Instituts* 106: 261-95.

Bingöl, O. 1998. *Magnesia am Mäander.* Ankara: Dönmez.

Bonnefond-Coudry, M. 1989. *Le sénat de la Republique Romaine.* Paris: Boccard.

Cain, H.-U. 1985. *Römische Marmorkandelaber.* Mainz: Philipp von Zabern.

Caprino, C., A.M. Colini, G. Gatti, M. Pallolino und P. Romanelli. 1955. *La colonna di Marco Aurelio.* Studi e materiali del Museo dell'Impero Romano 5. Rom: L'Erma di Bretschneider.

Ciotti, U. 1950. „Rilievo romano e plutei medioevali ritrivati a Castel S. Elia." *Bolletino d'arte* 35: 1-8.

Coarelli, F. 1968. „La porta trionfale e la via dei trionfi." *Dialoghi di Archeologia* 2: 55-103.

—. 1983. „Il Pantheon, l'apoteosi di Augusto e l'apoteosi di Romolo." In *Città e architettura nella Roma imperiale.* Analecta Romana Istituti Danici, Suppl. 10: 40-6.

—. 1999a. „Statua: Marsyas." In *Lexicon Topographicum Urbis Romae*, Band 4, 364-5.

—. 1999b. „Tigillum Sororium." In *Lexicon Topographicum Urbis Romae*, Band 5, 74-5.

—. 1999c. *La colonna Traiana.* Rom: Colombo.

Döbler, C. 1999. *Politische Agitation und Öffentlichkeit in der späten Republik.* Frankfurt am Main: Peter Lang.

Fless, F. 1995. *Opferdiener und Kultmusiker auf stadtrömischen historischen Reliefs.* Mainz: Philipp von Zabern.

Gasparri, C. 1979. *Aedes Concordiae Augustae.* Rom: Istituto di Studi Romani.

Gazda, E.K. 1991. *Roman Art in the Private Sphere.* Ann Arbor: The University of Michigan Press.

Hassel, F.J. 1966. *Der Trajansbogen in Benevent.* Mainz: Philipp von Zabern.

Hesberg, H. v. 2005. *Römische Baukunst.* München: C.H. Beck.

Hölscher, T. 1990. „Homonoia /Concordia." In *Lexicon Iconographicum Mythologiae Classicae*, Band 5, 479-98.

44 Oben Anm. 19.
45 Caprino u. a. 1955, tav. XXX fig. 61.
46 Coarelli 1999c, tav. 35.

—. 1995. *Formen der Kunst und Formen des Lebens*, herausgegeben von T. Hölscher und R. Lauter. Ostfildern-Ruit: Cantz.

—. 2000. „Augustus und die Macht der Archäologie." In *La revolution Romaine après Ronald Syme*, herausgegeben von A. Giovannini und F. Millar, 237-81. Entretiens sur l'Antiquite Classique 46. Genf: Fondation Hardt.

—. 2001. „Die Alten vor Augen. Politische Denkmäler und öffentliches Gedächtnis im republikanischen Rom." In *Institutionalität und Symbolisierung. Verstetigungen kultureller Ordnungsmuster in Vergangenheit und Gegenwart*, herausgegeben von G. Melville, 183-211. Köln u. a.: Böhlau.

—. 2002. „Bilder der Macht und Herrschaft." In *Traian*, herausgeben von A. Nünnerich, 127-44. Mainz: Philipp von Zabern.

—. 2004. „Provokation und Transgression als politischer Habitus in der späten römischen Republik." *Mitteilungen des Deutschen Archäologischen Instituts Rom* 111: 83-104.

—, im Druck a. „La cultura della memoria negli spazi pubblici di Roma antica." In *Urbs* (Scuola Olandese di Roma).

—, im Druck b. „Das Dorum Romanum und die monumentale Geschichte Roms." In *Erinnerungsorte der Antike. Rom und sein Imperium*, herausgegeben von K.-J. Hölkeskamp und E. Stein-Hölkeskamp. München: C.H. Beck.

—, im Druck c. „Geräte und Gefäße für Rauchopfer." *Thesaurus Cultus et Rituum Antiquorum* Band 5 (2006).

Kern, O. 1900. *Die Inschriften von Magnesia am Mäander.* Berlin: Spemann.

Kockel, V. 1995. „Forum Augustum." In *Lexicon Topographicum Urbis Romae*, Band 2, 289-95.

Köb, I. 2000. *Rom – ein Stadtzentrum im Wandel. Untersuchungen zur Funktion und Nutzung des Forum Romanum und der Kaiserfora in der Kaiserzeit.* Hamburg: Kovač.

Koeppel, G. 1985. „Die historischen Reliefs der römischen Kaiserzeit III. Stadtrömische Denkmäler unbekannter Bauzugehörigkeit aus traianischer Zeit." *Bonner Jahrbücher* 185: 143-213.

—. 1986. „Die historischen Reliefs der römischen Kaiserzeit IV. Stadtrömische Denkmäler unbekannter Bauzugehörigkeit aus hadrianischer bis konstantinischer Zeit." *Bonner Jahrbücher* 186: 1-90.

—. 1990. „Der Bogen des Septimius Severus, die Dezennalienbasis und der Konstantinsbogen." *Bonner Jahrbücher* 190: 1-64.

La Rocca, E. 1995. „Sul circo Flaminio." *Archeologia Laziale* 12: 103-19.

L'Orange, H. P. und A. v. Gerkan. 1939. *Der spätantike Bildschmuck des Konstantinsbogens.* Berlin: de Gruyter.

Maier, J. 1985. *Architektur im römischen Relief.* Bonn: Habelt.

Mommsen, Th. 1887-8. *Römisches Staatsrecht.* 3 Bände. Handbuch der römischen Altertümer 2. Leipzig: S. Hirzel.

Nash, E. 1961. *Bildlexikon zur Topographie des antiken Rom.* 2 Bände. Tübingen: Wasmuth.

Quante-Schöttler, D. 2002. *Ante aedes. Darstellung von Architektur im römischen Relief.* Hamburg: Kovač.

Rüdiger, U. 1973. „Die Anaglypha Hadriani." *Antike Plastik* 12: 161-73.

Rüpke, J. 1995. *Kalender und Öffentlichkeit.* Berlin: de Gruyter.

Ryberg, I.S. 1955. *Rites of the State Religion in Roman Art.* Memoirs of the American Academy in Rome 22. Rom: American Academy.

—. 1967. *Panel Reliefs of Marcus Aurelius.* New York: Archaeological Institute of America.

Seelentag, G. 2004. *Taten und Tugenden Traians.* Wiesbaden: Franz Steiner.

Stemmer, K., Hrsg. 1995. *Standorte. Kontext und Funktion antiker Skulptur.* Berlin: Freunde und Förderer der Abguss-Sammlung antiker Plastik e. V.

Strocka, V.M. 2005. „Das Fassaden-Motiv des Venus Genetrix-Tempels in Rom. Bedeutung und Nachwirkung." In *Omni pede stare. Saggi architettonici e circumvesuviani in memoriam Jos de Waele*, herausgegeben von S. T. A. M. Mols, 153-67. Studi della Sopraintendenza Archeologica di Pompei 9. Rom: L'Erma di Bretschneider.

Taylor, L. und R. Scott. 1969. „Seating Space in the Roman Senate and the Senatores Pedarii." *Transactions of the American Philological Association* 100: 529-86.

Ulrich, R.B. 1993. „Julius Caesar and the Creation of the Forum Iulium." *American Journal of Archaeology* 97: 49-80.

—. 1994. *The Roman Orator and the Sacred Stage. The Roman Templum Rostratum.* Brüssel: Latomus.

Weinstock, S. 1937. „Transvectio equitum." In *Realencyclopädie der classischen Altertumswissenschaft*, Band VI A, 2178-87.

Winterling, A. 2003. *Caligula.* München: C.H. Beck.Zanker, P. 1970. *Forum Augustum.* Tübingen: Wasmuth.

—. 1972. *Forum Romanum. Die Neugestaltung durch Augustus.* Tübingen: Wasmuth.

—. 1979. „Zur Funktion und Bedeutung griechischer Skulptur in der Römerzeit." In *Le classicisme à Rome aux Iers siècles avant et après J.-C.*, herausgegeben von Th. Gelzer und H. Flashar, 282-314. Entretiens sur l'Antiquite Classique 25. Genf: Fondation Hardt.

—. 2004. *Die Apotheose der römischen Kaiser.* München: Carl Friedrich von Siemens Stiftung.

Ziołkowski, A. 1992. *The Temples of Mid-Republican Rome and Their Historical and Topographical Context.* Rom: L'Erma di Bretschneider.

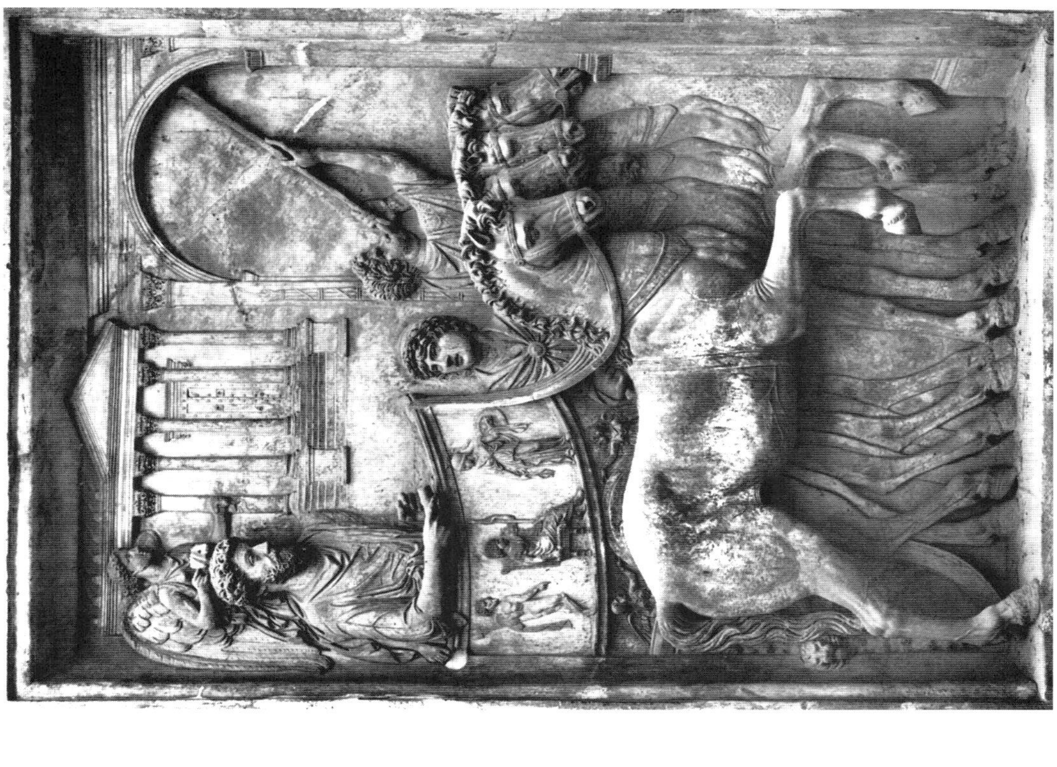

1. Rom, Palazzo dei Conservatori. Relief mit Triumphzug des Kaisers Marc Aurel (176 n. Chr.). Nach: Ryberg 1967, Taf. IX.

2. Rom, Palazzo dei Conservatori. Relief mit Triumphopfer des Kaisers Marc Aurel (176 n. Chr.). Nach: Ryberg 1967, Taf. XV.

1. Castel S. Elia, Relief mit Theaterfassade und Prozession. Aufnahme: Gabinetto Fotografico, Roma, E 27686.

2. Rom, Museo della Civiltà Romana. Relief mit Fassade des Tempels des Mars Ultor (Gipsabguss, Rekonstruktion) (ca. 41-56 n. Chr.). Nach: Rüdiger 1973, Abb. 2.

3. Sesterz des Caligula mit Einweihungsopfer des Tempels des Divus Augustus (37 n. Chr.). Aufnahme: Chr. Pietereck nach Gipsabguss, British Museum, London.

4. Sesterz des Tiberius mit Tempel der Concordia (35-36 n. Chr.). Aufnahme: Ashmolean Museum, Oxford.

5. Rom, Musei Vaticani. Sarkophag mit Ehepaar beim Opfer (190-200 n. Chr.). Aufnahme: Deutsches Archäologisches Institut Rom, 36540.

1. Rom, Curia des Senats. Relief mit Ansprache des Kaisers Traian auf dem Forum. Anfang 2. Jh. n. Chr. Aufnahme: Deutsches Archäologisches Institut Rom, 68/2785.

2. Rom, Curia des Senats. Relief mit Verbrennung von Schuldtafeln auf dem Forum. Anfang 2. Jh. n. Chr. Aufnahme: Institut für Klassische Archäologie der Universität Heidelberg.

3. Rom, Konstantins-Bogen. Relief mit Ansprache des Kaisers Konstantin auf dem Forum. 315 n. Chr. Aufnahme: Anderson.

Figuren des Imaginären. Imagination und Architektur in karolingischer Zeit

CARSTEN JUWIG

Das künstliche Gedächtnis besteht bekanntlich aus Örtern (locis) und Bildern (imaginibus). Als Örter wollen wir etwas bezeichnen, das bündig, vollständig und, aus sich selbst heraus oder fremdbestimmt, deutlich derart abgegrenzt ist, daß wir es mit dem natürlichen Gedächtnis leicht erfassen und behalten können [...]. Denn die Örter sind einer Wachstafel oder einem Papierblatt vergleichbar, die Bilder Buchstaben, die Einteilung und Anordnung der Bilder der Schrift und der Vortrag dem Lesen. [...] Die Vorstellungskraft kann nämlich jedes beliebige Gebiet in sich fassen und in ihm die Anlage eines bestimmten Ortes nach Gutdünken herstellen (fabricari) und errichten (architectari). [...] Wenn wir uns der Einrichtung der Grundformen (formarum dispositione) und kluger Bildzeichen bedienen, so können wir uns, sooft wir wollen, an eine Sache erinnern und können, was immer wir wollen, leicht im Gedächtnis wiederfinden. [...] Die Kunst soll also die Natur nachahmen, soll herausfinden, wessen die Natur bedarf, und dem Weg folgen, den sie weist. [...] Deshalb möge jeder nach seinem Bedarf Bilder zusammenstellen[1].

Rhetorica ad Herennium 3.16-23.

ABSTRACT

This essay aims at contextualizing Carolingian architecture in the comprehensive concepts of art and media set out in contemporary literature. Therefore, the discussion does not focus on preserved buildings, but rather on representations of architecture in other media. Since any architecture is based on an imagined or drawn plan and imaginative agency, particular attention is paid to the relationship of architecture and image.

Hardly any other artefact is as closely linked to the human body as architecture. Buildings are experienced bodily through physical movement: the arrangement of rooms, architectural forms and the staging

Der vorliegende Beitrag reflektiert Zwischenergebnisse des laufenden Dissertationsprojekts *Zwischen imago und Imagination. Bilddiskussion und Medienpraxis am Hofe Karls des Großen*. Für die großzügige und inspirierende Förderung des Vorhabens sei Herrn Prof. Dr. J. Maran, dem Altertumswissenschaftlichen Kolleg Heidelberg und dessen Teilnehmern herzlich gedankt. Gewinn bringenden Anteil an der Anfertigung des Beitrages nahmen auch Herr Prof. Dr. B. Reudenbach und Frau V. Diemand M.A. Auch ihnen gebührt großer Dank.

1 *Constat igitur artificiosa memoria ex locis et imaginibus. Locos appellamus eos qui breuiter, perfecte, insignite aut natura aut manu sunt absoluti, ut eos facile naturali memoria comprehendere et amplecti queamus* [...]. *Nam loci cerae aut cartae simillimi sunt, imagines litteris, dispositio et conlocatio imaginum scripturae, pronuntiatio lectioni.* [...] *Cogitatio enim quamuis regionem potest amplecti et in ea situm loci cuiusdam ad suum arbitrium fabricari et architectari.* [...] *et, quotiescumque rem meminisse uolemus, si formarum dispositione et imaginum diligenti notatione utemur, facile ea quae uolemus memoria consequemur.* [...] *Imitetur ars igitur naturam et quod ea desiderat, inueniat, quod ostendit, sequatur;* [...] *Quare sibi quemque suo commodo conuenit imagines conparare* (*Rhetorica ad Herennium* 3.16-23). Übersetzung nach: Berns 2003, 115-123. S. hierzu Blum 1969; Yates 2001; Carruthers 2002.

of light ritualize individual movement and the subjective gaze. But in its entirety, a building is conceived only in the individual imagination. In framing the performance of social meaning, architecture and individual buildings correspond to the human body, since it is only in the latter that this social meaning becomes real through sensual perception, imagination and cognition.

This interplay of body and embodiment, which was of central importance for medieval Christianity, had already been described by the apostle Paul in his *First Epistle to the Corinthians*. Similarly, Isidore of Seville, building on traditional concepts of rhetorics and the *ars memorativa*, compared the exegesis of Holy Scripture with the erection of a building within the human body. He borrowed the terms *constructio* and *dispositio* from Vitruv's *Ten Books on Architecture* and referred to the memorizing which follows reading as *machina*. Transmitted by Irish and Anglo-Saxon monks, the tradition of the *artes liberales* flourished anew in the Frankish kingdom and was fundamental for comprehensive reforms in liturgy, education and government under the reign of Charlemagne. A treatise on the soul by Alcuin of York, who was perhaps the most influential theologian at the royal court, shows that sensual perception and cognition can be understood as a process of *poiesis* underlying any act of cultural production and, hence, also the production, reception and interpretation of architecture in Carolingian times.

I.

Die Passagen des anonymen römischen Rhetoriklehrers, die das Mittelalter der Autorität Ciceros zuschrieb[2], ähneln raumsoziologischen Überlegungen, wie sie jüngst Martina Löw vorstellte. Als „relationale (An)Ordnung von Lebewesen und sozialen Gütern“[3] basiere Raum auf zwei nur analytisch zu scheidenden Handlungsprozessen: Dem Platzieren von Körpern und Gütern, woraus objektivierte, symbolisch aufgeladene Orte resultierten, und subjektiven Syntheseleistungen, wie Wahrnehmung oder Erinnerung, die durch sozial ritualisierte Anordnungsprozesse und Symboliken geprägt werden[4].

Die Schlussfolgerung Löws, der menschliche Körper fungiere als Medium „zwischen den virtuellen und erdschweren Räumen“[5], konkretisiert der römische Rhetor durch die Bezeichnung des Gedächtnisses als *thesaurus*. Ihre Symbolik erhalten die abzuschreitenden Gedächtnisorte durch eine endogene Bildproduktion – die Imagination –, die wie die *ars memorativa* selbst, auf natürlichen Erinnerungsprozessen basiert; das Erinnern gleicht einem endogenen Sehprozess[6]. Die nur in ihrem Gebrauch existenten *imagines* besitzen spezifische *formae*, *notae* oder *simulacra* des zu Erinnernden[7]. Dauerhafte Präsenz sichern den *imagines agentes* erkennbare Ähnlichkeit und affektives Potenzial auf der Grundlage individuellen Wissens und sozialer Symboliken – hierin entsprechen sich in Funktion und Gestaltung imaginative *imagines* und rhetorischer Vortrag[8]. Nicht nur aktiviert jeweils eine *actio* die *imagines*, son-

2 Nüßlein 1998, 328.

3 Löw 2001, 154.

4 Löw 2001, 158-9.

5 Löw 2001, 113.

6 *Docet igitur nos ipsa natura, quid oporteat fieri. Nam si quas res in vita videmus parvas, usitatas, cottidianas, meminisse non solemus, proterea quod nulla nova nec admirabili re commovetur animus; at si quid videmus aut audimus egregie turpe, inhonestum, inusitatum, magnum, incredibile, ridiculum, id diu meminisse consuevimus* (*Rhetorica ad Herennium* 3.22).

7 *[N]am imagines, sicut litterae, delentur ubi nihil utimmus* (*Rhetorica ad Herennium* 3.18). *Imagines sunt formae, quaedam et notae et simulacra eius rei quam meminisse uolumus* [...] (*Rhetorica ad Herennium* 3.16). Differenziert werden *imagines* für Geschehnisse, die an einem einzigen Ort bildlich kontaminiert werden, und jene für Worte, denen jeweils ein einzelnes Bild – respektive ein gesonderter *locus* – zugeordnet werden: *Quoniam ergo rerum similies imagines esse oportet et ex omnibus verbis nosmet nobis similitudines eligere debemus, duplices igitur similitudines esse debent, unae rerum, alterae verborum. Rerum simlitudines exprimuntur, cum summatim ipsorum negotiorum imagines conparamus; verborum similitudines constituuntur, cum unius cuiusque nominis et vocabuli memoria imagine notatur* (*Rhetorica ad Herennium* 3.20).

8 *Imagines igitur nos in eo genere constituere oportebit, quod genus in memoria diutissime potest haberi. Id accidet, si quam maxime notatas similitudines constituemus; si non mutas nec vagas, sed aliquid agentes imagines ponemus; si egregiam pulcritudinem aut unicam turpitudinem eis adtribuemus* (*Rhetorica ad Herennium* 3.22). Peter Parshall (1999, 467) spricht hier treffend von einem „interplay between originality and convention“. Die Parallelität von rhetorischer *actio* und Bildschöpfung offenbart die Definition der *actio* durch Johannes Bilstein. Er charakterisiert sie (Bilstein 2005, 71) als eine „körperlich-reale Durchführung der Rede, die leibliche Performanz einer vorher entworfenen, strukturierten,

dern in der Ausdrucks- und Darstellungsform des Körpers medialisieren sich die Bilder der Innenwelt in der Außenwelt, um vom Rezipienten einverleibt zu werden[9]. Dabei besitzt die Bildproduktion einen ikonoklastischen Zug, da sie den Prototyp jeweils durch eine Überschreibung oder Überzeichnung einer spezifischen Funktion und individuellem Wissen anpasst[10]. Zentrales Problem von *ars memorativa* und performativer Rhetorik – von Bildproduktion und Rezeption – ist somit „how to offer a general instance that would nevertheless register to each respondent individually"[11].

Überträgt man das bisher Ausgeführte auf mittelalterliche Architekturen, so lässt sich konstatieren, dass erst eine performative *actio* einen spezifischen Sinngehalt aktiviert – somit überlagern sich an einem Ort unterschiedliche, durch den jeweiligen Handlungskontext konstituierte Räume. Dem entspricht, dass „Bauformen und Bauteile nicht grundsätzlich fixfertige Inhalte propagieren"[12]. So ist retrospektiv kaum entschlüsselbar, ob primär ästhetische Vorlieben oder konkrete Sinngehalte Baugestalten prägten, welche selbst einer spezifischen Medialität unterliegen[13].

Die Medialität von Architektur definiert sich u.a. durch ihre Körperlichkeit: Ihre Dimensionen werden erst vor der Matrix des menschlichen Körpers fassbar; Raumabfolgen, Bauformen und Ausstattung leiten Bewegung und Blick; Beleuchtungsakzentuierungen und Akustik transformieren alltägliche Sinneswahrnehmungen. Baukörper werden mit ihrer Ausstattung stets performativ erfahren und sind in ihrer Ganzheit allein imaginativ re-präsentierbar, so dass ihre Medialität Reflexionen über Wahrnehmungs- und Körpererfahrungen stimuliert[14]. Wie andere Artefakte erhalten sie ihre sozialen Sinnhorizonte in einem intermedialen Handlungskontext, der Deutungsmuster kollektiver Imaginationen subjektiviert. Die performative Vor*führung* erzeugt ein „In-Erscheinung-Treten"[15] im Spannungsfeld von leiblicher Wahrnehmung und reflexiver Erfahrung; diese Inszenierung von Präsenz konstituiert Raum und dessen Bedeutungshorizonte[16]. In ritualisierten Akten „leiblicher Kopräsenz"[17] werden über körperlich-mimetische Prozesse Sinnhorizonte nicht nur normiert, sondern in der subjektiven Synthese re-präsentiert – das sukzessive Geschehen wird von spezifischen Zeigehandlungen präsentiert und über Wahrnehmung und Nachvollzug mimetisch einverleibt[18].

Auf ähnlichen Prämissen entwarf Gottfried Boehm eine Bildtheorie, die die „ikonische Differenz" fokussiert[19] – d.h. den im zweidimensionalen Bildobjekt präsentierten Grundkontrast von simultan ansichtiger Gesamtfläche und sukzessiv zu betrachtender Binnenstruktur. Dieser durch die Präsentationslogik betonte Kontrast evoziert eine Präsenz des Dargestellten im nachvollziehenden Sehprozess und „bewirkt den Übergang von der materiellen Vorhandenheit ins Erscheinen"[20]. Hieraus resultiert einerseits, dass das Bild – ebenso wie der architektonische Ort – stets einen performativen Charakter

ausgearbeiteten und memorierten sprachlichen Handlung." Rüdiger Campe (1997, 223) resümiert: „‚Rhetorik' kann man als Namen für die unauflösbare Doppelung von Sprache und medialer Technik nehmen".

9 Wulf und Zirfas 2005b, 27.

10 „The object to be remembered is privately overwritten with an image that absorbs and subordinates its prototype, a case of the signifier overwhelming the signified" (Parshall 1999, 458).

11 Parshall 1999, 467.

12 Brenk 2002, 158.

13 Brenk 2002, 151. Brenks Argumentation richtet sich hauptsächlich gegen eine auf benennbare politische Ansprüche zielende Architekturinterpretation. Die hierbei entstehenden methodischen Probleme sind durch kritische und perspektivreiche Einzeluntersuchungen wiederholt aufgegriffen worden (Reudenbach 1980; Traeger 1980; Untermann 1989; Binding 1996).

14 Unter Performanz sei hier im Anschluss an Christoph Wulf und Jörg Zirfas (2005b, 7) der prozessuale, wirklichkeitskonstituierende „Aufführungscharakter menschlichen Handelns" und die „Inszenierung [...] des menschlichen Körpers" (Wulf 2005, 35) verstanden. „Performative Handlungen gelingen, wenn sie ritualisiert sind" (Wulf und Zirfas 2005b, 9). Die Untersuchung der performativen Dimension sozialen Handelns richtet ihr Augenmerk vor allem auf die sinnstiftende Form und ästhetische Wirkung sozialer Arrangements (Wulf und Zirfas 2005b, 13). Performative Handlungen gelten als selbstreferenziell, selbstidentifizierend und selbstexemplikativ. Zur Diskussion um den Performanzbegriff s. Fischer-Lichte 1998, Wirth 2002.

15 Fischer-Lichte 2004, 173.

16 Gumbrecht 2004, 11, 34, 59.

17 Wulf und Zirfas 2005b, 14.

18 Boehm 2001b, 6.

19 Boehm 1994, 29-36.

20 Boehm 2001b, 13: „Wenn Repräsentationen vor allem Präsenzen begründen wollen, dann erfüllt sich der Sinn der Bilder im Akt der Wahrnehmung, dann, wenn sie dem Betrachter eine Mitpräsenz ermöglichen, wenn, was wir ansehen auch uns ansieht, der Blick dem Blick begegnet".

besitzt, weil es in seiner Struktur „die Bedingungen und Strategien [seiner] Verwirklichung“[21] präsentiert; andererseits besteht eine Differenz zwischen dem im Sehakt verkörperten Bild und seinem medialen Bildträger – wie es bereits der römische Rhetor betonte, existieren Bilder nur, weil sie in einem Medium verkörpert und einverleibt werden[22].

Der Verkörperungsakt gelingt durch die menschliche Einbildungskraft, die das Gesehene in die imaginative Bildwelt überführt und es dort verortet[23]. Geformt werden diese endogenen mimetischen Prozesse durch kulturelle Lernprozesse, die Imaginationen an kollektive Leitbilder binden[24] F. Bildwahrnehmung und -produktion sind – ebenso wie Raumwahrnehmung und -produktion – symbolische Akte performativer Animation[25].

Unter diesen Prämissen soll im Folgenden die karolingische Architektur exemplarisch in ein zeitgenössisches Kunst- und Medienverständnis eingebettet werden. Um das Spannungsfeld interdependenter Medien zwischen Körper und Verkörperung zu skizzieren, werden zunächst nicht Bauwerke, sondern ihre Medialisierungen betrachtet. Besonderes Augenmerk gilt dem Verhältnis von Architektur und Bild, da jede Architektur auf einem imaginativen oder gezeichneten Entwurf und einer bildhaften Wirkung basiert.

II.

Die Wechselwirkung von Bild, Imagination und Bauwerk findet sich bereits bei Vitruv. Er nennt als ästhetische Grundbegriffe *ordinatio*, *dispositio*, *eurythmia*, *symmetria*, *decor* und *oikonomia*[26]. Bezeichnet *ordinatio* die adäquate Abmessung des Bauwerks und der Proportionen seiner Glieder im Verhältnis zu seiner Symmetrie[27], so differenziert sich die *dispositio* in *ichnographia* (die maßstabsgerechte Grundrisszeichnung), *scaenographia* (die perspektivische Zeichnung der Fassade) und *orthographia*[28]: *Orthographia autem est erecta frontis imago modiceque picta rationibus operis futuri figura*[29].

Die zeichnerischen Entwürfe basieren auf der *cogitatione et inventione* des Architekten, dessen Tätigkeiten mit rhetorischen Praxiskategorien verbunden werden[30]. Dies verdeutlichen die Begriffe *inventio*

21 Wulf 2005, 17.

22 Es besteht somit eine „Differenz zwischen dem, *was* bildhaft sichtbar wird, und dem Medium, *worin* es sichtbar wird“ (Waldenfels 2001, 15). S. auch Wulf 2005, 40; Belting 2001.

23 Wulf 2005, 37.

24 Hans Belting (2001, 20-2) schreibt: „Die Bildproduktion hat immer eine Standardisierung der individuellen Bilder bewirkt, und doch schöpfte sie ihrerseits aus einer zeitgenössischen Bilderwelt ihrer Betrachter, die eine kollektive Wirkung überhaupt erst ermöglicht hat. [...] Die Bildmacht wird von den Institutionen, die über die Bilder verfügen, durch das aktuelle Medium und seine Attraktivität ausgeübt: mit dem Medium wirbt man für das Bild, das man den Empfängern einprägen will“.

25 Belting 2001, 13, 20. Ein Beispiel für die angeführten Zusammenhänge ist die Wahrnehmung von Wandmalereien in Sakralbauten. Wird die Bewegung des Blickes zunächst durch die sukzessive, ritualisierte Bewegung der Körper geleitet, so entspricht dieser die prozessuale Blickführung durch einzelne Bildfelder, die auf die Wandfläche übertragen wird. Diese kinästhetische Wahrnehmung führt zur Einverleibung des Ortes und konstituiert Raum durch imaginative Bildfolgen. S. hierzu Wenzel 1999, 549-50; Juwig (im Druck).

26 Vitruv *De architectura* 1.2.

27 *Ordinatio est modica membrorum operis commoditas separatim universeque proportionis ad symmetriam comparatio* (Vitruv *De architectura* 1.2.2).

28 *Dispositio autem est rerum apta conlocatio elegansque compositionibus effectus operis cum qualitate. Species dispositionis* [...] *sunt hae: ichnographia, orthographia, scaenographia. Ichnographia est circini regulaeque modice continens usus, e qua capiuntur formarum in solis arearum descrptiones.* [...] *Item scaenographia est frontis et laterum abscedentium adumbratio ad circinique centrum omnium linearum responsus* (Vitruv *De architectura* 1.2.2).

29 Vitruv *De architectura* 1.2.2.

30 *Hae nascuntur ex cogitatione et inventione. Cogitatione est cura studii plena et industriae vigilantiaeque effectus propositi cum voluptate. Inventio autem est quaestionum obscurarum explicatio ratioque novae rei vigore mobili reperta* (Vitruv *De architectura* 1.2.2). Jaś Elsner (1995, 78) erkennt die funktionale Gestaltung eines römischen Wohnhauses als „representation of the structure of Roman rhetoric“ und ihrer visualisierenden Erinnerungstechnik. Nicht nur sei die Rhetorik architektonisch, sondern die Architektur ebenso rhetorisch geprägt. In seinem Werk *De oratore* (3.179-81) bezieht sich Cicero hinsichtlich der Ordnung der Rede auf die Architektur und den menschlichen Körper: *Referte nunc animum ad hominum vel etiam ceterarum animantium formam et figuram. Nullam partem corporis sine aliqua necessitate adfictam totamque formam quasi perfectam reperietis arte, non casu.* [...] *Columnae templa et porticus sustinent; tamen*

und *figura*; letzterer meint im angeführten Zitat die imaginative Erscheinung des Bau*körpers*, der über den *figura*-Begriff an die Matrix des *hominis bene figurati*[31] als Exempel proportionaler Symmetrie gebunden wird[32]. Medialisiert sich der kognitiv-imaginative Akt der *inventio* zunächst in einer Zeichnung, so wundert sich Vitruv über das menschliche Sehvermögen und den ihm inhärenten Projektionsakt, da das Auge anhand der zweidimensionalen Zeichnung die *figura* des Baukörpers imaginiere: *Quem ad modum etiam in scaenis pictis videntur columnarum proiecturae, mutulorum ecphorae, signorum figurae prominentes, cum sit tabula sine dubio ad regulam plana*[33].

III.

Die älteste erhaltene Handschrift des Architekturtraktats stammt aus dem fränkischen Raum des 9. Jahrhunderts[34]. Ebenfalls aus dem fränkischen Reich der ersten Hälfte des 9. Jahrhunderts stammen die frühesten Grundrisszeichnungen des Mittelalters; überliefert sind sie in den Abschriften des Buches *De locis sanctis*, das Adomnanus, Abt von Iona, um 688 verfasste[35].

Laut Adomnanus basiert seine Schrift auf den Erzählungen des fränkischen Bischofs Arculf, der während einer Pilgerreise Jerusalem, Palästina, Damaskus, Alexandria, Konstantinopel und das Mittelmeergebiet bereiste[36]. Neuere Forschungen bezweifeln die Authentizität des Pilgerberichtes, der in großem Umfang patristische und historiografische Texte rezipiert[37]. Der vermeintliche Pilger sei, so Thomas O'Loughlin, eine fiktive Figur, die den primär exegetischen Gehalt des Werkes durch eine fingierte Augenzeugenschaft authentisiere[38]. David Woods vermutet hinter dem sog. Arculf einen aus Gallien stammenden und vielleicht in Angelsachsen beheimateten Bischof namens Arnulf. Woods argu-

habent non plus utilitatis quam dignitatis: Capitoli fastigium illud et ceterarum aedium non venustas, sed necessitas ipsa fabricata est; [...] *Hoc omnibus item partibus orationis evenit, ut utilitatem ac prope necessitatem suavitas quaedam et lepos consequatur* [...]. Die Übersetzung nach Harald Merklin (2003, 558-9) lautet: „Betrachtet nun Erscheinung und Gestalt der Menschen oder auch der anderen Geschöpfe! Ihr werdet finden, daß kein Teil des Körpers ohne eine zwingende Notwendigkeit gebildet ist und die Gestalt im ganzen gleichsam ein Kunstwerk, nicht ein Werk des Zufalls ist. [...] Tempel und Hallen stützen sich auch auf Säulen, doch liegt in ihnen ebensoviel Würde wie Nützlichkeit. Nicht Schönheit, sondern zwingende Notwendigkeit schuf den berühmten Giebel des Kapitols und der übrigen Tempel. [...] Das trifft auch auf alle Teile der Rede zu, daß Nützlichkeit und fast Notwendigkeit eine gewisse Art von Reiz und Anmut im Gefolge hat". S. hierzu Bilstein 2005, 70.

31 Vitruv *De architectura* 3.1.1

32 Reudenbach 1992, 173-4.

33 Vitruv *De architectura* 6.2.2. Die Übersetzung nach Fensterbusch (1964, 270-1) lautet: „Z.B. sieht man auch bei gemalten Szenen das Hervortreten der Säulen, die Ausladungen der Mutuli und die Figuren der Bildsäulen hervortreten, obgleich doch das Bild ohne Zweifel nach der Richtschnur eben ist."

34 Zum sog. Codex *Harleianus 2767* s. Fensterbusch 1964, 11; Schuler 1999, 135. Wie es Bibliothekskataloge aus karolingischer Zeit nahe legen, wurde der Text Vitruvs zunächst nicht als Einführung in die Baukunst, sondern in die *artes liberales* geschätzt. So befand sich der Architekturtraktat in der Reichenauer Klosterbibliothek zunächst neben Schriften Cassiodors und anderer Kirchenväter (Schuler 1999, 49, 114-6).

35 Zur Textüberlieferung von Adomnanus' *De locis sanctis* s. Bieler 1958, 30-4; McKitterick 2002, 126. Beda Venerabilis berichtet in seiner *Historia Ecclesiastica* 5.15, dass Adomnanus sein Werk König Aldfrith von Northumberland persönlich überreichte. Als *terminus ante quem* für die Fertigstellung des Berichts gilt somit das Jahr 688. Zur Datierung s. Meehan 1958; Wilkinson 1977, 10; O'Loughlin 1996, 98.

36 In der *Praefatio* von Adomnanus' *De locis sanctis* heißt es: *Arculfus sanctus episcopus gente Gallus diuersorum longe remotorum peritus locorum uerax index et satis idoneus in Hierusolimitana ciuitate per menses nouem hospitatus et loca sancta cotidianis uisitationibus peragrans mihi Adomnano haec uniuersa quae infra craxanda sunt experimenta diligentius percunctanti et primo in tabulis describenti fideli et indubitabili narratione dictauit; quae nunc in membranis breui textu scribuntur.* Die Übersetzung nach Donner (2002, 312) lautet: „Arkulf, ein heiliger Bischof gallischer Herkunft, verschiedener weit entfernter Orte kundig, ein wahrhaftiger und vollkommen zuverlässiger Berichterstatter, der sich in der Stadt Jerusalem neun Monate besuchsweise aufgehalten und die heiligen Orte täglich aufgesucht hat, hat mir – dem Adomnanus – alle unten beschriebenen Erfahrungen nach gründlicher Erkundigung diktiert. Ich habe seine getreuliche und verläßliche Erzählung zunächst auf Tafeln geschrieben, die jetzt auf Pergament in Form einer kurzen Abhandlung übertragen werden".

37 O'Loughlin 1994, 1997. O'Loughlin rekonstruierte insgesamt 27 sicher benennbare Quellen, wie u.a. *De civitate Dei* des Augustinus, das *Onomastikon* des Hieronymus, Schriften des Vergil, Hegesippus, Iuvencus, Josephus und des Ps. Eucherius. S. hierzu O'Loughlin 1994, 35; Woods 2002, 27; Meehan 1958, 11-8; Wilkinson 1977, 10.

38 O'Loughlin 1992, 1997.

mentiert u.a. mit dem Fehlen weiterer Zeugnisse zu Arculf und der *Gesta abbatum Fontanellensium*, die für das Abatiat des Austrulf den Fund einer Kiste mit Reliquien im Hafen von Portbail überliefert, die ein in Seenot geratenes Schiff verloren habe[39]. Da Adomnanus berichtet, Arculf sei durch einen Sturm nach Iona gelangt, schließt Woods, dass dieser ein Begleiter der Reliquienüberführung gewesen sei, der einige Dokumente aus Konstantinopel und Syrien gerettet habe, die die Authentizität der Reliquien belegten. So gelangten u.a. syrische Mirakelberichte nach Angelsachsen, wo sie kopiert und später von Adomnanus exzerpiert wurden[40]. Ebenso wie die Namensverwechslung von Arnulf zu Arculf sei das Missverständnis von Translation und Pilgerfahrt einem Lese- oder Kopierfehler geschuldet[41].

Adomnanus' exegetische Intention steht außer Frage, doch war die Authentisierung der Hl. Schrift traditionell eine wichtige Motivation des Pilgerwesens[42]. Adomnanus wählte somit bewusst die Form des Pilgerberichts, um durch eine spezifische Rhetorik eine imaginative Augenzeugenschaft zu evozieren; dieser *intentio* dient die rhetorische Figur Arculf, die der Leser in der Lektüre verkörpert.

Auffällig ist die polarisierende *dispositio* der Pilgerroute, die in dem von Gott errichteten und geweihten Jerusalem beginnt[43]: *Hinc ergo non neglegenter annotandum est quanti uel qualis honoris haec electa et praedicabilis ciuitas in conspectu aeterni genitoris habeatur, qui eam sordidatam diutius remanere non patitur, sed ob eius unigenti honorificantiam citius eam emundat, qui intra murorum eius ambitum sanctae crucis et resurrectionis ipsius loca habet honorifica*[44]. Konterkariert wird dies irdische Abbild der himmlischen Sphäre[45] am Ende des Berichts durch den vor Sizilien liegenden *Uulganus mons* [...] *quasi tonitruum totis diebus et noctibus in tantum intonat ut Siciliae terra longius positae terrifico termore submoueri putetur, sed maius sexta feria et sabbato intonare uidetur. Qiu omni tempore noctibus flammare monstratur, diebus uero fumare*[46].

Seine *evidentia* verdankt der Pilgerbericht den Sinneserfahrungen Arculfs[47]. Neben der optischen und akustischen besitzt die haptische Wahrnehmung einen besonderen Stellenwert: Arculf berührte Reliquien[48] und vermaß eigenhändig die Jerusalemer Anastasis und das Grab Christi.

39 Woods 2002, 43-6 mit Quellenbeleg.

40 Zu diesen Schriftstücken, so Woods (2002, 43, 51), habe auch eine unbekannte Vita Konstantins d. Gr. gehört.

41 Woods 2002, 52.

42 S. hierzu Kötting 1988.

43 *Nam Hierusolimitanus ipse situs a supercilio aquilonali montis Sion incipiens ita est molli a conditore Deo dispositus cliuo usque ad humiliora aquilonalium orientaliumque murorum loca ut illa pluuialis exuberantia nullo modo in plateis stagnantium aquarum in similitudinem supersedere possit sed instar fluuiorum de superioribus ad inferiora decurrat. Quae scilicet caelestium aquarum inundatio per orientalis influiens portas et omnia secum stercuralia auferens abhominamenta uallem Iosaphat intrans torrentem Cedron auget, et post talem Hierusolimitanam baptizationem continuatim eadem pluuialis exuberatio cessat* (Adomnanus *De Locis sanctis* 1.1.11-2). Die Übersetzung nach Donner (2002, 316) lautet: „Denn die Lage Jerusalems ist durch Gott, den Schöpfer, von der Nordanhöhe des Berges Zion beginnend in sanfter Abwärtsneigung bis zu den tiefer gelegenen Orten der nördlichen und östlichen Mauern so eingerichtet worden, daß jene Regenfülle, die auf keine Weise mit den sonst in den Straßen sich stauenden Wassern verglichen werden kann, nach Art von Flüssen von den höher gelegenen Teilen zu den tieferen herabfließt. Diese Überschwemmung mit Himmelswasser – muß man wissen – durchfließt die Osttore, trägt allen abscheulichen Schmutz mit sich fort, tritt in das Tal Josaphat und läßt den Bach Kidron anschwellen; doch sogleich nach dieser Jerusalemtaufe geht die Regenmenge wieder zurück".

44 Adomnanus *De locis sanctis* 1.1.13. Die Übersetzung nach Donner (2002, 316) lautet: „So kann man denn nicht unterlassen anzumerken, wie groß und von welcher Art die Bedeutung ist, die diese auserwählte und preiswürdige Stadt in den Augen des ewigen Schöpfers hat, der nicht duldet, daß sie längere Zeit schmutzig bleibe, sondern sie wegen der seinem eingeborenen Sohn gebührenden Ehre alsbald reinigt, da sich ja in ihrem Mauerring die ehrwürdigen Orte des hl. Kreuzes und der Auferstehung befinden".

45 O'Loughlin 1996, 119.

46 Adomnanus *De locis sanctis* 3.6.1-2.

47 So schreibt Adomnanus (*De locis sanctis* 3.6.3) zum *Uulganus mons*: *Haec mihi Arculfus scribenti de eodem dictauit monte, qui propriis illum oculorum aspexit abtutibus noctu ignitosum diae uero fumosum, eiusque tonitrualem sonitum propriis aurium audiuit auditibus in Sicilia per aliquot hospitatus dies*. Die Übersetzung nach Donner (2002, 394) lautet: „Das hat Arkulf mir, dem Schreiber, über diesen Berg diktiert: er sah ihn mit eigenen Augen nachts feurig und am Tage rauchend und hörte mit eigenen Ohren auch den Donnerschall, als er einige Tage in Sizilien zu Gast war". Zur Autorität der Sinneseindrücke vgl. auch die *Praefatio*.

48 *Inter illam quoque Gologothanam basilicam et martirium quaedam inest exedra, in qua calix Domini, quem a se benedictum propria manu in caena pridiae quam pateretur ipse conuiua apostolis tradidit conuiuantibus;* [...] *Quem sanctus Arculfus uidit, et per illius scrinioli ubi reconditus habetur operculi foramen pertusi manu tetigit propria osculatus* (Adomnanus *De locis sanctis* 1.7.1-3).

In der Ekphrasis der Grabeskirche kulminiert die eschatologische Interpretation Jerusalems[49]. Sie beginnt mit einem Zitat Arculfs: *Arculfus itaque de ipsius ciuitatis habitaculis a nobis interrogatus respondens ait: Memini me et uidisse et frequentasse multa ciuitatis eiusdem edificia plurimasque domus grandes lapideas per totam magnam ciuitatem intra moenia circumdata mira fabricatas arte sepius considerasse.* [...] *De quibus diligentius sanctum interrogauimus Arculfum, praecipuae de sepulchro Domini et eclesia super illud constructa, cuius mihi formulam in tabula cerata Arculfus ipse depinxit*[50] (Abb. 1). Es folgt eine detaillierte architektonische Beschreibung[51], die mit einem Hinweis auf weitere Grundrisszeichnungen endet: *Supradictae igitur rotundae eclesiae formulam cum rotundo tegoriolo in eius medio collocato* [...], *subiecta declarat pictura, nec non et trium aliarum figuras eclesiarum* [...]. *Has itaque quaternalium figuras eclesiarum iuxta exemplar quod mihi* [...] *sanctus Arculfus in paginola figurauit cerata depinximus, non quod possit earum similitudo formari in pictura sed ut Dominicum monumentum licet tali uili figuratione in medietate rotundae eclesiae constitutum monstretur aut quae huic proprior eclesia uel quae eminus posita declaretur*[52].

Das hier zugrundeliegende Bildverständnis verdeutlichen zwei weitere Beschreibungen von Bildobjekten: In Jerusalem sah Arculf ein von der Gottesmutter gewebtes *lintanem, in quo uidelicet* [...] *duodecim apostolorum formulae habentur intextae et ipsius Domini imago figurata*[53]. In Konstantinopel hörte er von einer *imago beatae Maria in breui tabula figurata* [...] *quod esset sanctae Mariae semper uirginis figura*[54]. Bei beiden *imagines* handelt es sich um wunderwirkende Ikonen, die eine körperliche Präsenz des Göttlichen bargen, wie es die Begriffe *figura* bzw. *figurare* nahe legen[55]. Zugleich verkörpert die Marienikone den abstrakten Sinngehalt ewiger Jungfräulichkeit.

Diese Differenzierungen von Bildlichkeit prägen auch Status und Funktion der Kirchengrundrisse. Unterschieden werden *forma* und *figura* des Baukörpers; letztere könne die *pictura* zwar erklären, jedoch nicht re-präsentieren[56]. Dass dies erst dem intermedialen Spannungsfeld von Schrift, Zeichnung und Imagination gelingt, verdeutlicht eine Sentenz aus Beda Venerabilis' *De locis sanctis*. Dort heißt es als Fazit der Ekphrasis des Zentralbaus der Eleonakirche: *Et huius basilice figuram pre oculis depingere placuit*[57].

49 U.a. interpretiert Adomnanus detailliert die Symbolik von zwölf Leuchtern im Grab Christi – ein Ausstattungsdetail, das keine der von ihm benutzten Quellen überliefert (O'Loughlin 1997, 141): *In quo utique sepulchro dudenae lampades iuxta numerum duodecim sanctorum apostolorum semper die ac nocte ardentes lucent, ex quibus .iiii. in imo illius lectuli sepulchralis loco inferius positae, aliae uero bis quartenales super eius marginem superius conlocatae ad latus dexterum oleo nutriente praefulgent* (Adomnanus *De locis sanctis* 1.2.12). Verbinden lässt sich die Betonung der Leuchter mit der spätestens seit dem 4. Jahrhundert allabendlich in der Anastasis vollzogenen Zeremonie des *Lucernare*; Wilkinson (2003, 109, 111) erkennt in ihr eine liturgische Anbindung an den jüdischen Tempel, der als von Gott selbst erbaut und als Abbild des himmlischen Tempels galt. Ähnlich deutet O'Loughlin (1996, 118) die Ekphrasis Jerusalems: „The Jerusalem that he [Adomnanus] describes is not only the city in Palestine but the wondrous city that was a motif in Christian belief and a forerunner of heavenly life".

50 Adomnanus *De locis sanctis* 1.2.1-2. Die Übersetzung nach Donner (2002, 317-8) lautet: „Ferner hat Arkulf, von uns über die Wohnungen der Stadt befragt, folgendes mitgeteilt: ‚Ich erinnere mich, daß ich viele Bauwerke der Stadt gesehen und besucht, auch zahlreiche große Steinhäuser durch die ganze Stadt innerhalb der umgebenden Mauern oftmals betrachtet habe, die überaus kunstvoll errichtet sind.' [...] Über dieses haben wir den heiligen Arkulf genau befragt, insbesondere über das Grab des Herrn und die darüber errichtete Kirche, deren Plan mir Arkulf selbst auf eine Wachstafel gezeichnet hat".

51 Adomnanus *De locis sanctis* 1.2.3.-1.4.3.

52 Adomnanus *De locis sanctis* 1.2.14-5.

53 Adomnanus *De locis sanctis* 1.10.2.

54 Adomnanus *De locis sanctis* 5.5.2-3.

55 Belting 1991.

56 Hinsichtlich der Zeichnungen der überlieferten Handschriften von Adomnanus' *De locis sanctis* ist bisher ungeklärt, ob sie auf Vorlagen basierten, die Arculf – falls er denn existierte – mit sich führte, oder ob er sie, wie es Adomnanus impliziert, aus der Erinnerung zeichnete. Da die überlieferten Pläne teils sehr detailliert sind, wurde vermutet, dass Arculf bzw. Adomnanus bereits Planzeichnungen kannten. Eine *pictura* von Jerusalem nennt Hieronymus in seinem Werk *Onomasticon*. Marina Smyth (1998, 514-6) verwies auf sog. *mensurae*, mit denen Pilger die Hl. Stätten vor Ort vermessen konnten und die als Berührungsreliquien mitgeführt wurden. Eine Auswahl von Abbildungen der überlieferten Zeichnungen bieten Heisenberg 1908, Wilkinson 1977.

57 Beda Venerabilis *De locis sanctis* 7. Wandhoff (2003, 5) schreibt: „Das Besondere an der Ekphrasis kann aus der intermedialen Perspektive darin gesehen werden, daß hier ein gemeinhin als nicht-visuell eingestuftes Medium, die Sprache, durch eine verbale Abbildung von räumlich-visuellen Kunstwerken selbst visuelle Bilder hervorbringen kann – wenn auch nur in der Imagination der Hörer und Leser".

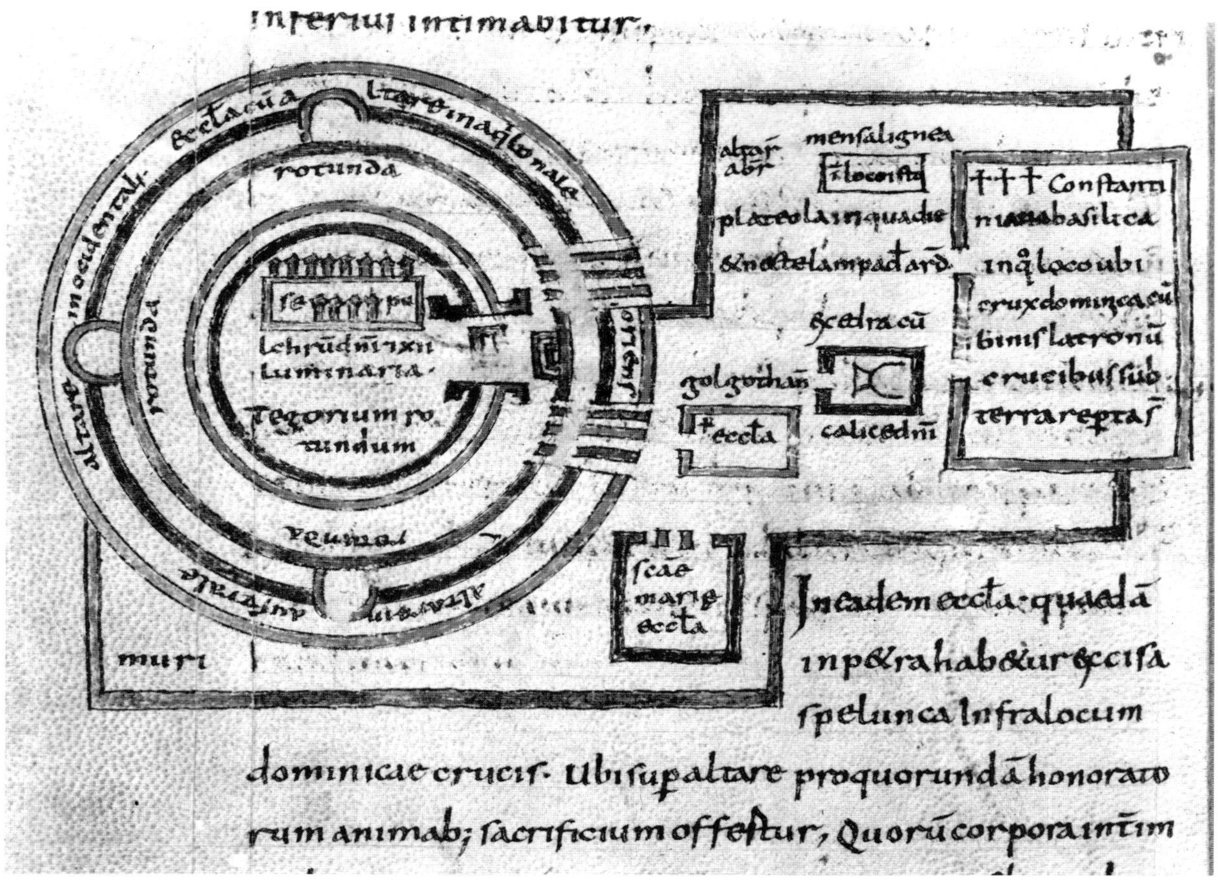

Abb. 1. Adomnanus, *De locis sanctis libri tres* (Cod. Vindobenesis 458.). Jerusalem, Grabeskirche (fol. 4v.), Mitte 9. Jahrhundert. Wien, Österreichische Nationalbibliothek.

Die Verbindung von *figura* und Imagination erschließt sich aus der rhetorischen *enargeia* (*evidentia*). Sie bezeichnet den höchsten Grad des *ornatus* und ein Vor-Augen-Stellen, das jeden Denkakt begleitet und bereits von Aristoteles mit dem Zeichnen verglichen wurde[58]. Als „aktuales Bildgeben"[59] basiert sie auf der *inventio* und *dispositio*, dem *ductus* und *ornatus* des Zeigemediums[60]. Adomnanus inszeniert dies imaginativ-vergegenwärtigende Potenzial durch die Autorität der Sinneswahrnehmungen Arculfs und verweist hierin auf die Tradition spätantiker Pilgerberichte, die seit dem 4. Jahrhundert einen „shift in the use of the senses at the holy places"[61] widerspiegeln. Erfuhren die Pilger an den Hl. Stätten eine göttliche Präsenz und Vergegenwärtigung der Heilsgeschichte an*hand* von Reliquien oder lebenden Heiligen[62], re-präsentieren die Schriften diese Sinnlichkeit im Leseakt durch ihre visualisierende Rhetorik[63]. Auffällig ist die Interdependenz von haptischer und visueller Wahrnehmung, die auf traditionellen Optikkonzepten und dem physischem Kontakt zwischen Auge (bzw. Sehstrahlen) und Objekt beruht[64]. Überliefert wurden diese Theorien u.a. durch die rhetorische *ars memorativa*. So liest sich Ciceros

58 Campe 1997, 216 mit den entsprechenden Nachweisen. Zur *enargeia* s. Campe 1997, 217-9; Boehm 1995, 35; Graf 1995, 145.

59 Campe 1997, 217.

60 Boehm 1995, 35; Morse 1991, 63.

61 Frank 2000, 32.

62 Frank 2000, 29.

63 James 2003.

64 Frank (2000, 125, 132-3) resümiert: „It is significant […], that the most enduring theories were those that incorporated notions of contact, penetration, and even collision. The idea of continuous contact between the viewer and the object explains a great deal about why vision was considered to ensure unmediated knowledge. […] the pilgrims extended a hand that embodied the visual ray of optics. To see and touch, then, were not exclusive activities but rather convergent senses […] Sight was not replaced by touch; it had always been a form of touch. […] The haptic function allowed vision

Ausführung zur Gedächtniskunst wie ein Kommentar des Pilgerberichts: „Wir können uns dasjenige am deutlichsten vorstellen, was sich uns durch die Wahrnehmung unserer Sinne mitgeteilt und eingeprägt (*impressa*) hat; der schärfste unter allen unseren Sinnen ist aber der Gesichtssinn (*sensum videndi*). Deshalb kann man am leichtesten behalten, wenn das, was man durch das Gehör oder durch Überlegung aufnimmt, auch noch durch die Vermittlung der Augen ins Bewußtsein dringt. So kommt es, daß durch eine bildhafte und plastische Vorstellung (*imago et figura*) Dinge, die nicht sichtbar und dem Urteil des Gesichts entzogen sind, auf solche Art bezeichnet werden, daß wir etwas, das wir durch Denken kaum erfassen können, gleichsam durch Anschauung behalten"[65].

Laut Cicero basieren imaginative Visualisierung und performative *actio* auf einer feststehenden Abfolge objekthafter Vorstellungen, die Wachstafel und Buchstaben ersetzten. Dem entspricht die *dispositio* einzelner *loci* im Pilgerbericht, dessen exegetische *intentio* sich auf Ciceros Diktum bezieht, dass Dinge und Sachverhalte, die nicht sichtbar bzw. durch das rationale Denken kaum fassbar sind, imaginiert werden. Evoziert wird dies durch das *ornamentum orationis* – fingierte Personen oder detaillierte Beschreibungen[66]. Dies erklärt die Funktion der exponierten Ekphrasis der Jerusalemer Grabeskirche und die evidente Rhetorik des Pilgerberichts, der den Leser imaginativ zu den Pilgerstätten führt. Diente die Gedächtniskunst dem Einverleiben artifizieller Erinnerungsmedien, so medialisierte Arculf sein Körpergedächtnis in Wachstafeln. Die Grundrisszeichnungen (Abb. 1) unterstützen als memorierende *ornamentae* die imaginative Re-Präsentation der sensuellen Erfahrungen Arculfs. So lobte Beda das Werk Adomnanus' als nützlich für diejenigen, die die Hl. Stätten nicht aus eigener Anschauung kannten[67].

Ihre *elocutio* erhält Adomnanus' Schrift durch die „textinterne Beobachterfigur"[68] Arculf; bereits Isidor von Sevilla schied die erdachte *fabula* von der durch einen kodifizierten Augenzeugenbericht verbürgten *historia*[69]. Vielleicht diente der Pilgerbericht der monastischen Meditation, wie es seine exegetische Intention nahe legt[70]. Als „micro-narrative"[71] birgt die Ekphrasis der Anastasis die Gesamtintention des Pilgerbericht – nicht nur fungiert sie in ihrer, durch Adomnanus plastisch vor Augen geführten, geschlossenen Form als Memorialbild[72], sondern das Grab Christi steht im Zentrum der Welt und Heilsgeschichte. In Funktion, Produktion und Rezeption orientieren sich somit auch die beigefügten Zeichnungen an rhetorischen Praxiskategorien[73].

to reach into the past and sanctity the present". Zur Tradition der Optikkonzepte s. Frank 2000, 113-29; Lindberg 1978; Nelson 2000a.

65 *Vidit enim [...] ea maxime animis effingi nostris, quae essent a sensu tradita atque impressa; acerrimum autem ex omnibus nostris sensibus esse sensum videndi; qua re facillime animo teneri posse ea, quae perciperentur auribus aut cogitatione, si etiam commendatione oculorum animis traderentur; ut res caecas et ab aspectus iudicio remotas conformatio quaedam et imago et figura ita notaret, ut ea, quae cogitando complecti vix possemus, intuendo quasi teneremus* (Cicero *De oratore* 2.357). Übersetzung nach: Merklin 2003, 435.

66 *Nam et commoratio una in re permultum movet et inlustris explanatio rerumque, quasi gerantur, sub aspectum paene subiectio; quae et in exponenda re plurium valent et ad inlustrandum id, quod exponitur, et ad amplificandum; ut eis, qui audient, illud, quod augebimus, quantum efficere oratio poterit, tantum esse videatur;* [...] *personarum ficta inductio vel gravissimum lumen augendi* (Cicero *De oratore* 3.202-5).

67 *Fecitque opus, ut dixi, multis utile, et maxime illis qui longius ab eis locis in quibus patriarchae et apostoli Apostoli erant, secreti, ea tantum de his quae lectione didicerint, norunt* (Beda Venerabilis *Historia Ecclesiastica Gentis Anglorum* 5.15). Dass Beda selbst mit Ciceros *De inventione* – oder zumindest Marius Victorinus' Kommentar zu diesem Werk – vertraut war, zeigte Roger Ray (1997). Mit dem Konzept der rhetorischen *inventio* selbst lässt sich auch Adomnanus' Quellenexegese rechtfertigen. S. hierzu generell Morse 1991.

68 Wenzel 1999, 550.

69 Wandhoff 1999, 589.

70 Die Charakterisierung der Ekphrasis von James und Webb (1991, 11) deutet dies an: „But by articulating things which cannot be seen with the physical eyes, it also reaches beyond art, into the realm of spirituality".

71 Wandhoff 2003, 7.

72 Wandhoff 1996, 218. Das Streben der Ekphrasis nach einer plastischen Form garantiere, so Wandhoff (2003, 6, 22), nicht nur dem Text selbst Dauer und Erinnerbarkeit, sondern bilde gleichzeitig „räumlich markierte Zonen des Verweilens und der Meditation", die eine „Reflexion über Sinn und Bedeutung des Wortkunstwerks" stimulierten.

73 Starkey 2005, 4: „Images and texts thus functioned similarly and were perceived as complementary means by which one might achieve the same results". Mario Klarer (1999, 35) betont hinsichtlich der Ekphrasis methodische Konsequenzen: „Many medieval allusions to pictures actually deal with mental images thereby self-reflexively drawing on privileged modes of medieval representation. [...] When analysing representational concepts in the Middle Ages, it is appropriate to

IV.

Die Interdependenz von Medialität und Imagination findet sich ebenfalls in einer Schrift Alkuins von York, des wohl einflussreichsten Theologen am Hofe Karls des Großen[74]. Geboren um 730 in Northumberland, wirkte Alkuin zunächst an der Kathedralschule zu York, bis er nach einem Treffen mit Karl in Parma (781) die Leitung der neubegründeten Hofschule übernahm. 796 wurde er Abt des Klosters zu Tours. In seiner Schrift *De animae ratione liber ad Eulaliam virginem* (801/4), die er der Schwester des Abtes Adalhard von Corbie und Cousine Karls des Großen widmete, entwirft Alkuin eine bildliche Kognitionstheorie, die sich an den Werken des Augustinus und der durch Cicero überlieferten Mnemotechnik und Rhetorik orientiert[75]: „Die Seele hat also [...] in ihrer Natur das Bild (*imago*) der heiligen Dreifaltigkeit dadurch, dass sie Verstand, Willen und Gedächtnis hat. [...] Was sie durch diese [die fleischlichen Sinne] gewissermaßen wie durch Boten an sinnlichen Dingen – bekannten und unbekannten – empfängt, formt (*format*) sie [....] zu Bildern (*figuras*) und bewahrt diese [...] in der Schatzkammer (*thesaurus*) ihres Gedächtnisses auf. So bildet (*fingit*) etwa jemand, der Rom sieht, in seinem Geist (*animo*) ein Bild Roms und formt (*format*) es so ab, wie es ist. Wenn er nun den Namen Rom hört oder erinnert, so wendet sich sein Geist sofort zum Gedächtnis zurück, wo er Roms Bild (*formam*) abgelegt hat [...]. Noch wunderbarer aber ist, daß die Seele selbst von unbekannten Dingen, wenn sie nur gelesen oder mit den Ohren gehört werden, sich sogleich ein Bild (*figuram*) der unbekannten Sache zurechtformt (*format*). So hat jeder von uns irgendein Bild Jerusalems in seiner Seele, obwohl das [wirkliche Bild], wenn man es sieht, ganz anders sein mag, als die Seele es sich vorstellt. [...] So geht der Geist des Menschen bei jeder Sache vor: nach bekannten gestaltet (*fingit*) er sich unbekannte, wobei er sie alle als Gestalten (*species*) in sich trägt“[76].

Alkuins Text liest sich durch seine Beispiele und die konstitutive Funktion der visuellen Wahrnehmung für den Kognitionsprozess wie eine Erläuterung der *enargeia* des Pilgerberichts. Wie Augustinus und zeitgleiche byzantinische Theologen impliziert er das Konzept der Extramission, nach der das Auge Sehstrahlen aussende, die die Form des Wahrgenommen abtasten und in den Körper zurückführen[77]. Gleich Adomnanus bezeichnet Alkuin die Vorstellungen als *figurae*, der Begriff *imago* bleibt einer göttlichen Präsenz vorbehalten, die der Seele ihre kognitive Imaginationsfähigkeit verleiht[78]. Formt der Geist durch das Einverleiben des Wahrgenommenen mimetische *figurae*, dient bei medialer Vermittlung das subjektive Wissen als Matrix der Imagination; im Schnittpunkt von reflexiver *memoria* und sinnlicher Wahrnehmung tritt mit der *figura* die Essenz des Wahrgenommenen vor Augen.

Implizit differenziert Alkuin zwischen Imagination und Fantasie. Er wundert sich, dass „jener lebendige und himmlische Sinn, der Verstand oder Geist genannt wird, derart beweglich ist, daß er selbst dann

divert the focus of attention from the described artefact as such to an analysis of the interaction between the object and its observer“. Zur monastischen Meditation s. Carruthers 2000.

74 Bullough 2004.

75 S. hierzu auch Juwig (im Druck) mit weiterer Literatur.

76 *Habet igitur anima in sua natura, ut diximus, imaginem sanctae Trinitatis in eo quod intelligentiam, voluntatem, et memoriam habet.* [...] *Nunc autem consideremus miram velocitatem animae in formandis rebus, que percipit per carnales sensus, a quibus quasi per quosdam nuntios, quidquid rerum sensibilium cognitarum vel incognitarum percipit, mox in seipsa earum ineffabili celeritate format figuras, informatasque in suae thesauro memoriae recondit. Sicut enim qui Romam vidit, Romam enim fingit in animo suo, et format qualis sit. Et dum nomen audierit vel rememorat Romae, statim recurrit animus illius ad memoriam, ubi conditam habet formam illius, et ibi recognoscit, ubi recondidit illam. Et adhuc mirabilius est, quod incognitarum rerum, si lectae vel auditae erunt in auribus, anima statim format figuram ignotae rei. Sicut forte Jerusalem quisquam nostrum habet in anima sua formatam, qualis sit: quamvis longe aliter sit, quam sibi anima fingit, dum videtur.* [...] *Sic de omni re facit animus hominis, ex cognitis fingit iincognita, habens has omnes species in se* (Alkuin *De animae ratione liber ad Eulaliam virginem* 6-7, 10). Die Übersetzung folgt Berns (2003, 507, 509). Alkuin rezipiert in dieser Passage die Ausführungen Augustinus' in *De trinitate*.

77 R.S. Nelson (2000b, 150) charakterisiert diese Extra- oder Emissionstheorie: „[O]ptical rays emerge from the eye, extend to the object of vision, touch it, and return to the eye bearing ‚the essence of the thing seen', which is conveyed to the mind and to the memory“. S. hierzu Lechterman 2003, 96. Zu Augustinus s. Miles 1983; Bumke 2001, 35-9. Bisher nicht diskutiert wurden die Parallelen in den Argumentationen Alkuins und denen des Johannes von Damaskus.

78 *Est quoque anima imagine et similitudine sui Conditoris in principali sui parte, quae mens dicitur, excellenter nobilitata. Quae imago tandem in ea clara et pulchra es, si toto Deo Conditori desiderio vincta est.* [...] *Habet igitur anima in sua natura, ut diximus, imaginem sanctae Trinitatis in eo quod intelligentiam, voluntatem, et memoriam habet* (Alkuin *De animae ratione liber ad Eulaliam virginem* 5-6).

nicht, wenn er schläft, auch wirklich ruht; [...] daß ihm schließlich alles, was ihm beliebt [...], sich selbst denkend vor Augen führt"[79].

Bezeichnet die Fantasie die Selbsttätigkeit des Geistes, so besitzt der figurative Denkakt stets ein präsentisches Erfahrungspotential – sei es durch die direkte Wahrnehmung oder durch die Erinnerung an Wahrgenommenes. Nach Alkuins Ausführungen bildet der performative Sehakt die Welt nicht ab, sondern diese gelangt als Bild in den Körper, wo sie zu *figurae* geformt wird[80]. Die *figurae* bergen als Objektivierung des Wahrgenommenen dessen Essenz und speichern das Abwesende. Bei indirekter Wahrnehmung durch mediale Vermittlung wird das Nicht-Sichtbare über die Matrix des individuellen Wissens re-präsentiert[81]. Der ‚erinnernde' Sehprozess ist als „exegetic viewing"[82] somit ein poietisches Verfahren[83].

V.

Dem entsprechen Bildobjekte der Hofschule Karls des Großen. So präsentiert eine um 800 in Aachen entstandene und heute in Oxford aufbewahrte Elfenbeinplatte (Taf. 31) im zentralen Bildfeld einen dem Betrachter frontal zugewandten *Christus triumphans*, der in Anlehnung an Psalm 91 Löwen und Drachen niedertritt[84]. Um das mittlere Bildfeld gruppiert sich ein zwölfteiliger Bildzyklus, der mit der Darstellung des Propheten Jesaja beginnt und elf Episoden des Lebens Christi zeigt.

Die Kleinplastik offenbart sich als Medialisierung einer *figura*, da der Bildschnitzer ein je fünfteiliges, weströmisches Diptychon des 5. Jahrhunderts als Vorlage benutzte, dessen Fragmente sich heute in Berlin, Paris und Nevers befinden (Abb. 2). Trotz stilistischer und motivischer *imitatio* diente das Modell der *inventio* eines neuartigen Bildobjekts: Innovativ sind die szenische *dispositio*[85], die Transformation des Polyptichons zu einem Bildobjekt und dessen Funktion – vielleicht erstmals wurden im Umfeld der Hofschule Codices mit Bildtafeln geschmückt[86]. Die *intentio* dieser Neuerung gründet in der von Karl initiierten Liturgiereform und einer spezifischen Medienpraxis.

Die Liturgiereform zeichnete sich durch eine neuartige Verkettung von Ritualsequenzen aus und allegorisierte einzelne liturgische Gebärden mit Episoden aus Leben und Passion Christi. Durch diese Synchronisierung von historischem Geschehen und Messfeier re-präsentierte der Ritus das Heilsgeschehen im imaginativen Nachvollzug der meist lateinunkundigen Gläubigen[87]. Dieser performativ evozierten *enargeia* ähnelt eine Bildpraxis, die Beda Venerabilis für die italienischen Malereien überliefert, die Benedict Biscop in der Klosterkirche zu Wearmouth angebracht hatte. So *erinnerten* die Mönche die dargestellten Szenen, als ob das Geschehen *vor Augen stände*[88]. Ebenso wie Beda die Funktion der

79 *Nec etiam aliquis potest satis admirari, quod sensus ille vivus atque coelestis, qui mens vel animus nuncupatur, tantae mobilitatis est, ut ne tum quidem, cum sopitus est, conquiescat: tantae celeritatis, ut uno temporis puncto coelum collustret, si velit, maria pervolet, terras et urbes peragret: omnia denique, quae libuerit, quamvis longe lateque submota sint, in conspectu sibi ipse cogitando constituat* (Alkuin *De animae ratione liber ad Eulaliam virginem* 8). Aus anthropologischer Sicht differenziert Wulf (2005, 45): „Phantasie bezeichnet eher die wildwüchsige Seite, Imagination die Bilderwelt und Einbildungskraft die Vorstellungskraft, mit der Neues erzeugt wird".

80 Wulf und Zirfas 2005b, 15.

81 Wandhoff (2003, 31): „Imagination und Gedächtnis sind deshalb so eng zusammen zu denken, weil die Erinnerung – nicht nur im Mittelalter – fundamental auf eine Re-Imagination der gespeicherten Wissensvorräte angewiesen ist".

82 Elsner 1995, 78.

83 Zum ‚erinnernden Sehen' Peter Matussek (1999, 639): „Das Re-Medium des visuellen Gedächtnisses, das dessen Mortifikation rückgängig macht, ist diesem artverwandt: Es ist das erinnernde Sehen".

84 Oxford Bodleian Library, Ms. Douce 179. S. hierzu Kötzsche 1965; Steenbock 1965; Fillitz 1966; Mayr-Harting 1992, 58-69; Nees 1995, 195-202; Kahsnitz 1999.

85 Bei Nees (1995, 198) heißt es hierzu: „The Carolingian artist has in fact ‚corrected' his late antique pictorial model by recourse to appropriate textual source".

86 Vgl. hierzu die Materialsammlung von Frauke Steenbock 1965.

87 Angenendt 2001, 136-9; Suntrup 1978, 50.

88 So heißt es in Beda Venerabilis' *Vita sanctorum abbatum monasterii in Uyramutha et Gyruum* (6): *[I]magines visonum apocalypsis beati Iohannis, quibus septentrionalem aeque parietem ornaret, quatenus intrantes ecclesiam omnes etiam literarum ignari, quaquaversum intenderent, vel semper amabilem Christi sanctorumque eius, quamvis in imagine, contemplarentur aspectum; vel Dominicae incarnationis gratiam vigilantiore mente recolerent; vel extremi discrimen*

Bildmedien in der Rhetoriklehre verankert, verwendet er in seiner Beschreibung der Meditationspraxis die Begriffe *ornare* und *decorare*, die den Verlauf der ritualisierten Imagination bestimmten[89].

Dem entsprechen Adomnanus' Pilgerbericht und das Bildprogramm der Elfenbeinplastik (Taf. 31). Ihr Bildzyklus beginnt mit dem alttestamentarischen Propheten Jesaja, der dem Betrachter einen Rotulus mit den Worten *Ecce Virgo Conc(ipiet)* präsentiert. Wurde Jesaja mit diesen Worten das Heilsgeschehen in einer göttlichen Vision vorhergesagt[90], leitet die Inschrift wörtlich die folgende Verkündigungsszene ein. Einen ebenso beredten Einstieg bietet die bildsyntaktische *dispositio*: Der Blick folgt dem Zeigegestus des Propheten in das folgende Bildfeld, wo ihn der Gestus des Verkündigungsengels aufnimmt[91].

In *actio* und Funktion gleicht die Prophetenfigur Adomnanus' fingiertem Pilger: Im Sehakt verkörpert der Betrachter die Figur des Propheten, wie es die Aufforderung *Ecce* expliziert. Da der alttestamentarische Prophet die Heilsgeschichte in einer von Gott eingegebenen Vision imaginierte, spiegelt das Bildprogramm die zeitgenössische liturgische Praxis. Die zum Buchdeckel gehörende Handschrift entstand im Konvent zu Chelles, dem eine Schwester Karls vorstand[92]. Als Evangelistar beinhaltet der Codex Evangelienexzerpte zur liturgischen Rezitation. Da die Liturgiereform anstrebte, das Heilsgeschehen in der Imagination der Gläubigen zu re-präsentieren, reflektiert Jesajas Aufforderung die rituelle Funktion des Codex, wobei die imaginierende *memoria* das artifizielle Gedächtnismedium ersetzt[93].

In der alttestamentarischen Prophetenfigur, dem Leben Christi und der Darstellung des *Christus triumphans* vereint der Buchdeckel drei heilsgeschichtliche Zeitalter. Dies weist auf die Überlieferung des *figura*-Begriffs in der christlichen Präfigurationstheorie und ihren Ursprung in der klassischen Rhetoriklehre[94].

VI.

Etymologisch besitzt der *figura*-Begriff haptische Konnotationen[95]. Hierin entspricht er dem griechischen σχῆμα, mit dem bereits Aristoteles die äußere Form bezeichnete[96]. Auch Adomnanus unterschied hinsichtlich des Jerusalemer Tuchbildes und der Anastasis *figura* und *forma*. Da die Konstantinopler

examinis, quasi coram oculis habentes, districtius se ipsi examinare memenissent. Zitiert nach: Carruthers 2000, 338, Fn. 77. S. hierzu Carruthers 2000, 203-5; Meyvaert 1979.

89 Carruthers 2000, 116-8, 205. An anderer Stelle bezeichnet Beda die *pictura* als *viva scriptura* (Rehm 2002, 442).

90 Jes. 7.14.

91 Das Zitat Jesajas wurde im Evangelium des Lukas (1.38) aufgenommen, so dass bereits die Patristik in der verbalen Verkündigung einen illokutionären Handlungsakt erkannte, in dem sich die Inkarnation Christi verwirklichte. Erhielt in karolingischer Zeit das Fest der Empfängnis Mariens einen wichtigen Status innerhalb des Kirchenjahres, so ließ bereits Papst Johannes VII. (705-707) in seinem Oratorium im römischen Lateranspalast eine Verkündigungsszene anbringen, in der die inschriftlich wiedergegebene Botschaft des Engels der performativen Rezitation und subjektiv-imaginativen Vergegenwärtigung der Heilsgeschichte diente. S. hierzu Wenzel 1993, 25; van Dijk 1999. Zum illokutionären Handlungsakt s. Krämer 1998.

92 Kahsnitz 1999. Während Kötzsche (1965) Buchdeckel und Handschrift voneinander schied, erkennt Nees (1995, 200) sie als zusammengehörig. Als Argument gegen die ursprüngliche Verbindung wird die Erneuerung des Buchdeckels im 17. Jahrhundert angeführt. Doch handelte es sich hierbei nur um eine Restaurierung des ursprünglichen Zustands, wie es auch Fillitz (1966) impliziert. Nees (1995, 200) sieht Alkuin, der im brieflichen Kontakt mit der Äbtissin zu Chelles stand, als Auftraggeber für die am Hofe entstandene Elfenbeinplatte.

93 Mayr-Harting (1992, 64) schreibt zur Funktion der Buchdeckel: „These ivories performed a function in relation to private prayer and meditation, and in so far as the books they adorned were liturgical books [...], this function could actually be better performed when the book was closed [...]. [...] Let me suggest that the covers of the Gospel book could be used for the lightning meditation of a priest or deacon or abbess immediately before mass". So erhalten die Bildobjekte nicht nur eine ähnliche Funktion, wie sie Beda Wandmalereien zuschrieb, sondern das Buch „in welches der Augenzeugenbericht eingespeichert ist, wird in seiner sichtbaren Körperlichkeit selbst zum (Ersatz-) Gegenstand authentizitätssichernder Augenwahrnehmung" (Wandhoff 1999, 588). Wenzel (1993, 38) setzt das Buch mit dem Leib Mariens gleich: „Als Leib, der den Logos umhüllt, wird Maria selbst zum Buch, in dem das Wort Gottes präsent ist".

94 Auerbach 1944.

95 Bereits bei Varro findet sich die Lösung des *figura*-Begriffs aus dem Kontext der Bildhauerei, in dem es mit dem Verb *fingere* verbunden war, hin zur Bezeichnung einer plastischen Vorstellung (Auerbach 1944, 12; Dierse 1972, 948).

96 Auerbach 1944, 14; Dierse 1972, 948. Auerbach (1944, 15) bezeichnet die *figura* im Gegensatz zum σχῆμα-Begriff als „Element der Bewegung und Verwandlung". Dies erinnert an den *imago*-Begriff des *Auctor ad Herennium*.

Abb. 2. Rechter Seitenstreifen eines fünfteiligen Diptychons. Weströmisch, Beginn 5. Jahrhundert. Berlin Staatliche Museen zu Berlin – Preußischer Kulturbesitz, Museum für Spätantike und Byzantinische Kunst, Inv. Nr. I. 2719.

Marienikone auch als *figura* der ewigen Jungfräulichkeit gedeutet wurde, verkörpert sie einen stets präsenten, abstrakten Sinngehalt. Cicero nennt die *figura* zunächst im allgemeinen Kontext sinnlicher Erscheinungen, wobei sie sich meist auf das darstellende Medium – wie die stilistische Ausschmückung der Rede – bezieht und nicht auf dessen Inhalt[97]. Da jedoch der Stil der Redepraxis abstrakte Inhalte figurativ vor Augen führt, gründet die imaginative *enargeia* in der sinnlich-äußeren Gestaltung eines performativ verwendeten Mediums.

Die christliche Präfigurationslehre bezeichnet mit der *figura* eine historische Person oder ein geschichtliches Ereignis als Verkörperung einer anderen geschichtlichen Tatsache[98]. Dies entspricht dem Gebrauch des *figura*-Begriffs in Alkuins Kognitionskonzept, in dem die *figura* nicht nur eine plastische Dimension besaß, sondern Abwesendes re-präsentiert. Die Welt wird zwar sinnlich wahrgenommen, die

97 Auerbach 1944, 17-20. Mit Cicero und dem *Auctor ad Herennium* wird der *figura*-Begriff erstmals als *terminus technicus* der Rhetoriklehre benutzt, wobei Cicero jedoch noch an dem Begriff *forma* für die umschreibend-figürlichen Redeweisen festhält und sich dabei an der Tradition des σχῆμα-Begriffes orientiert. Da die Schriften Quintilians erst ab dem 12. Jahrhundert rezipiert wurden (Fried 1997, IX), bleiben seine Ausführungen hier unberücksichtigt.

98 Auerbach 1944: „Die Figuraldeutung stellt einen Zusammenhang zwischen Geschehnissen oder Personen her, in dem eines von ihnen nicht nur sich selbst, sondern auch das andere bedeutet, das andere hingegen das eine einschliesst oder erfüllt. Beide Pole der Figur sind zeitlich getrennt, liegen aber beide, als wirkliche Vorgänge oder Gestalten, innerhalb der Zeit“.

in ihr konkretisierten heils-geschichtlichen *figurae* werden jedoch erst durch den Intellekt entschleiert. Hierin entsprechen sich Alkuins Kognitionskonzept, Rhetoriklehre und christliche Exegese[99].

Vor dem Hintergrund der Präfigurationstheorie erklärt sich auch die Funktion der alttestamentarischen Prophetenfigur der Elfenbeinplastik, die den zukünftigen Verlauf der Heils-Geschichte voraussieht[100]. Zwischen Ver- und Enthüllung (*velatio* und *revelatio*) steht die *figura* als sinnlich-konkreter Bedeutungsträger – nur das intellektuelle Erkennen der Figur, das Entschleiern ihrer Erfüllung, bleibt ein abstrakter Deutungsakt[101]. Hierin unterscheidet sich die innergeschichtliche Präfigurationstheorie als Auslegungstechnik von allegorisch-moralischen Interpretationen wie der Lehre des vierfachen Schriftsinns[102]. Bereits Augustinus empfahl die figurale Interpretation des Alten Testaments zur Missionierung und Predigt, da sie durch ihren sinnlichen Gehalt verständlicher sei als abstrakt-allegorische Interpretationen und den Erlösungsgedanken in der gelebten Historie verorte[103]. Dies nutzte auch die karolingische Liturgiereform, die die Heilsgeschichte performativ vor Augen stellte und die rituelle Inkarnation Christi als Erfüllung des Alten Bundes vergegenwärtigte. Wichtig ist hinsichtlich des Oxforder Buchdeckels, dass innergeschichtliche Verheißung und Erfüllung nur vorläufig sind, da sich erst im endzeitlichen Gericht die sinnlich-erfahrbare Heilsgeschichte einer geistigen Schau eröffnet.

VII.

Einher ging die karolingische Liturgiereform mit umfassenden Bildungsreformen auf Grundlage der *artes liberales*[104]. Im Zuge der Bemühungen *errata corrigiere*, *superflua abscindere* und *recta cohartare*[105], wurden u.a. vom Papst Musterkodizes erbeten und ein für jede Kirche verbindlicher Kanon liturgischer Handschriften verfügt; ihre Pragmatik und Lesbarkeit gewährleistete die Einführung der karolingischen Minuskel[106]. Amts- und Liturgiesprache war Latein.

Den wichtigen Stellenwert der *artes liberales* verdeutlicht exemplarisch das Wirken Alkuins, der neben theologischen Traktaten eine grammatikalisch korrigierte Vulgatafassung und Lehrbücher zum artistischen Trivium verfasste, in denen er u.a. Cicero, Boethius, Isidor von Sevilla und Augustinus rezipierte[107]. In seinem Rhetoriklehrbuch verknüpfte Alkuin die Rhetorik mit den vier Kardinaltugenden und der Ausübung politischer Ämter, wobei Karl als gelehriger Schüler und idealtypisches Exempel fun-

99 In seinem 1. Brief an die Thessaloniker (5.23) unterscheidet Paulus zwischen *corpus*, *anima* und *spiritus* des Menschen. Diese Triade wird von Augustinus aufgenommen und auf die menschliche Wahrnehmung übertragen. In seinem auch für das karolingische Bildverständnis grundlegenden Werk *De genesi ad litteram* unterscheidet er drei Stufen des Sehens: das irrationale körperliche und spirituelle Sehen, das exogene Bilder aufnimmt und endogene Bilder erzeugt und die reflexiv-intellektuelle Schau, in der die göttliche Wahrheit bewusst werde. S. hierzu u.a. Brinkmann 1980, 245; Kessler 2000, 22, 174.

100 Auerbach 1944, 29: „Die prophetische Figur ist sinnlich-geschichtliche Tatsache, und sie wird durch sinnlich-geschichtliche Tatsachen erfüllt".

101 Auerbach 1944, 30; Oster 2002.

102 Brinkmann 1980.

103 Auerbach 1944, 34-50.

104 Dass diese umfassenden Reformen mit einem spezifischen Ethos verbunden waren, zeigt bereits der gegen 784/5 u.a. von Alkuin mitverfasste Bildungsbrief *Epistola de litteris colendis*, der, obwohl ursprünglich an den Fuldaer Konvent gerichtet, allen Bischofskirchen und Klöstern übersandt wurde. Zitiert sei die Übersetzung einer Passage durch Günther Binding (1996, 110 mit Quellennachweisen): „Deswegen fordern wir euch auf, das Studium der Wissenschaften nicht nur nicht zu vernachlässigen, sondern in der Tat mit ergebenster und Gott gefälliger Anstrengung das eifrig zu lernen, damit ihr leichter und richtiger den Inhalt der heiligen Schrift zu durchdringen vermögt. Wenn nämlich in der Heiligen Schrift die Wendungen, der bildliche Gebrauch und die übrigen ihnen eingefügten Ähnlichkeiten erkannt werden, ist es kein Zweifel, daß jeder, der diese liest, um so schneller geistlich versteht, je gründlicher er zuvor in der Fähigkeit der Wissenschaften unterrichtet worden ist". S. hierzu auch Angenendt 1995, 314; McKitterick 1997. Wichtigen Einfluss nahmen angelsächsische Gelehrte und Missionare. David Rollason (2001, 23) sieht in der Kirchengeschichte Bedas, die im 9. Jahrhundert nachweislich in Fulda, Mainz, Würzburg, St. Gallen und auf der Reichenau vorhanden war, „a kind of blueprint" für die Kirchenreform.

105 Angenendt 1995, 322.

106 Angenendt 1995, 304-52; Schieffer 1989.

107 Haase 2005.

giert[108]. Doch galt die Hofgesellschaft insgesamt als moralisches Vorbild, so dass im frühen 9. Jahrhundert, als Aachen lokales Zentrum geworden war, junge Adlige zur Unterweisung hierher kamen[109]. Ihre Ausbildung bestand nicht aus einem formalen Unterricht, sondern höfische Verhaltensmodelle wurden durch Imitation und Disziplin erlernt[110]. Auch wurden bei Hofe, teils in Anwesenheit des Herrschers, Gedichte und Epen vorgetragen – Quellen, die wohl nicht erst heute der Interpretation von Kunstwerken dienen[111].

VIII.

Die *artes liberales* prägten neben dem höfischen Selbstverständnis auch das Verständnis materieller Bildwerke, wie es das *Opus Caroli regis contra synodum* (im Folgenden: OC) verdeutlicht[112]. Anlass seiner Anfertigung war das zweite Konzil von Nicäa (787), das den seit den 720er Jahren in Byzanz virulenten Bilderstreit durch das erneute Einsetzen der Bildverehrung kurzzeitig beilegte[113]. Initiiert von Kaiserin Irene wurde das Konzil durch die Anwesenheit des Papstes und trotz Abwesenheit fränkischer Abgesandter als universalkirchlich propagiert. Nach ihrer Übersetzung am päpstlichen Hof gelangten die Konzilsakten nach Aachen[114]. Im Namen Karls verfasste Theodulf, der aus Hispanien stammende Abt von Orléans, das *Capitulare adversus synodum*, das die Verehrung von Bildwerken ablehnte und Papst Hadrian übersandt wurde. Nach dessen Antwortschreiben wurde die endgültige Fassung des OC spätestens 793 abgeschlossen. Ein Jahr später verwarf das Frankfurter Konzil die in Nicäa getroffenen Beschlüsse offiziell in Anwesenheit päpstlicher Legaten[115]. Dennoch wurde das OC nicht veröffentlicht[116]. Überliefert ist das am Hof diskutierte Arbeitsexemplar, das Kommentare Karls als Marginalien enthält[117]. Obwohl das OC als ‚Staatsschrift' charakterisiert wurde, besaß es keinen rechtsverbindlichen Status[118]. Celia Chazelle nannte es treffend eine „isolated proclamation of theology"[119].

Grundsätzlich kritisiert das OC sowohl die Verehrung als auch die Zerstörung von Bildwerken. Hatte die Übersetzung der Konzilsakten noch *adorare* für Anbetung und Verehrung von Bildwerken verwendet[120], beharrten die Karolinger auf der alleinigen Anbetung Gottes und einer memorierenden und schmückenden Funktion der Bildwerke: *sed solum Deum adorantes et eius sanctos venerantes secundum antiquam patrum et ecclesiasticam traditionem eas in ecclesia ornamento et memoria rerum gestarum, si libet, habeamus*[121].

Die Argumentation des OC folgt einer lehrbuchhaften Rhetorik[122]. So wird nicht nur die undifferenzierte Wortwahl der vermeintlich byzantinischen Kontrahenten kritisiert, sondern ihre generelle

108 Haase 2005. Bereits Cicero differenzierte in seinem Werk *De inventione* die Tugend in *prudentia, iustitia, fortitudo* und *temperantia*. Die *prudentia* wiederum bildeten *memoria, intelligentia* und *providentia* (Yates 2001, 26). Aus einem Gedicht Alkuins über York lässt sich erschließen, dass die dortige Bibliothek Werke Ciceros besaß (Ray 1997, 7). So lässt sich vermuten, dass nicht nur die Werke Ciceros – hier vor allem das von ihm in *De inventione* entworfene Kulturideal –, sondern auch die Cicero rezipierenden Werke Bedas und Augustinus' das von Alkuin mitentwickelte karolingische Reformethos beeinflussten.

109 Innes 2003, 68.

110 Innes 2003, 67-75.

111 Zur Vortrags- und Zirkulardichtung s. Schaller 1995. Auch bildeten sich bei Hofe philosophische Diskussionszirkel junger Adliger (Nelson 2003, 49).

112 S. hierzu Chazelle 1986; Jeck 1993; Saurma-Jeltsch 1994; Thümmel 1997; Freeman 1998; Nagel 1998; Chazelle 2001; Ommundsen 2002.

113 Belting 1991; Freeman 1998.

114 Noble 1995, 231.

115 Zur Textgeschichte s. Freeman 1998; Nagel 1998; Thümmel 1997.

116 Ommundsen 2002, 196.

117 Cod. Vaticanus lat. 7207.

118 Noble 1995, 236.

119 Chazelle 2001, 41.

120 Thümmel 1997, 968-9; Chazelle 1986, 164.

121 *Opus Caroli regis contra synodum* 2.31.

122 Ommundsen 2002, 187: „The Carolingian practice and didactic use of the liberal art, in combination with their criticism of the Byzantine language, leads to a clear-cut contrast: The Carolingians are masters of grammar, rhetoric and dialectic and the interpretation of Scripture".

Unkenntnis der *artes liberales*, da sie die Hl. Schrift nur wörtlich interpretierten[123]. Da sich Gott selbst der *artes liberales* in der Hl. Schrift bedient habe, müsse diese auf deren Grundlage wissenschaftlich ausgelegt werden, um die in ihr verborgenen *mysticas figuras* zu entschleiern[124].

Konterkariert werden von Menschenhand geschaffene Bildwerke mit den gottgewollten Offenbarungsmedien der *res sacratae* – der Hl. Schrift, dem Sakrament der Eucharistie, den liturgischen Gefäßen, dem Kreuz und der Bundeslade[125]. War die von Mose auf Gottes Weisung gefertigte Bundeslade noch eine Präfiguration[126], konkretisierte sich die Vereinigung von himmlischer und irdischer Sphäre im Kreuzestod Christi[127]. Erhielt das materielle Kreuz seine heils-geschichtliche Bedeutung durch die Berührung Christi, so sind auch die liturgischen Gefäße und das eucharistische Sakrament von ihm selbst eingesetzt.

Die *res sacratae* bezeichnen somit liturgische Requisiten, die eine rituelle Segnung empfangen, welche die heils-geschichtlichen Präfigurationen aktualisieren[128]. Ihre rituelle ‚Spiritualisierung' scheidet sie grundsätzlich von Bildwerken, die nur der körperlichen Sinneswahrnehmung zugängig seien und das Auge durch materielle Qualitäten erfreuten[129]. Der spirituelle Gehalt der Sakramente hingegen sei dem inneren Auge erfahrbar[130]. Hier rekurriert das OC wiederum auf ein Optik- und Imaginationskonzept: *Corporale igitur est, quod fit per corpus; spiritale, cum imagines eorum, quae videmus, in memoria condimus; intellectuale nempe, cum ea, quae corporaliter videmus et imaginaliter in memoria retinemus, intellectu discernimus. Intellectu igitur discernimus, quod illud sit corpus, illud similitudo corporis.* [...] *Vident et ipsa per corpus, et eorum, quae vident, imaginaliter spiritus informantur.* [...] *Postremo corporalis ista visio sine spiritali esse non potest. Ergo cum avertimus oculos ab eis, quae vidimus, imagines eorum, quae non videmus, in memoria retinemus. Spiritalis vero visio sine corporali esse potest.* [...] *Intellectu nec corpus videmus nec imaginem corporis; per hunc quippe videtur iustitita, caritas, ipse Deus, ipsa mens homnis, quae nullum corpus habet, nullam soliditatem corporis*[131].

Die von der optischen Wahrnehmung evozierte memorierende Imagination ist jedoch nur Vorstufe der intellektuellen Schau unkörperlich-immaterieller Wesenheiten[132]. Bemerkenswert ist die Feststellung des OC, dass Heilige – weil sie eine *imago* Gottes seien – nicht adäquat in leblosen Bildwerken darstellbar sind: *Ecce quam subtiliter quamque salubriter sancti viri hominem ad imaginem et simi-*

123 Mit den entsprechenden Quellennachweisen Thümmel 1997, 971.

124 *Esto, mundane sapientiae et saecularis scolae quemquam amor oblectat, accedat ad divinae legis armaria, quae sapientes mundi sicut meritorum celsitudine, ita etiam tempore praecedit, et liberalium studiorum profunditates, quas scit, cognovisse, et quas nescit, invenisse se gaudeat. Illic inveniet et recte loquutionis decorem, ethimologias nominum, schematum varietates, tropicas perplexiones.* [...] *Inveniet etiam historias, metra, quae omnia proprie artis grammaticae sunt* (*Opus Caroli regis contra synodum* 2.30). Dies kommentiert Ommundsen (2002, 178-9): „The original source for the arts is the Bible, and God is their creator. The language of the Bible is in fact built on the liberal arts, following the rules of grammar, rhetoric and dialectic, the trivium. [...] When scripture is the only means of communication between God and man, knowledge of the liberal arts, especially the trivium, becomes crucial".

125 Chazelle 1986, 165-6.

126 *Fecisse sanctus Moyses praecipiente Domino propitiatorium et arcam testamenti et duos cherubim aureos nec non excidisse tabulas lapideas legitur, non tamen adorare iussisse; nec ea ob praeteritarum quarundam rerum memoriam, sed ob futurorum mysteriorum sacratissimam praefigurationem creditur condidisse* (*Opus Caroli regis contra synodum* 1.15).

127 *In cruce namque, non in imaginibus, pretium mundi pependit.* [...] *Hoc est nostri regis insigne, non quedam pictura, quod nostri exercitus indesinentur aspiciunt legiones. Hoc est signum nostri imperatoris, non conpaginatio colorum, quod ad proelium nostre sequuntur cohortes.* [...] *Per crucis lignum, non per imagines, antiqui illius sceleris facinus diluitur, quod in protoplasto per ligni aesum contractum est* (*Opus Caroli regis contra synodum* 2.28; diese Passage ist mit der Marginalie *bene* versehen). S. hierzu Chazelle 2001, 51.

128 Chazelle 1986, 167, 181. Hinsichtlich der liturgisch-performativen Vergegenwärtigung des Heilsgeschehens ist hier nicht unbedeutend, dass in karolingischer Zeit die Altarmensa als Propitiatorium und somit als Antitypos der Bundeslade bezeichnet wurde (Braun 1993, 280).

129 *Opus Caroli regis contra synodum* 3.24. S. hierzu Chazelle 1986, 165.

130 *Multum igitur, et ultra quam mentis oculo prestringi queat, distat sacramentum Dominici corporis et sanguinis ab imaginibus pictorum arte depictis, cum videlicet illud efficiatur operante invisibiliter spiritu Dei, hae visibiliter manu artificis; illud consecretur a sacerdote divini nominis invocatione, hae pingantur a pictore humane artis eruditione* (*Opus Caroli regis contra synodum* 2.27).

131 *Opus Caroli regis contra synodum* 3.26. S. hierzu auch Chazelle 1986, 175.

132 S. hierzu Chazelle 1986, 172. Deutlich bezieht sich diese Differenzierung auf die in Fn. 101 angeführten Überlegungen des Augustinus.

litudinem Dei factum esse, imaginem videlicet in anima, in qua est intellectus, voluntas et memoria, similitudinem in moribus, id est in caritate, iustitia, bonitate et sanctitate, quae omnia incorporea sunt, intellegentes disseruere![133]

Nur (schriftliche) Zeichen vermittelten das Immaterielle dem Intellekt[134]. Bildobjekte verweisen somit generell auf die Verhüllung des Unsichtbaren durch Sichtbares, da sie vergangene Handlungen zeigen, in denen sich immaterielle Tugenden veräußerten[135]. Dem entspricht die Bezeichnung Christi als *imago* und *figura*: *Est etiam imago Dei* [...]*; ideo figura, quia suscipiens formam servi operum virtutumque similitudine Patris in se imaginem atque similitudinem designavit*[136]. Bezeichnet die *imago* nichtsichtbare Qualitäten, so werden diese durch die figurierte Verkörperung sichtbar. Wiederum vereint die *figura* immaterielles Prinzip und sinnliche Form: Christus verkörperte den per*forma*tiven Dienst an Gott, in dem sich dessen *virtus* vergegenwärtigte.

Hinsichtlich Alkuins Kognitionskonzept und den jeweiligen *imago*-Definitionen argumentiert das OC stringent gegen die Anbetung von Bildwerken, denen eine an den rhetorischen Praxiskategorien orientierte Erinnerungs- und Schmuckfunktion zugestanden wird; ihre Deutung erfolgt durch die Dialektik.[137]

Diesen Grundsätzen entspricht die Oxforder Elfenbeinplatte (Taf. 31). Die Aufforderung *Ecce* des ‚impliziten Betrachters'[138] Jesaja verwehrt die *adoratio*[139]. Seine *actio* lenkt den Blick auf die performative Inkarnation des Gotteswortes, die der Redegestus des Engels visualisiert. Die *virtus* der menschlichen *forma* offenbaren die rahmenden Wunderszenen. Die Narrativität dieser *imagines agentes* konterkariert die fixierende Darstellung des Auferstandenen, deren symmetrische Frontalität durch die Binnenrahmen aus Architektur und Tiergestalten intensiviert wird. Die imaginierende Syntax der Historienbilder wird im Bildzentrum zu einer fixierenden Reflexivität umgeformt. Steht die zukünftige Erlösung im Zentrum der Heils-Geschichte, so befindet sich die Christusfigur im kompositorischen Mittelpunkt, wobei der nahezu horizontale Kreuzstab Kompositionslinien der seitlichen Felder aufnimmt – kehrt der erste Blick die Heilsgeschichte um, so lenkt ihn die Bildsyntax in historische Bahnen.

Betont das OC die äußerliche Ähnlichkeit von Bildobjekten, so imitierte der Bildschnitzer ein frühchristliches Relikt, um dem im ‚rechtgläubigen' Ritus benutzten Evangelistar ein adäquates *decorum* zu verleihen. Dies entspricht nicht nur dem Kognitionskonzept Alkuins, sondern auch den karolingischen Reformbestrebungen und der Rhetoriklehre, die der *imitatio* von Rednern und literarischen Modellen einen wichtigen Stellenwert beimaß. Dem Grundsatz, dass allein die *inventio* die *imitatio* übertreffe, folgt die innovative Gestaltung und Funktion der Plastik[140].

Die poietischen Grundsätze finden eine weitere Entsprechung in den Äußerungen des in Aachen tätigen irischen Dichters Modoin. Dieser konstatierte hinsichtlich des künstlerischen Schaffensprozesses, dass zunächst die *historia* durch ihre schriftliche Kodifizierung gesichert werden müsse, damit ihr in einem Akt „geistige[r] Durchdringung"[141] *verba figure* unterlegt werden könnten, um die inhärente *veritas* und den *mysticus ordo* zu entschleiern[142]. In den Schreibkünsten bezeichnet die *figura* ebenso

133 *Opus Caroli regis contra synodum* 1.7. S. hierzu Jeck 1993, 100-2.

134 Jeck 1993, 181.

135 Chazelle (1986, 178): „Hence while the sight of an ordinary artistic rendering may arouse a mental vision of the prototype's existence in reality, even within this vision his spiritual qualities remain as imperceptible as they were when he actually existed, except whenever they were manifested to the outside world through his physical body, by his words and deeds".

136 *Opus Caroli regis contra synodum* 1.23.

137 Ommundsen 2002, 184. Chazelle (1986, 173) resümiert die Funktion eines Bildwerks: „[I]t can induce the viewer to recall not merely the prototype's appearance but the real existence of that person or thing […]. The man-made image is able to have this effect because, the LC indicate, in addition to being a material likeness of the prototype it is its sign; as such the work of art provokes the viewer to think of the prototype as it in its own rights exists or existed, outside of the artistic representation".

138 Iser 1994.

139 Die Abkehr von der Idolatrie ist bereits ein wichtiges Element der Prophezeiung Jesajas.

140 Petersen 2000, 68.

141 Binding 1996, 24.

142 *Versibus egregiis decursum clarus Arator Carmen apostolicis cecinit insigne coronis, Historiamque prius preponens cautus ubique Substituit tipice sensatim uerba figure. Lingua canora bonum testatur iure poetam, Mysticus ingenium sic indicat ordo profundum* (Modoin v. Autun *Versus Iohannis Foldensis Didascali* 5). Zitiert nach: Dümmler 1875, 67-8.

die „visuelle Isoliertheit des Wortes" bzw. seine Anordnung, die Les- und Memorierbarkeit gewährleistete[143]. Sind es laut dem OC gerade die (Schrift-)Zeichen, die dem Intellekt Undarstellbares vermitteln, so vereinigt die *figura* analog der Definition Ciceros geistige Inhalte und äußere Form.

IX.

Rhetorik und Imagination prägen auch Hrabanus Maurus' Gedichtzyklus *In honorem sanctae crucis*. Als Novize des Fuldaer Klosters verbrachte Hraban seine Lehrzeit bei Alkuin in Tours, bevor er 822 Abt zu Fulda und 25 Jahre später Erzbischof zu Mainz wurde. Zu seinen überlieferten Schriften zählt neben exegetischen Werken die klerikale Lehrschrift *De clericorum Institutione*. Die *artes liberales* prägen sein Verständnis des liturgischen Ritus, den eine „Analogiefähigkeit des sichtbaren Aktes und des dabei gebrauchten Materials" konstituiert[144]. Das Sakrament erkennt Hraban als dynamische „Beziehung zwischen Vorgängen, nicht [...] Dingen" und als „religiöse[n] Verweiszusammenhang, in dem man durch einen liturgischen Akt Einsicht gewinnt"[145]. Wirke der Priester im sakramentalen Vollzug auf die sichtbare Materie, erfülle Gottes Wort diese spirituell[146].

Der Gedichtzyklus *In Honorem Sanctae Crucis* entstand um 810[147]. Überliefert sind insgesamt 15 Exemplare, deren ältestes im zweiten Viertel des 9. Jahrhunderts in Fulda gefertigt und dort aufbewahrt wurde[148]. Laut der ersten Widmung sandte Hraban ein Exemplar nach Tours als Dank für die dortige Pflege der *artes liberales*[149]. Der Zyklus besteht aus 28 *carmina figurata* auf den jeweiligen *verso*-Seiten der Handschriften; ein erläuternder Kommentar begleitet sie auf den gegenüberliegen *recto*-Seiten. Interpretationen der Gedichte in Prosaform bilden den zweiten Teil (*Liber II*) des Gesamtwerks[150].

Die Figurengedichte selbst zeigen meist abstrakt-zeichenhafte Kreuzfigurationen, fünfmal jedoch auch figurative Darstellungen: Hraban in der Proskynese vor einem Kreuz (*cap. 28*), kreuzförmig arrangierte Blüten (*cap. 16*), das Lamm mit den vier apokalyptischen Wesen (*cap. 15*) und in *cap. 4* jeweils vier Cherubim und Seraphim. Den Auftakt bildet eine *imago Saluatoris* (*cap. 1*; Taf. 32). Die geöffneten Augen und das Fehlen von Wundmalen und Kreuzbalken verdeutlicht, dass es sich bei der Darstellung nicht um einen Kruzifixus handelt[151]. Der Figur eingeschrieben ist der Textcorpus, wobei einzelne Buchstaben Augen, Brustwarzen und Nabel Christi bilden[152]. Nennt der Text 60 Christusnamen und -symbole[153], so erläutert der Beginn des Kommentars programmatisch die imaginative Praxis des Codex: *Ecce imago Saluatoris membrorum suorum positione consecrat nobis saluberrimam, dulcissimam et amantissimam sanctae crucis formam, ut in eius nomine credentes et eius mandatis oboedientes, per eius passionem spem uitae aeternae habemus; ut quotiescumque crucem aspiciamus, ipsius recordemur, qui pro nobis in ea passus est, ut eriperet nos de potestate tenebrarum*, deglutiens quidem mortem, ut uitae aeternae heredes efficeremur, *profectus in caelum subiectis sibi angelis et potestatibus et uirtutibus*[154].

143 Ganz 1996, 24. So heißt es zur *figura* in einem Corpus Glossarum des 9. Jahrhunderts: *conformatio dictionis quam ostentationem et habitum possumus nuncupare*. Zitiert nach: Ganz 1996, 24.

144 Picker 2001, 165.

145 Picker 2001, 164-5.

146 Picker 2001, 167.

147 Zur Datierung s. Holter 1996, 159; Becht-Jördens 1996, 336.

148 Das Exemplar befindet sich heute in der Biblioteca Apostolica Vaticana (Cod. reg. lat 124.) Zur Textüberlieferung s. Holter 1996.

149 Ernst 2003, 17.

150 Becht-Jördens (1996, 344): „Bei Hraban hat die Prosaversion im zweiten Buch vor allem die Funktion, den durch die technischen Zwänge des Figurengedichts extrem verknappten und sprachlich bis zur Unverständlichkeit verdunkelten Sinn der Grundtexte expandierend und supplierend zu paraphrasieren".

151 Reudenbach 1986, 27; Ernst 2003, 25.

152 Chazelle 2001, 103.

153 Zu diesem programmatischen Auftakt schreibt Becht-Jördens (1996, 339-40): „Wie die 60 Christusnamen und -symbole in der *expositio* zu *figura I* bilden daher auch die 28 *figurae* im ganzen, unter ihnen auch das Bild des Gekreuzigten, einen Zyklus, mit dem Hraban das Problem der *imago Christi* und letztlich der *imago Dei* umschreitet".

154 Hrabanus Maurus *In honorem sanctae crucis* C1.

Im gleichen Kommentar findet sich eine aus dem OC bekannte Passage über Christus als *imago* und *figura*: *Imago dicitur propter parem similitudinem Patris. Figura, quod suscipiens formam serui, per operum uirtutumque similitudinem, Patris in se imaginem atque inmensam magnitudinem designauit*[155]. Somit verzichtet die bildliche Darstellung konsequent auf materielle Relikte der Passion und zeigt allein eine per*forma*tive *actio*, die die Kreuzform segnet und die Heils-Geschichte imaginativ vergegenwärtigt[156]. Das Einschreiben der göttlichen *virtus* in den Körper explizieren die Lettern *D-E-O* der Brustwarzen und des Nabels[157].

Hraban verweist in seinen Kommentaren stets auf die den Inhalten angemessene *dispositio*, *distributio* und *expositio* der *figurae*[158]. Dies bezieht sich sowohl auf die Form als auch den Status der Darstellungen, deren Inhalt die intermediale Symbiose von Zeichen, Zeichnung und Imagination re-präsentiert. Ausgangspunkt ist hierbei wiederum die sinnliche Wahrnehmung, die durch (Schrift-)Zeichen zu spirituellen Inhalten abstrahiert wird[159]. So sollen, wie es im Kommentar des zweiten Gedichts heißt, die *figurae* zu einer intellektuellen Schau der Heilsmysterien mit den *oculi sanae fidei* (*Prologus*) führen. Dies reflektiert die Bildsyntax (Taf. 32): Erfasst der erste Blick die figurative Zeichnung, so erschließt sich über den Text-*Corpus* der *versus intexti* sukzessive der Gedichtstext. Die ikonische Differenz von „synchrone[r] visio und sukzessive[r] lectio“[160] offenbart sich, ebenso wie in der Oxforder Elfenbeinplatte (Taf. 31), als grundlegendes Prinzip medialer Gestaltung, das aus dem performativen Kognitionskonzept Alkuins ableitbar ist, das direkte Wahrnehmung und reflexives Erkennen als zwei Phasen unterscheidet. Dies erklärt auch die Ambiguität der *figura*, die Sinnliches und Abstraktes vereint. Diese grundlegende Ikonizität reflektieren sowohl Hraban als auch das OC in der jeweiligen Gleichsetzung von Bildbetrachtung und Leseprozess – der sensuellen Wahrnehmung des ‚ersten Blicks’ folgt eine intellektuelle, auf einen spezifischen Sinnhorizont ausgerichtete Reflexion[161]. Konzeptuell entspricht dies der von Modoin beschriebenen poietischen Produktion. So kommentiert auch Hraban das Figurengedicht nicht Wort für Wort, sondern Sinneinheit für Sinneinheit[162].

Die Gliederung der Handschrift offenbart diese als ‚Sehschule‘: schrittweise wird der sensuelle Sehprozess abstrahiert, um eine intellektuelle Einsicht der mystischen Figuren zu ermöglichen. Der kontemplativen Funktion und Pragmatik des Gedichtzyklus, die heils-geschichtlichen Mysterien sukzessive zu entschleiern, entsprechen die im ersten Kommentar explizierte Medienpraxis und die Nutzung verschiedener Schriftformen, die eine Memorierung erleichtern[163].

Bemerkenswert ist die Bildfolge der *carmina figurata*: Sie beginnt mit der Darstellung einer Per*formanz*, die Christus als *figura* und *imago* Gottes auszeichnet und die Kreuzform segnet. Die folgenden *carmina* abstrahieren die *actio* Christi über zeichenhafte Kreuzfigurationen, um die liturgische Kreuzverehrung zu legitimieren – das letzte Bildfeld zeigt Hraban in Proskynese vor einem Kruzifix. Ist der

155 Hrabanus Maurus *In honorem sanctae crucis* C1.

156 Chazelle (2001, 115-6): „a visible repetition of the form of the cross may be considered sacred. [...] There is no cross in the poem’s figure, since the purpose is not only to recall that he was crucified, but to teach viewers that the crucified humanity exemplified the cross’s shape and thereby sanctified it“. S. hierzu Reudenbach 1986, 27.

157 Chazelle 2001, 117.

158 Reudenbach 1986, 30; Chazelle 2001, 112.

159 Laut Chazelle (2001, 196) betone Hraban „the central role to corporeal sight in contemplation of the mysteries revealed through the form of the cross“.

160 Ernst 2003, 25.

161 Im *Opus Caroli regis contra synodum* (2.30) heißt es: *[S]ed oculis tantummodo faveant, per quos quasi per quosdam legatos gestarum rerum memoriam cordibus mandent.* In einem Brief schreibt Hraban: *Sed claritatem eius et maiestatem perpetuam, laudibus quibuscumque possum, conservis meis praedic, ut saepius eam legentes ac sedulo conspicientes nostram in ea redemptionem assidue cogitemus.* Zitiert nach: Ferrari 1996, 512, Fn. 42.

162 Ulrich 2003, 19.

163 Ernst 2003, 21; Becht-Jördens 1996, 337. Ob die Figuren allein „im Dienst der verbalen Verkündigung“ (Ernst 2003, 28) stehen, bleibt fraglich, da der Codex, ebenso wie der Pilgerbericht des Adomnanus und die von Beda beschriebenen Bildwerke, als intermedial ausgerichtetes Kontemplationsobjekt diente. Das Kloster Fulda wurde vom angelsächsischen Missionar Bonifatius gegründet und der insulare Einfluss zeigt sich im 9. Jahrhundert auch in der Buchmalerei des Klosters (Ferrari 1996, 119; Mütherich 2004). Zwar werden die Darstellungen im Sinne des OC an die Schrift gebunden, doch erhalten sie eine ihr vergleichbare Funktion (Becht-Jördens 1996, 341). Becht-Jördens (1996, 340) vermutet hier den Einfluss Alkuins auf die Bilddiskussion, „die unter weitgehender Integration der bildkritischen Argumente gleichwohl zur Einsicht in die spirituellen Möglichkeiten des Bildes gelangt war und die Voraussetzungen sowohl für Hrabans Figurengedichtzyklus als auch für die Bildprogramme der Evangeliare der Hofschule und der Touroner Bibeln bildet“.

Körper Christi Ausgangspunkt der Kontemplation, so wird er schließlich imaginativ auf das körperlose Kreuzzeichen projiziert. Dies belegt ein Zitat Einhards – einst selbst Novize in Fulda –, der 836 auf eine Frage Lupus' von Ferrières zur Kreuzverehrung antwortete: *Illud tamen nosse debes, quod Greci inter orationem et adorationem talem differentiam faciunt, ut orationem proséuchin, adorationem proschínusin appellent, idque huiuscemodi differentia demonstari, quod horum alterum ad mentis, alterum ad corporis spectat officium.* [...] *Et quoniam haec differentia quod alicui rei licenter possit aptari, manifestum est, iam liquere puto, quod adoratio sanctae cruci non sit deneganda, quin potius, ut beatus Hieronimus de sancta Paula Hierosolimam veniente commemorans: ‚prostarta', inquit, ‚ante crucem, quasi pendentem Dominum cerneret, adorabat', hoc et nobis credamus esse faciendum, ut prosternamur videlicet ante crucem et eum, qui in ea pependit interioribus oculis intuentes adoremus*[164].

Einhards Verweis auf die Autorität des Hieronymus ist bemerkenswert: Nachdem Kaiserin Helena Passionskreuz und Grab Christi aufgefunden hatte, überbaute Kaiser Konstantin zwischen 325 und 335 das Grab mit einer monumentalen Rotunde, der Anastasis[165]. Unter ihrer Kuppelöffnung lag der freistehende Grabbau Christi (*tugurium*), dessen vergoldetes Dach von einem Kreuz bekrönt wurde[166]. Umgeben wurde er von einem Zentralbau mit Stützenstellung und drei mit Altären versehenen Apsiden im Norden, Süden und Westen. Östlich war dem Memorialbau eine Vorhalle vorgelagert, in der das Golgothaheiligtum lag. Die Kreuzigungsstätte trug ein Memorialkreuz[167]. Vielleicht fiel hier Paula nieder, ‚als wenn sie den Herrn dort hängen sah'[168]. Wie in Hrabans Gedichtzyklus würde somit die Imagination die körperliche Absenz Christi kompensieren , die ja erst die heils-geschichtliche Bedeutung des leeren Grabes konstituierte[169]. Medienpraxis und vergegenwärtigende Performanz verweisen auf den Pilgerbericht des Adomnanus, der auf der sensitiven Wahrnehmung und der *actio* ihres Protagonisten basierte und die Heils-Geschichte in der Imagination der Leser, die fern der Hl. Stätten weilten, vergegenwärtigte[170].

X.

Die „älteste sicher benennbare ‚Kopie' der Jerusalemer Anastasis"[171] erbauten in den Jahren 820-822 Abt Eigil und Hrabanus Maurus auf dem Mönchsfriedhof des Fuldaer Klosters (Taf. 33.1 und 33.2). Vom Ursprungsbau erhalten ist die unterirdische Krypta. Das Obergeschoss wurde im 11. Jahrhundert erneuert, besaß aber einen überwölbten Zentralraum, den acht Säulen von einem Umgang trennten[172]. Auch die durch einen separaten Eingang[173] begehbare Krypta besitzt einen Zentralraum, der sich durch

164 „Denn Du mußt immerhin wissen, daß die Griechen zwischen Gebet und Anbetung folgenden Unterschied machen, daß sie nämlich Gebet, ‚proséuchin', Anbetung ‚proschínusin' nannten und durch eine derartige Unterscheidung gezeigt wird, daß die eine Handlung den Geist, die andere den Körper betrifft. (...) Und weil es offenbar ist, daß dieser Unterschied jedwelchem Ding nach Belieben angepaßt werden kann, halte ich schon für klar, daß die Anbetung dem heiligen Kreuz nicht zu verweigern sei; und um so eher – als der selige Hieronymus von der hl. Paula bemerkt, wie sie nach Jerusalem kam: ‚zu Boden geworfen vor dem Kreuz betete sie an, als wenn sie den Herrn dort hängen sah' – sollen wir dies auch für richtig halten, daß wir uns nämlich vor dem Kreuz niederwerfen und den, der an ihm hing, mit den inneren Augen schauend anbeten". Zitat und Übersetzung nach: Hauck 1974, 216. S. hierzu Chazelle 2001, 124, 297.

165 Untermann 1989, 53-4.

166 Wilkinson 2003; Röwekamp 2000, 50-9.

167 Röwekamp 2000, 54; Schüppel 2005, 199. Die eigentliche Kreuzreliquie befand sich in einem vergoldeten Reliquiar und wurde während der Karfreitagsliturgie zur Verehrung ausgesetzt (Röwekamp 2000, 57).

168 Peers (2004, 41) schreibt hierzu: „This idea of mimesis and assimilation was central to experiencing a Christian reality, and it is clearest perhaps in the description of Holy Land pilgrimage from the fourth to the seventh century".

169 Die performative Vergegenwärtigung der Heils-Geschichte im Ritus der Anastasis verdeutlicht der spätantike Pilgerbericht der Egeria. Sie beschreibt, dass jeden Sonntag, „the clergy carried censers into the tomb to perform the actions of the three woman who brought spices to embalm Christ's body, and the bishop, standing at the door of the tomb, took the role of the angel and proclaimed Christ's resurrection" (van Dijk 1999, 430).

170 Die performative *actio* aktualisiert hierin das subjektive Wissen, das die Hl. Schrift und Pilgerberichte vermittelten: „In gazing at a cross, the Christian is made mindful of the miracle of redemption that is the source of its consecration and revelation of sacred wisdom, as recorded in scripture" (Chazelle 2001, 116).

171 Untermann 1989, 54.

172 Ellger 1989, 12; Untermann 1989, 55; Binding 1996, 17.

173 Becht-Jördens 1994, LI, Fn. 112.

vier an den Himmelrichtungen orientierte Zugänge zu einem Umgang öffnet. Das Gewölbe des Zentralraumes trägt eine Säule.

In der Krypta befand sich die Grablege Eigils und ca. 20 Jahre nach dessen Tod veranlasste Abt Hraban den Mönch Brun Candidus, einen Schüler Einhards, die Vita des Kirchengründers anzufertigen. Brun verfasste nicht nur anhand zahlreicher architektonischer Fachbegriffe eine detaillierte Ekphrasis des Baus, sondern interpretierte ihn auch[174]. Nach der Beschreibung des Baukörpers resümiert er den Entwurfsprozess: *Hoc siquidem aedificium pater* [Eigil] *iste uenerandus ac supra commemoratus magister* [Hraban] *cum sociis nescio quid magni fingentes Diuino magisterio docti, quod tamen ipse salua fide Christi et ecclesiae puto praesignari posse figuram*[175].

Es folgt eine detaillierte Deutung in Anlehnung an den ersten Brief Paulus' an die Korinther[176]: Die *figura* sei als *ecclesia spiritualis* aus den lebendigen Steinen der Heiligen und Gläubigen errichtet. Christus sei ihr Bauherr, Fundament, tragende Säule und ihr Schluss- bzw. Eckstein. Die acht Säulen des Obergeschosses versinnbildlichten die acht Seligpreisungen der Bergpredigt[177], die Kreisform des *templum* die ewige Macht Gottes und das ewige Leben[178].

Brun kennzeichnet die Deutung explizit als subjektiv, so dass es unklar bleibt, ob sie bereits den Entwurfsprozess beeinflusste[179]. Die Übertragung des Vitentextes auf das Bauwerk ist somit nicht nur aufgrund der jeweiligen Gattungskonventionen problematisch[180]. Die Vita richtete sich, wie ihre einstigen Dedikationsbilder zeigten, an die Fuldaer Mönche[181]. Im Sinne Modoins unterlegt Brun der Baugestalt *typice verba figure*[182]. Innerhalb der Vita birgt die Ekphrasis – ebenso wie Adomnanus' Beschreibung der Anastasis – als *micro-narrative* oder „topographisches Binnengedächtnis"[183] die Intention und Struktur des Gesamtwerks. Eigil errichtete als Medium göttlichen Willens zur *memoria* der Fuldaer Mönche die Kirche, in der er in einem Akt göttlicher Eingebung seine eigene Grabstätte fand. So figuriert in der Ekphrasis die Rotunde den Fuldaer Konvent, der als *ecclesia Christi ex lapidibus vivis* seiner heilsgeschichtlichen Bestimmung durch Eigil zugeführt wird[184]. Die Vita diente aber nicht nur der *memoria* Eigils, sondern war eine dezidierte Stellungnahme zu innerklösterlichen Konflikten, die unter Eigils Vorgänger Ratger begannen. Dieser hatte gegen den Willen der Mönche u.a. das tägliche Gebet für den Kaiser, sowie Verehrung und Totengedenken eingeschränkt[185]. Eigil nahm, wie Brun betont, diese Einschränkungen zurück, so dass die Michaelskirche in Funktion und literarischer Exegese ein Exempel identitätsstiftender *memoria* ist.

Bruns Text bietet jedoch auch konkretere Anhaltspunkte für eine Annäherung an die Baugestalt. Im Anschluss an Ekphrasis und Deutung überliefert er drei von Hraban verfasste Altartituli, die wohl an

174 *Pater namque monasterii dehinc sedulus addiscens communis uitae gaudia cum consilio et fratrum consensu ecclesiam paruam aedificauit rotundam, ubi defuncta corpora fratrum sepulturae tradita requiescunt, quam cimiterium uocant, quod Graece dicitur KOIMHTHPION, Latine uero dormitorium interpretatur. Cuius etiam aedificii structura subtus terram, ubi peruium circuit antrum, ab una columna lapidea in medio posita arcubus hinc et inde in eandem compaginatis ualenter exsurgit. Supra uero octonis subrigitur columnis atque in summitate operis lapide concluditur uno* (Brun Candidus *Vita Aegil abbatis Fuldensis* 17.1-2).

175 Brun Candidus *Vita Aegil abbatis Fuldensis* 1.17.3.

176 1. Kor. 3.17-8.

177 Math. 5.3-10.

178 Brun Candidus *Vita Aegil abbatis Fuldensis* 1.17.4-7. S. hierzu Untermann 1989, 57; Binding 1996, 20.

179 Untermann (1989, 50) bezeichnet Bruns Überlegungen als „nachträglich und spekulativ", so dass sie „nicht erkennbar auf Bauentwurf und Wahl von Bauformen eingewirkt" hätten. Günther Binding (1996, 21) konstatiert, „daß bei der Formfindung und Gestaltung theologische Vorstellungen grundlegend waren, die die Formen zum Zeichen machten und dem Zeichen eine Bedeutung gaben. Da diese zumeist vom Bauherrn nicht schriftlich fixiert wurden, mußten jüngere Autoren aus der Kenntnis der Zeit und aus ihren eigenen Vorstellungen eine Interpretation für die Gründe zur Formwahl beibringen".

180 Reudenbach 1980, 351.

181 Becht-Jördens 1993.

182 In einer späteren Passage nutzte Brun die literarische *enargeia*, um mit dem Leser die Fuldaer Klosterkirche imaginativ zu durchschreiten. Der Rundgang beginnt in der Ostkrypta der sog. Ratgerbasilika und endet in der Westkrypta; an jedem Altar erfolgt ein Gebet. Gereon Becht-Jördens (1994, XXI, Fn. 38) erkennt in der Route einen liturgischen Prozessionsweg, den der Leser imaginativ nachschreitet.

183 Wandhoff 2003, 32.

184 Becht-Jördens 1993, 89-93; 1994, XXV.

185 Ellger 1989, 163, 173; Becht-Jördens 1994.

den Altären des Obergeschosses angebracht waren[186]. Der des Hauptaltares beginnt: *Hoc altare Deo dedicatum est maxime Christo/ cuius hic tumulus nostra sepulchra iuuat. Pars montis Sinai, Moysi et memoratio digna,/ hic Christi Domini est et genitale solum. Hic Michael princeps Domini et symmysta Ioannes/ victoresque foci tres simul et pueri*[187].

Hieran anschließend werden weitere Reliquien von Märtyrern und Heiligen aufgeführt, so dass der Hauptaltar materielle Relikte der heils-geschichtlichen Zeitalter barg[188]. Bemerkenswert ist die Bezeichnung der Michaelskirche als *tumulus* Christi[189].

Per formam vereint die Baugestalt zwei konkrete Vorbilder: Mit der Jerusalemer Anastasis teilt sie die Zentralbauform mit drei Altären, einem Säulenumgang und einem abgesonderten Grabbereich; der Ausrichtung der Apsiden an den Himmelsrichtungen entspricht in Fulda die Disposition der Zugänge zum Zentralraum der Krypta. Vermittelt wurden die Charakteristika der Anastasis vielleicht durch Adomnanus' Pilgerbericht, den ein Fuldaer Bücherverzeichnis des 15. Jahrhunderts aufführt[190]. Die achtteilige Säulenstellung mit Architraven des Obergeschosses rezipiert den Zentralraum des Lateransbaptisteriums. Hier tragen die Architrave eine Inschrift, die die Taufe als Präfiguration der endzeitlichen Wiedergeburt deutet, deren Quelle die Passion Christi sei[191].

In ihrer architektonischen Disposition ähnelt die Michaelskirche den vom *Auctor ad Herennium* beschriebenen *imagines agentes*, die stets einen Handlungskontext zu einem Bild verdichten: „Da nun also den Vorgängen die Bilder (*imagines*) ähnlich sein müssen und wir aus allen Vorgängen für uns Ähnlichkeiten auswählen müssen, müssen die Ähnlichkeiten doppelt sein, zum einen mit den Vorgängen, zum anderen mit den Worten. Ähnlichkeiten mit den Vorgängen werden zum Ausdruck gebracht, wenn wir insgesamt für die Handlungen selbst Bilder (*imagines*) zurechtlegen; Ähnlichkeiten mit den Worten werden aufgestellt, wenn die Erinnerung an jede einzelne Benennung und jedes einzelne Wort durch ein Bild kenntlich gemacht wird. Die Erinnerung an den ganzen Vorgang halten wir durch ein einziges Kennzeichen und ein einfaches Bild fest“[192].

Eine ähnliche Bildrhetorik konstatiert das OC, laut dessen unbelebte Bildobjekte allein vergangene Handlungen als Verkörperungen unsichtbarer Tugenden visualisierten. Festzuhalten bleibt, dass die sinnstiftende Vergegenwärtigung der Gedächtnisbilder erst über die Per*forma*nz des Redners und die imaginative Rezeption des Zuhörers erfolgt.

186 Ellger 1989, 82; Untermann 1989, 57.

187 Brun Candids *Vita Aegil abbatis Fuldensis* 2.22.1.

188 Ellger 1989, 83.

189 Untermann 1989, 58; Binding 1996, 21.

190 Das Bücherverzeichnis (Hs. Basel F III 42) nennt neben Werken Ciceros auch Vitruvs Architekturtraktat (Schrimpf 1992, 98-171).

191 So heißt es in der Inschrift: *Virgineo faetu genitrix ecclesia natos,/ quos spirante deo concipit, amne parit./ Insons esse volens isto mundare lavacro,/ seu patrio premeris crimine seu proprio./ Fons hic est vitae, qui totum diluit orbem/ sumens de Christi vulnere principium./ Caelorum regnum sperate, hoc fonte renati;/ non recipit felix vita semel genitos.* Zitiert nach: Underwood 1950, 55.

192 *Quoniam ergo rerum similes imagines esse oportet et ex omnibus verbis nosmet nobis similitudines eligere debemus, duplices igitur similitudines esse debent, unae rerum, alterae verborum. Rerum similitudines exprimuntur, cum summatim ipsorum negotiorum imagines conparamus; verborum similitudines constituuntur, cum unius cuiusque nominis et vocabuli memoria imagine notatur* (*Rhetorica ad Herennium* 3.20). Übersetzung nach: Nüßlein 1998, 170-1. Der *Auctor* gibt ein bemerkenswertes Beispiel, das verdeutlicht, wie Handlungsprozesse und Sinnzusammenhänge auf der Grundlage sozial etablierter Wissenshorizonte zu einer *imago* verdichtet werden: „Die Erinnerung an den ganzen Vorgang halten wir oft durch ein einziges Kennzeichen und ein einfaches Bild fest, z.B. auf folgende Weise, wenn der Ankläger sagt, von dem Angeklagten sei ein Mensch mit Gift getötet worden, und ihn beschuldigt, die Tat sei um einer Erbschaft willen begangen worden, und weiterhin sagt, dafür gebe es viele Zeugen und Mitwisser. Wenn wir uns daran erinnern wollen, damit es uns für die Verteidigung dienlich sei, werden wir am ersten Ort ein Bild des ganzen Vorganges gestalten (*in primo loco rei totius imaginem conformabimus*); wir werden den Menschen selbst, um den es geht, uns krank im Bett liegend vorstellen, wenn wir sein Aussehen festhalten (*si formam eius detinebimus*); wenn wir ihn nicht kennen, werden wir irgendeinen Kranken, und zwar nicht aus dem niedrigsten Stande, nehmen, damit er uns schnell in den Sinn kommen kann, und wir werden den Angeklagten an sein Bett stellen, wie er in der Rechten den Giftbecher, in der Linken das Testament und am Ringfinger die Hoden eines Widders hält [Die *testiculi* dienten als Geldbeutel]. Auf diese Weise können wir die Erinnerung an Zeugen, die Erbschaft und den durch Gift getöteten behalten“. (*Rhetorica ad Herennium* 3.33.) Übersetzung nach: Nüßlein 1998, 171, 173. Die *Rhetorica ad Herennium*, die bereits Hieronymus als Werk Ciceros bezeichnete, ist durch Handschriften des 9. Jahrhunderts überliefert. U.a. hat Lupus von Ferrières, der mit Einhard über Fragen der Kreuzverehrung korrespondierte, den Text emendiert (Nüßlein 1998, 342).

Die architektonische Formenwahl in Fulda erinnert an den von Modoin beschriebenen poietischen Schaffensprozess; ebenso wie Alkuin verband Brun die *figura* mit dem Verb *fingere*, wobei die entwerfende *cogitatio* auf göttlicher Unterweisung beruhte. Dieser Topos findet sich in der Hl. Schrift im Kontext des Salomonischen Tempelbaus – dem folgt die Bezeichnung der Michaelskirche als *templum*[193]. Verbindet man Alkuins *figura*-Begriff mit dem des angeführten Glossariums – also der visuellen Isoliertheit des Wortes –, so fügt die *dispositio* der Michaelskirche unterschiedliche, historisch gesicherte architektonische *figurae* mit einem gemeinsamen Sinnhorizont zusammen. Dem entspräche die *figura*-Definition in Hrabans Gedichtzyklus, der Brun inspirierte[194]. Die *imago Saluatoris* des ersten Kreuzgedichts (Taf. 32) vereint *per forma* die historischen Ereignisse Tod und Auferstehung; die *actio* Christi verkörpert die göttliche *virtus*. Diese Ikonizität von Immanenz und Transzendenz birgt auch die Jerusalemer Anastasis als architektonische Figur, da das leere Grab die göttliche *actio* bezeugt. Segnete in Hrabans *imago Saluatoris* die Kreuzform des Körpers die liturgische Kreuzverehrung als Akt memorierender Meditation sowie die unterschiedlichen Kreuzformationen, so ist dies auf die Zentralbauform und den in ihr performativ vergegenwärtigten Sinnhorizont übertragbar[195].

Bezüglich der Handlungskontexte der Bauwerke in Jerusalem, Rom und Fulda ist bemerkenswert, dass in ihnen stets Übergangsriten vollzogen wurden[196]. Kreuzigung und Auferstehung aus dem Grab, das im Zentrum der Anastasis verortet war, präfigurieren die an Ostern vollzogene Taufe und das Auftauchen aus dem *tegurium* des Taufbeckens im Zentrum des Lateransbaptisteriums[197]. Bruns Bezeichnung der Michaelskapelle als *dormitorium* verdeutlicht deren transitiven Charakter. Zwar lässt sich ihre rituelle Nutzung kaum erschließen, doch legt die architektonische Disposition nahe, dass sich die Mönchsgemeinschaft zur rituellen *memoria* im Zentralraum der Kapelle versammelte (Taf. 33.1); dem entspricht, dass der Erzengel Michael, dessen Patrozinium die Kirche trägt, von Alkuin als Übermittler der Fürbitten gesehen wurde[198]. Diese Anbindung an die Offenbarung des Johannes[199] legt eine rituelle Vergegenwärtigung der endzeitlichen *Ecclesia spiritualis* nahe. So überliefert auch ein Fuldaer Sakramentar zum Totengedächtnis die „Hoffnung, daß auf dem Friedhof [...] beim Schall der Posaune die verstreuten Glieder und Knochen wieder ‚ad iuncturas corporum ac liniamenta nervorum', also zu ganzen Körpern zusammengefügt werden"[200]. Die Körpermetapher verweist auf den *corpus mysticum* der *Ecclesia*, der in den Reliquien der Altäre präsent ist[201]. Eine Anbindung an die Offenbarung prägte auch das monastische Totengedenken: Sah Johannes die Toten vor dem endzeitlichen Thron Gottes stehen, wo über sie nach ihren im Buch des Lebens verzeichneten Taten gerichtet wurde[202], wurden in karolingischer Zeit zahlreiche Nekrologien angefertigt, in denen die Namen Lebender und Verstorbener zu liturgischen Rezitation aufgezeichnet waren[203]. Da die Fuldaer Nekrologien nur örtliche Ordensmitglieder führten, offenbart sich die rituell vergegenwärtigte Gemeinschaft der Lebenden und Verstorbe-

193 In seinem *De templo* (1.1) deutet Beda Venerabilis Salomos Tempel, *quam aedificavit* [...] *in Hierusalem in figuram facta est sanctae universalis ecclesiae quae a primo electo usque ad ultimum qui in fine mundi nasciturus est cotidie per gratiam regis pacifici sui videlicet redemptoris aedificatur quae partim adhuc peregrinatur ab illo in terris partim evasis peregrinandi aerumnis cum illo iam regnat in caelis ubi percato ultimo iudico tota est regnatura cum illo.* Zitiert nach: Binding 1996, 382.

194 Becht-Jördens 1994, XXI, Fn. 39, XXII.

195 Es ist mit Blick auf die *imago Saluatoris* in Hrabans Gedichtzyklus auffällig, dass Brun den Zentralbau der Kapelle nicht nur als Symbol der ewigen Macht Gottes, sondern auch als *figura Christi* deutet. Galt Vitruv der menschliche Körper als Exempel idealtypischer Symmetrie, so betont Brun, dass Christus Fundament, Schlussstein und tragende Säule des Baukörpers sei. Die ewige Macht Gottes bezieht sich dabei auf die menschliche und göttliche Natur, die Christus nicht zuletzt durch seine Auferstehung verkörperte. So könnte die Darstellung des Gedichtzyklus (Taf. 32) gleichsam eine idealtypische Proportionsstudie sein, die mit der *figura*-Definition des Kommentars zum ersten Kreuzgedicht kongruierte, da die *figura* hier auf einer spezifischen *forma* basiert.

196 Turner 1995.

197 Zum Taufritus und der Überlieferung des *teguriums* s. Underwood 1950, 45; Chazelle 2001, 21, 172.

198 Ellger 1989, 71.

199 Apk. 12.7-9.

200 Ellger 1989, 96.

201 Zum Auferstehungsgedanken in karolingischer Zeit mit zahlreichen Quellen aus dem OC s. Chazelle 2001, 171.

202 Apk. 20.12-5.

203 Schmenk 2003.

nen als konstitutive Identitätsstiftung[204]. Die Performanz des heilsgeschichtlichen Sozialkörpers reflektiert Bruns Deutung der *lapides vivi*, die das Fundament der *Ecclesia spiritualis* bildeten[205].

Dem Spannungsfeld zwischen Immanenz und Transzendenz – zwischen Wahrnehmung und Reflexion – entspricht die Tradition des *figura*-Begriffs: Bezeichnete Vitruv mit ihm noch die imaginative Re-präsenz eines gezeichneten Baukörpers, so deutet Augustinus in seinen *Enarrationes in psalmos* den Tempel Salomos als *figura futurae ecclesiae et corporis Domini*[206]. Die auf der *cogitatio* basierende, imaginative *figura* Vitruvs wird über das ‚exegetische Sehen' der *oculis mentis* zur *mystica figura* der Heils-Geschichte.

XI.

In seinem 1. Brief an die Korinther[207] bezeichnet Paulus nicht nur das Innere des Menschen als *aedificium*, sondern sich selbst in seiner Funktion als Vermittler des Gotteswortes als Bauherrn, der das Fundament lege, auf dem die Gläubigen durch ihre Lebensführung aufbauen. In dieser Tradition wurde die Auslegung der Hl. Schrift mit der Errichtung eines Gebäudes im Inneren des Menschen parallelisiert[208]. Bereits Isidor von Sevilla entlehnte von Vitruv u.a. die Begriffe *constructio* und *dispositio*; als *machina* bezeichnete er die der Lektüre folgende Memorierung[209]. Der poietische Prozess der Architektur- und Textkonstruktion als (An-)Ordnung von Elementen entspricht der subjektiven Synthese von Wahrnehmung, Imagination und Reflexion. Die angeführten Wahrnehmungskonzepte haben gezeigt, dass die Wahrnehmung kein Abbilden der Welt ist, sondern ein Akt des Fingierens – der poetischen Doppelung, die eine Simultanpräsenz der äußerlich-objektivierten und endogen-virtuellen Welten ermöglicht[210]. Der Funktion der Baukörper als Rahmen performativer Vergegenwärtigungen sozialer Sinnhorizonte entspricht dabei der menschliche Körper, in dem sich durch Imagination und Reflexion diese Sinnwelten erst verwirklichen.

Bibliografie

Angenendt, A. 1995. *Das Frühmittelalter. Die abendländische Christenheit von 400 bis 900*. 2. Auflage. Stuttgart: Kohlhammer.

—. 2001. *Liturgik und Historik. Gab es eine organische Liturgie-Entwicklung?* Quaestiones Disputate 189. Freiburg u.a.: Herder.

204 Karl Schmid (1998, 14) schreibt hierzu: „Daher wurde die Gemeinschaft der lebenden und verstorbenen Brüder als eine Wirklichkeit betrachtet, die im Aufruf der Namen ihrer Mitglieder, das heißt durch ihre Vergegenwärtigung bei den liturgischen Handlungen am Altar oder im Kapitel praktiziert worden ist". In einem Nekrolog der Reichenau heißt es: „Du mögest, Herr, diejenigen, deren Namen im liturgischen Lebensbuch aufgeschrieben sind, auch in deinem himmlischen Lebensbuch aufschreiben". Zitiert nach: Schmid 1998, 20.

205 In gleicher Weise deutete Hrabanus Maurus in seinen *Commentaria in libros Regum* (3.5) das Fundament des Tempels (Binding 1996, 278-9).

206 Mit den entsprechenden Quellennachweisen Binding 1996, 369. In seinem in karolingischer Zeit intensiv rezipiertem Werk *De civitate Dei* (15.26) deutet Augustinus in Anlehnung an Vitruv die Arche Noah als *figura peregrinatis in hoc saeculo civitatis Dei, hoc est ecclesia*. Zitiert sei die Übersetzung nach Binding (1996, 401): „[D]enn auch die Maße selbst ihrer Länge, Höhe und Breite bezeichnen den menschlichen Körper, in dessen Wirklichkeit der Erlöser zu kommen verheißen war und in der Tat gekommen ist. Denn die Länge des menschlichen Körpers vom Scheitel bis zur Sohle beträgt das Sechsfache der Breite von einer Seite zur anderen, und das Zehnfache der Höhe, seitlich gemessen vom Rücken bis zum Bauch. Wenn man nämlich einen hingestreckt auf dem Rücken liegenden Menschen mißt, wird er sechsmal so lang sein vom Kopf bis zu den Füßen, als er in der Breite mißt von rechts nach links oder umgekehrt, und zehnmal so lang, als er hoch ist vom Erdboden aus. Und nach diesem Maß ist die Arche gemacht worden, 300 Ellen in der Länge, 50 in der Breite und 30 in der Höhe". S. hierzu Reudenbach 1980, 312.

207 1. Kor. 3.9-17.

208 Brinkmann 1980, 230.

209 Schuler 1999, 45; Carruthers 1993, 896. Carruthers (1993, 899) resümiert: „Making the scheme is a creative task. When the master builder raises his tropes on the foundation-stones of an actual text [...] he must smooth, scrape, chip off, and in other ways shape the dicta et facta memorabilia he is using as materials".

210 Zu den Begriffen ‚Fingieren' und ‚Fiktionalität' s. Iser 1993, 144-5.

Auerbach, E. 1944. „Figura." In *Neue Dantestudien*, 11-71. Istanbuler Schriften 5. Istanbul: Basimevi.

Becht-Jördens, G. 1993. „Text, Bild und Architektur als Träger einer ekklesiologischen Konzeption von Klostergeschichte. Die karolingische Vita Aegil des Brun Candidus von Fulda (ca. 840)." In *Hagiographie und Kunst. Der Heiligenkult in Schrift, Bild und Architektur*, herausgegeben von G. Kerscher, 75-106. Berlin: Reimer.

—, Hrsg. 1994. *Vita Aegil abbatis Fuldensis a Candido ad modestum edita prosa et versibus. Ein Opus Geminum des IX. Jahrhunderts*. Marburg: Selbstverlag.

—. 1996. „Litterae Illuminatae. Zur Geschichte eines literarischen Formtyps in Fulda." In Schrimpf 1996, 325-64.

Belting, H. 1991. *Bild und Kult. Eine Geschichte des Bildes vor dem Zeitalter der Kunst*. Unveränderter Nachdruck der 2. Auflage. München: C.H. Beck.

—. 2001. *Bild-Anthropologie. Entwürfe für eine Bildwissenschaft*. München: Fink.

Berns, J.J., Hrsg. 2003. *Gedächtnislehren und Gedächtniskünste in antike und Frühmittelalter [5. Jahrhundert v. Chr. bis 9. Jahrhundert n. Chr.]. Dokumentsammlung mit Übersetzung, Kommentar und Nachwort*. Documenta Mnemonica 1.1. Tübingen: Max Niemeyer.

Bieler, L. 1958. „The Text Tradition." In Meehan 1958, 30-4.

Bilstein, J. 2005. „Gestischer Lakonismus." In Wulf und Zirfas 2005, 59-83.

Binding, G. 1996. *Der früh- und hochmittelalterliche Bauherr als* sapiens architectus. Veröffentlichungen der Abteilung Architekturgeschichte des Kunsthistorischen Instituts der Universität zu Köln 61. Köln: Abteilung des Kunsthistorischen Institutes der Universität.

Blum, H. 1969. *Die antike Mnemotechnik*. Spudasmata 15. Hildesheim u.a.: Olms.

Boehm, G. 1994. „Die Wiederkehr der Bilder." In *Was ist ein Bild?*, herausgegeben von G. Boehm, 11-38. München: Fink.

—. 1995. „Bildbeschreibung. Über die Grenzen von Bild und Sprache." In Boehm und Pfotenhauer 1995, 23-40.

—, Hrsg. 2001a. *Homo Pictor*. Colloquium Rauricum 7. Leipzig und München: Saur.

—. 2001b. „Repräsentation – Präsentation – Präsenz. Auf den Spuren des homo pictor." In Boehm 2001a, 3-13.

Boehm, G. und H. Pfotenhauer, Hrsg. 1995. *Beschreibungskunst – Kunstbeschreibung. Ekphrasis von der Antike bis zur Gegenwart*. München: Fink.

Braun, J. 1993. Nachdruck. „Propitiatorium." In *Liturgisches Handlexikon*, 280. 2. Auflage. München: Mäander. Originalausgabe, Regensburg: Kösel & Pustet, 1924.

Brenk, B. 2002. „Legitimation – Anspruch – Innovation. Zur Herrschaftskunst der Karolinger." In Ehlers 2002, 149-76.

Brinkmann, H. 1980. *Mittelalterliche Hermeneutik*. Tübingen: Niemeyer.

Bullough, D.A. 2004. *Alcuin. Achievement and Reputation*. Education and Society in the Middle Ages and Renaissance 16. Leiden u.a.: Brill.

Bumke, J. 2001. *Die Blutstropfen im Schnee. Über Wahrnehmung und Erkenntnis im ‚Parzival' Wolframs von Eschenbach*. Hermeia. Germanistische Forschungen NF 94. Tübingen: Niemeyer.

Campe, R. 1997. „Vor-Augen-Stellen. Über den Rahmen rhetorischer Bildgebung." In *Poststrukturalismus. Herausforderungen and die Literaturwissenschaft*, 208-25. Germanistische Symposien Berichtsbände 18. Stuttgart u.a.: Metzler.

Carruthers, M. 1993. „The Poet as Master Builder. Composition and Locational Memory in the Middle Ages." *New Literary History* 24: 881-904.

—. 2000. *The Craft of Thought Meditation, Rhetoric, and the Making of Images, 400-1200*. Cambridge Studies in Medieval Literature 34. Cambridge: University Press.

—. 2002. *The Book of Memory. A Study of Memory in Medieval Culture*. 10. Auflage. Cambridge: University Press.

Chazelle, C. 1986. „Matter, Spirit, and Image in the *Libri Carolini*." *Recherches Augustiniennes* 21: 163-84.

—. 2001. *The Crucified God in the Carolingian Era. Theology and Art of Christ's Passion*. Cambridge: University Press.

Cubitt, C., Hrsg. 2003. *Court Culture in the Early Middle Ages. Proceedings of the First Alcuin Conference*. Studies in the Early Middle Ages 3. Turnhout: Brepols.

Dierse, U. 1972. „Figur.“ In *Historisches Wörterbuch der Philosophie*, herausgegeben von J. Ritter, Band 2, 948-9. Darmstadt: Wissenschaftliche Buchgesellschaft.

Donner, H., Hrsg. und Übers. 2002. *Pilgerfahrt ins Heilige Land. Die ältesten Berichte christlicher Palästinapilger (4.-7. Jahrhundert.)*. 2. durchgesehene und ergänzte Auflage. Stuttgart: Verlag Katholisches Bibelwerk.

Dümmler, E., Hrsg. 1875. „Gedichte des Naso.“ *Zeitschrift für Deutsches Alterthum* 18: 58-70.

Eastmond, A. und L. James, Hrsg. 2003. *Icon and Word. The Power of Images in Byzantium. Studies presented to Robin Cormack*. Aldershot u.a.: Ashgate.

Ehlers, J., Hrsg. 2002. *Deutschland und der Westen Europas im Mittelalter*. Vorträge und Forschungen 56. Stuttgart: Thorbecke.

Ellger, O. 1989. *Die Michaelskirche zu Fulda als Zeugnis der Totensorge. Zur Konzeption einer Friedhofs- und Grabkirche im karolingischen Kloster Fulda*. Veröffentlichungen des Fuldaer Geschichtsvereins 55. Fulda: Parzeller.

Elsner. J. 1995. *Art and the Roman Viewer. The Transformation of Art from the Pagan World to Christianity*. Cambridge Studies in New Art History and Criticism. Cambridge: University Press.

Ernst, U. 2003. „Die Kreuzgedichte des Hrabanus Maurus als multimediales Kunstwerk. Textualität – Ikonizität – Numeralität.“ In Schmitz und Wenzel 2003, 13-37.

Fensterbusch, C., Hrsg. und Übers. 1964. *Zehn Bücher über die Baukunst*. Darmstadt: Wissenschaftliche Buchgesellschaft.

Ferrari, M. 1996. „Hrabanica. Hrabans *De laudibus sanctae crucis* im Spiegel der neueren Forschung.“ In Schrimpf 1996, 493-526.

Fillitz, H. 1966. „Die Elfenbeinreliefs zur Zeit Karls des Großen.“ *Aachener Kunstblätter* 32: 14-45.

Fischer-Lichte, E., Hrsg. 1998 *Kulturen des Performativen*. Paragrana 7. Berlin: Akademie-Verlag.

—. 2004. *Ästhetik des Performativen*. Frankfurt am Main: Suhrkamp.

Frank, G. 2000. *The Memory of the Eyes. Pilgrims to Living Saints in Christian Late Antiquity*. Berkeley u.a.: University of California Press.

Freeman, A., Hrsg. 1998. *Opus Caroli regis contra synodum (Libri Carolini)*. Monumenta Germaniae Historica. Concilia Tomus 2, Supplementum 1. Hannover: Hahnsche Buchhandlung.

Fried, J. 1997. „Vom Nutzen der Rhetorik und Dialektik für das Leben.“ In *Dialektik und Rhetorik im frühen und hohen Mittelalter*, herausgegeben von J. Fried, VII-XX. Schriften des Historischen Kollegs, Kolloquien 27. München: Oldenbourg.

Ganz, D. 1996. „Temptabat et scribere. Vom Schreiben in der Karolingerzeit.“ In *Schriftkultur und Reichsverwaltung unter den Karolingern. Referate des Kolloquiums der Nordrhein-Westfälischen Akademie der Wissenschaften am 17./18. Februar 1994 in Bonn*, herausgegeben von R. Schieffer, 13-33. Abhandlungen der Nordrhein-Westfälischen Akademie der Wissenschaften 97. Opladen: Westdeutscher Verlag.

Graf, F. 1995. „Ekphrasis. Die Entstehung der Gattung in der Antike.“ In Boehm und Pfotenhauer 1995, 143-55.

Gumbrecht, H. U. 2004. *Diesseits der Hermeneutik. Die Produktion von Präsenz*. Frankfurt am Main: Suhrkamp.

Haase, F.-A. 2005. „Rhetoric as a Praise of the Emperor and Applied Politics of an Education Concept. The ‚tres publica litteraria‘ inside the Monarchy. Alcuin of York and Rhabanus Maurus as Representatives of the Early Rhetoric in Germany during the Renaissance of Charlemagne and the Manuscript *Albinus ad Regem*.“ *Concilium medii aevi* 8: 1-25. http://www.cma.d-r.de/dr,cma,008,2005,a,01.pdf (5. September 2005).

Hauck, K. 1974. „Versuch einer Gesamtdeutung des Einhard-Kreuzes.“ In *Das Einhardkreuz. Vorträge und Studien der Münsteraner Diskussion zum arcus Einhardi*, herausgegeben von K. Hauck, Anhang 2, 211-16. Abhandlungen der Akademie der Wissenschaften in Göttingen. Philologisch-Historische Klasse 3. Folge 87. Göttingen: Vandenhoek & Ruprecht.

Heisenberg, A. 1908. *Grabeskirche und Apostelkirche. Zwei Basiliken Konstantins*. Band 1. Leipzig.

Holter, K. 1996. „Kommentar.“ In *Buchkunst – Handschriften – Bibliotheken. Beiträge zur mittelalterlichen Buchkultur vom Frühmittelalter bis zur Renaissance*, Band 1, 157-86. Linz: Oberösterreichischer Musealverein et al.

Innes, M. 2003. „‚A Place of Discipline‘. Carolingian Courts and Aristocratic Youth.“ In Cubitt 2003, 59-76.

Iser, W. 1993. *Das Fiktive und das Imaginäre. Perspektiven literarischer Anthropologie*. Frankfurt am Main: Suhrkamp.

—. 1994. *Der implizite Leser. Kommunikationsformen des Romans von Bunyan bis Beckett*. 3. Auflage. München: Fink (UTB).

James, L. 2003. „Art and Lies. Text, Image and Imagination in the Medieval World." In Eastmond und James 2003, 59-71.

James, L. und Webb. R. 1991. „‚To understand Ultimate Things and Enter Secret Places'. Ekphrasis and Art in Byzantium." *Art History* 14: 1-17.

Jeck, U.R. 1993. „Gott in der Materie darstellen? Zum Grundverständnis des Kultbildes in *Libri Carolini*." *Hermeneia* 2: 95-108.

Juwig, C. Im Druck. „Ort der Imagination. Visualität und Bildlichkeit der Aachener Pfalzkapelle." In *Orte der Herrschaft – Places of Power – Lieux de pouvoir*, herausgegeben von C. Ehlers. Göttingen: Vandenhoek & Ruprecht.

Kahsnitz, R. 1999. „Buchdeckel mit triumphierendem Christus." In *799. Kunst und Kultur der Karolingerzeit. Karl der Große und Papst Leo III. in Paderborn*, herausgegeben von C. Stiegemann und M. Wemhoff, Band 2, 696-8. Mainz: von Zabern.

Kessler, H.L. 2000. *Spiritual Seeing. Picturing God's Invisibility in Medieval Art*. Philadelphia: University of Pennsylvania Press.

Klarer, M. 1999. „*Ekphrasis*, or: The Archeology of Historical Theories of Representation. Medieval Brain Anatomy in Wernher der Gartenaere's *Helmbrecht*." *Word & Image* 15: 34-40.

Kötting, B. 1988. *Ecclesia peregrinans. Das Gottesvolk unterwegs*. 2 Bände. Münsterische Beiträge zur Theologie 54. Münster: Aschendorff.

Kötzsche, D. 1965. „Buchdeckel mit triumphierendem Christus." In *Karl der Große. Werk und Wirkung*, 335-6. Düsseldorf.

Krämer, S. 1998. „Sprache – Stimme – Schrift. Sieben Thesen über Performativität als Medialität." In Fischer-Lichte 1998, 33-57.

Lechterman, C. 2003. „Nebenwirkungen: Blick-Bewegungen vor der Perspektive." In Schmitz und Wenzel 2003, 93-111.

Lindberg, D.C. 1978. „The Science of Optics." In *Science in the Middle Ages*, herausgegeben von D. C. Lindberg, 338-68. Chicago u.a.: University of Chicago Press.

Löw, M. 2001. *Raumsoziologie*. Frankfurt am Main: Suhrkamp.

Matussek P. 1999. „Der selbstbezügliche Blick. Ein Merkmal des erinnernden Sehens und seine medialen Metamorphosen." *Zeitschrift für Germanistik* NF 9: 637-54.

Mayr-Harting, H. 1992. „Charlemagne as a Patron of Art." In *The Church and the Arts. Papers Read at the 1990 Summer Meeting and the 1991 Winter Meeting of the Ecclesiastical History Society*, herausgegebenen von D. Wood, 43-77. Oxford u.a.: Blackwell Publishing.

McKitterick, R., Hrsg. 1997. Nachdruck. *Carolingian Culture. Emulation and Innovation*. Cambridge: Cambridge University Press. Originalausgabe, Cambridge: Cambridge University Press, 1994.

—. 2002. „Kulturelle Verbindungen zwischen England und den fränkischen Reichen in der Zeit der Karolinger. Kontexte und Implikationen." In Ehlers 2002, 121-48.

Meehan, D., Hrsg. und Übers. 1958. *Adamnan's De locis sanctis*. Scriptores Latini Hiberniae 3. Dublin: Dublin Institute for Advanced Studies.

Merklin, H., Hrsg. und Übers. 2003. *De oratore*. 5. Auflage. Stuttgart: Philipp Reclam jun.

Meyvaert, P. 1979. „Bede and the Church Paintings at Wearmouth-Jarrow." *Anglo-Saxon England* 8: 63-77.

Migne, J.-P., Hrsg. 1861. *Venerabilis Bedae, Anglo-Saxonis presbyteri, opera omnia*. Band 6 Patrologiae Latinae 95. Paris: Selbstverlag.

—, Hrsg. 1863. *B. Flacci Albini seu Alcuini abbati et Caroli Magni imperatoris magisteri opera omnia*. Band 2. Patrologiae Latinae 101. Paris: Selbstverlag.

Miles, M. 1983. „Vision. The Eye of the Body and the Eye of the Mind in Saint Augustine's *De trinititate* and *Confessiones*." *Journal of Religion* 63: 125-42.

Morse, R. 1991. *Truth and Convention in the Middle Ages. Rhetoric, Representation, and Reality*. Cambridge u.a.: Cambridge University Press.

Mütherich, F. 2004. „Die Fuldaer Buchmalerei in der Zeit des Hrabanus Maurus.“ In *Studies in Carolingian Manuscript Illumination*, 374-416. London: Pindar Press.

Nagel. H. 1998. *Karl der Große und die theologischen Herausforderungen seiner Zeit.* Freiburger Beiträge zur mittelalterlichen Geschichte 12. Frankfurt am Main u.a.: Lang.

Nees, L. 1995. „Carolingian Art and Politics.“ In Sullivan 1995, 186-226.

Nelson, J.A. 2003. „Was Charlemagne's Court a Courtly Society?“ In Cubitt 2003, 39-57.

Nelson, R.S., Hrsg. 2000a. *Visuality before and beyond the Renaissance. Seeing as Others Saw.* Cambridge: University Press.

—. 2000b. „To Say and to See. Ekphrasis and Vision in Byzantium.“ In Nelson 2000a, 143-68.

Noble, T.F.X. 1995. „Tradition and Learning in Search of Ideology.“ In Sullivan 1995, 227-60.

Nüßlein, T., Hrsg. und Übers. 1998. *Rhetorica ad Herennium.* 2. Auflage. Düsseldorf u.a.: Artemis und Winkler.

O'Loughlin, T. 1992. „The Exegetical Purpose of Adomán's *De Locis Sanctis*.“ *Cambridge Medieval Latin Celtic Studies* 24: 37-53.

—. 1994. „The Library of Iona in the late Seventh Century. The Evidence from Adomnán's De Locis Sanctis.“ *Eriu* 45: 33-52.

—. 1996. „The View from Iona. Adomnán's Mental Maps.“ *Peritia* 10: 98-122.

—. 1997. „Adomnán and Arculf. The Case of an Expert Witness.“ *The Journal of Medieval Latin* 7: 127-46.

Ommundsen. Å. 2002. „The Liberal Arts and the Polemic Strategy of the Opus Caroli Regis Contra Synodum (Libri Carolini).“ *Symbolae Osloenses* 77: 175-200.

Oster, P. 2002. *Der Schleier im Text. Funktionsgeschichte eines Bilder für die neuzeitliche Erfahrung des Imaginären.* München: Fink.

Parshall, P. 1999. „The Art of Memory and the Passion.“ *Art Bulletin* 81: 456-72.

Perrin, M., Hrsg. 1997. *Rabani Mauri In honorem sanctae crucis.* Corpus Christianorum. Continuatio mediaevalis 100. Turnhout: Brepols.

Pers, G. 2004. *Sacred Shock. Framing Visual Experience in Byzantium.* University Park: Pennsylvania State University Press.

Petersen, J.H. 2000. *Mimesis – Imitatio – Nachahmung. Eine Geschichte der europäischen Poetik.* München: Fink (UTB).

Picker, H.-Ch. 2001. *Pastor Doctus. Klerikerbild und karolingische Reformen bei Hrabanus Maurus.* Veröffentlichungen des Instituts für europäische Geschichte Mainz 186. Mainz: von Zabern.

Ray, R. 1997. *Bede, Rhetoric, and the Creation of Christian Latin Culture.* Jarrow Lecture. Jarrow on Tyne: Rectory.

Rehm, U. 2002. „Der Körper der Stimme. Überlegungen zur historischen Initiale karolingischer Zeit.“ *Zeitschrift für Kunstgeschichte* 65: 441-59.

Reudenbach, B. 1980. „Säule und Apostel. Überlegungen zum Verhältnis von Architektur und architekturexegetischer Literatur im Mittelalter.“ *Frühmittelalterliche Studien* 14: 310-51.

—. 1986. „Imago – figura. Zum Bildverständnis in den Figurengedichten von Hrabanus Maurus.“ *Frühmittelalterliche Studien* 20: 25-35.

—. 1992. „Die Gemeinschaft als Körper und Gebäude. Francesco di Giorgios Stadttheorie und die Visualisierung von Sozialmetaphern im Mittelalter.“ In *Gepeinigt, begehrt, vergessen. Symbolik und Sozialbezug des Körpers im späten Mittelalter und in der frühen Neuzeit*, herausgegeben von K. Schreiner und N. Schnitzler, 171-98. München: Fink.

Rollason, D. 2001. *Bede and Germany.* Jarrow Lecture. Jarrow on Tyne: Rectory.

Röwekamp, G., Hrsg. und Übers. 2000. *Itinerarium – Reisebericht.* 2. verbesserte Auflage. Fontes Christiani 20. Freiburg u.a.: Herder.

Saurma-Jeltsch. L. 1994. „Zur karolingischen Haltung gegenüber dem Bilderstreit.“ In *794 – Karl der Große in Frankfurt am Main. Ein König bei der Arbeit*, herausgegeben von Johannes Fried, 69-72. Sigmaringen: Thorbecke.

Schaller, D. 1995. „Vortrags- und Zirkulardichtung am Hof Karls des Großen.“ In *Studien zur lateinischen Dichtung des Frühmittelalters*, 87-109. Quellen und Untersuchungen zur lateinischen Philologie des Mittelalters 11. Stuttgart: Hiersemann.

Schieffer, R. 1989. „„Redeamus ad fontem‘. Rom als Hort authentischer Überlieferung im frühen Mittelalter." In *Roma caput et fons. 2 Vorträge über das päpstliche Rom zwischen Altertum und Mittelalter*, 45-70. Gerda Henkel Vorlesung. Opladen: Westdeutscher Verlag.

Schmenk, H. 2003. *Die frühmittelalterlichen Gedenkbücher des Bodenseeraums*. Marburg: Tectum Verlag.

Schmid, K. 1998. „Die Reichenauer Fraternitas und ihre Erfoschung." In *Die Reichenauer Mönchsgemeinschaft und ihr Totengedenken im frühen Mittelalter*, von R. Rappmann und A. Zettler, 11-34. Sigmaringen: Thorbecke.

Schmitz, U. und H. Wenzel, Hrsg. 2003. *Wissen und neue Medien. Bilder und Zeichen von 800 bis 2000*. Philologische Studien und Quellen 177. Berlin: Erich Schmidt.

Schrimpf, G., Hrsg. 1992. *Mittelalterliche Bücherverzeichnisse des Klosters Fulda und andere Beiträge zur Geschichte der Bibliothek des Klosters Fulda im Mittelalter*. Fuldaer Studien 4. Frankfurt am Main: Knecht.

—, Hrsg. 1996. *Kloster Fulda in der Welt der Karolinger und Ottonen*. Fuldaer Studien 7. Frankfurt am Main: Knecht.

Schuler, St. 1999. *Vitruv im Mittelalter. Die Rezeption von ‚De architectura' von der Antike bis in die frühe Neuzeit*. Pictura & Poesis 12. Köln u.a.: Böhlau.

Schüppel, K.C. 2005. *Silberne und goldene Monumentalkruzifixe. Ein Beitrag zur mittelalterlichen Liturgie- und Kulturgeschichte*. Weimar: VDG.

Smyth, M. 1998. „Perceptions of Physical and Spiritual Space in Early Christian Ireland." In *Raum und Raumvorstellungen im Mittelalter*, herausgegeben von J.A. Aertsen und A. Speer, 505-24. Miscellana Mediaevalia 25. Berlin u.a.: de Gruyter.

Starkey, K. 2005. „Visual Culture and the German Middle Ages." In *Visual Culture and the German Middle Ages*, herausgegeben von K. Starkey und H. Wenzel, 1-12. New York u.a.: Palgrave Macmillan.

Steenbock, F. 1965. *Der kirchliche Prachteinband im frühen Mittelalter. Von den Anfängen bis zur Gotik*. Jahresgabe des Deutschen Vereins für Kunstwissenschaft. Berlin: Deutscher Verlag für Kunstwissenschaft.

Sullivan, R.E., Hrsg. 1995. *‚The Gentle Voices of Teachers'. Aspects of Learning in the Carolingian Age*. Columbus: Ohio State University Press.

Suntrup, R. 1978. *Die Bedeutung der liturgischen Gebärden und Bewegungen in lateinischen und deutschen Auslegungen des 9. bis 13. Jahrhunderts*. Münsterische Mittelalter-Schriften 37. München: Fink.

Thümmel, H.G. 1997. „Die fränkische Reaktion aus das 2. Nicaenum 787 in den ‚Libri Carolini'." In *Das Frankfurter Konzil von 794. Kristallisationspunkt Karolingischer Kultur*, herausgegeben von R. Berndt, Band 2, 965-80. Quellen und Abhandlungen zur mittelrheinischen Kirchengeschichte 80. Mainz: Selbstverlag der Gesellschaft für mittelrheinische Kirchengeschichte.

Tobler, T. und A. Molinier, Hrsg. 1966. Nachdruck. *Itinera Hierosolymitana et descriptiones terrae sanctae: Bellis sacris anteriora et Latina lingua exarata*. Publications de la Société de l'orient latin 2,1.2. Osnabrück: Zeller. Originalausgabe, Genf: Fick, 1879-85.

Traeger, J. 1980. *Mittelalterliche Architekturfiktion. Die Allerheiligenkapelle am Regensburger Domkreuzgang*. München et al.: Schnell & Steiner.

Turner, V. 1995. *The Ritual Process. Structure and Anti-Structure*. New York: Aldaine de Gruyter.

Ulrich, E. 2003. „Die Kreuzgedichte des Hrabanus Maurus als multimediales Kunstwerk. Textualität – Ikonizität – Numeralität." In Schmitz und Wenzel 2003, 13-37.

Underwood, P.A. „The Fountain of Life in Manuscripts of the Gospels." *Dumbarton Oaks Papers* 5: 41-138.

Untermann, M. 1989. *Der Zentralbau im Mittelalter. Form – Funktion – Verbreitung*. Darmstadt: Wissenschaftliche Buchgesellschaft.

van Dijk, A. 1999. „The Angelic Salutation in Early Byzantine and Medieval Annunciation Imagery." *The Art Bulletin* 81: 420-36.

Waldenfels, B. 2001. „Spiegel, Spur und Blick. Zur Genese des Bildes." In Boehm 2001a, 14-31.

Wandhoff, H. 1996. *Der epische Blick. Eine mediengeschichtliche Studie zur höfischen Literatur*. Philologische Studien und Quellen 141. Berlin u.a.: de Gruyter.

—. 1999. „*velden* und *visieren*, *blüemen* und *florieren*: Zur Poetik der Sichtbarkeit in den höfischen Epen des Mittelalters." *Zeitschrift für Germanistik* NF 9: 586-97.

—. 2003. *Ekphrasis. Kunstbeschreibungen und virtuelle Räume in der Literatur des Mittelalters*. Trends in Medieval Philology 3. Berlin et al.: Springer.

Wenzel, H. 1993. „Die Verkündigung an Maria. Zur Visualisierung des Wortes in der Szene, oder: Schriftgeschichte im Bild.“ In *Maria in der Welt. Marienverehrung im Kontext der Sozialgeschichte 10.-18. Jahrhundert*, herausgegeben von C. Opitz, H. Röckelein, G. Signori und G.P. Marchal, 23-52. Zürich: Chronos.

—. 1999. „Visualität. Zur Vorgeschichte der kinästhetischen Wahrnehmung.“ *Zeitschrift für Germanistik* NF 9: 549-56.

Wilkinson, J. 1977. *Jerusalem Pilgrims before the Crusades*. Warminster: Aris Phillips.

—. 2003. „Picturing New Jerusalem.“ In Eastmond und James 2003, 105-18.

Wirth, U., Hrsg. 2002. *Performanz. Zwischen Sprachphilosophie und Kulturwissenschaften*. Frankfurt am Main: Suhrkamp.

Woods, D. 2002. „Arculf's Luggage: The Sources for Adomnán's De Locis Sanctis.“ *Eriu* 52: 25-52.

Wulf, Ch. 2005. „Zur Performativität von Bild und Imagination.“ In Wulf und Zirfas 2005a, 35-49.

Wulf, Ch. und J. Zirfas, Hrsg. 2005a. *Ikonologie des Performativen*. München: Fink.

—. 2005b. „Bild, Wahrnehmung und Phantasie.“ In Wulf und Zirfas 2005a, 7-31.

Yates, F.A. 2001. *Gedächtnis und Erinnern. Mnemotechnik von Aristoteles bis Shakespeare*. 6. Auflage. Acta humaniora. Berlin: Akademie Verlag.

Buchdeckel mit triumphierendem Christus. Hofschule Karls des Großen, Aachen um 800. Oxford, Bodleian Library, Ms. Douce 176.

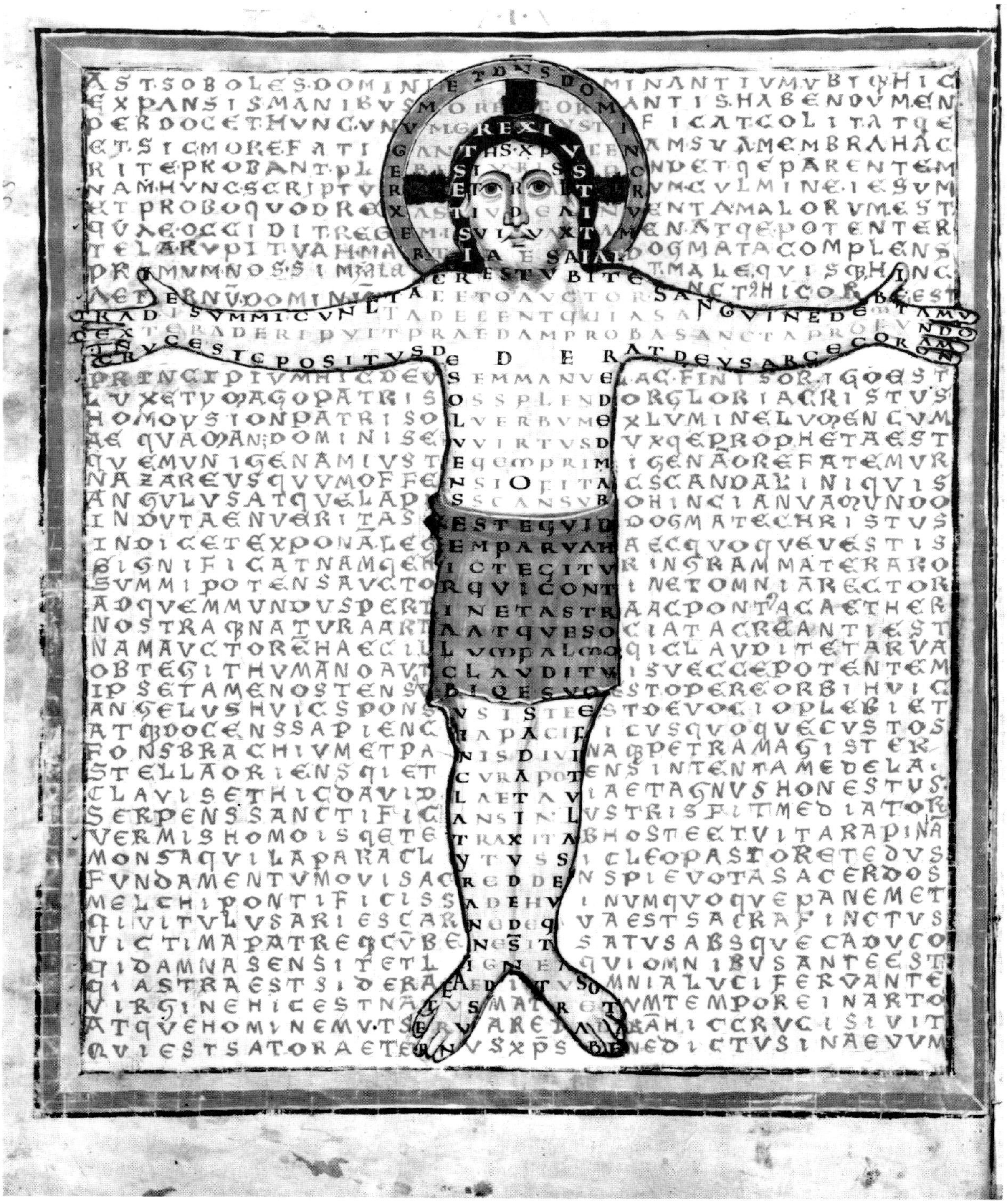

Hrabanus Maurus, In honorem sanctae crucis (Reg. Lat. 124.) Imago salvatoris (fol. 8v.) Fulda, um 825.
Rom, Biblioteca Apostolica Vaticana.

1. Fulda, St. Michael, Erdgeschoss. Neubau des 11. Jahrhunderts. Marburg, Bildarchiv Foto Marburg.

2. Fulda, St. Michael, Krypta. um 820. Marburg, Bildarchiv Foto Marburg.

Bauwerk und Bedeutungsträger
Französische Residenzarchitektur und Königsherrschaft im 14. Jahrhundert

BERND CARQUÉ

ABSTRACT

Art-historical studies of the contents and intentions of the representation of late medieval rulers have always tended to focus on the physical shape of buildings and the representational contents of works of pictorial art. Underlying this is the tacit assumption that a former meaning can immediately be read from the outward form and appearance of monuments, from building forms and pictorial motifs. Accordingly, the methods of architectural iconology and of iconography are held to suffice for deciphering the messages of monuments representing rulership. This approach, however, is based upon two questionable premises: it assumes, that the monuments themselves – through their specific material and formal characteristics – generated certain meanings, which for this reason are to be understood as objectifiable and invariable. Furthermore, the approach takes for granted the reliability of reconstructions of monuments a majority of which has been lost. As is demonstrated with reference to 19th century examples, efforts at reconstruction soon reach limits which can only be overcome by recourse to hypotheses, the results of which remain contingent upon their time and context. In the same way, late medieval depictions – such as the miniatures of the *Très Riches Heures* – do not provide authentic representations of the monuments shown, but visualize an understanding contingent upon its time and context. To escape the resulting interpretative dead end, research will have to pay more attention to sources which offer information about actual forms of use and perception of monuments. With this in mind, the paper turns to a state visit paid by emperor Charles IV to the court of king Charles V in Paris at the turn of the year 1377-1378, as the protocol of and politico-social practices associated with this occasion permit a recognition of how the perception of the monuments was systematically organized and how situation-specific meanings were ascribed to works of architecture and art through their presentation and explanation. This observation provides the grounds for introducing the notion of 'meaning' as something variable and only contextually objectifiable into research concerning the monumental representation of rulership in late medieval Paris.

EIN GALGEN OHNE GEHENKTEN UND DEUTUNGEN OHNE ZUSAMMENHANG

„*Une potence sans pendu, c'est un pommier sans pomme.*"[1] – Mit diesem drastischen Vergleich brachte ein anonymer Kommentator der *Exposition universelle de Paris* im Jahre 1900 sein Bedauern darüber zum Ausdruck, dass einer besonders effektvollen Inszenierung mittelalterlicher Königsmacht kein Erfolg beschieden war: Nach Entwürfen des Zeichners und Schriftstellers Albert Robida war zur Weltausstellung der Jahrhundertwende am Ufer der Seine das monumentale Architekturcapriccio *Le Vieux Paris* errichtet worden (Abb. 1), das mit Nachbauten der Porte Saint-Michel, eines Turms des Château du Louvre oder der Grand'Salle des Palais de la Cité auch verlorene königliche Bauwerke des 14. Jahrhunderts zur Anschauung brachte[2]; und dort hatte man – um das herrschaftliche Privileg der Hochgerichtsbarkeit sinnfällig vor Augen zu führen – an exponierter Stelle, nämlich am alles überragenden Louvre-Turm, die lebensgroße Puppe eines Gehenkten aufgeknüpft. Nach heftigen Protesten

1 Exposition 1900, 3: 47.
2 Robida 1900; zuletzt Emery 2005.

Abb. 1. Exposition universelle de Paris 1900, Le Vieux Paris. Photographie. Nach: Meier-Graefe 1900, 38.

einer schockierten Öffentlichkeit musste dieses pikante Requisit des *Vieux Paris* freilich alsbald wieder entfernt werden[3].

So anekdotisch diese Begebenheit erscheinen mag, wirft sie doch ein bezeichnendes Licht auf das historische Verständnis der Monumente. Denn offenkundig hatte die Baugestalt allein zu genügen, um mittelalterliche Königsherrschaft anschaulich zu vergegenwärtigen – signifikante Details der Herrschafts*praxis* fielen dagegen den Empfindlichkeiten eines Publikums zum Opfer, das aus der Literatur zur ‚architecture civile et militaire' gelernt hatte, herrschaftliche Macht in den Monumenten selbst repräsentiert zu sehen. Als narratives Beiwerk fielen die *ephemeren* Ausprägungen dieser Macht unter die ‚mœurs et usages' und damit in den Zuständigkeitsbereich der ‚histoire de la civilisation', während es Aufgabe der Kunst- und Architekturgeschichte war, die *dauerhaften* ‚Zeichen der Herrschaft' zu entziffern. Dabei befleißigte man sich seit den Anfängen der systematischen Materialerschließung im zweiten Viertel des 19. Jahrhunderts und verstärkt in den szientistisch geprägten Dezennien um 1900 einer nüchtern klassifizierenden Bestandsaufnahme der Gebäudetypen, Bauformen und Bildmotive[4], um von dort aus ohne Umschweife zur Ebene der Bedeutung vorzudringen. Denn – so lautete die unausgesprochene Prämisse dieser Vorgehensweise – Bedeutung sei unmittelbar an den Gestalteigenschaften der Bauwerke und an den Darstellungsinhalten der Bildwerke abzulesen; da sie stets an die Materialität der Werke zurückgebunden bleibe, müsse sie als ein objektivierbares und invariables Merkmal der Monumente begriffen werden.

Inmitten der weitläufigen, bald typologisch, bald chronologisch oder topographisch angelegten Registraturen materieller Relikte begegnen daher unvermittelt Deutungen, die – an der bloßen Formerscheinung abgelesen – etwa den Donjon des Château de Coucy als „un emblème de la puissance et de la fierté de ces barons"[5] bestimmen, Deutungen, die nach dem eingeübten Muster der Ikonographie

3 Bildlich überliefert ist der Gehenkte allein durch eine Zeichnung Albert Robidas; Exposition 1900, 3: 48.

4 Repräsentativ für diese Art der Erfassung von Profanarchitektur sind: De Caumont 1830-41, Bd. 5; Viollet-le-Duc 1854-68 (eine bemerkenswerte Funktionsgeschichte der Wehrarchitektur liegt freilich vor mit Viollet-le-Duc 1874); Enlart 1929-32; im deutschsprachigen Bereich vor allem Piper 1912; exemplarisch zum Umgang mit den Bildkünsten: Hennin 1856-63, Maumené und Harcourt 1928-32.

5 De Caumont 1830-41, 5: 295, ähnlich 345.

des Sakralbaus einer vermeintlichen *lingua franca* des Profanbaus abgelauscht scheinen: „*Si l'église romane traduit avec une douceur sévère, et l'église gothique avec une somptueuse fantaisie, le caractère grave et sublime du dogme évangélique, il faut également reconnaître que le château fait parler haut, en quelque sorte, l'âpre et farouche sentiment d'autorité féodale dont il est à la fois l'instrument et le symbole [...], ce n'est pas sans une sorte d'éloquence audace que les tours, les donjons s'élancent, s'échelonnent, se commandent, se soutiennent*"[6].

In weithin ungebrochener Tradition stellt die Rekonstruktion der Bau- und Motivgestalt daher bis heute die maßgebliche und oft auch einzige Grundlage der Bedeutungsforschung dar, gelten Bau- und Motivgestalt vielerorts in der Literatur zu den französischen Höfen und Residenzen des Spätmittelalters *per se* als Bedeutungsträger[7]. Wo ihr Aussagegehalt nicht aus sinnstiftenden Zusammenhängen – etwa aus den Bedürfnissen und Interessen der Auftraggeber, den Zweckbestimmungen und Gebrauchsweisen der Monumente oder den Wahrnehmungs- und Deutungsmustern ihrer Besteller und Betrachter – hergeleitet oder zumindest wahrscheinlich gemacht wird[8], scheint Bedeutung gleichwohl – und *a priori* – gegeben. Entsprechend wird der in den sechziger Jahren des 14. Jahrhunderts errichtete Donjon des Schlosses von Vincennes (Taf. 35.1) als Symbol königlicher Macht schlechthin, gar als „französisches Hoheitszeichen" gedeutet[9], ohne dass je danach gefragt worden wäre, ob er tatsächlich als ein solches ‚Zeichen der Herrschaft' intendiert oder rezipiert wurde, wer seine Adressaten, wer die Betrachter waren und welche Sicht- und Verständnisweisen bei diesen möglicherweise eine Rolle spielten. Bautypus und Bedeutung scheinen einander ohne weiteres selbst zu erklären. Der idealtypischen Definition von Herrschaftsrepräsentation[10] gehorchen offenbar auch die Statuen Karls V. und seiner Gemahlin Jeanne de Bourbon vom Ostportal des Louvre (Taf. 37.1)[11], denn mit ihnen habe der König ein dauerhaftes Bild seiner selbst in Amt und Würden vermittelt und damit zugleich die Institution, deren Haupt er war, in ihrer Bedeutung stellvertretend vergegenwärtigt. Bestimmungsort und Bildmotiv[12] bleiben freilich die einzigen Anhaltspunkte dieser im Allgemeinsten verharrenden Deutung.

Da sie auf weiterreichende Kontextualisierungen gewöhnlich verzichten, laufen solche Interpretationen beständig Gefahr, einem argumentativen Kurzschluss zu erliegen: Bau- und Bildwerke, die im Auftrag von Herrschaftsträgern entstanden sind, die im Rahmen der Herrschaftspraxis genutzt wurden oder darin in Erscheinung traten, deren Motive auf diesen Zusammenhang verweisen – solche Bau- und Bildwerke dienten, so die reduktionistische Folgerung, notwendig und wesentlich der medialen Konstruktion von Macht und der Repräsentation von Herrschaft. Entsprechende Nachweise bleibt die Literatur indes schuldig, da sie den Zusammenhang von Monument und Bedeutung über die vorgebliche Selbstevidenz der Bau- und Motivgestalt meint herstellen zu können. Was Bildwerke wie die Statuen vom Ostportal des Louvre anbelangt, so muss deren Sinngehalt damit freilich bemerkenswert unbestimmt bleiben; ebenso bleibt unergründet, wodurch sie im einzelnen Bedeutung hervorgebracht und auf welchen Wegen sie diese vermittelt haben. Im Fall der Bauwerke – namentlich der Donjons in Vincennes oder am Louvre in Paris – werden funktionale und ideelle Aspekte in wechselseitiger Verschränkung aufeinander bezogen, Gebrauchswert und Symbolwert in eins gesetzt – wobei man einen Grad der inhaltlichen Codierung von Bauformen ungeprüft als allgemein gültig unterstellt, wie ihn *so*

6 Lacroix 1877, 377-8.

7 Unvermittelte architekturikonographische Deutungen im Kontext positivistischer Bautypologie und Formenkunde begegnen beispielsweise bei Mesqui 1991-3, bes. 1: 219-20; ähnlich auch Bove 2003; die allein an der gegenständlichen Motivgestalt der Bildkünste orientierte Bedeutungsforschung etwa bei Erlande-Brandenburg (1988, 356-82) oder in den Beiträgen zu Pleybert 2001.

8 Für die Plazierung und Gestaltung der *estude* des Schlosses von Vincennes hat dies beispielhaft Liebenwein (1977, 37-44) unternommen.

9 Albrecht 1986, 21-2, 36; vollends zum Prinzip erhoben findet sich der allein auf den Donjon fixierte Blick in: Ausstellung Französische Donjons 2001. – Zum Château de Vincennes zuletzt: Chapelot 1994; Chapelot und Lalou 1996; Vincennes 2003-4; speziell zum Donjon auch Whiteley 1994.

10 Unter Hinweis auf die einschlägige Literatur zusammenfassend Michalsky 2000, 22-31.

11 Baron 1996, 150 (mit Lit.).

12 Abzusehen ist dabei freilich von der sinnentstellenden, zwischen 1848 und 1852 vorgenommenen Ergänzung der Attribute; zur ursprünglichen Motivgestalt s. unten.

nur die mittelalterliche Allegorese des Kirchenbaus und seiner Ausstattung[13] oder aber die normative Architekturtheorie seit dem 16. Jahrhundert[14] überliefern.

Beide Deutungstraditionen waren geeignet, den Eindruck einer universellen, die Grenzen des jeweiligen Gegenstandsbereichs oder der Zeitstellung überschreitenden Semantik der Formerscheinung zu erwecken. Was die Architekturallegorese in höchster Komplexität für den Sakralbau postuliert hatte, wurde dem Prinzip nach bedenkenlos auf den Profanbau übertragen, was die Architekturtheorie in der Frühen Neuzeit konzeptualisiert hatte, wurde ohne Zögern auch für die Residenzarchitektur des Mittelalters geltend gemacht – dass nämlich dem Vokabular jener Bauformen, die man zum Zwecke der Herrschaftsrepräsentation ins Werk gesetzt habe, eine geradezu lexikalisch präzise Bedeutung zukomme und die moderne Forschung daher die Monumente ohne weiteres verschlagworten und übersetzen könne[15]. Übersehen wurde dabei freilich, dass eine ‚Zeichensprache der Architektur', wie man sie dem mittelalterlichen Profanbau nur allzu bereitwillig unterstellte, erst anhand der Quellen zur neuzeitlichen Residenzarchitektur überzeugend nachgewiesen werden konnte[16] und deshalb etwa die moderne Burgenforschung zum kritischen Blick auf die Überlieferungssituation mahnt, um nicht leichtfertig und assoziativ von den pragmatischen Aspekten der Wehrarchitektur auf programmatische Aspekte einer Repräsentationsarchitektur zu schließen[17]. Wo die Quellen über zeitgenössische Wahrnehmungs- und Deutungsmuster schweigen, berechtigen erst die Einsichten von Bauforschung und Militärgeschichte in die wehrtechnische Funktionslosigkeit von Türmen, Schießscharten oder Zinnen zu der Annahme, die betreffenden Bauglieder seien in einem solchen Fall aus anderen denn aus fortifikatorischen Gründen zum Einsatz gekommen.

Kurzum, es sind Zweifel angebracht – Zweifel nicht nur an der historischen Angemessenheit und Plausibilität gängiger Verknüpfungen von Gestalt und Bedeutung oder an der pauschalisierenden Interpretation der Monumente als ‚Zeichen der Herrschaft'[18], sondern Zweifel auch und zuerst am allzu großen Vertrauen in die vorgeblich objektivierende Aneignung der Bau- und Motivgestalt durch Rekonstruktionen, von denen die Deutung der Monumente in der Regel ihren Ausgang nehmen muss. Denn gerade das, was Herrschaft im spätmittelalterlichen Paris[19] sichtbar verkörpert und ihr zu dauerhafter Präsenz im Stadtbild verholfen zu haben scheint – die Bauwerke der Residenzen und Fortifikationen, die Bildwerke ihrer Fassaden und Portale –, gerade diese Medien entziehen sich heute weitgehend der unmittelbaren Anschauung. Noch bevor unter dem Gesichtspunkt der ‚Konstruktion der Macht' die gesellschaftliche Wirkungsweise von Architektur im *Mittelalter* näher in den Blick genommen werden kann, stehen uns daher jene Wirkungen vor Augen, die das historische Material in den Imaginationen der *Moderne* entfaltet hat.

13 Exemplarisch: Sauer 1924; Simson 1956; Reudenbach 1980.

14 Zu den Anfängen einer *architettura parlante* und der ihr eigentümlichen normativen Architektursprache Kruft 1985, 55-143.

15 Während Bandmann 1951 – einer der Klassiker der Architekturikonographie – noch die Nähe der Quellen sucht und in jedem einzelnen Fall um Kontextualisierung und Plausibilität bemüht ist, verfährt etwa Reinle 1976 weitgehend assoziativ und generalisierend.

16 So bei von Moos 1974; Schütte 1994, 141-70, 233-43; Imesch 2003; Müller 2004; ohne auch nur den Versuch einer Herleitung zu unternehmen, setzen hingegen Prinz und Kecks (1994, 19-58) beispielsweise den in mittelalterlicher Tradition „immer als Herrschaftssymbol gesehenen Donjon" (35) apodiktisch voraus.

17 Zeune 1996, 13-57; Deutsche Burgenvereinigung 1999, 1: 16-37, 2: 42-109; zu den stets auch rekonstruktions- und deutungsrelevanten Imaginationen der Burg in Neuzeit und Moderne außerdem Laß 2002; Zeune 2004; eine der wenigen älteren Deutungen, die sich der historischen Quellen versichert, bei Meyer 1976.

18 Über den gegenwärtigen Stand der Diskussion um Macht und Monumente orientieren: Auzépy und Cornette 2003; Schwandner und Rheidt 2004; Paravicini 2005; Ehlers (im Druck).

19 Zur Geschichte der Stadt im Spätmittelalter Cazelles 1972; Favier 1974; 1997, 78-82, 271-8, 767-95; Pleybert 2001; Roux 2003.

Abb. 2. La Bastille. Lithographie nach der Vorlage von Fédor Hoffbauer. Nach: Hoffbauer 2001, Taf. nach 552.

Vexierbilder der Baugestalt

Durch die revolutionäre Schleifung weitestgehend ihrer Materialität beraubt, ist etwa die Bastille zum Paradigma Respekt heischender Herrschaftsarchitektur aufgestiegen und wurde als ein solches wie vor allem als *das* architektonische Emblem des Ancien Régime schlechthin zur Weltausstellung 1889, zum Centenarium der Revolution in monumentalem Maßstab nachgebaut[20]. Bereits um 1880 hatte Fédor Hoffbauer die Kavalierperspektive der klassischen Vedute eingenommen, um die Bastille, die Porte Saint-Antoine und die *enceinte de Charles V*[21] aus spärlich ergrabenen Resten und einer Vielzahl mitunter erheblich voneinander abweichender Bildzeugnisse zu einem Idealbild ihrer einstigen Größe zu verdichten (Abb. 2)[22] – wobei er sich mangels geeigneter spätmittelalterlicher Befunde im monumentalen Gleichmaß der Stadtbefestigung unverkennbar an jenem Inbegriff einer hochmittelalterlichen Stadt orientierte, den Architekten und Restauratoren in der zweiten Hälfte des 19. Jahrhunderts beispielsweise in Carcassonne[23] idealtypisch ins Werk gesetzt haben. Dort wie auch in den bildlichen Darstellungen der Pariser Stadtbefestigung begegnen daher nicht die rekonstruierten Monumente des Mittelalters, sondern zuallererst die konstruierten Imaginationen der Moderne.

Von jenem Louvre des späten 14. Jahrhunderts, den Karl V. zur fortifikatorisch gut gesicherten Residenz und zum wichtigsten Standort des königlichen Haus- und Hofhalts hatte um- und ausbauen lassen, konnten 1866 und erneut 1983-86 in der Cour Carrée des neuzeitlichen Louvre nur mehr Teile der Substruktionen freigelegt werden[24]. Gleichwohl steht uns der Gebäudekomplex auch in seinen aufgehenden Teilen vielerorts unübersehbar vor Augen. Nach einer Vorlage des Schlachtenmalers Alphonse de Neuville bringt ihn ein Holzstich zu François Guizots *Histoire de France* mit der dramatischen Bildrhetorik und den motivischen Versatzstücken des romantischen Nachtstücks in malerischer Unbestimmtheit zur Anschauung (Taf. 34.1)[25] – als schaudererregende Trutzburg feudaler Herrschaft, deren

20 Journal 1888; Exposition 1900, 1: 161.
21 Zu diesen Monumenten zuletzt Pleybert 2001, 76-90.
22 Hoffbauer 2001, Taf. nach 552.
23 Viollet-le-Duc 1878.
24 Zur Geschichte des mittelalterlichen Louvre sowie zu den Grabungskampagnen Berty u.a. 1866-97, 1: 123-99, 2: 109-68; Louvre des rois 1986.
25 Guizot 1873-6, 2: 141.

Anmutungen noch die theatralische Lichtregie der aktuellen Grabungspräsentation im Untergeschoss des Musée du Louvre zu evozieren versucht. In Eugène-Emmanuel Viollet-le-Ducs *Dictionnaire raisonné de l'architecture française* begegnet der Louvre hingegen aus der nüchtern strukturanalytischen Vogelschau des rationalistischen Architekten und gibt in detailreicher Feinzeichnung die Disposition der Baukörper und Mauerzüge, vor allem aber den hoch aufragenden, bereits um 1200 unter Philipp II. Augustus errichteten Donjon zu erkennen (Taf. 34.2)[26].

Ob dieser Donjon freilich auf derart symbolträchtige Weise in Erscheinung trat und deshalb „zum mittelalterlichen Staatssymbol par excellence geworden ist“[27], muss offen bleiben, denn auf bildlichen Darstellungen des 15. Jahrhunderts – so auf dem *Retable du Parlement de Paris* von etwa 1453/5 (Taf. 34.3) oder auf der gegen 1500 entstandenen *Piétà de Saint-Germain-des-Prés*[28] – ist sein Kegeldach inmitten der umfassenden Gebäudeflügel und ihrer Dachaufbauten kaum auszumachen – entweder, weil er sie tatsächlich kaum überragte oder aber, weil ihm die betreffenden Tafelmaler keine überragende Bedeutung beimaßen. Einzig auf einer möglicherweise schon um 1415 begonnenen, doch erst zwischen 1438 und 1442 vollendeten Miniatur im Kalender der *Très Riches Heures* des Duc de Berry findet er sich – modernen Erwartungen an sein Erscheinungsbild eher entsprechend – sichtlich hervorgehoben (Taf. 34.4)[29]. Dort nimmt der Baukörper des Château du Louvre zusammen mit dem horizontalen Riegel der Vorburgbefestigung exakt das mittlere Register des Kalenderbildes ein. Im unteren Drittel erscheinen die dem Wechsel der Jahreszeiten unterworfenen Verrichtungen des bäuerlichen Alltags, während im oberen Drittel der entsprechende Zeitabschnitt des Jahreslaufs schematisch zur Darstellung kommt. Als formales Bindeglied zwischen beiden Sphären verkörpert der Gebäudekomplex gleichsam das statische, dem Zeitlauf enthobene Zentrum inmitten steten Wandels. In solch monumentaler Dauerhaftigkeit beherrscht er sinnfällig den sozialen Raum der Bauern und ragt zugleich mit der Dachbekrönung des genau auf der Mittelachse des Bildes platzierten Donjon' bis in den kosmischen Raum des Jahreskreises, bis zu jenem Wolkenband empor, auf dem das Gespann des Helios vorüberzieht. Nur vermöge dieser Bildordnung aber markiert der Louvre die physisch-metaphysische Sinnmitte der Herrschafts- und Lebensordnung, denn nicht die Baugestalt an sich, sondern erst die Art und Weise, in der ihre Erscheinung und Wahrnehmung bildlich organisiert und kontextualisiert wird, bringt hier Bedeutung hervor.

Ähnlich verhält es sich mit jenen Monumenten, die in konkreten Handlungszusammenhängen und Rezeptionssituationen dargestellt wurden. Auch deren Baugestalt findet sich variabel ins Bild gesetzt, auch an ihnen wird der Blick erst aus dem Zusammenhang heraus sinnstiftend fokussiert. So genügten in einer um 1455-60 von Jean Fouquet illuminierten Handschrift der *Grandes Chroniques de France*[30] die Statuen des hl. Dionysius und seiner Märtyrergefährten Rusticus und Eleutherius, um die Wiedererkennbarkeit der Porte Saint-Denis zu gewährleisten. Bei der Darstellung der *entrée* Karls V. nach der Weihe und Krönung in Reims 1364 befleißigte sich Fouquet der weitgehenden Sachtreue gegenüber den Örtlichkeiten des Zeremoniells, denn in topographisch verbürgter Folge erscheinen neben der Porte Saint-Denis im weiteren Verlauf der Stadtmauer die Porte Saint-Martin, der Temple und im Hintergrund die Bastille (Taf. 35.3). Als Schauplatz der Zusammenkunft Karls V. mit Kaiser Karl IV. im Jahre 1377 begegnet die Porte Saint-Denis einige Folia weiter erneut (Taf. 35.4) – wobei sie nun jedoch die aus der ersten Miniatur vertraute Baugestalt der Porte Saint-Martin angenommen hat und daher einzig anhand ihres Skulpturenschmucks präzise zu benennen ist. Denn im Kontext der feierlichen *entrée* markierte dieser allein unmissverständlich jenen Ort, an dem die Einziehenden die Hauptstadt des Reiches betraten und sich unter den Schutz des *patronus regis et regni* begaben. Die konkrete Baugestalt des Stadttores hatte dem nichts Sinntragendes hinzuzufügen und konnte daher getrost vernachlässigt werden.

Mithin erlauben Darstellungen wie diejenigen der *Très Riches Heures* oder der *Grandes Chroniques* auch nur sehr allgemeine Aussagen über das einstige Erscheinungsbild der Monumente. Jeder Versuch, ihre Sachtreue zu überprüfen, läuft Gefahr, sich in den selbstreferentiellen Verweisungen von Repräsentationen zu verlieren, die allesamt ein leeres Zentrum umkreisen. Denn wo sich das *tertium comparationis* – die originäre Bausubstanz – nicht erhalten hat oder durch spätere Überformungen zum

26 Viollet-le-Duc 1854-68, 3: 137.
27 Albrecht 1986, 21.
28 Pleybert 2001, 194-5; zum *Retable du Parlement de Paris* auch Lorentz 1998; 2004.
29 Chantilly, Musée Condé, ms. 65, fol. 10v. – Zu dieser Handschrift zuletzt: Très Riches Heures 2004.
30 Bibliothèque nationale de France, Mss, Fr. 6465. – Avril 2003, 219-48.

Verschwinden gebracht wurde, ist über die Wirklichkeitsnähe einer Darstellung schlechterdings nicht zu befinden. Wie die Bild gewordenen Imaginarien der Moderne – die ‚Rekonstruktionen' eines Fédor Hoffbauer oder Viollet-le-Duc –, so führen uns auch zeitgenössische Ansichten die Residenzen und Fortifikationen als relationale Objekte vor Augen – unaufhebbar eingelassen in spezifische Sicht- und Verständnisweisen und gebunden an entsprechende Modi der Visualisierung.

Die Darstellungen der *entrées* in den *Grandes Chroniques* geben außerdem zu bedenken, dass neben den genuin bildnerischen Mitteln einer aspekthaften, perspektivischen und konstruktiven Aneignung der Monumente weitere, außerbildliche Faktoren ihrer Rezeption in Betracht zu ziehen sind. Denn sie zeigen, dass Bau- und Bildwerke im Kontext *bestimmter* politisch-sozialer Praktiken auf *bestimmte* Art und Weise wahrgenommen und verstanden wurden. Dieser Umstand legt nahe, dass sich ihr jeweiliger Sinn erst über die im Angesicht der Monumente vollzogenen Handlungen näher erschloss, dass also die Bedeutungen, als deren Träger sie die Forschung zu interpretieren versucht, nicht *per se* gegeben waren, sondern situativ hergestellt und präzisiert wurden. ‚Bedeutung' ist demnach kein Merkmal, das sich ohne weiteres am materiellen Erscheinungsbild der Objekte – an den Gestalteigenschaften der Bauwerke oder den Darstellungsinhalten der Bildwerke – ablesen ließe und entsprechend als objektivierbar und invariabel zu begreifen wäre. Vielmehr muss sie als eine kontextabhängige und daher variable Größe verstanden werden.

Daher ist es auch nicht damit getan, nach bautypologisch klassifizierbaren und architekturikonologisch interpretierbaren Erscheinungsformen oder nach der gegenständlichen Motivgestalt und ihrem Aussagegehalt zu fragen. Und es reicht ebenso wenig aus, die so gewonnene Deutung mit der von den Auftraggebern intendierten und von den Zeitgenossen rezipierten Bedeutung gleichzusetzen. Da spätmittelalterliche Bildmedien das ‚Gehäuse der Macht'[31] überwiegend in zeremoniell strukturierten Kontexten[32] zur Anschauung bringen, ist genauer nach den dort vorherrschenden Wahrnehmungsbedingungen konkreter Betrachter zu fragen, ist noch vor der unspezifischen Wahrnehmung einer idealtypischen ‚breiten Öffentlichkeit' – über deren Formen wir mangels geeigneter Quellen kaum Näheres in Erfahrung bringen können – die spezifische Wahrnehmung einer repräsentativen Öffentlichkeit in den Blick zu nehmen. Denn nur dort besteht Aussicht, den Diskursen der Bedeutungszuweisung, den Medien und Praktiken der Sinnerzeugung im Angesicht der Monumente auf die Spur zu kommen.

Esse est percipi – und was man als König dafür tun musste

Als besonders aufschlussreich erweist sich in dieser Hinsicht jene Reise, die Kaiser Karl IV. zur Jahreswende 1377/78 an den Hof seines königlichen Neffen nach Paris unternahm, um mit Karl V. drängende politische Probleme – die Thronfolge in Ungarn und Polen, den Wunsch Frankreichs nach dem Recht des Vikariats im Arelat, die Frage einer kaiserlichen Unterstützung im Kampf gegen England – zu verhandeln. Das in der zeitgenössischen Historiografie, namentlich in den königlichen *Grandes Chroniques* ausnehmend detailreich geschilderte Ereignis ist von der Forschung stets mit großer Aufmerksamkeit bedacht und in jüngerer Zeit besonders unter dem Aspekt der Visualität erörtert worden[33]. Denn die Texte erzählen von einer umfassenden Semiotisierung jener Bereiche der städtischen und höfischen Lebenswelt, die vorübergehend zu Schau- und Handlungsräumen des Besuchszeremoniells wurden. An ihnen hat die Forschung die Zeichensysteme von Wappen und Devisen, Livreen und Pferden, von Sitzordnung, Rang- und Reihenfolge aufgewiesen, hat deren Funktion und Bedeutung im Kontext performativer Herrschaftsrepräsentation scharfsichtig erhellt.

Kaum Beachtung gefunden hat dagegen der Umstand, dass sich das Itinerar dieser Reise auch als ein Inventar jener Repräsentationsräume königlicher Herrschaft lesen lässt, die nicht von ephemeren Zeichen, sondern von solchen dauerhafter Präsenz, nicht von den mobilen Medien des Zeremoniells,

31 Paravicini 2005.

32 So unternimmt denn auch die jüngere Residenzenforschung vermehrt Vorstöße, Fragen der Herrschaftsrepräsentation mit architektonischen Mitteln stärker an die Funktionsforschung und den Nachweis entsprechender Gebrauchsweisen zurückzubinden; dazu etwa Paravicini 1997; Schmitt und Oexle 2002, 307-62.

33 Den zentralen Quellentext stellt Delachenal (1910-20, 2: 193-277) bereit; unter den jüngeren Arbeiten sind hervorzuheben (jeweils mit Hinweisen auf die umfangreiche ältere Literatur) Autrand 1995; Strubel 2000.

sondern von ortsfesten Bau- und Bildwerken erfüllt waren. Auch deren Wahrnehmung blieb nach Ausweis der Quellen nicht dem Zufall überlassen, wurde vonseiten des Gastes eingefordert, aufseiten des Gastgebers mit Bedacht organisiert und war dabei in spezifische Erwartungs- und Verständnishorizonte eingelassen. Wenngleich nicht mit letzter Sicherheit zu entscheiden ist, welchen Anteil an den Schilderungen der *Grandes Chroniques* die protokollarische Fiktion, welchen das Ereignisprotokoll besitzt, lässt deren Bericht doch die zentrale Bedeutung erkennen, die man im Angesicht der Monumente geordneten Wahrnehmungsbedingungen und unmissverständlichen Bedeutungszuweisungen beimaß.

Von Tangermünde kommend, reiste Karl IV. über Aachen, Brüssel und Cambrai zunächst nach Saint-Denis. Mit der Königsabtei besuchte der Kaiser – noch bevor er auf dem sich anschließenden Weg nach Paris mit Karl V. zusammentraf – den ersten herausragenden Ort im Repräsentationsraum königlicher Herrschaft. Dort war zunächst der Reliquienschatz des Klosters erklärtes Ziel des kaiserlichen Schauverlangens, der Devotion und Berührung: [...] *il se dementa de veoir les reliques de leanz, et se fist porter ou tresor en une chaiere, et là vit les reliques, les couronnes, joyaus, et s'i tint moult longuement, en y prenant tres grant plaisir, si comme il sembloit à sa chiere, par le rapport de ceuls qui près de lui estoient.* [...] *Si se fist porter en l'eglise de monseigneur Saint-Denis, devant les corps sains, et là fist ses devocions, et se fist porter entour les chaces, et baisa les reliques, le chief, le clou et la couronne* [...][34]. Durch Wappen und Inschriften aber waren einige der Reliquiare als königliche Stiftungen ausgewiesen, andere Objekte des Schatzes gaben sich durch Typus und Beschaffenheit als Teil der im Kloster verwahrten Krönungsinsignien zu erkennen, die vereinzelt – etwa im Fall der erwähnten *couronne*, der *corona spinae domini* oder *grande couronne s. Louys*, die Johann II. 1350 für seine Krönung hatte verwenden und aus diesem Anlass restaurieren lassen – ihrerseits Reliquienträger waren[35].

Neben der Verehrung der Reliquien ist es freilich auch die dynastische Gedächtnispflege gewesen, die den Kaiser dazu bewogen hat, Werke der königlichen Hofkunst näher in Augenschein zu nehmen, denn er *demanda à veoir les sepultures des roys, et par especial du roy Charles et de la royne Jehanne, sa femme, du roy Phelippe et de la royne Jehanne de Bourgoigne sa femme, qu'il disoit que en leurs hostelz il avoit esté nourris en sa jonesce et que moult de biens li avoient faiz. Et aussi voult veoir la sepulture du roy Jehan, et fist assembler l'abbé et le couvent et leur requist tres affectueusement que ilz vousissent Dieu prier pour ses bons seigneurs et dames, qui gisoient là*[36]. Mithin waren es neben den 1329 beziehungsweise gegen 1372 vollendeten *sepultures* Karls IV. (Taf. 36.3) – eines Onkels – und seiner dritten Gemahlin Jeanne d'Évreux[37] auch die im Auftrag Karls V. 1364-6 entstandenen Grabmäler Philipps VI. (Taf. 36.4) und seiner ersten Gemahlin Jeanne de Bourgogne sowie Johanns II. (Taf. 36.4) – eines Schwagers –[38], an denen Kaiser Karl IV. der engen familiären Verbindungen der Luxemburger zu den Kapetingern wie zu den Valois gedachte.

Da das Protokoll der Reise ein späteres Zusammentreffen von Kaiser und König vorsah, kam Karl IV. in der Abtei noch nicht in den Genuss jenes Privilegs, von dem Christine de Pisan 1404 in ihrem *Livre des fais et bonnes meurs du sage Roy Charles* berichtet. Als Zeichen der besonderen Ehrerbietung habe der König Gäste zuweilen persönlich nach Saint-Denis geführt, um ihnen dort eigenhändig Truhen und Schränke zu öffnen und die darin geborgenen Reliquien, Paramente und Insignien zu zeigen: [*L*]*à leur faisoit moustrer les reliques, le tresor et les richeces, qui là sont, les riches chasubles, aournemens d'aultelx, les beaulx paremens et abiz en quoy les roys sont sacrez, dont il en fist faire de tous neufs, et les plus riches qui oncques y eussent esté veus, que on sache, tous les abiz ouvrez à ffines et grosses perles, et meismement les souliers; ouvrir les riches armoires, où des joyaulx de grant valeur a à merveilles, où est la riche couronne du sacre, qu'il fist faire, en laquelle a un gros balei au bout, du pris de .xxx. mille frans, et d'autres pierrerie moult fine, et vault la couronne merveilles d'avoir, et les autres estranges choses, qui y sont, de moult grant richece*[39].

Besondere Leitung und Lenkung vonseiten des Königs erfuhr die kaiserliche Wahrnehmung der Monumente offenbar erst, als nach dem feierlichen Einzug in die Stadt – *c'estoit noble et merveilleuse*

34 Delachenal 1910-20, 2: 206-7.
35 Trésor de Saint-Denis 1991; speziell zu den Insignien auch Gaborit-Chopin 1987.
36 Delachenal 1910-20, 2: 207-8.
37 Zu jener 1329 vollendeten Gruppe von Monumenten, der die Liegefigur Karls IV. entstammt, Carqué 2004, 512-3.
38 Carqué 2004, 282-321 passim.
39 Solente 1936-40, 2: 87.

Abb. 3. Très Riches Heures du duc de Berry. Chantilly, Musée Condé, ms. 65, fol. 6v (Auschnitt). Nach: Sainte-Chapelle de Bourges 2004, 27.

chose à veoir[40], wie die *Grandes Chroniques* nicht müde werden zu betonen – der Regierungs- und Verwaltungssitz der Krone und damit zugleich das funktionale und ideelle Zentrum des Reiches, der Palais de la Cité (Taf. 36.1)[41], erreicht war. Die dort vom Kaiser und seinem Gefolge betretenen Bereiche und Gemächer *estoient partout tres richement parées et ordenées*[42], Augenzeugen des Geschehens *furent moult merveilliez, qui autrefoiz n'avoient veue tele ne si bonne ordenance de tele multitude, si pou de desroy ne de presse*[43]. Der König habe seinen Gast zwischen eigens errichteten Abschrankungen hindurch über den Hof des Palais, durch die Galerie Mercière in die Grand'Salle geleitet.

In illa monarchie Francorum illustrissima sede, insigne quoddam regalis magnificentie signum, gloriosissimum palatium constructum est – so preist Jean de Jandun in seiner Eloge *Tractatus de laudibus Parisius* von 1323 den Palais de la Cité[44]. Diese überragende Bedeutung erlangte der Gebäudekomplex jedoch nur schrittweise – jeweils begleitet von gezielten architektonischen und bildkünstlerischen Hervorhebungen. Unter den königlichen Residenzen ausgezeichnet wurde er von Ludwig IX. 1241 bis 1248 durch den Bau einer neuen Palastkapelle – der Sainte-Chapelle –, die auch und vor allem als Aufbewahrungsort der in Konstantinopel erworbenen Passionsreliquien diente und dergestalt den in einzigartiger Weise geheiligten Mittelpunkt der Monarchie markierte[45]. Im Zuge der Zentralisierung des Herrschaftsapparates unter Philipp IV. wurde sodann in den Jahren um 1300 die Grand'Salle als wichtigster Schau- und Handlungsraum königlicher Macht, als Ort von Rechtsakten, Gesandtschaftsempfängen und Hoffesten, neu aufgeführt[46]; die Galerie Mercière, der Verbindungstrakt zwischen Sainte-Chapelle und

40 Delachenal 1910-20, 2: 220.
41 Dessen Geschichte grundlegend und umfassend bei Guérout 1949-51, 1996.
42 Guérot 1996, 226.
43 Guérot 1996, 222.
44 Le Roux de Lincy und Tisserand 1867, 48.
45 Guérout 1949-51, 1: 157-74; Sauerländer 1977; Trésor de la Sainte-Chapelle 2001.
46 Guérout 1949-51, 2: 128-43; Bennert 1992.

Abb. 4. Charles Meryon, Grand'Salle, 1855. Radierung nach der Vorlage des Jacques Ier Androuet du Cerceau von etwa 1580. Nach: Charles Meryon 1975, 136.

Grand'Salle, wurde ausgebaut und erhielt das über eine monumentale Freitreppe zugängliche Hauptportal des Gebäudes[47].

So erheblich spätmittelalterliche Darstellungen des Palais de la Cité im Detail wie im Ganzen voneinander abweichen[48], stimmen sie doch darin überein, dass sie den markanten Doppelgiebel der Grand'Salle stets mit einer Bauzier zeigen, die dem älteren Sakralbau, namentlich aber der benachbarten Sainte-Chapelle nachempfunden ist (Abb. 3). Zudem überliefern die sonst stark divergierenden Ansichten der neuzeitlichen Reliefpläne von Paris für die westliche Stirnseite des Gebäudes einhellig zwei mächtige, beinahe die gesamte Fassadenfläche einnehmende spitzbogige Maßwerkfenster[49]. Auch an der zur Grande Cour hin gelegenen Fassade der Galerie Mercière (Taf. 36.2) ließ Philipp IV. mit wimpergüberfangenen Zwillingsfenstern, Blendmaßwerk, schlanken Fialen und Figurentabernakeln gezielt Schmuckformen aufgreifen[50], die – namentlich in den Couronnements – engste Übereinstimmungen mit jener Formensprache aufweisen, die fünf Jahrzehnte früher etwa an der Nordquerhausfassade der Kathedrale Notre-Dame oder an der Sainte-Chapelle und ihrem zweigeschossigen Anbau, der die Sakristei und den Trésor des Chartes barg, ins Werk gesetzt worden war. Vor allem aber entstand ein im profanen Kontext gänzlich voraussetzungsloses Figurenportal, das mit der Statue Philipps IV. am Trumeau erstmals den regierenden Monarchen, mit der Statue des Enguerran de Marigny im Gewände zur Linken[51] erstmals einen ranghohen Amtsträger des königlichen Herrschaftsapparates – nach dem Beispiel sakraler Bildkunst – im Medium der Monumentalskulptur zur Darstellung brachte.

Auch im Inneren der Grand'Salle begegnen Anzeichen einer bewußten Verschränkung weltlicher Herrschaft mit der Sphäre des Sakralen. Denn dort fanden sich an den Wandvorlagen der Längsseiten und an den Pfeilervorlagen der Mittelstützen die überlebensgroßen *ydola cunctorum regum Francie* auf-

47 Guérout 1949-51, 2: 87-93.

48 Selbst innerhalb der *Très Riches Heures* erscheint der Gebäudekomplex dreifach auf je verschiedene Weise – abweichend in der Anordnung der Gebäude wie in den Einzelheiten ihrer Baugestalt; Chantilly, Musée Condé, ms. 65, fol. 5v (Monatsbild Mai), 6v (Monatsbild Juni; hier Abb. 3) und 51v (Begegnung der Hl. Drei Könige).

49 Boutier 2002.

50 Die turmartig aufragenden Gaubenfenster der Mansarde wurden dagegen erst unter Johann II. um 1350/5 errichtet.

51 Da Enguerran de Marigny nach des Königs Tod hingerichtet und seine Statue vom Portal entfernt wurde, zeigt die *Crucifixion du Parlement de Paris* nur mehr im Gewände zur Rechten eine Figur, die möglicherweise den Sohn und Nachfolger Philipps IV., Ludwig (X.), darstellte.

gestellt (Abb. 4). Ihre auf stete Ergänzung und Aktualisierung hin angelegte Reihe inschriftlich bezeichneter Herrschergestalten ließ durch gezielte Auslassungen die ungebrochene Geschlechterfolge von den Merowingern über die Karolinger bis zu den Kapetingern sinnfällig werden und reihte Philipp IV. in die Kontinuität der herrscherlichen Familien- und Amtsgenealogie seit Pharamond ein. Gattungsspezifische Äquivalente besaß dieses Statuenensemble um 1300 einzig in den Königsgalerien der Kathedralen zu Paris, Chartres oder Reims wie freilich auch in jenem Apostelzyklus, der in der Sainte-Chapelle an den Gurtbogendiensten der Oberkapelle aufgestellt war.

Die von Philipp IV. offenbar zielstrebig betriebene Anverwandlung der weltlichen Funktionsbereiche des Palais de la Cité an die Charakteristika des Sakralbaus entsprach dem unter seiner Herrschaft vehementer denn je entfalteten Selbstverständnis einer Monarchie, deren Träger als Nachfahren und Nachfolger Ludwigs des Heiligen von der Aura der Geblütsheiligkeit umgeben waren, die mit dem von Gott gesandten Öl der Sainte Ampoule gesalbt wurden und die Gabe der wundertätigen Skrofelheilung empfingen[52]. Markierte die Sainte-Chapelle bereits den Aufbewahrungsort der Heiltümer der Krone und damit das durch die Passionsreliquien in einzigartiger Weise geheiligte Zentrum des Reiches, so setzten Galerie Mercière und Grand'Salle nun flankierende Zeichen einer wesentlich sakral verstandenen Herrschaft.

Und an eben diesen Orten konzentrierte siebzig Jahre später Karl V. – der sich in vielerlei Hinsicht Philipp IV. wie vor allem Ludwig dem Heiligen anzugleichen suchte –[53] den zeremoniellen Ablauf des kaiserlichen Besuches. Freitreppe und Portal der Galerie Mercière waren Schauplatz des feierlichen Einzugs in den Palais. In der Grand'Salle fand jenes berühmte Festbankett statt, dem die Buchmaler des königlichen Exemplars der *Grandes Chroniques* eine der wenigen beinahe ganzseitigen Miniaturen gewidmet haben[54]. Karl IV. und sein Gefolge wurden im Verlauf dieses Banketts nicht nur Zeugen einer szenischen Darstellung der Eroberung Jerusalems durch Godefroy de Bouillon, sondern gewahrten auch zahlreiche, zum Teil auf separaten Tischen arrangierte Tafelaufsätze und – hoch über den Köpfen der Festgesellschaft – die monumentale Genealogie der französischen Könige.

Da man die Grand'Salle aus Anlaß des Festes mit Bildteppichen geschmückt hatte, sah sich der Autor des betreffenden Abschnitts der *Grandes Chroniques* dazu veranlaßt, nachdrücklich auf die uneingeschränkte Sichtbarkeit der Statuen und also auf ihre unverminderte Wahrnehmbarkeit hinzuweisen: *Et est assavoir que la sale du grant Palais estoit continuée et parée de tapiz de hault liche à ymages tout au tour, si bien ordenez et si à point mis que les roys, qui sont de pierre tout autour, n'estoient point occupez ne empeschiez de veoir*[55]. Womöglich kam bei dieser Gelegenheit auch die bestechende Lebendigkeit der Statuen zur Geltung, von der Jean de Jandun im *Tractatus de laudibus Parisius* berichtet: *Pro inclite vero recordationis honore, ydola cunctorum regum Francie, qui hactenus precesserunt, sunt ibidem adeo perfecte representationis proprietate formata, ut primitus inspiciens ipsa fere judicet quasi viva*[56]. Denn durch den Herrscherornat und eine entsprechende Farbfassung fand sich die dauerhafte Präsenz des Königs im Bild seiner ephemeren Erscheinung im Zeremoniell angeglichen.

Auch im Rahmen der Gottesdienste, denen der Kaiser in der Sainte-Chapelle beiwohnte, spielte die Visualität eine beherrschende Rolle: *Et fist le service l'arcevesque de Rains, et fu la Sainte-Chapelle si noblement aournée, et l'autel si richement et grandement garny de joyaux d'eglises et de reliques, et telement enluminée, que c'estoit belle et merveilleuse chose à veoir*[57]. Verwandelte in diesem Fall die Liturgie den Kirchenraum in einen durch sakrales Gerät und Beleuchtung visuell organisierten Schau- und Handlungsraum, so scheint bereits die Sainte-Chapelle selbst nach Ausweis des *Tractatus de laudibus Parisius* vor allem über Eindrücke des Gesichtssinnes erfahren worden zu sein: *Sed et illa formosissima capellarum, capella regis, infra menia mansionis regie decentissime situata, integerrimis et indissolubilibus solidissimorum lapidum gaudet structuris. Picturarum colores electissimi, ymaginum deauratio preciosa, vitrearum circumquaque rutilantium decora pervietas, altarium venustissima para-*

52 Carqué 2004, 514-6, 529-31.

53 Carqué 2004, 422-3, 485-92, 514-43.

54 Bibliothèque nationale de France, Mss, Fr. 2813, fol. 473v; der Text weist hier eigens auf die ihn begleitende bildliche Darstellung hin: [...] *comme il est figuré en l'ystoire, ci après pourtraite et ymaginée.*

55 Delachenal 1910-20, 2: 237.

56 Le Roux de Lincy und Tisserand 1867, 48.

57 Delachenal 1910-20, 2: 229.

menta, sanctuariorum virtutes mirifice, capsularum figurationes extranee gemmis adornate fulgentibus, tantam utique illi orationis domui largiuntur decoris yperbolem, ut, in eam subingrediens, quasi raptus ad celum, se non immerito unam de Paradisi potissimis cameris putet entrare[58].

Die unmittelbare Nähe, ja die Berührung der Passionsreliquien suchte Karl IV. außerhalb des Gottesdienstes in kleinem Kreis: [...] *l'Empereur fist prier au Roy qu'il li pleust celui jour monstrer les saintes reliques, et que, celui jour, avoit devocion de les veoir et soy faire apporter* [...][59]. Durch seine schwere Gichterkrankung kaum mehr des Laufens fähig, musste der korpulente Kaiser unter großen Schmerzen eine der engen Wendeltreppen zur Reliquientribüne im Chorpolygon der Sainte-Chapelle hinaufgetragen werden – *par les braz et jambes*, da der sonst für ihn verwendete Tragestuhl hier nicht eingesetzt werden konnte: *Et quant il fu amont et le Roy ot ouverte la sainte chasse, le dit Empereur osta son chaperon et joint les mains, et comme en lermes fist là son oroison longuement, en tres grant devocion, et puis se fist soustenir et aporter baisier les saintes reliques. Et li monstra et devisa le Roy toutes les pieces qui sont en la dite chasse. Et après ce que les princes, qui avec lui estoient, orent baissié, le Roy tourna la dite chasse devers la chapelle, et laissa à garder ycelle les evesques de Beauvaiz et de Paris, revestus en pontifical de mictres et de crosses. Et quant l'Empereur fu raporté aval, il ne voult pas estre mis en l'oratoire, que le Roy li avoit fait appareillier, mais volt estre en la chaiere où le tresorier de la dite chapelle a acoustumé à seoir, pour mieux et plus longuement veoir les dites saintes reliques et estre mieulx à l'opposite du front de la dite chasse*[60].

Mit der *sainte chasse* ist in den *Grandes Chroniques* jener drehbar gelagerte Reliquienschrein angesprochen, der unter einer hoch aufragenden Baldachinarchitektur auf der Tribüne hinter dem Hauptaltar den Reliquienschatz der Sainte-Chapelle barg[61]. Die Türen dieses Schreins ließ sich mit den in der Obhut des Königs befindlichen Schlüsseln öffnen und gab so den Blick auf die darin verwahrten Reliquiare frei – entweder exklusiv für die hinter dem Schrein auf der Tribüne stehenden Betrachter oder aber, nach vollzogener Drehung, für die vom Kirchenraum aus Emporblickenden. Mit der Reliquienweisung, deren Adressat und Augenzeuge der Kaiser nebst seinem Gefolge und den anwesenden Bischöfen in der Sainte-Chapelle wurde, gehorchte Karl V. einem monarchischen Rollenbild, das auf keinen Geringeren als Ludwig IX. selbst, also den Käufer der Reliquien und den Initiator ihres Kultes zurückging, denn schon dieser König hatte die einzigartigen Heiltümer der französischen Krone in eigener Person gegenüber höchsten weltlichen und geistlichen Würdenträgern zur Schau gestellt[62]. Vor allem aber ließ Karl V. mit der Öffnung der Grande Châsse und der minutiösen Erläuterung ihres Inhalts sinnfällig werden, was seine gelehrte Entourage in ihren Traktaten zur politischen Theologie des Königtums nicht müde wurde zu betonen: Zeigten die himmlischen Zeichen um den König – Sainte Ampoule und Fleurs de lis, Oriflamme und die Gabe der Skrofelheilung –, dass *Diex l'a fait et ordoné son vicaire en la temporalité*[63], so hätten die Passionsreliquien der Sainte-Chapelle den *rois très chrétien* zum *magister sacrorum scriniorum* werden lassen. Daher *doit estre le paÿs de France appellé la Saincte Terre, sur tous aultres princes seculiers, ce Roy et son pueple sont de Diex esleüs*[64].

Erst über die Präsentation der Heiltümer, über ihre gelenkte und kommentierte Wahrnehmung erschloss sich demnach, worauf schon Jean de Jandun im *Tractatus de laudibus Parisius* anspielt, wenn er den Palais de la Cité als den bedeutendsten Sitz der französischen Monarchie, als *insigne quoddam regalis magnificentie signum*, und die *capella regis* als einen paradiesesgleichen Ort bezeichnet – dass der Palais nicht nur das funktionale, sondern auch und vor allem das ideelle, den inkommensurablen Status göttlicher Auserwähltheit verkörpernde Zentrum des Reiches war.

Nach ihrem Aufenthalt im Palais de la Cité fuhren König und Kaiser in einem eigens zu diesem Zweck gefertigten Prunkschiff Seineabwärts zum Louvre: *Ainsi arriverent au Louvre, et fu apporté le dit Empereur en sa chaiere, et le Roy estoit tousjours costé lui, jusques à ce qu'il fu dedenz le dit chastel, et li monstra et fist monstrer, au dehors et dedenz, le nouvel edifice que il y avoit fait, dont l'Empereur*

58 Le Roux de Lincy und Tisserand 1867, 46.
59 Delachenal 1910-20, 2: 232.
60 Delachenal 1910-20, 2: 233.
61 Trésor de la Sainte-Chapelle 2001, 107-37.
62 De Mély 1904, 165-440.
63 Schnerb-Lièvre 1982, 1: 51.
64 Schnerb-Lièvre 1982, 1: 325-6.

par semblant prenoit tres grant plaisir[65]. Wiewohl uns der Text nähere Einzelheiten dieser Besichtigung schuldig bleibt, ist anzunehmen, dass Karl IV. dabei auch jene überlebensgroßen Statuen des Königspaares zu Gesicht bekam, die weithin sichtbar am Ostportal aufgestellt waren (Taf. 37.1). Wie von der Literatur zutreffend bemerkt, brachten sie den König ursprünglich in vollem Krönungsornat, angetan mit allen statusbezeugenden *regalia*, zur Anschauung – in einem Typus also, den eine um 1305 bis 1310 entstandene Statue Ludwigs des Heiligen aus dem Schloss des königlichen Finanzverwalters Enguerran de Marigny in Mainneville[66] hinsichtlich der Gewandung und ihrer Farbigkeit, eine Miniatur des Heiligen im *Registre des ordonnances de l'Hôtel du roi* von 1320 (Taf. 37.4)[67] darüber hinaus auch hinsichtlich der Insignien, des Szepters und der Main de justice, überliefert.

Verborgen geblieben ist dem ikonographisch fixierten Blick indes, dass Karl V. mit seiner Statue am Ostportal des Louvre nicht nur den von Philipp IV. um 1300 eingeführten Typus der Königsdarstellung aufgegriffen hat, sondern bewusst auch dessen betont schlichtes, auf wenige, plastisch ausgebildete Einzelformen beschränktes Erscheinungsbild – wie es in charakteristischer Ausprägung ein skulptiertes Giebelfragment vor Augen führt, das wahrscheinlich vom Grabmal der Blanche de France, einer 1320 verstorbenen Tochter Ludwigs IX., bei den Cordeliers zu Paris stammt (Taf. 37.3)[68]. An diesem der Hofkunst Philipps IV. verpflichteten Werk findet sich der ausgesprochen voluminöse Gewandstil der Louvre-Statue ebenso vorgebildet wie etwa die mächtigen Schüsselfalten, zu denen der sonst glatt fallende Mantel über der Mittelachse des Körpers aufgeworfen ist. Mit dieser Prägnanz und Schlichtheit der Formensprache hielten die Werke der Bildhauerkunst am Hof Karls V. ein Deutungsangebot bereit, dessen monumentale Zusammenhänge Karl IV. bereits bei seinem Aufenthalt in Saint-Denis erfahren haben könnte.

Denn dort galt das Totengedenken des Kaisers mit Karl IV. und Johann II. zwei Königen, deren Liegefiguren ihrem stilistischen Erscheinungsbild nach in denkbar schärfstem Kontrast auseinander treten. Während der ältere, um 1329 geschaffene Gisant des letzten Kapetingers ein feingliedrig-ornamentreiches Gewandsystem aufweist (Taf. 36.3), legen die 1364-66 im Auftrag Karls V. entstandenen Figuren der ersten Valois größte formale Bescheidenheit an den Tag (Taf. 36.4). Wie auch an programmatischen Verlautbarungen des Hofes und öffentlichkeitswirksamen Auftritten des Königs zu ersehen ist, propagierte Karl V. in alledem das Bild eines dem christlichen Herrscherideal der *humilitas* in besonderem Maße verpflichteten Monarchen[69]. Denn nach der wohl schwersten französischen Niederlage des Hundertjährigen Krieges in der Schlacht bei Poitiers 1356 und den sich anschließenden außen- wie innenpolitischen Konflikten um die Thronrechte der Valois und die Autorität der Krone schien das Leitbild des demütigen und bescheidenen Herrschers geeignet, der massiven, auch gewaltsam artikulierten Kritik an der politisch-gesellschaftlichen Führungsschicht des Landes entgegenzuwirken[70]. Außerdem signalisierte dieses Bild eine Form der Lebensführung und Herrschaftspraxis, mit der Karl V. dem Beispiel und Vorbild Ludwigs des Heiligen gleichkam – dem Ideal eines Königs, der für ein von Bußverlangen und barmherzigen Werken bestimmtes asketisches Leben stand und wie kein zweiter die Sorge um das Gemeinwohl, um Gerechtigkeit und finanzpolitische Stabilität verkörperte[71].

Während seines Aufenthalts im Hôtel Saint-Pol wird der Aufmerksamkeit des Kaisers die in unmittelbarer Nachbarschaft gelegene Coelestinerkirche nicht entgangen sein. Und dort, am Stifterportal der 1370 geweihten Kirche (Taf. 37.2), fanden sich Karl V. und seine Gemahlin Jeanne de Bourbon erneut und unmissverständlich in den Sinnzusammenhang der *humilitas* eingelassen. Denn die den Louvre-Statuen aufs engste verwandten Standbilder des Königspaares flankierten die am Trumeau aufgestellte Figur des heiligen Papstes Coelestin V. Dieser aber galt aufgrund seiner noch im Jahr der Papstwahl 1294 vollzogenen Abdankung als Inbegriff christlicher Demut, der von ihm begründete Orden trat durch ein klösterliches Leben hervor, das durch vollkommene individuelle Armut, äußerst strikte Fastenregeln

65 Delachenal 1910-20, 2: 245.
66 Mainneville, Saint-Pierre. – Art au temps des rois maudits 1998, Nr. 51.
67 Paris, Archives nationales, JJ 57, fol. 20. – France de Saint Louis 1970, Nr. 213.
68 Paris, Musée Carnavalet. – Art au temps des rois maudits 1998, Nr. 50.
69 Carqué 2004, 556-60.
70 Zu den Konfliktlinien im Überblick Carqué 2004, 498-503.
71 Das überkommene christliche Herrscherideal der *humilitas* hatte sich zuletzt im hagiografischen Bild Ludwigs des Heiligen mächtiger denn je erneuert; Le Goff 1996, 595-641.

und strenge Bußübungen gekennzeichnet war[72]. Die von Karl 1352 noch als Dauphin gegründete Niederlassung der Coelestiner in Paris stand hoch in der Gunst des Königshauses, denn auch politisch besaß die Gestalt Coelestins gesteigerte Signifikanz. Philipp IV. hatte den Orden im Jahr 1300 mit Bedacht auch gegen den hierokratischen Anspruch Bonifaz' VIII. in Frankreich eingeführt, und im eschatologischen Denken der Franziskanerspiritualen wurde der 1313 kanonisierte Papst mit jenem endzeitlichen Engelpapst identifiziert, der zusammen mit dem französischen König der Welt den Frieden bringen würde.

Das von Karl V. konsequent entfaltete Herrscherbild der *humilitas* war, da es wesentlich auf innenpolitische Konflikte wie den radikalen ständischen Widerstand reagierte, der sich in den gewaltsamen Aufständen der Pariser Bürger um Étienne Marcel und der Bauern in der Jacquerie artikuliert hatte, zuallererst für die Augen einer breiten Öffentlichkeit bestimmt. Entsprechend prägte es vor allem jene Bildmedien, deren Wahrnehmung keinerlei Beschränkungen unterlag. Waren die Bilder hingegen nur der repräsentativen Öffentlichkeit des Hofes zugänglich, so befleißigten sie sich einer unvermindert aufwendigen, an den ornamentreichen Stilidiomen der späten kapetingischen Hofkunst orientierten Formensprache[73]. Träger dieses ungleich exklusiveren Betrachterbezugs standen dem Kaiser bei seinem Besuch in Paris vielfach vor Augen, denn sein erklärtes Interesse galt den in Hofkreisen zirkulierenden Codices ebenso wie der Ausstattung der Residenzen.

Mit dem Château de Vincennes vor den Toren der Stadt besuchte der Kaiser schließlich einen Ort königlicher Herrschaft, der diesen gruppenspezifischen Wahrnehmungshorizont gleichsam architektonisch umschrieb. Denn die annähernd sechs Hektar umfassende Schlossanlage (Taf. 35.2) hatte Karl V. nach den Worten Christine de Pisans als *ville fermée* konzipiert: [...] *dehors Paris, le chastel du bois de Vincennes, qui moult est notable et bel, et avoit entencion d'y faire ville fermée, et là avoit establie en beaulz manoirs la demeure de plusieurs seigneurs, chevaliers et aultres ses mieulz amez* [...][74]. Demnach sollte Vincennes mit dem eigens befestigten Donjon (Taf. 35.1), den Wohntürmen der Umfassungsmauer und den Gebäuden des älteren kapetingischen *manoir* den weiteren Haus- und Hofhalt – die königliche Familie und Vertreter der politisch-gesellschaftlichen Führungsschicht – in seinen Mauern aufnehmen. War schon die fortifikatorische Struktur des Château du Louvre geeignet, die königliche Residenz nicht nur gegen einen Angriff der Stadt von außen, sondern auch gegen Angriffe aus dem Inneren von Paris zu verteidigen, so konnte sich die Herrschaftselite des Reiches nun vollends aus dem Gefahrenbereich der Hauptstadt zurückziehen und in der Wehranlage von Vincennes Zuflucht suchen.

Da ein Herrschaftszentrum solchen – auch architektonischen – Zuschnitts ohne Beispiel und Vorbild war, bedurfte es in besonderem Maße des näheren Einblicks und der Erläuterung. Entsprechend hatte man dem Kaiser im Donjon die *chambre du roi* im zweiten Obergeschoss zur Verfügung gestellt, und am Tag nach der Ankunft *se fist porter le dit Empereur tout au tour de la chambre dessus dite, pour veoir par les fenestres le circuite du chastel, pour ce qu'il n'y povoit aller*[75]. Aus diesem Grund war der Kaiser nicht zugegen als *celuy jour fist monstrer au roy des Romains* [Wenzel IV.; B. C.] *et aus autres princes et chevaliers la tour, les estages, garnison et abillemens d'icelle, et furent jusques au hault; les quelz la tenoient à la plus bele et merveilleuse chose que onques més eussent veue*[76]. Angesichts einer derart gründlichen Besichtigung des Donjon' und eingedenk der dem gichtkranken Kaiser ermöglichten Vogelschau über die Befestigungsanlagen ist anzunehmen, dass man aufseiten des Gastgebers einmal mehr dafür Sorge getragen hatte, dass die Gäste auch in Vincennes Bau- und Bildwerke im gewünschten Sinne wahrgenommen und verstanden haben.

72 Herde 1981.
73 Carqué 2004, 544-61.
74 Solente 1936-40, 2: 40.
75 Delachenal 1910-20, 2: 263.
76 Delachenal 1910-20, 2: 265.

ERFAHRUNGS- UND VERSTÄNDNISHORIZONTE

In den politisch-sozialen Praktiken dieses Staatsbesuches zeichnen sich Formen umfassend gesteuerter Rezeption ab, die es nicht dem Zufall überlassen haben, wie Orte und Zeichen der Herrschaft wahrgenommen und verstanden wurden. Das Spektrum rezeptionslenkender Mittel und Wege reichte dabei von der umsichtigen Schaffung geeigneter Wahrnehmungsbedingungen über die Stillung des wiederholt artikulierten Schauverlangens bis hin zur gezielten, von Erläuterungen begleiteten Besichtigung und Präsentation. Einiges spricht dafür, dass solche Mittel und Wege der Blickführung ihre beabsichtigte Wirkung nicht verfehlt haben – so vor allem die vielfach wiederkehrenden Hinweise auf ergreifende oder gar überwältigende Sinneseindrücke, auf eine *belle* oder *noble et merveilleuse chose à veoir*, die *tres grant plaisir* bereitet habe, auf Orte und Objekte, die *les plus belles* oder *les plus riches* gewesen seien, die man je gesehen habe.

Derartige Zeichen der Bewunderung geben zu erkennen, dass Blickführung und Rezeption in denselben gruppenspezifischen Erfahrungs- und Verständnishorizont eingelassen waren. Mithin konnte sich der Hof Karls V. auf die Wirksamkeit jener grundlegenden Wahrnehmungs- und Deutungsmuster verlassen, die Bau- und Bildwerke im Schlüsselbegriff der *magnificentia* als Form der Sorge um das Gemeinwohl und zugleich als Ausdruck herrscherlicher Prachtentfaltung bestimmten[77]. Die Fürstentugend der *providentia* kehrt Évrard de Trémaugon hervor, als er im Prolog des *Songe du Vergier* auf die Bauunternehmungen Karls V. zu sprechen kommt: [*L*]*e grant tresor que tu assambles et que tu elargis en murs, en fossés et en chastiaux reparer et redrecer, et aucuns faire de novel, car en edifices de palais et de chastiaux nul n'est plus soutif ne de plus grant magnificence que tu soies; et tout ce fais pour la pais du peuple, et le garder d'opprission et deffendre*[78].

Neben diesen aus der antiken philosophischen wie aus der mittelalterlichen theologischen Tradition herrührenden ethischen Normen[79] sind es jedoch auch standesspezifische Anspruchs- und Aufwandsnormen gewesen, denen die Kunstaufträge des Hofes zu genügen hatten. Denn der ethischen Hoheit in Tat und Gesinnung entsprach, da sie sich der Öffentlichkeit wesentlich über die Mittel und Wege symbolischer Kommunikation und Repräsentation mitteilte, die Großartigkeit im Erscheinungsbild – einem Erscheinungsbild freilich, das zuallererst für die repräsentative Öffentlichkeit des Hofes bestimmt war. Denn neben ihrer allgemeinen politisch-gesellschaftlichen Dimension, der Verpflichtung des Königs zu Freigebigkeit und Fürsorge gegenüber dem Gemeinwesen, besaß die *magnificentia* auch eine weitaus exklusivere, schichtspezifische Komponente. Sie war ein zentrales Merkmal hochadliger Lebenswelt, dessen jeweilige Ausprägung sich – wie bei Froissart oder in den *Grandes Chroniques* vielfach belegt[80] – nach dem *estat* und *degré*, der *poissance* und *rikèce* seiner Träger bemaß – mithin nach der gesellschaftlichen Stellung wie nach den jeweiligen Möglichkeiten ihrer Repräsentation. Entsprechend mangelte es auch beim Besuch des Kaisers in Paris nicht an ranggerechten Wertsignalen, waren Gemächer *tres richement parées et ordenées*, Reliquiare *tres richement garni* oder Insignien *de moult grant richece*.

Schließlich war den Medien der *magnificentia* auch eine prospektive Zweckbestimmung zugedacht. Denn als in die Gegenwart wie in die Zukunft wirkende Manifestationen sollten sie helfen, *memoria* zu begründen. Pracht und Würde der zeremoniellen Erscheinung des Königs seien – so vermerkt Christine de Pisan im *Livre des fais et bonnes meurs* – inszeniert worden, *pour garder, maintenir et donner exemple à ses successeurs à venir que par solemnel ordre se doit tenir et mener le tres digne degré de la haulte couronne de France, à laquelle toute magnificence souveraine est deue, pertinent et redevable*[81]. Und nach dem Kommentar des Nicole Oresme zur Nikomachischen Ethik waren gerade die größten Aufwendungen zur Demonstration von *magnificentia* über jeden moralischen Zweifel erhaben, da sie dem Andenken zu besonderer Dauerhaftigkeit verhalfen: *C'est trop plus grant magnificence et meilleur chose de faire un temple ou un palais longuement durable de quoy il est aussi comme perpetuel memoire*

77 Das vielförmige und vielschichtige Imaginarium der *magnificentia* im Überblick bei Paravicini 2001; Franke 2004.

78 Schnerb-Lièvre 1982, 1: 6-7.

79 Zentrale antike Referenz ist die *Nikomachische Ethik* des Aristoteles gewesen, die am Hof Karls V. in der Übersetzung Nicole Oresmes vorlag; Menut 1940, bes. 241-7.

80 Carqué 2004, 450-1.

81 Solente 1936-40, 1: 51.

de celuy qui l'a fait et proffit au bien publique, que de faire une tele chose bele et jolie et de petite duree. Mais se elle estoit belle et durable, ce seroit tres bien[82].

Materielle Dauerhaftigkeit und öffentlichkeitswirksame Sichtbarkeit sicherten den Bau- und Bildwerken schließlich auch höchste Autorität und Glaubwürdigkeit. Darüber gibt ein Prozess Auskunft, in dem Bildwerke als Beweismittel in den Zeugenstand gerufen wurden. Vor den Schranken des obersten Gerichtshofs der Krone trafen sich im Jahre 1410 die Mönche von Saint-Denis und die Domherren von Notre-Dame, die einander den Besitz der wahren Schädelreliquie des hl. Dionysius streitig machten. Im Zuge dieses lang schwelenden Konflikts hatten sich illustre Parteien gebildet, deren Zusammensetzung unschwer erkennen lässt, dass der Kampf um den *patronus regis et regni* eine Angelegenheit von nationalem Interesse gewesen ist. Denn auf Seiten der Mönche standen Karl VI. und Louis d'Orléans, auf der des Kapitels Jean de Berry, Jean Gerson, der Kanzler der Universität, und selbstredend der Bischof Pierre d'Orgemont, ein Sohn des gleichnamigen Kanzlers und mutmaßlichen Autors der *Grandes Chroniques* unter Karl V. In den Stellungnahmen vor Prozessbeginn legte das Domkapitel dar, dass die in seinem Besitz befindliche Schädel*kalotte* die wahre Reliquie sei, da allein diese Form des Martyriums – und nicht die vollständige Enthauptung – bezeugt werde *de grans et anciens ymages de pierre et en lieux patens et publiques, au veu et sceu de tous ceulx qui l'ont volu veoir* [...][83].

Wahrnehmungs- und Deutungsmuster wie die Sakralität von Herrschaft, die christliche Fürstentugend der *humilitas*, das gesellschaftliche Pflichtgebot der *magnificentia* oder die Legitimation qua Sichtbarkeit markieren den weiteren Horizont jener Bedeutungszuweisungen, die in den konkreten Handlungszusammenhängen und Rezeptionssituationen des Staatsbesuches greifbar wurden. Gerade in diesen flüchtigen Momenten aktiver Sinnproduktion scheint die Kunstgeschichte den historischen Bedeutungsdimensionen und Wirkungsweisen von Bau- und Bildwerken näher zu kommen als über die bloße Wiedergewinnung ihrer verlorenen Sichtbarkeit, von deren epistemologischen Unschärfen eingangs die Rede war. Denn nicht die Bau- oder Motivgestalt an sich, sondern erst die Art und Weise, in der ihre Wahrnehmung organisiert und kontextualisiert wurde, ließ Bau- und Bildwerke zu Bedeutungsträgern werden, brachte Wirkungen hervor und trug damit zur monumentalen Konstruktion der Macht bei.

BIBLIOGRAFIE

Albrecht, U. 1986. *Von der Burg zum Schloß. Französische Schloßbaukunst im Spätmittelalter*. Worms: Wernersche Verlagsgesellschaft.

Art (L') au temps des rois maudits. Philippe le Bel et ses fils, 1285-1328. 1998. Ausstellungskatalog Paris, Galeries nationales du Grand Palais. Paris: Éditions de la Réunion des Musées Nationaux.

Ausstellung Französische Donjons. 2001. Aachen: Selbstverlag Bernhard Siepen.

Autrand, F. 1995. „Mémoire et cérémonial. La visite de l'empereur Charles IV à Paris en 1378 d'après les 'Grandes Chroniques de France' et Christine de Pizan." In *Une femme de lettres au Moyen Age. Études autour de Christine de Pizan*, herausgegeben von L. Dulac und B. Ribémont, 91-103. Orléans: Paradigme.

Auzépy, M.-F. und J. Cornette, Hrsg. 2003. *Palais et Pouvoir. De Constantinople à Versailles*. Saint-Denis: Presses Universitaires de Vincennes.

Avril, F., Hrsg. *Jean Fouquet. Peintre et enlumineur du XVe siècle*. Ausstellungskatalog Paris, Bibliothèque nationale de France. Paris: Hazan.

Bandmann, G. 1951. *Mittelalterliche Architektur als Bedeutungsträger*. Berlin: Gebr. Mann.

Baron, F. 1996. *Sculptures françaises I. Moyen Âge*. Musée du Louvre, département des sculptures du Moyen Âge, de la Renaissance et des temps modernes. Paris: Éditions de la Réunion des Musées Nationaux.

Bennert, U. 1992. „Art et propagande politique sous Philippe IV le Bel. Le cycle des rois de France dans la Grand'salle du palais de la Cité." *Revue de l'art* 97: 6-59.

82 Menut 1940, 246.
83 Delaborde 1884, 399.

Berty, A., H. Legrand und L.-M. Tisserand. 1866-97. *Topographie historique du vieux Paris*. Histoire générale de Paris. 6 Bände. Paris: Imprimerie Impériale/Nationale.

Boutier, J. 2002. *Les Plans de Paris des origines (1493) à la fin du XVIIIe siècle*. Paris: Bibliothèque nationale de France.

Bove, B. 2003. „Les palais royaux à Paris au Moyen Âge (XIe-XVe siècles).“ In Auzépy und Cornette 2003, 45-79.

Carqué, B. 2004. *Stil und Erinnerung. Französische Hofkunst im Jahrhundert Karls V. und im Zeitalter ihrer Deutung*. Göttingen: Vandenhoeck & Ruprecht.

Cazelles, R. 1972. *Nouvelle histoire de Paris. De la fin du règne de Philippe Auguste à la mort de Charles V, 1223-1380*. Paris: Hachette.

Chapelot, J. 1994. *Le château de Vincennes. Une résidence royale au Moyen Âge*. Paris: Éditions du CNRS.

Chapelot, J. und E. Lalou, Hrsg. 1996. *Vincennes aux origines de l'État moderne*. Paris: Presses de l'Ecole Normale Supérieure.

Charles Meryon. Paris um 1850, Zeichnungen – Radierungen – Photographien. 1975. Ausstellungskatalog Frankfurt am Main, Städelsches Kunstinstitut und Städtische Galerie. Frankfurt am Main: Städelsches Kunstinstitut und Städtische Galerie.

Châtelet, A. 2000. *L'âge d'or du manuscrit à peintures en France au temps de Charles VI et les Heures du Maréchal Boucicaut*. Dijon: Éditions Faton.

De Caumont, A. 1830-41. *Cours d'antiquités monumentales. L'art dans l'ouest de la France, depuis les temps les plus reculés jusqu'au XVIIe siècle*. 6 Bände. Paris: Lance/Derache.

Delaborde, H. F. 1884. „Le procès du chef de saint Denis en 1410.“ *Mémoires de la Société de l'Histoire de Paris et de l'Ile-de-France* 11: 297-409.

Delachenal, R., Hrsg. 1910-20. *Chronique des règnes de Jean II et de Charles V (Les Grandes Chroniques de France)*. 4 Bände. Paris: Renouard.

De Mély, F. 1904. *Exuviae Sacrae Constantinopolitanae III. La Croix des premiers croisés, la sainte Lance, la sainte Couronne*. Paris: E. Leroux.

Deutsche Burgenvereinigung, Hrsg. 1999. *Burgen in Mitteleuropa. Ein Handbuch*. 2 Bände. Stuttgart: Konrad Theiss.

Ehlers, C., Hrsg. (im Druck). *Orte der Herrschaft – Places of Power – Lieux de pouvoir*. Göttingen: Vandenhoeck & Ruprecht.

Emery, E. 2005. „Protecting the Past. Albert Robida and the ›Vieux Paris‹ Exhibit at the 1900 World's Fair.“ *Journal of European Studies* 35: 65-85.

Enlart, C. 1929-32. *Manuel d'archéologie française depuis les temps mérovingiens jusqu'à la Renaissance II: Architecture civile et militaire*. 2 Bände. 2. Auflage. Paris: Picard.

Erlande-Brandenburg, A. 1988. *Triumph der Gotik, 1260-1380*. Universum der Kunst 34. München: C.H. Beck.

Exposition (L') de Paris (1900). 1900. Encyclopédie du Siècle. 3 Bände. Paris: Librairie Illustrée.

Favier, J. 1974. *Nouvelle histoire de Paris. Paris au XVe siècle, 1380-1500*. Paris: Hachette.

—. 1997. *Paris. Deux mille ans d'histoire*. Paris: Fayard.

France (La) de Saint Louis. 1970. Ausstellungskatalog Paris, Salle des gens d'armes du Palais. Paris: Les presses artistiques.

Franke, B. 2004. „Magnifizenz. Die Tugend der Prachtentfaltung und die französische Kunst um 1400.“ In *Dortmund und Conrad von Soest im spätmittelalterlichen Europa*, herausgegeben von Th. Schilp und B. Welzel, 141-61. Bielefeld: Verlag für Regionalgeschichte.

Gaborit-Chopin, D. 1987. *Regalia. Les instruments du sacre des rois de France. Les ›Honneurs de Charlemagne‹*. Paris: Éditions de la Réunion des Musées Nationaux.

Guérout, J. 1949-51. „Le Palais de la Cité à Paris des origines à 1417. Essai topographique et archéologique.“ *Mémoires de la Fédération des Sociétés historiques et archéologiques de Paris et de l'Ile-de-France* 1: 57-212, 2: 21-204, 3: 7-101.

—. 1996. „L'hôtel du roi au palais de la Cité à Paris sous Jean II et Charles V.“ In Chapelot und Lalou 1996, 219-88.

Guizot, F. 1873-6. *Histoire de France depuis les temps les plus reculés jusqu'en 1789, racontée à mes petits enfants*. 5 Bände. Paris: Hachette.

Hennin, M. 1856-62. *Les Monuments de l'Histoire de France. Catalogue des productions de la sculpture, de la peinture et de la gravure, relatives à l'histoire de la France et des Français*. 10 Bände. Paris: Delion.

Herde, P. 1981. *Cölestin V. (1294). (Peter von Morrone) Der Engelpapst*. Päpste und Papsttum 16. Stuttgart: Hiersemann.

Hoffbauer, F. 2001. Reprint. *Paris à travers les âges. Aspects successifs des monuments et quartiers historiques de Paris depuis le XIIIe siècle jusqu'à nos jours, fidèlement restitués d'après les documents authentiques*. Zuerst in Lieferungen 1875-82. Paris: Bibliothèque de l'Image.

Imesch, K. 2003. *Magnificenza als architektonische Kategorie*. Oberhausen: Athena-Verlag.

Journal officiel de la Bastille et de la rue Saint-Antoine. Faits rétrospectifs de 1789. 1888. Paris.

Kruft, H.-W. 1985. *Geschichte der Architekturtheorie*. München: C.H. Beck.

Lacroix, P. 1877. *Les Arts au Moyen Âge et à l'époque de la Renaissance*. Paris: Firmin-Didot.

Laß, H., Hrsg. 2002. *Mythos, Metapher, Motiv. Untersuchungen zum Bild der Burg seit 1500*. Alfeld an der Leine: Coppi-Verlag.

Le Goff, J. 1996. *Saint Louis*. Paris: Gallimard.

Le Roux de Lincy, A. und L.-M. Tisserand, Hrsg. 1867. *Paris et ses historiens aux XIVe et XVe siècles. Documents et écrits originaux recueillis et commentés*. Paris: Imprimerie Impériale.

Liebenwein, W. 1977. *Studiolo. Die Entstehung eines Raumtyps und seine Entwicklung bis um 1600*. Berlin: Gebr. Mann.

Lorentz, Ph. 1998. „À propos du ›réalisme‹ flamand. La ›Crucifixion du Parlement de Paris‹ et la porte du beau roi Philippe au Palais de la Cité." *Cahiers de la Rotonde* 20: 101-24.

—. 2004. *La crucifixion du Parlement de Paris*. Paris: Éditions de la Réunion des Musées Nationaux.

Louvre (Le) des rois. Les fouilles de la Cour Carrée. 1986. Archéologia. Dossiers Histoire et archéologie 110. Fontaine-lès-Dijon: Archéologia.

Maumené, Ch., und L. de Harcourt. 1928-32. *Iconographie des rois de France*. Archives de l'Art français, nouv. pér. XV-XVI. 2 Bände. Paris: Colin.

Meier-Graefe, A. J., Hrsg. 1900. *Die Weltausstellung in Paris 1900*. Paris und Leipzig: F. Krüger.

Menut, A. D., Hrsg. 1940. *Nicole Oresme, Le Livre de Ethiques d'Aristote*. New York: Stechert.

Mesqui, J. 1991-3. *Châteaux et enceintes de la France médiévale. De la défense à la résidence*. 2 Bände. Paris: Picard.

Meyer, W. 1976. „Die Burg als repräsentatives Statussymbol. Ein Beitrag zum Verständnis des mittelalterlichen Burgenbaues." *Zeitschrift für Schweizerische Archäologie und Kunstgeschichte* 33: 173-81.

Michalsky, T. 2000. *Memoria und Repräsentation. Die Grabmäler des Königshauses Anjou in Italien*. Göttingen: Vandenhoeck & Ruprecht.

Müller, M. 2004. *Das Schloß als Bild des Fürsten. Herrschaftliche Metaphorik in der Residenzarchitektur des Alten Reichs (1470-1618)*. Göttingen: Vandenhoeck & Ruprecht.

Moos, S. v. 1974. *Turm und Bollwerk. Beiträge zu einer politischen Ikonographie der italienischen Renaissancearchitektur*. Zürich: Atlantis.

Paravicini, W., Hrsg. 1997. *Zeremoniell und Raum*. Residenzenforschung 6. Sigmaringen: Thorbecke.

—. 2001. „Die zwölf ›Magnificences‹ Karls des Kühnen." In *Formen und Funktionen öffentlicher Kommunikation im Mittelalter*, herausgegeben von G. Althoff, 319-95. Stuttgart: Thorbecke.

—, Hrsg. 2005. *Das Gehäuse der Macht. Der Raum der Herrschaft im interkulturellen Vergleich. Antike, Mittelalter, Frühe Neuzeit*. Mitteilungen der Residenzen-Kommission der Akademie der Wissenschaften zu Göttingen, Sonderheft 7. Kiel: Christian-Albrechts-Universität.

Piper, O. 1912. *Burgenkunde. Bauwesen und Geschichte der Burgen*. 3. Aufl. München: Piper.

Pleybert, F., Hrsg. 2001. *Paris et Charles V. Arts et architecture*. Paris: Action Artistique de la Ville de Paris.

Prinz, W. und R. G. Kecks. 1994. *Das französische Schloß der Renaissance. Form und Bedeutung der Architektur, ihre geschichtlichen und gesellschaftlichen Grundlagen*. 2., erweiterte Auflage. Berlin: Gebr. Mann.

Reinle, A. 1976. *Zeichensprache der Architektur. Symbol, Darstellung und Brauch in der Baukunst des Mittelalters und der Neuzeit*. Zürich u. a.: Verlag für Architektur Artemis.

Reudenbach, B. 1980. „Säule und Apostel. Überlegungen zum Verhältnis von Architektur und architekturexegetischer Literatur im Mittelalter.“ *Frühmittelalterliche Studien* 14: 310-51.

Robida, A. 1900. *Exposition universelle de 1900. Le Vieux Paris, guide historique, pittoresque et anecdotique*. Paris: Imprimerie Artistique.

Roux, S. 2003. *Paris au Moyen Âge*. Paris: Hachette.

Sainte-Chapelle (La) de Bourges. Une fondation disparue de Jean de France, duc de Berry. 2004. Ausstellungskatalog Bourges, Musée du Berry. Paris: Somogy.

Sauer, J. 1924. *Symbolik des Kirchengebäudes und seiner Ausstattung in der Auffassung des Mittelalters*. 2. Auflage. Freiburg im Breisgau: Herder.

Sauerländer, W. 1977. „Die Sainte-Chapelle du Palais Ludwigs des Heiligen.“ *Jahrbuch der Bayerischen Akademie der Wissenschaften* 92-115.

Schmitt, J.-C. und O.G. Oexle, Hrsg. 2002. *Les tendances actuelles de l'histoire du Moyen Âge en France et en Allemagne*. Paris: Publications de la Sorbonne.

Schnerb-Lièvre, M., Hrsg. 1982. *Le Songe du Vergier. Édité d'après le manuscrit royal 19 C IV de la British Library*. 2 Bände. Paris: Éditions du CNRS.

Schütte, U. 1994. *Das Schloß als Wehranlage. Befestigte Schloßbauten der frühen Neuzeit im alten Reich*. Darmstadt: Wissenschaftliche Buchgesellschaft.

Schwandner, E.-L. und K. Rheidt, Hrsg. 2004. *Macht der Architektur – Architektur der Macht*. Diskussionen zur Archäologischen Bauforschung 8. Mainz: Philipp von Zabern.

Simson, O. v. 1956. *The Gothic Cathedral. The Origins of Gothic Architecture and the Medieval Concept of Order*. London: Routledge & Kegan Paul.

Solente, S., Hrsg. 1936-40. *Christine de Pisan, Le Livre des fais et bonnes meurs du sage Roy Charles*. 2 Bände. Paris: Champion.

Strubel, A. 2000. „Le ›chevauchier‹ de Charles V. Christine de Pisan et le spectacle de la majesté royale.“ In *Penser le pouvoir au Moyen Âge (VIIIe-XVe siècle). Études d'histoire et de littérature offertes à Françoise Autrand*, herausgegeben von D. Boutet und J. Verger, 385-99. Paris: Éditions Rue d'Ulm.

Très Riches Heures (Les) du duc de Berry et l'enluminure en France au début du XVe siècle. 2004. Ausstellungskatalog Chantilly, Musée Condé. Paris: Éditions de la Réunion des Musées Nationaux.

Trésor (Le) de Saint-Denis. 1991. Ausstellungskatalog Paris, Musée du Louvre. Paris: Éditions de la Réunion des Musées Nationaux.

Trésor (Le) de la Sainte-Chapelle. 2001. Ausstellungskatalog Paris, Musée du Louvre. Paris: Éditions de la Réunion des Musées Nationaux.

Vincennes. Du manoir capétien à la résidence de Charles V. 2003-4. Dossiers d'Archéologie 289. Dijon: Éditions Fanton.

Viollet-le-Duc, E.-E. 1854-68. *Dictionnaire raisonné de l'architecture française du XIe au XVIe siècle*. 10 Bände. Paris: Bance/Morel.

—. 1874. *Histoire d'une forteresse*. Paris: Hetzel.

—. 1878. *La cité de Carcassonne (Aude)*. 2. erweiterte Auflage. Paris: Morel.

Whiteley, M. 1994. „La grosse tour de Vincennes, résidence de Charles V.“ *Bulletin monumental* 152: 313-35.

Zeune, J. 1996. *Burgen – Symbole der Macht. Ein neues Bild der mittelalterlichen Burg*. Regensburg: Pustet.

—. 2004. „Vom »echten Styl« deutscher Burgen. Das Bild der Burg im 19. Jahrhundert.“ *Burgen und Schlösser* 45: 8-17.

1. Château du Louvre. Holzstich nach der Vorlage von Alphonse de Neuville.

2. Château du Louvre. Holzstich nach der Vorlage von Viollet-le-Duc.

3. La Crucifixion du Parlement de Paris (Ausschnitt). Paris, Musée du Louvre. Nach: Lorentz 2004, 36.

4. Très Riches Heures du duc de Berry. Chantilly, Musée Condé, ms. 65, fol. 10v. Nach: Châtelet 2000, 154.

1. Château de Vincennes, Donjon. Ansicht von Südosten. Nach: Pleybert 2001, 75.

2. Le château de Vincennes vers 1400. Rekonstruktionszeichnung von Jean-Claude Golvin und Florence Babled. Nach: Chapelot 1994, vordere Umschlagabbildung.

3. Grandes Chroniques de France. Bibliothèque nationale de France, Mss, Fr. 6465, fol. 417. Nach: Avril 2003, 243.

4. Grandes Chroniques de France. Bibliothèque nationale de France, Mss, Fr. 6465, fol. 444. Nach: Avril 2003, 245.

1. Der Palais de la Cité um 1350-60. Rekonstruktion des Grundrisses. Nach: Cazelles 1972, 350.

2. La Crucifixion du Parlement de Paris (Ausschnitt). Paris, Musée du Louvre. Nach: Pleybert 2001, 125.

3. Liegefigur Karls IV. Saint-Denis, ehem. Abteikirche. Archiv des Verfassers.

4. Liegefiguren Johanns II. und Philipps VI. Saint-Denis, ehem. Abteikirche. Archiv des Verfassers.

1. Statuen Karls V. und der Jeanne de Bourbon. Paris, Musée du Louvre.

2. Portal der Coelestinerkirche. Nach: A. L. Millin, Antiquités Nationales, 1790-8.

3. Giebelfragment vom Grabmal der Blanche de France. Paris, Musée Carnavalet.

4. Registre des ordonnances de l'Hôtel du roi. Paris, Archives nationales, JJ 57, fol. 20.

Liturgical Space as a Social Product
Anthropological Aspects of the Early Modern Maiestas Pontificia in the Sistine Chapel

TRISTAN WEDDIGEN

SOCIAL SPACE, SACRED AND PROFANE

Human societies organise themselves spatially and impose social structures and meanings upon their physical environment – in the words of Henri Lefèbvre (1905–91): "(social) space is a (social) product"[1]. According to Émile Durkheim (1858–1917), societies are only possible if they are partitioned and structured into different and classified groups which communicate and interact with each other; organised societies thus manifest themselves spatially[2].

Conversely, structured environments express equivalent forms of society. In his study on the court society of the Ancien Régime, Norbert Elias (1897–1990) considered the structure of dwellings as indicators of social configurations, a view that is still valid for the socio-historical analysis of architecture and its decoration[3]. As Elias shows, different spatial situations provide information about the different social groups who create and inhabit the various spaces at court: members of the court, driven by an essential desire for prestige, aesthetically transform their architectural surroundings in accordance with their social standing[4]. Thus constructed and decorated or even just depicted spaces can be seen as signs or 'symbolic forms' that designate social relationships[5]. In the early modern period the correspondence between social structures and their aesthetic appearance is based above all on the social, rhetorical and art theoretical ideal of *decorum* or appropriateness, in other words on a socially accepted differentiation of ordered human interrelationships[6].

Elias' model of the Baroque court can indeed be used for the analysis of the role of the arts at the early modern papal court. In fact, the absolutist court modelled its ceremonial on that of the early modern Roman Curia, which – as the *monarchia Christi* – was renowned for its strict social structure and distinction. Jörg Jochen Berns argues that from the early Cinquecento the papacy, as the "energetic core of European ceremonial", operated a kind of 'ceremonial imperialism' that had a decided influence on the efforts of secular courts to sacralise their own ceremonial[7].

This contribution is drawn from my forthcoming book *Raphael's Parrot Room – Ritual, Functions and Decorations at the Vatican Palace of the Renaissance.* The translation of the present text was provided by Fiona Healy.

1 Lefèbvre 1991, 26.

2 Durkheim 1968, 632: "Celle-ci [la société] n'est possible que si les individus et les choses qui la composent sont répartis entre différents groupes, c'est-à-dire classés les uns par rapport aux autres. La société suppose donc une organisation consciente de soi qui n'est autre chose qu'une classification. Cette organisation de la société se communique naturellement à l'espace qu'elle occupe."

3 Elias 1983, 42–65. Cf. Paravicini 1997a, 14; Asch 1991. See also Daniel 2001, 254–69: on Elias' role in cultural studies. Kempers 1994, 6–9: on the social history of art. Aulinger 1992: on the sociology of art. Cf. Schneider 1996.

4 Elias 1983, 43: "And so the precipitate of a social unit in terms of space and indeed, more narrowly, in terms of rooms, is a tangible and – in the literal sense – visible representation of its special nature. In this sense the kind of accommodation of court people gives sure and very graphic access to an understanding of certain social relationships characteristic of court society."

5 Cf. Panofsky 1964: on perspective as a 'symbolic form'. Bertelli, Cardini, and Zorzi 1986: on court culture. Signorotto and Visceglia 2002: overview of research on papal court culture.

6 Cf. Elias 1983, 57: e.g. the use of canonical column orders according to social standing. Cf. Rutherford and Mildner 1996–2001; Grassi and Pepe 1978, 1: 144–5: on *decorum*. Weddigen 2003: on functionalism.

7 Cf. Kerscher 2000, 182–3: on the use of courtly ceremonial at the Curia of Avignon. Kerscher 1995: on the sacralisation of court ceremonial. Berns 1995, 160: the growing interest in ceremonial in Rome at the beginning of the sixteenth century can be understood "zum einen als Anzeichen dafür, dass man das Zeremoniell gefährdet sah und dass man seine Uneinheitlichkeit bekämpfen wollte; zum anderen als Anzeichen dafür, dass man die Möglichkeit einer zentripetalen

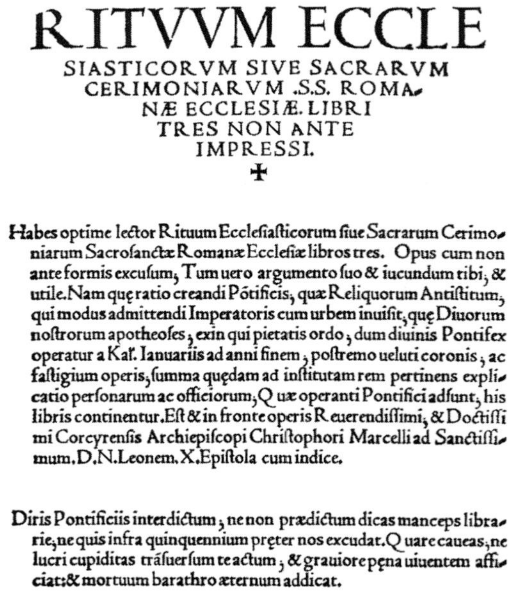

RITVVM ECCLE
SIASTICORVM SIVE SACRARVM
CERIMONIARVM .S.S. ROMA-
NÆ ECCLESIÆ. LIBRI
TRES NON ANTE
IMPRESSI.
✠

Habes optime lector Rituum Ecclesiasticorum siue Sacrarum Cerimoniarum Sacrosanctæ Romanæ Ecclesiæ libros tres. Opus cum non ante formis excusum, Tum uero argumento suo & iucundum tibi, & utile. Nam quę ratio creandi Pōtificis, quæ Reliquorum Antistitum, qui modus admittendi Imperatoris cum urbem inuisit, quę Diuorum nostrorum apotheoses, exin qui pietatis ordo, dum diuinis Pontifex operatur a Kal. Ianuariis ad anni finem, postremo ueluti coronis, ac fastigium operis, summa quędam ad institutam rem pertinens explicatio personarum ac officiorum, Quæ operanti Pontifici adsunt, his libris continentur. Est & in fronte operis Reuerendissimi, & Doctissimi Corcyrensis Archiepiscopi Christophori Marcelli ad Sanctissimum. D. N. Leonem. X. Epistola cum indice.

Diris Pontificiis interdictum, ne non prædictum dicas manceps librarie, ne quis infra quinquennium pręter nos excudat. Quare caueas, ne lucri cupiditas trāsuersum te actum, & grauiore pęna uiuentem afficiat: & mortuum barathro æternum addicat.

Abb. 1. Frontispice from: Agostino Patrizi Piccolomini. 1516. *Rituum ecclesiasticorum sive sacrarum cerimoniarum s. s. romanae ecclesiae: Libri tres non ante impressi*. Venice. After: Piccolomini 1965.

Because of its staunch awareness of the traditions of the Catholic Church's institutions and the extraordinary stability of its rituals, the Vatican could rely on clearly defined and long-standing social structures and groupings, all of which found expression in a correspondingly traditional use of particular architectural spaces and forms of decoration. The dual function of the *pontifex maximus* as Monarch of the Church State *and* as the Vicar of Christ means his office combines both sacred *and* worldly powers[8]. As the office of the pope is expressed through clearly defined rituals in pre-determined locations, these same rituals are simultaneously both religious *and* profane in character. This leads to a corresponding connection between sacred and worldly spatial forms and so distinguish papal palaces from the residences of secular rulers.

What is Ceremony?

Life at the papal court was defined and structured by binding and institutionalised rituals that were codified over the centuries. These rituals governed the areas of *liturgy* and *ceremonial*[9], though the boundaries between the two remain more or less indistinguishable during the early modern period, as for instance is evident from the title of the most significant codification of papal ceremonies: *Rituum ecclesiasticorum sive sacrarum cerimoniarum s. s. romanae ecclesiae libri tres* (Abb. 1)[10]. This text describes the rules for both liturgy and court ceremonial and was written by Agostino Patrizi Piccolomini (1430/40–94) around 1488, but published only in 1516 by Cristoforo Marcello (sixteenth century), who however failed to

Vereinheitlichung des Zeremoniells historisch erstmals für gegeben erachtete und erstmals die Chance eines Romzentrierten *Zeremoniellimperialismus* sah." Berns and Rahn 1995a, 652: "Denn die Römische Kurie ist das energetische Zentrum des europäischen Zeremoniells. Vom Papsthof breitet sich das Amt [of the master of ceremonies] im Laufe des 16. Jahrhunderts auf fast alle europäischen Höfe aus." Klapisch-Zuber 1985, 138: "ces interférences entre rituels liturgiques et rituels royaux révèlent la place capitale qu'occupe le sacré dans l'essence et la manifestation du pouvoir politique." Da Castiglionchio 1999, 102: *Christi monarchia*. Chatenet 2002, 79–80: *corte romana* known for its *cerimonie e distinzione,* and the French court for its *disordine e confusione.*

8 Cf. Prodi 1982; Muir 1997, 260; Fernández 1999, 141–2.

9 Burke 1987, 168–82; Stinger 1998, 46–59. Adamson 1999a: on court culture and ceremonial. Schimmelpfennig 1999; Fernández 1999; Kerscher 2000, 28–30: on papal ceremonial and liturgy.

10 Piccolomini 1965, title page.

acknowledge Piccolomini's authorship. So despite the growing polarisation of secular and worldly matters in early modern society, no clear differentiation of the historical terms *ritus* and *caeremonia* was undertaken until the sixteenth century[11]. Around 1517, Paride de Grassi (ca. 1460–1528), Piccolomini's successor as Master of Ceremonies, answered the rhetorical question of the meaning of 'ceremony' – *quid sit caeremonia* – as follows: "Ceremony is the art of implementing appropriately the cult of the sacred, and it is performed either by man for God or because of God for man"[12].

Whereas for Piccolomini liturgical *ritus* and *caeremonia,* irrespective of whether sacred or courtly, meant one and the same thing, de Grassi, some thirty years later, considered the generic term *caeremonia* to have a purely religious significance. Therefore, he based his – never published – *Book of Ceremonies* on the paradigmatic papal liturgy in the Sistine Chapel. Though artificial, distinguishing the *rites* of the *liturgy* from the *rituals* of the *court ceremonial* has the decided advantage of allowing papal representation to be divided into its separate components of the *religious-liturgical* and the *secular-ceremonial.* Only in this way does it become possible to speak, for instance, of political iconography in sacred space. As the anthropologist Ronald L. Grimes so succinctly put it: "*A* liturgy or *the* liturgy is not purely liturgical"[13].

On the Origins of Rites by Means of Supernatural Selection

What meaning did the papal Masters of Ceremonies around 1500 attach to *caeremonia*? Piccolomini is the first to provide a quasi 'anthropological' definition of the term. He recognises that the regulations and the implementation of ritual in liturgy and ceremonial bestow authority and spirituality on the deity, the ruler and the elite. In order to win God's mercy, he postulates the need for pure, chaste and appropriate ceremonies. It is only fitting for both the apostolic majesty *(maiestas)* and the authority and dignity of the holy Senate that everything is carried out in proper order and with the pertinent rites. In this way, each receives the fitting degree of honour and reverence[14]. Thus the form of such rites is constituted by their appropriateness, and their content serves to create hierarchies of power.

Cristoforo Marcello also provided a religious anthropology of sorts in his dedication to Pope Leo X de' Medici (1475–1521) of Piccolomini's appropriated *Book of Ceremonies.* It is generally known, he states, that the ancient structure of the holy ceremonies originated and evolved together with religion. However, without appropriate and enhancing ceremonies religion appears barbaric, formless and without any beauty whatsoever. Recognition gives pleasure to princes and munificence pleases. But, he continues, homage is considerably more satisfying when it is accompanied by gestures of honour, eloquent speech and eulogies. The most powerful and benevolent King sits on an elevated throne, surrounded by

11 Glei et al. 1971–95: *liturgy* a late term, *ordo* and *ritus* earlier. Möseneder 1983, 70–1: definition of *ceremonial* in the Baroque. Carlen 1993, 6: at the Curia, liturgy and ceremonial were difficult to separate. Blanco 1995, 47–8: states that, from the beginning, ceremonial was profane as well as sacred.

12 De Grassi 1514–25, fol. 1r–3r: *Quid sit caerimonia, et unde dicatur*; fol. 1r: [gloss: *Caerimonia quid sit*] *Hinc et beatus Thomas, caerimoniae, inquit, opera sunt exteriora ad cultum Dei pertinentia. Igitur caerimonia est sacri cultus benegerendi scientia, quae vel Deo ab homine, vel propter Deum quandoque homini exhibetur, ex quo illud exodi ad Moisem.* Cf. Dykmans 1986, 287; Cornides 1967, 9. Cf. Firmani [16th c.], fol. 63v, cit. Fosi 1997, 89: *Cirimonia nihil aliud est quam honor debitus Deo aut hominibus propter Deum*; from Piccolomini, cit. Dykmans 1980–82, 1:31*. Cf. Kempers 2003.

13 Grimes 1995, 51: "liturgies [...] contain motifs that are ceremonious, magical, and decorous. *A* liturgy or *the* liturgy is not purely liturgical."

14 Piccolomini 1965, unpag. dedication: *Cogitavit sane circumspectissima beatitudo tua [pope Innocent VIII], & recte quidem, plurimum ad divinam clementiam nobis propitiandam pertinere, si puris, castis, congruisque caeremoniis illa colatur, nec minus spectare ad majestatem apostolicam, sacrique senatus auctoritatem venerationemque praeservandam atque augendam, si suo ordine, rituque decenti omnia peragantur; si rerum, temporum, personarum ratio habeatur; si cuique reddantur debitus honor, & propria reverentia, quae quidem omnia hac una disciplina continentur, suggerentur, administranturque.* Cf. Dykmans 1980–82, 1: 27*.

Abb. 2. *Papal Mass and Pizza,* Holy Year, photograph, Rome, Swiss Institute. Photograph: author.

divine spirits, who approach him successively according to their status. This pious *Book of Ceremonies* contains the divine spirit, the chaste prayer, the image of the heavenly abode, the holiest rites and the prefiguration of secret mysteries[15].

To explain the liturgical forms of homage, Marcello takes as his model the secular definition of the relationship between the ruler and his subjects[16]. It is therefore hardly surprising that, conversely, liturgy can be imbued with political values. Norms of behaviour that are politically effective and ensure social discipline – recognition of a higher power, physical force and the omniscience of the ruler as well as the maintenance of hierarchies, consensus and unity – are expressed though the rites and rituals, are thus displayed and exercised, and in the end sanctified and imbued with an aura that makes them unalterable. Catherine Bell sees the socially disciplining function of rites and rituals as being above all applicable to societies that place great importance on social unity and on restrictive verbal and symbolic communication, that show a preference for the hierarchical rather than the individual and require a strong socially binding consensus – much like male clerical groups within the Catholic Church[17].

The political function of the *caeremonia* is confirmed *ex negativo* by de Grassi's protest against Marcello's piracy and unauthorised publication of Piccolomini's *Caeremoniale.* De Grassi considers the betrayal of the ceremonial's secret protocols and rules to the laity is tantamount to a debasement and vulgarisation of the mystery of the rites, thereby not only jeopardising the effectiveness and integrity of the *caeremonia,* but also calling into question the authority and veneration of the pope himself. A

15 Piccolomini 1965, unpag. dedication by Marcello to Leo X: *Vetustissimam sacrarum cerimoniarum observationem beatissimus pater, & una cum ipsa religione ortam esse conspicuum est. Velut enim haec mortalibus semper optima, ac summopere necessaria extitit, ut pote: qua deos immortales suspicerent, admirarentur, & colerent, ita sine debito cerimoniarum ornatu inculta est, informis, ac omni pulchritudine vacua. Placet recognitio principi. Benevolentia placet. At multo magis gratum obsequium, si & gestuum veneratione, & compositione verborum, & munerum blandimentis afficiatur. Sedet in sublimi solio rex omnium optimus, circumstant divinae mentes, quae certatim se illi gratas reddunt, diversis agitationibus coeli moventur.* Cf. da Castiglionchio 1999, 129: "worship and veneration are usually pleasing, whoever carries them out. This is also most wisely established by our divine laws: that every sacrifice, even if it is made by the most corrupt of priests, provided that the ritual is done correctly *[modo rite factum],* is a sacrifice that is true, integral, absolute, intact, and inviolate and is to be deemed as accepted in the eyes of God."

16 Cf. Vec 1998, 333: on *Psalm* 82, where rulers are called *gods,* used as a justification for princely splendour in the eighteenth century. Cf. Bölling 2004, 154: according to Piccolomini the difference of rank between a cardinal bishop and cardinal deacon is to be compared with the difference between father and son.

17 Bell 1992, 178–9. Cf. Boyer 2001, 255: "Rituals do not *create* social effects but only the illusion that they do".

comparable de-mystification of the divine and a reduction in the power of religion occurs through the technical reproducibility of ritual (Abb. 2). When physical presence in a particular location is no longer essential to participation in a collective rite, then the binding force and socially disciplining power of that rite are diminished[18].

For Marcello, the ceremonial and liturgical presentation of the worldly church reflects that of the Kingdom of Heaven. He believes the aesthetic plays an integral part in transmitting the church's religious and political values and is thus politically indispensable. If the use of magnificence, pomp, splendour and beauty is adequate when worshipping God like a worldly ruler, then it is just as appropriate for venerating the pope like a divine monarch.

Ritual Bonds and Bodies

How does religion unfold in space? Being a communicative and social event, rites occupy space[19]. According to Jean Cazeneuve, rites acquire real or imagined functionality[20]. A stable, repetitive rite can thus establish itself in a spatial or architectural form and transform that space into a container, frame or stage for ritual functions[21]. One of the primary types of ritual activity to assume a spatial form is that of separation. Common to all religions – so Durkheim's commonplace – is the ability to radically divide the world into profane and sacred areas, something that is also suggested by the etymology of *sanctus* and *profanum*[22]. The result is a complementary definition of the *sacred* as that which is inaccessible to all that is worldly and the *profane* as that which is excluded from the consecrated area – as Durkheim put it: sacred things are those which interdicts protect and isolate; profane things are those to which these prohibitions apply and which have to be kept at a distance from the former[23].

It is this ritual delineation of boundaries that characterises the profane and the sacred. Crossing a holy border, that is from a profane to a sacred area or situation, and vice versa, is accompanied, so Arnold van Gennep (1873–1957), by specific *rites de passage* – an example is the opening of the *porta sancta* at the beginning of a Holy Year[24]. Institutionalised rites of passage can assume material form and thus become *passages matériels,* for example thresholds or barriers, platforms or textiles. Material rites of passage can however also involve physical changes to a person, such as the obligatory shaving and tonsure, or the papal paraliturgical donning of vestments prior to the celebration of mass[25].

18 Dykmans 1980–82, 1: 40*–1*. Cf. Catalano 1750–51, 1: XIII–XVII. Cf. Cornides 1967, 16. Cf. Muir 1997, 269–75: on desacralisation and the end of ritual.

19 Gehlen 1988–98, 389–91: on space, society, and religion. Grimes 1995, 26–7: on the space of ritual.

20 Cazeneuve 1996, 17. Bell 1997, 46–52: "magic, religion, and science", on the difference between practical activities and seemingly non-functional rituals.

21 Cf. Gehlen 1988–98, 391–6.

22 Durkheim 1968, 50: "Toutes les croyances religieuses connues, qu'elles soient simples ou complexes, présentent un même caractère commun: elle supposent une classification des choses, réelles ou idéales, que se représentent les hommes, en deux classes, en deux genres opposés, désignés généralement par deux termes distincts que traduisent assez bien les mots de *profane* et de *sacré*"; cf. 454–5: on the difference between *profane* and *sacred.* Cf. Bell 1997, 24–6: on Émile Durkheim. Cf. Widengren 1969, 20-45; Glei et al. 1971–95; Casajus and Dumas 1999.

23 Durkheim 1968, 56: "Mais ce qui est caractéristique du phénomène religieux, c'est qu'il suppose toujours une division bipartite de l'univers connu et connaissable en deux genres qui comprennent tout ce qui existe. Les choses sacrées sont celles que les interdits protègent et isolent; les choses profanes, celles auxquelles ces interdits s'appliquent et qui doivent rester à distance des premières. Les croyances religieuses sont des représentations qui expriment la nature des choses sacrées et les rapports qu'elles soutiennent soit les unes avec les autres, soit avec les choses profanes. Enfin, les rites sont des règles de conduite qui prescrivent comment l'homme doit se comporter avec les choses sacrées." Cf. Bell 1992, 101–4: "ritual oppositions and hierarchies"; criticises Durkheim's conceptual dichotomy. Cf. Bauer and Rahn 1997.

24 Van Gennep 1960, 1: "So great is the incompatibility between the profane and the sacred worlds that a man cannot pass from one to the other without going through an intermediate stage." Cf. Sindzingre 1999. Cf. Grimes 1995, 72: "The ways we cross boundaries of founded places say who we are." Bell 1997, 36–8: on Arnold van Gennep; 94–102: on rites of passage. Stinger 1998, 45: *porta sancta.* Bynum 1996, 30: on liminality in the case of breaking with norms and rules.

25 Van Gennep 1960, 18: "this symbolic and spatial area of transition may be found in more or less pronounced form in all the ceremonies which accompany the passage from one social and magico-religious position to another"; cf. 192: "it seems important to me that the passage from one social position to another is identified with a *territorial passage,* such as the entrance into a village or a house, the movement from one room to another, or the crossing of streets and squares".

The form of sacred space corresponds to the internal subdivision and hierarchy of the sacred group. The liturgy of the mass is an exchange, one that involves the humanising glorification of God on one hand and the sanctification of man on the other[26]. Religion bestows 'exclusive' sanctity – in the true sense of the word – on the clerical community by binding its members to the heavenly and divine Father while using an esoteric practice to elevate them above the lay state of the sons and daughters[27].

Recurring rites and ceremonies give a community its identity, both internally and externally, by helping it to practice and memorise social structures[28]. Rites create on the one hand an integrating collective awareness and sense of unity among the clergy, while the liturgy on the other expresses, actualises and strengthens the internal classification and hierarchy of its members according to the status of their offices[29]. Internal differentiation or exclusion is expressed for example by a member's place in a procession, the seating order in the choir or the material value of vestments.

The controlled interplay of forms of inclusion and exclusion allows for a spatial and decorative counter-image of the clerical social body as the organically functioning mystical body of Christ that is shrouded in an anthropomorphic sacred space and focused on the bodily incarnation of the Lord in the Eucharist[30]. The use of allegory and typology for the liturgy and for the physical structure of the church and its offices, as found, for example, in the twelfth-century *Mitrale* by Sicardus and in Durandus' *Rationale* of the following century, allows the social body to present itself as the worldly spatial counter-image of the hierarchically structured, harmonious and heavenly Ecclesia[31].

This projection of the ideal image of the community occurs as part of the liturgical ceremony that veils reality and suggests a degree of certainty or social commitment that tends to be independent of its worldly surroundings[32]. Rites serve to shape an image of the world by simplifying, framing, systemati-

Möseneder 1983, 67–9: on the representation of state order and of social differences by the means of courtly dress codes. Schütze 1997: on the ritual meaning of architectural borders. The donning of the vestments, the so-called *praeparatio ad missam pontificalem* is treated more extensively in my forthcoming *Raphael's Parrot Room*.

26 Cf. 3 *Moses* 20.7–8: *sanctificamini et estote sancti quia ego dominus deus vester | custodite praecepta mea et facite ea ego dominus qui sanctifico vos*. Martimort 1963, 1: 201: "Die Doppelbewegung der Liturgie: Verherrlichung Gottes und Heiligung des Menschen."

27 Durkheim 1968, 65: "Une religion est un système solidaire de croyances et de pratiques relatives à des choses sacrées, c'est-à-dire séparées, interdites, croyances et pratiques qui unissent en une même communauté morale, apelée Église, tous ceux qui y adhèrent". Bell 1997, 136: "It appears that ritual is used in those situations in which certain values and ideas are more powerfully binding on people if they are deemed to derive from sources of power outside the immediate community."

28 Cf. Burkert 1972, 33–4. Cf. Gebauer and Wulf 1998, 97: "Über die Mimesis institutioneller Gesten werden die Machtansprüche von Institutionen wahrgenommen und aufrechterhalten."

29 Muir 1997, 4: on ritual as social binding and solidarity beyond consensus. Kertzer 1988, 10: on actualisation and identification.

30 Durandus 1995–2000, 1: 17: on the comparison between church buildings and the human body. Cf. e.g. Pastor 1891–1933, 3.2: 849–50: at the first meeting of the Lateran Council on 10 May 1512, the Church is being called an organic machine, which schismatics are to be excluded from. Ullmann 1960, 3–6: on the uniform body of the Church. Bagliani 1994, 87–9: on cardinals as part of the papal body; 93–4: on the pope as the head of the Church's body. Muir 1997, 232: reference to the *Epistle to the Romans* 12,4–5, *sicut enim in uno corpore multa membra habemus omnia autem membra non eundem actum habent; ita multi unum corpus sumus in Christo singuli autem alter alterius membra*. Kerscher 2000, 319: in the *Leges palatinae,* the human body and its organs are used as an example for the hierarchy of offices. Frings 1998, 347–9: on anthropomorphism as a model for the Church and the state and for their buildings. Koschorke 2002, 78: "In der Tradition des abendländischen Staatsdenkens hat besonders das Bild des sozialen Körpers diese Funktion der imaginären Ganzheitsstiftung mitsamt der dazu komplementären Ausgrenzungen versehen".

31 Cf. e.g. Pastor 1891–1933, 3.2: 850: at the Lateran Council 1512, Rome and the Church is mentioned as the body and image of the heavenly Church. Möseneder 1983, 72: "So wie die Staatsordnung und die kosmische Ordnung, so ahmt das Zeremoniell die staatliche Ordnung nach und verweist wieder auf die vorbildhafte Ordnung zurück. Zeremoniell ist also darstellende Aktualisierung des staatlichen Gemeinschaftslebens in vollem Umfang." D'Amico 1983, 219: the papal confessor Pietro Colonna Galatino, in his manuscript *Libellus de re publica christiana pro vera eiusdem rei publicae reformatione* of about 1521 dedicated to Leo X und Hadrian VI: "it organizes reform around the concept of the Church as the mystical body of Christ"; every member and garment is part of Christian society; weakness causes discord amongst Christians and strengthens the infidel. Spiess 1997: on seating order as an image of social order. Vec 1998, 157–62: on the unity of cosmic and political order in the eighteenth century. Stinger 1998, 46: in the sermons of the Sistine Chapel, the Curia is said to be an image of the heavenly hierarchy. Cf. Schimmelpfennig 1992.

32 Bell 1997, 24: on ritual as a sacralising self-projection of society; 66: on rituals and religious symbols as idealising images which, in the ritual, fuse with reality.

sing and stylising complex and changeable reality, by reducing it to a miniaturised model of the world and society – an ideal model which can be applied to as many different situations as possible, as Catherine Bell has shown in relation to non-European rituals[33].

Papal Majesty Embodied

An engraving by Étienne Dupérac (ca. 1525–1604) is an excellent document for the liturgical uses of architecture and decoration to spatially distinguish social groups (Taf. 38). Published in 1578 as part of Antoine Lafréy's (1512–77) *Speculum romanae magnificentiae,* this famous sheet depicts a papal mass in the Sistine Chapel during the pontificate of Gregory XIII Boncompagni (1502–85). Generally such masses were celebrated once a week, and the participants depicted have been studied in depth by the historian of liturgy Niels Krogh Rasmussen[34].

According to the inscription, the engraving provides an "exact depiction of the papal majesty (*maiestas pontificia*) during the celebration of the divine mass in the Sistine Chapel"[35]. The print is to be understood as part of the efforts of Gregory XIII to restructure the rites and ceremonies of the *capella papalis* and to return to the old tradition and, most importantly, to abolish the *abusi,* the abuses of the order of precedence by secular dignitaries[36]. The print is symptomatic of papal propaganda on the one hand and on the other of the pan-European fascination – be it early anthropological or 'tourist' curiosity – with liturgical and ceremonial matters.

The inclusion of an enumerated legend makes it possible to identify the individual officials and participants. The beholder of the print has the additional privilege of being able to 'participate' in the theatrically choreographed celebration of the Eucharist from an elevated position, whereas the laity actually attending such services in the chapel, as if seated in a *cavea,* had to be content with the impaired view through the metal grille of the choir screen[37].

These visitors – exclusively male and drawn from the bourgeoisie and the lower clergy – are prevented from entering the sacred area of the choir by two rows of Swiss Guards (nr. 55), who receive instructions from the Master of Ceremonies (nr. 46)[38]. Then – as indeed now – it was the responsibility of the Guards to silence the reverberating chatter of lay visitors while on the other side of the screen, the *mazzieri* (nr. 54), ensured those in the choir space maintained the necessary degree of silence, respect and contemplation[39].

33 Sullivan 1986: on the performative character of rituals. Bell 1997, 161: "the ritual-like nature of performative activities appears to lie in the multifaceted sensory experience, in the framing that creates a sense of condensed totality, and in the ability to shape people's experience and cognitive ordering of the world. In brief, performances seem ritual-like because they explicitly model the world. They do not attempt to reflect the real world accurately but to reduce and simplify it so as to create more or less coherent systems of categories that can be projected onto the full spectrum of human experience." Muir 1997, 5: "Many rituals work like models. They present a standard or a simplified miniature for society to follow." Houseman 2001, 49: "Rituale erzählen weniger Geschichten, sondern stellen bestimmte *Wahrheiten* dar"; the linguistic model is not adequate for ritual rules.

34 Rasmussen 1983. Cf. Adalbert Roth in Kruse 1999, 496–7, nr. 186; Visceglia 1997, 130–3. De Grassi 1514–25, fol. 15v; Dykmans 1985, 400: about fifty high papal masses per year. Cf. Roth 1999, 163: about forty *capellae papales* per year.

35 *Maiestatis pontificiae dum in capella Xysti sacra peraguntur accurata delineatio.*

36 Visceglia 1997, 130: "per ridurre le cerimonie all'uso antico et levar gli abusi trascorsi nella venuta de principi, come de loro ambasciatori et di molt'altre cose"; 131: "sino da principio del suo pontificato [he had] volto l'animo a riordinare i riti e le cerimonie della cappella pontificia la quale n'havea molto bisogno"; 132: on the congregation of rites. Bölling 2003, 60–1: 22 January 1588, founding of the *Sacra congregatio caeremonialis.*

37 Cf. Bell 1997, 160: "By virtue of [...] framing, performance is understood to be something other than routine reality; it is a specific type of demonstration."

38 Rasmussen 1983, 142: visitors comprise lower clergy, servants of the cardinals, laymen, but no women; in 1573, the master of ceremonies Francesco Mucanzio excludes, with the help of the Swiss Guard, unauthorised laymen from the choir and the *loco retro sedilio cardinalium.*

39 De Grassi 1514–25, fol. 146r–7v: *De universali silentio, ac veneratione et contemplatione omnium mysteriorum in capella papali.* Cf. Dykmans 1986, 293–4; Minnich 1993, 394: on silence in the chapel. Dykmans 1982, 442; Quednau 1984, 87: on the *mazzieri.*

The *Book of Ceremonies* devotes an entire chapter to the complex rules of admittance to and exclusion from the papal chapel[40]. Excluded from the *corpus* of the chapel were physical or mental outcasts, criminals, syphilitics, jugglers and mimics who would, presumably, have threatened the sacred fiction, pets such as lapdogs and parrots, as well as transvestites and women in men's clothing, i.e. prostitutes, and, not least, women, with the exception of the Empress on the occasion of her coronation provided she was not menstruating[41]. The place of each member of the Curia assembled on the other side of the marble *cancellata* was determined by his duties and privileges, all of which were minutely described in the *Book of Ceremonies*[42].

SCREENING POWER

According to Durkheim, the secular and sacred are clearly and unmistakably separated by classifying signs[43]. However, being interdependent, this separation involves controlled communication between the two, and this in turn makes the elevation of the sacred above the secular and by the secular possible[44]. An example of such a classifying division is the rood screen of the Sistine Chapel: by controlling communication between the sacred and secular, the screen articulates the social differences and inter-dependence of the two areas[45].

The ceremonial master and humanist Paris de Grassi traced the origins and meaning of the rituals back to ancient times, when the *cancelli* separated the senate from the common people[46]. By preventing the laity from entering the choir and allowing only a partial view of the forbidden space, the Sistine choir screen conveys the privileged status of the clergy[47].

Such a socially distinguishing visual exchange was possible because the upper part of the rood screen has metal grilles. The view into the Holy of Holies and of the incarnation of Christ is the Christian innovation that replaced the impenetrable curtain of the Tabernacle of Moses and of the Temple of Solomon in Jerusalem, from which Sicardus derived the origin of choir screens, and which according to St Matthew's Gospel was torn in two forever by Christ's sacrifice on the cross[48]. The openings in the choir screen also permitted the laity to hear the word of God being spoken and to visually partake in

40 De Grassi 1514–25, fol. 51r–3r: *De his qui admitti consueverunt intra capellam papalem, et de excludendis ab eadem*; on admission into and exclusion from the Sistine Chapel. Cf. Dykmans 1986, 292.

41 De Grassi 1514–25, fol. 52r–v: *cavendum quoque permaximé ne animalium, et mansuetorum et nobilium genus aliquod intromittatur, ut sunt catellae, et damulae, et qua pro delitijs habentur, nec minus avium, ut sunt accipitres, psitacive*, which distract the spirit from contemplation; at the imperial coronation of Nicolas V in 1542, *ad id coronationis munus in crastinum peragendum es superventu repentino menstrui dilatus est catus in diem ab inde sextum, et dicta ipsa Leonora demum coronata fuit; sed nec vir muliebri modo ornatus, neque e contra mulier virili habitu transformata, | ut plenique meretrices solent, vel quia impudentes*; fol. 23r–v: on the *corpus* of the chapel. Randolph 1997, 18: "Orthodoxy denied menstruating women entry to the church."

42 Piccolomini 1965, fol. 122v–4v: *De ordine sedendi in capella papae*. Cf. Dykmans 1986, 296–7. De Grassi 1514–25, fol. 53v–65r: on the seating order in the *capella papalis*. Cf. Dykmans 1977–85, 3:311–2: on the seating order in Avignon.

43 Durkheim 1968, 55: "L'opposition de ces deux genres vient, d'ailleurs, se traduire au dehors par un signe visible qui permet de reconnaître aisément cette classification très spéciale, partout où elle existe. Parce que la notion du sacré est, dans la pensée des hommes, toujours et partout séparée de la notion du profane, parce que nous concevons entre elles une sorte de vide logique, l'esprit épurge invinciblement à ce que les choses correspondantes soient confondues ou simplement mises en contact".

44 Durkheim 1968, 55: "La chose sacrée, c'est, par excellence, celle que le profane ne doit pas, ne peut pas impunément toucher. Sans doute, cette interdiction ne saurait aller jusqu'à rendre impossible toute communication entre les deux mondes; car, si le profane ne pouvait aucunement entrer en relations avec le sacré, celui-ci ne servirait à rien."

45 Thomas et al. 1996, 290: "Barrier for the subdivision of a church into areas of differing function and liturgical significance." Cf. Jung 2001: on social differentiation by the means of rood screens.

46 De Grassi 1514–25, fol. 14v–5r: *Cancelli, repagula, aut crates intermedij | sunt, qui senatum à populo distinguunt*. Cf. Moroni 1840–79, 8:221. Cf. Randolph 1997, 30: on the rood screen as a social boundary. Constant 1903, 329: de Grassi refers back to the antique rites of the Roman *pontifex maximus*.

47 Burkert 1972, 39: "Ritus, als Mitteilung, ist eine Art Sprache"; its complexity activates social differences. Möseneder 1983, 74: in the baroque festivities, the beholder becomes an element of the body political.

48 *St Matthew's Gospel* 27.50–1. Cf. *Epistle to the Hebrews* 6.19, 10.19. Cf. Shearman 1972, 71. Thomas et al. 1996, 290: "The division of churches into several zones by screens (as well as steps and different paving) is associated with the increasing tendency in the Middle Ages to understand churches in terms of the Temple of Jerusalem, with its separate

the celebration of mass. Although the Catholic Church recommended the removal of rood screens in the later Cinquecento, the screen in the Sistine Chapel remained in place; clearly, it was permeable enough, and perhaps without the screen the security of the pope could not be ensured in a chapel that consisted of only a single nave.

TYPOLOGICAL TOPOGRAPHY

Although it is here impossible to deal with the complex decoration of the Sistine Chapel, to which extensive study has been devoted, one example deserves mention, especially as it demonstrates the relevance of such embellishments for the ritual of the liturgy: the ten magnificent tapestries after designs by Raphael (Taf. 39). Traditionally known as *The Acts of the Apostles,* nine of the ten were used solely for the adornment of the choir space, thus providing yet another indication of the privileged status of the clergy. The choice of *ten* pieces is moreover an iconographical reference to the Tabernacle of Moses, which God ordained be made of ten curtains[49]. Such an obvious visual association between the Tabernacle – as the prefiguration of the Temple of Salomon and accordingly of every Christian Church – and the Sistine Chapel provided, at the dawn of Reformation, some theological and rhetorical justification for the horrendous cost of the tapestries[50].

But the tapestries' iconography also relates to the liturgical function of the space: John Shearman (1931–2003) has shown how the content and composition of *St Paul Preaching at Athens* (Abb. 3), the only tapestry to hang in the area reserved for the laity, reflects the functional context of the ritual and space[51]. Following the example of the Greek philosophers assembled on the Areopagus to hear the apostle's sermon, the humanistically educated laity should attend the words spoken from the chancel in the Sistine Chapel and embrace Christianity with the fervour of the Neo-Platonist Dionysius the Areopagite, seen in the lower left of the tapestry ascending *ex abysso* to become Paul's disciple. The Renaissance credited him with the authorship of two highly valued and complementary texts: *The Heavenly Hierarchy* and *The Ecclesiastical Hierarchy.* The latter is identified as a material counter-image, analogy or symbol of the harmonious and heavenly order[52]. As a counter-image of divine beauty, the heavenly and ecclesiastical hierarchies strive to become closer to God himself. The figure of Dionysius in the tapestry is therefore an explicit reference to the assembly in the choir of the *capella papalis* as the earthly mirror of the harmonious heavenly order. As in the external ceremonies, which Dionysius called "the beautiful wall paintings in the entrance to the shrine", the tapestry in the lay space serves to convey a sensuous experience of the divine[53].

ORGANISING THE BODY RELIGIOUS

Although the architecture and decoration of the Sistine Chapel create a social division between the clerics and the laity, a few of the more privileged lay visitors did nevertheless gain admittance to the choir, as can be seen in Dupérac's engraving (Taf. 38) where some nobles and church ambassadors take their

courts and areas and their ascending holiness. The sanctuary thus became the equivalent of the Holy of Holies. The separation and ritual protection of these zones were affected by the various screens (as well as by *ciboria* and hangings)." Hall 1978, 1974: on rood screens in Italy.

49 *Exodus* 26.1.

50 This aspect will be studied in depth elsewhere.

51 Shearman 1972, 73; Stinger 1998, 314: on the harmony between antique philosophy and Christian theology.

52 Areopagita 1911, 3–4: "Deshalb hat auch die heilige Satzung [...] *unsere* heiligste | (kirchliche) Hierarchie in *der* Form gewährt, dass sie dieselbe einer überweltlichen Nachahmung der himmlischen Hierarchie würdigte und diese eben erwähnten immateriellen Hierarchien in materiellen Gestalten und zusammengesetzten Gebilden auf mannigfach verschiedene Weise darstellte. [...] die Rangstufen der irdischen (kirchlichen) Ordnungen als einen Abglanz des harmonischen und wohlgeordneten Verhältnisses zum Göttlichen"; cf. 19–20; 93–5: on the analogy between the ecclesiastical and heavenly hierarchy.

53 Areopagita 1911, 122–3: "Dieses Äussere (der Zeremonien) also [...], die schönen Wandbilder in der Vorhalle des Heiligtums, wollen wir den noch Unvollendeten zu einer | für sie ausreichenden Betrachtung überlassen."

Abb. 3. Workshop of Pieter van Aelst after Raffaello Santi, *Paul Preaching at Athens,* ca. 1518, tapestry, 490 x 520 cm, Vatican City, Vatican Museums. After: Fermor 1996, 39 fig. 15.

places within the *quadratura* and opposite the pope[54]. The Senator (nr. 30), the Conservators (nr. 31) and the Roman aristocracy (nr. 32) are seated, in descending order, on the steps of the pontifical *solium* and of the *presbyterium,* thereby expressing their special relationship with the pope and, simultaneously, their obsequiousness. The pope for his part could honour nobles and relatives by assigning them a more important location[55].

The choreography of space during the liturgy is based on the physical coordinates of the protagonists: *above* and *below, left* and *right*[56]. At the very beginning of his *Caeremoniarum opusculum,* de Grassi takes the measurements of the chapel, as if it were a stage, so as to ensure that the seating order follows the rules of *symmetria*[57]. Resistance to the rules governing seating and dress was seen by the Master of Ceremonies, and indeed by the cardinals and participants themselves, as a conscious disregard for

54 Rasmussen 1983, 141, nr. 10: "Duces".

55 Rasmussen 1983, 140–1, nr. 30 and 31: "senator romanus" and "conservatores Urbis". Bölling 2004, 183: on the higher status of the right side of the papal throne.

56 Cf. Schütte 1995, 422: "Liturgie und Zeremoniell zeigen eine Segmentierung der rituellen, zeitlich definierten Handlung nach Stellung der Beteiligten an bestimmten Orten. Der Ablauf ist räumlich horizontal und vertikal strukturiert";"die unmittelbare rituelle Praxis nimmt dabei räumlich-körperliche Muster auf." Suntrup 1978, 198–224: on top, bottom, right, and left in the mass. Elze 1991; Paravicini 1997a, 24–5: on left and right.

57 De Grassi 1514–25, fol. 23r–v: *De simetria totius capellae papalis*; especially in the seating order; on the measuring of the Sistine Chapel. Cf. Dykmans 1986, 289: de Grassi organises mass of the *capella papalis* in Bologna and Ravenna.

decorum and social order and something which could disrupt the ceremony[58]. The liturgical social order in the choir is structured not only accordingly to horizontal and vertical symmetry, but has in addition two centres: foremost the altar (nr. 1), with the papal throne (nr. 2) as the second, subordinate centre[59]. *Vertically,* steps elevate the choir above the lay space as well as the presbytery from the *quadratura* and the altar from the throne[60]. *Horizontally,* the privileged proximity to the pope is expressed in the concentric rows of seats and in the floor patterns of the *quadratura,* which however are not illustrated in the print. Just like a playing field, the Cosmatesque design of the pavement aids each player in finding his particular starting position and indicates the rules of the game.

The clerics sit on benches, their exact position determined according to a system based on official rank and social status, whereby the most privileged sit to the right of the pope. De Grassi described this system of reverence as a type of cosmology of respect towards God and the different social classes of men, from *latria* to *incurvatio*[61]. The hierarchy should appear harmonious not only through the seating and clothing of the various groups, but also through the singing of the papal choirs, just like Dionysius in his *Ecclesiastical Hierarchy* interpreted the chanting of the psalms as a means of achieving universal unity[62].

The social structure of the Curia is reflected in the character of the liturgy. That the physical disposition of those in the choir was intended to give an accurate image of the curial hierarchy is evident from the fact that the pope could bestow additional honour on a person or an official body by making changes in the seating arrangements or by granting permission to enter the choir area[63]. The anthropologist David I. Kertzer has shown how small changes and adjustments to rites, which by their very nature are conservative, possess a strong political message[64].

CHOREOGRAPHIES OF POWER

Rites transmit traditional images of the world, but can also serve to establish new traditions[65]. Hierarchy only becomes reality when anchored by the rituals of the ceremonial. Liturgy can be compared with the practiced etiquette that Norbert Elias described as a self-presentation of courtly society in as far as part of the ceremonial rite is the public examination and confirmation of the dignity and prestige of each and every member of court society[66].

58 See e.g. O'Reilly 1972, 85–6: 25 November 1512, cardinal Matthäus Lang refuses to don the cardinal's gown which is understood as an act of arrogance.

59 Dykmans 1986, 293: according to de Grassi, the altar should be standing higher than the papal throne; therefore, Leo X eliminated three steps from the throne.

60 Staubach 2004a: on the levelling under Leo X. See supra n. 59.

61 De Grassi 1514–25, fol. 144r–6r: *Quid sit latria, quid dulia, quid cultus, quid reverentia, quid obedientia, quid genuflexio humiliatio, et inclinatio, ac incurvatio, et à quibus huiusmodi fiunt, ac qualiter, et ante quos fieri respective debeant.* Dykmans 1986, 292: "Toutes les nuances du respect dû à Dieu et à ses créatures seront parcourues." Dykmans 1982, 458: "Les règles d'étiquette sont de plus en plus fines."

62 Sherr 1982: on music in the *capella papalis.* Cf. infra n. 68. Areopagita 1911, 127: "durch den Einklang der göttlichen Lieder die Eintracht der Herzen mit dem Göttlichen, mit uns selbst und mit unsern Nebenmenschen gleichwie in *einem* übereinstimmenden Reigenchor geregelt." Sherr 1994: on polyphony in the papal chapel as a tribute to the Church and the pope.

63 Rasmussen 1983, 136: Gregory XIII grants a new and higher position to a French archbishop within the seating order of the Sistine Chapel; 137: in 1568, the Dominican Pius V grants the Dominicans precedence over other Orders; 138: in 1574, Gregory XIII grants the *abbreviatores de parco maiori* a place within the choir of the Sistine Chapel.

64 Kertzer 1988, 12: "It is because people create and alter rituals that they are such powerful tools of political action"; cf. 12 and 42: "Paradoxically, it is the very conservatism of ritual forms that can make ritual a potent force in political change."

65 Moore and Myerhoff 1977, 7–8.

66 Elias 1983, 101: "The practice of etiquette is, in other words, an exhibition of court society itself. Each participant, above all the king, has his prestige and his relative power position confirmed by others. Social opinion, which constitutes the prestige of the individual, is expressed by reciprocal behaviour within a communal action according to certain rules. And in this communal action each individual's existential bond to society is directly visible. Without confirmation of one's prestige through behaviour, this prestige is nothing. The immense value attached to the demonstration of prestige and

Abb. 4. *The Fifth Lateran Council*, woodcut, from: Antonio del Monte, ed. 1521. *Sanctum lateranensum concilium*. Rome: Giacomo Mazzocchi. After: Kruse 1999, 116 fig. 94.

The corporate body of the pontifical court celebrates its structure in the Sistine Chapel and by doing so presents itself as the concentrically arranged Curia before the eyes of the clergy and the laity, in much the same way as the citizens of Rome perceived themselves in the ancient circus. Rites present and actualise existing social structures[67]. Dupérac's engraving (Taf. 38) depicts the social hierarchy of the Curia and the church much like a pyramid, as shown, for example, in a depiction of the Lateran Council of 1521 (Abb. 4) where the pope, crowned by the Holy Ghost, thrones above the hierarchy. The bird's-eye view of Dupérac's print bears no relation of course to the actual perspective of the participants; the image was intended to convey a propagandistic ideal that enthrones the pope in the vanishing point, and which locates the imagined viewpoint at the base of the (social) pyramid. The rationalised distance of the quasi-photographic view of a systematically arranged scene points to an attempt to give a 'scientific' explanation of liturgy and ceremonial. But, although the imagined viewer is placed at the end of the social hierarchy, he is granted a superior viewpoint. Much like Marcello's controversial publication of the *Book of Ceremonies,* Dupérac's ambivalent codification may thus be seen as a secularisation or even profanation of sacred rites that were intended to be experienced in their full majesty.

the observance of etiquette does not betray an attachment to externals, but to what was vitally important to individual identity." Cf. Möseneder 1983, 66: on ceremonial as an image of the absolutist order of the state and of the relationships of power and law. Gaston 1987, 114: on the social history of mass liturgy as a *desideratum* in research.

67 See supra n. 31: on actualisation. Muir 1997, 7: rites make conditions present and actual. Cf. Houseman 2001, 51: "Mithilfe von vorgeschriebenen Verhaltensmustern, die gleichzeitig höchst evokative (vielschichtige) und grundsätzlich vieldeutige Beziehungen abbilden (was die Kondensierung von Gegensätzen zur Folge hat), gewährleisten rituelle Handlungen den Teilnehmern unmittelbare Erfahrungen von neuen, höchst integrativen, ausserordentlichen Wirklichkeiten, unterstützt von Selbstbezogenheit und unter Einführung von bestimmten Handelnden sowie spezifischen Redewendungen (Symbolik); dadurch vermitteln sie unerschütterliche Zusammenhänge für die konventionelle Neubewertung der aufeinander abgestimmten Beziehungen, aus denen die soziale Welt der Teilnehmenden besteht. Amen."

The sacredness, invariance and venerability of liturgy and the decoration of the chapel became aureate attributes of the papacy as a social form. When the sublimation of power advances from its original physical violence to a more effective symbolic *pars pro toto* – were it a prohibitive sign or the Eucharist – a decisive role is played by the aesthetic and artistic, be it clothing, choreography, wall painting etc. Power thus also becomes an aesthetical construct that is created and transmitted. Despite the aesthetic sublimation of pure violence, rites remain structured by bodily coordinates. Rituals require no architecture, for every ritual meeting, for example a papal procession, creates its own physical, hierarchical and spatial structure by the means of the mere choreography of bodies. However, in the context of the papal liturgy, texts, above all the codified standardisation of the transmitted rites and practices in the *Book of Ceremonies,* also play a role in defining the spatial stage, and accordingly the macro-structure of the architecture.

As the inscription in Dupérac's *Papal Mass* suggests, the *maiestas pontificia*, namely the size, dignity and majesty of the papacy, depends to a large extent on the ordered and splendid depiction of the court as a hierarchically structured and musically harmonised *capella papalis*[68]. The papal mass as a multimedia event or ritual *Gesamtkunstwerk* was the focal point of the Roman *theatrum mundi*[69].

BIBLIOGRAPHY

Adamson, J. 1999a. "Introduction: The Making of the Ancien-Régime Court 1500–1700." In Adamson 1999b, 7–42.

—, ed. 1999b. *The Princely Courts of Europe: Ritual, Politics and Culture under the Ancien Régime 1500–1750.* London: Weidenfeld & Nicolson.

Areopagita, P.-D. 1911. *Des heiligen Dionysius Areopagita angebliche Schriften über die beiden Hierarchien.* Bibliothek der Kirchenväter 1. Edited by J. Stiglmayr. Kempten: Kösel.

Asch, R.G. 1991. "Introduction." In *Princes, Patronage, and the Nobility: The Court at the Beginning of the Modern Age c. 1450–1650*, edited by R.G. Asch and A.M. Birke, 1–38. Studies of the German Historical Institute London. Oxford: Oxford University Press.

Aulinger, B. 1992. *Kunstgeschichte und Soziologie: Eine Einführung.* Berlin: Dietrich Reimer.

Bagliani, A.P. 1994. *Il corpo del papa.* Biblioteca di cultura storica 204. Turin: Einaudi.

Bauer, M., and T. Rahn, eds. 1997. *Die Grenze: Begriff und Inszenierung.* Berlin: Akademie.

Bell, C. 1992. *Ritual Theory, Ritual Practice.* Oxford: Oxford University Press.

—. 1997. *Ritual: Perspectives and Dimensions.* Oxford: Oxford University Press.

Berns, J.J. 1995. "Luthers Papstkritik als Zeremoniellkritik: Zur Bedeutung des päpstlichen Zeremoniells für das fürstliche Hofzeremoniell der Frühen Neuzeit." In Berns and Rahn 1995b, 157–73.

Berns, J.J., and T. Rahn. 1995a. "Zeremoniell und Ästhetik." In Berns and Rahn 1995b, 650–65.

—, eds. 1995b. *Zeremoniell als höfische Ästhetik in Spätmittelalter und Früher Neuzeit.* Frühe Neuzeit: Studien und Dokumente zur deutschen Literatur und Kultur im europäischen Kontext 25. Tübingen: Niemeyer.

Bertelli, S., F. Cardini, and E.G. Zorzi, eds. 1986. *Italian Courts of the Renaissance.* London: Facts on File. Original edition, *Le corti italiane del Rinascimento*. Milano: Mondadori, 1985.

Blanco, M. 1995. "Cérémonie." In *Dictionnaire raisonné de la politesse et du savoir-vivre du Moyen Âge à nos jours*, edited by A. Montandon, 47–72. Paris: Seuil.

68 Da Castiglionchio 1999, 131. O'Malley 1979, 10–1: in the papal chapel, *auctoritas*, *dignitas*, *honor* are important; the earthly liturgy and hierarchy corresponds to the heavenly; strict topographical hierarchy. Cf. Muir 1997, 230: "Political ritual or ritualized politics tends to camouflage tensions, especially by representing more political *harmony* than may actually exist". Cf. Quednau 1984, 94: singers' choir in the Stanza dell'Incendio as a symbol of political harmony.

69 Da Castiglionchio 1999, 161: "But this is the greatest and most esteemed of theaters *[theatrum],* and many peoples have come here to watch. Nothing admirable can be done here that does not draw everyone's notice and is not illuminated by everyone's praises." Da Castiglionchio 1999, 173: "Well then, anyone who is especially moved by the visual must feel a marvelous pleasure, owing to these things, which are so many, so great, so varied, and so diverse." Cf. Seidler 1995, 14–5: *corte di Roma/pontificia* not equal to *sede apostolica.*

Bölling, J. 2003. "Vide apostillam: Eine unbeachtete Quelle zur Geschichte des frühneuzeitlichen Papstzeremoniells." *Miscellanea Bibliothecae Apostolicae Vaticanae* 10: 51–73.

—. 2004. "Causa differentiae: Rang- und Präzedenzregelungen für Fürsten, Herzöge und Gesandte im vortridentinischen Papstzeremoniell." In Staubach 2004b, 147–96.

Boyer, P. 2001. *Religion Explained: The Evolutionary Origins of Religious Thought.* New York: Basic Books.

Burke, P. 1987. *The Historical Anthropology of Early Modern Italy: Essays on Perception and Communication.* Cambridge: Cambridge University Press.

Burkert, W. 1972. *Homo necans: Interpretation altgriechischer Opferriten und Mythen.* Religionsgeschichtliche Versuche und Vorarbeiten 32. Berlin: Walter de Gruyter.

Bynum, C.W. 1996. *Fragmentierung und Erlösung: Geschlecht und Körper im Glauben des Mittelalters.* Edition Suhrkamp 731. Frankfurt: Suhrkamp.

Carlen, L. 1993. *Zeremoniell und Symbolik der Päpste im 15. Jahrhundert: (Vortrag vom 22. Mai 1991).* Freiburger Veröffentlichungen aus dem Gebiete von Kirche und Staat 39. Fribourg: Universitätsverlag.

Casajus, D., and A. Dumas. 1999. "Sacré." In Le Manh 1999.

Catalano, G. 1750–51. *Sacrarum caeremoniarum sive rituum ecclesiasticorum sanctae romanae ecclesiae libri tres ab Augustino Patricio ordinati, et a Marcello Corcyrensi archiepiscopo primum editi. Nunc vero tandem in duos tomos distributi, ac innumeris pene mendis purgati, et commentariis aucti ad sanctissimum patrem Benedictum XIV. pontificem maximum.* 2 vols. Rome: De Rossi.

Cazeneuve, J. 1996. *La sociologia del rito.* Milano: Saggiatore. Original edition, *Sociologie du rite.* Paris: Presses universitaires de France, 1971.

Chatenet, M. 2002. "Etiquette and Architecture at the Court of the Last Valois." In *Court Festivals of the European Renaissance: Art, Politics and Performance*, edited by J.R. Mulryne and E. Goldring, 76–100. Aldershot: Ashgate.

Constant, G.L.M.J. 1903. " Les maîtres de cérémonie du XVIe siècle: Leurs diaires." *Mélanges d'archéologie et d'histoire de l'École française de Rome* 23: 161–229, 319–43.

Cornides, E. 1967. *Rose und Schwert im päpstlichen Zeremoniell: Von den Anfängen bis zum Pontifikat Gregors XIII.* Wiener Dissertationen aus dem Gebiet der Geschichte 9. Wien: Geyer.

da Castiglionchio, L. 1999. "Lapi Castelliunculi 'De Curiae Commodis' Diologus / Lapo da Castiglionchio's Dialogue 'On the Benefits of the Curia'." In *Renaissance Humanism and the Papal Curia: Lapo da Castiglionchio the Younger's De curiae commodis*, edited by C.S. Celenza, 102–227. Papers and Monographs of the American Academy in Rome 31. Ann Arbor: University of Michigan Press.

d'Amico, J.F. 1983. *Renaissance Humanism in Papal Rome: Humanists and Churchmen on the Eve of the Reformation.* Johns Hopkins University Studies in Historical and Political Science 101. Baltimore: Johns Hopkins University Press.

Daniel, U. 2001. *Kompendium Kulturgeschichte: Theorie, Praxis, Schlüsselwörter.* Suhrkamp-Taschenbuch Wissenschaft 1523. Frankfurt am Main: Suhrkamp.

de Grassi, P. 1514–25. "Caeremoniarum opusculum." Manuscript in the Biblioteca Apostolica Vaticana, Vaticano latino 5634/1.

Durandus, G. 1995–2000. *Rationale divinorum officiorum*, edited by A. Davril and T.M. 3 vols. Thibodeau Corpus christianorum, continuatio mediaevalis 140–B. Turnhout: Brepols.

Durkheim, É., 1968. *Les formes élémentaires de la vie religieuse : Le système totémique en Australie.* Bibliothèque de philosophie contemporaine. 5th ed. Paris: Presses universitaires de France.

Dykmans, M. 1977–85. *Le cérémonial papal de la fin du Moyen Âge à la Renaissance.* 4 vols. Bibliothèque de l'Institut historique belge de Rome 24–7. Rome: Institut Historique Belge de Rome.

—. 1980–82. *L'oeuvre de Patrizi Piccolomini ou le cérémonial papal de la première Renaissance.* 2 vols. Studi e Testi 293–4. Vatican City: Biblioteca Apostolica Vaticana.

—. 1982. "Paris de Grassi." *Ephemerides liturgicae: Commentarium bimestre de re liturgica* 96: 407–82.

—. 1985. "Paris de Grassi." *Ephemerides liturgicae: Commentarium bimestre de re liturgica* 99: 383–417.

—. 1986. "Paris de Grassi." *Ephemerides liturgicae: Commentarium bimestre de re liturgica* 100: 270–333.

Elias, N. 1983. *The Court Society.* Translated by Edmund Jephcott. Oxford: Basil Blackwell. Orginal edition, *Die höfische Gesellschaft: Untersuchungen zur Soziologie des Königtums und der höfischen Aristokratie.* Darmstadt: Luchterhand, 1969.

Elze, R. 1991. "Rechts und links: Bemerkungen zu einem banalen Problem." In *Das Andere Wahrnehmen: Beiträge zur europäischen Geschichte: August Nitschke gewidmet*, 75–82. Köln: Böhlau.

Fermor, S. 1996. *The Raphael Tapestry Cartoons: Narrative, Decoration, Design*. London: Scala.

Fernández, H.D. 1999. "The Patrimony of St Peter: The Papal Court at Rome c. 1450–1700." In Adamson 1999b, 141–64.

Firmani, G.F. [16th c.]. "Collecta." Manuscript in the Biblioteca Apostolica Vaticana, Vaticano latino 12285.

Fosi, I. 1997. "'Parcere subiectis, debellare superbos': L'immagine della giustizia nelle cerimonie di possesso a Roma e nelle legazioni dello Stato Pontificio nel Cinquecento." In Visceglia and Brice 1997, 89–115.

Frings, M. 1998. *Mensch und Maß: Anthropomorphe Elemente in der Architekturtheorie des Quattrocento*. Weimar: Verlag und Datenbank für Geisteswissenschaften.

Gaston, R. 1987. "Liturgy and Patronage in San Lorenzo, Florence, 1350–1650." In *Patronage, Art, and Society in Renaissance Italy*, edited by F.W. Kent, P. Simons and J.C. Eade, 111–33. Canberra et al.: Humanities Research Centre et al.

Gebauer, G., and C. Wulf. 1998. *Spiel – Ritual – Geste: Mimetisches Handeln in der sozialen Welt*. Rowohlts Enzyklopädie 55591. Reinbek: Rowohlt.

Gehlen, R. 1988–98. "Raum." In *Handbuch religionswissenschaftlicher Grundbegriffe*, edited by H. Cancik, vol. 4, 377–98. Stuttgart: Kohlhammer.

Glei, R.F., S. Natzel, C. Sigrist, and T. Grimm. 1971–95. "Ritus." In *Historisches Wörterbuch der Philosophie*, edited by J. Ritter, vol. 8, 1052–9. Darmstadt: Wissenschaftliche Buchgesellschaft.

Grassi, L., and M. Pepe, eds. 1978. *Dizionario della critica d'arte*. 2 vols. Turin: UTET.

Grimes, R.L. 1995. *Beginnings in Ritual Studies*. 2nd ed. Columbia: University of South Carolina Press.

Hall, M.B. 1978. "The Italian Rood Screen: Some Implications for Liturgy and Function." In *Essays Presented to Myron P. Gilmore*, edited by S. Bertelli and G. Rakamus, 213–8. Florence: La Nuova Italia.

Houseman, M. 2001. "Was ist ein Ritual?" In *Altäre: Kunst zum Niederknien*, edited by J.-H. Martin, 48–51. Ostfildern-Ruit: Hatje Cantz.

Jung, J.E. 2001. "Beyond the Barrier: The Unifying Role of the Choir Screen in Gothic Churches." *The Art Bulletin: A Quarterly Published by the College Art Association* 82: 622–57.

Kempers, B. 1994. *Painting, Power and Patronage: The Rise of the Professional Artist in the Italian Renaissance Kunst*. Translated by Beverley Jackson. London: Penguin. Original edition, *Kunst, macht en mecenat: Het beroep van schilder in sociale verhoudingen 1250–1600*. Amsterdam: Arbeiderspers, 1987.

—. 2003. "Ritual and Its Images. Paris De Grassis, Raphael and the 'Signatures' in the Vatican Stanze." In Weddigen et al. 2003, 71–93.

Kerscher, G. 1995. "Das mallorquinische Zeremoniell am päpstlichen Hof: Comederunt cum papa rex maioricarum…" In Berns and Rahn 1995b, 125–49.

—. 2000. *Architektur als Repräsentation: Spätmittelalterliche Palastbaukunst zwischen Pracht und zeremoniellen Voraussetzungen: Avignon – Mallorca – Kirchenstaat*. Tübingen: Wasmuth.

Kertzer, D.I. 1988. *Ritual, Politics and Power*. New Haven: Yale University Press.

Klapisch-Zuber, C. 1985. "Rituels publics et pouvoir d'état." In *Culture et idéologie dans la génèse de l'état moderne : Actes de la table ronde organiée par le Centre national de la recherche scientifique et l'École française de Rome*, edited by J.-C.M. Vigueur and C. Pietri, 135–144. Collection de l'École française de Rome 82. Rome: École française de Rome.

Koschorke, A. 2002. "Macht und Fiktion." In *Des Kaisers neue Kleider: Über das Imaginäre politischer Herrschaft: Texte, Bilder, Lektüren*, edited by T. Frank, A. Koschorke, S. Lüdemann, and E. Matala de Mazza, 73–84. Frankfurt am Main: Fischer.

Kruse, P., ed. 1999. *Hochrenaissance im Vatikan 1503–1534*. Kunst und Kultur im Rom der Päpste 1. Ostfildern-Ruit: Hatje Cantz.

Lefèbvre, H., 1991. *The Production of Space*. Translated by Donald Nicholson-Smith. Oxford and Cambridge: Blackwell 1991. Original edition, *La production de l'espace*. Paris: Anthropos, 1974.

Le Manh, P., ed. 1999. *Encyclopaedia universalis* (CD-ROM). Vers. 5.1.2. Paris: Encyclopaedia universalis.

Martimort, A.-G., ed. 1963. *Handbuch der Liturgiewissenschaft*. 2 vols. Freiburg im Breisgau: Herder. Original edition, *L'Église en prière: Introduction à la liturgie*. Tournai: Desclee 1961.

Minnich, N.H. 1993. "Paride De Grassi's Diary of the Fifth Lateran Council." In *The Catholic Reformation: Council, Churchmen, Controversies*, 370–460. Aldershot: Variorum. Originally published in *Annuarium historiae conciliorum: Internationale Zeitschrift für Konziliengeschichtsforschung* 14 (1982) 370–460.

Moore, S.F., and B.G. Myerhoff. 1977. "Introduction: Secular Ritual: Forms and Meanings." In *Secular Ritual*, edited by S.F. Moore and B.G. Myerhoff, 3–24. Amsterdam: Gorcum.

Moroni, G. 1840–79. *Dizionario di erudizione storico-ecclesiastica*. 103 vols. Venice: Tipografia emiliana.

Möseneder, K. 1983. *Zeremoniell und monumentale Poesie: Die 'Entrée solennelle' Ludwigs XIV. 1660 in Paris*. Berlin: Gebrüder Mann.

Muir, E. 1997. *Ritual in Early Modern Europe*. Cambridge: Cambridge University Press.

O'Malley, J.W. 1979. *Praise and Blame in Renaissance Rome: Rhetoric, Doctrine and Reform in the Sacred Orators of the Papal Court, c. 1450–1521*. Durham: Duke University Press.

O'Reilly, C. 1972. "'Maximus Caesar et Pontifex Romanus': Giles of Viterbo Proclaims the Alliance between Emperor Maximilian I and Pope Julius II." *Augustiniana* 22: 80–117.

Panofsky, E. 1964. "Die Perspektive als 'symbolische Form'." In *Aufsätze zu Grundfragen der Kunstwissenschaft*, edited by H.Oberer and E.Verheyen, 99-168. Berlin: Hessling.

Paravicini, W. 1997a. "Zeremoniell und Raum." In Paravicini 1997b, 11–27.

—, ed. 1997b. *Zeremoniell und Raum: 4. Symposium der Residenzen-Kommission der Akademie der Wissenschaften in Göttingen*. Residenzforschung 6. Sigmaringen: Thorbecke.

Pastor, L. v. 1891–1933. *Geschichte der Päpste seit dem Ausgang des Mittelalters*. 8th-13th ed. 16 vols. Freiburg im Breisgau: Herder.

Piccolomini, A.P. 1965. Reprint. *Caeremoniale romanum of Agostino Patrizi, Piccolomini: The First Edition, Venice 1516, to which is Appended Patrizi's Original Preface, Rediscovered by Jean Mabillon and Published by him in the Second Volume of his Museum Italicum, Lutetiae Parisiorum 1689*. Ridgewood: Gregg. Original edition, *Rituum ecclesiasticorum sive sacrarum cerimoniarum s. s. romanae ecclesiae: Libri tres non ante impressi*, edited by C. Marcello. Venice: Leonardo Lauredano, 1516.

Prodi, P. 1982. *Il sovrano pontefice: Un corpo e due anime: La monarchia papale nella prima età moderna*. Saggi 228. Bologna: Mulino.

Quednau, R. 1984. "Päpstliches Geschichtsdenken und seine Verbildlichung in der Stanza dell'Incendio." *Münchner Jahrbuch der bildenden Kunst* 35: 83–128.

Randolph, A.W.B. 1997. "Regarding Women in Sacred Space." In *Picturing Women in Renaissance and Baroque Italy*, edited by G.A. Johnson and S.F.M. Grieco, 17–41. Cambridge: Cambridge University Press.

Rasmussen, N.K. 1983. "Maiestas pontificiae: A Liturgical Reading of Étienne Dupérac's Engraving of the Capella Sixtina from 1578." *Analecta romana instituti danici* 12: 109–48.

Roth, A. 1999. "Liturgische Musik im Dienste der maiestas papalis in re divina." In Kruse 1999, 162–70.

Rutherford, I., and U. Mildner. 1996–2001. "Decorum." In *Historisches Wörterbuch der Rhetorik*, edited by G. Ueding, vol. 2, 423–52. Tübingen: Niemeyer.

Schimmelpfennig, B. 1992. "Die Bedeutung Roms im päpstlichen Zeremoniell." In *Rom im hohen Mittelalter: Studien zu den Romvorstellungen und zur Rompolitik vom 10. bis zum 12. Jahrhundert: Reinhard Elze zur Vollendung seines 70. Lebensjahres gewidmet*, edited by B. Schimmelpfennig and L. Schmugge, 47–61. Sigmaringen: Thorbecke.

—. 1999. "Vatikanpalast und Zeremoniell." In Kruse 1999, 154–9.

Schneider, N. 1996. "Kunst und Gesellschaft: der sozialgeschichtliche Ansatz." In *Kunstgeschichte: Eine Einführung*, edited by H. Belting, H. Dilly, W. Kemp, W. Sauerländer, and M. Warnke, 306–35. Berlin: Reimer.

Schütte, U. 1995. "Höfisches Zeremoniell und sakraler Kult in der Architektur des 17. und 18. Jahrhunderts. Ansätze zu einem strukturellen Vergleich." In Berns and Rahn 1995b, 410–31.

Schütze, S. 1997. "Stadttor und Hausschwelle: Zur rituellen Bedeutung architektonischer Grenzen in der frühen Neuzeit." In Paravicini 1997b, 305–24.

Seidler, S.M. 1995. *Il teatro del mondo: Diplomatische und journalistische Relationen vom römischen Hof aus dem 17. Jahrhundert.* Beiträge zur Kirchen- und Kulturgeschichte 3. Frankfurt am Main: Peter Lang.

Shearman, J. 1972. *Raphael's Cartoons in the Collection of Her Majesty the Queen and the Tapestries for the Sistine Chapel.* London: Phaidon.

Sherr, R. 1982. "The Singers of the Papal Chapel and Liturgical Ceremonies in the Early Sixteenth Century: Some Documentary Evidence." In *Rome in the Renaissance: The City and the Myth: Papers of the Thirteenth Annual Conference of the Center for Medieval and Early Renaissance Studies*, edited by . P.A. Ramsey, 249–64. Medieval and Renaissance Texts and Studies 18. Binghamton: Center for Medieval & Early Renaissance Studies.

—. 1994. "Speculations on Repertory, Performance Practice, and Ceremony in the Papal Chapel in the Early Sixteenth Century." In *Collectanea II: Studien zur Geschichte der päpstlichen*, edited by B. Janz, 103–22. Capellae apostolicae sixtinaeque collectanea acta monumenta 4. Vatican City: Biblioteca Apostolica Vaticana.

Signorotto, G., and M.A. Visceglia. 2002. "Introduction." In *Court and Politics in Papal Rome, 1492–1700*, edited by G. Signorotto and M.A. Visceglia, 1–7. Cambridge Studies in Italian History and Culture. Cambridge: Cambridge University Press.

Sindzingre, N. 1999. "Rites de passage." In Le Manh 1999.

Spiess, K.-H. 1997. "Rangdenken und Rangstreit im Mittelalter." In Paravicini 1997b, 39–61.

Staubach, N. 2004a. "'Honor dei' oder 'Bapsts Gepreng'? Die Reorganisation des Papstzeremoniells in der Renaissance." In Staubach 2004b, 91–136.

—, ed. 2004b. *Rom und das Reich vor der Reformation.* Frankfurt a.M.: Peter Lang

Stinger, C.L. 1998. *The Renaissance in Rome.* 2nd ed. Bloomington: Indiana University Press.

Sullivan, L.E. 1986. "Sound and Senses: Toward a Hermeneutics of Performance." *History of Religions: An International Journal for Comparative Historical Studies* 26:1–33.

Suntrup, R. 1978. *Die Bedeutung der liturgischen Gebärden und Bewegungen in lateinischen und deutschen Auslegungen des 9. bis 13. Jahrhunderts.* Münstersche Mittelalter-Schriften 37. München: Fink.

Thomas, J., K. Kavan, J.N. Lupia, and C.M.E. Guth. 1996. "Screen." In *The Dictionary of Art*, edited by J. Turner, vol. 28, 290–8. London: Macmillan.

Ullmann, W., ed. 1960. *Die Machtstellung des Papsttums im Mittelalter: Idee und Geschichte.* Edited by G. Möser-Mersky. Graz: Styria. Original edition, *The Growth of Papal Government in the Middle Ages: A Study in the Ideological Relation of Clerical to Lay Power.* London: Methuen, 1955.

van Gennep, A. 1960. *The Rites of Passage.* Translated by M.B. Vizedom and K. Paul. London: Routledge & Kegan. Original edition, *Les rites de passage: Étude systématique des rites: De la porte et du seuil, de l'hospitalité, de l'adoption, de la grossesse et de l'accouchement, de la naissance, de l'enfance, de la puberté, de l'initiation, de l'ordination, du couronnement, des fiançailles et du mariage, des funérailles, des saisons, etc.* Paris: Nourry, 1909.

Vec, M. 1998. *Zeremonialwissenschaft im Fürstenstaat: Studien zur juristischen und politischen Theorie absolutistischer Herrschaftsrepräsentation.* Studien zur europäischen Rechtsgeschichte 106. Frankfurt am Main: Klostermann.

Visceglia, M.A. 1997. "Il cerimoniale come linguaggio politico: Su alcuni conflitti di precedenza alla corte di Roma tra Cinquecento e Seicento." In Visceglia and Brice 1997, 117–76.

Visceglia, M.A., and C. Brice, eds. 1997. *Cérémonial et rituel à Rome (XVIe–XIXe siècle).* Collection de l'École française de Rome 231. Rome: École française de Rome.

Weddigen, T. 1999. "Tapisseriekunst unter Leo X. – Raffaels 'Apostelgeschichte' für die Sixtinische Kapelle." In Kruse 1999, 268–84.

—. 2003. "Zur Funktionsgeschichte." In Weddigen et al. 2003, 9–25.

Weddigen, T., S. de Blaauw and B. Kempers, eds. 2003. *Functions and Decorations: Art and Ritual at the Vatican Palace in the Middle Ages and the Renaissance.* Capellae apostolicae sixtinaeque collectanea acta monumenta 9, collectanea 5. Vatican City et al.: Biblioteca Apostolica Vaticana et al.

Widengren, G. 1969. *Religionsphänomenologie.* Berlin: Walter de Gruyter. Original edition, *Religionens värld.* 2nd rev. ed. Stockholm: Svenska, 1953.

Étienne Dupérac, *The Exact Depiction of the Papal Majesty During the Celebration of the Divine Mass in the Sistine Chapel*, 1578, etching, 51 x 36 cm. Vatican City, Biblioteca Apostolica Vaticana.

Reconstruction of the hanging of the *Acts of the Apostles* in the Sistine Chapel, ca. 1521 (Weddigen/Trogisch). After: Weddigen 1999, 270 fig. 2.

Houses, Power and Everyday Life in Early Modern England

MATTHEW JOHNSON

In this paper, I want to examine some changes in the patterns of architecture and material life in England between the late medieval and early modern periods. My argument will be that to understand how power was constructed through ordinary buildings, we need to take a contextual and holistic view of social power. In particular, we need to compare patterns of architecture and power between realms often considered as separate discursive domains – religious and domestic, ceremonial and everyday. We also need to reflect on the constitution of power and its relationship to agency – to put it crudely, to take a 'bottom-up' as well as a 'top-down' view of power and the way that power is materialised and expressed in architecture.

I will first offer some theoretical reflections on the nature of power, and then move on to consider the layout and meanings of the late medieval house in England. I will then turn to the social and ideological changes of the sixteenth century, sketching out a 'top-down' view of religious and political reformation. Finally, I will consider the reaction of the socially middling to these changes, in their patterns of building and living in ordinary houses.

SOCIAL POWER, THE MATERIAL, AND THE EVERYDAY

The recognition of agency has been one of the most important developments in the human sciences over the last thirty years. By agency, I am referring to something very simple: that social and material structures are constantly being created and recreated by the actions of human beings. When we are attempting to explain the construction of power in buildings, then, we must look in part to an understanding of the intentions of actors from all social levels rather than simply refer to abstract processes.

Of course, an understanding of the individual social agent was never far from the thinking of the founders of the human sciences, most notably Max Weber; and the tradition of micro-sociology, most notable exemplified in the work of Erving Goffman, has seen agency as a central issue. It is nevertheless the case that thinking about agency and structure has been crystallised in the last generation. I would pick out two developments here. The first is the work of Anthony Giddens in drawing together insights from Bourdieu, Geertz, Goffman and others into a coherent and systematic framework for the understanding of agency, structure and contradiction[1]. The second is the intellectual and cultural impact of feminist thought. The impact of feminism has been such that never again can we talk of relations between husband and wife, patterns of household and community activity, as somehow 'innocent' or apart from questions of social power[2].

Such an exploration of agency leads directly to the conception of the everyday. The mundane and the 'normal' are sites of the most important concentrations of social and cultural power, precisely because of their mundane, taken-for-granted nature. The essentials of a cultural system, then, are to be revealed most profoundly in what it takes for granted: the rhythms and processes of food preparation, eating, where people sleep, notions of privacy, the different domains of women and men, the care of children.

The power of architecture lies, in this view, in its materialisation of what is normal or taken for granted. Buildings, insofar as they are arrangements of space designed to 'facilitate' a way of living that is

I would like to thank the organisers, particularly Prof Joseph Maran and Ulrich Thaler, for their invitation to the conference, and for their hospitality and friendship during my time in Heidelberg.

1 Giddens 1984. In my own thinking, I have been particularly inspired by the work of Erving Goffman.
2 Ardener 1981; Moore 1986, 1988. It has to be said that much traditional architectural history of both polite and vernacular buildings is still written not in refutation of the feminist critique, but as if it had never happened.

'taken for granted', are material expressions of the way the world is held to work. As such, buildings are always and immediately ideological: they seek to give legitimation and authority to something which is arbitrary. Such ideology might at one level be obvious and vulgar, as seen for example in the Nuremburg buildings (this volume). At other levels it is more subtle.

Architectural historians have tended to concentrate on the meanings of 'polite' or elite building. This is an understandable and intuitive move. A medieval castle or Renaissance palace is clearly and self-evidently about power: it stands at the apex of society. As I write these words and look around me, it is the Heidelberg Schloss that comes to mind when I look for expressions of power, not the buildings of the Altstadt. Such great buildings are also, frequently, the subject of written texts, such as those of the Classical world (Vitruvius) or of the early modern world (Palladio, Bentham). These texts appear to refer directly to the relationship between buildings and power, even if their reading or interpretation is problematic. However, I want to stress in this paper that *ordinary buildings are just as much embedded in relations of power as their monumental or elite counterparts*. If agency theory shows us that everyday activity is in part about power relations, then the ordinary and quotidian nature of that activity makes it no less powerful.

Several methodological and theoretical factors militate against the view of ordinary or vernacular buildings as materialising the construction of power, and make a view that links questions of vernacular building, agency, and power counter-intuitive. It is worth considering what these factors are, and why they are potentially misleading.

First, the lower the social level and the more mundane the building, the less likely it is to be the subject of overt written discourse. Contemporaries wrote about Palladian villas, but they did not write in the same overt way about ordinary houses and cottages. The inhabitants of ordinary buildings were frequently illiterate, and therefore the buildings they dwelt in are in a sense effectively prehistoric. This absence of direct textual information can make scholars reluctant to push the boundaries of interpretation beyond technology and economy into questions of social power. In this view, we can talk about power in elite (documented) buildings, but not with regard to vernacular (undocumented) buildings. However, the idea that oral or written testimony gives the scholar more 'direct' or 'positive' information about social relations than the material record does is, in my view, completely illusory. There is nothing inherently superior about the documentary as opposed to the archaeological record. John Moreland has shown how the perception of documentary information as superior or more direct has its origin in medieval religious doctrine, in particular the primacy of the Word of God over the material world[3].

Second, despite the appreciation of agency discussed above, there is a lingering perception that social power is an exclusively top-down process. Elites have power and express it in elite building; peasants or the lower social orders do not have power. Stated so baldly, such a position seems absurd, but it nevertheless lingers on. For example, a recent book on 'the archaeology of power' discusses palaces, castles, great houses, but not peasant buildings[4]. Clearly, there is great inequality of power between social classes and genders, but this does not mean that power is not always and already a two-way process, as the most cursory reading of Foucault will indicate[5].

Third, traditional models of the behaviour of lower social orders have tended to understress their agency. The classic example is that of 'social emulation'. It is often assumed that when ordinary people adopted new patterns of behaviour and lifestyle, they must have done so in order to emulate or imitate their social 'betters' or superiors. Thus, improvements in houses, changes in house style, or better furnishings, must in this view be the result of a desire to move up the social scale. Such a view often finds support in the texts of the time. The late medieval and early modern literate elite spent much of their time complaining that their lifestyles were being 'aped' by their social 'inferiors', for example in dress but also in building style. The elite even passed 'sumptuary legislation' against this perceived process, forbidding those below a certain status from wearing certain clothing materials or consuming certain goods. However, as critical scholars, we do not have to accept these elite complaints at face value. Anxiety about social position and the perception of threats to it tell us more about the anxieties of the

3 Moreland 2001.
4 Steane 2001.
5 Foucault 1977 being the most obvious example.

elite than they do about the 'reality' of ordinary behaviour. Colin Campbell has pointed out, for example, that tea-drinking among the lower social orders in eighteenth century Britain may not be due to a desire to imitate elite tea-drinking; it may be rather that people liked to drink tea. Following Campbell, we can suggest that it may be that ordinary people rebuilt their houses in a certain style because they liked that style, not because they sought to imitate anybody or to rise up the social scale.

THE NATURE OF VERNACULAR BUILDING

In my view, the homes of people below the elite should be understood in terms of their own agency, their own view of the world. In this view, the story of vernacular architecture is "the study of people acting. It shows us people [...] engaged with their surroundings in a critical way, people making their own histories in the face of authorities trying to make it for them"[6].

'Vernacular' is, of course, a concept that has to be understood relationally and dialectically. In other words, the category of 'vernacular' only makes sense if it is understood in terms of a totality that includes 'polite' or elite building. Relatively humble dwellings can only exist alongside relatively ostentatious ones. In this sense, societies that lack marked social differentiation do not have either vernacular or polite architecture; rather, they have a single category of building tradition, which in the past would have been called 'primitive'.

In England, and indeed in many areas of Europe, thousands of vernacular buildings from the late medieval and early modern period still stand today, albeit heavily modified, and continue to be occupied as family homes. I will discuss their changing form below. Their pattern of construction, the technical systems that they embody, their decoration, are all distinctive in terms of their relatively humble social status, and are strongly differentiated regionally. For example with respect to timber framing, Richard Harris has spoken of a national "language" or "grammar" of carpentry techniques, a set of rules which specify how the raw timber from the living tree is first to be sawn and chopped, and then assembled into a timber skeleton that is prefabricated and held together by carpentered joints and pegs. He goes on to show how, within this national language, there exist what he calls "dialects", particular kinds of decoration or choice of building materials that mark a vernacular building out in regional terms[7]. As a result of this combination of language and dialect, an observer can accurately 'place' a building to within 40 or 50 kilometres in the English countryside by observations of its choice of building materials, construction details and style.

How old are these houses? In many regions of the English countryside, particularly in the south and east, there are literally thousands of surviving houses that date in origin to the later Middle Ages, that is, the period 1350 to 1550. They have invariably been heavily modified over the generations to meet the needs of modern living, and their original form often needs a great deal of 'detective work', clambering about in the loft and examining exposed timbers, to elucidate. However, the fact that such numbers have survived for 500 to 600 years is an interesting observation in itself. It suggests that the later Middle Ages saw a rise in the numbers and wealth levels of socially middling farmers and an increased inclination on their part to rebuild their houses in 'permanent' form.

Such a bald statement must be qualified in two ways. First, there is a methodological problem in the comparison of the evidence of medieval peasant houses from excavation on the one hand, and the remains of standing houses on the other. It may well be that much of our perception of 'improvement' of building is illusory – that the difference that existed in the past between houses destined to survive, and houses destined to fail to survive and then to be excavated by archaeologists, is not actually all that great, and may even be non-existent. Second, numbers of houses standing in a given area of the English countryside today may be as much the product of contingent factors of survival as it is of a 'real' process in the past, for example fire and indeed subsequent prosperity. This village may have suffered extensively from fire, and remaining medieval houses may have been torn down and rebuilt in modern style when its inhabitants grew rich on nineteenth century agricultural improvements, while that village

6 Upton and Vlach 1986, xxiii.
7 Harris 1989.

Abb. 1. A reconstructed medieval house from Kent in South-East England, Weald and Downland Museum: the hall is open to the roof, with doors at one side leading into its upper end. Photograph: author.

may have been free from episodes of fire and have stagnated during the nineteenth century, its medieval houses therefore surviving. It may be therefore that the 'appearance' of such surviving peasant houses from the later Middle Ages may be at the very least the result of a longer-term process. My own view is that these peasant houses do represent a break from existing traditions, though the evidence is too complex to go into here[8].

However, I want to concentrate here on the *form* of the later medieval houses (Abb. 1). While their framing and decoration varies regionally, the basic plan of many of these houses is strikingly uniform. It is invariably centred on a room open to the rafters, termed the 'hall'. The hall was heated by an open hearth rather than a fireplace and chimneystack, sited in the middle of the room. The smoke from this hearth rose to the roof, where it exited through a louvre or, more commonly, would simply disperse amidst the thatch[9]. While an open space, the hall was divided by the hearth position into 'upper' and 'lower' ends. The upper end would be lit by a large window, and have the bench and table for the master of the house and his wife. Often, this bench was fixed against the wall at the upper end, and the peg-holes and mortises for this attachment can still be seen.

'Below' the hearth, a pair of external doors gave access to the outside world; as a result, not only was the lower end draughtier, but it was also more dimly lit. As a result, a visitor to the house is immediately placed in a certain relationship to the peasant farmer at the upper end. He or she enters through one of the doors, their eyes only gradually becoming accustomed to the darkness and straining to see through the smoke; the master of the house rises from his seat at the other end of the hall, whether to welcome

8 See Currie (1988) for the argument that present patterns are partly contingent rather than 'real', and Dyer (1986) for the more general argument, from documentary evidence, that surviving peasant houses from the Later Middle Ages are not significantly different from those that have not survived.

9 Many such roofs are still blackened from the rising soot, and many still have the original blackened thatch: Letts et al. 2000.

the guest and invite them to the upper end, or to direct those of lower status to the service rooms at the lower end.

The form of the medieval peasant house thus encoded and enforced social power at a very basic and everyday level. The meanings of the system were apparent every time someone entered or left the hall, apparent in where they sat at mealtimes, even in the placement of a log on the fire. They were reinforced in other ways. First, the technical system of the house emphasised the upper over the lower ends. The pegs that fixed the timber frame in place would be 'faced in' to the bench at the upper end of the hall; that is, they would be driven in so that their flat faces were towards the master's seat, while the sharp ends of the pegs faced away. The hall itself would generally be of two bays or structural divisions[10], with an open truss between creating a visual focus and directing the eye upwards. The 'upper' bay was often slightly longer, by one rafter, than the lower – a small detail that only the builder of the house may have been aware of.

Second, they were reinforced by the close correspondence between the form and arrangement of the peasant hall with that of the halls of social superiors. The basic form – open to the roof, with opposed doors and service area at the lower end, large window lighting the upper end – was a common system or structure at different levels of English medieval society. Halls at a higher social level frequently had fireplaces and chimneystacks, though many, for example Gainsborough Old Hall, did not. They would also have the upper ends slightly raised on a step, in the form of a 'dais', and the opposed doors at the lower end were frequently set behind screens, forming a 'screens passage'. Benches often ran the length of these larger halls, and one's status within the great medieval household was reflected in the order people sat, those especially favoured being closer to the lord, that is, farther towards the upper end of the hall.

The meanings of such halls are clear at a general level. Late medieval England saw itself as a 'corporate community', with common principles running up and down the social scale. The hall was a piece of theatre: the body of the lord was on display, and the opportunity given to show lordship on the one side and deference on the other. The power of the hall lay also in its use in other contexts, when the benches would be moved back and an open space created – for example, in holding court and administering justice. And a similar code existed in the medieval peasant house. Just as the lord ruled, so did the socially middling peasant farmer, over his wife, his children and the few servants or farm labourers who were also part of even quite humble households.

It is clear that much of the ideological power of the open hall lay in its reference to a system of meanings that lay at the heart of medieval society. The preference of the late medieval peasant for buildings of this kind is striking, given that the technology of chimneystacks was well known and, to judge from the impressive size of the houses they built, they could clearly have afforded them. Instead, peasant households opted invariably for a space that was cold, draughty, full of smoke, because of the central importance of what it meant to them and for their view of their world.

THE GREAT REBUILDING

And yet… a century later, the open hall was no more. The building of open halls at a peasant level declined after 1500, particularly in southern and eastern England. By 1550, very few open halls were constructed. Where new houses were now built, they abandoned the plan open to the roof; instead, new houses were built with brick chimneystacks[11]. Additionally, older open-hall houses were converted; a ceiling was inserted into the old hall, and a brick chimneystack placed in the space. The new space created was much warmer, less draughty, and less prone to risk of sparks from the open fire setting the house alight. However, the new hall was smaller; it lacked the spatial system created by the opposing

10 A few halls in surviving smaller houses are of one bay only.

11 There is a variety of forms that might be classified as transitional between the open hall and the ceiled hall with chimneystack, including 'smoke bays', smoke hoods, and timber-and-plaster chimneystacks, each with its own regional distribution. Such forms may have been more common in the past, as fire risk and subsequent modernisation of houses has removed the vast majority of examples.

Abb. 2. The postmedieval house, Cranborne, in Dorset in south-west England: the position of the windows indicates a house of two full storeys throughout; the hall is now much smaller, with a ceiling rather than open to the roof. Photograph: author.

doors; and no longer was the eye drawn upwards to the roof. By the early seventeenth century, most open halls had been 'ceiled over' (Abb. 2).

At the same time, there was a continued impetus in house building at a middling social level. Earlier scholars talked of the period 1560 to 1640 being one of a 'Great Rebuilding', in which much of the English countryside saw a dramatic rise in the numbers of new houses being built and in the general standard of living and number and quality of material goods. The contemporary observer William Harrison, for example, quoted in his testimony the recollections of the old people of his Essex parish. Harrison wrote that the "old men yet dwelling in the village where I remain" cite "three things to be marvellously altered in England within their sound remembrance": the replacement of the open hearth with fireplaces and chimneystacks, the "great amendment of lodging" including the replacement of straw mattresses with featherbeds, the use of a bolster or pillow instead of a "good round log", and changes in furniture. Harrison's elderly informants also cited a general rise in the number and standards of moveable goods, for example the exchange of wooden tableware for that of metal – "for so common were all sorts of treen stuff in old time, that a man should hardly find four pieces of pewter [...] in a good farmer's house"[12].

More recent scholarship has tended to underplay the idea of a Great Rebuilding in this period, stressing instead a wider degree of variation between regions of England in the chronology and pace of housing improvements, or seeing the period 1560-1640 not as a moment of critical change, but rather as part of a much longer process of rebuilding that started with the later medieval houses discussed above and went on to the rise of Georgian architecture and the so-called 'death of vernacular' in the eighteenth century[13]. Nevertheless, the Great Rebuilding thesis has proved strikingly durable.

12 Edelen 1968, 200-1. For a fuller discussion of Harrison's comments, and an attempt to place them within early modern discourses of status, domesticity and masculinity, see Johnson 1996, 157-60. Harrison was cited as supporting evidence for the Great Rebuilding by Hoskins (1953).

13 Machin 1977; Johnson 1993b.

It is certainly the case that a more qualified version of the Great Rebuilding thesis can be advanced. Across many regions of England, between the Reformation of the mid-sixteenth century and the English Revolution of the 1640s, great numbers of socially middling farmers, who would have described themselves as lesser gentry, yeomen and husbandmen chose to rebuild their houses. Further, their houses also changed in form with the loss of the open hall and the steady rise in levels of privacy and material comfort.

The question then arises: why did they do so? What triggered the choice not just for greater investment in domestic housing, but a change in form that such housing took?

HOUSES AND PROTESTANTISM

So far, this paper has followed a well-trodden path. I outlined the form of medieval peasant houses, and the archaeological evidence for what that form meant, some years ago. In that work, I went on to describe the changes associated with the Great Rebuilding in one area of England[14].

To account for the transformation in the form of houses, I looked contextually not just at domestic space, but the whole pattern and rhythm of people's lives, and the way that pattern and rhythm was changing. I pointed out that early abandonment of the open hall occurred in the southern and eastern areas of England, particularly in East Anglia. Further, rebuilding was carried out by the socially middling classes. I linked this rebuilding and improvement to what was going on in the rural landscape as a whole, particularly the widespread abandonment of the open field system and an ongoing enclosure of the landscape. So, just as the house was becoming more segregated and privatised, so it was with the landscape as a whole. This link between houses and the wider landscape has been criticised[15], but it is one that I would maintain. Houses in the English countryside were, in the main, working farms. Their builders and owners might sometimes have other professions such as carpenter or clothier listed in their wills and inventories, but a farm was generally maintained 'on the side'. The link between changes in the spheres of the domestic and of the agrarian, then, is demonstrable; it is a view that seeks to impose *a priori* divisions between them, that is, a modern, ethnocentric imposition of a split between work and leisure. I called this common process one of 'closure'.

I sought an explanation for the process of closure in the content of Protestant and specifically Puritan religious belief. Radical Protestantism, retrospectively defined by its political and religious enemies as Puritanism, gained an increasing number of adherents in the later sixteenth and early seventeenth centuries. These adherents were often men of the 'middling sort', and tended to come from precisely those areas of England that also saw the rebuilding of large numbers of houses from an early period. In this argument, I was following the lead set by Max Weber over a century ago, but also the work of British historians, the socialist Richard Tawney and Marxist Christopher Hill in particular[16]. The male, Puritan head of household drew from his religion a heightened sense of self and of discipline. This discipline was to be extended over one's own person, over one's wife and family, over the household as a whole, including servants, over the village community, and over the wider social and natural landscape as a whole. Such an account of the central role of Puritanism went along with a wider view of social, cultural and economic change. In this view, Puritanism was closely linked to the rise of the 'middling sort', and the increased cultural and political assertiveness of the middling sort led to the English Revolution of the 1640s. The English Revolution, then, was in part a bourgeois revolution that sought to free English society and economy from its old feudal chains.

Again, I would defend such an account, with the same proviso as Weber himself made originally. Weber saw the link between religious ethic and the spirit of capitalism as one side of a many-sided causal chain, and similarly I suggest that Puritan belief, changes in ordinary houses, and wider cultural

14 Johnson 1993a.

15 Williamson (2000) offers the most sustained and serious critique, seeing the link made as "mystical". I contend that a view which sees the realms of the domestic and the agrarian as quite separate domains of experience would be alien, and as such 'mystical', to the early modern farmer.

16 Weber 1958; Tawney 1926; Hill 1964.

developments are linked, but in a more complex way than simple cause-and-effect. It does not imply that all house builders were Puritans, or that there was a precise one-to-one correlation between house building, enclosure and religious radicalism.

In the rest of this paper, then, I want to look at some of the other factors that should be involved in a fuller account of changes in domestic space and their cultural context. Specifically, I want to argue that a valid criticism of this earlier model of change is that it stressed change in the *content* of religious belief at the expense of changes in *form*. As such, it led the argument away from themes that can most fruitfully be addressed through the material evidence, towards ones that were less immediately accessible. To put it another way, archaeologists will always find it difficult or at least epistemologically problematic to penetrate the 'inner life' of individuals, and to demonstrate a link between that inner life and outward show; after all, it was such a link between the 'inner man' and 'outward man' that the Puritans themselves sought to question. However, we can say very precisely and directly what the parish church in a village community looked like, what participants in village life would have seen as they walked to and from house, church and alehouse. The forms of household and village life are, in this sense, much easier terrain for the scholar than their meaning-content. So, instead of looking at the content of Protestant belief, I want to look instead at its material manifestations, in the changes brought about by the English Reformation.

THE LATE MEDIEVAL CHURCH

The parish church stood, and in most cases continues to stand, at the physical and social heart of virtually every local community in the English countryside. Since the work of Emile Durkheim, it is an anthropological commonplace that when a community worships God it is also worshipping society, that religious observation always takes a form distinctive to that society[17]. The physical fabric of the church, then, is not simply or solely a record of changing religious belief. It is also and at the same time a complex record of the changing social and cultural composition of the local community[18].

The physical fabric of a typical parish church is of medieval origin. The walls are often a complex palimpsest of building, rebuilding, changes, subdivisions, additions, remodelling. To wander round such a church, then, is to see inscribed in its fabric the complex story of the parish community, just as to look at a house is to see the complex story of the family and household. Towards the end of the Middle Ages, as with vernacular houses, many parish churches were extensively or completely rebuilt. The financing of such rebuilding sometimes had little direct relationship with the overall wealth of the community. Many 'wool churches', for example, were built from the profits from the wool and cloth trade of the landlords and wealthier peasants, and were far larger and grander than the local community actually needed.

A key element of recent scholarship on the late medieval English church has been to stress its complexity and richness of meaning, and to examine its close ties with patterns of everyday life in the local and regional communities of which it was a part[19]. A late medieval peasant saw the church as the largest and most important building in the local community, rivalled only by the manor house or local residence of the lord. Work in the fields, and the everyday rhythm of the working day and week, was regulated by the tolling of the church bell. The tower of the church was often visible from the furthest reaches of the parish territory; in some areas of lowland England it is possible to see six or more church towers from neighbouring parishes at any one time, and difficult to walk across the landscape without having sight of such towers. Ordinary people began their lives by being christened in the church font, and ended their lives by being buried in the churchyard. To traverse the churchyard on the way to church every Sunday was to pass by and even over the bones of their ancestors.

The internal fabric and texture of the church gave material expression to the values of the community. Just as in the open fields, the space represented a complex structuring of rights and responsibilities, the

17 Durkheim 1912; see also Turner 1974.
18 Glassie (2000) provides an evocative description of the English parish church.
19 In what follows I draw on various recent works, including French et al. 1997; Kumin 1996; Duffy 1992, 2001.

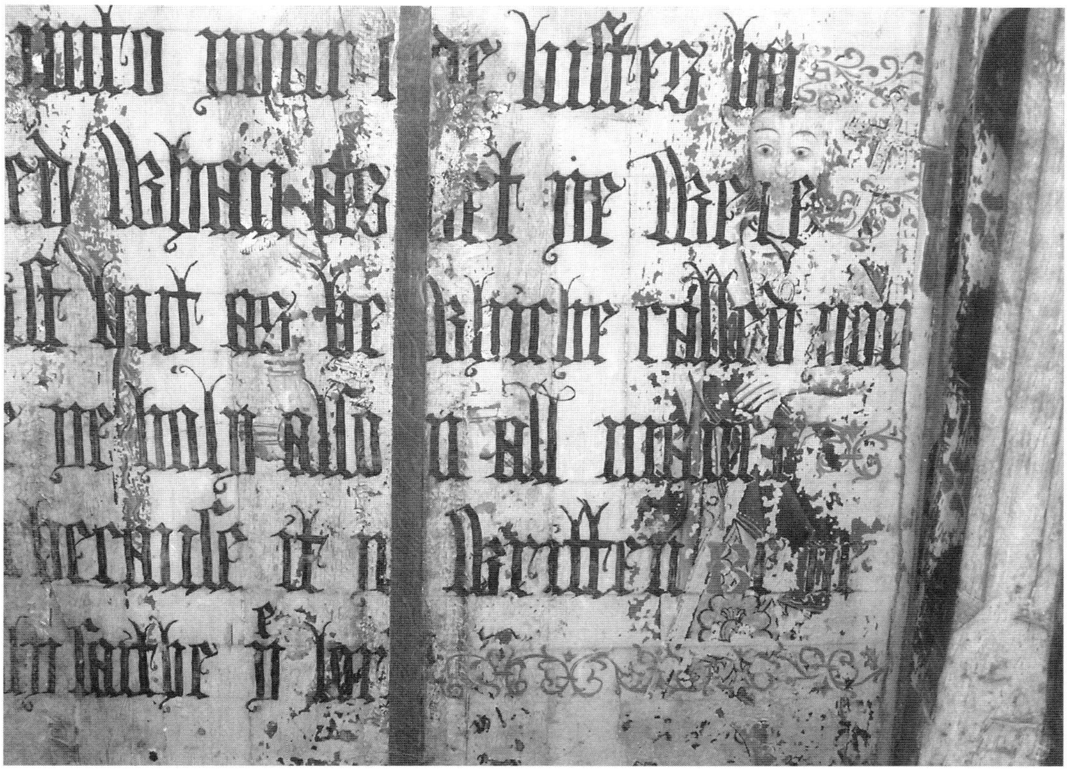

Abb. 3. Binham Priory, Norfolk: fragment of the old rood screen; medieval painted figures have been painted over with biblical texts. Photograph: author.

chancel for example being the responsibility of the priest and the nave that of the parish respectively. The walls of the church were covered with pictures (Abb. 3). These were of Biblical scenes, and/or had moral and allegorical content that attempted to give guidance for people's everyday lives and which reflected the construction of power in the medieval village – scenes of women 'gossips', portrayals of saints, a plough to be blessed at ploughing time, and so on. Frequently there would be graphic depictions of Purgatory and Hell, depicting in an age before photography precisely what fate awaited the sinful. Such images were repeated in the stained glass windows, filling the church with coloured light.

It should be remembered that the vast majority of the congregation was illiterate, with literacy biased by gender as well as class. Consequently, the visual imagery of the church, and the performance of liturgy, played a pivotal role. The performance of the Mass by the priest was only seen indistinctly by the congregation through the openings in the rood screen dividing nave and chancel; the words, spoken in Latin rather than the vernacular, added to this mysterious quality. Pam Graves has emphasised the power of this architecture and this performance, and the richness of meaning it held for both priest and congregation; but she has also stressed how ordinary people had their own understandings of what was going on around them in church[20].

It is difficult not to see a close link between the experience of domestic space and experience of religious space, and common principles structuring both. Where the hall was divided into upper and lower ends, the church was divided into nave and chancel. The altar was in the position of the bench and table in the hall, and stood on a raised platform, just as the dais end was in larger halls. The visitor to both church and house entered at the lower end, and turned towards either altar or high table. And the liturgy of the Mass, whatever the doctrinal debates among the literate clergy over its precise meaning, was experienced by the congregation in a way that brought to mind the ritual of eating within the hall.

20 Graves 2000. It should be noted that where historians have tended to concentrate on the 'official' doctrinal histories of the late medieval church and its reformation, Graves' training as an archaeologist makes her sensitive to alternative readings, and less hesitant in discerning symbolic linkages where there is an absence of documentary 'evidence'.

Literate discourse emphasises division between the domestic and the religious; there is almost no comment on such a link and its possible meanings either in contemporary documents or in the commentaries of modern historians. Yet the formal, archaeological parallels in physical pattern, and the linkage and cross-referencing of both in the corporate community of the late medieval world, can hardly be denied.

THE ENGLISH REFORMATION

It was this immensely powerful configuration of religious and social power that the English Reformation sought to deconstruct and reassemble[21]. The immediate context of reformation was a top-down process, driven by the character of the King, and later by the religious convictions of the wealthy and powerful, and enforced by the growing bureaucratic and physical power of the sixteenth century State. Its first impetus were the personality and dynastic ambitions of the monarch Henry VIII, but once started, the power and momentum of reformation was gained from preceding and parallel developments in continental Europe. Henry broke with Rome and declared himself Head of the Church of England, and proceeded to dissolve the great monasteries and seize their wealth. Rebellion and resistance, most notably the Pilgrimage of Grace, was crushed.

After Henry's death, the protectors of his young son Edward proceeded to give the Reformation a distinctively Protestant character and to extend reform into the parish church. In this way, the power of the English State was extended outwards and downwards into every local community in the realm, even to what Puritans were later to call 'the dark corners of the land'. The death of Edward, the subsequent accession and death of the Catholic Mary, and the coronation of the Protestant Queen Elizabeth, saw a succession of changes in religious preferences of the monarch, each of whom attempted to impose a new 'settlement' on the Church. And each new 'settlement' was felt in every parish church in the kingdom.

The impact of religious reform on any local parish church was quite sudden. The architectural fabric was left, but the experience of the internal space was abruptly transformed (Abb. 4). Chantry chapels and other fixtures and fittings were removed and destroyed. Images of the Virgin Mary and of other saints were seen as idolatrous and smashed. Stained glass was destroyed. The internal walls of the church had their pictures covered over; the whole church was whitewashed (Abb. 3).

It should be noted that the perceptual transformation produced by these changes hinged on text, in an age when, as we have noted, the majority of the population could not read. The whitewashed walls were covered with the words of the Ten Commandments and the Royal coat of arms set up at the upper end of the church; thus, when the congregation faced the altar, they faced the Royal Coat of Arms as well. In the official doctrinal view, the Word of God was to be disseminated into hearts and minds not through visual imagery but by preaching. The liturgical mystery was reduced or abandoned – the rood screen with its pictures of saints cut down or dismantled, the view to the altar made clearer or the alter even moved into the nave, the orientation of the altar changed according to religious preference.

These changes were top-down; they were enforced by the power of the State. Local communities resisted passively or actively. The physical evidence of Reformation is very clear; much of the documentary evidence comes from extensive and systematic surveys, commissioned by the State through the apparatus of the established Church. Local priests were directed to comply and ensuing correspondence details enforcement where priests and communities were less than willing.

REFORMING THE HOUSE

What were the reactions of ordinary people to these changes? An elderly yeoman in 1570 would have seen, over the course of his life, a cataclysmic change in the ordering and reordering of the most important element of his community, the church. He would have seen, first, the dissolution of local monasteries; the destruction of chantry chapels; an assault on elements of the landscape such as holy wells

21 See Duffy (1992, 2001) for passionate accounts of the process as it affected local experience, and Macculloch (2001) for a different view.

and wayside crosses; the destruction and remodelling of the interior of the church; the restoration of traditional practices under Mary and yet another new settlement under Elizabeth.

Archaeologists and historians often agonise over the limits to our knowledge; it is often claimed that we cannot access the inner mentalities of people, or that if we can, we have to use the evidence of written texts. I reject both of these views. If we cannot access people's mental worlds, we cannot attempt any meaningful analysis of historical process unless we adopt the most vulgar ecological or technological determinism in which those mental worlds are seen as of no or little significance. If, alternatively, we grant privileged status to the written text over the archaeological evidence, we repeat the same error that medieval theology made when privileging the Word of God over the material world[22]. Both material world and the documentary realm are products of social action. As such, they are meaningful constructions, and as such, both offer avenues however problematic methodologically for understanding the thoughts and actions of past peoples.

However, for this paper, let us grant that the inner thoughts of our elderly yeoman are hard to guess; after all, this was an age when overt expressions of religious or political disloyalty were habitually punished in quite graphic ways. What we can do is note a series of changes or processes that characterised the century during and after the later Reformation, and think about these changes in terms of the agency of ordinary people.

First, an increased consciousness of the State and of nation. Ordinary people, after all, had seen an overt intrusion of the Tudor State into their everyday lives. One of the ideological implications of the late medieval corporate community was that order and authority at the level of the King and the Lord was echoed by, and derived support from, authority at the household level. Each household was 'a little commonwealth'; offences against that commonwealth, for example in overly assertive behaviour by wives, were matters of public concern and punishable as such. However, the changes of the sixteenth century left the middling sort in a position of much greater willingness to intervene in the other direction, both in terms of buttressing political authority through participation in local politics and in questioning it. The later fifteenth and sixteenth centuries saw a series of major and minor 'rebellions'; the later sixteenth and seventeenth centuries saw the steady development of a wider political consciousness and a willingness to identify with class in wider political debate[23].

Second, a reluctance to put any more money into the Church. The rebuilding and adornment of the late medieval church had been a matter of lay patronage, as we have seen. Walking around a medieval parish church today, the visitor will see relatively little rebuilding dating from the early sixteenth century onwards. A typical church may well have a fine collection of individual funerary monuments from the sixteenth to eighteenth centuries, and there may well have been much sixteenth and seventeenth century expenditure on church furnishing that has subsequently been swept away by later generations of Victorian reformers. However, the basic fabric of the church received very little investment after the Reformation. In part, the reluctance of the middling sort to finance further rebuilding of the Church was due to the abolition of the doctrine of Purgatory. The late medieval sinner had been offered the prospect of a speedier passage to Heaven through the purchase of pardons, to Luther's famous disgust, and through patronage of the Church. Nevertheless, a simpler and more basic motive for the reluctance of the middling sort to contribute to the Church may be found in their simple observation of what had happened since the 1530s – the repeated pillaging of the goods and furnishings, the removal of costly church plate, the requirement to finance yet another new set of religious regalia according to the religious preferences of the monarch.

Third, a desire to understand the new emphasis on the Word, and the texts now written on the whitewashed fabric of the church, which our illiterate yeoman cannot read, while they understand their power and authority only too well. The reaction of many socially middling families was to send their sons to grammar school[24]. After a fall in the mid-sixteenth century, possibly due to the abolition of Church institutions, levels of literacy rose steadily. It has been argued that rising levels of literacy led to a rise in the practice of solitary reading, most obviously of the Bible, and this in turn was related to a rise in

22 Moreland (2001) gives a discussion of this issue which, to my mind, is unanswerable.

23 Demos (2000) on the 'commonwealth' in Puritan colonies; Fletcher and Macculloch (1997) on rebellion. Malcolmson and Suzuki (2002) give an overview of debates over gender relations.

24 Cressy 1975.

Abb. 4. Binham Priory, Norfolk, eastern England: before the Reformation, this church like many others was shared between the local parish community and the monks. After the Reformation, the eastern part formerly used by the monks fell into ruin, while the western part continued in use and is still standing. Photograph: author.

'privacy' that we have noted architecturally[25]. They also led to a greater engagement in the affairs of the nation discussed above.

Fourth, a new impetus in the rebuilding of houses (Abb. 2). When the medieval peasant had a succession of good harvests, the money might well be donated to the Church, for the good of his soul; after the Reformation, the money might go in other directions, for example towards purchase or enclosure of land, or the construction of a new home. That new home was to be constructed in a new form. It still had a hall, and the hall still retained much of its power and meaning. However, the hall was now smaller, and had lost its centrality to the circulation pattern of the house.

So we see three generations of rebuilding in the English countryside after 1560 – but in a manner which is not a complete rejection of earlier architectural models, nor is it complete acceptance of what was prescribed for the middling sort by their social superiors. The later sixteenth and seventeenth centuries saw the production and circulation of printed books of different genres, getting steadily cheaper in price. One of these genres was the advice book, often written by a man of the gentry classes, but explicitly addressed to both women and men of the middling sort. The gentry were free in dispensing advice on farming, household affairs, the management of family life, table manners. One such writer was Gervase Markham, who wrote on how to be a gentleman's servant, how to be a housewife, garden design, the art of horsemanship, and the practice of 'husbandry' (a word that in the seventeenth century denoted not just farming but also the management of the household)[26].

Markham's *The English Husbandman* included an idealised plan of a farmhouse. In size, Markham's drawing is appropriate to a gentry house rather than a house of the middling sort, and in form, it remains steadfastly traditional, with a central hall, chimneystack placed to one side, and extensive and rambling wings. Socially middling farmers read Markham's advice and proceeded to build houses that expressed

25 Jagodzinski 1999.
26 Markham 1648. See Johnson (1996, 83-7) for a discussion of such books and 'husbandry' as a discourse.

their view of their world, not that prescribed for them. It was not a rejection of Markham's model, but neither was it complete acceptance. Their houses tended to be more compact, in part a function of their lesser size and status, but also a choice on their part – plenty of late medieval houses had had Markham's rambling wings.

CONCLUSION

The construction of power is a bottom-up as well as a top-down process. It involves questions of agency and social meaning. The study of power and its construction overflows and runs away from simple questions of elite authority. It is revealed as a much deeper and wider terrain than that covered by what bureaucrats and clerics chose to write down in texts. In late medieval and early modern England, we see a vernacular construction of power, an expression by the middling sort of people of their view of their world. Such a view is not easily approximated to either an unquestioning acceptance of the construction of authority, but neither is it a complete rejection. The top-down changes of the Reformation led to changes in the constitution of that authority; the bottom-up response was active, and led to unintended consequences and patterns of change.

These consequences and patterns were complex ones, and shaped, albeit indirectly, the world we live in today. The historical fashion is to stress contingency over historical processes, and specifically to emphasise a diversity of factors and processes at work in early modern England. The old view of the English Revolution as a class conflict between the old order and a newly culturally and politically assertive 'middling sort' has to be at the very least heavily qualified. The underlying Marxist narrative of bourgeois revolution leading to nascent capitalism, again, cannot be sustained in its original form.

Nevertheless, a century after the first English Reformation, the Commons of England, led by a group of regicides derided by their political opponents as the middling sort of people, put a king on trial and proceeded to engage in public condemnation and execution of the monarch. The regicides chose not to follow the medieval pattern of having the king quietly murdered and installing a successor in his place; instead, the king was publicly tried and executed, and a 'Commonwealth' or republic put in his place. Such an action would have been culturally and politically quite inconceivable a century earlier. It is a truism to state that it was made conceivable, in part, by changing constructions of power. And it is also a truism to state that changes in that construction of power were as much about the agency of ordinary people, for example in building and rebuilding their homes, as they were about the actions of kings and princes. It is a challenge to our imagination and intellect to discern the links up and down the social scale between the actions of ordinary men and women and the construction of power at the grandest level, and it is not a challenge that will go away[27].

BIBLIOGRAPHY

Ardener, S., ed. 1981. *Women and Space: Ground Rules and Social Maps*. New York: St. Martin's Press.

Cressy, D. 1975. *Education in Tudor and Stuart England*. London: Edward Arnold.

Currie, C. 1988. "Time and Chance: Modeling the Attrition of Old Houses." *Vernacular Architecture* 19: 1-9.

Demos, J. 2000. *A Little Commonwealth: Family Life in Plymouth Colony*. Oxford: Oxford University Press.

Duffy, E. 1992. *The Stripping of the Altars: Traditional Religion in England 1400-1580*. New Haven: Yale University Press.

—. 2001. *The Voices of Morebath: Reformation and Rebellion in an English Parish*. New Haven: Yale University Press.

27 Sharpe (2000) offers the best summary and assessment of revised views of the English Revolution, and makes a powerful case for the importance of meaning and representation, although the agencies of ordinary people are largely absent from his account.

Durkheim, E. 1912. *Les formes élémentaires de la vie religieuse: Le système totémique en Australie*. Paris: Alcan.

Dyer, C.C. 1986. "English Peasant Building in the Later Middle Ages: The Documentary Evidence." *Medieval Archaeology* 30: 19-45.

Edelen, G., ed. 1968. *The Description of England by William Harrison*. Ithaca: Cornell University Press.

Fletcher, A.J., and D. Macculloch. 1997. *Tudor Rebellions*. London: Longman.

Foucault, M. 1977. *Discipline and Punish: The Birth of the Prison*. London: Allen Lane.

French, K.L., G.G. Gibbs, and B. Kumin. 1997. *The Parish in English Life 1400-1600*. Manchester: Manchester University Press.

Giddens, A. 1984. *The Constitution of Society: Outline of the Theory of Structuration*. Berkeley: University of California Press.

Glassie, H. 2000. *Vernacular Architecture*. Bloomington: University of Indiana Press.

Graves, C.P. 2000. *The Form and Fabric of Belief: An Archaeology of the Lay Experience of Religion in Medieval Norfolk and Devon*. British Archaeological Reports, British Series 311. Oxford: British Archaeological Reports.

Harris, R. 1989. "The Grammar of Carpentry." *Vernacular Architecture*. 20: 1-8.

Hill, C. 1964. *Society and Puritanism in Pre-Revolutionary England*. London: Secker and Warburg.

Hoskins, W.G. 1953. "The Rebuilding of Rural England, 1570-1640." *Past and Present* 4: 44-59.

Jagodzinski, C.M. 1999. *Privacy and Print: Reading and Writing in 17th Century England*. London: University of Virginia Press.

Johnson, M.H. 1993a. *Housing Culture: Traditional Architecture in an English Landscape*. London: University College London Press.

—. 1993b. "Rethinking the Great Rebuilding." *Oxford Journal of Archaeology* 12(1): 117-25.

—. 1996. *An Archaeology of Capitalism*. Oxford: Blackwell.

Kumin, B. 1996. *The Shaping of a Community: The Rise and Reformation of the English Parish c.1400-1560*. Aldershot: Scolar Press.

Letts, J.B., J. Moir, D. Smith, D. deMoulins, and P.D.S. Caligari. 2000. *Smoke Blackened Thatch: A Unique Source of Late Medieval Plant Remains from Southern England*. London: English Heritage.

Macculloch, D. 2001. *The Later Reformation in England, 1547-1603*. Basingstoke: Palgrave.

Machin, R. 1977. "The Great Rebuilding: A Reassessment." *Past and Present* 77: 33-56.

Malcolmson, C., and M. Suzuki. 2002. *Debating Gender in Early Modern England, 1500-1700*. Basingstoke: Macmillan.

Markham, G. 1648. *A Way to Get Wealth: The First Five Books Gathered by G.M., the Last by Master W.L.* 7th ed. London: Jon Harrison.

Moore, H. 1986. *Space, Text and Gender*. Cambridge: Cambridge University Press.

—. 1988. *Feminism and Anthropology*. Cambridge: Polity.

Moreland, J. 2001. *Archaeology and Text*. London: Duckworth.

Sharpe, K. 2000. *Remapping Early Modern England*. Cambridge: Cambridge University Press.

Steane, J. 2001. *The Archaeology of Power: England and Northern Europe, AD800-1600*. Stroud: Tempus.

Tawney, R.H.1926. *Religion and the Rise of Capitalism: A Historical Study*. London: John Murray.

Turner, V. 1974. *The Ritual Process: Structure and Anti-Structure*. Harmondsworth: Penguin.

Weber, M. 1958. *The Protestant Ethic and the Spirit of Capitalism*. Translated by T. Parsons. New York: Charles Scribner.

Williamson, T. 2000. "Understanding Enclosure." *Landscapes* 1(1): 56-79.

Der Architekt, der Ökonom, das Theater und die Sterne – der Raum der Physiokratie und der Raum der Architektur. Studien zu einer denkwürdigen Gleichung

Christopher Schlembach

Kunst gibt nicht das Sichtbare wieder, sondern macht sichtbar.

Paul Klee, Schöpferische Konfession

Damit die Gesellschaft sich ihrer bewusst werden kann und dem Gefühl, das sie von sich hat, den nötigen Intensitätsgrad vermitteln kann, muss sie versammelt und konzentriert sein.

Emile Durkheim,
Die elementaren Formen des religiösen Lebens

Abstract

The late *Ancien Régime* of eighteenth century France gave birth to the so-called 'revolutionary architecture'[1], to political economy and to a new notion of social order, which comes to be seen as describable in terms of space. This essay investigates the relationship between 'revolutionary architecture' and the social sciences, both of which arose against the background of the seventeenth century scientific revolution and a changing notion of space, which was no longer seen as a body, but as containing bodies – bodies in space constituting social order.

Starting from Durkheim's sociology and his concept of 'social space', I try to show that the constitution of abstract categories (time, space, force) describing nature in its social aspects (social time, social space and social force) has its counterpart in physiocratic concepts, which derive these social forms from an evident natural order. As becomes obvious in the more popular writings of Le Mercier de la Rivière, the physiocrats interpret the soul in juridical terms and conceive of social subjects in terms of a mathematized nature.

A corresponding transformation of space can be traced by comparing Quesnay's brief text on *droit naturel* of 1765 and one of the most important projects of 'revolutionary architecture', the saltworks town of Chaux, designed by Claude-Nicolas Ledoux and built between the villages of Arc and Senans from 1775 to 1779. Quesnay constructs a history of the genesis of economic space by interpreting, in different stages of natural law, the respective spatial relationship between human beings and subsistence goods. Economic space in the physiocratic sense becomes possible when political space, which is the territory of a state etc., is related to astronomical space, which is the domain of navigation and, in consequence, of trade and calculable exchanges within functionalized space and time. Ledoux, on the other hand, bases his design of the saltworks town of Chaux on the groundplan of a Roman theatre; thus, he integrates the physiocratic space of production and trade within the concept of an 'industrial theatre'. By becoming an element of this theatre, human labour finds its place in society. At the same time, Ledoux defines a new position of art and the artist in society, which mirrors the position of economy and the economist. Like the physiocrats, the artist claims to make nature visible as a model for social life, so that it can be inscribed into the body of society. In the industrial theatre, workers participate in the play of nature. In his later drafts, Ledoux transforms the city into a cosmic theatre of Newtonian symbolism. Ledoux' ideas concerning moral and social reforms are driven by the same hopes and fears as the reform

1 Kaufmann 1952.

plans of political and administrative writers. They can be interpreted as responses both to an open time, in which it is no longer certain whether the human species will exist until the end of time, and an open space, which to inhabit demands new means of administration and politics as well as of building.

VORBEMERKUNG

Der hier vorgestellte soziologische Essay soll etwas über den Zusammenhang von Soziologie und Architektur vor dem Hintergrund der historischen Formierung der Soziologie selbst zur Sprache bringen. Er handelt von der machtvollen Geste einer neuen Wissenschaft, durch die sie sich in das politische Wissen und in die Seelen (das Gewissen) der Menschen einschrieb und beide neu formierte. Es ist eine Geschichte, die von den frühen Vertretern einer sozio-ökonomischen Wissenschaft, den Physiokraten des 18. Jahrhunderts, und von einem Architekten und Zeitgenossen der Physiokraten, Claude-Nicolas Ledoux (1736–1806), handelt. An ihm soll anschaulich und greifbar werden, wie der Gegenstand der Soziologie, die Gesellschaft, in das Licht der Rationalität eintritt und in deren Raum auftritt. Die tektonischen Bewegungen dieses Ereignisses können wir heute kaum mehr wahrnehmen. In der technischen Sprache der Profession vibrieren sie nur mehr sanft. Die sozialen Ordnungen, die seit Johannes von Salisbury allgemein in der Metaphorik des politischen Körpers beschrieben werden konnten, wurden vor dem Hintergrund der wissenschaftlichen Revolution des 17. Jahrhunderts in Körper im Raum transformiert und damit Gegenstand einer ‚politischen Geometrie'. Im 18. Jahrhundert wurden diese Körper Gegenstand einer ‚politischen Physik' und eines neuen Typs sozialer Gesetzmäßigkeit. Architektur wirft das Problem des Raumes auf und so bitte ich die LeserInnen um Verständnis, wenn dem eigentlichen Thema eine umfangreichere Ausführung darüber vorangeht, wie bestimmte Konzepte von Raum und sozialer Ordnung zueinander in eine Beziehung treten, durch die hindurch ich auf den Punkt blicken möchte, an dem sich Architektur, Ökonomie und deren Soziallehre im 18. Jahrhundert treffen.

VOM RAUM DER SOZIOLOGIE UND DER SOZIOLOGISIERUNG DES RAUMES

Anders als durch die Zeit werden im Raum die ‚Kräfte' eines Zeitalters sichtbar. Wie aber konnte sich diese abstrakte Beziehung als beobachtbares Phänomen formieren, die in einem bestimmten Moment der Geschichte das Feld der Sichtbarkeit zu bestimmen begann? Gegen Ende des 19. Jahrhunderts stellte Emile Durkheim die wissenssoziologische These auf, dass es die Gesellschaft ist, die in kollektiver Anstrengung alle abstrakten Kategorien hervorbringt. Raum, Zeit und Kraft seien also auf die sozialen Formen dieser Kategorien rückführbar, in denen die Gesellschaft sich selbst formiert und umgekehrt seien diese kollektiven Gestalten Modelle für die Anwendung dieser Kategorien auf die gesamte – auch außergesellschaftliche – Wirklichkeit. Für Durkheim war es „der Rhythmus des sozialen Lebens"[2], der eine Fassung für die Kategorie der Zeit bietet und „der Raum, den die Gesellschaft einnimmt, hat den Stoff für die Kategorie des Raumes geliefert; die kollektive Kraft wurde der Prototyp des Begriffs der wirksamen Kraft, damit eines der wesentlichen Elemente der Kategorie der Kausalität"[3]. Durkheim hatte Nietzsches Wissenschafts- und Religionskritik sowie die Ansätze des amerikanischen Pragmatismus studiert und daraus die Anschauung gewonnen, dass kollektives menschliches Handeln und die Bestimmung von Wissen als eines ‚Willens zur Macht' den Untergrund für Strukturen der Rationalität darstellen, die sich in den jeweiligen Systemen von Ideen artikulieren. Ideen allerdings bedürfen der Symbolisierung, um soziale Verbindlichkeit zu gewinnen und dies ist der Punkt, an dem er sich von der ökonomischen Analyse als Basis sozialer Ordnung weg bewegt und auf das Feld religiöser Ausdrucksformen wechselt. Erst im Register der Religion und deren idealer Ordnungen war es möglich, den Inbegriff von Wissenschaft zu begreifen, dessen Totalität das Korrelat wissenschaftlichen Denkens darstellt: die Welt. Und in diesem Moment ereignet sich in der Denkbewegung Durkheims ein Übergang oder vielmehr eine Vermischung, in welcher ein neuer Gegenstand auftaucht, der allerdings nicht

2 Durkheim 1994, 588.
3 Durkheim 1994, 588.

mehr in der Welt enthalten ist, sondern vielmehr selbst die Welt enthält: die Gesellschaft als ‚sozialer Raum'. Der soziale Raum ist vom Raum gewöhnlicher sinnlicher Erfahrung ebenso unterschieden, wie der physikalische Raum der Naturwissenschaften seiner Zeit, der gerade entgegen sinnlicher Erfahrung konstruiert werden kann: „Aber wenn die Welt in der Gesellschaft enthalten ist, dann vermischt sich der Raum, den sie einnimmt, mit dem Gesamtraum. In der Tat haben wir gesehen, wie jedes Ding seinen Platz im sozialen Raum hat. Was deutlich zeigt, wie sehr sich dieser Gesamtraum von den konkreten Anschauungen unterscheidet, die uns unsere Sinne wahrnehmen lassen, ist, daß diese Lokalisierung ganz idealistisch ist und in nichts dem ähnlich, was sie wäre, wenn sie uns allein durch unsere sinnhafte Erfahrung diktiert worden wäre"[4].

Durkheim steht in einer langen Tradition soziologischen Denkens, die bis zu den Physiokraten des 18. Jahrhunderts zurückreicht. Die Physiokraten suchten in der Natur die Gesetze der sozialen Ordnung zu enthüllen und gingen damit spiegelbildlich zu seinen fundamentalen soziologischen Thesen vor. Trotzdem waren es deren Engführungen von Raum und Gesellschaft, die es dem spätgeborenen Soziologen erlaubten, eine ‚soziologische Gleichung' aufzustellen, die nicht die soziale Struktur im Raum, sondern den Raum in einer sozialen Struktur begreift. Durkheim hätte nicht die Natur als Spiegelung der Gesellschaft interpretieren können, wenn nicht die Gesellschaft den Physiokraten eine Spiegelung der Natur gewesen wäre. Der Hintergrund für Durkheims Einsicht, dass der Raum (aber auch die Zeit und die Kraft) einem Schema der sozialen Ordnung entspricht, waren die gewaltigen Technisierungen der Lebenswelt, die einen neuen Zugang zur Natur als Gegenstand der Gestaltung von Welt eröffneten und damit die Naturwissenschaften zu einem neuen konstruktiven ‚Geist' führten. Im 20. Jahrhundert begannen Architekten und Künstler diese neuartige Synthese zu dechiffrieren, genauso wie es Architekten des 18. Jahrhunderts waren, die begonnen hatten, in den ästhetischen Registern ihrer Kunst die von Durkheim bemerkte Vermischung von Raum und Gesellschaft zu realisieren. An diesen zwei Spiegelungen möchte ich ansetzen, um den Raum in seiner soziologischen Bedeutung zu ermessen und um auf ein anderes Problem aufmerksam zu machen: Es bedarf der Symbolisierung, der Konstitution von Bedeutung und für die Modernen eines Zusammenhangs von Wissenschaft und Ästhetik, damit es gelingen kann, wissenschaftliche Konzepte in die soziale Welt zu übersetzen, um *diese* Welt allererst hervorzubringen. Denn was Durkheim in genialer Einsicht erfasste, dass hinter einer statistischen Regelmäßigkeit des gesellschaftlichen Lebens (und des gesellschaftlichen Todes) eine soziale Tatsache steckt, war tatsächlich Ausdruck einer Macht, die sich im 18. Jahrhundert formierte und die einen neuartigen sakralen Charakter erhielt[5]. Diese Macht drückte sich auch in der Sprache der Architektur aus und machte damit zugleich die Funktionsweise sozialer Tatsachen in ihrer objektivierbaren Kraft sichtbar. Der Architekt Claude-Nicolas Ledoux entwarf seine architektonische Umsetzung sozialer Ordnung im Rahmen der Planung einer Salzmanufaktur, der Salinenstadt Chaux. Das ist die Vorstufe jenes Orts, von dem aus Durkheim überhaupt soziale Tatsachen konstruieren konnte: die Fabrik, der Ort, an dem sich Funktionsbeziehungen, Disziplin und Technik zu einem neuen Leben der ‚organischen Solidarität' verselbstständigen konnten[6].

Die ‚Kräfte', die den Raum beherrschen und die Zusammenhänge, die diesen Raum konstituieren, wurden bald nach Durkheims Tod 1917 in Wissenschaft und Kunst thematisch. In den 1920er-Jahren begann Oskar Schlemmer als Mitglied des Bauhauses, die Beziehungen zwischen dem zweidimensionalen Raum der Malerei und dem dreidimensionalen Raum des Theaters zu untersuchen. Ihn interessierte der Zusammenhang zwischen einem Raumschema, zum Beispiel der abstrakten Notation von Bewegungen, und einem realen Raum, in dem diese Bewegungen ausgeführt werden sollen. Was passiert dazwischen? Was passiert mit der Bewegung menschlicher Körper, die in ein rigides Schema und eine leere Form unendlicher Möglichkeiten eingespannt waren? Welcher Raum entsteht unter diesen Bedin-

4 Durkheim 1994, 590-1.

5 Paolo Prodi (2003, 283-6) hat auf eine chiasmische Bewegung aufmerksam gemacht, wodurch es im 18. Jahrhundert gegenläufig zur Verrechtlichung der Moral zu einer Sakralisierung des Rechts kommt. Das Recht, welches Sakralität verkörpert, ist Basis für ein selbstreferentiell organisiertes positives Recht. An diesem Kreuzungspunkt der beiden Bewegungen zwischen einem rechtsförmigen Gewissen und einem Rechtswissen, an das man glaubt, an dieser neuen Einheit von Wissen und Gewissen, entfaltet sich die 'Gesetzeskraft' der Soziologie. Der dargestellte Zusammenhang ist auch die Basis, auf der Durkheims Vorlesungen zur *Physik der Sitten und des Rechts* operieren (Durkheim 1999).

6 Durkheim 1993.

gungen? Welche Spannungen und Kräfte bauen sich auf? Für Schlemmer bedeutete diese Beziehung zugleich jene von Theorie und Praxis, von konstruktiver Raumanschauung und sinnlicher Raumerfahrung. Im leeren Raum des Theaters sollten die Kräfte, die den menschlichen Körper beherrschen, sichtbar gemacht werden. Der zweidimensionale Raum umfasst Bilder, Zeichen und deren Verkettungen, in denen symbolische Ordnungen darstellbar sind. Über ihre Aufführung werden sie zu Bestandteilen eines Geschehens in Raum und Zeit. Diese Arbeiten führten zur Entwicklung dessen, was man heute einen ‚performativen Raum' nennen kann: er enthält zugleich räumliche und ideale Dimensionen, nicht nur im Sinne von Zonen, die Bedeutung tragen, signifikanten Orten und Übergängen zwischen ihnen. Die ideale Dimension meint auch abstrakte Handlungsregeln und -schemata, die den Raum wie Fasern durchziehen. Es handelt sich um eine sehr präzise Analyse der Phänomene, die Durkheim in seiner Soziologie untersuchte. Doch Schlemmer drang in die stillschweigenden Voraussetzungen dieser Soziologie vor. Inspiriert von der Gestaltpsychologie, die nach den subjektiven Korrelaten zu den objektiven Räumen der Wissenschaft suchte, befasste er sich mit den Wegen, welche die psychologische Dimension der *Raumempfindung* analysierbar machen sollte. Um diese Frage ästhetisch bearbeiten zu können, überlagerte er den leeren Theaterraum mit einem Bewegungsschema, das nun in diesem Raum sichtbar wurde und ihn strukturierte. In der Bühnenaufführung *Tanz im Raum* bewegte sich ein Darsteller auf einer Grundfläche, die durch orthogonale Achsen und Diagonalen strukturiert und von einem Kreis umschlossen war. Seile, die vom Boden aus durch den leeren Raum gespannt waren, definierten die Struktur seines Volumens. Entlang dieser Struktur bewegte sich nun der Tänzer und die Raumempfindung sollte dadurch spürbar werden, dass die Figur durch eine widerständige Substanz hindurch dringen würde, welche ihre Bewegungen hemmte. Der Raum, den Schlemmer sichtbar machte, war voller Spannungen und Kräfte, es war eine Art Kraftfeld.

Im 20. Jahrhundert hatte die Mechanisierung der Lebenswelt die konstruktivistische Analyse des Menschen im Raum möglich gemacht und die Suche nach den Gesetzen angeregt, die diesen Raum beherrschten und den Schlemmer in seinem Theater-Labor darzustellen versuchte. Was Schlemmer in der künstlerischen Analyse mit luzider Einsicht gelang, war eine Offenlegung dessen, wie Menschen mit Hilfe schematisierter Bewegungen und Gesten sich in einem Kräftefeld zu bewegen begannen, in dem die Signatur der mechanischen Welt dem menschlichen Leib ihre Prägung verlieh, sich auf ihn legte und ihn bekleidete. Wenn das Bewegungsgesetz im Raum sichtbar gemacht werden konnte, so war damit das Schema der Raumerzeugung von der Realisierung dieses Raumes gelöst.

Dieses Auseinandertreten von Raum als Ordnungsschema oder von geometrischem Raum und konkretem Raum war für die Erfassung dessen, was mit dem Raum passiert war, noch nicht hinreichend. Für den Phänomenologen Jan Patocka war es ein wichtiger Schritt der Analyse, doch es war zu wenig und in diesem Sinn reduktiv. Patocka kehrt die Blickrichtung um, damit er die Konstitution von Raumschemata klären kann, indem er sein Augenmerk auf die Realisierung eines Schemas, weniger auf das Schema selbst richtet. Das Raumschema ist das Produkt einer langsamen und hartnäckigen Arbeit, die von den nicht-geometrischen Anteilen des Raumes abstrahiert: „Der Raum ist eine formale Struktur und qualitative Realisierung, ein Konkretum mit dessen struktureller Gesetzmäßigkeit. [...] Wenn wir über den Raum als Konkretum etwas erfahren möchten, müssen wir die Aufmerksamkeit statt auf die Beziehungsstruktur, die Geometrie, auf die Realisierung richten. Nicht die Geometrie schafft die Realisierung, sondern die Realisierung schafft die Geometrie. Die Geometrie wurde in der atomistisch-newtonschen Auffassung hypostasiert. Diese Auffassung erwies sich als nicht haltbar. Der Raum ist nicht als realer universeller Rahmen, in dem das reale Geschehen stattfindet, zu verstehen, sondern als die formale Struktur dieses realen Geschehens selbst“[7].

Die Verdinglichung der newtonschen Geometrie, die der Rückblick bemerkt, ließ diese für einen Augenblick zum großen ‚Durchblick' in die Ordnung der Dinge werden, in der sich eine Welt öffnete, die durchgängig gesetzmäßig strukturiert erschien, gerade weil das Ordnungsschema nicht vom Raum getrennt war und weil dieser geordnete Raum um die Mitte des 18. Jahrhunderts mit Evidenz erkannt werden konnte. Für einen Augenblick hatte ein auf der sinnlichen Mannigfaltigkeit liegendes Erkenntnisraster Ruhe gefunden. Diese perfekte Deckung und Einheit von Raum und Raumschema ist der Berührungspunkt von Natur und Gesellschaft, von Naturgesetz und positivem Recht und von archi-

7 Patocka 1991, 87-8.

tektonischem Raum und dem Raum der Natur. Im 18. Jahrhundert wird Gesellschaft zugleich erkannt und realisiert. Es gibt Einsichten in ihre Ordnung und zugleich den Willen zu deren Reform.

DIE MENSCHEN WERDEN WENIGER: DIE GESELLSCHAFT DER PHYSIOKRATIE UND DIE ANTRIEBE FÜR REFORMEN

Birger Priddat hat die Physiokratie als eine „Transformationsphilosophie des 18. Jahrhunderts" bezeichnet und zugleich als ein „misslungenes Experiment", das suchend und tastend zwischen Antike und Moderne stand[8]. Tatsächlich war das französische Ancien Régime in der Mitte des 18. Jahrhunderts tiefgreifenden Transformationen unterworfen, die in Wirtschaft und Gesellschaft, in Politik und Wissenschaft Ausdruck fanden, was auch Ausdruck dafür war, dass sich die absolutistische Staatskonstruktion und die Legitimation ihrer Herrschaft in einer tiefen Krise befanden. Noch zu Beginn des Jahrhunderts wurde Chastel de St. Pierre aus der *Académie française* ausgeschlossen, weil er in seinem *Discours sur la Polysynodie* die verdeckte soziale Logik des Absolutismus aufgedeckt hatte, indem er das absolutistische Regime mit der literarischen Fiktion einer ‚orientalischen Despotie' verglich[9]. Das war dreißig Jahre später ein Topos der politischen Rhetorik. Die Spannung zwischen despotischer Willkür und der Einsicht in soziale Gesetzmäßigkeiten hatte politisch enorme Sprengkraft, denn einerseits öffnete sie in der Vorstellungswelt der reformwilligen Kräfte ein nahezu grenzenloses Feld an Entwicklungsmöglichkeiten, andererseits hatten die politischen Institutionen ihre Voraussetzungen und Geltungszusammenhänge, an deren Grundlagen die oft radikalen Reformprojekte rüttelten.

Der von d'Amilaville für Diderots *Encyklopédie* verfasste Artikel *Bevölkerung*, der schon aufgrund seiner Thematik wissenschaftliche, sozialreformerische und politische Themen miteinander verband, macht die prekäre Situation deutlich. D'Amilaville geht von einer Hypothese aus, die um die Mitte des 18. Jahrhunderts allgemein geteilt wurde: Die Bevölkerung der Erde würde kontinuierlich abnehmen. Doch selbst wenn er Montesquieus pessimistische Prognose aufgreift, dass aufgrund anhaltenden Bevölkerungsschwundes die Welt dereinst eine Einöde sein würde, so kann d'Amilavilles religiös-spekulatives Empfinden in probabilistischen Andeutungen der Vorstellung einer nachmenschlichen Weltzeit nicht zustimmen. Denn „höchstwahrscheinlich wird es, solange die Erde fortbesteht, auch Menschen geben, die sie bewohnen. Vielleicht sind für ihr Dasein Menschen ebenso notwendig, wie die Erde für das Dasein des Universums notwendig ist"[10]. Montesquieu war in den Perserbriefen viel weiter gegangen. Im 112. persischen Brief lässt er Rhedi an Usbek über das demographische Problem berichten. Dieser schreibt, dass er seinen Aufenthalt in Europa zum Studium der Geschichtsschreiber nutzt „und vor allem richte ich meine Aufmerksamkeit auf die großen Veränderungen, die die Zeiten voneinander unterscheiden, so dass die Erde sich selbst kaum noch gleicht"[11]. Was aber im historischen Blick das Gesicht der Erde verwandelt, was die Katastrophe ausmacht, die er zu sehen vermeint, ist „die im Innern versteckte Krankheit, das heimliche Gift, das Siechtum, dem die Menschennatur anheimgefallen ist"[12]. Usbek wiederum ist ein feinsinniger Zweifler, der auch vor der kosmischen Tragweite seiner Skepsis nicht halt macht. Die Auslöschung der Menschheit durch Kräfte der Natur ist ihm jederzeit möglich. In der Geschichte war es ein sehr schmaler Grad, der Leben und Tod der Menschengattung voneinander trennte, und die Beunruhigung durch diesen schmalen Grad war ihm auch durch die Gesetze des Himmels nicht zu beseitigen. Nicht nur der Wandel in der Geschichte war unvorhersehbar und von zahllosen Ursachen bestimmt. Dasselbe galt für die den Sternkundigen zugängliche Beobachtung der Himmelskörper. Und weil weder Erde noch Himmel vor dem Verderben sicher waren, gab es für die persischen Briefschreiber auch keinen Rückzugsort mehr, der Beständigkeit versprach. Dafür war allerdings ein Naturverständnis grundlegend, das der Welt eine allgemeine – wiewohl gesetzmäßige – Bewegung unterstellte, aber keine Bewegung, die mit der fraglosen Existenz des Menschen in ihr zusammenge-

8 Priddat 2001, 7.
9 Brian 2001, 6.
10 D'Amilaville 1985, 685.
11 De Montesquieu 1988, 194.
12 De Montesquieu 1988, 196.

stimmt war: „Die Welt, mein lieber Rhedi, ist gegen kein Verderben gefeit, nicht einmal die Himmel sind es. Die Sternenkundigen sind die Augenzeugen ihres Wandels, und dieser ist eine ganz natürliche Folge der allgemeinen Bewegtheit der Materie. Die Erde unterliegt wie die anderen Planeten den Gesetzen des Wandels; sie ist in ihrem Inneren einem beständigen Kampf ihrer Elemente ausgesetzt. Das Meer und das Festland scheinen sich in einem fortwährenden Krieg miteinander zu befinden; jeder Augenblick bringt neue Konstellationen hervor. Die Menschen, die einen so wandelbaren Planeten bewohnen, sind nicht besser daran; zahllose Ursachen können sich vernichtend auswirken, erst recht natürlich ihre Zahl vermehren oder verringern“[13].

Montesquieu ließ metaphysisch die Möglichkeit eines Scheiterns der Menschheit zu und übergab sie dem Spiel der Kontingenz. Er machte sie für die Welt zu einem Unternehmen, dessen Ausgang ungewiss und offen war. Dass damit eine Analogie zum ökonomischen Denken des Risikos gezogen wurde, mag ihm nicht entgangen sein. Vielleicht sah er auch, dass es die Möglichkeit geben könne, dieses Risiko zu kalkulieren. Denn in diesem Wandel und trotz aller Unbeständigkeit zeichnet sich für den persischen Reisenden eine Gesetzmäßigkeit der Natur in Form einer ‚ökonomischen Ordnung‘ ab. Die natürlichen Faktoren von Krankheit und Seuchen waren eine Sache, doch erst der Verstoß gegen die natürliche Gesetzmäßigkeit hätte zu Niedergang und Entvölkerung geführt und dadurch setzt der Mensch seine Existenz aufs Spiel. Der Grund für diese metaphysische Angst liegt in einem menschlichen Verhalten, das die Kräfte der Natur durch eine widernatürliche soziale Ordnung verschwenden und verausgaben würde: „Die Natur geht immer langsam und ohne Kräfteverschwendung vor: sie überstürzt nichts, sie verlangt Mäßigung in allen Hervorbringungen, sie kennt weder Regellosigkeit noch Maßlosigkeit. Wenn man sie forciert, erschlaffen ihre Kräfte alsbald. Dann braucht sie ihre ganze Energie, um sich zu erhalten, sie verliert ihre Produktivität und Zeugungsgewalt“[14].

Montesquieu hatte damit eine Analyse der islamischen und der christlichen Gesellschaften im Auge, deren Heiratsregeln und die damit verbundenen Institutionen und sozialen Ordnungen zu jener Verschwendung natürlicher Kräfte geführt hätten, die ihm als Ursache der Entvölkerung erschienen.

Im Artikel *Bevölkerung* werden die metaphysischen Konsequenzen zwar abgeschwächt, die politischen aber verschärft. D'Amilaville greift vor allem eine Steuerpolitik an, welche die Möglichkeiten der Völker übersteigt. Die Verschwendung der Kräfte, von der Montesquieu geschrieben hatte, wird am zeitgenössischen höfischen Verhalten aufgezeigt und zur Ursache von Kriegen wie von Entvölkerung gemacht. D'Amilavilles politisch-physikalische Konzeption besteht letztlich aus zwei fundamentalen Behauptungen. Erstens entsprechen die Bedürfnisse der Völker stets den Bedürfnissen ihrer Staaten, weil die Staaten Institutionen sind, welche Völker im Interesse ihrer Bedürfnisse eingerichtet haben. Zweitens verwirklichen sich in den Bedürfnissen der Völker zugleich die Ziele der Natur und nach diesen Zielen muss jede institutionelle Ordnung ausgerichtet werden: „Die Natur hat nur zwei große Ziele: die Erhaltung des Individuums und die Fortpflanzung der Gattung. Wenn es aber wahr ist, daß alles danach strebt, zu leben oder Leben zu schenken; wenn es wahr ist, daß wir das Leben nur empfangen haben, um es weiterzugeben, so müssen wir wohl zugeben, daß jede Institution, die uns von diesem Ziel zu entfernen sucht, nicht gut ist und der Ordnung der Natur widerspricht“[15].

Folgt der Mensch der natürlichen Ordnung, so stimmen der Wille des Volkes und der des Staates zusammen und dies gewährt zugleich das Wachstum der Bevölkerung. Umgekehrt ist das Wachstum der Bevölkerung das Zeichen dafür, dass die staatlichen Institutionen der natürlichen Ordnung folgen: „Wenn die Bedürfnisse des Staats zugleich diejenigen der Völker sind, dann werden sie die notwendigen Steuern entrichten, diese werden mäßig sein, der Staat wird mächtig sein, Landwirtschaft und Handel werden blühen, und die Menschen werden zahlreich sein, weil sie sich immer im Verhältnis zu dem Wohlstand vermehren, dessen sie sich erfreuen“[16].

13 De Montesquieu 1988, 196-7.
14 De Montesquieu 1988, 199.
15 D'Amilaville 1985, 688.
16 D'Amilaville 1985, 686-7.

Die Physiokratie: Soziologisierung der Seele über den Raum

In dieser Stimmung, die von d'Amilaville scharf und polemisch zugespitzt wurde, entfaltet sich die physiokratische Soziallehre, die damit nicht nur eine ökonomische Analyse darstellt, sondern auch als sozialpolitisches Reformprogramm erscheint. Physiokratie heißt, dass die politische Ordnung und ihre positiven Institutionen mit der natürlichen Ordnung in Übereinstimmung gebracht werden müssen, damit der Mensch das Ziel der Natur – dem zuwider zu handeln ihm seine Freiheit allerdings ermöglicht – verwirklichen kann. Mercier de la Rivière nannte es den *ordre essentiel*; in ihm sind die Mittel formuliert, die zur Verwirklichung der natürlichen Zwecke notwendig sind: „Was ich *wesentliche Ordnung* nenne ist im Allgemeinen eine Verkettung der Mittel, ohne die es nicht möglich ist, das vorgegebene Ziel zu erreichen. Weil also das Glück und die Vermehrung der Menschen das *letzte* Ziel der Formierung einzelner Gesellschaften sind – so, wie wir es in den Absichten ihres ersten Stifters wahrnehmen – ist es evident, dass die essentielle Ordnung der Gesellschaft *in vollkommener Übereinstimmung mit den sozialen Institutionen steht, ohne die das Glück und diese Vermehrung nicht stattfinden können*"[17].

Was war die Bedingung, unter der Mercier diese Übereinstimmung finden konnte? Was ermöglichte eine derartige politische Physik und worin bestand sie? Den Physiokraten war es um eine juristische Interpretation einer mathematisierten Natur zu tun, die zugleich teleologisch aufgefasst wurde, indem sie die Zweckreihen, die in diesen beiden Ordnungen enthalten waren, zur Deckung brachten. Die juristische und die physikalische Ordnung ließen sich an einem absoluten Punkt aufeinander beziehen, an dem sich Recht und Notwendigkeit verbinden konnten: „Es ist lange her, dass wir aus dem römischen Recht den Satz *Jus constituit necessitas* übernommen haben und dass wir sagen, ohne die Kraft und die Gerechtigkeit dieser Redeweise zu verstehen, *dass die Notwendigkeit das Gesetz macht*. Dieses Axiom enthält jedoch eine große Wahrheit. Es lässt uns verstehen, dass das, was von *absoluter* Notwendigkeit ist, auch von *absoluter* Gerechtigkeit ist"[18].

Die physiokratische Ökonomie war nun nichts anderes als eine solche Verschränkung von Recht und Natur, indem sie die Menschen als Körper in Raum und Zeit begriff und indem sie einen Kodex natürlichen Rechts auf dem Grund der Seele entdeckte. Das cartesianische Konzept der Evidenz klärte für die Physiokraten nicht nur das Verhältnis von Subjekt und Welt in der Wahrnehmung, sondern auch das Verhältnis von positivem und natürlichem Gesetz. Die Evidenz dessen, was gerecht und notwendig ist, erfasst den Geist unmittelbar, ohne Vermittlung durch äußere Zeichen. Mercier de la Rivière versteht diesen Zusammenhang als Gesetzbuch (*code*) der Natur, das der Mensch mit Hilfe des natürlichen Lichts zu lesen vermag: „Die Gerechtigkeit und die Notwendigkeit dieser essenziellen und universellen Naturgesetze sind von solcher Evidenz, dass sie sich in allen Menschen manifestieren, ohne die Hilfe eines sinnlichen Zeichens. Sie sind auch nicht in die gewöhnlichen Gesetzessammlungen aufgenommen. Sie finden sich im Gesetzbuch (*code*) der Natur selbst aufgeschrieben und wir lesen sie dort alle deutlich (*distinctement*) mit Hilfe der Vernunft, jenes Lichts, das *illuminat omnem hominem venientem in hunc mundum*"[19].

Auf ihrem Höhepunkt, den die Buchdruckkultur im 18. Jahrhundert erreicht hatte, konnte über die alles durchdringenden Linien der Schrift eine Verbindung zwischen dem natürlichen und dem positiven Recht hergestellt werden und das setzte tatsächlich voraus, dass die Seele verrechtlicht und vertextet

17 Le Mercier de la Rivière 1910, 19: „Ce que j'appelle un *ordre essentiel* est, en général, un enchaînement de moyens sans lesquels il est impossible de remplir l'objet qu'on s'est proposé. Ainsi l'objet *ultérieur* de la formation des sociétés particulieres, tel que nous l'appercevons dans les intentions de leur premier Instituteur, étant le bonheur et la multiplication des hommes, il devient évident que l'ordre essentiel des société est l'*accord parfait des institutions sociales sans lesquelles ce bonheur et cette multiplication ne pourroient avoir lieu*".

18 Le Mercier de la Rivière 1910, 9: „Il y a long-tems que nous avons adopté l'axiome du droit Romain, *Jus constituit necessitas,* et que sans connoître la force et la justice de cette façon de parler, nous disons que *la nécessité fait la loi.* Cet axiome cependant renferme une grande vérité; il nous apprend ce qui est d'une nécessité *absolue,* est aussi d'une justice *absolue*; […]".

19 Le Mercier de la Rivière 1910, 56: „La justice et la nécessité de ces loix naturelles, essentielles et universelles, sont d'une telle évidence, qu'elles se manifestent à tous les hommes, sans le secours d'aucun signe sensible: aussi ne sont-elles point insérées dans les recueils ordinaires des loix; c'est dans le code même de la nature qu'elles se trouvent écrites, et nous les y lisons tous distinctement à l'aide de la raison, de cette lumiere qui *illuminat omnem hominem venientem in hunc mundum*".

wurde. Die Seele wurde in dem Maße juridisch, als das Subjekt natürlich wurde und damit war der Gehorsam der Untertanen (*sujets*) nicht mehr durch eine Geste der Unterwerfung, sondern durch einen Akt der Einsicht in das eigene Wesen begründet. Es ist ein neuer Zusammenhang von Wissen und Gewissen (im Französischen bezeichnet *conscience* beides) der an jener Stelle auftrat, an der sich die Zweifel an der absolutistischen Ordnung regten. Doch die Deckung positiver und natürlicher Gesetze war nicht genug, wenn die Einsicht in die Notwendigkeit ihrer Kongruenz nicht in den Seelen der Menschen verankert werden konnte. Mercier hatte auch dafür einen Begriff mit weitreichenden Konsequenzen gefunden: die „Religion des internen Forums", Religion eines zugleich individuellen und kollektiven Wesens, das sein internes Forum, sein Gewissen, zum Ort der sozialen Ordnung macht: „Es reicht nicht aus, dass die positiven Gesetze den natürlichen und essenziellen Gesetzen der Gesellschaft exakt konform gehen: Diese erste Bedingung verlangt für ihre Sicherung eine konstante Unterwerfung. Wenn die erste erfüllt ist, bedarf es noch einer zweiten Bedingung, diese ist, wie wir noch sehen werden, dass diese Konformität in einer Weise erkannt werden muss, dass niemand daran zweifeln kann. Denn die Gesetze können nur *durch die Religion des internen Forums* getreulich beachtet werden, eine Religion, die sich nur durch unzweifelhafte Erkenntnis (*connoissance*) ihrer Gerechtigkeit und Notwendigkeit etablieren kann"[20].

Das interne Forum war also ein Ort des Gesetzes und eines rationalisierten Glaubens geworden, aber zur Erfassung sozialer Ordnung musste es sich zugleich in den Raum der Gesellschaft ausdehnen. Diesen Raum suchten die Physiokraten schematisch zu erfassen. Damit deckten sie die Ordnung eines neuartigen Raumes auf, den sie als Funktionszusammenhang mit Bezug auf den menschlichen Körper zu beschreiben begannen.

Was Mercier und andere damit zu schaffen hofften, war eine Deckung von Macht und Wahrheit, die sich im König als einem absoluten geometrischen Ort der Vergesellschaftung verschränken und verkörpern sollte. Raum, Zeit und Kraft erhielten im König zugleich einen Ort des Ausdrucks, denn im König wurde die Einheit der natürlichen Ordnung und ihrer Gesetze sichtbar, und ein Schema des Handelns, denn der König war durch seine Gesetzgebung das Exekutivorgan dieser Ordnung. Und dies war deswegen möglich, weil das Raumschema und der soziale Raum innerhalb der empiristischen Epistemologie des Zeitalters nicht differenzierbar waren.

Wir finden diese neuartige Verschränkung von Raum, Zeit und menschlicher Kraft in einer kleinen Schrift zum Naturrecht von François Quesnay aus dem Jahr 1765. „Das Naturrecht der Menschen," so fängt Quesnay an, „unterscheidet sich darin vom legitimen Recht oder vom Recht, das durch menschliche Gesetze festgelegt wird, dass es mit Evidenz durch das Licht der Vernunft erkannt werden kann. Und durch diese Evidenz alleine ist es verbindlich, unabhängig von jeglichem Zwang"[21]. Das Wissen um das Naturrecht ist für Quesnay in eine natürliche Theologie eingebunden, die um den göttlichen Autor des Naturrechts weiß[22].

Naturrecht ist das Recht des Menschen auf Dinge, von denen er Genuss (*jouissance*) bekommen kann. Aber dieses Recht ist sehr begrenzt. Es „ist dem einer jeden Schwalbe auf alle Fliegen ähnlich, die sich in der Luft befinden, aber die sich in der Realität auf jene beschränken, die die Schwalbe durch ihre Arbeit fassen kann oder durch die nach ihrem Bedürfnis geordnete Suche"[23]. Quesnay hat hier bereits einen Raum bestimmt, in dem er gemäß Heidegger das Vorhandene und das Zuhandene differenziert. Arbeit wird darin nicht als Produktion verstanden, sondern als Beziehung zu den Dingen, die

20 Le Mercier de la Rivière 1910, 61: „Ce n'est point assez que les loix positives soient exactement conformes aux loix naturelles et essentielles de la société: cette premiere condition requise pour leur assurer une soumission constante, étant remplie, il en faut encore une seconde, qui est, comme on vient de le voir, que cette conformité soit connue de maniere que personne ne puisse en douter; car elles ne peuvent être fidelement observées que *par religion de for intérieur*, religion qui ne peut s'établir que sur une connoissance indubitable, de leur justice et leur nécessité".

21 Quesnay 1991, 72: „Le droit naturel des hommes diffère du droit légitime ou du droit décerné par les lois humaines, en ce qu'il est reconnu avec évidence par les lumières de la raison, et que par cette évidence seule, il est obligatoire indépendamment d'aucune contrainte; [...]".

22 Quesnay 1991, 72: „Souvent le droit *légitime* restreint le droit naturel, parce que les lois des hommes ne sont pas aussi parfaites que les lois de l'Auteur de la nature, [...]".

23 Quesnay 1991, 73: „Car *son droit à tout* est semblable au droit de chaque hirondelle à tous les moucherons qui voltigent dans l'air, mais qui dans la réalité se borne à ceux qu'elle peut saisir par son travail ou ses recherches ordonnées par le besoin".

sich im Raum des Zuhandenen befinden. Diese Beziehungen messen den Raum aus und bestimmen seine Gestalt. Alle Lebewesen erschließen sich durch ihre Arbeit Räume. Der Mensch unterscheidet sich von ihnen aber darin, dass die Arbeit und der durch sie bestimmte Raum eine Geschichte haben. Diese Geschichte stellt Quesnay in einer Abfolge von Stadien dar, in denen der Mensch im Bezug auf sein Naturrecht betrachtet werden kann.

Im Stand der reinen Natur oder der vollständigen Unabhängigkeit machen die Menschen nur durch Arbeit und Suche Gebrauch von ihrem Naturrecht auf die benötigten Dinge. Das Naturrecht aller auf alles reduziert sich auf das, was sich der Einzelne durch die Aktivitäten des Jagens, Fischens oder Sammelns pflanzlicher Nahrung verschaffen kann. Der erste Raum, der durch die Arbeit der Einzelnen solcherart geöffnet wird, könnte als eindimensionaler nomadischer Raum bezeichnet werden. Die Menschen folgen den Spuren von Tieren, sie suchen nach Orten, an denen Früchte wachsen oder sie folgen den Flüssen auf der Suche nach Fischgründen.

Im nächsten Stand wird das Naturrecht der Menschen in Bezug aufeinander betrachtet, also im Zustand der Menge. Für Quesnay gibt es in diesem Moment noch keine positiven Gesetze, welche die Menge zu einer Gesellschaft unter einer souveränen Autorität organisieren würden. Er betrachtet diese Ordnung als „Stamm von Wilden in der Wildnis, die dort von der natürlichen Produktion des Territoriums leben und wo sie sich notwendigerweise den Gefahren der Räuberei aussetzen“[24]. In diesem Stand können sich die Menschen nicht mit jenen Reichtümern versorgen, die ihnen aus Landwirtschaft und Viehzucht erwachsen würden, weil es keine Schutzmacht (*puissance tutélaire*) gibt, die ihr Eigentum sichert, um diesen Tätigkeiten nachgehen zu können. Hier tauchen im Text zum ersten Mal die Begriffe Territorium und Reichtümer auf, sowie die Sicherung des Eigentums, eine zentrale Kategorie aller Physiokraten. Das Territorium ist ein zweidimensionaler Raum, in dem sich Familien lose bewegen. Auch wenn die Menschen in diesem Territorium durch Arbeitsteilung mehr an Gütern erarbeiten können als im reinen Naturzustand, so können sie kaum Reichtümer anhäufen, da sie ständig der Gefahr des Raubs ausgesetzt erscheinen.

Im dritten Stand wird nun das Naturrecht der Menschen beschrieben, die unter einer souveränen Autorität zur Gesellschaft vereint sind. Quesnay geht es nicht um die souveräne Autorität selbst. Sie kann demokratisch, aristokratisch oder monarchisch verfasst sein. Die Regierungsform reduziert sich nur auf die positiven Gesetze und berührt nicht die Essenz des Naturrechts. Durch die Abfolge von Reichen und Regierungsformen zieht sich als transzendente Größe der reine Naturstand des Menschen und damit sein Naturrecht. Reiche vergehen, wenn sie dem Naturrecht zuwider handeln. Das reine Naturrecht ist hier die elementare Form, die durch Analyse gewonnen werden kann, und befindet sich an der Schnittlinie des Empirischen und des Transzendentalen, wie Foucault sagt. Und genau an diesem Punkt wendet Quesnay den Blick von den unvorhersehbaren Bewegungen in der Geschichte der Reiche zu den Bewegungen der Himmelskörper, um dort das Maß und die Bestimmung von Ort und Zeit in einem dritten Raum zu finden: „Um die Ordnung der Zeiten und der Räume zu erkennen, um die Navigation zu steuern und den Handel sicherzustellen, wurde es notwendig, mit Präzision die Bewegungsgesetze der Himmelskörper zu beobachten (auch: zu beachten: *observer*) und zu berechnen. Um die Reichweite des Naturrechts der Menschen, die zu einer Gesellschaft vereinigt sind, zu erkennen, muss man sich auch nach den Naturgesetzen der bestmöglichen Regierung richten. Die Regierung, unter welche die Menschen gebracht werden müssen, besteht also aus der natürlichen Ordnung und aus derjenigen positiven Ordnung, die für die Menschen, die zur Gesellschaft vereinigt sind, am vorteilhaftesten ist“[25].

Dieser Raum, in dem Handel und Navigation stattfinden und der zugleich durch die Sicherungsmacht des Souveräns geschützt werden soll, ist der dreidimensionale ökonomische Raum der Physiokratie. In ihm nimmt der Ökonom den Rang eines Philosophen ein, der im Himmelsbetrachter, im *contemplator*

24 Quesnay 1991, 80: „[...], il faut les envisager comme des peuplades de sauvages dans des déserts, qui y vivraient des productions naturelles du territoire, ou qui s'exposeraient par nécessité aux dangers du brigandage, [...]“.

25 Quesnay 1991, 82-3: „Pour connaître l'ordre des temps et des lieux, pour régler la navigation et assurer le commerce, il fallu observer et calculer avec précision les lois du mouvement des corps célestes; il faut de même, pour connaître l'étendue du droit naturel des hommes réunis en société, se fixer aux lois naturelles constitives du meilleur gouvernement possible. Ce gouvernement auquel les hommes doivent être assujettis consiste dans l'ordre naturel et dans l'ordre positif, les plus avantageux aux hommes réunis en société“.

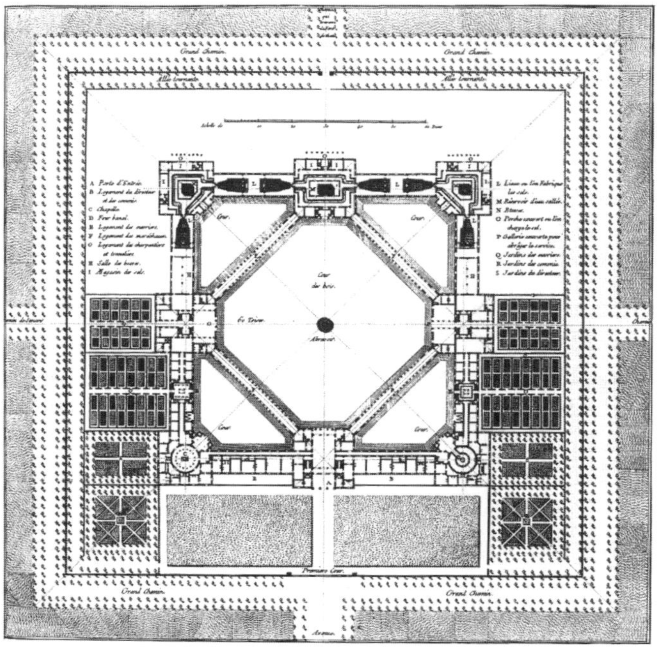

Abb. 1. Claude-Nicolas Ledoux: Erster Entwurf für die Saline von Chaux. Nach: Kruft 1989, Abb. 108.

coeli, seit Thales seinen Prototyp hatte[26]. In der dritten Dimension stehen also sowohl der Souverän, der die Schutzmacht auszuüben hat, als auch der Sternenbeobachter, der in den Bewegungen der Himmelskörper die Gesetze erkennt, die innerhalb dieses gesicherten Raumes nachzuahmen sind. Das ist in einer anderen Formulierung die Bedingung, um das natürliche und das positive Gesetz zur Deckung zu bringen. Die Identifikation der politischen und der astronomischen Achse eröffnet den ökonomischen Raum.

Mit der physiokratischen Ökonomie formuliert Quesnay keine politische Metaphysik als Grundlage des Staats mehr, wie sie in der barocken Konstruktion des Sonnenkönigs eine Fassung erhielt, sondern eine politische Physik. Politische Ökonomie taucht in jenem Moment der Geschichte auf, als der Staat über seine neue analytisch-geometrische Bestimmung als verwaltbares Territorium gefasst wird. Mit politischer Ökonomie lässt sich der Staat machen und die Macht des Staats messen. Sie verzichtet auf das übernatürliche Licht als Symbol für die Teilhabe am mystischen Körper des Königs, sondern orientiert sich vielmehr am natürlichen Licht der Sterne, das Bewegungsgesetze einsehbar macht. Die Physiokraten hatten einen sozialen Raum konstituiert, in dem der Fixsternhimmel und seine geometrischen Bewegungen Vorbild für eine Naturgesetzlichkeit wurden, die durch den Ökonomen erkannt und durch den König verwirklicht werden sollte. Im König verkörperte sich keine Allegorie, sondern das Gesetz der Gesellschaft selbst. Seine absolute Position sollte es möglich machen, dass sich absolute Notwendigkeit und absolute Gerechtigkeit bündeln und über das Konzept der Evidenz in jedes einzelne Subjekt ausstrahlen konnten.

Raum und Gesetz in der Architektur: Die Salinenstadt Chaux

Dieser Raum, wie er im Übergang der barocken politischen Welt des Absolutismus zu einer ebenso absolutistischen ‚Verwaltungslandschaft' konstituiert wird, lässt sich selbst nicht sichtbar machen. Wir können ihn nur anhand seiner Materialisierungen kennen lernen und uns plastisch vor Augen führen. Die führenden Architekten des Zeitalters machen an den Bauformen deutlich, was die Verwaltungsbeamten in ihren formalen Operationen für die Staatskonstruktion umzusetzen suchen. Ihre Ideen und

26 Blumenberg 1987.

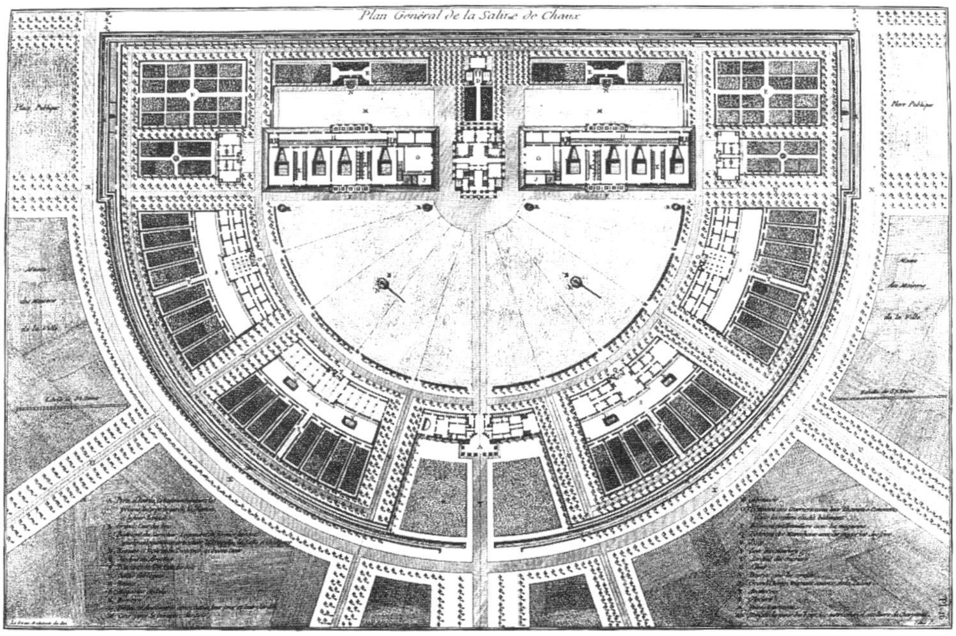

Abb. 2. Claude-Nicolas Ledoux: Plan der Saline von Chaux. Nach: Kruft 1989, Abb. 109.

Programme kreuzen sich an den Beziehungen jeweiliger Auftraggeberschaft und bearbeiten den Raum von ihrer jeweiligen ‚sozialen Perspektive' aus. Am Beispiel des Architekten Claude-Nicolas Ledoux werden diese Kreuzungspunkte sichtbar. Ledoux ist einerseits Hofbeamter. Als Architekt war er für die staatliche Forstbehörde (*Service des Eaux et Fôrets*) sowie für die Brücken und Wegebehörde (*Ponts et Chaussées*) unter Leitung des Ingenieurs Jean-Rodolphe Perronet tätig, dessen Assistent er 1771 wurde. Er arbeitete auch für reformorientierte Administratoren wie die Trudaines und Turgot, den Intendanten des Limoges und späteren *Controleur Générale des Finances*. Auf der anderen Seite versteht sich der Architekt als Schöpfer einer neuen Welt, der Modernisierungen wie Industrie, öffentliche Wirtschaft, staatliche Planung und das Begreifen dieser Momente als Funktionen von Raum zu integrieren hatte.

Architektur, so hat Eugen Rosenstock-Huessy einmal bemerkt, ist gefrorene Soziologie[27]. Das stimmt für die Architektur Ledoux' insofern, als sie in derselben Konjunktur steht, in der die Sozialwissenschaften im 18. Jahrhundert Gestalt annehmen. Architektur ist in dieser Formulierung nicht nur eine Verortung und Verräumlichung des Sozialen, gleichsam gefrorene Gesellschaft, sondern gefrorene Gesellschaftslehre, ein Korpus von Wissen über die Gesellschaft. Diese Ausgangslage ist der Hintergrund für die vielleicht wichtigste Schöpfung des Architekten Ledoux, da sie auch im Zentrum seines architekturtheoretischen Schaffens steht: die Salinenstadt Chaux. Die architekturtheoretischen Überlegungen hatte Ledoux in seinem Buch *L'Architecture considérée sous le rapport de l'art, des mœurs et de la législation* festgehalten, das er in der Zeit seiner Inhaftierung 1793 zu schreiben begonnen und erst 1804 publiziert hatte. An ihr wird die Eigenart einer vorrevolutionären ‚Soziologie' sichtbar, die ein „revolutionärer Architekt"[28] zu verwirklichen sucht. Der Architekt wird der Lenker der sozialen Entwicklung, der sich als Rivale Gottes neben den König stellt und Architektur als eine Führungswissenschaft durch Kunst begreift: „Als Rivale Gottes, der die runde Masse erschaffen hat, hat er mehr als dieser gemacht. Er hat Berge eingeebnet, die Furcht erregten. Er hat Schluchten ausgehöhlt, um das klare Wasser frei hindurch strömen zu lassen. Er hat die Wildnis beschönigt (*embelli*)"[29].

27 Rosenstock Huessy 1958, 18.

28 Der Begriff ‚revolutionärer Architekt' stammt von Emil Kaufmann, mit der er eine Gruppe von Architekten in der zweiten Hälfte des 18. Jahrhunderts charakterisieren wollte, welche ihm die politische Revolution vorwegzunehmen schienen.

29 Ledoux 1804, 103: „Rival du dieu qui créa la masse ronde, il aura plus fait que lui, il l'aura comblé les montagnes qui effraient la timidité; il aura creusé les ravins pour faire coule librement les eaux limpides; il aura embelli les déserts".

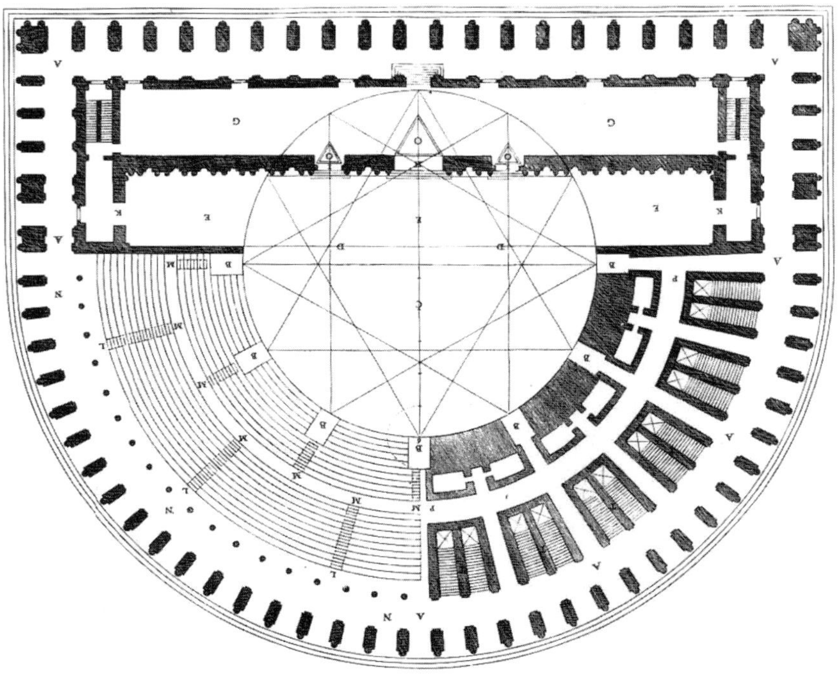

Abb. 3. Claude Perrault: Rekonstruktion des römischen Theaters nach Vitruv (1684). Nach: Kruft 1989, Abb. 111.

Architektur scheint dazu berufen, gerade die sich im Laufe des Jahrhunderts entwickelnden politischen und sozialen Wissensformen zu bündeln und zu ordnen. Der Architekt ist sozusagen dem Ideal der Gelehrsamkeit gemäß der enzyklopädische Mensch: „Was sage ich? Gibt es etwas, das ihm fremd sein sollte? Diese Kunst, die alle Kenntnisse in sich versammelt. Ist sie nicht durch fühlbare Anziehung mit der allgemeinen Verwaltung, mit der höfischen Politik, mit den allgemeinen und den besonderen Sitten, mit den Wissenschaften, mit der Literatur, mit der ruralen Ökonomie [d.i. die physiokratische Ökonomie, Ch.S.], mit dem Handel verbunden?“[30]

Das Projekt der Salinenstadt Chaux vereinigt nun all diese Kenntnisse und führt damit auch die Räume zusammen, die mit ihnen verbunden sind: den politischen Raum, den Raum der physiokratischen Ökonomie, den des Handels und letztlich einen sozialen Raum. Die verschiedenen Entwurfsstadien machen eine Entwicklung der Absichten und Konzepte Ledoux' deutlich[31]. Der erste Entwurf (Abb. 1) ist vor dem Tod Ludwig LV. im Jahr 1774 entstanden. Er orientiert sich noch ganz an der Hospital-Tradition und der abgeschlossenen Manufakturanlagen der Zeit Colberts. Ledoux unterwarf die Anlage einer strengen geometrischen Ordnung und suchte die Wege zwischen den einzelnen Arbeitsstationen möglichst kurz zu halten und damit einer Ökonomisierung von Zeit und Raum zu unterwerfen.

Der zweite Entwurf (Abb. 2, Taf. 40), welcher tatsächlich zur Ausführung gelangte, geht nun deutlich andere Wege. Ledoux entschied sich diesmal, die Anlage halbkreisförmig zu planen und den kompakten Block in eine Reihe von Pavillons aufzulösen. Verantwortlich dafür war gewiss die seit den 1770er-Jahren geführte Auseinandersetzung um die Konstruktion von Krankenhäusern, die sich vor allem um Fragen der Hygiene und Durchlüftung drehte. In diesem Rahmen setzte sich die Auflösung der Blöcke in Pavillons durch. Ledoux folgte diesen Diskussionen aufmerksam und nahm auch darauf Bezug. Der Grund für die Wahl der halbkreisförmigen Anlage war jedoch ein anderer. Der Architekt wollte damit

30 Ledoux 1904, 17: „Que dis-je? est-il quelque chose qui lui soit étranger? Ce art qui rassemble toutes les connoissances, n'est il pas lié par des attractions sensible, à l'administration générale, à la politique des cours, aux mœurs publiques et particulières, aux sciences, à la littérature, à l'économie rurale, au commerce?“

31 Zum Verhältnis der publizierten Entwürfe zur tatsächlich realisierten Stadt und damit zu Ledoux' Stellung zwischen Ancien Régime und Revolution s. Kruft 1989, 112-26.

die Empfindung evozieren, dass es sich bei der Salinenstadt um ein großes Theater handle. Ledoux besaß die Vitruv-Übersetzung Perraults, die die Rekonstruktion eines römischen Theaters enthielt (Abb. 3)[32]. An ihr konnte er sich orientieren. Anthony Vidler hat darauf hingewiesen, dass die Arbeiten am Entwurf von Chaux mit der Gestaltung eines richtigen Theaters parallel liefen, das in Besançon errichtet werden sollte. Dieses Theater stellte eine mikrokosmische Variante zum ‚Industrie-Theater' von Chaux dar[33]. Das Theater kann sowohl als Analogie der Gesellschaft als auch als Allegorie von Ledoux' sozialreformerischen Plänen verstanden werden. In Chaux führen der Direktor und die Arbeiter das Stück der Salzproduktion auf. Das Beispiel der Arbeit soll Antrieb moralischen Fortschritts sein. Entsprechend der physiokratischen Wirtschaftstheorie wird Arbeit in ihrer moralischen und nicht in ihrer produktiven Qualität verstanden. Indem Ledoux aber der Arbeit den Status eines Elements des Theaterspiels verleiht, gibt er ihr auch die Würde, ein Bestandteil der Gesellschaft zu sein, die sich in diesem Spiel erkennt. Neu ist nun, dass die Zuseher des Stücks zugleich diejenigen sind, die es aufführen. Das Theater ist nichts anderes als ein Schema, das die Umsetzung des Entwurfs in den sozialen Raum zu leiten hatte. Es organisierte die Blicke und Handlungen, es klärte die Positionen und Bewegungen.

Die mehrschichtige Verbindung von Industrieraum und Theater zum Industrie-Theater hat Ledoux in einem allegorischen Bild gefasst. Dieses Bild klärt die Funktionsweise des Übergangs vom zweidimensionalen Entwurf zum dreidimensionalen Theaterraum. Das Bild zeigt das Auge des Direktors, in dem sich der leere, doch gegliederte Zuschauerraum widerspiegelt. Aus dem Hintergrund des Auges dringt ein Lichtstrahl in die Tiefe des Raumes. Bezogen auf Chaux ist das Auge dort positioniert, wo sich das Haus des Direktors befindet. Anthony Vidler schreibt, dass es eine Beziehung zwischen dem Direktor der Saline und den Arbeitern ebenso wiedergibt, wie jene zwischen einem Gesetzgeber und seinem Volk, wie Rousseau es im *Contrat Social* dargelegt hatte[34]. Vor dem Hintergrund der Überlegungen zur Physiokratie und der Beziehung, die sie zwischen der Verrechtlichung der Seele und der politisch-physikalischen Konstitution des ökonomischen Raumes durch die Schutzmacht des Königs zu etablieren suchte, wird aber auch deutlich, dass das Theater-Auge und der Raum, den es durch sein Licht erschließt, eine zu Quesnays ökonomischem Raum analoge Konstruktion eröffnet. Das natürliche Licht und die Position des Direktors und damit letztlich des Königs werden in eins gesetzt. Da Ledoux seit 1771 *Inspecteur des Salines de Franche-Comté* und damit selbst ein Funktionär der absolutistischen Verwaltung war, hatte er eine Position inne, von der aus er diese Konstruktion nicht nur entwerfen, sondern auch umsetzen konnte.

In der barocken Konstruktion war es das metaphysische Licht des Königs, das sich regelmäßig abgestuft auf alle ergoss, die am mystischen Körper des Königs Teil hatten. Der Lichtkörper des Königs war der politische Raum. Nun ist es das natürliche Licht der Aufklärung, das sich nicht nur den Sternen zuwendet, sondern auch der im (Industrie)-Theater versammelten Gesellschaft. Um die Position des Architekten zu verstehen, müssen wir ihn in dieser Krise des barocken Symbolismus und der allegorischen Repräsentation des Königs erkennen. Der Architekt muss dort eine neue symbolische Struktur erschaffen, einen neuen symbolischen Raum stiften und ausleuchten, wo das Licht der politischen Metaphysik dunkel wurde.

Was waren aber die Voraussetzungen in der Kunst, damit Ledoux' Projekt gelingen konnte? Was verlieh seinem Entwurf die ‚Gesetzeskraft', von der die Physiokraten sprachen? In seiner Schrift *L'Architecture* sucht Ledoux den Schnittpunkt zwischen Natur und Gesellschaft zu bestimmen, indem er zwei Verträge konstruiert, die erst zusammen diese Vermittlung leisten sollten. Diese Verträge entwirft er in der besonderen Form stiller Verträge, *contrats tacites*. Es sind Verträge, die auf einer stillschweigenden Übereinkunft oder Gewohnheit beruhen. Der erste Vertrag bezieht sich auf jenes Problem, das sich aus der Diskussion der Charaktere im Rahmen der ‚sprechenden Architektur' (*architecture parlante*) ergibt: Ist die Beziehung zwischen dem äußerlich Dargestellten und dem innerlich Intendierten auch aufrichtig? Warum soll man daran glauben? Diese Konstruktion zeigt an, dass die Repräsentation von Bedeutung nicht mehr selbstverständlich ist und nach einer neuen Legitimation verlangt. An dieser Stelle setzt Ledoux den Vertrag der Einbildung oder der Einbildungskraft (*imagination*) ein: „Die Ein-

32 Kruft 1989, 114.
33 Vidler 1987, 39-40
34 Vidler 1987, 40.

Abb. 4. Claude-Nicolas Ledoux: Perspektivische Ansicht der Saline von Chaux. Nach: Kruft 1989, Abb. 122.

bildungskraft ist ein stiller Vertrag zwischen demjenigen, der wahrnimmt und dem Künstler, der ihm zu denken gibt"[35].

Diese Vorstellung war gerade in der Welt des Theaters nicht ungewöhnlich, in der die aufrichtige Darstellung eines Charakters Teil eines stillschweigenden Übereinkommens zwischen Publikum und Schauspieler war. Der Charakter ist auch in der physiokratischen Soziallehre eine Schwelle oder ein Siegel, das natürliche und positive Gesetze miteinander verknüpft. Er soll sicher stellen, dass sich hinter der positiven Ordnung keine willkürlichen Setzungen befinden, die doch nur Anlass zu Widersprüchen und Konflikten innerhalb einer Gesellschaft sind. Er ist aus der Sicht der Physiokraten aber nur dann gewährleistet, wenn er sich in einem Zusammenhang mit der unmittelbar gegebenen Evidenz befindet: „Aber wie die gesetzgebende Macht nur durch die Einrichtung guter positiver Gesetze eingesetzt werden kann, Gesetze, deren letzter Grund darin besteht, dass Gott selbst sie diktiert hat und gemäß denen die ganze Gesellschaft regiert werden soll, so ist diese Macht im Gesetzgeber nicht mehr als *das exklusive Recht, durch sinnliche Zeichen anderen Menschen die Resultate der natürlichen und wesentlichen Gesetze der Gesellschaft erfahrbar zu machen, nachdem diese Macht ihm evident geworden ist und sie mit dem Siegel seiner Autorität versehen wurde, um ihnen einen Charakter einzuprägen, der für alle Geister und alle Willen der Fixpunkt ihrer Vereinigung sein soll*"[36].

Der Künstler ist nun derjenige, der für die Stimmigkeit dieses Ereignisses bürgt, weil er sich nicht auf einen regionalen Brauch beruft, sondern auf die Natur, die er dank seines Genies nachzuahmen berufen ist. Wie der Gesetzgeber, also der König, wird der Architekt zu einem Punkt der Einheit, der die Gesetze der Natur sichtbar machen soll. Der König vermittelt die sichtbaren Zeichen, die aus der Kodifikation im Rahmen seines positiven Rechts erwachsen. Der Architekt vermittelt sie in den sichtbaren Zeichen

35 Ledoux 1804, 78: „L'imagination est un contrat tacite entre celui qui conçoit et l'artiste qui donne à penser".

36 Mercier de la Rivière 1910, 81-2: „Mais comme le pouvoir législatif ne peut être institué que pour établir de bonnes loix positives, des loix dont la raison primitive soit dans celle que Dieu nous a dictées lui-même, et selon lesquelles toute société doit être gouvernée, ce pouvoir n'est plus dans le Législateur que *le droit exclusif de manifester par des signes sensibles aux autres hommes, les résultats des loix naturelles et essentielles de la société, après qu'ils lui sont devenu évidents, et de le sceller du sceau de son autorité, pour leur imprimer un caractère qui soit pour tous les esprits et toutes les volontés le point fixe de leur réunion*".

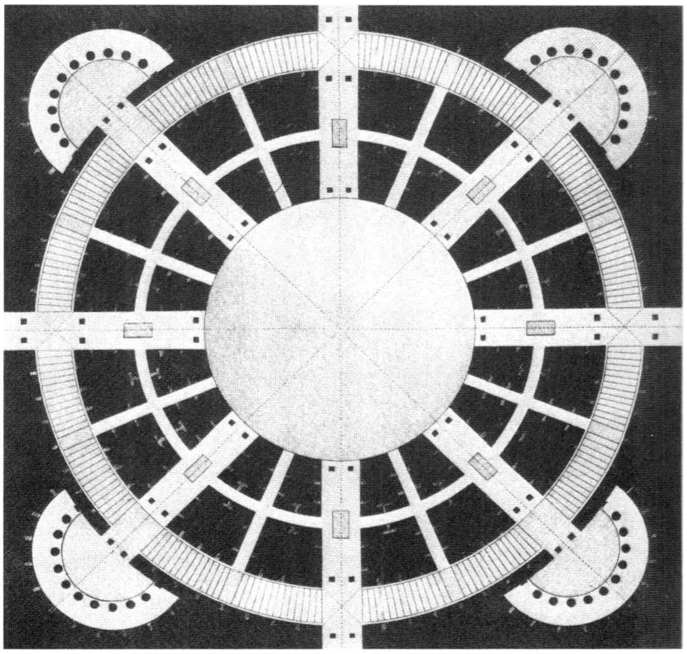

Abb. 5. Claude-Nicolas Ledoux: Grundriss des Friedhofs von Chaux. Nach: Gallet 1983, 242 Abb. 425.

seiner Bauprogramme. Und wie die positiven Gesetze nur aus Kalkülen folgende Resultate der einfachen und evidenten Naturgesetze der Gesellschaft sind, so sind auch die Bauformen Ledoux' Effekte der einfachen natürlichen Formen. Eine Reihe von Entwürfen ergeben sich etwa daraus, dass er ein einfaches Schema von neun Quadraten horizontal und vertikal abwandelte.

Die Referenz des Stücks ist die Darstellung der Natur und damit der sozialen Ordnung, weshalb Ledoux noch einen zweiten *contrat tacite* einführt. Dieser Vertrag eröffnet eine vertikale Dimension und kreuzt so die erste zwischen Künstler und Betrachter. In ihm wird die Stadt Chaux ein Ort, eine von der Welt isolierte Welt und insofern eine Natur in der Natur, in der die stillschweigenden Voraussetzungen der natürlichen Ordnung anerkennbar werden sollen. Der Mensch soll darin in der Arbeit jenem Versprechen genüge tun, das die Natur ihm in ihrer Fruchtbarkeit angekündigt hat: „Es ist eine von der Welt isolierte Welt; es ist ein arbeitsames Volk, das alle Samen sich entwickeln und aufblühen lässt, welche die Natur in ihrem stillen Vertrag mit den Menschen fruchtbar macht“[37].

In der doppelten Beziehung zwischen Natur und Mensch einerseits, zwischen Mensch und Künstler andererseits übersetzt der Architekt die wissenschaftlichen Einsichten aus dem Naturvertrag in ästhetische Symbole des Vertrags der Einbildungskraft und diese setzt er in Architektur um, damit sie sich in die Gesellschaft einschreiben können. Gesellschaft wird in Chaux zu theatralisierter Natur. Dafür ist das Industrie-Theater Symbol.

Diese letzte Konsequenz fand in Ledoux' utopischer Weiterführung des Salinenprojekts Ausdruck, in der er nicht die Position des Direktors und das natürliche Licht zusammenführt wie im Theater-Auge, sondern in der er dem Direktor und letztlich dem Architekten selbst die Position des philosophischen *contemplator coeli* zugewiesen hat. Dieser Entwurf ist allerdings so utopisch geblieben wie der Anspruch des Architekten auf universales Leitungswissen der Gesellschaft.

Im dritten Entwurf, der auch noch auf die Zeit vor der Revolution zurückgeht, wird der erste Halbkreis um einen zweiten ergänzt und die Stadt in eine Ellipse verwandelt (Abb. 4). Damit gewinnt die Salinenstadt eine neue raumzeitliche und kosmische Dimension. Sie erscheint als Steigerung des englischen Landschaftsgartens zur Gartenstadt erweitert, die im Zentrum sich schneidender Straßenzüge steht und überhaupt im Schnittpunkt aller Märkte des Königreichs liegen sollte. Dieses Zentrum nun fasst Ledoux

37 Ledoux 1804, 74: „C'est un monde isolé du monde; c'est un peuple laborieux qui développe et fait éclore tous les germes que la terre, dans son contrat tacite avec les humains, a promis de féconder“.

Abb. 6. Claude-Nicolas Ledoux: Schnitt des Friedhofs von Chaux. Nach: Gallet 1983, 243 Abb. 426.

in Anspielung auf das Zentralgestirn und die Sternenbahn. Die newtonsche Symbolisierung im Zeichen der Astronomie ersetzt die theatralische Repräsentation der barocken Form. Kaufmann hat im Aufgeben der barocken Emblematik den Schritt hinaus und das Hervortreten des revolutionären Architekten erblickt[38]. Die barocken Naturallegorisierungen waren für Ledoux nur mehr schlechtes Theater. Doch dann spielte der König auch nur mehr schlechtes Theater oder „Deadly Theatre“ wie Peter Brook es in seinem Buch *The empty space* nennt[39]. Ledoux musste ein neues „Heiliges Theater“[40] erfinden, das eine neue Beziehung zwischen dem Sichtbaren und dem Unsichtbaren errichtet.

Das Verhältnis zwischen dem Sichtbaren und dem Unsichtbaren erhält seinen Ausdruck innerhalb der Sichtbarkeit in einer neuen Verteilung von hellem und ‚dunklem Raum‘[41]. Den dunklen Raum des Todes, die Nekropole von Chaux (Abb. 5 u. 6), hatte Ledoux als Spiegel zur Stadt der Lebenden konzipiert – Spiegel und zugleich Schatten und dunkle Seite einer Welt, die in den transparenten Räumen der Aufklärung gegenwärtig und wirksam war[42].

Dreigeschossige unterirdische Galerien führen radial von Katakombenräumen mit halbkreisförmigem Grundriss in einen kugelförmigen Raum von etwa siebzig Metern Durchmesser. Diese sind wiederum durch kreisrunde Gänge miteinander verbunden. Die untere Halbkugel des zentralen Raumes ist durch gewölbte Fenster zu den Galerien hin offen. Die obere Hälfte, die aus der Erde herausragt, ist vollkommen glatt und sollte dem Betrachter „ein Bild des Nichts“[43] vermitteln. Die Kugel selbst hat

38 Kaufmann 1952, 514: „Commenting on the fountains, Ledoux inveighs against Baroque animism and illusionism, as ‚les tromperies de l'art'. He ridicules theatrical statuary, e.g. a Thetis pressing the water from her hair, or a Neptune whose mighty trident brings forth from the rock a poor rivulent. All this is to him bluff, ‚Tout est imposture.' What had seemed ‚natural' to the Baroque, was bad theatre to the revolutionary“.

39 Brook 1996, 9: „The Deadly Theatre can at first sight be taken for granted, because it means bad theatre“.

40 Brook 1996, 42: „I am calling it the Holy Theatre for short, but it could be called The Theatre of the Invisible – Made – Visible: the notion that the stage is a place where the invisible can appear has a deep hold on our thoughts“.

41 Vidler 1994.

42 Ich folge der Interpretation von Anthony Vidler (1994, 172), der hier die Grenzen von Foucaults Analyse des Zusammenhangs von Macht, Raum und Licht benennt: „Here the limits of Foucault's interpretation of Enlightenment space become evident. Still tied to the Enlightenment's own phenomenology of light and dark, clear and obscure, his insistence of the operation of power through *transparency,* the panoptic principle, resists exploration of the extent to which the paring of transparency and obscurity is essential for power to operate. For it is in the intimate associations of the two, their uncanny ability to slip from one to the other, that the sublime as instrument of fear retains its hold – in that ambiguity that stages the presence of death in life, dark space in bright space. In this sense, all the radiant spaces of modernism, from the first Panopticon to the Ville Radieuse, should be seen as calculated not on the final triumph of light over dark but precisely on the insistent presence of the one in the other“.

43 Ledoux 1804, 195 Fn 1: „[...], l'image du néant ne pouvoit offrir aux yeux ni bois, ni prés, ni vallons, ni fleuves, encore moins les bienfaits du soleil qui vivifie la nature“.

keine Funktion und ist auch nicht zu betreten. Nur durch die Fenster sollte man von den Galerien aus Einblick in ihr unheimliches Dunkel gewinnen. Einzig im Zenit der Kugel lässt eine Öffnung Tageslicht eindringen, das sich zwielichtig im Dunkel verliert. Von außen sollte die Halbkugel als Symbol des Unendlichen einsam in die Landschaft ragen.

Ledoux hatte in seinem Kommentar dazu die göttliche Ordnung der Sterne, die Vorbild für die geistige Welt des Menschen ist, mit apokalyptischen Bildern in Verbindung gebracht, die das Zulaufen des Menschen auf das Nichts darstellen. Er hatte damit dem burkeschen Erhabenen eine neue Bedeutung für die Gesellschaft gegeben. Für Burke ist das Erhabene die Vorstellung der eigenen Vernichtung vor Gott, also eine religiöse Vorstellung angesichts eines unermesslichen Objekts oder Geschehens[44] und diese Vorstellung wollte Ledoux als möglichen Ausgang der Geschichte in seiner Architektur sichtbar machen: „Gott prägte auf das Antlitz dieser Sterne die Dankbarkeit des Menschen, welche die Nacht der Zeiten in ihrem Schleier verschließt. Die Schöpfung breitet ihre Gaben aus. Die geistige Welt, für die dieser gemacht wurde, bietet euch eine Stufenleiter dar, welche die Fülle der Wesen beinhaltet, die durch das himmlische Feuer beseelt sind. Sie bietet euch ihre göttlichen Geister an, die sich ganz oben auf dem Himmelsrund erheben. Der Architekt ist da, umgeben von Stürmen und Wolken, die mit ihm um die Überlegenheit der Himmel streiten. Er sieht Schatten unter seinen Füßen, welche die Erde verdunkeln und die Trauer der Zeiten belasten. Die Bäume sind laublos, die Seen, gerade noch mit flüssigem Reichtum erfüllt, sind ausgetrocknet. Zerstörende Winde verbreiten Krankheit, Hunger, alles Unglück, das die Reiche vernichtet. Ein unabänderliches Schicksal scheint ihr Ende festgesetzt zu haben. Die Erde schließt sich ein. Der verschreckte Mensch weicht zurück vor dem Anblick dieses fürchterlichen Gewölbes, das die Trümmer der Menschheit bedeckt. Eine abscheuliche Politik gewöhnt sich an das Verbrechen, häuft die Gifte und Dolche. Vergeltungen, Ungerechtigkeiten und hochfahrende Leidenschaften erschüttern die unwandelbare Ordnung. Laster häuft sich auf Laster und erstickt die Tugenden. Die bewegenden Kräfte lasten auf den beiden Polen. Die tödlichen Erschütterungen erregen das Blut, das seine Ansteckung entfaltet. Alles ist hier durcheinander. Die Natur ist gescheitert. Der moralische Mensch existiert nicht mehr“[45].

Zwischen dem Ausblick auf das Ende und das Nichts und der Einrichtung von Gesellschaft gemäß der göttlichen Ordnung steht der Architekt, der angesichts seines eigenen Todes seinen Auftrag an die kommenden Generationen weiterzugeben sucht. Die Menschen sollen den Tugenden Tempel errichten und ihre Motive auf dem universellen Vertrag gründen, „der alle Tugenden zum Wohl aller vereint“[46]. Andernfalls, wenn der Mensch der Natur zuwiderhandelt, wäre sie für uns ein riesiger Friedhof. Die Nekropole ist der Ort eines Schreckens, eines Nichts, das in die Welt der Aufklärung eindringt und ihr als Möglichkeit stets gegenwärtig bleibt. Es ist die andere Seite der Evidenz, die nicht nur durch ihre fraglose Gültigkeit zwingt, sondern auch durch die Drohung des Scheiterns der Natur. Sowohl in der Physiokratie und ihrer Idee einer der Vernunft geoffenbarten natürlichen Ordnung, als auch in der Architektur von Ledoux, gibt es ein eschatologisches Moment. Dieses endzeitliche Gericht, das in der Angst der Aufklärung vorweggenommen wird und das in Ledoux' dunklem Raum erscheint, ist die Kraft, durch die sich das Gesetz in die Seele einschreiben soll. Im Moment des Erhabenen, dort, wo sich Licht

44 Burke 1989, 104: „Indem wir uns das unermeßliche Objekt, das sich uns dabei darbietet, in der Hand der Allmacht und überall von Allgegenwart erfüllt vorstellen, schrumpfen wir zu der Winzigkeit unserer eigenen Natur zusammen und werden gewissermaßen vor Gott vernichtet“.

45 Ledoux 1804, 155: „Dieu imprima sur le front de ces étoiles la gratitude de l'homme que la nuit des temps enferme encore dans ses voiles. La création déploie ses largesses. Le monde intellectuel pour lequel celui-ci a été fait vous offre une échelle graduée qui reçoit l'affluence des êtres électrisés par la flamme céleste; il vous offre ces divins génies qui s'élèvent au sommet de la voûte éthérée: l'Architecte est là, entouré de tourbillons, de nuages qui disputent qui disputent avec lui la prééminence des cieux; il voit sous ses pieds ses ombres qui obscurcissent la terre e la chargent du deuil des saisons. Les souffles destructeurs vomissent l'épidémie, la faim, les malheurs qui détruisent les empires: l'invariable destin semble avoir décrété leur fin. La terre s'isole; l'homme épouvanté recule à la vue de cette voûte redoutée qui va couvrir les décombres de l'humanité: la hideuse politique se familiarise avec le crime, amoncèle les prisons, les poignards; les vengeances, les injustices, les passions ambitieuses, l'ordre immuable s'agitent, les vices entassés sur les vices étouffent les vertus; les puissances motrices pèsent sur les deux pôles; les secousses meurtrières remuent la sange qui déploie sa contagion. Tout ici se confond, la nature est ébranlée; l'homme moral n'est plus“.

46 Ledoux 1804, 196: „[…]; appuyez vos motifs sur les bazes du pacte universel qui fait concourir les vertus de tout genre au bien-être de tous“.

und Dunkel berühren, wird die kosmische Ordnung durchlässig, enthüllt sich zugleich das Gesetz und dessen Sanktion.

DER PLATZ DES ARCHITEKTEN

In *Les Mots et les Choses* hat Michel Foucault die Frage gestellt, wer den Platz des Königs einnehmen wird. In diesem Sinn ist der Platz des Königs leer. Ein leerer Raum hat sich aufgetan und dieser Raum ist nicht unendlich in sich gefaltet wie der barocke Raum, sondern unendlich weit. In diesem Raum soll der König einen neuen Ort finden und dabei hilft ihm der Architekt. Dessen Person hält die soziale Ordnung in zwei Dimensionen zwischen Naturbetrachtung und deren Symbolisierung in der Kunst zusammen. Er wird zu einer Figur, durch die hindurch erst Wissenschaft und Kunst vermittelt werden. Ledoux, man darf es nicht vergessen, hat seinen Text nach 1789 verfasst, als auch er diese Position nicht mehr bekleidete. Sein Denken und Schaffen in dieser Zeit sind die Rückdatierung einer Möglichkeit, die das Ancien Régime gehabt hatte.

Anders als Quesnay, der aus der Himmelsbetrachtung Gesetzmäßigkeiten erkennbar machen wollte, sollte der Architekt durch sein Schaffen die Sterne in die Welt bringen und damit das Licht der Aufklärung als Orientierungsmöglichkeit königlicher Herrschaft einrichten. „Die Architektur", schreibt er in der Linie jener Doppeldeutigkeit, welche die ganze Aufklärung begleitet, „ist den wohltätigen Sternen ähnlich, welche die Welt erhellen"[47]. Die Krise der Metaphysik und somit auch der politischen Metaphysik hatte eine Krise dieser symbolischen Systeme zur Folge, welche die soziale und politische Ordnung konstituieren. Ledoux antwortet darauf mit ästhetischen Konzepten wie der Theatralisierung der Gesellschaft und einer aus Naturbetrachtung abgeleiteten Symbolik. Im Industrietheater von Chaux kombiniert er diese Elemente. Ledoux mag als Vorläufer der französischen Revolution erscheinen, aber er war weder glühender Anhänger ihrer Ideale, noch Bürokrat oder moderner Techniker, sondern er war ein Künstler, der die Unruhe und den Wunsch des 18. Jahrhunderts zu verwirklichen versuchte, dass die Wahrheit in der Macht erscheinen kann, dass Freiheit und Notwendigkeit zusammen bestehen können.

BIBLIOGRAFIE

Blumenberg, H. 1987. *Das Lachen der Thrakerin. Eine Urgeschichte der Theorie*. Frankfurt am Main: Suhrkamp.

Brian, É. 2001. *Staatsvermessungen. Condorcet, Laplace, Turgot und das Denken der Verwaltung*. Wien u.a.: Springer.

Brook, P. 1996. *The Empty Space*. New York: Touchstone.

Burke, E. 1989. *Vom Erhabenen und Schönen*. Hamburg: Meiner.

D'Amilaville, É.-N. 1985. „Bevölkerung". In *Artikel aus Diderots Enzyklopädie*, herausgegeben von M. Naumann, 685-91. Frankfurt am Main: Röderberg.

De Montesquieu, C. 1988. *Perserbriefe*. Frankfurt am Main: Insel.

Durkheim E. 1993. *Über soziale Arbeitsteilung. Studie über die Organisation höherer Gesellschaften*. Frankfurt am Main: Suhrkamp.

–. 1994. *Die elementaren Formen des religiösen Lebens*. Frankfurt am Main: Suhrkamp.

–. 1999. *Physik der Sitten und des Rechts. Vorlesungen zur Soziologie der Moral*. Frankfurt am Main: Suhrkamp.

Gallet, M. 1983. *Claude-Nicolas Ledoux. Leben und Werk des französischen „Revolutionsarchitekten"*. Darmstadt: Wissenschaftliche Buchgesellschaft.

Kaufmann, E. 1952. „Three Revolutionary Architects, Boullée, Ledoux, and Lequeu." *Transactions of the American Philosophical Society* 43/3, 431-564.

Kruft, H.-W. 1989. *Städte in Utopia. Die Idealstadt vom 15. bis zum 18. Jahrhundert*. München: C.H. Beck.

47 Ledoux 1804, 7: „L'Architecture est semblable aux astres bienfaisants qui éclairent le monde".

Le Mercier de la Rivière, P.-P. 1910. *L'ordre naturel et essentiel des sociétés politique*. Paris: Librairie Paul Geuthner.

Ledoux, C.-N. 1804. *L'Architecture considérée sous le rapport de l'art, des mœurs et de la législation*. Paris: H.L. Perroneau.

Patocka J. 1991. „Der Raum und seine Problematik." In *Die Bewegung der menschlichen Existenz. Phänomenologische Schriften II*, herausgegeben von K. Nellen, 63-131. Stuttgart: Klett-Cotta.

Priddat, B.P. 2001. *Le Concert universel. Die Physiokratie. Eine Transformationsphilosophie des 18. Jahrhunderts*. Marburg: Metropolis.

Prodi, P. 2003. *Eine Geschichte der Gerechtigkeit. Vom Recht Gottes zum modernen Rechtsstaat*. München: C.H. Beck.

Quesnay, F. 1991. „Droit naturel." In *Physiocratie. Droit naturel, Tableau économique et autres textes*, herausgegeben von J. Cartelier, 67-86. Paris: Flammarion.

Rosenstock-Huessy, E. 1958. „Das Geheimnis der Universität." In *Das Geheimnis der Universität. Wider den Verfall von Zeitsinn und Sprachkraft. Reden und Aufsätze aus den Jahren 1950-1957*, herausgegeben und eingeleitet von Kurt Ballerstedt, 17-34. Stuttgart: Kohlhammer.

Vidler, A. 1987. „The Theater of Industry. Claude-Nicolas Ledoux and the Factory-Village of Chaux." In *The Writing of the Walls. Architectural Theory in Late Enlightenment*, 35-49. Princeton: Architectural Press.

–. 1994. „Dark space." In *The Architectural Uncanny. Essays in the Modern Unhomely*, 167-75. Cambridge: MIT-Press.

Ansicht der Saline von Chaux. Nach: Kruft 1989, Abb. 109.

La Tour d'horizon

Zur Ikonographie von Teufel, Turm und Panorama

Michael Diers

[...] der aus Strichen sich bildende Eiffelturm.

Franz Kafka [1]

Es ist wirklich eine Landkarte, ohne merkliche Höhenunterschiede. Alles ist auf dem Punkt. Der Fluß fließt auf der Höhe des Berggipfels.

Félix Tournachon, gen. Nadar[2]

Abstract

In his book on the Eiffel tower, Roland Barthes writes, "The Eiffel tower watches over Paris."[3] This paper examines this metaphor and attempts to reconstruct the history of inspiration of this technical building, which, to the present day, continues to function as an anthropomorphic cipher. I aim to demonstrate that the shape of the tower can be understood as a distant reflection of a mythological figure, which, in the panoramatic nineteenth century, embodied the idea of a view from above and hence of an overview.

Vol d'oiseau – Zwischen April 1843 und Dezember 1845 erschien in Form von Lieferungen bei dem Verleger Jules Hetzel unter dem Titel *Le Diable à Paris*[4] eine zeitgenössische Stadt- und Sittengeschichte der Metropole. Nach Abschluss der Subskription, in zwei Bänden zusammengefasst, hielt der Käufer eine Enzyklopädie erzählerischen und illustrativen Charakters in Händen, die im Untertitel versprach, von „moeurs et coutumes, caractères et portraits des habitants de Paris" zu handeln und ein „tableau complet de leur vie privée, publique, politique, artistique, littéraire, industrielle etc., etc."[5] zu liefern. Als Autoren steuerten unter anderem Honoré de Balzac, Théophile Gautier, Alfred de Musset und George Sand Erzählungen und Feuilletons bei; als Hauptillustratoren für die rund 200 Tafeln und über 800 Textvignetten wurden Paul Gavarni und Bertall verpflichtet. In der auf Louis Sebastièn Mercier zurückgehenden Tradition des *Tableau de Paris* enthalten die beiden Bücher neben historischen, statisti-

Die grundlegende Idee des Aufsatzes verdankt sich der anregenden Parallellektüre zweier materialreicher Bücher, dem Paris-Band von Karlheinz Stierle (Stierle 1993) sowie dem von Bodo von Dewitz und Werner Nekes edierten Ausstellungskatalog des Museum Ludwig in Köln *Ich sehe was, was Du nicht siehst! Sehmaschinen und Bilderwelten. Die Sammlung Werner Nekes.* (Dewitz und Nekes 2002).

1 Kafka 1990, 977.
2 Zitiert nach Weiß 1992, 23.
3 Barthes 1970, 38.
4 Le Diable à Paris 1845/6. Ein Reprint der Originalausgabe ist 1992 im Verlag der Editions Paris-Musées erschienen.
5 Le Diable à Paris, Titelblatt.

schen und geographischen Fakten insbesondere literarische Essays, Geschichten und Dialoge sowie das überaus reiche Bildprogramm der Holzstiche.

Die Rahmenerzählung handelt vom Teufel, der sich in der Hölle langweilt, auf seinem Thron räkelt und schließlich aufbricht, um in Paris wieder einmal nach dem Rechten zu sehen. Bertall als Illustrator der Teufelsgeschichten spinnt diese Episoden genrehaft aus. Das Frontispiz (und damit das Auftakt- und Programmbild der Bände) stammt aus der Feder von Gavarni, der um die Jahrhundertmitte zu den populärsten Grafikern neben Daumier zählte[6], und hat wenig mit den eher naiven Drolerien des Kollegen gemein (Taf. 44.1)[7]. Es setzt den Drucktitel anschaulich ins Bild und liefert einen visuell überzeugenden ‚Begriff' des gesamten Unternehmens, so dass die Zeichnung mit Recht als ein Meilenstein der Buchillustration der Epoche gilt[8]. In seiner ikonographischen, mediengeschichtlichen und theoretischen Qualität ist das Blatt allerdings noch nicht hinreichend gewürdigt worden; einige Hinweise dazu finden sich nachfolgend.

Schattenwerfend steht der riesenhafte, zeitgenössisch gewandete Teufel im Tal der Seine – richtiger: er steht auf einem Plan der Stadt Paris, der in Borges'scher Manier im Maßstab 1:1 wie eine Decke über die gesamte Region ausgebreitet ist. Nur die Höhen von Montmartre mit ihren Windmühlen und einer Wäscheleine bleiben von dieser Bedeckung ausgespart. An die Stelle der Stadt nebst Weichbild ist die Karte gerückt, statt einer topographischen Ansicht mit Landmarken wird ein zur Erdoberfläche gewandeltes, in leichter Aufsicht dargebotenes abstraktes Kartenbild präsentiert; um im Bild zu bleiben, ein teuflisch-verzwicktes, modernes Ideogramm, das den geläufigen Blick aus der Vogelschau völlig neu auffasst und auch andere Versuche summierender Synthetisierung eines Stadtbildes hinter sich zurücklässt. So bediente sich zum Beispiel noch die Titelillustration des 1852 erschienenen *Tableau de Paris* von Edmond Texier kumulierend und collagierend des üblichen heraldischen, allegorischen, architektonischen und anekdotischen Zeichenvorrats, um zu seinem Programmbild von Paris zu gelangen (Taf. 44.2)[9]. Bereits sieben Jahre zuvor aber ist mit Gavarni eine geradezu kopernikanische Wende eingeleitet worden, indem dieser paradigmatisch den „kartographischen Blick"[10] illustriert, wobei es dem Künstler spielerisch gelingt, die Märchenfigur des Teufels überzeugend in den eminenten Mediensprung zu integrieren[11].

Eine eindringliche Beschreibung der Gavarnischen Teufelsgestalt hat Karlheinz Stierle geliefert: „Der donquijotesk magere Teufel der Stadtbeobachtung, gleichsam Gestalt gewordener Mythos des Auges, in dem die Stadt sich selbst spiegelt, wächst zur schwarzgekleideten imaginären Riesengestalt, die sich zur Stadt hinunterbeugt, die unter ihren Füßen, zum Stadtplan verkleinert, liegt und auf die er mit seinem winzigen Monokel herabschaut. Die Stadtplan gewordene Stadt erscheint mit hieroglyphischen Bildzügen von Straßen, Plätzen, Bauwerken als Bild der Oszillation zwischen Lesbarkeit und Unlesbarkeit. Die linke Hand hält den unendlich dünnen Spazierstock, in dem die gebrechlichen Riesenbeine ein ironisches Echo haben, und eine Laterne, die an die Laterne des Diogenes erinnert; auf dem Rücken aber trägt die phantastische Gestalt einen Korb, bis zum Überlaufen angefüllt mit den Manuskripten jener Pariser, die ihm ihre Beobachtungen und Erfahrungen anvertraut haben, die Manuskripte zugleich jenes ‚Diable à Paris', den der Leser in Händen hält und dessen Titel er auf der gegenüberliegenden Seite liest"[12].

Nur an einer einzigen, im vorliegenden Zusammenhang allerdings wesentlichen Stelle ist die zitierte Darstellung ungenau[13], denn Gavarnis Teufel trägt keine einfache (Licht-)Laterne mit sich herum, sondern vielmehr eine Laterna Magica (Taf. 44.3), einen mechanischen Bildprojektor, wie er um die Mitte des 19. Jahrhunderts bereits als Spielzeug populär war. In Text (vgl. die Manuskripte im Korb) *und* Bild

6 Vgl. L'oeuvre de Gavarni 2002.

7 Auch das Subskriptionsplakat warb mit der Teufelsgestalt von Gavarni.

8 Vgl. Fünf Jahrhunderte Buchillustration 1987, 176f.; Bilderwelten 1985, 126-8 (Nr. 54).

9 Siehe auch die vergleichbare Vignette des Kapitels *Géographie de Paris* in Le Diable à Paris 1845/6, Band 2, 1.

10 Siehe zu diesem Begriff Buci-Glucksmann 1997.

11 Fast möchte man diese Kehrtwende auch sprachlich in der Formulierung des Titels wiederfinden, die nicht, wie dem Genre nach üblich, auf „Tableau de", sondern wie in einem lautmalerischen Echo auf „Le Diable à" setzt.

12 Stierle 1993, 267f.

13 Anmerken ließe sich noch, dass der Spazierstock des Teufels eine Pike ist, wie sie Lumpen- und Papiersammler damals als Werkzeug benutzten; der Teufel hält die Pike mit dem Haken nach oben gekehrt. Vgl. auch die Darstellung des Chiffonier in Finke 1972, Abb. 74, 75.

(vgl. die Lichtbilder der Laterna Magica), demnach durch Beschreibung *und* Illustration, möchte die angezeigte aktuelle Ausgabe eines *Tableau de Paris* seine Leserschaft mittels einer Gesamt- und Zusammenschau charakteristischer Phänomene unterrichten und unterhalten. In der ebenso emblematischen wie realistischen, auf (Blick-)Erfahrung basierenden Darstellung der zu seinen Füßen ausgebreiteten Karte fallen in einer Schrift/Text und Grafik/Bild vermittelnden Gattung beide Ansprüche wie in einer Synthese zusammen[14].

Dass Gavarni zur Stellvertretung des Mediums Bild in seinem Frontispiz darüber hinaus auf das optische Instrument der Laterna Magica zurückgreift, scheint nicht zuletzt durch die seit dem Spätmittelalter geläufige Vorstellung inspiriert, es handele sich bei der 'Zauberlaterne' und ihren Projektionen um Magie und Teufelswerk. Jedenfalls tritt der Teufel in den entsprechenden Darstellungen seit alters vielfach als eine übergroße Erscheinung auf (Taf. 44.4). Bei Gavarni wird die schlichte Blechlaterne zum Attribut des (Bild-)Reportage-Teufels. Dessen Komposit-Ikonographie lässt sich zur einen Hälfte aus der Figur des fahrenden Laterna Magica-Gesellen (Taf. 45.1)[15] und zur anderen Hälfte aus der im Kontext der Gattung *Tableau de Paris* als Vorbild naheliegenden literarischen Gestalt des ‚Hinkenden Teufels' herleiten, wie sie Alain-René Lesage in seinem Roman *Le Diable Boiteux* (1707) zum Titelhelden gemacht hat[16]. Als Dank für die Befreiung aus dem Kerker einer Phiole im Dachzimmer eines Magiers eröffnet der Teufel seinem studentischen Retter bei Lesage einen Blick hinter die Kulissen der Großstadt, indem er mit leichter Hand die Dächer der Häuser lüftet und ihm dadurch ein Panorama des grellbunten Lebens der Bewohner erschließt: „‚Ich möchte Euch alles zeigen, was in Madrid [i.e. Paris] geschieht; und da ich in diesem Viertel hier beginnen will, könnte ich für meinen Zweck keinen geeigneteren Standort finden [als den Turm von San Salvador]. Ich werde, kraft meiner Teufelsgewalt, die Dächer von den Häusern abheben; und trotz der nächtlichen Finsternis wird sich ihr Inhalt Euren Augen öffnen.' Bei diesen Worten tat er nichts weiter, als seinen rechten Arm aus[zu]strecken, und sofort verschwanden die Dächer. Sogleich sah der Student wie am hellen Mittag das Innere der Häuser, ‚geradeso' – sagt Luiz de Guevara – ‚wie man den Inhalt einer Pastete erblickt, wenn man die Kruste abnimmt.' Der Anblick war zu ungewohnt, um nicht seine ganze Aufmerksamkeit zu fesseln. Er ließ seine Augen überall hinwandern, und die Vielfalt der Ereignisse, die ihn umgaben, hielt seine Neugier gefangen"[17]. Wieder ist es der Blick von oben, der den spektakulären Schauplatz einer Welt als Puppenhaus erschafft.

Im selben Jahr wie Gavarnis Teufel-Illustration kamen in Paris auch die Holzstiche von Gustave Doré zu Rabelais' *Gargantua und Pantagruel* heraus, darunter auch jene Darstellung, die den Riesen zeigt, wie er vor dem „gaffsüchtigen Volk von Paris" (Lesage) flieht und sich zwischen den Türmen von Notre Dame verschanzt – allerdings nur, um die Umstehenden von dort aus mittels persönlicher „Brunzsintflut" (Lesage) zu besudeln und zu ersäufen (Taf. 45.2). Kathedralarchitektur und Riese verschmelzen zu einer einzigen Gestalt und die Fassade des Wahrzeichens von Paris wird zu deren Hosenlatz.

An diese und verwandte Traditionen der Teufel- und Riesenmärchen knüpft Gavarni mit seinem elegant über dem Plan der Stadt verweilenden Giganten an. In Szene gesetzt wird durch diesen Protagonisten der suchend-prüfende, technisch gestützte Blick von hoch oben auf die Karte zu den Füßen weit unten. Der Topos der Stadtbetrachtung aus der Vogelschau ist insbesondere für Paris bildlich und literarisch stark ausgeprägt. Ein prominentes Dokument stellt Victor Hugos Roman *Der Glöckner von Notre Dame* (1831) dar, dessen drittes Buch sich im zweiten Kapitel dem Nachdenken über dieses „Schauspiel ganz eigener Art" widmet[18]. Immer wieder ist von den Türmen und der von dort aus dem Blick sich bietenden grandiosen Stadtlandschaft die Rede, die sich im Blick von oben in ihrer Fülle ebenso wie in

14 Dieses Argument lässt sich vielleicht noch dadurch bekräftigen, dass die Druckbögen eines Buches, bevor sie zu Lagen gefaltet und anschließend geheftet werden, grundsätzlich nicht anders aussehen als eine ausgefaltete Karte, die ihre Bogengestalt bewahrt, während aus Druckbögen im Laufe der Wandlung zum Buch einzelne Seiten werden (wie sie z.B. in den losen Blättern im Korb des Teufels auszumachen sind).

15 Aufschlussreich ist der Umstand, dass die Außenseiten der Laterna Magica im angeführten Holzstich (Taf. 45.1) Teufelszenen zeigen. Vgl. auch die sog. *Diablerie-Laterna Magica* (Frankreich um 1880) aus der Sammlung Werner Nekes; auch hier zeigen die gestanzten Außenseiten der Blechlaterne Teufelsszenen (Dewitz und Nekes 2002, 131); siehe hier auch das Glossar s.v. Diablerien (Dewitz und Nekes 2002, 434.)

16 Vgl. zum Motiv und seiner literarischen Tradition allgemein den entsprechenden Eintrag in Kindlers Literatur Lexikon (Einsiedel und Woerner 1974, Band 7, 2627-8).

17 Alain-René Lesage, Der hinkende Teufel; zitiert nach Klotz 1969, 533.

18 Vgl. das Hugo-Kapitel *Stadtschau und Schaustadt* in Klotz 1969, 92ff.

ihren Strukturen erschließen lasse. Als Beispiel für die bildliche Umsetzung einer solchen Vogelschau sei ein wenig bekanntes Riesentableau aus dem Jahr der ersten Pariser Weltausstellung angeführt (Taf. 45.3). Victor Navlets Panoramalandschaft entstand nach Skizzen, die der Maler von einem Fesselballon aus angefertigt und anschließend im Atelier kompiliert hat. Bis heute eine atemberaubende Darstellung, die in ihrem Panoramaeffekt und Detailreichtum kaum zu überbieten ist, stellt es den Abschluss der Tradition der gemalten Weltlandschaft dar. Wenig später schwingen sich bereits die Fotografen in die Höhe, um die Vogelschau mit ihren technischen Aufzeichnungsgeräten zu fixieren. Der berühmteste fotografierende Luftpionier der Zeit ist zweifellos Nadar, dessen Paris-Aufnahmen vom Korb aus Epoche gemacht haben (Taf. 46.1). Kaum zufällig war sein Ballon, mit dem er vom Champ de Mars aufzusteigen pflegte, auf den Namen *Le Géant* („Der Riese") getauft[19].

Point de vue – So qualitätvoll und bedeutend Gavarnis Titel-Illustration für sich betrachtet und aus der Tradition heraus verstanden bereits ist, ein ganz besonderer Rang erwächst dieser künstlerischen Invention dadurch, dass man sie als ein Voraus-Bild oder aber modellhaftes Vor-Bild für eine Pariser Institution begreifen kann, die rund vierzig Jahre später projektiert wird, rasch Gestalt gewinnt und umgehend zum neuen, überaus modernen Wahrzeichen der Stadt und darüber hinaus zu einem Jahrhundertbau avanciert (Taf. 46.2-3)[20]. Wie es scheint, haben all die Phantasmagorien und Imaginationen, die Gavarnis Entwurf bündelt, in den zeichnerischen Entwurf und damit in die technische Konstruktion des Eiffelturms sowie in dessen Funktion als Ansichts- und Aussichtsturm Eingang gefunden[21].

Nicht ausgeschlossen, dass dem Schüler Gustave Eiffel (1832-1923) die hagerdunkle Gestalt des Teufels beim Stöbern in einer Ausgabe des *Diable de Paris* oder durch einen Plakataushang als prägnante Bildformel begegnet ist. Jedenfalls könnte die Erinnerung an diese Figur den Entwurf seines Turmes dem Schema und der Kontur nach beeinflusst haben. Dass der kolossale Bau, von vielen Zeitgenossen als hässliches Teufelswerk oder „wahrhaft tragischer Laternenpfahl"[22] verspottet, fast an eben jener Stelle zu stehen kam, wo der Teufel auch bei Gavarni gerade Halt gemacht hat, und zwar nahe dem Märzfeld, spricht ebenfalls für diese Spur. Dass der gezeichnete Riese schließlich, seine Schattenbeine mitgezählt, ebenfalls auf vier mageren ‚Pfeilern' steht, ließe sich überdies zur Stärkung des Arguments anführen. Man vergleiche aber auch die feine Durchbrucharbeit des Weidenkorbgeflechtes sowie die filigrane Textur des Rockes in Gavarnis Zeichnung mit der ‚gestrichelten' Gitterstruktur der Eisenkonstruktion[23].

Vergleiche hinken, insbesondere solche mit dem Teufel. Aber es geht weniger um den Nachweis unmittelbaren Einflusses, als vielmehr um den Aufweis eines offenbar durchaus begrenzten Vorrats sinnfälliger visuell-visionärer Topoi, auf welche die Fantasie, will sie Neues imaginieren, zurückgreifen kann. Es geht um Ähnlichkeit, Transformation und Metamorphose und um einen Versuch der Erklärung einer augenfälligen strukturellen Verwandtschaft zweier Gestalt gewordener Epochen-Einbildungen. Walter Benjamin, der im *Passagen-Werk* verschiedentlich auf den Eiffelturm zu sprechen kommt, würdigt in den begleitenden erkenntnistheoretischen Notizen dieses Phänomen durch den Begriff der ‚Korrespondenz': „Daß zwischen der Welt der modernen Technik und der archaischen Symbolwelt der Mythologie Korrespondenzen spielen, kann nur der gedankenlose Betrachter leugnen. Zunächst wirkt das technisch Neue freilich allein als solches. Aber schon in der nächsten kindlichen Erinnerung ändert es seine Züge. Jede Kindheit leistet etwas Großes, Unersetzliches für die Menschheit. Jede Kindheit

19 Edouard Manet hat dem Nadarschen Ballon in seinem Weltausstellungs-Gemälde von 1867 (Oslo, Nationalgalerie) ein 'vielsagendes' Denkmal gesetzt: Vom Boden aus betrachtet, wirkt der Fotografen-Ballon in den Lüften wie der freischwebende Augapfel eines Zyklopen, das säkularisierte Gottesauge, das ab jetzt dem Fotografen eignet. Vgl. Steinhauser 1994, 27ff.

20 Vgl. allgemein Eiffel 1900, 1902; Giedion 1992, 196ff. u. passim; Loyrette 1992; sowie die nachfolgend zitierte Literatur zum Thema.

21 Zum medialen Charakter von Turmbauten vgl. Engell 1999.

22 Léon Bloy, zitiert nach Lemoine 1988, 96.

23 Bemerkenwert ist auch die Tatsache, dass die figürlich geprägte Deckelillustration der Originalausgabe um die Gavarnische Teufelsgestalt herum in einer Vignettenbordüre vier Pariser Bauwerke und Monumente zitiert, und zwar oben die Assemblée nationale, unten die Börse und zu Seiten des Riesen links die Vendôme-Säule und rechts den Obelisken der Place de la Concorde; dass gerade die beiden prominenten Vertikal-Monumente dem Teufel unmittelbar vergleichend zur Seite gestellt werden, spricht für die wahrgenommene Formverwandtschaft.

bindet in ihrem Interesse für die technischen Phänomene, ihre Neugier für alle Art von Erfindungen und Maschinerien die technischen Errungenschaften an die alten Symbolwelten"[24]. Während Benjamin die produktive Verwandlung und Rückbindung erst in der Erinnerung am Werk sieht, steht im vorliegenden Fall der Vorausentwurf und damit die Idee der Antizipation einer prägenden Form zur Debatte.

Den Eiffelturm mit an Gavarni geschulten Augen als anthropomorphe Chiffre zu bestimmen (und vice versa seine Teufelsgestalt als technische Struktur und Utopie zu dechiffrieren), führt dazu, den avancierten konstruktiven Entwurf des Turms als fernen Reflex einer atavistischen mythologischen Figur anzusehen, die in ihrer zeitgenössischen künstlerischen Fasson keine dämonische Angst mehr verbreitet und schließlich als Architektur keine andere Aufgabe mehr hat, als Anblick und Ausblick zu gewähren und Bilder bereit zu stellen – sei es für den Ausschau haltenden Besucher, sei es für die Übertragung durch nachrichtentechnische Einrichtungen wie Funk und Radar (Taf. 47.1).

Von Gavarnis Protagonisten hieß es weiter oben, er repräsentiere den „Mythos des Auges" (Stierle). Ähnlich hat bereits Roland Barthes in seinem Buch *La Tour Eiffel* den eintausend Fuß hohen Turm („tour de mille pieds") mit dem edelsten der menschlichen Sinne begabt, wenn es dort kurz und bündig heißt: „Der Eiffelturm betrachtet Paris"[25]. Dieses Bild ist nicht nur seinem poetischen Gehalt nach zutreffend, sondern auch der dem Turm vorausliegenden, im Wortsinn fantastischen Bildidee sowie seiner technischen Funktion nach (Taf. 47.2). Ob der Karikaturist des *Punch* im Jahr 1889, dem Jahr der Einweihung und der Jahrhundertfeier der Französischen Revolution, diese Zusammenhänge geahnt hat, als er dem Bau die Person des Architekten leibhaftig eingezeichnet hat, mag dahingestellt bleiben (Taf. 47.3)[26].

Als Nachtrag zur Wahlverwandtschaft der Ikonographien von Teufel, Turm und Panorama sei auf ein Spielzeug hingewiesen. Gleich nach der Eröffnung des Turms kam eine Laterna Magica 'in forma turris' auf den Markt (Taf. 47.4). Sie zeigt den Turm durchstoßen vom Objektiv des Projektors, und es ist keine Frage, dass die zugehörigen Glasbilder unter anderem Ansichten von Paris darboten. Selbst als porzellanenes Schreibtischset wurde diese Idee in Miniaturformat umgesetzt. Die Motive des Bildprojektors und des Turms werden miteinander konjugiert und (er-)zeugen so jenen Kitsch, in dem schöpferische Ideen sich gelegentlich niederschlagen, um in einer Trivialgestalt verborgen zu überdauern.

Gavarnis Teufel-Skizze wird Architektur und diese zum Wahrzeichen. Der kartographische oder ikarische Blick des Teufels wird technisch installiert, touristisch institutionalisiert und damit zugleich demokratisiert. Wenn es noch einer Bestätigung dieser Herleitung bedürfte, genügte ein Blick in den Michelin-Reiseführer *Paris*, wo es heißt: „Von der 3. Etage [des Eiffelturms] kann die Sicht, die eine Stunde vor Sonnenuntergang am besten ist, bis zu 67 km weit reichen [...]. Paris erscheint dann mit seinen Vororten wie eine gigantische Reliefkarte"[27]. Dieses Relief verflacht bekanntlich in dem Maße, in dem man höher steigt – demnach mindestens auf die hier gebotene Kopfhöhe des Teufels gelangt, der sich bereits wesentlich früher am Tag auf seine Wanderung durch Paris begeben hat, wie der gen Norden gerichtete Schattenwurf seiner Gestalt anzeigt.

Seit kurzem kann man übrigens den Eiffelturm selbst leichterdings aus der Vogelschau betrachten. Die Satellitenbild-Software *Google Earth*, die „jeden Personal Computer in einen digitalen Globus [verwandelt], wie ihn die Welt noch nicht gesehen hat"[28], zoomt aufs Stichwort Paris/Eiffelturm das Bauwerk in Windeseile heran[29]. Am Bildschirm lässt sich der herbeigezauberte Ausschnitt des Stadtbildes um die eigene Achse drehen oder horizontal schwenken, und zwar solange, bis die gewünschte Perspektive, zum Beispiel diejenige Gavarnis, samt Schatten rekonstruiert ist (Taf. 48.1).

24 Benjamin 1993, 576.

25 Barthes 1970, 38.

26 Vgl. auch die Karikatur aus Le Central, Nr. 4, 1889, die Eiffel neben seinem Turm und der winzigen Cheopspyramide zeigt; die Beischrift lautet: „A la grandeur, on mesure la grandeur de l'homme." Abbildung in Lemoine 1989, 63.

27 Paris 1979, 52.

28 Lemm 2005; vgl. auch Lüber 2005.

29 S. im World Wide Web unter http://earth.google.com.

„Von der 110. Etage des World Trade Centers sehe man auf Manhattan. Unter dem vom Wind aufgewirbelten Dunst liegt die Stadt-Insel. [...] Für einen Moment ist die Bewegung durch den Anblick erstarrt."

Michel de Certeau[30]

Coup d'oeil – Ein dem Bau des Eiffelturms vergleichbar spektakuläres und ambitioniertes Projekt stellt für die Gegenwart die Errichtung jenes New Yorker Turmbaus dar, der das am 11. September 2001 zum Einsturz gebrachte World Trade Center ersetzen soll. Der international diskutierte Entwurf von Daniel Libeskind, der inzwischen durch Einreden der Investoren bis zur Unkenntlichkeit entstellt wurde, sah ursprünglich einen 1776 Fuß hohen Turm vor, dessen Gestalt in abstrahierter Form die Freiheitsstatue in Erinnerung ruft und somit ebenfalls auf eine Figur der französischen Kunst des späten 19. Jahrhunderts Bezug nimmt (Taf. 48.2)[31]. Diesmal sollte ein Gebäude dem Schemen nach explizit eine menschliche Gestalt assoziieren lassen, um mittels bildhafter Züge Architektur in ihrem Symbolgehalt leichter ‚lesbar' und einprägsam zu machen. Dass in diesem Fall die Personifikation der Freiheit als (Vor-)Bild diente, resultiert aus der tragischen Vorgeschichte des Bauplatzes. Der 530 Meter-Wolkenkratzer, der als höchster Turm der Welt zugleich als Monument konzipiert war, sollte in der Libeskindschen Fassung an die Opfer der Terroranschläge ebenso wie an die amerikanische Unabhängigkeit und Freiheit gemahnen[32]. Dass in der New Yorker Freiheitsstatue des französischen Bildhauers Auguste Bartholdi als Armierung ein von Raymond Koechlin und Gustave Eiffel entworfenes Eisenskelett steckt, das dem des Eiffelturms eng verwandt ist, sei nur noch am Rande vermerkt.

BIBLIOGRAFIE

1889 – La Tour Eiffel et l'exposition Universelle. 1989. Ausstellungskatalog Museé d'Orsay, Paris. Paris: Biro.

Bartetzko, D. 2003. „Guter Wein. Das neue World Trade Center." In *Frankfurter Allgemeine Zeitung* vom 28. Februar 2003, 37.

Barthes, R. 1970. *Der Eiffelturm.* München: Rogner & Bernhard.

Buci-Glucksmann, C. 1997. *Der kartographische Blick der Kunst.* Berlin: Merve.

Benjamin, W. 1993. *Das Passagen-Werk,* herausgegeben von R. Tiedemann. Band 1. Frankfurt am Main: Suhrkamp.

Bilderwelten. *Französische Illustrationen des 18. und 19. Jahrhunderts. Aus der Sammlung von Kritter.* 1985. Ausstellungskatalog Museum für Kunst und Kulturgeschichte, Dortmund. Dortmund: Cramers Kunstanstalt.

Bode, U., Hrsg. 1984. *Paris – Belle Époque 1880-1914,* Ausstellungskatalog Villa Hügel, Essen. Recklinghausen: Bongers.

De Certeau, M. 1988. *Kunst des Handelns.* Internationaler Merve-Diskurs 140. Berlin: Merve.

Dewitz, B. v. und W. Nekes, Hrsg. 2002. *Ich sehe was, was Du nicht siehst! Sehmaschinen und Bilderwelten. Die Sammlung Nekes.* Ausstellungskatalog Museum Ludwig Köln. Göttingen: Steidl.

Eiffel, G. 1900. *La Tour de trois cents mètres.* Paris: Guyot.

—. 1902. *La Tour Eiffel en 1900.* Paris: Masson.

Einsiedel, W. v. und G. Woerner, Hrsg. 1974. Kindlers Literatur-Lexikon im dtv. 25 Bände. München: Deutscher Taschenbuch-Verlag.

Engell, L. 1999. „Der Turm als Medium, oder: Ausfahrt nach Babylon." *In Der Turm von Jena. Architektur und Zeichen,* herausgegeben von M. Diers, S. Grohé und C. Meurer, 147-51. Minerva. Jenaer Schriften zur Kunstgeschichte 9. Jena: Kunsthistorisches Seminar.

Finke, U., Hrsg. 1972. *French 19th Century Painting and Literature.* Manchester: University Press.

Forberg, G., Hrsg. 1975. *Gustave Doré. Das graphische Werk.* Band 1. München: Rogner & Bernhard.

30 De Certeau 1988, 179.

31 Bis heute steht unweit des Eiffelturms eine verkleinerte Variante der Freiheitsstatue am Seine-Ufer.

32 Vgl. zum ursprünglichen Konzept Mejias 2003; Bartetzko 2003. Zu den geänderten Plänen vgl. Ouroussoff 2005.

Fünf Jahrhunderte Buchillustration. Meisterwerke der Buchgraphik aus der Bibliothek Otto Schäfer. 1988. Ausstellungskatalog Germanisches Nationalmuseum Nürnberg und Bayerische Staatsbibliothek München. Nürnberg: Germanisches Nationalmuseum.

Giedion, S. 1992. *Raum, Zeit und Architektur.* Die Entstehung einer neuen Tradition. 5. Auflage. Zürich u.a.: Verlag für Architektur Artemis.

Hoffman, D. und A. Junker. 1982. *Laterna Magica. Lichtbilder aus Menschenwelt und Götterwelt.* Berlin: Frölich & Kaufmann.

Kafka, F. 1990. *Tagebücher*, herausgegeben von H.-G. Koch, M. Müller und M. Pasley, Band 1: Reisetagebuch vom September 1911. Frankfurt am Main: S. Fischer.

Klotz, V. 1969. *Die erzählte Stadt. Ein Sujet als Herausforderung des Romans von Lesage bis Döblin.* München: Hanser.

Le Diable à Paris. Paris et les Parisiens. 1845/6. 2 Bände. Paris: J. Hetzel.

L'Œuvre de Gavarni. 2002. Erweiterter Neudruck. *L'Œuvre de Gavarni. Catalogue Raisonne of the Graphic Work*, herausgeben von J. Armelhaut und E. Bocher. San Francisco: Wofsy Fine Arts. Originalausgabe: Paris: Plon. 1873.

Lemm, K. 2005. „Reisen auf dem digitalen Globus." In *Stern* vom 14. Juli 2005, 102.

Lemoine, B. 1988. *Gustave Eiffel.* Basel u.a.: Birkhäuser.

—. 1989. *La Tour de Monsieur Eiffel.* Découvertes Gallimard 62. Paris: Gallimard.

Loyrette, H. 1992. „La Tour Eiffel." In *Les Lieux de Mémoire*, herausgegeben von P. Nora, Band 3, 474-503. Paris: Gallimard.

Lüber, K. 2005. „Der Traum vom Fliegen. Aus den Schluchten Manhattans zu den Füßen der Sphinx." In *Süddeutsche Zeitung* vom 09./ 10. Juli 2005, 156.

Mejias, J. 2003. „Fundamente der Widerstandskraft. Noch ist nicht entschieden, ob Daniel Libeskind oder das Team um Rafael Vinoly Ground Zero bauen." In *Frankfurter Allgemeine Zeitung* vom 3. Februar 2003, 40.

Ouroussoff, N. 2005. „A Tower of Impregnability, the Sort That Politicians Love." In *The New York Times*, Beilage der *Süddeutsche Zeitung* vom 18. Juli 2005, 15.

Paris. 1979. Michelin Reiseführer. Karlsruhe: Michelin Reifenwerke.

Steinhauser, M. 1992. „Der inszenierte Blick des Flaneurs. Manet und Baudelaire." In *Konstruktionen der Moderne*, 9-40. Im Blickfeld 1. Jahrbuch der Hamburger Kunsthalle.

Stierle, K. 1993. *Der Mythos von Paris. Zeichen und Bewußtsein der Stadt.* München: Deutscher Taschenbuchverlag.

Stuffmann, M., Hrsg. 1975. *Charles Meryon. Paris um 1850. Zeichnungen, Radierungen, Photographien.* Ausstellungskatalog Städelsches Kunstinstitut und Städtische Galerie Frankfurt am Main und Hamburger Kunsthalle. Frankfurt am Main: Städelsches Kunstinstitut und Städtische Galerie.

Weiß, S. 1992. „Paris aus der Vogelschau. Modernität im Zweiten Kaiserreich." Magisterarbeit, Kunstgeschichtliches Seminar der Universität Hamburg.

Wittkop-Menardeau, G. und J.F. Wittkop. 1978. *Paris – Prisma einer Stadt. Eine illustrierte Kulturgeschichte.* Zürich u.a.: Atlantis.

1. Gavarni, Frontispiz zu „Le Diable à Paris", Holzstich von Henri Brugnot, 1845. Archiv des Verfassers.

2. Edmond Texier, Tableau de Paris, Paris 1852/53, Bd.I, Titelillustration. Nach: Stuffmann 1975, 16.

3. Laterna Magica, Blechlaterne mit eingeschobenem Glasbildstreifen, 18. Jahrhundert. Nach: Hoffmann und Junker 1982, 24.

4. Lichtbildprojektion einer Teufelsgestalt, Federzeichnung aus Giovanni da Fontana, Bellicorum instrumentorum liber, Manuskript um 1420, Cod. icon. 242, Bayerische Staatsbibliothek, München. Nach: Hoffmann und Junker 1982, 14.

1. Pégard, *La Lanterne Magique*, um 1850, Holzstich. Nach: Dewitz und Nekes 2002, 127.

2. Gustave Doré, *Der Riese Gargantua*, Holzstich von Sotain, aus: François Rabelais, Oeuvres de François Rabelais contenant la vie de Gargantua et celle de Pantagruel, Paris 1854. Nach: Forberg 1975, 39.

3. Victor Navlet, *Vue générale de Paris, prise de l'Observatoire*, 1855 (INV. 20094) Paris, musée d'Orsay.

1. Nadar im Ballonkorb, Atelierfoto um 1865. Nach: Wittkop-Menardeau und Wittkop. 1978, 370.

2. Der Eiffelturm um 1889. Nach: Wittkop-Menardeau und Wittkop. 1978, 281.

3. Paris-Panorama mit Eiffelturm und Trocadéro („pris en ballon"), Postkarte, Fotografie von J.H. Deposé, Musée Carnavalet, Paris. Nach: Bode 1984, 28.

1. 25 Jahre Eiffelturm: Aktuelle Nutzung zur drahtlosen Telegraphie, Illustration aus „Le Petit Journal", 1914. Nach: Lemoine 1989, 72.

2. George Garen, *Illumination des Eiffelturms anläßlich der Weltausstellung von 1889*, 1889, Aquarell, Musée d'Orsay, Paris. Nach: 1889 – La Tour Eiffel et l'exposition Universelle, Paris 1989, 34.

3. Karikatur auf Gustave Eiffel aus „Punch", 1889. Nach: Lemoine 1989, 144.

4. Eiffelturm-Laterna Magica, Hersteller Louis Aubert, Frankreich 1889, Slg. Werner Nekes, Mülheim/ Ruhr. Nach: Dewitz und W. Nekes 2002, 133.

1. Blick auf Paris von Südwesten, Google Earth-Satellitenbild, screenshot 2005.

2. Blick auf die Skyline von New York mit geplantem Ground Zero-Turmhochhaus von Daniel Libeskind, 2003, Computersimulation. Nach: Die Welt vom 28. Februar 2003, Titelseite.

Zur Inszenierung der totalen Herrschaft: Ursprungskult bei den Reichsparteitagen der NSDAP

Yvonne Karow

Abstract

This study is intended to reflect on the function of cult and on what it transmits. The question is raised to what extent the *National Socialist movement* stages itself as a cult, which means are used to facilitate this staging and which function it fulfills, i.e. to channel the physical and emotional movement of individual participants. If the *Reichsparteitag* is understood as a cultic event, then the *Reichparteitagsgelände* is the cult locale, in which the rite is practiced. The description of the function of the associated ritual canon is developed in three steps. Firstly, the ties entered or established in the festive act are demonstrated, their functions and meanings explored. The ritual evocation, e.g., of those who fell in World War I or as *blood-witnesses* of the *movement* forms, in prescribed ritual form, a regular and central element of the *Reichsparteitage*. In this way, the world of the heroic dead is integrated in the world of the living and the heroes' fate offered as an example to be followed. This tie to the world of the dead, which is acknowledged as better than the one of the living, is intended to foster power and strength and allow to regain them. Ritual practice (e.g. the touching of the *Blutfahne*) permits to approach this world. What is held to be life's aim, i.e. to *sacrifice* life for the *movement*, is incorporated in the events and thus aggrandized. The ties entered by each participant establish a closeness to the *movement's* roots and engender a readiness for sacrifice.

In dealing with the second aspect, the cultic staging of power is considered. This power is the *movement's* power, which permeates the *Volksgemeinschaft*, the community of the people. The argument is developed through reference to the architecture of the *Parteitagsgelände*, which is characterized as an architecture of death by its monolithic and antivital character and its borrowings from sepulchral architecture. Its sole purpose is to help the staging of the *movement*, a function which is identified as a specifically National Socialist trait. Building materials evoking eternal duration, the buildings themselves and the routes prescribed by the architecture have to be understood as functions and cult paraphernalia of a ritual act and its staging.

Liturgical activity is not only expressive and staged, but also encompasses representation. As a democratic form of parliamentary representation is rejected, the question arises how to represent what is expressed and staged at the *Reichsparteitage*. Party formations marching or standing to attention come to stand for the people; *sacrifice* can be identified as the content of representation. Hitler represents *Germany*, an empty phrase which signifies the *Ursprungsmacht*, an original force or power, and attains its function in the self-submission of the individual. In the ritual act, the individual sacrifices itself to this "origin", an act affirmed by specific rites (*Blutfahne*) and oaths. At the outbreak of World War II in 1939, this representative act of the people becomes redundant as it is replaced by actual *sacrifice* in battle.

Die Reichsparteitagsveranstaltungen als kultische Inszenierungen zu deuten, ist nicht neu. Bereits Hans-Jochen Gamm und Klaus Vondung hoben den kultischen Charakter dieser als politisch ausgegebenen Veranstaltungen hervor[1]. In dieser kleinen Abhandlung soll darüber reflektiert werden, was eigentlich die Funktion von Kult ist und was hier transportiert wird. Gefragt wird, inwieweit sich die nationalsozialistische Bewegung kultisch inszeniert, welcher Hilfsmittel sie dazu bedarf und welche Funktion dies letztlich ausübt, nämlich die Bewegtheit jedes Einzelnen zu kanalisieren. Wird der Reichsparteitag als kultische Veranstaltung interpretiert, so gilt das Reichsparteitagsgelände als Kultort, wo der Ritus vollzogen wird. Da wir es mit der Sphäre des Mythos zu tun haben, denn in den Kulten sucht man die Bindung zu einer mythischen Urvergangenheit, von der man Identität und Mächtigkeit für den Alltag bezieht, sollen hier auch spezifisch religionswissenschaftliche Kategorien verwendet werden, wie sie der Religionswissenschaftler und -philosoph Paul Tillich generiert hat. In diesem Sinne wird besonderes Augenmerk auf den Inhalt des Kultus gelegt, i.e. in der Tillichschen Begriffsnomenklatur spezifischer Ursprungsort, spezifische Ursprungszeit und Ursprungsbedeutung in Hinblick auf eine Ursprungsnähe.

Wenn man fragt, was als kultische Inszenierung gelten kann, so muss nach dem entsprechenden rituellen Regelwerk gefragt werden. Denn der Ritus zeigt den spezifischen Ort, die spezifische Zeit und die spezifische Bedeutung eines Kultus an. Diese Bindungen verweisen – meist genealogisch hergeleitet – auf eine imaginierte begründende Vergangenheit und stiften Identität und Sinn. Die Reichsparteitage werden zum Thema gemacht, weil unterstellt wird, dass bestimmte religiöse Vorstellungen als Schubkräfte für die nationalsozialistische Massenbewegung fungierten, die an ihnen, da sie die objektivierte Spitze der NS-Ideologie darstellten, abzulesen sind[2]. Hier inszeniert sich der NS am aufwendigsten und am konsequentesten. So wird insbesondere die Binnensicht des nationalsozialistischen Veranstaltungsgeschehens dargestellt. Das kultische Geschehen beinhaltet Ausdruck (der Ursprungsbindung), Inszenierung (der ‚Bewegung') und Repräsentation (des Volkes). Da in dieser Abhandlung besonderer Wert auf die Inszenierungsseite gelegt wird, werden Ausdrucks- und Repräsentationsseite nur so weit dargestellt, wie es zum Verständnis der Argumentationsstruktur geboten erscheint. Für eine ausführliche Darstellung verweise ich auf meine Monographie *Deutsches Opfer*[3]. Zur Beantwortung der Frage, wie diese produktive Inszenierungsseite der Bewegung rezipiert worden ist, d.h. inwieweit die Bevölkerung die nationalsozialistische Mythenbildung durch die eigene Wunsch- und Bedürfnisstruktur unterstützt und getragen hat, sei ebenfalls die genannte Monographie zur Lektüre empfohlen.

1. Anbindung an die mythische Ursprungswelt: Imagines von ewigem Ort, ewiger Zeit und ewigem Volk

Fragt man nach dem Ausdruck, so muss nach den Bindungen gefragt werden, die im Kultus eingegangen werden, und welche Funktion sie haben. Z.B. gehört die Anrufung der im Ersten Weltkrieg oder für die Bewegung gefallenen Blutzeugen zum festen und zentralen Bestandteil der Reichsparteitage[4]. Damit wird die Welt der Heldentoten in die der Lebenden eingebunden und deren Schicksal der Nachahmung anempfohlen[5]. Von der Bindung an die Welt der Toten, die als eine bessere anerkannt wird, erhofft man sich Kraft und Stärke. An sie sucht man sich im Vollzug des Rituals (z.B. durch Berührung mit der Blutfahne[6]) anzunähern. Das ideologische Ziel des Lebens, dieses für die Bewegung zu opfern, wird in die Feierveranstaltung eingebunden und damit kultisch überhöht. Zudem werden u.a. alle geographischen

1 Gamm 1962, Vondung 1971.

2 Siehe hierzu ausführlich Karow 1997.

3 Karow 1997.

4 Zu Beginn der Eröffnungsveranstaltung werden die Namen „der Nationalsozialisten, die im Kampf um die Macht gefallen sind, die [...] ihr Leben für Großdeutschland hingaben, die im Ausland wegen ihrer Gesinnung bolschewistischer Mordgier zum Opfer fielen" (zitiert nach Kerrl 1938, 39) verlesen. Zum Ablauf des Rituals vgl. Kerrl 1938, 38f. Rituelle Totenehrungen wurden in ähnlicher Form bei allen Aufmärschen vorgenommen.

5 Vgl. Kerrl 1938.

6 Die *Blutfahne* soll beim Marsch auf die Feldherrnhalle 1923 mit dem Blut der bei dem Putschversuch umgekommenen oder verletzten Mitstreiter der Bewegung getränkt worden sein. Aufgrund des magischen Aktes der Berührung glaubte man, Anteil an der Heldenkraft der Toten zu haben – eine rituell eingeübte Identifizierung, die auf eine ausgeprägte Opferhaltung und -bereitschaft schließen lässt.

Bereiche, repräsentiert durch die vorgeführten Standarten, die stellvertretend für die Volksgemeinschaft stehen, aufgerufen und beschworen. Sie erhalten ebenfalls durch die Berührung mit der Blutfahne kultische Einbindung. Diese Bindungen, die von jedem Einzelnen eingegangen werden, erzeugen Bindung an die imaginierte Vergangenheit oder, im Sinne Tillichs, an ‚Ursprungsnähe' und ‚Opferbereitschaft'. Dieser imaginierte Ursprung, an den man sich anzunähern sucht und von dem man seine Kraft zu beziehen glaubt, wird als spezifisch ‚deutsch' imaginiert.

Nürnberg erschien im 19. Jahrhundert aufgrund bestimmter Faktoren gleichsam als Verkörperung vaterländischer Ideale und Symbol deutscher Kultur. Seit 1219 mit dem Status als freie Reichsstadt privilegiert, war Nürnberg zudem seit 1356 Austragungsort des ersten Reichstages eines jeden neu gewählten Königs. Die Stadt hatte eine wirtschaftliche und kulturelle Blüte im 15. und 16. Jahrhundert und eine große politische Bedeutung während der Reformationszeit. Der als ursprünglich ‚deutsch' geltende Charakter ihrer Architektur und das Aufkommen der Tradition der Meistersinger im 16. Jahrhundert taten ein Übriges, Nürnberg im Zuge des romantischen Interesses am ‚Altdeutschen' wiederzuentdekken. Ihren exponierten Ausdruck fanden diese Bestrebungen in Richard Wagners germanisches Mythenmaterial verarbeitendem Werk *Die Meistersinger von Nürnberg*[7].

Der mittelalterlichen Stadt zugeordnete Attribute, wie Unabhängigkeit und Freiheit sowie wirtschaftliche Stärke und eine dementsprechende kulturelle Leistungsfähigkeit, verbunden mit der Vorstellung, hier manifestiere sich ursprüngliches Deutschtum, bildete ein Amalgam für das Bedürfnis nach Anknüpfung an den ‚Ursprung'[8] spezifisch ‚deutscher' Geschichte. Zum Rückbindungsort wird also im Kontrast zur ‚seelenlosen Großstadt' ein Zentrum der Provinz, ungeachtet der modernen Technologieanwendungen wie beispielsweise in der dortigen Spielzeugindustrie. Die aus vielen unterschiedlichen Faktoren zusammengesetzte Gemengelage, die zur Wahl Nürnbergs als Stadt der Reichsparteitage geführt hatte, diente der identitätsbildenden Funktion, sich mit einem spezifisch 'deutsch' gedachten ‚Ursprungsort', ausgedrückt durch die Metapher ‚Nürnberg', eins zu wissen.

Die mythische Zeitvorstellung, die sich im Ritus zum Ausdruck bringt, ist zyklisch und mit Ewigkeitsmetaphern konnotiert. Der Septemberbeginn als Zeitraum der jährlich wiederkehrenden Reichsparteitage bindet diese an den deutschen Sieg über die Franzosen am 2. September 1870 – eine Synthese, die Teilhabe an einem Triumph verleiht, der dem drängenden Bedürfnis nach Tilgung der erlittenen ‚Schmach' durch den verlorenen Ersten Weltkrieg zur Kompensation verhilft. Die periodisch-zyklische, den irreversiblen Verlauf der Zeit und somit die Geschichte überwindende und Einheit mit dem Ursprung versinnbildlichende Rhythmisierung des Kultus ist durchgängiges Ausdrucksmittel der Reichsparteitagsinszenierungen und spiegelt die inszenatorische Absicht, die Bewegung mit der steten rhythmischen Wiederkehr natürlicher Prozesse (das ‚ewige Stirb und Werde') in eins zu setzen und ihr somit Ewigkeitswert und damit Ursprungsnähe zu verleihen. Nicht nur der Parteitag als Ganzes findet seine zyklische Wiederholung (die insgesamt zehn Veranstaltungen von 1923 bis 1938 unterscheiden sich formal nicht wesentlich voneinander), sondern auch dessen Einzelveranstaltungen sind streng durchformalisiert. Unterlegt ist das rhythmische Geschehen mit dumpfem Trommelwirbel, der nahezu jedes Ritual einleitet oder dessen Höhepunkt kennzeichnet. Ursprünglich den Takt der Marschierenden angebend, wird der Trommelschlag nicht nur bei den Aufmärschen, sondern auch bei anderen Feierformen zum beherrschenden Stilelement des Geschehens und zum Ausdruck gleicher Gesinnung und Tat[9]. Neben den Elementen der Feiergestaltung – Trommelwirbel, Musik, Tanz und Spiele – drücken die rhythmische Praxis der chorischen Wechselreden bei Bekenntnisformeln und Treuegelöbnissen[10], das exzessive Aufmarschieren im Gleichschritt sowie das stereotype Insistieren auf die Mechanisierung der Bewegungsformen, durch die das Feiergeschehen zum ‚Ornament der Masse'[11] gerinnt, die erstrebte Überwindung der Zeit und das Eintauchen in eine mythische Urzeit aus. Die Anbindung an eine mythische Urzeit und an einen mythischen Ursprungsort dient somit der Einbettung in eine problemfreie Zone, d.h. in einen von Raumproblemen freien Raum und in eine von Zeitproblemen freie Zeit.

7 Vgl. u.a. Burden 1967, 11f.; Täubrich 1993, 16-9; Zelnhefer 1993.

8 zur Terminologie vgl. Tillich 1948.

9 Z.B. zum Auftakt des zentralen Totenrituals am Sonntag. S. hierzu Offizieller Bericht 1938, 298. Zur Feierstunde des RAD vgl. Offizieller Bericht 1938, 96f.

10 Vgl. z.B. das Gelöbnis des RAD in Offizieller Bericht 1938, 96f.

11 Kracauer 1977.

Zu den Imagines von (deutschem) Ursprungsort und ewiger Zeit gehört eine spezifische Ursprungsgesellschaft, die rituell als ewig und mächtig gekennzeichnet ist. Durch den Aufmarsch aller Gliederungen der Partei wird eine eigene, formierte, neuständische und hierarchisch gegliederte Ritualgesellschaft unter Auslassung der realen gesellschaftlichen Differenzierung[12] als geschlossene Gesamtheit präsentiert. Die nationalsozialistischen Gefolgschaftsgruppierungen werden als Ganzes vorgeführt und kultisch verarbeitet. Damit soll zum Ausdruck gebracht werden, dass die einzelnen Verbände in das nationalsozialistische Ganze legitim eingebunden seien: Das Führungskorps steht für den nationalsozialistischen Staat selbst, die Politischen Leiter für dessen Amtsapparat, der Reichsarbeitsdienst (RAD) für die Gruppe der Werktätigen; Hitlerjugend (HJ), Bund deutscher Mädel (BDM) und Pimpfe repräsentieren die Jugend; die Nationalsozialistische Frauenschaft verkörpert den weiblichen Teil der Volksgemeinschaft; Sturmabteilung (SA) und Schutzstaffeln (SS) stehen für das innerparteiliche Soldatentum und bilden mit den Einheiten der Luftwaffe, Marine, des Heeres und der Polizei sowie des Nationalsozialistischen Fliegerkorps (NSFK) und des Nationalsozialistischen Kraftfahrkorps (NSKK) die Exekutive. Ihrer besonderen Funktion innerhalb der nationalsozialistischen Gesellschaft gemäß, werden den Verbänden der RAD, HJ, SA, der Wehrmacht und denen der Politischen Leiter eigene, besonders ausgearbeitete Feierformen zugeordnet. Diese Gesellschaft wird im Kultus als inszenatorischer Ersatz mit Realcharakter anstelle der realhistorischen Erfahrungen gesellschaftlicher Differenzierungen und Zerfallserscheinungen gesetzt. Die einzelnen geographischen Bereiche des Reiches, repräsentiert durch die bei jedem Aufmarsch zahlreich mitgeführten Fahnen und Standarten der Gaue und Städte, müssen aus Sicht der Partei ebenfalls rituell integriert werden. Alle den NS-Staat formierenden gesellschaftlichen Gruppierungen sowie alle dem Reich zugehörigen Regionen werden somit in das rituelle Geschehen eingebunden[13].

1.1 URSPRUNGSNÄHE DURCH OPFERHALTUNG

Der zentrale Gemeinschaft stiftende Ritus ist (neben dem Aufmarsch) die Fahnenweihe, in deren Mittelpunkt die Berührung mit der Blutfahne, dem Hauptkultrequisit der Reichsparteitage, steht. Als Banner des fehlgeschlagenen Novemberputsches von 1923, das mit dem Blut der Märtyrer der Bewegung getränkt sei, steht sie für die Welt der Heldentoten, speziell derer, die für die Bewegung gefallen sind und dadurch ihre Opferbereitschaft ‚erwiesen' haben, eine Haltung, die zur Nachahmung anempfohlen wird. Dies alles wird durch die Berührung auf gleichsam magische Weise übertragen. Damit wird die Welt der Heldentoten in die der Lebenden eingebunden und ihr Opferschicksal mit dem der Traditionsträger verknüpft. Man wird so des Märtyrerstatus'[14] der Parteimitglieder der ersten Generation teilhaftig.

Eigentlich kommen die Toten mit den Lebenden nur in Berührung, so legen es Sagen, Volkslieder und Balladen nahe, um jene zu sich holen. Wenn nun die Lebenden die Toten beschwören, wie in dem bekannten Refrain des *Horst-Wessel-Liedes*: „Kam'raden, die Rotfront und Reaktion erschossen,/ marschier'n im Geist in unsern Reihen mit!“[15], verweist dies auf die Gleichsetzung von Totenheer und Lebendenheer im dem Sinne, dass man die Toten bei sich mitmarschieren lässt. Sie werden aufgenommen um der Stärkung willen: sich selbst den Toten weihen, um zu siegen und dabei in der Regel den Tod zu finden[16]. Wenn man dies ertragen kann, ist man gleichsam selbst ein Toter. Die andere, feindliche Seite weiß, dass sie jetzt durch die Beschwörung der Toten gleichsam mit einem Totenheer zu kämpfen hat, was dessen Schlagkraft auf unerhörte Weise verstärkt. Die Totenkopfzeichen der SS drücken dies am augenfälligsten und extremsten aus: Wir sind eigentlich ein Totenheer, wir sind immer schon dem Tode geweiht, wir haben die Toten mit uns und sind eigentlich selbst Tote. Dies hilft, die Angst vor dem Tod zu bewältigen, denn Tote haben keine Angst, verbreiten sie aber[17]. Die mit vollem Marschgepäck ausgerüsteten, Dominanz ausstrahlenden

12 Die realhistorische Situation steht im diametralen Gegensatz zur kultisch vorgeführten geschlossenen Volksgemeinschaft.

13 Rudolf Heß bei der Kongresseröffnung (S. hierzu Kerrl 1938, 40).

14 Er drückt sich aus im Begriff ‚Blutzeuge'.

15 Zitiert nach dem *Liederbuch des Reichsarbeitsdienstes.*

16 Vgl. u.a. die klassischen historischen Beispiele in Livius' Ab urbe condita, in dem der römische Feldherr in einer aussichtslos erscheinenden Situation die andere Seite dennoch besiegen will, indem er sich und sein Heer den Toten weiht.

17 Klaus Heinrich in einem Gespräch am 06.12.1991.

geschlossenen Kohorten, die durch das Parteitagsgelände und die Stadt marschieren, sind die sichtbare Verkörperung dieses angstfreien Kampfeswillens und der entschlossenen Opferbereitschaft.

Wie nun die gesuchte und durch den Opferstatus erkaufte Ursprungsnähe im Sinne des nationalsozialistischen Staatsmythos inszenatorisch umgesetzt wird, soll am Beispiel der architektonischen Gestaltung des Reichsparteitagsgeländes aufgezeigt werden.

2. Die Reichsparteitagsbauten als Inszenierung des Ursprungs

Die Bühnen und Dekorationsarchitekturen[18] auf dem Parteitagsgelände dienen ausschließlich als Inszenierungshilfe für den Kultus, eine Funktion, die als NS-spezifische bestimmt werden kann. Dafür spricht, dass das Reichsparteitagsgelände ein Areal sein sollte, das ausschließlich für die Reichsparteitagsfeierlichkeiten konzipiert wurde und somit bereits als kultische Sphäre gekennzeichnet ist. Allein die Luitpoldarena mit Gefallenenehrenmal sowie das Zeppelinfeld und die Große Straße wurden fertig gestellt; alle anderen Bauwerke, wie Deutsches Stadion, Kongreßbau und Märzfeld, haben den Projektstatus nicht überschritten bzw. zeugten als Bauruinen vom Ende des Tausendjährigen Reiches. Auskunft über den Inszenierungscharakter der Parteitagsbauten geben aus der nationalsozialistischen Binnensicht vornehmlich die Äußerungen Hitlers[19], die des von ihm für die Parteitagsbauten beauftragten Architekten Paul Ludwig Troost und, nach dessen Tod 1934, die Albert Speers[20].

Das ewige Haltbarkeit verbürgende Baumaterial (wie Granit), die Aufbauten und die Straßenführungen sind als kultische Funktionen und Kultkulissen zu werten[21], die bereits auf den Ewigkeitscharakter der Bewegung hindeuten. Neben vereinzelten ägyptisierenden Elementen[22] sind die frühesten architektonischen Bezüge Reminiszenzen an die griechische und teilweise römische Antike[23]. Diese werden ästhetisch in Dienst genommen, da man der Meinung war, die Antike gehe im Grunde genommen auf germanische Wurzeln zurück. Die Bauwerke stehen somit für die ästhetische Demonstration und Beschwörung der mythischen, als spezifisch ‚deutsch' verstandenen Urzeit[24], von der aus man eine universale, Raum und Zeit transzendierende Geltung der Bewegung genealogisch zu legitimieren sucht.

In ihrem Aufsatz über die Antikenrezeption der Speer'schen Reichsparteitagsbauten konstatiert Yasmyn Doosry zum Grundriss des 1937 fertiggestellten Zeppelinfeldes[25] (Abb. 1): viereckiger Platz mit vorbeiführender Straße, stilistische Adaptionen einer griechischen Agora[26], speziell der von Priene.

Die Haupttribüne entspreche der dortigen Heiligen Halle, da sie wie jene über ansteigende Stufenreihen, abschließende Pfeilerhallen, eine Niveauerhöhung gegenüber der Platzfläche und eine vorgelagerte große Freitreppe verfüge[27]. Albert Speer selbst, der 1934 von Hitler den Auftrag erhielt, die damals vorhandene provisorische Holztribüne durch eine steinerne Anlage zu ersetzen[28], bezieht sich auf die griechische Antike, da er seinen Tribünenentwurf von der Formensprache des Pergamonaltars (ca. 181 v.

18 Benno von Arent, künstlerischer Ausstatter von Opern und Operetten, wurde von Hitler zum Reichsbühnenbildner ernannt und zur Ausführung seiner Bühnenbildideen nach dem traditionellen Muster Wagnerscher Opern herangezogen. Er inszenierte z.B. *Die Meistersinger von Nürnberg*. Von ihm stammen auch die Pläne, große Straßen mit Pylonen zu säumen. S. hierzu Speer 1978, 154f., 199.

19 So Adolf Hitler in der Speer'schen (1978a, 155) Erinnerung. Vgl. auch Teut 1967, 13, 91f., 188f.

20 Vgl. Troost 1938/43. Zu Speer s. u.a. Speer 1943, 1976, 1978a, 1978b.

21 Vgl. u.a. Hitlers Äußerungen über Architektur und Städtebau in Teut 1967, 181f.

22 Barbara Miller Lane (1973, 343, fig. 4, 5) sieht eine ästhetische Verbindung zwischen der Zeppelinfeldtribüne und dem Grabmal der Königin Hatshepsut at Deir-el-bahari; vgl. die Kritik Scobies (1990, 87, 90), laut derer die hellenistischen Elemente die Architektur deutlich beherrschen. Vgl. Bartetzko 1986, 1849.

23 Auf eine architekturtheoretische Diskussion der Stilelemente wird verzichtet, da sie für die Analyse des Inszenierungscharakters der Reichsparteitagsarchitektur nur von marginaler Bedeutung ist (vgl. z.B. die Neoklassizismus-Debatte in Schäche 1979, Koch 1978, Larsson 1978).

24 Die Dorer waren, so die herrschende Rassenideologie, germanischen Ursprungs.

25 Doosry 1979, 110f.; Ogan und Zelnhefer 1986, 5; Dehlinger 1951, 54f.; Arndt 1973, 10-2.

26 vgl. Radt 1988, 106-18, bes. 112-8.

27 Doosry 1979, 112.

28 Speer 1976, 67f.

Abb. 1. Zeppelinfeld, zeitgenössische Postkarte, Sammlung Karow.

Chr.) ableitete[29]. Doosry wiederum bestätigt die Komparabilität in Bezug auf die breite Freitreppe und die Pfeiler- bzw. Säulenhallen, ordnet diese Elemente jedoch nicht bestimmten antiken Bauten zu, da sie in der zeitgenössischen Architektur allgemein verbreitet gewesen seien. Vielmehr vergleicht Doosry den Mitteltrakt der Tribünenrückfront (die Wandgliederung durch vier bzw. drei Türen, die Rhythmisierung durch eine vertikale Gliederung sowie durch Vor- und Rücksprünge) und die Vorderseite des Mitteltraktes der Ehrentribüne (zehn Wandpfeiler auf Stufensockel) mit dem Tempel von Didyma. Die Tür in der Mitte der Zehnpfeilerfront sei mit der Tempeltür von Didyma vergleichbar, die bereits im Dritten Reich als Erscheinungstür des Gottes und als Verkündigungsort des priesterlichen Orakels interpretiert wurde[30]. Dennoch scheint die ästhetisch-assoziative Verbindung zum Pergamonaltar für die kultische Szenerie von größerer Bedeutung. Mit Hilfe dieser Reminiszenz werden die dem Pergamonaltar zugeordneten kultischen Elemente aus der griechischen Antike ästhetisch-archaisierend auf die Zeppelinfeldtribüne und die ihr zugeordneten Feierhandlungen übertragen und in die Gegenwart geholt. Zu diesen assoziativ aus dem Pergamonkult in das Reichsparteitagsgeschehen übertragenen Elementen gehören[31]: die überdimensionierte Gestaltung und Funktionalisierung der Zeppelinfeldtribüne als Opferaltar, deren Weihe an die Hauptgöttin von Pergamon, die siegbringende (*nikephoros*) Stadtgöttin Athena und ihren Vater, den obersten Herrscher über das Pantheon und Kämpfer gegen die Mächte der Finsternis, sowie der Bezug zu den hohen Stadtopferfesten, den Nikephorien[32], bei denen die geschlachteten Opfertiere zum Teil verbrannt und die Reste des Fleisches an die Festteilnehmer verteilt wurden. Die auf dem *Großen Fries* dargestellten Kämpfe zwischen Göttern und Giganten stehen für die Verteidigung der griechischen Kultur gegen die Barbaren. Pergamon stilisierte man als zweites Athen und als Vorkämpferin der griechischen Freiheit sowie der traditionellen griechischen Werte, während das Königsgeschlecht von Pergamon mit dem siegreichen Göttergeschlecht des Zeus intentional identifiziert wurde.

29 1936 nach Entwürfen aus dem Jahr 1934 fertiggestellt (s. hierzu Speer 1976, 68). Zur Collagierung von Stilelementen s. auch Koch 1978, 139f.

30 Doosry 1979, 112f.; zu den Architekturzitaten aus dem Formenfundus des Schinkelschen Alten Museums in Berlin (diese betreffen den Vorbau) vgl. Koch 1978, 141.

31 Für den Pergamonaltar im folgenden nach: Radt 1988, 190-206.

32 Begleitet von musischen, gymnischen und hippischen Wettkämpfen. S. hierzu Radt, 1988, 271f.

Abb. 2. Deutsches Stadion (Modell), abgedruckt mit freundlicher Genehmigung der Bildstelle des Hochbauamtes Nürnberg.

Die Zeppelinfeldtribüne ist somit als Opferaltar einer siegreichen Stadtgottheit – die Assoziation an Athena wirft ein Licht des Sieges und der Stärke auf den Ursprungsort Nürnberg – ästhetisch gekennzeichnet. Die Stadt, der Opferaltar und der Sieg werden durch die pergamenischen Formadaptionen aufeinander bezogen, wobei die übersteigerten Maße der Tribüne die Bedeutung dieses Verhältnisses außerordentlich überhöhen. Der überdimensionierte Opferaltar, der hier in dem extrem pointierten architektonischen Tribünengewand erscheint, fordert gleichsam überwältigend und mit Nachdruck zum Opfer an den Ursprung (metaphorisch: Nürnberg) auf, ein Opfer, das – so die Binnensicht – der kulturbringenden ‚Bewegung der Herrenrasse' zum endgültigen Sieg über die barbarischen Mächte der Finsternis, wie ‚Juden, Bolschewisten, Demokraten' etc., verhelfen soll. Hitler, durch die Führerkanzel ins Zentrum des Geschehens gerückt, wird in diesem Licht als oberster Opferer markiert: Göttergleich wie Zeus wird er, so macht das Bauwerk assoziativ deutlich, einen siegreichen Kampf gegen die bedrohlichen Mächte der Finsternis führen.

Neben Adaptionen aus dem Formenkanon antiker griechischer Architektur bezieht sich Speer mittels eines Größenvergleichs der Tribünenanlage mit den Caracalla-Thermen in Rom – es ist für ihn von großer Wichtigkeit, sie um „fast das Doppelte"[33] übertroffen zu haben – gleichzeitig auf die römische Antike. Eine ästhetische Verbindung zum Zweiten Reich wird durch ein dekoratives Versatzstück geknüpft, das auf die jüngste Vergangenheit verweist: Die Ausfachungen der Pfeilerreihen mit Hakenkreuzflaggen sind in leuchtendem Rot gehalten. Zusammen mit dem kontrastierenden weißen Jurakalkstein erinnern sie an die alten Reichsfarben der Hohenzollernzeit[34].

Die architektonische Formgebung des Tribünenbaus steht somit bereits für das Bestreben, die gesamte Geschichte auf die Partei zu vereinen und in Besitz zu nehmen. Der Bogen wird gespannt von der grauen Vorzeit ägyptischer Königsdynastien über die griechisch-römische Antike und das Kaiserreich bis zum *Dritten*, dem *Tausendjährigen Reich*, wobei auch Anleihen an die französische Revolutionsarchitektur[35] gemacht werden. Auch die anderen Parteitagsbauten folgen diesem Konzept assoziativer Übertragungen.

Im Deutschen Stadion (Abb. 2), das nicht über die Projektionsphase hinaus gediehen war, amalgamieren, so Doosry, zwei antike Bauformen: die des griechischen Stadions mit der typischen Form des

33 Speer 1976, 68.

34 Die Fahnen selbst bilden mit dem schwarzen Hakenkreuz in der Mitte eines weißen Kreises auf rotem Grund die Trikolorefarben des Kaiserreiches ab (vgl. Thöne 1979, 27); zum symbolischen Zusammenhang zwischen der Farbe Rot sowie Blut und Feuer vgl. Thöne 1979, 24: „Während der Nürnberger Reichsparteitage konnte am ‚Tag der politischen Leiter' der nächtliche Einmarsch von 30.000 angestrahlten Fahnenträgern [...] so erlebt werden, als ob ein riesiger Organismus durch einen belebenden, gleichsam ‚befeuernden' Blutstrom zu neuer Kraft kommt".

35 Vgl. Vogt 1970, 358.

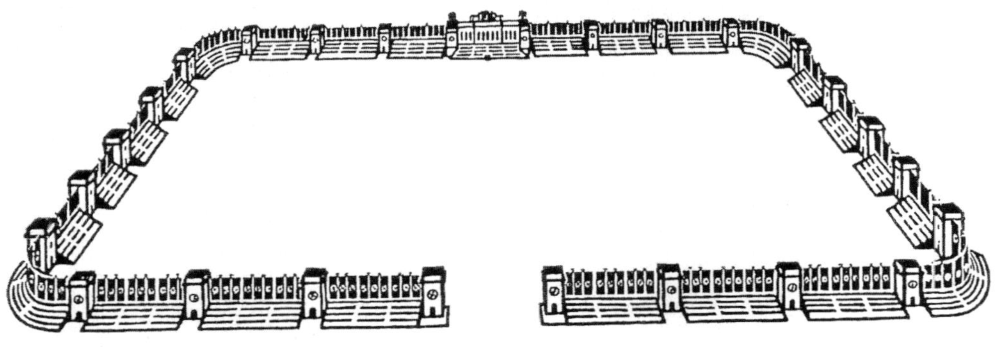

Abb. 3. Märzfeld (Zeichnung), abgedruckt mit freundlicher Genehmigung von Prof. Weiß, Nürnberg.

langgestreckten Hufeisens – Speer nennt das Athener Stadion des Herodes Atticus, das ihn bei seinem Besuch 1935 tief beeindruckte, als architektonisches Vorbild[36] – und die des antiken Theaters, wofür die gedrungenen, dem Grundriss einer Cavea vergleichbaren Proportionen und die Ähnlichkeit der dem Stadion zugekehrten Seite des Standartenheiligtums mit einer griechischen Bühnenfront sprechen.

Die Außenfront des Stadions mit ihren extrem hohen Pfeilerarkaden bildet Formelemente römischer Aquädukte nach und die Straßenseite der Standartenhalle erinnert an eine griechische Tempelfront mit hohem Stufensockel[37]. Hitlers Vorhaben, nach der 1940 in Tokio stattfindenden Olympiade die gesamten olympischen Wettkämpfe für alle Zeiten im Deutschen Stadion austragen zu lassen – ungeachtet dessen nicht-olympischer Abmessungen[38] – weckt Assoziationen von Weltherrschaftsbestrebungen, wie sie in der Antike mit den zyklisch veranstalteten sportlichen Wettkämpfen verbunden wurden. Pangermanische Wettkämpfe hätten dann die panathenäischen ersetzt[39].

Auch das nur partiell fertiggestellte und 1967 gesprengte Märzfeld (Abb. 3) weise, so Doosry, ästhetische Bezüge zur antiken Tradition auf.

Der rechteckige Grundriss, die regelmäßige Umschließung mit Türmen und die Große Straße, die senkrecht auf das Haupttor zuführe, adaptierten die Grundformen eines römischen Lagers – möglicherweise die des Diokletianpalastes in Split[40]. Zudem erinnere die Bezeichnung Märzfeld nicht nur an die Wiedereinführung der Wehrpflicht im März 1935, sondern auch an den römischen Kriegsgott Mars und den Campus Martius, i.e. die Heeresversammlung der Römer und Franken[41]. So ist das Feld der Wehrmachtsübungen und nationalsozialistischen Kampfspiele intentional sowohl dem römischen Kriegsgott Mars, als auch – darauf weist die bekrönende Tribünenskulpturengruppe – der griechischen Siegesgöttin Nike[42] geweiht[43].

Der bei Einstellung der Arbeiten erst im Rohbau fertiggestellte Kongreßbau[44] (Abb. 4) weist ebenfalls antike Bezüge auf, da er Formelemente des römischen Colosseums zitiert[45].

Gleichzeitig erinnere seine geschlossene Hufeisenform an ein römisches Theater, wie beispielsweise das des Marcellus[46].

36 Speer 1976, 76, 81. Hier äußert Speer – ebenso wie Hitler – eine Vorliebe für die dorische Welt.
37 Doosry 1979, 113; vgl. Koch 1978, 141; Scobie 1990, 75f. Nach Scobie überwögen die römischen über die griechischen Elemente und das Stadion erinnere mehr an den Circus Maximus als an das Stadion des Herodes Atticus.
38 Speer 1976, 84.
39 vgl. Scobie 1990, 79f.
40 Doosry 1979, 113.
41 Speer 1978b, 10.
42 Förster 1985, 169-82.
43 Dies Konglomerat aus griechischen und römischen Stilementen wird durch Formenadaptionen aus der mittelalterlichen Fortifikationsarchitektur erweitert.
44 Entwurf: Ludwig und Franz Ruff, Beginn der Bauarbeiten: 1935. Vgl. Dehlinger 1951, 64f., Arndt 1973, 12f.
45 Dehlinger 1951, 65; Ogan und Zelnhefer 1986, 6.
46 vgl. Rodenwaldt 1943, Abb. 71, 73.

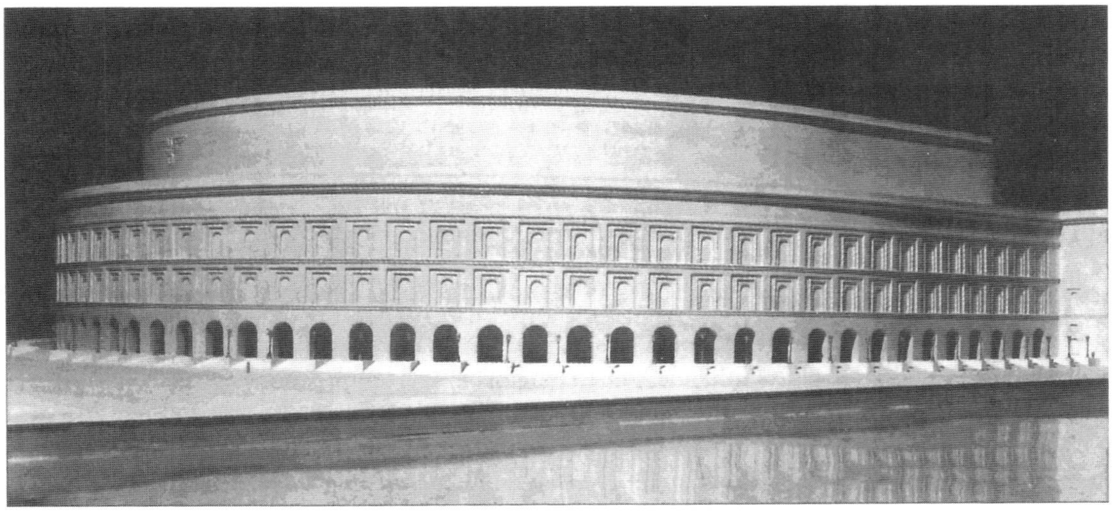

Abb. 4. Kongreßbau (Modell), abgedruckt mit freundlicher Genehmigung der Bildstelle des Hochbauamtes Nürnberg.

2.1 DAS *NEUE GERMANISCHE REICH* VERBUNDEN MIT DER MÄCHTIGKEIT DES URSPRUNGS

Mit der Ausrichtung der zwei Kilometer langen und nahezu hundert Meter breiten Großen Straße[47] vom Märzfeld zur Kaiserburg der Hohenzollern – durch sie wird ein baulicher und (bei guten Sichtverhältnissen) optischer Bezug zwischen Aufmarschfeld und Burg hergestellt – wird die erstrebte Bindung der Partei an die nationale Geschichts- und Kulturtradition architektonisch sinnfällig. Die Kaiserburg der Hohenzollern, Symbol des Reichsgedankens und Kristallisationspunkt des Ursprungsortes, wird durch die Große Straße mit dem Aufmarschgelände der Wehrmacht, dem symbolischen Zentrum der nationalsozialistischen (immer zugleich militärisch verstandenen) Herrschaft ästhetisch verknüpft. Damit wird der Aufmarsch der Wehrverbände auf dem Märzfeld, dem architektonischen und zeremonialen Schlusspunkt des Reichsparteitagsgeländes, zu einer feierlich inszenierten, demonstrativen Besetzung des Ursprungsortes und zur Legitimierung eigener Herrschaftsansprüche. Diese ästhetische Okkupation spezifisch ‚deutscher' Geschichte korreliert mit der erstrebten Bindung an die griechisch-römische Antike[48], da man den Griechen, Römern und Germanen gemeinsame rassische Wurzeln zuschrieb[49]. Die architektonisch inszenierte Einheit von Kaiserburg und Reichsparteitagsbauten als Rezeptionen antiker Tempel und Arenen entspricht der Anschauung Hitlers, zwischen Germanen und Griechen bestünde eine ungebrochene völkische Linie. Speer berichtet: „Die Kultur der Griechen bedeutete für Hitler auf jedem Gebiet die höchste Vollendung. Ihre Lebensauffassung, so wie sie sich beispielsweise in der Architektur äußerte, sei ‚frisch und gesund' gewesen. [...] Mit den Griechen meinte er die Dorer. Natürlich war die von Wissenschaftlern seiner Zeit genährte Vermutung dabei im Spiel, daß der von Norden eingewanderte dorische Volksstamm germanischen Ursprungs und daher seine Kultur nicht der mediterranen Welt zugehörig gewesen sei"[50].

Der ästhetisch in Szene gesetzten Anbindung an den als ursprünglich ‚deutsch' gedachten Ursprung entsprang auch die Idee, rund um den Dutzendteich einen Eichenhain anzulegen[51]. Er kennzeichnet das Reichsparteitagsgelände als Opferstätte, da ein Heiliger Hain zum Inventar zahlreicher Kulte gehört[52]. Die

47 Die Fahrbahn nimmt eine Breite von 60m ein; die Gesamtbreite einschließlich der beidseitigen Gehsteige und Standtribühnen beträgt 98,80m. Vgl. Speer 1976, 81.

48 Der Inszenierungscharakter dieser Rückbindung wird deutlich, wenn man bedenkt, dass die Germanen niemals romanisiert wurden und traditionellerweise als Feinde der *Pax Romana* galten. S. hierzu Scobie 1990, 92.

49 Hitler 1934, 26f. Vgl. Thies 1976, 73.

50 Speer 1976; 110; vgl. Hitlers Tischgespräch vom 18.01.1942 (Picker 1989, 85).

51 S. hierzu den entsprechenden Beitrag in Speer 1978b, 10; vgl. Hitler 1935, 27.

52 Das Heiligtum der siegbringenden Athena, das Nikephorion in Pergamon, war ebenfalls von einem Heiligen Hain umgeben. S. hierzu Radt 1988, 272.

projektierte Bepflanzung mit der deutschen Eiche muss in diesem Zusammenhang als szenische Einbringung von Ursprungssymbolen germanischer Tradition in das Kulissenensemble der Kultbühne verstanden werden.

Mittels der Reichsparteitagsbauten wird nicht nur die gesuchte Nähe zu einer Urvergangenheit, die man sich in der griechischen und römischen Antike sowie in der mit dieser eng verbundenen, spezifisch ‚deutschen' Geschichte dachte, inszeniert, sondern man greift, eine Kreisbewegung beschreibend, gleichzeitig auch auf die Okkupation der, ebenfalls spezifisch ‚deutsch' gedachten, Zukunft aus. Den Ursprungsort bezeichnend und durch Entspringen aus ihm auf ihn zurückverweisend, gelten die Bauwerke zugleich als Metapher für die Rückkehr zum Ursprung, insofern sie für ein neues germanisches Reich stehen. Die Vorstellung vom rhythmisch wiederkehrenden Entstehen und Vergehen sowie erneutem Entstehen als Ausdruck ewigen Pulsierens manifestiert sich hier architektonisch und verleiht der Bewegung die Aura von Unsterblichkeit und zeitloser Gültigkeit[53]. Die sich jährlich wiederholende rhythmische Wiederkehr der Parteitagsdekorationen verstärkt abermals das In-Szene-Setzen einer ewigen, pulsierenden Bewegung. Sie ist die Bewegungsform des Ursprungs, die Martin Heidegger als ‚Ursprung in actu' bezeichnet. Dessen konvulsivische Pulsationsbewegungen findet in der ästhetischen Parteitagskulisse Ausdruck und Spiegelung.

2.2 SEPULKRAL-, MEMORIAL- UND FORTIFIKATIONSARCHITEKTUR IM DIENST DES OPFERGEDANKENS

Untersucht man die Konzeption des Reichsparteitagsgeländes zwischen Kaiserburg und Märzfeld im Hinblick auf ihre symbolische Funktion, so ergibt sich eine ästhetisch-assoziative Richtung von mythischer Urvergangenheit zum Endsieg: Die Kaiserburg repräsentiert den mit deutscher Geschichte in eins gedachten Ursprung; die Luitpoldarena – am Beginn des baulichen Kulissenarrangements Stätte der Eröffnungsfeierlichkeiten – symbolisiert mit dem Ehrenmal als Stätte der Gefallenenehrung die Verbundenheit der Lebenden mit den Heldentoten; das Märzfeld, als größte bauliche Anlage mit der Siegesgöttin Nike bekrönt, bildet den Abschluss des Ensembles und steht als Ort der Wehrübungen und Kampfspiele für den siegreichen soldatischen Einsatz im Krieg. Die Gesamtanlage kann somit als bauliche Inszenierung nationalsozialistischer mythischer Vorstellungen verstanden werden, da sie einen ästhetischen Spannungsbogen zwischen Ursprungsnähe, Gemeinschaftsbildung – untereinander und mit den Heldentoten – und, als Zielpunkt und Hinwendung allen Geschehens, kultisch antizipierter Opferung im Krieg beschreibt. Die architektonische Gesamtanlage des Geländes bildet gleichsam den kultisch vorab quasireal beschrittenen und realhistorisch noch zu beschreitenden Weg zwischen Entspringen (aus der Welt der Heldentoten) und Zurückfallen in den Ursprung und damit die endgültige Rückbindung an die Welt der Heldentoten (Opferung im Krieg) ab. Im Mitvollzug der Veranstaltungen[54] und im Beschreiten der baulichen Anlage wird diese ideologische Vorgabe für den Beteiligten real erfahrbar und von der Volksgemeinschaft als Kultgemeinde rituell vollzogen.

So zeigen alle baulichen In-Szene-Setzungen deutliche Bezüge zum nationalsozialistischen Totenkult, der bei allen Feierveranstaltungen von zentraler Bedeutung war. Schon der Ausgangspunkt der kultischen Prozession, die Luitpoldarena, wird mit der Welt der Heldentoten in einen engen ästhetischen Bezug gesetzt. Das von der Stadt Nürnberg zwischen 1927 und 1930 erbaute Mahnmal für die Gefallenen des Ersten Weltkrieges wird durch eine 240m lange und 18m breite Straße in die architektonische Gestaltung der Luitpoldarena einbezogen. Ehrenmal und Führertribüne liegen sich, durch eine Aufmarsch- bzw. Prozessionsstraße eindeutig ästhetisch verknüpft, innerhalb des Platzrechtecks gegenüber. Der architektonisch inszenierte Bezug zwischen Staats- und mit sepulkralen Konnotationen versehenem Memorialbau findet sich innerhalb der gesamten Reichsparteitagsarchitektur wieder. Die Vorstellung von einem sozialen Neuaufbau durch die Zusammenschweißung der vom Zerfall bedrohten Nachkriegsgesellschaft sucht

53 „Die deutsche Nation hat doch bekommen ihr germanisches Reich." So hat sich Hitler zum Abschluss des Reichsparteitags 1937, auf dem der Grundstein des Deutschen Stadions gelegt wurde, geäußert (Hitler 1938a, 103; vgl. Speer 1976, 83). Vermutlich drückt sich hier eine Vision aus, die Hitler Speer (1976, 93) gegenüber wenig später spezifizierte: „Wir werden ein großes Reich schaffen. Alle germanischen Völker werden darin zusammengefaßt sein. Das fängt in Norwegen an und geht bis Norditalien. Ich selbst muß das noch durchführen."

54 Wie der Feierablauf zeigt, ist die Totenehrung am Sonntagvormittag der Höhepunkt der Veranstaltungen. Den Abschluss der Feierlichkeiten bilden – so die Planungen für die Zeit nach dessen Fertigstellung – die Wehrdemonstrationen auf dem Märzfeld.

man mittels gemeinschaftsstiftender, memorialer Symbole, die man einer fernen (besseren) Vergangenheit zuordnet[55].

Der sepulkrale Charakter der Gesamtanlage wird zusätzlich hervorgehoben durch die zahlreichen Feuerschalen[56], die auf die Bauwerke gesetzt sind. Der Aufbahrungstradition[57] entlehnt, kennzeichnen sie die Parteitagsbauten ästhetisch als Grabesarchitektur. Die im bisherigen analytischen Befund aufgewiesenen memorialen Konnotationen der Reichsparteitagsarchitektur sind – und dies wird von der Forschung bestätigt – für den NS symptomatisch. Demnach besteht eine enge Affinität der Denkmalsarchitektur zur Sepulkral- und Fortifikationsästhetik[58]. Der Kunsthistoriker Berthold Hinz zitiert das Tannenberg-Denkmal, 1927 errichtet und 1945 gesprengt, als Präfiguration eines Bauens, das memorialen Habitus „unter dem Aspekt des Kriegs-Todes fortifikatorisch" aufrüstete und dessen Grundmuster, Wehrtürme, skandierend in eine polygonale Anlage gesetzt und durch gleichmäßige bastionsartige Querriegel akzentuiert, an mittelalterliche Wehrbauten erinnerte und sie reaktivierte – ein Prinzip, das u.a. in Zeppelin- und Märzfeld erneut aufgenommen werde[59]. „Die hybrideste Synthese von Bastion und Grabmal aber zeichnete sich ab in dem Plan, mit einem Ring von 'Totenburgen' von der Atlantikküste bis in die ‚Weiten Russlands', von Norwegen bis nach Afrika die faschistische Einflusssphäre zu dokumentieren und ästhetisch zu 'sichern'"[60]. Die Entwürfe sind, so kommentiert der Architekturhistoriker Wolfgang Schäche, „eine logische Konsequenz und Entsprechung einer Politik, die die Lebenden auf die eigentliche Bestimmung, den ‚Tod für die Rassengemeinschaft' vorbereite. [...] Überall in den eroberten und unterjochten Gebieten sollten die ‚Ehrenmäler' von der Macht und Überlegenheit der deutschen Rassen künden, den Unterdrückten zur Warnung, den potentiellen Kriegern zum Ansporn"[61]. Das Opfer der Vorausgegangenen definierte auf diese Weise in den architektonischen Verkörperungen die Grenzen des Reiches und die Identität der Volksgemeinschaft. Für diese Volksgemeinschaft, die vom memorial symbolisierten Totenheer gleichsam umzingelt und vereinnahmt wird, ist – so wird sinnbildlich vermittelt – ein Leben nur im Opferstatus, in der imaginären Vorwegnahme des von jenen schon real vollbrachten Opfertodes, sinnvoll. In der Reichsparteitagsarchitektur kommt also manifest zum Ausdruck, was von der NS-Propaganda immer wieder verbal eingehämmert wird: das von jedem Einzelnen geforderte uneingeschränkte Opfer für die Bewegung. Die Opferhaltung, so geben die gigantischen Bauwerke eindrücklich zu verstehen, ist für die Gemeinschaftsbildung konstitutiv und gilt als das zentrale Lösungskonzept auf dem Wege zur ersehnten sozialen Synthesis. Das Opfer an den ‚Ursprung' ist daher das zentrale Verhandlungsthema des Reichsparteitagskultes. Auf die psychische Disposition des Einzelnen übertragen, meint dies die Überantwortung der eigenen Subjekthaftigkeit an eine höhere Macht, die man sich einer Urvergangenheit und einem Ursprungsort angehörig vorstellt. Man hat die Vorstellung, die Partei handle als deren Verkörperung oder doch zumindest im Auftrag dieser Ursprungsmacht. Aufgrund dieses Subjektwechsels zu einem unendlich mächtigeren, ursprünglichen Vitalsubjekt glaubt man sich mit der Welt des Ursprungs – es ist diejenige, in die das Totenheer bereits eingegangen ist – verbunden, eine Imagination, die Angstfreiheit, Unbesieg-

55 Hitler 1925/27, 289f.; vgl. Speer 1936, 77.

56 Feuerschalen befinden sich z.B. auf den flankierenden Pylonen der Zeppelinfeldtribüne, auf den Außentürmen und – den Abständen der Pfeiler angeglichen – auf dem Halbrund des Deutschen Stadions (vgl. Doosry 1979, 111). Mit Rauchpfannen sollte auch die Ehren- und Pressetribüne der Luitpoldarena ausgestaltet werden [so eine Niederschrift der Stadt Nürnberg über eine Besprechung mit Hitler am 25.4.1934 anlässlich der Ausgestaltung der Luitpoldarena, BA R 2/18722, Reichsfinanzministerium]. Zugleich sei an dieser Stelle auf die vielen Feuerspektakel (Fackelzüge, Feuerwerke, Illuminationen etc.) verwiesen, die ebenfalls starke sepulkrale Momente aufweisen.

57 Z. B. griechische Opferpfannen.

58 Der Denkmalscharakter der Reichsparteitagsbauten fügt sich in eine allgemein zu beobachtende Tradition des NS, Ehrenmäler zu errichten, ein. Das *Denkmal für die Gefallenen der Bewegung* am Münchener Königsplatz bildet kurz nach der Machtergreifung den Auftakt einer exzessiven Bautätigkeit mit memorialem Schwerpunkt. Politische Gliederungen wie RAD, SS und SA erhalten, ebenso wie z.B. Reichsautobahn und Westwall, ihre Mäler. Darüber hinaus sollen Totenburgen den nationalsozialistischen Einflussbereich ringförmig umschließen und kennzeichnen. Ein großer Teil der errichteten oder geplanten Bauten hat Sepulkralcharakter, so die Soldatenhalle von W. Kreis, die Langemarck-Halle des Berliner Olympiastadions oder die vielen Kaderausbildungsstätten, wie die Hohe Schule der NSDAP am Chiemsee. S. hierzu Hinz 1979, 217f. Vgl. Hinz 1974; 135; Teut 1967, Dok. 71, 222f.; vgl. Kunst 1971, 51f. Zur Neuen Reichskanzlei s. Schönberger 1981, bes. 171; für andere Bauwerke s. u.a. Arndt 1970, 48f.

59 Hinz 1974, 133f.; Hinz 1979, 223f.; Bartetzko 1985a, 74f., 82f.; vgl. die Verbindung von Wehr- und Memorialarchitektur beim Aachener Gefallenen-Ehrenmal (1935): Bartetzko 1985a, 80; Schrade 1939, 9f.

60 Hinz 1974, 135; vgl. Brenner 1963, 128f.

61 Schäche 1983b, 73; Petsch 1976, 139f.

barkeit und ewige Stärke zu verleihen verspricht. Nicht die Tradierung eines bestimmten Baustils wurde gesucht, dagegen spricht auch das collagierende Vorgehen, sondern die Inszenierung von Ordnung kontra Chaos, von Selbstbewusstsein kontra Ohnmacht, von Stärke kontra Schwäche und von Zeitlichkeit kontra zeitlichem Zerfall. Der propagierten Volksgemeinschaft zugeschrieben finden diese Idealvorstellungen in den errichteten und geplanten Bauwerken repräsentativen ästhetischen Ausdruck. Ihre Geschlossenheit und Einheit muss als steinerne Manifestation des nationalsozialistischen Gemeinschaftsideals verstanden werden. Die Todesarchitektur der Reichsparteitagsbauten steht jedoch für die Inszenierung eines Ideals, das einem Wunschdenken entspringt. Es spiegelt nicht die durch enorme Umwälzprozesse zerrissene historische gesellschaftliche Realität der Zwischenkriegszeit wider, sondern steht ihr – eine sehr starke Diskrepanz – diametral entgegen. Gemeinschaft wird gedacht als formierter Zusammenschluss soldatischer Prägung. Dies wird nicht nur mittels der architektonischen Kultkulissen ausgedrückt, sondern zeigt sich auch in den zahlreichen, während der Parteitagsveranstaltungen vorgeführten, Aufmärschen der Parteigliederungen. Als Teil eines nach militärischen Gliederungsstrukturen geordneten Kolonnenganzen wird der Mensch zum funktionalen Bestandteil der auf den Tod zielenden Architektur. In der Widerspiegelung der architektonischen Todeskulisse übereignet er sein Subjekt dem ‚Ursprung'[62] und folgt damit der symbolisch vorgeführten Bildsprache, die eine Gleichsetzung von formierten Stein- und Menschenmassen suggeriert. Die Unterordnung unter eine größere Einheit, die Wehrhaftigkeit und Sicherheit garantieren soll, wird als Modus des Zusammenschlusses zwischen Lebenden und Toten verstanden, dessen gemeinsame Ausrichtung, der Opfertod, von diesen bereits vollzogen, von jenen in der Nachfolge erwartet, bei den Reichsparteitagsveranstaltungen inszenatorische Realität gewinnt und idealiter antizipiert wird. Das Opfer wird dabei als Opferung des Subjektes verstanden, da die Beteiligten nicht real, sondern imaginär (in ihrem Subjektstatus) tot sind, indem sie ihre vollständige und uneingeschränkte Unterwerfung unter die Forderungen der Bewegung rituell beschwören, im Kultus scheinreal einüben und vollziehen und im feierlichen Initiationseid der Parteianwärter kollektiv besiegeln. Fortifikationsarchitektur und formierter Aufmarsch weisen dieselben Strukturelemente auf: Symmetrie, Axialität, Monumentalität und Massivität, sowie kubische bzw. blockhafte Geschlossenheit. Die in Kolonnen Angetretenen finden ihre steinerne Widerspiegelung in den geordneten Pfeilerreihen der sie umschließenden Bauwerke. Todesgleich erstarrte Lebende und steinerne Sepulkralarchitektur bilden, in eins verschmolzen, die ästhetische Antizipation einer propagierten und erstrebten Gemeinschaft der Lebenden mit den Toten. Diese Volksgemeinschaft präsentiert sich in der baulichen Verkörperung als einig, geschlossen, opfer- und kriegsbereit. Der Einzelne, im Opferstatus als subjektlose Hülle in sepulkrale Formen gepresst, bekundet so sein Verwertungsangebot an den Ursprung, die Welt der Heldentoten, eine Haltung, die innerhalb der Kultveranstaltung gleichsam erlebte Wirklichkeit wird.

2.3 ZENTRIERUNG AUF DEN *FÜHRER*: HITLER IN SZENE GESETZT ALS OBERSTES OPFER UND ALS OBERSTER OPFERER ZUGLEICH

Das gesamte Feiergeschehen der Reichsparteitage ist auf Hitler als den Führer der Volksgemeinschaft ausgerichtet. Er selbst hatte maßgeblichen, uneingeschränkten und auch kleinste Detailfragen betreffenden Einfluss auf die Planung und Fertigstellung der ästhetischen Kulisse[63]. Sein extraordinäres und leidenschaftliches Interesse für Architektur ist in zahlreichen eigenen Entwurfsskizzen dokumentiert[64]. Offensichtlich hatte die Inszenierungsseite bei der Planung und Erstellung der Bauwerke höchste Prio-

62 Der von Hitler repräsentiert und verkörpert wird.

63 Speer 1936, 72; Speer 1966b, 54; Speer 1976, 68, 152, vgl. 41; Teut 1967, 179; Arndt 1973, 22f.; Führung Reichsparteitag 1938, Stadtarchiv Nürnberg, C 32, 339a; vgl. March 1967, 204; vgl. Bonatz 1950, 179f.; für die Bildhauerarbeiten wurden weder Ausschreibungen noch Wettbewerbe veranstaltet (Förster 1985, 172, vgl. 162).

64 Z.B. Speer 1976, 41, 52, 54f., 88, 92f., 170, 186. Hitler verfügte jedoch nicht über die fachliche Kompetenz eines ausgebildeten Architekten; sein Anspruch, Baumeister zu sein, gilt als eigenkreierte Legende, die in Hitler 1925/27, 5, 15, 18f. bereits formuliert und von den Funktionären weitertradiert wurde (z.B. Speer 1936, 72f.). Hitler gründete einen Baustab, über dessen zunehmende Kompetenzen er uneingeschränkt verfügte (Teut 1967, 12f., 178f.; Speer 1966a, 48, 50, 54; dagegen legendenkonform Speer 1936, 75. S. hierzu auch Arndt 1965, 11; Arndt 1970, 47; Arndt 1973, 21f. mit einer detaillierten Diskussion über den Anteil Hitlers an den Reichsparteitagsbauten.) Vgl. die ausführliche Diskussion über Hitlers Tätigkeit als ‚Baumeister' bei Thies 1976, 36f.

rität, da die Frage nach der finanziellen Absicherung der Bauarbeiten stark vernachlässigt wurde[65] – ein Umstand, der aufgrund des angespannten Staatshaushaltes in den Dreißigerjahren auf ein nicht-rationales, ökonomisch unsinniges Vorgehen hinweist. Der kultisch inszenierten, die realhistorische Wirklichkeit ablösenden mythischen Welt scheint man für das Zusammenschweißunternehmen Volksgemeinschaft stärkere Wirkkraft zuzuerkennen, als dem rationalen Diskurs offengelegter sozioökonomischer Problemlagen. Offensichtlich ist Hitler als Symbolfigur und Verkörperung des geeinten ‚Deutschtums' von solch enormer Wirkmächtigkeit, dass alles andere seiner immensen Stilisierung und kultischen Erhöhung untergeordnet wurde, ‚koste es, was es wolle!'

Architektonisch in Szene gesetzt wird die Ausrichtung auf den Führer mittels der exponiert platzierten sowie eigens für ihn entworfenen und errichteten Führerbalkone[66], Führerlogen in Theatern[67] und Führertribünen. Die architektonische Exponierung der Führerkanzel gibt der Geschlossenheit und Einheit versprechenden inszenierten gemeinsamen Ausrichtung der Volksgemeinschaft manifesten ästhetischen Ausdruck. Während die Reichsparteitagsbauten gleichsam die Größe und Stärke der Bewegung sowie, in der Tradition des Ersten und Zweiten Reiches, die Größe des gesamten Tausendjährigen Reiches ausdrücken, dient die Rednertribüne dem speziellen Zweck, Hitler als den Mittelpunkt dieser gleichsam kosmischen Umwälzungsbewegungen und zugleich als Stellvertreter des Volkes architektonisch sinnfällig zu markieren. Dieser Überhöhung Hitlers zum Kultmittelpunkt, Zeremonienmeister und (stellvertretendem) oberstem Opferer[68] entspricht die Zentrierung auf der Zeppelinfeldtribüne, die als Opferaltar kenntlich gemacht ist. Das architektonische Gesamtensemble adaptiert römische Zirkus- und Theaterbauten und deren hervorgehobene Positionierungen für die Götter und Imperatoren als Spitze der sozialen Pyramide, von wo aus sie die Spiele auf dem Feld beobachteten und überwachten[69]. Indem Hitler ihren Platz einnimmt, stellt er sich in einen assoziativen Zusammenhang mit den römischen Göttern und Imperatoren, die wiederum, göttergleich, als Beherrscher der Welt galten und deren Triumph, Macht und Glanz mit den antiken Formadaptionen auf Hitler übergehen.

In der architektonischen Inszenierung ist Hitler also der Brennpunkt des Kultgeschehens und der Beherrscher der Welt. Seine ihm von der Propaganda zugewiesene Rolle als Oberhaupt der Nation und Führer der Volksgemeinschaft erhält dadurch kultische Weihe und unmittelbar erlebbaren, sinnfälligen und quasirealen Ausdruck. Das öffentlich inszenierte Zur-Schau-Stellen kontrastiert mit seiner Rolle als Privatperson, die nicht in Erscheinung tritt[70] – ein aus Heiligenlegenden vertrautes Phänomen, das seiner Stilisierung als gottgleicher Weltenregent dient und das zur Bildung des Staatsmythos beiträgt. Dieser steht im Dienst des sozialen Zusammenschweißunternehmens und muss als Herrschaftsinstrument des NS verstanden werden. So wirkt die ästhetisch vorgebildete gemeinsame Ausrichtung auf den Führer letztlich auf die Konstituierung und Befestigung der Volksgemeinschaft[71]. Der Einzelne erfasst in dem gewaltigen,

65 Nach Weisung Hitlers wehrte man die Forderung des Reichsfinanzministeriums nach einem verbindlichen Kostenvoranschlag für die Bebauung des Reichsparteitagsgeländes mehrfach ab; die notwendigen Summen wurden geheimgehalten (Speer 1976, 82, vgl. 184; s. auch Arndt 1973, 22f.)

66 An der Fassade des Reichskanzleianbaus wird auf Wunsch Hitlers eigens ein ‚historischer Balkon' angebracht, um ihm einen angemessenen Auftritt vor der versammelten Menge zu ermöglichen (Speer 1976, 47; vgl. Brenner 1963, 123).

67 Vorhandene Herrscherlogen werden für Hitler neu genutzt; wo sich keine befinden, werden neue errichtet – Maßnahmen, die nahezu alle deutschen Theater betreffen (s. hierzu Bartetzko 1985a, 93).

68 Als *Volkskanzler* handelt er im Auftrag und im Dienst des Volkes.

69 Z.B. fungierten der Circus Maximus und das Amphitheatrum Flavium (Colosseum) als Inszenierungsstätten der Imperatoren, die sich dort in starker Affinität zu den Göttern dem Volk als Weltherrscher präsentieren (s. hierzu Scobie 1990, 73f.).

70 Speer 1976, 72. Die Fotos für eine Neuauflage von Heinrich Hofmanns Veröffentlichung *Hitler, wie ihn keiner kennt* (Hofmann 1938) wählte Hitler selbst aus (Speer 1976, 97) – eine Tatsache, die ebenfalls als Indiz für den Inszenierungscharakter seiner Person zu werten ist. Seit 1939 entwickelte Hitler jedoch eine zunehmende Distanz zu der Bevölkerung, zeigte sich kaum noch vor Menschenmassen und bezog eine eher feindliche und abwehrende Haltung (Speer 1976, 173).

71 „Diese zwingende Ausrichtung der Massen durch die Anordnung der Architektur bewirkt, daß jeder Teilnehmer den gewaltigen Zusammenklang des Willens aller Beteiligten wie in einem großen Spiegel vor sich erblickt, als eine kraftvolle Zusammenfassung und Sinngebung des Geschehens." (Lotz abgedruckt in Teut 1967, Dok. 64, 193).Vgl. die mit ähnlichen Mitteln gestaltete Inszenierung des Herrschafts- und Führungsanspruchs Hitlers am Bau der Neuen Reichskanzlei (zum Arbeitszimmer als 'Thronsaal' s. Schönberger 1981, 110, 113). „Die Ausstattung des Arbeitszimmers ist allegorisch zu verstehen. [...] Die Überdimensionierung des Schreibtisches, die Schreibtischlampe, das vom Sessel aus nicht erreichbare Telefon, die dekorative Anordnung der Schreibtischutensilien und der Bücher an Stelle von Akten machen

auf den Führer zentrierten kultischen Bühnenspektakel unmittelbar assoziativ, dass er ihm gegenüber ein Nichts ist, eine Entleerungsbewegung des Subjekts, die ihn psychisch auf die endgültige Übergabe an den Ursprung vorbereitet. Er spürt, dass sich in Adolf Hitler diese Macht des Ursprungs nicht nur vermittelt und Ausdruck verschafft, sondern gleichsam leibhaftig verkörpert hat.

An dieser Stelle wird bereits der Übersprung deutlich, der sich an der Hitler-Figur vollzieht: Vom obersten Opferer wechselt er über zum obersten Opfer, das den Subjektwechsel bereits vollzogen hat und nunmehr ganz dem ‚Ursprung' gehört. Hitler wird demnach nicht nur als Mittler der Ursprungsmacht, sondern als deren Verkörperung stilisiert. Seine immense Macht ist also nicht nur vom Ursprung abgeleitet, sondern – und dies ist die totalitäre Spitze der Überhöhung – er ist die absolute Macht des Ursprungs selbst. Sich ganz und gar ihm zu überlassen, birgt die enorme Verlockung, ganz und gar an der absoluten Mächtigkeit des Ursprungs teilzuhaben und somit selbst absolut mächtig zu werden – eine Vorstellung, die vor dem Hintergrund der nationalen Ohnmachtsgefühle durch den verlorenen Ersten Weltkrieg geeignet ist, gesamtgesellschaftliche Wirkkraft zu erlangen.

Seiner exponierten Stellung als Staats- und Volksvertreter gemäß werden Hitlers Redekanzeln mit dem Hoheitszeichen[72] ausgestaltet. Als Symbol von Partei und Staat markiert das Hoheitszeichen die Usurpation des Ursprungsortes durch die Bewegung und ist damit unverzichtbarer Bestandteil der Einzelkulissen[73]. Als geplante Bekrönung des Märzfeldes[74] steht es gleichsam für den Endpunkt der Geschichte, die an der Kaiserburg ihren symbolischen Anfang nahm. Mit dieser spezifisch deutschen ‚Urzeit' ist man über die Große Straße geradlinig verbunden. Das Hoheitszeichen ist auch an der Führerkanzel der Luitpoldtribüne angebracht, die durch eine extrem niedrige Balustrade Hitlers schmächtige Gestalt zu korrigieren sucht. Sein Standort auf dem Zeppelinfeld ist durch Fahnentuch, Parteiemblem und Hakenkreuz im Eichenlaubkranz markiert[75].

Hitlers Gang zu den Heldentoten in der architektonischen Kulisse der Luitpoldarena eint – und dafür stehen die Staatssymbole – stellvertretend die Welt der Lebenden mit der Welt der Toten, indem sich die Lebenden der Totenwelt weihen. Die mythische Welt wird so in die reale eingebracht.

Im Reichsparteitagsgelände wird qua Architekturkulisse ein Prozess gesellschaftlicher Vereinheitlichung im Sinne von formierter, gepresster Zurichtung szenisch antizipiert. Sie zielt auf die gewünschte und propagierte gesamtgesellschaftliche Ausrichtung auf Hitler als dem Ursprungsmächtigen und die Opferung der Kultteilnehmer an den Ursprung. Hitler fungiert dabei in mehrfacher Hinsicht als zentrale Figur: Er bildet den Brennspiegel der geforderten Aktion, ist Mittler und Verkörperung der Ursprungsmacht, ihr erster und oberster Opferer und zugleich ihr erstes und oberstes Opfer. Hitler selbst verbalisiert diese Stilisierung in seiner Rede in der Kroll-Oper am 10. Februar 1939[76], in der er sich als Protagonist

deutlich, daß es sich um rein stillebenartige Arrangements handelt." (Schönberger 1981, 113). Die Neue Reichskanzlei suggeriert durch die Architektur nur den „Anschein von Arbeit"; wichtiger ist der architektonisch intendierte Eindruck von Autorität, „Vertrauen in die Macht des Staates" und „der persönlichen Repräsentation Hitlers. [...] Räume, in denen tatsächlich gearbeitet wurde, blieben anonym." (Schönberger 1981, 171) Der gesamte Bau diente „der Visualisierung des Führerprinzips und der Personalisierung von Machtpolitik [...] und entsprach auch dem Bedürfnis großer Teile der Bevölkerung nach Repräsentation von Macht und Identifikation mit ihr und diente der Hinwendung und Identifikation mit dem ‚Führer'. [...] So erweist sich der Bau der neuen Reichskanzlei in all seinen vielschichtigen Bezügen als einzigartiges Beispiel von Architektur der Macht, von Suggestion von Macht durch Architektur." (Schönberger 1981, 173.)

72 Neugestaltet in den Jahren 1935 und 1936. In einer *Verordnung über die Gestaltung des Hoheitszeichens des Reichs*, vom 7.3.1936, heißt es: „Das Hoheitszeichen des Reichs zeigt das Hakenkreuz, von einem Eichenkranz umgeben, auf dem Eichenkranz einen Adler mit geöffneten Flügeln. Der Kopf des Adlers ist nach rechts gewendet." [zitiert nach dem Zentralblatt der Bauverwaltung 56 (1936), 296.] Hitler hat an der Gestaltung der Partei- und Staatsabzeichen (z.B. Hakenkreuzfahne, Hoheitsadler, Feldzeichen der SA und SS) maßgeblichen Anteil; er gestaltet Kundgebungen und Aufmärsche und entwirft Saaldekorationen (s. hierzu Speer 1936, 73).

73 Die Hoheitszeichen auf der Haupttribüne und an den Tribünenendbauten des Zeppelinfeldes werden in reduzierter Version, Hakenkreuz in Eichenlaubkranz, 1938 fertig gestellt. 1935 überragt ein den Vorschriften entsprechendes Hoheitszeichen den Standplatz Hitlers auf dem (zu dieser Zeit) noch hölzernem Tribünenbau; zwischen den Türmen des Märzfeldes sollen Fahnenmasten aus Stahl oder Bronze befestigt werden, mit Kanneluren in Goldmosaik und mit vergoldeten Hoheitsadlern (s. hierzu Förster 1985, 162f., bes. Anm. 47, 175).

74 Lotz 1938, 265. Die Kaiserburg als Symbol des Reichs und das zu ihr in Beziehung gesetzte Hoheitszeichen verweisen auf die politische Formel, wonach das *Dritte Reich* die Fortsetzung des Ersten Reichs darstellt, und dienen der Proklamation des Herrschaftsanspruchs (s. hierzu Förster 1985, 175 mit Anm. 148).

75 Arndt 1973, 11, vgl. 16. Bereits der erste Entwurf, eine hölzerne Haupttribüne, trug den Hoheitsadler in der Mittelachse.

76 Sie wurde vor Vertretern der mittleren Führungsebene des Heeres gehalten.

nationalsozialistischer Opferideale und als legitimes militärisches und geistiges Oberhaupt vorführt, eine Vorreiterrolle, der jeder Einzelne in seiner Gänze zu folgen habe: „Dafür [für notfalls mit Waffengewalt durchzusetzenden Ziele Hitlers] fordere ich vom deutschen Volk die ungeheuersten Opfer, dafür habe ich den Befehl zum Aufbau unserer gewaltigen neuen Wehrmacht gegeben, dafür setze ich mich ein, dafür lebe ich, und ich brauche Ihnen nicht zu versichern, meine Herren, dafür würde ich persönlich auch jederzeit bereit sein, sofort zu sterben. [...] Sie dürfen in mir nicht nur den Obersten Befehlshaber der Deutschen Wehrmacht sehen, sondern Sie müssen in mir auch sehen Ihren obersten weltanschaulichen Führer, dem Sie ebenfalls auf Gedeih und Verderb verpflichtet sind“[77].

Die Parteitagsarchitektur muss also abschließend insofern als Inszenierungshilfe des nationalsozialistischen Staatsmythos verstanden werden, als durch sie die propagierte Volksgemeinschaft mit den erstrebten Epitheta wie Einheit, Ewigkeit, Wehrhaftigkeit, Opferbereitschaft, Größe und Stärke, verbunden mit deren Schattenseiten Unterordnung, Erstarrung, Entindividualisierung und Tod mit Hitler als dem gemeinschaftsstiftenden Bezugspunkt ästhetisch in Szene gesetzt und manifest wird.

Bei den Parteitagsveranstaltungen kultisch antizipiert und durch die Usurpation des Ursprungsortes auf ewige Zeit und auf das gesamte Volk bezogen, erhalten die mythisch verbrämten Wunschvorstellungen Realitätscharakter sowie gesamtgesellschaftliche Bedeutung und Weihe. Hitler erscheint in der ästhetischen Inszenierung als Symbol und Verkörperung des ewigen Tausendjährigen (Ursprungs-)Reiches, als römischer Imperator und Gottkönig, Beherrscher der Welt und, wenn man die ägyptisierenden Elemente berücksichtigt, auch als ägyptischer Pharao. Er erscheint aber auch ebenso als Deutschritter[78], ableitbar aus den mittelalterliche Burgen adaptierenden Formelementen, und als legitimer Nachfolger der deutschen Kaiser, ausgedrückt in der Überreichung der Reichsinsignien und der Wahl Nürnbergs als traditionellem Herrschaftssitz der Hohenzollern. Letztlich inszeniert er sich als neuer, ewiger und endgültiger Herrscher am Ende der Geschichte, in der die Vergangenheit restlos aufgeht. Alle diese die Gesamthistorie umgreifenden Elemente werden endgültig übertrumpft durch die unmittelbare Bindung an den Ursprung, durch seine Stilisierung als oberster Opferer und Kultzelebrant sowie als oberstes und erstes Opfer an den Ursprung. Im Kultus wird diese Anbindung beschworen und quasireal eingesetzt, was der steten Rückversicherung dient. Ihr zentrales Thema ist die Anbindung an Ewigkeitswerte, die Welt der Heldentoten, die nicht mehr vergehen kann, da sie – und darin liegt der große Trost – schon vergangen ist. Der Tod, als Bedrohung verstanden, hat damit seinen millionenfachen Schrecken, den er im Ersten Krieg gezeigt hat, imaginär verloren.

Nach Ausdruck und Inszenierung soll nun abschließend die Repräsentationsfunktion des Ritus innerhalb der Reichsparteitagsveranstaltungen aufgezeigt werden.

3. Kollektive Unterwerfung unter Hitler im Dienst des Opfers an den Ursprung: Zur Repräsentationsfunktion der Reichsparteitage.

Bereits zum Auftakt des Reichsparteitags *Großdeutschland* benennt Reichspressechef Otto Dietrich zwei der zentralen Repräsentationsinhalte der Feierveranstaltungen: soldatisch geprägte Männlichkeit und nationalsozialistische Gesinnung; in mythologischer Übersetzung bedeutet dies Verlöschensbereitschaft durch Einnahme des Opferstatus mit dem Ziel des ewigen Sieges. Die gesamte nationalsozialistische Gesellschaft wird in der kultischen Verarbeitung als eine vorrangig männliche Gesellschaft der Krieger repräsentiert. Die einer Kriegergesellschaft naturgemäß innewohnende strikte Differenzierung der Geschlechterrollen, die mit einer Marginalisierung der gesellschaftlichen Position der Frau verbunden ist, spiegelt sich in den spezifischen Darbietungen am Tag der Gemeinschaft kultisch wider: Soldatische Kampfspiele und „Mutproben“ wurden von den jungen Männern vorgeführt[79], Schautänze und gymnastische Übungen von den jungen Frauen[80].

77 Abgedruckt in Dülffer u.a. 1978, 312, vgl. 313.
78 Vgl. die Stilisierung Hitlers als hl. Ritter Georg in dem Gemälde von H. Lanzinger (Bartetzko 1985b, 159).
79 Vgl. Offizieller Bericht 1938, 176.
80 Offizieller Bericht 1938, 176f.; vgl. Kerrl 1938, 192.

Das nationalsozialistische Idealbild der Frau wird im kultischen Handeln durch die NS-Frauenschaft repräsentiert: Glaube an den Führer und Gehorsam, Selbstlosigkeit und uneingeschränkte Einsatzbereitschaft (als Mutter) – Eigenschaften, die mehr sein sollen als bloße Dienstleistung, da sie als göttliche Verpflichtung[81] im Kampf zwischen Gut und Böse verstanden wurden und somit von der Sphäre des Ursprungs her legitimiert, sanktioniert und schließlich, von dort her, mit Absolutheit eingefordert werden. Für die männliche Sphäre gelten die nationalsozialistischen Tugenden entsprechend, da sie beliebig und universal einsetzbar sind. Sie bezeichnen bloße Bewusstseinshaltungen ohne konkreten Inhalt, so dass diese Leerstellen mit beliebigen Handlungsanweisungen (seitens des Regimes) gefüllt werden können. Die Leermetapher nationalsozialistischer Tugenden schlechthin ist das Opfer. So fordert das Regime etwa Opferbereitschaft zugunsten des Winterhilfswerks, der Heimatfront, des Landeinsatzes, der Familie, des Volkes, Hitlers etc. Sogar der stets propagierte Eintopfsonntag wurde als Opfer für das Vaterland in Szene gesetzt[82].

Gemäß dem nationalsozialistischen mythischen Bild spielen die Einforderung und Beschwörung von Unterordnung und Gehorsam zum Zwecke der Konstituierung einer geeinten Volksgemeinschaft im Feierverlauf die zentrale Rolle. In diesem Sinne dienen die nationalsozialistischen Kampfspiele der Demonstration des geeinten Willens durch „gemeinsamen Rhythmus"[83] und der uneingeschränkten Einsatzbereitschaft durch „Sekundengehorsam"[84]. Dieses Gemeinschaftsideal, das sich definiert durch das Verlöschen des Subjektes im kollektiven Eintauchen in die – nicht näher definierte – Ursprungsmacht wird auf den Reichsparteitagen kultisch verarbeitet, d.h. stellvertretend für die Gesamtgesellschaft beschworen, quasireal eingesetzt und als ewig gültige und sakrosankte Wahrheit behandelt. So stehen alle Reichsparteitagsveranstaltungen im Dienste der Beschwörung und Repräsentation nationalsozialistischer Idealvorstellungen von gesellschaftlicher Einheit, wonach die Partei mit Hitler an der Spitze die unangefochtene Führungsrolle einnimmt[85]. Hitler wird als uneingeschränktes Oberhaupt der Gemeinschaft, als Krisenbewältiger und Retter der Nation proklamiert[86].

Gemäß der nationalsozialistischen Führungsidee stehen die aufmarschierten Verbände für die soziale Differenzierung und unterschiedliche Bewertung der einzelnen gesellschaftlichen Gruppen innerhalb des nationalsozialistischen Volkes. In der so repräsentierten nationalsozialistischen Gesellschaft werden ausschließlich parteiliche Gruppierungen vorgeführt, die sich alle in gleicher Weise dem Oberhaupt, Hitler, unterordnen. Der Reichsarbeitsdienst steht für den arbeitenden Bevölkerungsteil, die Hitlerjugend für den ideologischen Nachwuchs, die militärischen Verbände, wie SA, SS, Wehrmacht etc. für die Wehrpflichtigen usw. Ihrer unterschiedlichen Bedeutung für die nationalsozialistischen Kriegergesellschaft entspricht die spezifische Ausgestaltung sowie der besondere Zeitpunkt und Ort ihrer Feierformen. Als konstitutiver Bestandteil der mythischen Kriegergesellschaft wird die Wehrmacht in besonderer Weise kultisch hervorgehoben, indem sie den Höhepunkt und Abschluss des Reichsparteitagskultus gestaltet. Die Politischen Leiter, ihrer Funktion nach unverzichtbare Erfüllungsgehilfen des Regimes, werden durch die besonders effektvolle Feierform des Lichtdoms als zentrale Gruppe der NS-Gesellschaft sakral gekennzeichnet. Die Höhepunkte des Feierzyklus bilden die Treuegelöbnisse der Parteianwärter, Arbeitsmänner und Arbeitsmaiden, die als politischer Nachwuchs und Instrumentarium der Partei ebenfalls der Herrschaftsstabilisierung dienen. Stellvertretend für alle Werktätigen repräsentiert Reichsarbeitsführer Konstantin Hierl den „ersten Arbeiter der Nation". Seine aufmarschierten *Spatenträger* fungieren als „[...] die ideale Verkörperung des Arbeitsethos des neuen Deutschland"[87].

81 Vgl. Kerrl 1938, 232f. „[...] die deutsche Frau hat sich *bedingungslos an die Seite des deutschen Mannes gestellt*, als sie fühlte, was für ein Kampf ihr aufgetragen wurde, nämlich der *Kampf zwischen der göttlichen Ordnung und Sinngebung der irdischen Dinge und dem Versuch volkloser Menschheitsapostel, sich dieser ewigen Ordnung durch Willkür zu widersetzen*, d.h. den Kampf zwischen Gut und Bösen in der Welt." (Offizieller Bericht 1936, 165).

82 S. hierzu Zentner und Bedürftig 1985, 144.

83 Kerrl 1938, 191.

84 Offizieller Bericht 1938, 176.

85 Z.B. für SA, SS, NSFK und NSKK. Vgl. Kerrl 1938, 338, 342; Hitler 1938b, 53f.; vgl. Zelnhefer 1991, 70f., 182f. für die Reichparteitage 1932 und 1936.

86 Aus der Begrüßungsrede von Oberbürgermeister Liebel (Offizieller Bericht 1938, 30f.).

87 Offizieller Bericht 1938, 89.

Durch magische Vermittlung, das Berühren mit der Blutfahne[88], wird die Zugehörigkeit zum Ursprung und die persönliche Bindung an ihn rituell vollzogen und weitergegeben. Die so qua Initiation vollzogene Subjektübereignung ist notwendiges Konstituens und bleibender Garant des Gruppenkonsenses als imaginäre Totengemeinschaft (der Vorausgegangenen mit den Opferbereiten) im ‚Ursprung'. Von der Initiandenseite durch persönlichen Eid, von der Ursprungsseite durch magische Vermittlung, wird der Übergang in die esoterisch-mythische Ursprungsgesellschaft durchschritten. Die persönliche Verpflichtung gegenüber der Macht des Ursprungs wird durch den eindringlich-intimen Blick Hitlers direkt in die Augen der Initianden besiegelt, der hier als Verschlingungsmetapher fungiert. Man ist gewiss: „Er sieht allen ins Auge, sie werden den Eid halten!"[89]

Der Marsch der Gliederungen und Verbände aller deutschen Gaue durch das Parteitagsgelände und durch die Stadt dient der Repräsentation eines idealen geeinten Deutschlands, das, im Gegensatz zu der erlittenen Niederlage im Ersten Weltkrieg, seine wiedererlangte Größe und Stärke, seine Einsatzbereitschaft, seinen Opfermut und Kampfeswillen demonstriert. Im Vorbeimarsch an Hitler und in der Treuebekundung an ihn zeigt dieses Volk Geschlossenheit und uneingeschränkte Einsatzbereitschaft für Deutschland und Hitler – beide Begriffe müssen als Ursprungsmetapher verstanden werden, der sich der Einzelne bereitwillig selbstverlöschend unterzuordnen verspricht. Der pauschal beeidete, inhaltslose Gehorsam in Verpflichtung einer unbekannten, größeren Einheit kann für konkrete, dem System dienende Zwecke beliebig funktionalisiert werden – gleichermaßen antizipatorisch im Kult wie nachfolgend real im Krieg. So ist der Einzelne, subjektlos der geheimen Ursprungsmacht überantwortet, reduziert auf ein kalkulierbares, universell einsetzbares Verwertungsobjekt der nationalsozialistischen Herrschaft. Der Hintergrund dieser Verwertungsbereitschaft bleibt damit jedem rationalen Diskurs notwendig enthoben. Die irrationale Basis der selbstlosen Opferbereitschaft wird so zu einem Ermöglichungsgrund der kalkulierten Verwertung, hervorgerufen durch einen evozierten Subjektwechsel, bei dem der Einzelne seinen eigenen Willen gegen den des Führers eintauscht und sich somit der Bewegung uneingeschränkt zur Verfügung stellt. Als propagierte Verkörperung der Mächtigkeit des Ursprungs nutzt Hitler diese universelle und unkritische Handlungsbereitschaft im Sinne seines Regimes, und zwar – das bringt diese ursprungsmythische Bewusstseinslage mit sich – ohne Einspruchsmöglichkeit durch Kritik und Diskurs. Indem er Hitler diese absolute Mächtigkeit zuerkennt und totalisierend auf das ganze Volk überträgt, 'konstatiert' Rudolf Heß zur Eröffnung des Kongresses auf dem Reichsparteitag 1934: „Sie sind Deutschland. Wenn *Sie* handeln, handelt die Nation"[90].

Alles wird vom Ursprung abgeleitet, zu dem der Führer teils in medialem Verhältnis stehend, teils als dessen Verkörperung stilisiert und inszeniert wird – er schillert ständig zwischen beidem. Jede konkrete öffentliche Handlung erhält ihren Sinn und ihre Weihe durch den Bezug zum Ursprung. Jedwede Tätigkeit, z.B. die Erntehilfe durch die Partei, die Wehrmacht, den RAD und die HJ wird in diesem Sinne als Dienst am Führer verstanden und damit als eine Handlung, die mit der Mächtigkeit des Ursprungs versehen und somit gewiss siegreich ist. So werden auf den Ursprung, stellvertretend durch jede einzelne aufmarschierte Gliederung, alle gesellschaftlichen Gruppierungen eingeschworen[91], eine Treueverpflichtung, die in der Vereidigung der Parteianwärter ihren Höhepunkt findet: „Ich schwöre bei Gott diesen heiligen Eid: *Ich werde meinem Führer Adolf Hitler allezeit treu und gehorsam sein. Ich will als Parteigenosse im Dienst der Gemeinschaft des deutschen Volkes gewissenhaft und opferbereit meine Pflicht erfüllen für die Größe und die Ehre der deutschen Nation. So wahr mir Gott helfe*!"[92]

Das kultische Zeremoniell der Reichsparteitage repräsentiert nicht nur die ideale Volksgemeinschaft der Lebenden und Toten, sondern auch die als Heilsgeschichte interpretierte Vergangenheit und Zukunft. Im kultischen Handeln wird totalrepräsentativ und quasireal der erstrebte ideale Verlauf der Geschichte

88 „Durch die Berührung der Standarten mit der Blutfahne haben wir das Vermächtnis unserer Toten übernommen, unseren Kameraden, die einst in Reih und Glied mit uns marschierten, und die ihre Treue zur Idee und ihren Glauben an Sie, mein Führer, mit ihrem Blute besiegelten." (So der Stabschef Viktor Lutze vor den aufmarschierten *SA*-Männern laut Offizieller Bericht 1938, 303).

89 Bei der Vereidigung der *Parteianwärter* (Offizieller Bericht 1938, 221). Vgl. Kerrl 1938, 252f.

90 Offizieller Bericht 1935, 20.

91 Z.B. für die gesamte Führungsspitze der Partei (als Repräsentantin der Volksgemeinschaft) Rudolf Heß: „[...] Führer, wir folgen dir! Dir gilt unser Glaube auf dieser Welt, Führer, du bist unser und wir sind dein! Adolf Hitler – Sieg Heil!" (zitiert nach Kerrl 1938, 263).

92 Offizieller Bericht 1938, 221.

vorab durchgespielt, den man sich abhängig denkt von der Einsatzbereitschaft und dem Opferwillen des Einzelnen. Da der innerhalb der Heilsgeschichte als notwendig erachtete Opferprozess (Subjektwechsel) naturgemäß in der persönlichen Entscheidung des Einzelnen liegt, wird damit auch das Gelingen oder Missglücken der gesamten Geschichte unmittelbar von seinem Wollen und seinem Engagement abhängig gedacht. Der Einzelne gilt gleichsam als der Erfüllungsgehilfe des Schicksals, des Ursprungs, und trägt daher im nationalsozialistischen Denken unmittelbare Verantwortung für den Gang der Geschichte, die in der opferbereiten, als Heilsweg propagieren[93] Nachfolge Hitlers konkrete Gestalt annehmen soll. Die Forderung der kollektiven Unterwerfung unter die Herrschaft des Ursprungs kreiert eine Idealvorstellung von gesellschaftlicher Synthesis, die von Konformismus und Gehorsam durchdrungen ist und die an den Reichsparteitagen kultisch vorgeführt und antizipiert wird. Hier wird ein streng hierarchisches, nach mechanistischen Gesetzen funktionierendes Sozialsystem repräsentiert, in dem der Einzelne zu einem kalkulierbaren Faktor einer gigantischen Maschinerie reduziert ist. Oberste Autorität ist eine sich rationaler Vermittlung entziehende, durch Hitler verkörperte und durch ihn repräsentierte geheime Ursprungsmacht, für deren imaginäre Anforderungen der Einzelne, durch Subjekttausch willenlos übereignet – konkret: letztlich für den Kriegseinsatz – in Funktion gesetzt wird. Der totalen mechanistischen Verwertung anheim gegeben, gilt es, „den Rhythmus des Blutes mit dem Takt der Maschinen in Einklang“[94] zu bringen.

Das, was bei dem Reichsparteitagsveranstaltungen 1938 als kultische Wirklichkeit antizipiert und vorgeführt wird, findet einige Jahre später seine reale Entsprechung, grausam auf die Spitze getrieben und flächendeckend das gesamte besetzte Land markierend, in den mechanistischen Verwertungsbetrieben der nationalsozialistischen Konzentrationslager. Umspannt werden sollte das Ganze von einem Ring von Totenburgen bzw. Gefallenenmälern, der das ganze Land als Totenstätte kennzeichnete. Die Besetzung des Reichsparteitagsgeländes bzw. Nürnbergs steht für die Besetzung Gesamtdeutschlands (in der Totalisierung müssen Europa, die Welt bzw. der gesamte Kosmos mitgedacht werden) durch die Partei und der militärische Charakter der Veranstaltungen steht für Aufrüstung und Kriegsbereitschaft. In Nürnberg wird stellvertretend kultisch durchgespielt, was im Jahr darauf mit dem Überfall auf Polen, der den Beginn des Zweiten Weltkriegs einleitet, Wirklichkeit wird. Der Krieg gewinnt nach dem Gesagten gleichsam heilsgeschichtlichen Charakter: Die durch Subjektwechsel in den Dienst der geheimen Macht gestellten Mitglieder der Bewegung scheinen Teil zu haben an einem ursprungsmächtigen Rettungsunternehmen, durch das sie ihr beschädigtes nationales Selbstbewusstsein von einer schändlich erlittenen Niederlage in eine unüberwindbare Stärke umzuverwandeln suchen. Die Reichsparteitagsveranstaltungen dienen somit der heilsgeschichtlichen Begründung und der (kult)praktischen, da stellvertretenden Einübung des Kriegslebens. Die kultische Seite der Feierhandlungen führt also ein imaginäres mythisches Bild einer Idealgesellschaft quasireal vor, in der die Übergabe des Subjekts, das verlöschende Eintauchen in den Ursprung zum Garant des Gruppenkonsenses und zur nationalen Heilsvorstellung inszeniert, repräsentativ beschworen und totaleingesetzt wird. Diese so inszenierte und repräsentierte mythisch imaginierte Einheitsgesellschaft der Opferbereiten kann als psychische Vorbereitung für die uneingeschränkte kritiklose Verwertbarkeit des Einzelnen im Dienste des Regimes verstanden werden.

Das Ganzopfer des Subjekts verspricht also das ewige Verlöschen, das von der Last der Individuation befreit. Die Subjektlosigkeit erscheint als das eigentlich attraktive individuelle Ziel und der Eintritt in das Totenheer als das eigentlich kollektive[95]. Die Ursprungswelt gilt als die bessere Welt, denn hier herrscht ewige Ruhe und nicht das so bedrohliche Chaos des an einen bestimmten Ort und an eine bestimmte Zeit gebundenden Vergänglichen. Es ist daher nicht von Bedeutung. Damit zusammenhängend ist der auf den Reichsparteitagen beschworene und kultisch veranstaltete Sieg nicht der über die Völker, sondern der über das Dasein an sich. Er erhält durch die dem Begriff Opfer inhärente Sinnaufladung höhere Weihe. Daraus ergibt sich, daß die Siegesgöttin Nike gerade das Märzfeld krönt, denn es ist zugleich Exerzier- und Kampfstätte der militärischen Gliederungen und Schauplatz der kultischen Opferschlacht. Am ästhetischen und festlichen Finale der Veranstaltungen platziert, steht sie für den Sieg des Opfers durch Verlö-

93 „Was wäre aus Deutschland geworden, wenn im Jahre 1919 nicht ein unbekannter Soldat den Glauben gehabt hätte, durch Wehrhaftigkeit und Hingabe, durch Tapferkeit und Opferwillen die deutsche Nation dereinst von ihrem Verfall retten zu können?“ (Hitler auf dem Reichsparteitag 1936. Zitiert nach Offizieller Bericht 1936, 307).

94 Aus dem Rechenschaftsbericht des Reichsorganisationsleiters Ley auf der Jahrestagung der DAF auf dem Reichsparteitag 1938 (Offizieller Bericht 1938, 225; s. hierzu Kerrl 1938; 255f.).

95 Vgl. Canetti 1976, 184.

schen des Selbst. Hier wird deutlich, wie nahe beieinander das Selbstverlöschen und das Andere-zum-Verlöschen-Bringen liegen. Die eigene psychische Demontage geht der millionenfachen Depersonalisierung und Vernichtung Anderer voraus. Die Totalisierung des Opfergedankens resultiert aus der regressiven Bewusstseinsbewegung zum Ursprung hin, die im vollständigen Eintauchen durch Totalopfer gipfelt[96]. Es besteht keine Sphärentrennung mehr – wie in den Religionen – zwischen Alltagswelt und mythischer Welt, wo das Opferhandeln gleichsam ein ,Tun-als-ob' darstellt, indem das Fleisch der Opfertiere nicht tatsächlich der Gottheit übereignet, sondern an das Volk verteilt wird und stattdessen nur Fleisch und Knochen als Opfer für die Gottheit verbrannt werden (Opfersubstitution). Hier besteht die große Verlockung, sich ganz und gar hingeben zu wollen, sie besteht im Übertritt vom Reflexionssubjekt zum mächtigen kollektiven Vitalsubjekt: Aus Reflexion wird bloßer Reflex und aus bedrohlicher Distanz wird (illusionär) selige Verschmelzung. Der vielfach von außen beobachtete Aktivismus der Parteimitglieder erscheint in diesem Licht nur noch als das auf bestimmte Reize, hier: Befehle, reagierende Zucken der Entleerten, die ihren Selbstverlust, qua mythologischer Transformation, als Ausdruck größter Sinnstiftung frenetisch umjubeln. Im kultischen Handeln quasireal inszeniert, opfert sich der Einzelne, durch Ritus (Blutfahne) und Eid besiegelt[97], der Ursprungsmacht Hitler, ein stellvertretend vorgeführter Akt des Volkes, der in der beschriebenen kultischen Inszenierung die beste Vorbereitung gewesen sein mag für die 1939 durch den Beginn des Zweiten Weltkrieges nun real geforderte Opferung in der Schlacht.

BIBLIOGRAFIE

Arndt, K. 1965. *Das Wort aus Stein*. Göttingen: Institut für den wissenschaftlichen Film.

—. 1970. „Filmdokumente des Nationalsozialismus als Quellen für architekturgeschichtliche Forschungen." In *Zeitgeschichte in Film- und Tondokumenten. 17 historische, pädagogische und sozialwissenschaftliche Beiträge*, herausgegeben von G. Moltmann und K.F. Reimers, 39-68. Göttingen u.a.: Musterschmidt.

—. 1973. *Baustelle Reichparteitagsgelände 1938/39*. Göttingen: Institut für den wissenschaftlichen Film.

Bartetzko, D. 1985a. *Illusionen in Stein. Stimmungsarchitektur im deutschen Faschismus. Ihre Vorgeschichte in Theater- und Film-Bauten*. Reinbek bei Hamburg: Rowohlt.

—. 1985b. *Zwischen Zucht und Ekstase. Zur Theatralik von NS-Architektur*. Berlin: Gebr. Mann.

—. 1986. „Versteinerte Gefühle – NS-Architektur als Wunscherfüllung." *Bauwelt* 77.48: 1848-56.

Bonatz, P. 1950. *Leben und Bauen*. Stuttgart: Engelhornverlag Spellmann.

Brenner, H. 1963. *Die Kunstpolitik des NS*. Rowohlts deutsche Enzyklopädie 167/ 168. Reinbek bei Hamburg: Rowohlt.

Burden, H.T. 1967. *Die programmierte Nation. Die Nürnberger Reichsparteitage*. Gütersloh: Bertelsmann.

Canetti, E. 1976. „Hitler, nach Speer." In *Elias Canetti. Das Gewissen der Worte. Essays*,175-204. 2. erweiterte Auflage. München u.a.: Hanser.

Dehlinger, A. 1951. *Architektur der Superlative. Eine kritische Betrachtung der NS-Bauprogramme von München und Nürnberg*. 2 Bände. München: Institut für Zeitgeschichte. *Deutschland erwacht. Werden, Kampf und Sieg der NSDAP*. 1933. Hamburg: Cigaretten-Bilderdienst Hamburg.

Doosry, Y. 1979. „Formale und inhaltliche Aspekte der Antikenrezeption in der Architektur des Nürnberger Reichsparteitagsgeländes." *Hephaistos* 1: 109-20.

Dülffer, J., J. Thies und J. Henke. 1978. *Hitlers Städte: Baupolitik im Dritten Reich. Eine Dokumentation*. Köln u.a.: Böhlau.

Förster, K. 1985. „Staatsaufträge für das Reichsparteitagsgelände in Nürnberg." In *Entmachtung der Kunst. Architektur, Bildhauerei und ihre Institutionalisierung 1920-1960*, herausgegeben von M. Bushart, B. Nicolai und W. Schuster, 156-82. Berlin: Frölich & Kaufmann.

Gamm, H.-J. 1962. *Der braune Kult. Das Dritte Reich und seine Ersatzreligion. Ein Beitrag zur politischen Bildung*. Hamburg: Rütten & Loening.

96 Die Uneinlösbarkeit dieser Unternehmung wird an dieser Stelle nicht eigens reflektiert; s. hierzu Karow 1990.

97 Rudolf Heß als Vorsprecher bei der Vereidigung der Parteianwärter (s. Offizieller Bericht 1938, 221).

Hinz, B. 1974. *Die Malerei im deutschen Faschismus. Kunst und Konterrevolution.* München: Hanser.

—. 1979. „Das Denkmal und sein Prinzip." In *Kunst im 3. Reich: Dokumente der Unterwerfung*, herausgegeben vom Frankfurter Kunstverein und der Arbeitsgruppe des Kunstgeschichtlichen Institutes der Universität Frankfurt am Main, 217-229. Frankfurt am Main: Zweitausendeins.

Hitler, A. 1925/27. *Mein Kampf.* 2. Bände. München: Franz Eher Nachfolger. Parteitagsreden.

—. 1934. *Die Reden Hitlers am Reichsparteitag 1933.* München: Eher.

—. 1935. *Die Reden Hitlers am Parteitag der Freiheit 1935.* München: Zentralverlag der NSDAP Eher.

—. 1938a. *Reden des Führers am Parteitag der Arbeit 1937.* München: Zentralverlag der NSDAP Eher.

—. 1938b. *Reden des Führers am Parteitag Großdeutschland 1938.* München: Zentralverlag der NSDAP Eher.

Hofmann, H. 1938. *Hitler wie ihn keiner kennt. 100 Bilddokumente aus dem Leben des Führers.* Berlin: Zeitgeschichte Verlag.

Karow, Y. 1990. *„Bhagwan"-Bewegung und „Vereinigungskirche": Religions- und Selbstverständnis der „Sannyasins" und der „Munies".* Stuttgart u.a.: Kohlhammer.

—. 1997. *Deutsches Opfer. Kultische Selbstauslöschung auf den Reichsparteitagen der NSDAP.* Berlin: Akademie Verlag.

Kerrl, H. 1938. *Reichstagung in Nürnberg 1937. Der Parteitag der Arbeit.* Berlin: Weller.

Koch, G.F. 1978. „Speer, Schinkel und der Preußische Stil." In Speer 1978b, 136-50.

Kracauer, S. 1977. *Das Ornament der Masse. Essays.* Frankfurt am Main: Suhrkamp.

Kunst, H-J. 1971. „Architektur und Macht: Überlegungen zur NS-Architektur." In *1. Mitteilungen, Kommentare, Berichte der Philipps-Universität Marburg* 3: 51-2.

Larsson, L.O. 1978. „Klassizismus in der Architektur des 2. Jahrhunderts." In Speer 1978b, 151-75.

Lotz, W. 1938. „Das Reichsparteitagsgelände in Nürnberg." *Kunst im Dritten Reich* 9: 264-9.

March, W. 1967. „Die Bauten des Reichssportfeldes." In Teut 1967, 200-6.

Miller Lane, B. 1973. „The Architecture of Nazi Germany." *Journal of the Society of Architectural Historians* 32: 325-8.

Offizieller Bericht über den Verlauf des Reichsparteitages mit sämtlichen Kongressreden

—. 1935. *Der Kongress zu Nürnberg vom 5.-10. September 1934.* 2. Auflage. München.

—. 1936. *Der Parteitag der Ehre vom 8.-14. September 1936.* München.

—. 1938. *Der Parteitag Großdeutschland vom 5.-12. September 1938.* München.

Ogan, B. und W.W. Weiß, Hrsg. 1992. *Faszination und Gewalt: Zur politischen Ästhetik des Nationalsozialismus.* Nürnberg: Tümmels.

Ogan, B. und S. Zelnhefer. 1986. *Merkblätter zur Ausstellung „Nürnberg und der Nationalsozialismus" im ehemaligen Reichsparteitagsgelände.* Beiträge zur politischen Bildung 4. Nürnberg: Pädagogisches Institut der Stadt Nürnberg.

Petsch, J. 1976. *Baukunst und Stadtplanung im Dritten Reich: Herleitung – Bestandsaufnahme – Entwicklung – Nachfolge.* München u.a.: Hanser.

Picker, H.H.H. 1989. *Hitlers Tischgespräche im Führerhauptquartier.* Frankfurt am Main u.a.: Ullstein.

Radt, W.1988. *Pergamon. Geschichte und Bauten, Funde und Erforschung einer antiken Metropole.* DuMont Dokumente. Köln: DuMont.

Rodenwaldt, G. 1943. *Kunst um Augustus.* 2. Auflage. Berlin: De Gruyter.

Schäche, W. 1979. „Nationalsozialistische Architektur und Antikenrezeption: Kritik der Neoklassizismus-These am Beispiel der Berliner Museumsplanung." In *Berlin und die Antike. Architektur, Kunstgewerbe, Malerei, Skulptur, Theater und Wissenschaft vom 6. Jahrhundert bis heute*, herausgeben von W. Arenhövel und C. Schreiber, 557-70. Berlin: Wasmuth.

—. 1983a. „Architektur und Städtebau im Nationalsozialismus." *Bauwelt* 74.4: 119-25.

—. 1983b. „Die 'Totenburgen' des Nationalsozialismus." *Arch+* 71: 72-5.

Schönberger, A. 1981. *Die neue Reichskanzlei von Albert Speer. Zum Zusammenhang von nationalsozialistischer Ideologie und Architektur.* Berlin: Gebr. Mann.

Schrade, H. 1939. *Bauten des Dritten Reiches.* Meyers Bild-Bändchen 35. Leipzig: Bibliographisches Institut.

Scobie, A. 1990. *Hitler's State Architecture. The Impact of Classical Antiquity*. University Park u.a.: Pennsylvania State University Press.

Speer, A. 1936. „Die Bauten des Führers." In *Adolf Hitler. Bilder aus dem Leben des Führers*, herausgegeben vom Cigaretten-Bilderdienst, 72-7. Altona/Bahrenfeld: Cigaretten-Bilderdienst.

—, Hrsg. 1943. *Neue Deutsche Baukunst*. Amsterdam: Volk und Reich.

—. 1966a. „Fühlende Brust. Ein Interview." *Der Spiegel* 40: 44-61.

—. 1966b. „Die Bürde werde ich nicht mehr los. *Spiegel*-Gespräch mit Albert Speer und den Redakteuren Manfred W. Hentschel und Dr. Wolfgang Malanowski." *Der Spiegel* 46: 48-62.

—. 1976. *Erinnerungen*. 14. Auflage. Berlin: Propyläen.

—. 1978a. *Spandauer Tagebücher*. Frankfurt am Main u.a.: Ullstein.

—. 1978b. *Albert Speer. Arbeiten 1933-1942*. Frankfurt am Main u.a.: Ullstein.

Täubrich, H.-Chr. 1993. „Nürnberg vor 1933. Ansichten über eine deutsche Stadt." In *Unterm Hakenkreuz 1933*, 16-9.

Teut, A. 1967. *Architektur im Dritten Reich. 1933-1945*. Berlin u.a.: Ullstein.

Thies, J. 1976. *Architekt der Weltherrschaft. Die „Endziele" Hitlers*. 2. Auflage. Düsseldorf: Droste.

Thöne, A.W. 1979. *Das Licht der Arier: Licht, Feuer- und Dunkelsymbolik des Nationalsozialismus*. München: Minerva Publikation.

Tillich, P. 1948. Neudruck. *Die sozialistische Entscheidung. Schriften zur Zeit*. Offenbach am Main: Bollwerk-Verlag. Erstausgabe, Offenbach am Main: Bollwerk-Verlag, 1933.

Troost, G. 1938/43. *Bauen im Neuen Reich*. 2 Bände. Bayreuth: Gauverlag.*Unterm Hakenkreuz. Alltag in Nürnberg 1933-1945*. 1993. Centrum Industriekultur Nürnberg. München: Hugendubel.

Vogt, A.M. 1970. „Revolutions-Architektur und Nazi-Klassizismus." In *Argo. Festschrift für Kurt Badt zu seinem 80 Geburtstag am 3. März 1970*, herausgegeben von M. Gosebruch und L. Dittman, 354-63. Köln: DuMont Schauberg.

Vondung, K. 1971. *Magie und Manipulation. Ideologischer Kult und politische Religion des Nationalsozialismus*. Göttingen: Vandenhoek & Ruprecht.

Zelnhefer, S. 1991. *Die Reichsparteitage der NSDAP: Geschichte, Struktur und Bedeutung der größten Propagandafeste im nationalsozialistischen Feierjahr*. 2. Auflage. Nürnberg: Stadtarchiv Nürnberg.

—. 1993. „Die historische Kulisse: Bild und Selbstbild der Stadt der Reichsparteitage." In *Unterm Hakenkreuz 1993*, 32-41.

Zentner, F. und F. Bedürftig, Hrsg. 1985. *Das große Lexikon des Dritten Reiches*. München: Südwest Verlag.

World Systems, Global Cities and Global Elites:
An archaeological-sociological intervention

Hermann Schwengel

A new concept of the world system that could stimulate present debates can be developed by connecting a sociological and an archaeological view of globalisation. At first sight, both the sociological and the archaeological view owe little to the age of *nation building* in terms of their formation, despite their methodological nationalism, which is currently under siege by sociology[1]. However, this negative bit of common ground cannot be intellectually satisfactory, for it is very important to alleviate the weakness of one way of interpretation by adding another perspective. I understand sociological action theory as an addition to the more structuralist architecture of archaeological examination. That is why I want to use archaeological motifs in order to examine two crucial points, the importance of, firstly, global cities and, secondly, global elites for globalisation. It would be possible, of course, to consider the whole range of decades' worth of debates, such as that about world system and world systems[2], and to illuminate the complexity of globalisation by means of overview and synthesis. At this point, however, I want to pursue a more minimalist approach by considering the sociological and archaeological perspective in order to re-open a fundamentally political debate, which has come to a virtual standstill in a discussion of largely theoretical nature[3]. To achieve this, it is important, firstly, to (fully) understand how the idea of the world system, as introduced by Immanuel Wallerstein and further developed by others, can be challenged in a central point and, secondly, to use this central point as point of departure for an archaeo-logical-sociological intervention and to clarify which contribution it can offer to further debates about globalisation.

The World System

Since the early 70s – as many maintain, we are still in the middle of the 1970 crisis –, the real challenge of any meta-sociological theory of the world system has lain in the singularity of the world system. We need to distinguish the latter both from Braudel's empires and their world economies and from modern nation states and their economies. It is the system that makes the difference, not any primary distinction between modes of production or classes, although the modern world system is defined by capitalism. The difficulty is even more apparent if we do not follow definitions of the world system either as one system with one division of labour, many cultural systems and core-, semi-peripheral and peripheral sectors[4] or as a normative liberal balance of markets and governance, modernization and international relations.

What is more, a world system is not an agglomeration of world economy, world politics, world society and world culture, the functional systems of which tie together – as if controlled by an *invisible hand* – territorial, local, regional, national and global orders. It is a connection of a principally open capitalistic mode of accumulation[5] and a hegemonic order of states, differentiating between central, peripheral and semi-peripheral actors. Thomas Hobbes' *Leviathan* is often taken to be more than merely a historical-political analysis. Instead, it is read as an experiment of thoughts, aiming at an understan-

1 Beck and Grande 2004.
2 Hall 2000a.
3 For the breaking-up of constellations in teaching world history cf. Schissler and Soysal 2005.
4 Wallerstein 1983.
5 It is useful to differentiate between mode of accumulation and mode of production in order to avoid "the implication that only production processes are important for systemic logic" (Grimes 2000, 49 n. 1).

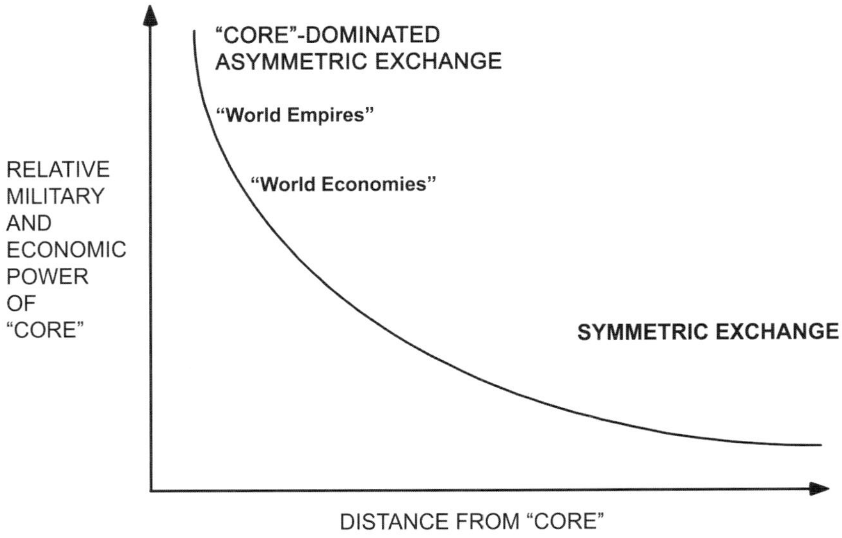

Abb. 1. Distance-Parity Model of Inter-Regional Interaction. After: Stein 1999, Fig. 4.1.

ding of the formation of treaties and rulership in its evolutionary natural state. Similarly, the notion of the world system can be understood as an experiment of thoughts which tries to examine the connection of accumulation and of hegemony in its natural state. To speak of one single world system remains a challenge to both archaeologists and sociologists. Both disciplines obviously have tried to deal with this challenge by differentiation. Despite the fact that world system theory seems to be much more current in archaeology than it is in the field of sociology, contributors to the discussion tend to speak of world systems rather than one world system. Sociological discourse tends to 'ethnologise' its objects in the process of differentiation. At this point, I want to point out the respective risk inherent in either approach: what remains are archaeological worlds without a system and sociological systems of action without the world. Therefore, I would like to discuss the archaeological and the sociological differentiation of the modern notion of a world system further.

At first, archaeologists dealing with the theory discover the enormous potential of the analysis of world systems – often only to be disappointed by the results they get. Chase Dunn and Hall recommended transforming the analysis of world systems under pre-capitalistic conditions into an empirical question. The discourse alternates between the continuity of 5000 years of globalisation and the fragmentation of this history into many discontinuous units without coherence. Military and political contacts and exchange both of luxury and prestigious goods and of knowledge are not all set in the same sphere in terms of a world system. One might add that previous world systems were subject to historical change; that type and meta-type are not easily distinguished; that they are extremely local and global – Afro-Eurasian – at the same time; that a capitalist production of goods did not generally exist prior to the rise of the Dutch bourgeoisie; and that the modern approach to world systems arises when the modern state is already in the making[6]. Last, but not least, the differentiation of the world system into more and more world systems leads to a loss of the coherence which to many archaeologists once was the most interesting aspect of Wallerstein's approach – worlds without a system. Hope for future studies does not seem to lie in defending classical world system theory but from considering through its perspective the long waves of globalisation in order to conceptualise the contemporary structural antagonisms. In this light, sharp intellectual-archaeological criticisms of the world systems approach[7] appear more fruitful than a defence of the political-sociological criticism of capitalism.

Looking at the sociological debates about globalisation, they seem to be subject to a similar dynamic. The differentiation between the objects of globalisation results in an increasing proliferation of different

6 Hall 2000b, esp. 10-3.
7 Stein 1999.

sociologies of globalisation, of which there were far too many in the first place. In attempting what German sociologists call the 'ethnologisation' of the globalisation debate[8], ethnologists hoped to be able to allow participants of globalisation to find their way through a multitude of objects of recognition, which is part of the globalisation of different spheres of life. Naturally, this attempt is not on the same level with the classical sociological theory of modernization which was compiled much earlier. Where the archaeologists have worlds without a system, ethnological sociologists have systems of action without the world. Despite these respective experiences of regression, archaeologists and sociologists are able to develop further the notion of a world system. Undoubtedly, however, the idea of a world system is as far from the idea of 'ethnological' globalisation as from the idea of a world-society, which relies too much on taken-for-granted notions of global functional differentiation, modern culture as a "shared and binding set of rules exogenous to any given society, and located not only in individual or elite sentiments, but also in many world institutions"[9] and global stratification codes.

Distance-Parity Variation and Global Cities

Archaeological criticism of the world system model uses three of the theory's constitutive assumptions as propositions which have to pass empirical testing: firstly, that the centre dominates, secondly, that there is an asymmetrical exchange between core and periphery, and thirdly, that trade represents the primary driving force. As Gil J. Stein argues, there is no point in 'softening' the world system model by adding more assumptions. By doing so, we may add, one would not do justice to either the model's coherence or the wealth of empirical data. Accordingly, Stein proposes a distance-parity model correlating the core's relative military-economical power with the distance from the core[10].

Stein explains: "The degree of core dominance, the extent of core control over the exchange system, and the degree to which interregional exchange structures peripheral polities are all highly variable. Under conditions of technological/demographic superiority or ease of access between two areas of differential social complexity, asymmetric core-periphery systems can develop along exactly the lines specified by Wallerstein in the world-system model. Thus, empires as generally defined (e.g. Sinopoli 1994) often have modes of interregional interaction that correspond closely to Wallerstein's world-empire type of world-system. Trade-diasporas in such networks would be expected to dominate their host communities. However, when these conditions are not obtained, then we would expect to see increasing parity with distance in core-periphery relations. Under the latter set of conditions, we would expect to see exchange systems organised through autonomous trade-diasporas."[11] At this point, we are unable to reconsider Stein's line of argument archaeologically, but we have to bear in mind some of his key notions: the relationship between core and periphery is marked by a process, which is *gradual, reversible, sometimes accelerating and sometimes decelerating*. Wallerstein's world systems are therefore stages within a continuous process, which can move in either direction.

We should not, however, let Stein's argument lure us into an analogical trap by using archaeological differentiation merely as a refutation of the idea of world system. Taking into account modern times, one should be cautious not to opt for either of two seemingly convenient solutions: the first solution would be to apply the archaeologist's gradualist perspective only to the *pre*-industrial states, thus avoiding the modern challenges of the industrial revolution – the modern nation-state and democracy. In contrast, a view accepting world economy and symmetrical exchange as extremes of a spectrum of open constellations is much more stimulating: it permits to ask whether and when a global world order is becoming imperial in character[12] or whether semi-peripheries are again strengthening their position and independence; or whether those excluded from global power structures are forming new institutions or whether a balance between global political forces can be observed. Each of these forms of global relationship is latently existent all the time. Shifts in how they are evaluated are frequent rather than exceptional.

8 Garhammer 2003.
9 Meyer 1980, 117.
10 Stein 1999, 62-4 .
11 Stein 1999, 64.
12 Münkler 2005.

In addition, a consideration of the forces that cause these shifts is of paramount importance. On Stein's graph, we would expect permanent shifts between imperial economic strategies and demands for symmetrical exchange with semi-peripheral rise and limited balances of power in the middle. Stein's curve would indicate structural instability, as many forces would be in a position to shift action parameters the curve, thus permanently keeping these in flux. Normatively, actors may hope that a trend to the middle will occur, for example that the rise of semi-peripheral powers – China, India and other global regions today – will be mediated by balancing power systems. But a middle ground between imperial desires and demands for symmetrical exchange is not easily defined.

The second convenient solution which has to be avoided is to argue that a distance-parity relation is no longer given in a globalised society, where transportation costs and the difficulties of transfers of technology have decreased to such an extent, that their effect is obscured by other parameters. Such an argument is to a large extent part of globalisation's ideology of communication and culture. In contrast to this position, I claim that the significance of Stein's graph (Abb. 1) should be even higher in a context of (modern) globalisation than in pre-industrial ones. If means of communication and transfer of knowledge resulting in a shared experience are available in a globalised world, then, as in the case of technological and demographic parity between two regions in an archaeological world, "a decline in core control over interregional change" may indeed cause "a shift from asymmetric to increasingly symmetric conditions of exchange" and one may expect "a progressive reduction in the importance of long-distance exchange relative to local exchange and subsistence production in the political economy of the periphery", "a progressive reduction in the exchange of bulk goods relative to the proportion of prestige goods due to the latter's high ratio of value to bulk/weight", "a progressive reduction in economic pressures/incentives toward the specialised production of surplus craft or subsistence goods for export", "a progressive restriction of core influence to peripheral elites, rather than the peripheral population as a hole", an "increasing restriction of the ability of the core to use its military, economic, and political influence in the periphery" and "a progressive decline in the degree to which interregional interaction affects the organisation and development of political systems in the periphery"[13]. Such variations of archaeological arguments could well be applied to the analysis of modern conflicts. From the archaeological point of view, one could learn that the struggle for centrality is permanent – exactly what urban sociology is teaching, too. The conflict concerning the nature of centrality in conjunction with an indisputable deterritorialisation increases the significance of the distance from the respective core. Expansive forces gain power precisely because the manner in which imperial order and equilibrium, semi-peripheral ascent and the hostile power of those excluded balance one another varies. Examples are, firstly, the formation of transnational states and regions like the European Union with its variable construction and open-endedness; secondly, the universe of global enterprises, which have taken on a political character through their strategic agendas and wide-ranging investments; thirdly, global sets of companies and technology, culture and media, which absorb, process and structure global economic 'landscapes'; and lastly, global cities, which form economical, cultural and political networks above as well as below the level of nation states and nation societies and which constitute technological circles, competition and order beyond national and international institutions. All these forms of order operate between the lines of traditional the traditional discourse of communities, cities, states and the world. Among these four forms of global order beyond international relations, it is the global cities which primarily represent and vitalise the eternal competition and eternal conflict for "centrality", as Saskia Sassen puts it[14]. It is not, however, a conflict between capitals, between financial centres, between metropoles or between media hubs. The conflict exists between types – sometimes within the same city – and between types and transnational associations, cultural scenes and global enterprises, which in themselves represent only rather vague areas of economical and political systems. This is how the struggle for centrality is defined, which accelerates and finally breaks down the dynamics of the distance-parity model. In the course of globalisation, centrality may become a dualistic structure. No longer is the variation of distance and parity normatively defined by the dialectic of rising semi-peripheral nations and the time and again stabilised balance of powers, as it was in the global order of national states and their

13 Stein 1999, 62-3.
14 Sassen 2000.

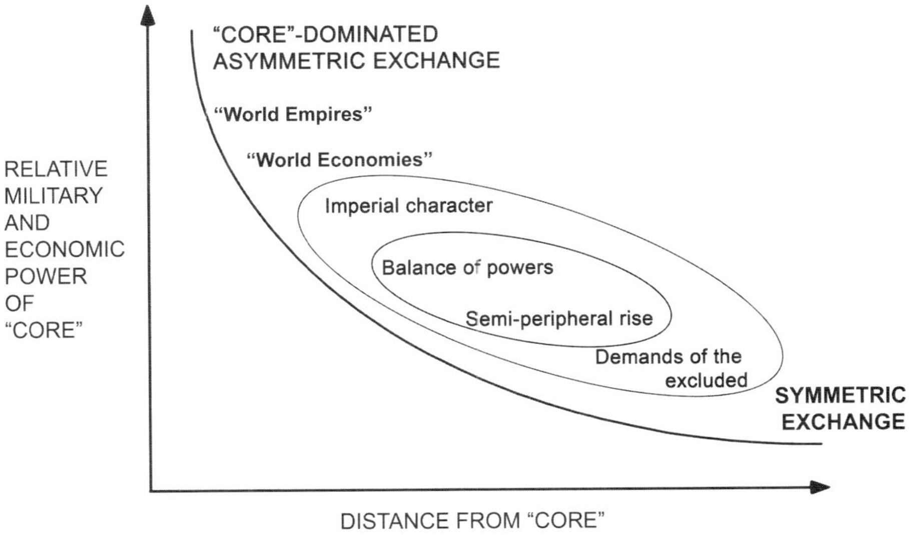

Abb. 2. Distance-Parity Model in a dynamic global order of states/economies. Modified from: Stein 1999, Fig. 4.1.

economies (Abb. 2), but by the dualistic structure of both aspirations to symmetric exchange and new imperial economies. If the vast literature on global cities does demonstrate anything, then this is that the concentration of leadership-functions, advanced middle-classes elaborating this global leadership and the cultural superstructures enabling people to be part of this leadership coexists in close geographical proximity with demands for symmetric exchange, for participation in globalisation and for regional political and social autonomy (Abb. 3).

In their most influential book, *Empire*, Negri and Hardt[15] carefully avoid telling us where the empire is actually located. It is nowhere, for the seat of power is permanently shifting, as is the identity of those in power, and only neo-conservative American and post-communist Chinese elites seem to believe they hold this position continually. One should not expect the place of the empire to be defined through any attacks on it in the future, although certain zones in the cities, central places of power, meetings of world leaders and symbolic places may offer some opportunities for attack. The neo-structural idea of the open circulating place of power itself is misleading – in the end, it is no more than the shadow of the ideology of open markets. It makes a difference whether the central global conflicts are located in the middle of Stein's curve between symmetric exchange and asymmetric exchange dominated by a core or whether the global spatial dynamics disintegrate into imperial and symmetric tendencies in certain places such as global cities or whether actors are able to bridge the spatial differences between symmetrical and asymmetrical exchange by constructing technological and demographic parities.

The Trade-Diaspora Model and Global Elites

Stein's model contains the empirical question to what extent means of communication and trade located in the core are able to settle down in the periphery, whether they are able to subjugate local elites symbolically – which they will, if there is an actual world system –, or whether local elites are able to use the core's distance to control the ascription of value to prestige goods and make possible and support conditions for symmetrical exchange. Undoubtedly, distance does not guarantee difference and does not necessarily bring about criticisms of homogeneity. But the reflection of spatial distance allows a reflection of difference which in itself makes a difference. In his modern cultural anthropology, Arjun

15 Hardt and Negri 2000.

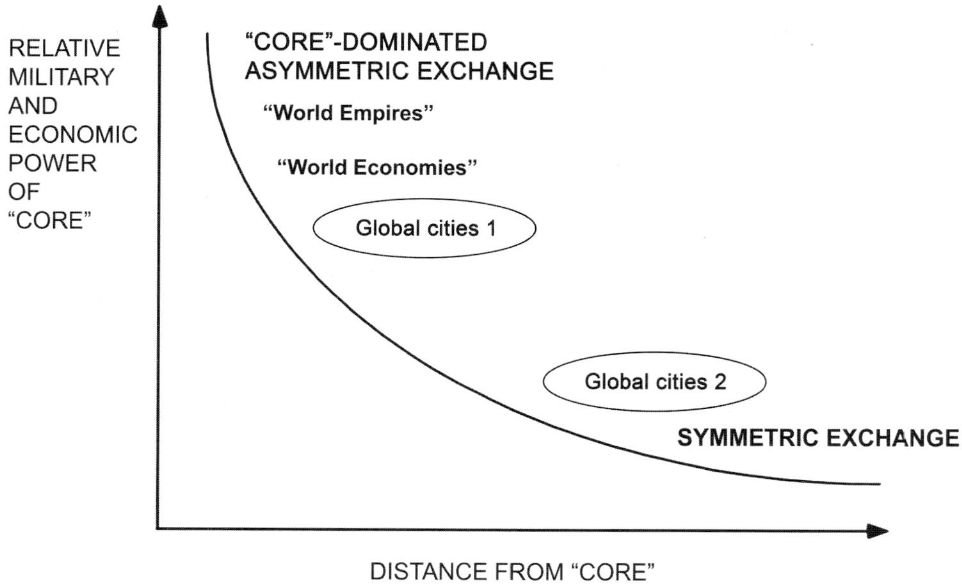

Abb. 3. Distance-Parity Model in antogonistic global ordering. Modified from: Stein 1999, Fig. 4.1.

Appadurai argues that a global society is determined by migration and media[16], and that a state of diaspora represents a regular occurrence in the post-national organisation of society. This is certainly an exaggeration, as is the idea that national societies casually turn into cosmopolitan societies, which dissolve the inconsistencies of 'diaspora' and 'home'. Similar to the eternal conflict over centrality, there exists a permanent conflict over the definition of 'own' and 'alien'. Whether this is played out in peaceful competition or whether it is allowed to explode into battle depends on the specific situation. Sociological theories of modernity are very often stuck in this permanent struggle on centrality and self because they have never adequately conceptualised or come to terms with either the experience of the south or the institutional economy of centrality. For a short time in intellectual history, modernisation seemed to represent some degree of unification of social structure and the politics of meaning, but this illusion faded decades ago. The idea of a reflexive modernisation is a mere umbrella term for an incredible variety of different actors and media of reflexivity; the idea of difference only notionally ties together countless declarations of cultural independence with the mode of consumption in advanced capitalism; the observation of social complexity and the flows of objects and subjects does not establish a mutual trust between players that they are playing the same game according to the same rules. There is too much reflexivity in the air to make a good life out of it. There is an open constellation unknown in historical modernity, which was always closer to the persistence of the old regime, to use Arno Mayer's famous phrase[17], than modern people believed.

This kind of open constellation calls for the interpretation of the elites. At least at first glance, archaeologists do not seem able to offer any help at this point, for archaeology does not reflect on the differentiation between ruling classes, power blocs and elites. For me, elites are defined by their way of decision-making, which – in open constellations – turns social fact, which itself influences the decisions of members of a given society, into meaning. Elites become superfluous when no decisions have to be made, because either the ruling classes rule or socio-technical inventions determine the future. Indirectly however, we can learn from the archaeologists' findings: the trade-diaspora model – or rather the communication-diaspora model – suggests looking carefully for relationships between local, regional, national and global elites and considering the way in which they contextualise global goods and create symbolical order. Local, regional and national elites are able to modify the meaning of goods and

16 Appadurai 1996.
17 Mayer 1981.

services on offer in border-neglecting markets, because in interaction with broad consumption patterns they define use values much more than under strict industrial conditions. The role of prestige goods, such as items of communication technology, fashion and design, is multi-facetted, i.e. these goods not only empower producers/providers allowing them a degree of control over the audience/recipients, but establish a basis for interaction between elites and masses in a different manner. The struggle over centrality – and meaning – is therefore much more open than analysts believe. If the hypothesis holds true that in one way or another global cities represent the struggle for centrality, the relationships between local, regional, national and global elites in these places is of decisive significance. The generalisation and global variation of the trade-diaspora model lets the continuous flow of things, persons, opinions and artefacts lead to a strong position of the elite, which controls the variations, selections and decisions made over the processes. These elites are to be distinguished from capitalists, rulers and 'stars' churned out by the culture industry. They are located close to economic empires as well as close to symmetrical exchange and, as is always the case, the split between the elites may provide the basis for the independence of the common people.

REPRESENTATION OF CENTRALITY AND ELITE POWER

If centrality and elite power coincide, this does by no means lead to the creation of a new empire – provided the above analysis is correct. What emerges is an area of permanent tension, which is perceived by the public and the media, which is intuitively recognised by most people and which then guides people's interests and passions. However, do not such interests and passions need central aesthetic places, such as palaces, industrial facilities, stations, squares or museums, and cultural production in order to work? Can the eternal struggle for centrality and the conflict between elites, which controls the flow of information, signs and meaning and was formerly expressed in absolutist, industrial or at least 'modern' places, objects or symbols, remain without representation? If the latter is the case, then there is nothing we can learn from the archaeologists and investing time into theoretical action reconstructions of archaeological signs of rulership will prove futile. This cannot be. Finally, I want to claim that within modern globalisation there are places of emergence, which can be investigated by means of archaeological imagination.

The eminent British sociologist John Urry speaks of emerging complex systems which organise flexible interdependencies between the local and the global, form ties between the world bank and CNN within the global network, and – most importantly in terms of representation – create signifiers of their emerging global order: the Blue Earth, the Olympic Flag, the sea, Nelson Mandela, whales, tigers and elephants, the sign of the International Red Cross, the rainforests along the Amazon, Mother Theresa etc. "These signifiers reflect and perform a global imagined community uniting different peoples, genders and generations. [...] Such images depict the globe through signifying certain iconic places, peoples, environments and animals. And such images also speak for the globe."[18] Roche in addition stresses the role played by planned mega-events such as world exhibitions, charity concerts, the Rio Summit, the destruction of the World Trade Centre, Princess Diana's death and funeral, Olympic Games, the World Women's Conference in Beijing, and calls them "social spatio-temporal hubs" and "switches that [...] channel, mix and re-route global flows"[19]. These symbols and events do not represent the order of balance; on the contrary, they themselves remain subject to the flow of symbols, but they represent the emergence of a global order, or rather a global ordering. Here too, elites attain their elite status by mediating between representation and the things represented and by creating alternatives. From this process emerges centrality, which is then again captured by global interdependence. Events interconnect and condense themselves until they offer a picture of politics, but no concept. Empire, municipality, global political scenes have a far shorter half-life than in previous history. This kind of fluidity is by no means harmless. For it is a social, economical, political and cultural struggle for the provision, organisation and definition of laboratories of global complexity[20]. There emerges the ambiguity of power as, at the same

18 Urry 2003, 81-2.
19 Roche 2000, 199.
20 Appadurai 1996.

time, an asymmetrical relationship between individuals, groups and classes and the ability to deal with others. The places where global laboratories are located are not just the result of emerging markets but also of emerging powers.

When historical and sociological thought met against the background of modernisation, it seemed – for a short while – that economics, politics, culture and society were separable as four historical systems, which was described as the socio-cybernetic view on the sociologists' side and as the socio-phenomenological view on the historians' side. This kind of order of things appeared to represent an epoch-making compromise in the seemingly 'gilded age' of a prospering post-war world, a compromise between democratic state and bourgeois society, capitalism and a rational ethics of economy, demonstrating to the world its future. Over the last few decades, the arrival of globalisation has shattered this picture on all levels. The heirs of the idea of modernisation operate on unstable grounds – historical functionalists deserve a renewed consideration: if you intend to continue to criticise capitalism, you have to concentrate on a critical composition of social, cultural and economical capital, which is losing social representatives. If you believe that cosmopolitical awareness is able to generate flexible spaces at least in Europe, the majorities in European societies have already been lost. If you want to think of society in terms of individuals, these have to face forces in the global network which master the game of differences without the individuals' consent. A communicable notion of world domination might be arrived at by looking at the flows in stock markets and global relational relationships. On the whole, it seems as if the reflection on modern spaces, spaces that are relevant in that they generate meaning, has nothing left to offer. The discourses of the modern age cannot explain the dimensions of globality adequately. Modernity and globality fall apart in a way that would have been unthinkable a decade ago. On the one hand, we have to pursue the phenomenology of things globally, on the other, we have to understand the archaeology of globalisation.

Bibliography

Appadurai, A. 1996. *Modernity at Large: Cultural Dimensions of Globalization.* Minneapolis: University of Minnesota Press.

Beck, U., and E. Grande. 2004. *Das kosmopolitische Europa: Gesellschaft und Politik in der Zweiten Moderne.* Frankfurt am Main: Suhrkamp.

Garhammer, M. 2003. "Die dritte Runde der Globalisierungsdebatte: Nach der Entdeckung des Globalen die Ethnographie des Lokalen." *Soziologische Revue* 26: 46-63.

Grimes, P. 2000. "Recent Research on World Systems." In Hall 2000b, 29-55.

Hall, T.D. 2000a. "World-Systems Analysis: A Small Sample from a Large Universe." In Hall 2000b, 3-27.

Hall, T.D., ed. 2000b. *A World-Systems Reader: New Perspectives on Gender, Urbanism, Cultures, Indigenous Peoples, and Ecology.* Lanham: Rowman and Littlefield.

Hardt, M., and A. Negri. 2000. *Empire.* Cambridge, Mass.: Harvard University Press.

Mayer, A.J. 1981. *The Persistence of the Old Regime: Europe to the Great War.* New York: Pantheon.

Meyer, J.W. 1980. "The World Polity and the Authority of the Nation-State." In *Studies of the Modern World-System*, edited by A. Bergesen, 109-37. New York: Academic Press.

Münkler, H. 2005. *Imperien: Die Logik der Weltherrschaft – vom Alten Rom bis zu den Vereinigten Staaten.* Berlin: Rowohlt.

Roche, M. 2000. *Mega-Events and Modernity.* London: Routledge.

Sassen, S. 2000. "On Concentration and Centrality in the Global City." In *World Cities in a World-System*, edited by P.L. Knox and P.J. Taylor, 63-75. Cambridge: Cambridge University Press.

Schissler, H., and Y.N. Soysal, eds. 2005. *Europe and the World: Textbooks and Curricula in Transition.* New York: Berghan Books.

Stein, G.J. 1999. *Rethinking World-Systems: Diasporas, Colonies, and Interaction in Uruk Mesopotamia.* Tuscon: University of Arizona Press.

Urry, J. 2003. *Global Complexity.* Cambridge: Polity.

Wallerstein, I. 1983. "Klassenanalyse und Weltsystemanalyse." In *Soziale Ungleichheiten*, edited by R. Kreckel, 301-20. Soziale Welt Sonderband 2. Göttingen: Otto Schwartz & Co.

Wobbe, T. 2000. *Weltgesellschaft*. Bielefeld: Transcript.

List of Contributors

PROF. DR. JOHN C. BARRETT

Department of Archaeology
Northgate House
West Street,
Sheffield, S1 4ET
United Kingdom
J.Barrett@Sheffield.ac.uk

DR. BERND CARQUÉ

Max-Planck-Institut für Geschichte
Hermann-Föge-Weg 11
D-37073 Göttingen
Deutschland
carque@mpi-g.gwdg.de

PROF. DR. MICHAEL DIERS

Hochschule für bildende Künste Hamburg
Lerchenfeld 2
D-22081 Hamburg
Deutschland
michael.diers@culture.hu-berlin.de

PROF. DR. MARLIES HEINZ

Albert-Ludwigs-Universität
Orientalisches Seminar
Postfach
D-79185 Freiburg
Deutschland
marlies.heinz@orient.uni-freiburg.de

PROF. DR. TONIO HÖLSCHER

Universität Heidelberg
Institut für Altertumswissenschaften
Seminar für Klassische Archäologie
Marstallhof 4
D-69117 Heidelberg
Deutschland
tonio.hoelscher@urz.uni-heidelberg.de

PROF. DR. MATTHEW H. JOHNSON

Archaeology
School of Humanities
University of Southampton
Avenue Campus, Highfield
Southampton SO17 1BF
United Kingdom
m.h.johnson@soton.ac.uk

CARSTEN JUWIG M.A.

Grögersweg 7
22307 Hamburg
Deutschland
Juwig@gmx.de

PRIV.-DOZ. DR. YVONNE KAROW

Religionswissenschaftliches Institut
Freie Universität Berlin
Altensteinstraße 40
D-14195 Berlin
Deutschland
yvonnekarow@compuserve.de

DR. ANDREA KUCHAREK

Handschuhsheimer Landstr. 35
D-69121 Heidelberg
Deutschland
akucharek@ix.urz.uni-heidelberg.de

PROF. DR. JOSEPH MARAN

Universität Heidelberg
Institut für Altertumswissenschaften
Seminar für Ur- und Frühgeschichte
Marstallhof 4
D-69117 Heidelberg
Deutschland
m17@ix.urz.uni-heidelberg.de

PROF. DR. THOMAS A. MARKUS

Flat 4/3, 6 Kingsborough Gate
Glasgow G12 9JZ
United Kingdom
t.a.markus@stratch.ac.uk

DR. MARIA GABRIELLA MICALE

Dipartimento di Scienze Storiche,
Archeologiche ed Antropologiche
dell'Antichità
Università degli Studi di Roma "la Sapienza"
Missione Archeologica Italiana in Siria
Via Palestro 63
00185 Roma
Italia
mgmlucy@libero.it

PROF. DR. DIAMANTIS PANAGIOTOPOULOS

Universität Heidelberg
Institut für Altertumswissenschaften
Seminar für Klassische Archäologie
Marstallhof 4
D-69117 Heidelberg
Deutschland
diamantis.panagiotopoulos@urz.uni-heidelberg.de

DR. MARINA PUCCI

Freie Universität Berlin
Institut für Vorderasiatische Altertumskunde
Hüttenweg 7
D-14195 Berlin
Deutschland
maripucci@hotmail.de

DR. CHRISTOPHER SCHLEMBACH

Schützplatz 2/15
1140 Wien
Östereich
christopher.schlembach@univie.ac.at

PROF. DR. HERMANN SCHWENGEL

Institut für Soziologie
der Albert-Ludwigs-Universität Freiburg
Rempartstr. 15
D-79085 Freiburg im Breisgau
Deutschland
hermann.schwengel@soziologie.uni-freiburg.de

ULRICH THALER M.A.

Deutsches Archäologisches Institut
Abteilung Athen
Fidiou 1
GR-10678 Athen
Griechenland
ulrich.thaler@gmx.de
thaler@athen.dainst.org

DR. TRISTAN WEDDIGEN

Institut für Kunstgeschichte
Universität Bern
Hodlerstrasse 8
CH-3011 Bern
Schweiz
weddigen@gmx.ch

PROF. DR. JAMES C. WRIGHT

Department of Classical and
Near Eastern Archaeology
Bryn Mawr College
Bryn Mawr, PA 19010-2899
USA
jwright@brynmawr.edu